Keys to Chinese
New HSK 1-6
Chinese-English Dictionary

1800 Essential Characters
Ordered by the
Traditional Radical Method

Compiled and edited by Jamie Hamilton

New HSK 2021 syllabus

键 KTC

Keys to Chinese Publishing
Farnham
Surrey
UK

Copyright © Jamie Hamilton 2022

ISBN 978-1-7391434-0-4

Keys to Chinese New HSK 1-6 Chinese-English Dictionary:
1800 Essential Characters Ordered by the Traditional Radical Method

Compiled and edited by Jamie Hamilton

键 KTC

Keys to Chinese Publishing *draws on the skills of English and Chinese educationalists to bring innovative learning products to print.*

www.keystochinese.co.uk

@ keys_to_chinese

Credits

HSK is an abbreviation of 汉语水平考试 *Hànyǔ Shuǐpíng Kǎoshì*, an organisation that runs the official, standard Chinese proficiency test (HSK tests 1-6). This is organised by *Hànbàn* which is part of the Ministry of Education of China. *Hànbàn* also runs the Confucius Institutes found worldwide.
Details of the new (2021) HSK 1-6 syllabus were taken from: http://www.chinesetest.cn. Exams based on this new syllabus will be rolled out in the coming years

This book uses information, with thanks, from the CC-CEDICT online dictionary. The link to this resource is: https://cc-cedict.org/wiki/#attribution. The contributors to the project were: Matic Kavcic, Richard Warmington, Julien Baley, Yves Candau, Feilipu, Craig Brelsford, Erik Peterson, and Paul Andrew Denisowski, the original creator of CEDICT. The use of this information here is licensed under a Creative Commons Attribution-Share Alike 3.0 License

Contents

Introduction	4
One Page Radical Index	11
Radical Index	12
Character Index	16
Main Entries	27
Pinyin Index	330

Notes

1. The following abbreviations for parts of speech are used in the Main Entries:

Noun	→	n.
Verb	→	vb.
Adjective	→	adj.
Adverb	→	adv.
Pronoun	→	pro.
Measure Word	→	m.w.
Affix	→	aff.
Conjunction	→	conj.
Number	→	num.
Interjection	→	intj.
Auxiliary	→	aux.
Phrase	→	phr.

2. The dictionary uses British English for the Main Entries.

Introduction

Welcome to a new style of Chinese language resource: a Chinese-English dictionary which is organised by the radicals. It presents 1800 characters essential for learning Chinese, but instead of ordering them in the standard "Pinyin-Alphabetical" style it orders them according to what radical they belong to.

This "Traditional Radical Method" of ordering the characters allows learners of all levels to better understand the logic and structure of written Chinese. It encourages a deeper and more enjoyable learning experience of the material. The 1800 characters enable the building of a solid base in the language. When ordered by the traditional radical method they become the "Keys to Chinese".

Who is the Dictionary for?

The dictionary is written to meet the needs of learners of Chinese who want to go deeper with their understanding of the writing system. The stage of learner that this will be of most use for is any point beyond complete beginner. The level of characters and words here is up to the new HSK 6 exam, meaning a very high level of Chinese proficiency.

This 2021 syllabus is broader and more challenging than before and aims to give an excellent level of language competence. Along with the characters are the 5456 words for HSK 1-6, plus parts of speech and English translation. Therefore, this dictionary can be used as a useful learning tool for students up to this advanced stage.

Radicals

In this work, the order of characters is by the "radical" first, then according to the number of strokes needed to make the character. This *Traditional Radical Method* of ordering characters is called 部首编排法 **bùshǒu biānpáifǎ** and is still used in some Chinese dictionaries. It seems to be a logical and useful way of ordering the language: showing connections between characters that improve our understanding of written Chinese. In fact, the radicals were first introduced as an educational tool to systematically order the characters.

The Chinese word for radical is 部首 **bùshǒu**, and these were best known as appearing in the famous dictionary brought out in the reign of the Emperor Kangxi in 1716, thus we have the name 康熙部首 *Kāngxī bùshǒu*. Modern dictionaries in China normally use an updated version of the radicals to order them, but all these versions are based on the original Kangxi set. There are 214 Kangxi radicals in all.

These days the Kangxi Radicals are used to order the characters in databases and are part of the official Unicode that define all characters. One key benefit of the using the Kangxi Radicals is that they link better to classical writing and then can help us understand the structure of older texts.

部首 **bùshǒu** means "headword" and should really be thought of as a chapter heading. There is a traditional order to them: thus 日 is in order the 72nd radical, and is called the "Radical 72". We can code a character by the radical that it "belongs" to and how many more strokes are needed to construct it. This is what we call the **Radical Code** and this is used to order the characters in the dictionary.

Characters and Words

This dictionary gives 1800 characters that head lists of words that contain these characters. In Chinese the "characters" are known in Chinese as 字 *zì* and the "words" as 词 *cí*. The 1800 characters and 5456 words in the Main Entries are those listed by the HSK organisation for exams at Levels 1-6.

Traditional Radical Method

Most modern Chinese and Chinese-English dictionaries now use Pinyin to alphabetically sort characters. This of course has some practical advantages, and naturally is not difficult for dictionary users who have European languages as their first language. With a pinyin system when we have a certain character, for instance the character for sun, 日 *rì*, we might expect the next entry to be something like 容 *róng*.

The next three entries following such a Pinyin-alphabetical method might look like this:

日 rì		sun
容 róng		to hold
肉 ròu		flesh
入 rù		to enter

In contrast we follow here the Traditional Radical Method, looking for other characters sharing the same radical. Thus the 日 *rì* entry plus the next three would be:

日 rì		sun
旦 dàn		dawn
旧 jiù		old
早 zǎo		early

Notice how the "sun" theme repeats itself... an image of the sun rising above the horizon [dawn], the sun (or a day) perhaps gone past something [old], the sun seen above a tree perhaps [early]. So, is this not a useful and logical way of organising things? So for instance 旦 *dàn* requires one extra stroke, while 早 *zǎo* needs two more, so 早 will come after 旦 in the ordering. It is only when the character has the same radical, and the same number of strokes, that the pinyin alphabetical system is used: thus returning to our original example 旦 *dàn* and 旧 *jiù* both need one stroke more (after the radical 日's four strokes) so all that separates them is the pinyin alphabetical system, thus *dàn* falls before *jiù* in the dictionary.

Radical Code

It is important to understand the Radical Code. It is applied to the 1800 characters and helps locate the character in the correct place in the Main Entries. As an example, let us look at the radical code for another character: 星 *xīng*. This character is another entry beloning to the sun 日 (*rì*) radical (Radical 72). Like the other examples discussed above, 星 *xīng* belongs this same "family" of 日 (*rì*) characters, and uses five extra strokes (in addition to the radical) to write it. To make the Radical Code we use the radical number 72 and the number of extra strokes separated by a dot. 星 *Xīng* then gets the code of 72.5. In addition, to aid recognition, the actual written form of the radical (here 日) is given as part of the radical code:

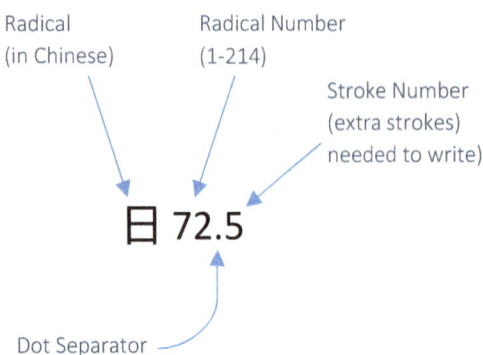

We can then use this character's radical code to locate it in the dictionary as belonging to the radical 72, or 日. Staying with the sun radical as an example, very often the radical appears to the left side as in:

晴 qíng

Less commonly it comes on the top:

早 zǎo

but often may come below as in:

春 chūn

Much less commonly we get the radical on the right as in:

旧 jiù

Sometime something is added to the radical to make it harder to recognise:

畅 chàng

Recognising the radical in any given character is usually straightforward, but like many skills in Chinese learning, it takes practice. Once one has become more familiar with the radicals themselves, it gets much easier to see them within characters. Radical Codes are also found in other places: in the app. Pleco the radical code for any character appears under the heading "RSUnicode". Incidentally, these English terms for the radicals are really more like names. They are sometimes translations, like "sun", "moon" or "mouth" but sometimes they are a word (or words) helping us remember the radical's appearance, for instance "down box" is the English term for Radical 13: 冂 *jiōng*.

Using the Main Entries section

The Main Entries section has all 214 Kangxi Radicals appearing like section headings. Most of the radicals appear as headings in bold, purple text, and come with Pinyin, English version and their radical number on the right. A typical radical entry looks like this:

Not all the 214 Kangxi Radicals have actual characters appearing with them. We felt that they should still be included in some places as they still provide information and interest. We call them "Orphans" and they appear in green, in the Radical Indexes.

To explore the radicals themselves further, have a look at the **One Page Radical Index** to get an overview, or the **Radical Index** which lists all the 214 radicals in turn. Both these Indexes include alternate forms of the radicals. In the main section, each radical then has the characters that belong to it, along with a list of all the words that have that character appearing in it.

Included in the word entries are "parts of speech", whether a noun, verb, adjective etc. using standard abbreviations, and HSK level for words and characters is also provided.

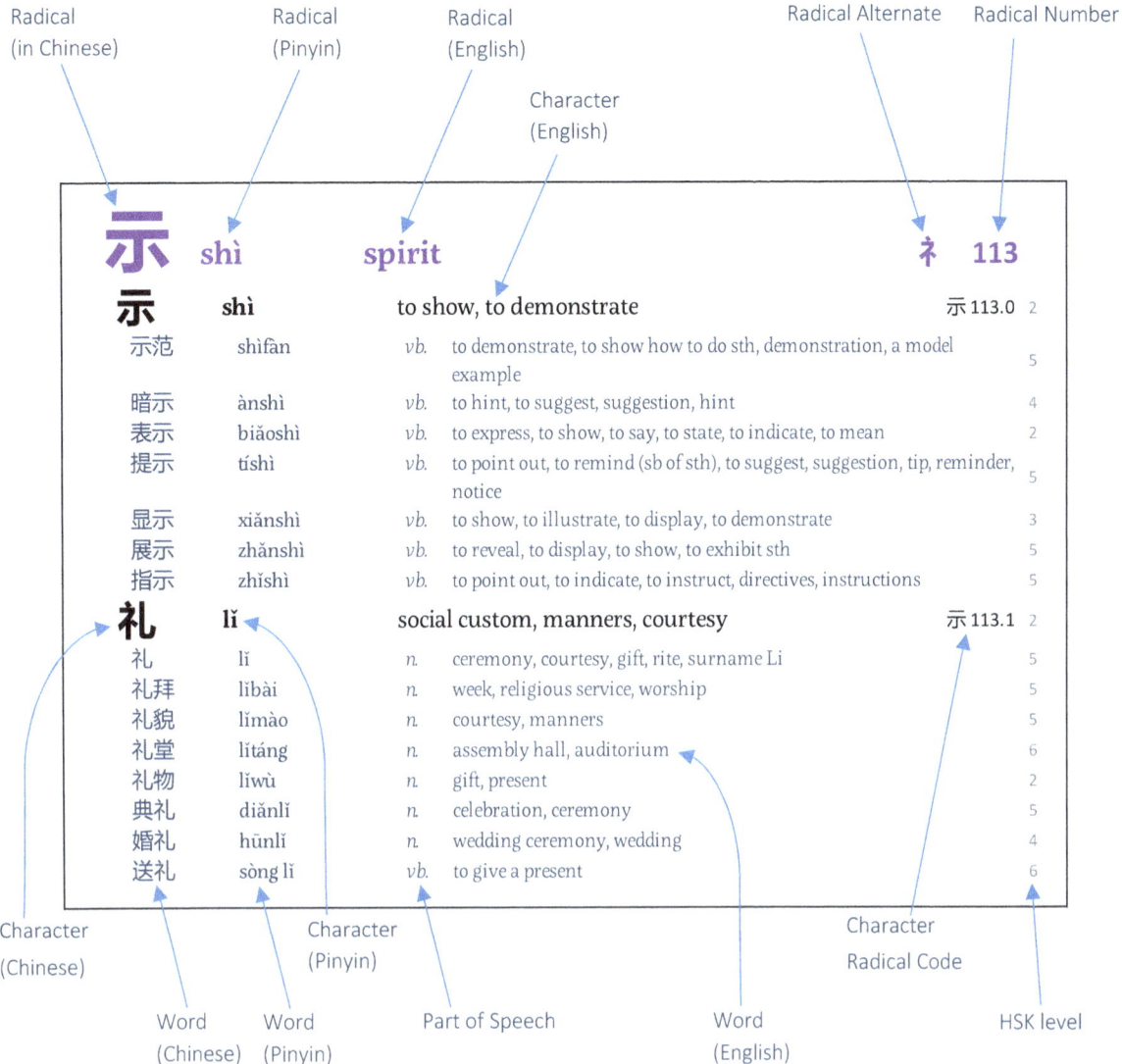

Above is an example of an entry for radical number 113, 示 *shì*, which is called "spirit" in English, and the first two characters that use it. Notice how we have the radical entry first, followed by the characters that use it (black type), with the words that use that character (blue type). For each character, first listed are the words where the character comes first, then second place and sometimes third and fourth place. Looking at the character 礼 *lǐ* as an example, we have first listed the words that start with 礼 *lǐ*: so 礼 *lǐ*, 礼 *lǐbài* etc. (these are listed in alphabetical order on the pinyin).

Second are the words that have 礼 *lǐ* contained, for instance 典礼 *diǎnlǐ*. Again these "second order" words are themselves ordered alphabetically. These entries in **dark blue** are formed from the list of 5456 words (字 *zì*) from the official lists provided by HSK. The **black** entries are of the 1800 characters (*cí*).

One may wonder why 礼 *lǐ* appears above as both a character and a word. This is because of the difference between the nature of words and characters. The "**words**" include simple one word character words in addition to two or more character words. The "**characters**" are those components in the language that are needed to construct the words, whatever the length. The Main Entries has *all* the characters needed to form the words (and no others).

Duo Yin Zi

In the Main Entries there are 74 characters that are Duo Yin Zi (DYZ) characters. 多音字 *duō yīn zì* means "many sounding character". This is where one character has more than one pronunciation and meaning. They appear in the Main Entries and Pinyin Index and the pinyin there is in **red-brown** with an asterisk ***** so they stand out.

Colour and word codes

Black is the main colour for characters, words are in dark blue. Special codes for words:
+ Alternative meaning by part of speech
- Pronunciation change
• Duo Yin Zi alternate

See text boxes below for more explanation. Below is another example of a Character Entry:

Character text (Pinyin) in **red-brown** and asterisk ***** shows a **Duo Yin Zi (DYZ:** One character, many pronunciations) with the alternate pronunciations (up to three)

Plus + sign for words show alternative meanings according to their parts of speech. These definitions are given by HSK as part of the 1-6 syllabus.

Character text (English) of a **Duo Yin Zi** separated by a semicolon show the alternate meanings

Character Radical Code

Words (Pinyin) with **dash -** show alternate pronunciation. This is due to one of the characters dropping their tone (here *chu* is in the 5th tone)

Words (Pinyin) with **bullet dots** • show that these are unusual pronunciations due to the presence of a **Duo Yin Zi** character in the word.

When a character is a DYZ then the *second* or *third* instance of it are considered the alternates. The words that are formed with that alternate character and have the bullet dot. Here with 好奇 *hàoqí*, 好·*hào* is the alternate meaning/ pronunciation, so it gets a dot to mark it out.

N.B. When a **Duo Yin Zi** word like this have two or more characters it will also be marked with a dot when listed under the other characters it belongs to. So also 好奇 *hàoqí* also appears is with a dot when listed under the character 奇 *qí*.

Dark blue for *words*.

HSK level for both words and characters

How the dictionary is structured

The dictionary has been designed to allow users to easily look up characters (and words) when they do not know their pinyin nor pronunciation. A common experience of Chinese learners is that they may see a character, and know that they have seen it before, but they cannot remember what it is. Unless we use an OCR mode in an app. like Pleco, we need to use a dictionary to find the character. Standard Chinese-English dictionaries also have this function, with indexes at the front for radicals and characters.

As explained before, where this dictionary is different is that when we go ahead to the main section where the character/ words are located, the order in not the standard pinyin-alphabetical one but ordered by the radicals. As a result it then helps with learning more about the radicals and the writing system. The order of the sections allows this look-up process to go ahead in a logical way:

1. One Page Radical Index
2. **Radical Index** Here we can locate a character's radical or explore the order that the radicals are found in
3. **Character Index** This helps confirm which radical a character is associated with and what the Radical Code will be
4. **Main Entries**
5. **Pinyin Index** This is put at the back, so that the logic of following from radicals to characters can be followed easily

Let us explore the dictionary sections in more detail:

One Page Radical Index

This gives a useful overview of the 214 radicals, alternates and orphans along with the radical number.

The Radical Index

An essential feature of the dictionary is the **Radical Index**. This shows all the 214 radicals and is organised by how many strokes comprise them. For instance, the first radical is 一 *yī*. Listed here are also the "variants" of the radicals that help identify them. These variants or "alternates" are usually small graphic elements that are used on the left side or underneath the main part of the character.

For example: 忄 is a variant for the heart radical 心 and is found in many characters, for instance: 忙 *máng*. We have listed these variants in the Radicals Index as if they were radicals themselves, i.e. by stroke number. So the 忄 variant, with its three strokes, is listed with the other three stroke radicals. To show they are variants we mark them with **light blue**. Having located the most likely radical for a character we can note the Radical Number to look up the Character in the next sections.

Character Index

This lists the 1800 characters for levels 1-6 in radical order. Having looked at the Radical Index we can have a good idea of what radical a character will belong to. To confirm this use the Character Index. Use the Radical Number to locate the right radical and look for the character under that radical.

If the character appears to not be there, then either it is not in the dictionary or else the radical we thought it belonged to was wrong. In that case go back a step to check for other possibilities for candidates for the radical.

The system of assigning characters to radicals can be confusing. It may be necessary to look at several radicals before we can locate the character. One possible pitfall when searching for a character's radical is that the character is itself a radical! For instance, we may be trying to look up a character like: 黄. It might appear to have a "grass" radical on the top, or an "eight" radical underneath? However it is not listed here as either as it is itself a radical: in this case radical 201, and of course this radical and character is 黄 *huáng* – yellow.

If we cannot find a character at all then it is because it is not there: not all characters one may encounter in advanced writing will be in this dictionary. Consider for a moment that there are 3500 characters considered by the Chinese government to be in "common use", so these 1800 characters given by the HSK organisation represent the most useful ones for learners.

From the Character Index we can confirm the radical, and also get the correct number of extra strokes needed to form the character. As explained before this makes the Radical Code and is used to look up the character in the Main Entries. Using the Character Index is optional: if one is sure of what radical a character belongs to and can easily count the number of extra strokes needed to form it, one can go straight to the Main Entries.

Main Entries

This is the main part of the dictionary with all 1800 characters and 5456 individual words. These appear in a total of just over ten thousand word entries. Note that this large number of word entries is because the words consisting of more than one character appear listed under different characters. For instance, a word like 一方面 *yīfāngmiàn* will appear listed in three different places under the characters 一 *yī*, 方 *fāng* and 面 *miàn*.

Pinyin Index

If you already know the pinyin of a character, you can use the **Pinyin Index** to "jump" straight into the correct entry. Each entry in the Pinyin Index also first gives the Chinese character to help identify it. From this index we get the radical code to then find the character in the Main Entries.

Keys to Chinese

The aim of the dictionary is to encourage students of Chinese to better explore and understand the structure behind the written form of Chinese.

Often learners find learning the characters to be forbidding, but it does not have to be that way. With a better understanding of the radical system we can see meaningful patterns emerge. The 1800 characters, when arranged in the radical order, are able to unlock the whole language: they can open the door to better understanding, more enjoyment in learning, and become real "Keys to Chinese".

Good luck with your learning and we hope this resource will help unlock that door!

One Page Radical Index

1 Stroke		3 Strokes		4 Strokes		4 Str. cont.		6 Strokes		7 Strokes		10 + Strokes	
一	1	口	30	尣	43	犬	94	竹	118	見	147	馬	187
丨	2	囗	31	心	61	王	96	竺	118	角	148	骨	188
丶	3	土	32	忄	61	玉	96	米	119	言	149	高	189
丿	4	士	33	戈	62	礻	113	糸	120	谷	150	髟	190
乙	5	夂	34	戶	63	耂	125	缶	121	豆	151	鬥	191
乛	5	夊	35	户	63	月	130	网	122	豕	152	鬯	192
乚	5	夕	36	戸	63	见	147	羊	123	豸	153	鬲	193
亅	6	大	37	手	64	贝	154	𦍌	123	貝	154	鬼	194
		女	38	扌	64			羽	124	赤	155		
2 Strokes		子	39	车	159	**5 Strokes**		老	125	走	156	魚	195
		宀	40	长	168			而	126	足	157	鳥	196
二	7	寸	41	风	182	歺	78	耒	127	𧾷	157	鹵	197
亠	8	小	42	支	65	母	80	耳	128	身	158	鹿	198
人	9	丷	42	攴	66	毋	80	聿	129	車	159	麥	199
亻	9	𭕄	42	攵	66	氺	85	肉	130	辛	160	麻	200
儿	10	尢	43	文	67	玄	95	臣	131	辰	161		
入	11	尸	44	斗	68	玉	96	自	132	辵	162	黃	201
八	12	屮	45	斤	69	瓜	97	至	133	邑	163	黍	202
冂	13	山	46	方	70	瓦	98	臼	134	酉	164	黑	203
冖	14	巛	47	无	71	甘	99	舌	135	釆	165	黹	204
冫	15	工	48	旡	71	生	100	舛	136	里	166		
几	16	己	49	日	72	用	101	舟	137	麦	199	黽	205
凵	17	巾	50	曰	73	田	102	艮	138			鼎	206
刀	18	干	51	月	74	疋	103	色	139	**8 Strokes**		鼓	207
刂	18	幺	52	木	75	疒	104	艸	140			鼠	208
力	19	广	53	欠	76	癶	105	虍	141	金	167		
勹	20	廴	54	止	77	白	106	虫	142	長	168	鼻	209
匕	21	廾	55	歹	78	皮	107	血	143	門	169	齊	210
匚	22	弋	56	殳	79	皿	108	行	144	阜	170		
匸	23	弓	57	毋	80	目	109	衣	145	隶	171	齒	211
十	24	彐	58	比	81	矛	110	襾	146	隹	172		
卜	25	彑	58	毛	82	矢	111	西	146	雨	173	龍	212
卩	26	彡	59	氏	83	石	112	覀	146	青	174	龜	213
巴	26	彳	60	气	84	示	113	页	181	非	175		
厂	27	忄	61	水	85	禸	114	齐	210	鱼	195	龠	214
厶	28	氵	64	火	86	禾	115			齿	211		
又	29	扌	64	灬	86	穴	116						
辶	149	犭	90	爪	87	立	117			**9 Strokes**			
辶	162	爿	94	爫	87	罒	122						
阝	163	糹	120	父	88	肀	129			面	176		
阝	170	艹	140	爻	89	衤	145			革	177		
		門	169	爿	90	钅	167			韋	178		
		飞	183	片	91	鸟	196			韭	179		
		饣	184	牙	92	龙	212			音	180		
		马	187	牛	93					頁	181	**Key:**	
				牜	93					風	182	Purple = Radical	
				牛	93					飛	183	Blue = Alt. rad.	
										食	184	Green = Orphan	
				cont...						首	185	Black = Rad. No.	
										香	186	Grey = Rad. No.	

Radical Index

- 214 Kangxi Radicals ordered by number of strokes and then traditional ordering.
- **Purple** is for standard radical entry. **Light blue** is for alternative, variant form.
- Follow the arrow to see the standard version of the variant.
- **Green** type shows "orphan" Radicals: radicals with no characters listed in Main Entries.
- Use the Radical Number to find a character in the Character Index or in the Main Entries.

STR	RAD	PIN	ENG	ALT	RAD No
1 Stroke					
1	一	yī	one		1
1	丨	gǔn	line		2
1	丶	zhǔ	dot		3
1	丿	piě	slash		4
1	乙	yǐ	second	㇈ ㄴ	5
1	㇈	yǐ	second	→ 乙	5
1	ㄴ	yǐ	second	→ 乙	5
1	亅	jué	hook		6
2 Strokes					
2	二	èr	two		7
2	亠	tóu	lid		8
2	人	rén	man	亻	9
2	亻	rén	man	→ 人	9
2	儿	ér	son, legs		10
2	入	rù	enter		11
2	八	bā	eight		12
2	冂	jiōng	down box		13
2	冖	mì	cover		14
2	冫	bīng	ice		15
2	几	jī	table		16
2	凵	qū	open box		17
2	刀	dāo	knife	刂	18
2	刂	dāo	knife	→ 刀	18
2	力	lì	power		19
2	勹	bāo	wrap		20
2	匕	bǐ	spoon		21
2	匚	fāng	right open box		22
2	匸	xǐ/xì	hiding enclosure		23
2	十	shí	ten		24
2	卜	bǔ	divination		25
2	卩	jié	seal	㔾	26
2	㔾	jié	seal	→ 卩	26
2	厂	hàn	cliff		27
2	厶	sī	private		28
2	又	yòu	again		29
2	讠	yán	speech	→ 言	149
2	辶	chuò	walk	→ 辵	162
2	阝	yì	city	→ 邑	163
2	阝	fù	mound	→ 阜	170
3 Strokes					
3	口	kǒu	mouth		30
3	囗	wéi	enclosure		31
3	土	tǔ	earth		32
3	士	shì	scholar		33
3	夂	zhǐ	go		34
3	夊	suī	go slowly		35
3	夕	xī	evening		36
3	大	dà	big		37
3	女	nǚ	woman		38
3	子	zǐ	child		39
3	宀	mián	roof		40
3	寸	cùn	inch		41
3	小	xiǎo	small	⺌ ⺍	42
3	⺌	xiǎo	small	→ 小	42

3	丷	xiǎo	small		→ 小	42	4	支	zhī	branch			65
3	尢	wāng	lame		尢	43	4	攴	pū	rap			66
3	尸	shī	corpse			44	4	攵	pū	rap		→ 攴	66
3	屮	chè	sprout			45	4	文	wén	script			67
3	山	shān	mountain			46	4	斗	dǒu	dipper			68
3	巛	chuān	river		川 巜	47	4	斤	jīn	axe			69
3	工	gōng	work			48	4	方	fāng	square			70
3	己	jǐ	oneself			49	4	无	wú	not		旡	71
3	巾	jīn	turban			50	4	旡	wú	not		→ 无	71
3	干	gān	dry			51	4	日	rì	sun			72
3	幺	yāo	short thread			52	4	曰	yuē	say			73
3	广	guǎng	dotted cliff			53	4	月	yuè	moon			74
3	廴	yǐn	long stride			54	4	木	mù	tree			75
3	廾	gǒng	two hands			55	4	欠	qiàn	lack			76
3	弋	yì	shoot			56	4	止	zhǐ	stop			77
3	弓	gōng	bow			57	4	歹	dǎi	death		歺	78
3	彐	jì	snout		彑	58	4	殳	shū	weapon			79
3	彑	jì	snout		→ 彐	58	4	毋	wú	do not		母	80
3	彡	shān	bristle			59	4	比	bǐ	compare			81
3	彳	chì	step			60	4	毛	máo	fur			82
3	忄	xīn	heart		→ 心	61	4	氏	shì	clan			83
3	扌	shǒu	hand		→ 手	64	4	气	qì	steam			84
3	氵	shuǐ	water		→ 水	85	4	水	shuǐ	water		氺 氵	85
3	爿	qiáng	half tree trunk		→ 丬	90	4	火	huǒ	fire		灬	86
3	犭	quǎn	dog		→ 犬	94	4	灬	huǒ	fire		→ 火	86
3	纟	mì	silk		→ 糸	120	4	爪	zhǎo	claw		爫	87
3	艹	cǎo	grass		→ 艸	140	4	爫	zhǎo	claw		→ 爪	87
3	门	mén	gate		→ 門	169	4	父	fù	father			88
3	飞	fēi	fly		→ 飛	183	4	爻	yáo	double x			89
3	饣	shí	eat		→ 食	184	4	爿	qiáng	half tree trunk		丬	90
3	马	mǎ	horse		→ 馬	187	4	片	piàn	slice			91
							4	牙	yá	fang			92
4 Strokes							4	牛	niú	cow		牜 䇂	93
							4	牜	niú	cow		→ 牛	93
4	尢	wāng	lame		→ 尢	43	4	䇂	niú	cow		→ 牛	93
4	心	xīn	heart		忄 忄	61	4	犬	quǎn	dog		犭	94
4	忄	xīn	heart		→ 心	61	4	王	yù	jade		→ 玉	96
4	戈	gē	halberd			62	4	玨	yù	jade		→ 玉	96
4	戶	hù	door		户 戸	63	4	礻	shì	spirit		→ 示	113
4	户	hù	door		→ 戶	63	4	耂	lǎo	old		→ 老	125
4	戸	hù	door		→ 戶	63	4	⺼	ròu	meat		→ 肉	130
4	手	shǒu	hand		扌 龵	64	4	见	jiàn	see		→ 見	147
4	龵	shǒu	hand		→ 手	64	4	贝	bèi	shell		→ 貝	154

4	车	chē	cart	→ 車	159
4	长	cháng	long	→ 長	168
4	风	fēng	wind	→ 風	182

5 Strokes

5	歹	dǎi	death	→ 歹	78
5	母	wú	do not	→ 毋	80
5	毋	wú	do not	→ 毋	80
5	氺	shuǐ	water	→ 水	85
5	玄	xuán	profound		95
5	玉	yù	jade	玊 王	96
5	瓜	guā	melon		97
5	瓦	wǎ	tile		98
5	甘	gān	sweet		99
5	生	shēng	life		100
5	用	yòng	use		101
5	田	tián	field		102
5	疋	pǐ	bolt of cloth	疋	103
5	疒	nè	sickness		104
5	癶	bō	dotted tent, legs		105
5	白	bái	white		106
5	皮	pí	skin		107
5	皿	mǐn	dish		108
5	目	mù	eye		109
5	矛	máo	spear		110
5	矢	shǐ	arrow		111
5	石	shí	stone		112
5	示	shì	spirit	礻	113
5	禸	róu	track		114
5	禾	hé	grain		115
5	穴	xué	cave		116
5	立	lì	stand		117
5	罒	wǎng	net	→ 网	122
5	聿	yù	brush	→ 聿	129
5	衤	yī	clothes	→ 衣	145
5	钅	jīn	gold	→ 金	167
5	鸟	niǎo	bird	→ 鳥	196
5	龙	lóng	dragon	→ 龍	212

6 Strokes

6	竹	zhú	bamboo	⺮	118
6	⺮	zhú	bamboo	→ 竹	118
6	米	mǐ	rice		119
6	糸	mì	silk	糹 纟	120
6	缶	fǒu	jar		121
6	网	wǎng	net	罒	122
6	羊	yáng	sheep	羋	123
6	羋	yáng	sheep	→ 羊	123
6	羽	yǔ	feather		124
6	老	lǎo	old	耂	125
6	而	ér	and		126
6	耒	lěi	plow		127
6	耳	ěr	ear		128
6	聿	yù	brush	肀	129
6	肉	ròu	meat	月	130
6	臣	chén	minister		131
6	自	zì	self		132
6	至	zhì	arrive		133
6	臼	jiù	mortar		134
6	舌	shé	tongue		135
6	舛	chuǎn	oppose		136
6	舟	zhōu	boat		137
6	艮	gēn	stopping		138
6	色	sè	color		139
6	艸	cǎo	grass	艹	140
6	虍	hū	tiger		141
6	虫	huǐ	insect		142
6	血	xuè	blood		143
6	行	xíng	walk enclosure		144
6	衣	yī	clothes	衤	145
6	襾	xī	west	西 覀	146
6	西	xī	west	→ 襾	146
6	覀	xī	west	→ 襾	146
6	页	yè	leaf	→ 頁	181
6	齐	qí	even	→ 齊	210

7 Strokes

7	見	jiàn	see	见	147
7	角	jiǎo	horn		148
7	言	yán	speech	言 讠	149

7	谷	gǔ	valley		150	9	飛	fēi	fly	飞	183
7	豆	dòu	bean		151	9	食	shí	eat	食饣	184
7	豕	shǐ	pig		152	9	首	shǒu	head		185
7	豸	zhì	badger		153	9	香	xiāng	fragrant		186
7	貝	bèi	shell	贝	154						
7	赤	chì	red		155						
7	走	zǒu	run	赱	156						
7	足	zú	foot	𧾷	157						
7	𧾷	zú	foot	→足	157						
7	身	shēn	body		158						
7	車	chē	cart	车	159						
7	辛	xīn	bitter		160						
7	辰	chén	morning		161						
7	辵	chuò	walk	辶辶	162						
7	邑	yì	city	阝阝	163						
7	酉	yǒu	wine		164						
7	釆	biàn	distinguish		165						
7	里	lǐ	village		166						
7	麦	mài	wheat	→麥	199						

10 + Strokes

10	馬	mǎ	horse	马	187
10	骨	gǔ	bone		188
10	高	gāo	tall	高	189
10	髟	biāo	hair		190
10	鬥	dòu	fight		191
10	鬯	chàng	sacrificial wine		192
10	鬲	lì	cauldron		193
10	鬼	guǐ	ghost		194
11	魚	yú	fish	鱼	195
11	鳥	niǎo	bird	鸟	196
11	鹵	lǔ	salt	卤	197
11	鹿	lù	deer		198
11	麥	mài	wheat	麦	199
11	麻	má	hemp		200
12	黃	huáng	yellow		201
12	黍	shǔ	millet		202
12	黑	hēi	black		203
12	黹	zhǐ	embroidery		204

8 Strokes

8	金	jīn	gold	金钅	167
8	長	cháng	long	镸长	168
8	門	mén	gate	门	169
8	阜	fù	mound	阝	170
8	隶	lì	slave		171
8	隹	zhuī	short-tailed bird		172
8	雨	yǔ	rain		173
8	青	qīng	blue	青	174
8	非	fēi	wrong		175
8	鱼	yú	fish	→魚	195
8	齿	chǐ	tooth	→齒	211

13	黽	mǐn	frog	黾	205
13	鼎	dǐng	tripod		206
13	鼓	gǔ	drum		207
13	鼠	shǔ	rat		208
14	鼻	bí	nose		209
14	齊	qí	even	齐	210
15	齒	chǐ	tooth	齿	211
16	龍	lóng	dragon	龙	212
16	龜	guī	turtle	龟	213
17	龠	yuè	flute		214

9 Strokes

9	面	miàn	face	面	176
9	革	gé	leather		177
9	韋	wéi	tanned leather	韦	178
9	韭	jiǔ	leek		179
9	音	yīn	sound		180
9	頁	yè	leaf	页	181
9	風	fēng	wind	风	182

Character Index

- Radicals in **purple** shown with radical number. "Orphan" type radical not shown.
- Characters (子 zì): In black type. Ordered by radicals. Duo Yin Zi in **red-brown**.
- +Str shows extra strokes needed to write character.
- Combine Rad. No. and Extra Strokes to make Radical Code, e.g Radical Code for 七: Rad. 1 + 1 extra stroke = 1.1. Use Radical code to look up characters in Main Entries.

R 子	Pinyin	+Str	R 子	Pinyin	+Str	R 子	Pinyin	+Str	R 子	Pinyin	+Str
一 yī		1	么	me	2	亮	liàng	7	优	yōu	4
一	yī	0	义	yì	2	赢	yíng	15	众	zhòng	4
七	qī	1	乌	wū	3	人 rén		亻 9	伴	bàn	5
三	sān	2	之	zhī	3	人	rén	0	但	dàn	5
上	shàng	2	乏	fá	4	亿	yì	1	低	dī	5
万	wàn	2	乎	hū	4	仓	cāng	2	佛	fó, fú	5
下	xià	2	乐	lè, yuè	4	从	cóng	2	估	gū	5
丈	zhàng	2	乘	chéng	9	介	jiè	2	何	hé	5
不	bù	3	乙 yǐ			仅	jǐn	2	你	nǐ	5
丑	chǒu	3	乙	yǐ	0	今	jīn	2	伸	shēn	5
与	yǔ, yù	3	九	jiǔ	1	仍	réng	2	似	shì	5
专	zhuān	3	飞	fēi	2	什	shén	2	体	tǐ	5
东	dōng	4	卫	wèi	2	代	dài	3	位	wèi	5
且	qiě	4	也	yě	2	付	fù	3	余	yú	5
世	shì	4	乱	luàn	6	令	lìng	3	住	zhù	5
业	yè	4	乳	rǔ	7	们	men	3	作	zuò	5
丢	diū	5	亅 jué		6	他	tā	3	侧	cè	6
夹	jiā	5	了	le, liǎo	1	仪	yí	3	供	gōng	6
亚	yà	5	予	yǔ	3	以	yǐ	3	佳	jiā	6
两	liǎng	6	争	zhēng	5	仔	zǐ	3	例	lì	6
严	yán	6	事	shì	7	传	chuán	4	使	shǐ	6
丨 gǔn		2	二 èr		7	仿	fǎng	4	依	yī	6
个	gè	2	二	èr	0	份	fèn	4	保	bǎo	7
丰	fēng	3	亏	kuī	1	会	huì, kuài	4	便	biàn, pián	7
书	shū	3	于	yú	1	伙	huǒ	4	促	cù	7
中	zhōng, zhòng	3	互	hù	2	价	jià	4	俩	liǎ	7
串	chuàn	6	井	jǐng	2	件	jiàn	4	侵	qīn	7
临	lín	8	五	wǔ	2	企	qǐ	4	俗	sú	7
丶 zhǔ		3	云	yún	2	任	rèn	4	信	xìn	7
为	wèi, wéi	3	些	xiē	5	伞	sǎn	4	倍	bèi	8
主	zhǔ	4	亠 tóu		8	伤	shāng	4	倡	chàng	8
丽	lì	7	亡	wáng	1	伟	wěi	4	倒	dào, dǎo	8
举	jǔ	8	交	jiāo	4	伍	wǔ	4	候	hòu	8
丿 piě		4	京	jīng	6	休	xiū	4	借	jiè	8
久	jiǔ	2	享	xiǎng	6	仰	yǎng	4	俱	jù	8

倾	qīng	8	冂	**jiōng**	**13**	刷	shuā	6	卩	**jié**	**巴 26**
修	xiū	8	册	cè	3	制	zhì	6	危	wēi	4
债	zhài	8	再	zài	4	剑	jiàn	7	印	yìn	4
值	zhí	8	冒	mào	7	前	qián	7	即	jí	5
偿	cháng	9	冖	**mì**	**14**	剧	jù	8	却	què	5
假	jià, jiǎ	9	写	xiě	3	副	fù	9	卷	juǎn, juàn	6
健	jiàn	9	农	nóng	4	剪	jiǎn	9	厂	**hàn**	**27**
偶	ǒu	9	冠	guān	7	剩	shèng	10	厂	chǎng	0
偏	piān	9	冫	**bīng**	**15**	力	**lì**	**19**	历	lì	2
停	tíng	9	习	xí	1	力	lì	0	厅	tīng	2
偷	tōu	9	冬	dōng	3	办	bàn	2	厉	lì	3
做	zuò	9	冰	bīng	4	劝	quàn	2	压	yā	4
傍	bàng	10	冲	chōng, chòng	4	功	gōng	3	厌	yàn	4
储	chǔ	10	决	jué	4	加	jiā	3	质	zhì	4
傅	fù	10	冻	dòng	5	动	dòng	4	厕	cè	6
傲	ào	11	况	kuàng	5	劲	jìn	5	厚	hòu	7
傻	shǎ	11	冷	lěng	5	劳	láo	5	厘	lí	7
像	xiàng	12	净	jìng	6	励	lì	5	原	yuán	8
儿	**ér**	**10**	凉	liáng	8	努	nǔ	5	厨	chú	10
儿	ér	0	准	zhǔn	8	助	zhù	5	厶	**sī**	**28**
元	yuán	2	减	jiǎn	9	势	shì	6	去	qù	3
允	yǔn	2	几	**jī**	**16**	勇	yǒng	7	县	xiàn	5
兄	xiōng	3	几	jǐ	0	勤	qín	11	参	cān	6
充	chōng	4	凡	fán	1	勹	**bāo**	**20**	又	**yòu**	**29**
光	guāng	4	凭	píng	6	勺	sháo	1	又	yòu	0
先	xiān	4	凵	**qū**	**17**	包	bāo	3	叉	chā	1
克	kè	5	凶	xiōng	2	匕	**bǐ**	**21**	反	fǎn	2
免	miǎn	5	出	chū	3	化	huà	2	及	jí	2
兔	tù	6	击	jī	3	北	běi	3	双	shuāng	2
党	dǎng	8	刀	**dāo**	**刂 18**	匚	**xǐ/xì**	**23**	友	yǒu	2
入	**rù**	**11**	刀	dāo	0	匹	pǐ	2	发	fā, fà	3
入	rù	0	分	fēn, fèn	2	区	qū	2	变	biàn	6
内	nèi	2	切	qiē, qiè	2	医	yī	5	艰	jiān	6
全	quán	4	刊	kān	3	十	**shí**	**24**	取	qǔ	6
八	**bā**	**12**	创	chuàng	4	十	shí	0	受	shòu	6
八	bā	0	刚	gāng	4	千	qiān	1	叔	shū	6
公	gōng	2	划	huà, huá	4	升	shēng	2	难	nán, nàn	8
六	liù	2	列	liè	4	午	wǔ	2	口	**kǒu**	**30**
共	gòng	4	则	zé	4	半	bàn	3	口	kǒu	0
关	guān	4	别	bié	5	华	huá	4	古	gǔ	2
兴	xìng	4	初	chū	5	协	xié	4	号	hào	2
兵	bīng	5	利	lì	5	卖	mài	6	叫	jiào	2
单	dān	6	判	pàn	5	丧	sàng	6	句	jù	2
典	diǎn	6	刺	cì	6	南	nán	7	可	kě	2
具	jù	6	到	dào	6	博	bó	10	另	lìng	2
其	qí	6	刮	guā	6	卜	**bǔ**	**25**	史	shǐ	2
养	yǎng	7	刻	kè	6	卡	kǎ	3	司	sī	2
总	zǒng	7	券	quàn	6	占	zhàn	3	台	tái	2

叹	tàn	2	哥	gē	7	垃	lā	5	夺	duó	3
叶	yè	2	哭	kū	7	坡	pō	5	买	mǎi	3
右	yòu	2	哪	nǎ	7	坦	tǎn	5	奋	fèn	5
召	zhào	2	哲	zhé	7	型	xíng	6	奉	fèng	5
只	zhǐ, zhī	2	啊	a	8	城	chéng	7	奈	nài	5
吃	chī	3	唱	chàng	8	埋	mái	7	奇	qí	5
吊	diào	3	啡	fēi	8	堆	duī	8	奔	bēn	6
各	gè	3	啦	la	8	基	jī	8	奖	jiǎng	6
合	hé	3	啤	pí	8	培	péi	8	类	lèi	6
后	hòu	3	商	shāng	8	堂	táng	8	牵	qiān	6
吉	jí	3	售	shòu	8	域	yù	8	奏	zòu	6
吗	ma	3	唯	wéi	8	堵	dǔ	9	套	tào	7
名	míng	3	喊	hǎn	9	塞	sāi	10	**女**	**nǚ**	**38**
同	tóng	3	喝	hē	9	塑	sù	10	女	nǚ	0
吐	tǔ, tù	3	喷	pēn	9	塔	tǎ	10	奶	nǎi	2
吓	xià	3	善	shàn	9	填	tián	10	妇	fù	3
向	xiàng	3	喂	wèi	9	境	jìng	11	好	hǎo, hào	3
吧	ba, bā	4	喜	xǐ	9	墓	mù	11	妈	mā	3
吵	chǎo	4	嘉	jiā	11	墙	qiáng	11	如	rú	3
吹	chuī	4	嘛	ma	11	墨	mò	12	她	tā	3
呆	dāi	4	嘴	zuǐ	12	增	zēng	12	妙	miào	4
吨	dūn	4	器	qì	13	壁	bì	13	姑	gū	5
否	fǒu	4	**囗**	**wéi**	**31**	**士**	**shì**	**33**	姐	jiě	5
告	gào	4	四	sì	2	士	shì	0	妹	mèi	5
含	hán	4	回	huí	3	壮	zhuàng	3	妻	qī	5
启	qǐ	4	团	tuán	3	声	shēng	4	始	shǐ	5
听	tīng	4	因	yīn	3	壶	hú	7	委	wěi	5
吞	tūn	4	困	kùn	4	**夂**	**zhǐ**	**34**	姓	xìng	5
吸	xī	4	围	wéi	4	处	chǔ, chù	2	娃	wá	6
呀	ya	4	园	yuán	4	务	wù	2	威	wēi	6
员	yuán	4	固	gù	5	备	bèi	5	姨	yí	6
和	hé, huo	5	国	guó	5	**夊**	**suī**	**35**	娘	niáng	7
呼	hū	5	图	tú	5	复	fù	6	娱	yú	7
咖	kā	5	圆	yuán	7	夏	xià	7	婚	hūn	8
命	mìng	5	圈	quān	8	**夕**	**xī**	**36**	婆	pó	8
呢	ne	5	**土**	**tǔ**	**32**	夕	xī	0	媒	méi	9
味	wèi	5	土	tǔ	0	外	wài	2	嫌	xián	10
周	zhōu	5	圣	shèng	2	多	duō	3	**子**	**zǐ**	**39**
哈	hā	6	场	chǎng	3	夜	yè	5	子	zi, zǐ	0
咳	ké	6	地	de, dì	3	够	gòu	8	存	cún	3
骂	mà	6	在	zài	3	**大**	**dà**	**37**	孙	sūn	3
品	pǐn	6	坏	huài	4	大	dà	0	字	zì	3
哇	wā	6	圾	jī	4	夫	fū	1	孤	gū	5
咸	xián	6	坚	jiān	4	太	tài	1	季	jì	5
响	xiǎng	6	均	jūn	4	天	tiān	1	学	xué	5
咬	yǎo	6	块	kuài	4	失	shī	2	孩	hái	6
咱	zán	6	址	zhǐ	4	头	tóu	2	**宀**	**mián**	**40**
咨	zī	6	坐	zuò	4	央	yāng	2	宁	níng	2

它	tā	2	尝	cháng	6	席	xí	7	弹	dàn, tán	8
安	ān	3	辉	huī	9	常	cháng	8	强	qiáng, qiǎng	9
守	shǒu	3	**尢 wāng**		**43**	幅	fú	9	**彐 jì**		**58**
宇	yǔ	3	尤	yóu	1	帽	mào	9	归	guī	2
宅	zhái	3	就	jiù	9	幕	mù	11	寻	xún	3
宏	hóng	4	**尸 shī**		**44**	**干 gān**		**51**	灵	líng	4
完	wán	4	尺	chǐ	1	干	gàn, gān	0	录	lù	5
宝	bǎo	5	尽	jǐn	3	平	píng	2	**彡 shān**		**59**
宠	chǒng	5	层	céng	4	年	nián	3	形	xíng	4
定	dìng	5	局	jú	4	并	bìng	5	须	xū	6
官	guān	5	尾	wěi	4	幸	xìng	5	彩	cǎi	8
审	shěn	5	届	jiè	5	**幺 yāo**		**52**	影	yǐng	12
实	shí	5	居	jū	5	乡	xiāng	0	**彳 chì**		**60**
宜	yí	5	屏	píng	6	幻	huàn	1	彻	chè	4
宗	zōng	5	屋	wū	6	幼	yòu	2	彼	bǐ	5
宫	gōng	6	展	zhǎn	7	幽	yōu	6	径	jìng	5
客	kè	6	属	shǔ	9	**广 guǎng**		**53**	往	wǎng	5
室	shì	6	**山 shān**		**46**	广	guǎng	0	征	zhēng	5
宣	xuān	6	山	shān	0	庆	qìng	3	待	dài, dāi	6
宾	bīn	7	岁	suì	3	庄	zhuāng	3	很	hěn	6
害	hài	7	岛	dǎo	4	床	chuáng	4	律	lǜ	6
家	jiā	7	岗	gǎng	4	库	kù	4	徒	tú	7
宽	kuān	7	岸	àn	5	序	xù	4	得	de, dé, děi	8
容	róng	7	峰	fēng	7	应	yīng, yìng	4	循	xún	9
宴	yàn	7	崇	chóng	8	底	dǐ	5	微	wēi	10
寄	jì	8	**工 gōng**		**48**	店	diàn	5	德	dé	12
密	mì	8	工	gōng	0	废	fèi	5	**心 xīn 忄⺗**		**61**
宿	sù	8	巨	jù	2	府	fǔ	5	心	xīn	0
富	fù	9	巧	qiǎo	2	度	dù	6	必	bì	1
寒	hán	9	左	zuǒ	2	庭	tíng	7	忆	yì	1
察	chá	11	巩	gǒng	3	座	zuò	7	忙	máng	3
赛	sài	11	差	chà, chā, chāi	7	康	kāng	8	忍	rěn	3
寸 cùn		**41**	**己 jǐ**		**49**	**廴 yǐn**		**54**	忘	wàng	3
寸	cùn	0	己	jǐ	0	延	yán	4	志	zhì	3
对	duì	2	已	yǐ	0	建	jiàn	6	忽	hū	4
导	dǎo	3	巴	bā	1	**廾 gǒng**		**55**	怀	huái	4
寺	sì	3	**巾 jīn**		**50**	开	kāi	1	快	kuài	4
寿	shòu	4	巾	jīn	0	异	yì	3	念	niàn	4
封	fēng	6	币	bì	1	弄	nòng	4	态	tài	4
射	shè	7	布	bù	2	弃	qì	4	忧	yōu	4
尊	zūn	9	市	shì	2	**弋 yì**		**56**	忠	zhōng	4
小 xiǎo ⺌⺍		**42**	帅	shuài	2	式	shì	3	怪	guài	5
小	xiǎo	0	师	shī	3	**弓 gōng**		**57**	急	jí	5
少	shǎo, shào	1	希	xī	4	引	yǐn	1	怜	lián	5
尔	ěr	2	帘	lián	5	弟	dì	4	怒	nù	5
当	dāng, dàng	3	带	dài	6	张	zhāng	4	怕	pà	5
尖	jiān	3	帝	dì	6	弯	wān	6	思	sī	5
尚	shàng	5	帮	bāng	7	弱	ruò	7	性	xìng	5

怨	yuàn	5	戴	dài	14	拍	pāi	5	援	yuán	9
怎	zěn	5	**户 hù　户户 63**			披	pī	5	摆	bǎi	10
恶	è	6	户	hù	0	抬	tái	5	搬	bān	10
恩	ēn	6	房	fáng	4	拖	tuō	5	搭	dā	10
恨	hèn	6	所	suǒ	4	押	yā	5	搞	gǎo	10
恢	huī	6	扁	biǎn	5	拥	yōng	5	摄	shè	10
恐	kǒng	6	扇	shān, shàn	6	择	zé	5	摇	yáo	10
恋	liàn	6	**手 shǒu　扌手 64**			招	zhāo	5	摩	mó	11
虑	lǜ	6	才	cái	0	按	àn	6	摸	mō	11
恰	qià	6	手	shǒu	0	持	chí	6	摔	shuāi	11
息	xī	6	扎	zhā	1	挡	dǎng	6	摘	zhāi	11
患	huàn	7	打	dǎ, dá	2	挂	guà	6	播	bō	12
悔	huǐ	7	扑	pū	2	挥	huī	6	撤	chè	12
您	nín	7	扔	rēng	2	挤	jǐ	6	撑	chēng	12
悄	qiāo	7	扣	kòu	3	括	kuò	6	撞	zhuàng	12
悟	wù	7	扩	kuò	3	拿	ná	6	操	cāo	13
悉	xī	7	扫	sǎo	3	拼	pīn	6	擦	cā	14
悬	xuán	7	托	tuō	3	拾	shí	6	**支 zhī 65**		
悲	bēi	8	扬	yáng	3	挑	tiāo, tiǎo	6	支	zhī	0
惨	cǎn	8	执	zhí	3	挖	wā	6	**攴 pū　攵 66**		
惯	guàn	8	把	bǎ	4	挣	zhèng	6	收	shōu	2
惠	huì	8	扮	bàn	4	指	zhǐ	6	改	gǎi	3
惊	jīng	8	报	bào	4	挨	āi, ái	7	攻	gōng	3
情	qíng	8	抄	chāo	4	捕	bǔ	7	放	fàng	4
惜	xī	8	承	chéng	4	换	huàn	7	政	zhèng	4
愁	chóu	9	扶	fú	4	捡	jiǎn	7	故	gù	5
愤	fèn	9	护	hù	4	捐	juān	7	效	xiào	6
感	gǎn	9	技	jì	4	损	sǔn	7	教	jiào, jiāo	7
想	xiǎng	9	抗	kàng	4	挺	tǐng	7	救	jiù	7
意	yì	9	扭	niǔ	4	振	zhèn	7	敏	mǐn	7
愉	yú	9	批	pī	4	捉	zhuō	7	敢	gǎn	8
慌	huāng	10	抢	qiǎng	4	措	cuò	8	散	sàn, sǎn	8
愿	yuàn	10	扰	rǎo	4	掉	diào	8	敬	jìng	9
慧	huì	11	投	tóu	4	接	jiē	8	数	shù	9
慢	màn	11	找	zhǎo	4	据	jù	8	敲	qiāo	10
慰	wèi	11	折	zhé	4	控	kòng	8	整	zhěng	11
懂	dǒng	13	抓	zhuā	4	排	pái	8	**文 wén 67**		
憾	hàn	13	拔	bá	5	授	shòu	8	文	wén	0
懒	lǎn	13	拜	bài	5	探	tàn	8	**斗 dǒu 68**		
戈 gē 62			抱	bào	5	掏	tāo	8	斗	dòu	0
戏	xì	2	拨	bō	5	推	tuī	8	料	liào	6
成	chéng	3	拆	chāi	5	掌	zhǎng	8	斜	xié	7
戒	jiè	3	抽	chōu	5	插	chā	9	**斤 jīn 69**		
我	wǒ	3	担	dān	5	揭	jiē	9	斤	jīn	0
或	huò	4	抵	dǐ	5	描	miáo	9	断	duàn	7
战	zhàn	5	拐	guǎi	5	搜	sōu	9	新	xīn	9
载	zài	6	拒	jù	5	提	tí	9	**方 fāng 70**		
截	jié	10	拉	lā	5	握	wò	9	方	fāng	0

施	shī	5	**月**	**yuè**	**74**	柱	zhù	5	死	sǐ	2
旅	lǚ	6	月	yuè	0	案	àn	6	残	cán	5
旁	páng	6	有	yǒu	2	档	dàng	6	殊	shū	6
旋	xuán	7	服	fú	4	格	gé	6	殖	zhí	8
族	zú	7	朋	péng	4	根	gēn	6	**殳**	**shū**	**79**
旗	qí	10	朗	lǎng	7	核	hé	6	段	duàn	5
无	**wú**	**无 71**	望	wàng	7	桥	qiáo	6	毁	huǐ	9
无	wú	0	朝	cháo	8	桃	táo	6	**毋**	**wú**	**母 80**
既	jì	5	期	qī	8	校	xiào	6	母	mǔ	1
日	**rì**	**72**	**木**	**mù**	**75**	样	yàng	6	每	měi	3
日	rì	0	木	mù	0	桌	zhuō	6	毒	dú	4
旦	dàn	1	本	běn	1	检	jiǎn	7	**比**	**bǐ**	**81**
旧	jiù	1	末	mò	1	梨	lí	7	比	bǐ	0
早	zǎo	2	术	shù	1	梁	liáng	7	毕	bì	2
时	shí	3	未	wèi	1	梅	méi	7	**毛**	**máo**	**82**
畅	chàng	4	朵	duǒ	2	梦	mèng	7	毛	máo	0
昌	chāng	4	机	jī	2	梯	tī	7	毫	háo	7
昏	hūn	4	权	quán	2	械	xiè	7	**氏**	**shì**	**83**
明	míng	4	杀	shā	2	棒	bàng	8	民	mín	1
旺	wàng	4	杂	zá	2	棵	kē	8	**气**	**qì**	**84**
易	yì	4	材	cái	3	棉	mián	8	气	qì	0
春	chūn	5	村	cūn	3	森	sēn	8	氛	fēn	4
是	shì	5	杆	gān	3	椅	yǐ	8	氧	yǎng	6
显	xiǎn	5	极	jí	3	植	zhí	8	**水**	**shuǐ**	**氵氺 85**
星	xīng	5	来	lái	3	楚	chǔ	9	水	shuǐ	0
映	yìng	5	李	lǐ	3	概	gài	9	永	yǒng	1
昨	zuó	5	束	shù	3	楼	lóu	9	汉	hàn	2
晒	shài	6	条	tiáo	3	榜	bǎng	10	汇	huì	2
晓	xiǎo	6	板	bǎn	4	横	héng	11	求	qiú	2
晕	yūn, yùn	6	杯	bēi	4	模	mó	11	汁	zhī	2
晨	chén	7	构	gòu	4	**欠**	**qiàn**	**76**	池	chí	3
晚	wǎn	7	果	guǒ	4	欠	qiàn	0	汗	hàn	3
景	jǐng	8	杰	jié	4	次	cì	2	江	jiāng	3
普	pǔ	8	林	lín	4	欢	huān	2	汤	tāng	3
晴	qíng	8	枪	qiāng	4	欣	xīn	4	污	wū	3
暑	shǔ	8	松	sōng	4	欲	yù	7	沉	chén	4
暂	zàn	8	析	xī	4	款	kuǎn	8	沟	gōu	4
智	zhì	8	枝	zhī	4	欺	qī	8	没	méi, mò	4
暗	àn	9	标	biāo	5	歇	xiē	9	汽	qì	4
暖	nuǎn	9	查	chá	5	歌	gē	10	沙	shā	4
暴	bào	11	柴	chái	5	歉	qiàn	10	波	bō	5
曰	**yuē**	**73**	柜	guì	5	**止**	**zhǐ**	**77**	法	fǎ	5
电	diàn	1	架	jià	5	止	zhǐ	0	泛	fàn	5
曲	qū, qǔ	2	栏	lán	5	正	zhèng	1	河	hé	5
更	gèng, gēng	3	某	mǒu	5	此	cǐ	2	泪	lèi	5
曾	céng	8	染	rǎn	5	步	bù	3	泥	ní	5
替	tì	8	柿	shì	5	武	wǔ	4	泡	pào	5
最	zuì	8	树	shù	5	**歹**	**dǎi**	**歺 78**	泼	pō	5

浅	qiǎn	5	漫	màn	11	**片**	**piàn**	**91**	甚	shèn	4
泉	quán	5	漠	mò	11	片	piàn	0	甜	tián	6
沿	yán	5	漂	piào	11	版	bǎn	4	**生**	**shēng**	**100**
泳	yǒng	5	演	yǎn	11	牌	pái	8	生	shēng	0
油	yóu	5	潮	cháo	12	**牙**	**yá**	**92**	**用**	**yòng**	**101**
治	zhì	5	潜	qián	12	牙	yá	0	用	yòng	0
注	zhù	5	激	jī	13	**牛**	**niú** 牜牛	**93**	**田**	**tián**	**102**
测	cè	6	澡	zǎo	13	牛	niú	0	甲	jiǎ	0
洞	dòng	6	**火**	**huǒ** 灬	**86**	牢	láo	3	申	shēn	0
洪	hóng	6	火	huǒ	0	物	wù	4	田	tián	0
活	huó	6	灭	miè	1	牲	shēng	5	由	yóu	0
济	jì	6	灯	dēng	2	特	tè	6	男	nán	2
洁	jié	6	灰	huī	2	牺	xī	6	画	huà	3
流	liú	6	灾	zāi	3	**犬**	**quǎn** 犭	**94**	界	jiè	4
浓	nóng	6	炒	chǎo	4	犯	fàn	2	留	liú	5
派	pài	6	炉	lú	4	状	zhuàng	3	略	lüè	6
洒	sǎ	6	炎	yán	4	狂	kuáng	4	番	fān	7
洗	xǐ	6	点	diǎn	5	犹	yóu	4	**疋**	**pǐ** 疋	**103**
洋	yáng	6	烂	làn	5	狗	gǒu	5	疑	yí	9
浮	fú	7	炼	liàn	5	独	dú	6	**疒**	**nè**	**104**
海	hǎi	7	炮	pào	5	狠	hěn	6	疗	liáo	2
浪	làng	7	炸	zhà	5	猜	cāi	8	疯	fēng	4
润	rùn	7	烦	fán	6	猛	měng	8	病	bìng	5
涉	shè	7	烤	kǎo	6	猴	hóu	9	疾	jí	5
消	xiāo	7	烈	liè	6	猫	māo	9	疼	téng	5
涨	zhǎng, zhàng	7	热	rè	6	献	xiàn	9	症	zhèng	5
淡	dàn	8	烧	shāo	6	猪	zhū	9	痛	tòng	7
混	hùn	8	烟	yān	6	**玄**	**xuán**	**95**	瘦	shòu	10
渐	jiàn	8	焦	jiāo	8	率	lǜ	6	**癶**	**bō**	**105**
清	qīng	8	然	rán	8	**玉**	**yù** 王	**96**	登	dēng	7
深	shēn	8	煮	zhǔ	8	王	wáng	0	**白**	**bái**	**106**
添	tiān	8	煤	méi	9	玉	yù	0	白	bái	0
液	yè	8	照	zhào	9	环	huán	4	百	bǎi	1
渡	dù	9	熊	xióng	10	玩	wán	4	的	de, dí, dì	3
港	gǎng	9	熟	shú	11	现	xiàn	4	皇	huáng	4
湖	hú	9	燃	rán	12	玻	bō	5	**皮**	**pí**	**107**
渴	kě	9	爆	bào	15	珍	zhēn	5	皮	pí	0
渠	qú	9	**爪**	**zhǎo** 爫	**87**	班	bān	6	**皿**	**mǐn**	**108**
湿	shī	9	爬	pá	4	珠	zhū	6	盆	pén	4
湾	wān	9	爱	ài	6	理	lǐ	7	监	jiān	5
温	wēn	9	**父**	**fù**	**88**	球	qiú	8	盐	yán	5
游	yóu	9	父	fù	0	琴	qín	8	益	yì	5
滑	huá	10	爷	yé	2	璃	lí	11	盗	dào	6
满	mǎn	10	爸	bà	4	**瓜**	**guā**	**97**	盖	gài	6
源	yuán	10	**爻**	**yáo**	**89**	瓜	guā	0	盒	hé	6
滴	dī	11	爽	shuǎng	7	**瓦**	**wǎ**	**98**	盘	pán	6
滚	gǔn	11	**爿**	**qiáng** 丬	**90**	瓶	píng	6	盛	shèng	7
漏	lòu	11	将	jiāng	6	**甘**	**gān**	**99**	盟	méng	8

目 mù		109	福 fú		9	简 jiǎn		7	绘 huì		6
目	mù	0	肉 róu		114	筷 kuài		7	结	jié, jiē	6
盲	máng	3	离	lí	6	签	qiān	7	绝	jué	6
直	zhí	3	禾 hé		115	管	guǎn	8	络	luò	6
盾	dùn	4	私	sī	2	算	suàn	8	绕	rào	6
看	kàn, kān	4	秀	xiù	2	箭	jiàn	9	绒	róng	6
盼	pàn	4	科	kē	4	篇	piān	9	统	tǒng	6
省	shěng	4	秒	miǎo	4	箱	xiāng	9	继	jì	7
相	xiāng, xiàng	4	秋	qiū	4	篮	lán	10	绩	jī	8
眠	mián	5	种	zhǒng, zhòng	4	籍	jí	14	绿	lǜ	8
真	zhēn	5	称	chēng	5	米 mǐ		119	维	wéi	8
眼	yǎn	6	积	jī	5	米	mǐ	0	绪	xù	8
着	zhe, zháo	6	秘	mì	5	粉	fěn	4	续	xù	8
督	dū	8	租	zū	5	粗	cū	5	综	zōng	8
睛	jīng	8	移	yí	6	粥	zhōu	6	编	biān	9
睡	shuì	8	程	chéng	7	粮	liáng	7	缓	huǎn	9
瞧	qiáo	12	稍	shāo	7	精	jīng	8	缘	yuán	9
矛 máo		110	税	shuì	7	糊	hú	9	繁	fán	11
矛	máo	0	稳	wěn	9	糕	gāo	10	缩	suō	11
矢 shǐ		111	稿	gǎo	10	糖	táng	10	缶 fǒu		121
知	zhī	3	穴 xué		116	糟	zāo	11	缺	quē	4
短	duǎn	7	究	jiū	2	糸 mì 丝		120	网 wǎng 罒		122
矮	ǎi	8	穷	qióng	2	系	xì, jì	1	网	wǎng	0
石 shí		112	空	kōng, kòng	3	纠	jiū	2	罚	fá	4
石	shí	0	穿	chuān	4	红	hóng	3	罢	bà	5
矿	kuàng	3	突	tū	4	级	jí	3	置	zhì	8
码	mǎ	3	窗	chuāng	7	纪	jì	3	罪	zuì	8
础	chǔ	5	立 lì		117	约	yuē	3	羊 yáng		123
破	pò	5	立	lì	0	纯	chún	4	羊	yáng	0
硕	shuò	6	产	chǎn	1	纷	fēn	4	美	měi	3
研	yán	6	亲	qīn	4	纲	gāng	4	群	qún	7
确	què	7	竞	jìng	5	紧	jǐn	4	羽 yǔ		124
硬	yìng	7	站	zhàn	5	纳	nà	4	羽	yǔ	0
碍	ài	8	竟	jìng	6	素	sù	4	翻	fān	12
碰	pèng	8	章	zhāng	6	索	suǒ	4	耀	yào	14
碎	suì	8	童	tóng	7	纸	zhǐ	4	老 lǎo 耂		125
碗	wǎn	8	端	duān	9	纵	zòng	4	考	kǎo	0
磨	mó	11	竹 zhú ⺮		118	经	jīng	5	老	lǎo	0
示 shì 礻		113	竹	zhú	0	累	lèi	5	者	zhě	4
示	shì	0	笔	bǐ	4	练	liàn	5	而 ér		126
礼	lǐ	1	笑	xiào	4	绍	shào	5	而	ér	0
社	shè	3	笨	bèn	5	细	xì	5	耐	nài	3
神	shén	5	第	dì	5	线	xiàn	5	耒 lěi		127
祝	zhù	5	符	fú	5	织	zhī	5	耗	hào	4
祖	zǔ	5	策	cè	6	终	zhōng	5	耳 ěr		128
票	piào	6	答	dá, dā	6	紫	zǐ	5	耳	ěr	0
祥	xiáng	6	等	děng	6	组	zǔ	5	聊	liáo	5
禁	jìn	8	筑	zhù	6	给	gěi, jǐ	6	职	zhí	5

联	lián	6	至	zhì	0	薪	xīn	13	**言** yán 讠言	**149**
聘	pìn	7	致	zhì	3	藏	cáng	14	言 yán	0
聚	jù	8	**舌** shé	**135**	薯	shǔ	14	订 dìng	2
聪	cōng	9	舌	shé	0	**虍** hū	**141**	计 jì	2
聿 yù 聿	**129**	舍	shě	2	虎	hǔ	2	认 rèn	2
肃	sù	4	敌	dí	4	虚	xū	5	记 jì	3
肉 ròu 月	**130**	舒	shū	6	**虫** huǐ	**142**	让 ràng	3
肉	ròu	0	辞	cí	7	虫	chóng	0	讨 tǎo	3
肌	jī	2	**舛** chuǎn	**136**	虽	suī	3	训 xùn	3
肠	cháng	3	舞	wǔ	8	蛋	dàn	5	讯 xùn	3
肚	dù	3	**舟** zhōu	**137**	蛇	shé	5	议 yì	3
肝	gān	3	般	bān	4	融	róng	10	访 fǎng	4
肥	féi	4	航	háng	4	**血** xuè	**143**	讲 jiǎng	4
肺	fèi	4	舰	jiàn	4	血	xuè	0	论 lùn	4
肤	fū	4	船	chuán	5	**行** xíng	**144**	设 shè	4
股	gǔ	4	**艮** gēn	**138**	行	xíng, háng	0	许 xǔ	4
肩	jiān	4	良	liáng	1	街	jiē	6	词 cí	5
肯	kěn	4	**色** sè	**139**	衡	héng	10	评 píng	5
胁	xié	4	色	sè	0	**衣** yī 衤	**145**	识 shí	5
育	yù	4	艳	yàn	4	衣	yī	0	诉 sù	5
肿	zhǒng	4	**艸** cǎo 艹	**140**	补	bǔ	2	译 yì	5
胞	bāo	5	艺	yì	1	表	biǎo	3	诊 zhěn	5
背	bèi, bēi	5	节	jié	2	衬	chèn	3	证 zhèng	5
胆	dǎn	5	花	huā	4	衫	shān	3	诚 chéng	6
胡	hú	5	苏	sū	4	被	bèi	5	该 gāi	6
胖	pàng	5	范	fàn	5	袋	dài	5	话 huà	6
胜	shèng	5	茄	qié	5	袜	wà	5	试 shì	6
胃	wèi	5	苦	kǔ	5	袖	xiù	5	诗 shī	6
脆	cuì	6	苹	píng	5	裁	cái	6	详 xiáng	6
胶	jiāo	6	若	ruò	5	裂	liè	6	询 xún	6
脑	nǎo	6	英	yīng	5	装	zhuāng	6	誉 yù	6
能	néng	6	草	cǎo	6	裤	kù	7	说 shuō	7
胸	xiōng	6	茶	chá	6	裙	qún	7	误 wù	7
脏	zàng	6	荣	róng	6	裹	guǒ	8	语 yǔ	7
脚	jiǎo	7	药	yào	6	**襾** xī 西覀	**146**	诞 dàn	8
脸	liǎn	7	获	huò	7	西	xī	0	调 diào, tiáo	8
脱	tuō	7	菜	cài	8	要	yào, yāo	3	读 dú	8
腐	fǔ	8	菌	jūn	8	**見** jiàn 见	**147**	课 kè	8
脾	pí	8	葡	táo	8	见	jiàn	0	谅 liàng	8
腰	yāo	9	营	yíng	8	观	guān	2	诺 nuò	8
腿	tuǐ	10	著	zhe, zhù	8	规	guī	4	请 qǐng	8
膜	mó	11	落	luò, là	9	视	shì	4	谁 shéi / shuí	8
臣 chén	**131**	葡	pú	9	觉	jué, jiào	5	谈 tán	8
卧	wò	2	蓝	lán	10	览	lǎn	5	谊 yì	8
自 zì	**132**	蒙	méng, měng	10	**角** jiǎo	**148**	诸 zhū	8
自	zì	0	蔬	shū	11	角	jiǎo, jué	0	谋 móu	9
臭	chòu	4	蕉	jiāo	12	触	chù	6	谓 wèi	9
至 zhì	**133**	薄	báo, bó	13	解	jiě	6	谐 xié	9

谦	qiān	10	**足 zú**	**⻊**	**157**	进	jìn	4	醋	cù	8
谢	xiè	10	足	zú	0	连	lián	4	醉	zuì	8
警	jǐng	13	跃	yuè	4	违	wéi	4	醒	xǐng	9
谷 gǔ		**150**	跌	diē	5	迎	yíng	4	**采 biàn**		**165**
谷	gǔ	0	践	jiàn	5	远	yuǎn	4	采	cǎi	1
豆 dòu		**151**	距	jù	5	运	yùn	4	释	shì	5
豆	dòu	0	跑	pǎo	5	这	zhè	4	**里 lǐ**		**166**
豕 shǐ		**152**	跟	gēn	6	迫	pò	5	里	lǐ	0
象	xiàng	5	跪	guì	6	述	shù	5	重	zhòng, chóng	2
豪	háo	7	跨	kuà	6	迷	mí	6	野	yě	4
豫	yù	9	路	lù	6	适	shì	6	量	liàng, liáng	5
豸 zhì		**153**	跳	tiào	6	送	sòng	6	**金 jīn**	**钅钅**	**167**
貌	mào	7	踩	cǎi	8	逃	táo	6	金	jīn	0
貝 bèi	**贝**	**154**	踏	tà	8	退	tuì	6	针	zhēn	2
贝	bèi	0	踢	tī	8	选	xuǎn	6	钢	gāng	4
负	fù	2	蹈	dǎo	10	追	zhuī	6	钟	zhōng	4
财	cái	3	蹲	dūn	12	递	dì	7	鉴	jiàn	5
贡	gòng	3	**身 shēn**		**158**	逛	guàng	7	铃	líng	5
败	bài	4	身	shēn	0	速	sù	7	钱	qián	5
购	gòu	4	躲	duǒ	6	通	tōng	7	铅	qiān	5
贯	guàn	4	躺	tǎng	8	透	tòu	7	铁	tiě	5
货	huò	4	**車 chē**	**车**	**159**	途	tú	7	钻	zuān	5
贫	pín	4	车	chē	0	造	zào	7	铜	tóng	6
责	zé	4	轨	guǐ	2	逐	zhú	7	银	yín	6
账	zhàng	4	军	jūn	2	逻	luó	8	锋	fēng	7
贷	dài	5	轮	lún	4	逼	bī	9	锅	guō	7
费	fèi	5	软	ruǎn	4	遍	biàn	9	铺	pù, pū	7
贵	guì	5	转	zhuǎn, zhuàn	4	道	dào	9	锁	suǒ	7
贺	hè	5	轻	qīng	5	遗	yí	9	销	xiāo	7
贸	mào	5	较	jiào	6	遇	yù	9	错	cuò	8
贴	tiē	5	辅	fǔ	7	遭	zāo	11	键	jiàn	8
资	zī	6	辆	liàng	7	遵	zūn	12	锻	duàn	9
赌	dǔ	8	辑	jí	9	避	bì	13	镇	zhèn	10
赔	péi	8	输	shū	9	邀	yāo	13	镜	jìng	11
赏	shǎng	8	**辛 xīn**		**160**	**邑 yì**	**⻏**	**163**	**長 cháng**	**长**	**168**
赖	lài	9	辛	xīn	0	那	nà	4	长	zhǎng, cháng	0
赚	zhuàn	10	辣	là	7	邻	lín	5	**門 mén**	**门**	**169**
赞	zàn	12	辩	biàn	9	邮	yóu	5	门	mén	0
赠	zèng	12	**辵 chuò**	**辶**	**162**	郊	jiāo	6	闪	shǎn	2
走 zǒu	**走**	**156**	边	biān	2	郎	láng	6	闭	bì	3
走	zǒu	0	达	dá	3	部	bù	8	闯	chuǎng	3
赶	gǎn	3	过	guò	3	都	dōu, dū	9	问	wèn	3
起	qǐ	3	迁	qiān	3	**酉 yǒu**		**164**	间	jiān, jiàn	4
超	chāo	5	迅	xùn	3	酒	jiǔ	3	闲	xián	4
趋	qū	5	迟	chí	4	配	pèi	3	闹	nào	5
越	yuè	5	返	fǎn	4	酱	jiàng	6	闻	wén	6
趣	qù	8	还	hái, huán	4	酷	kù	7	阅	yuè	7
趟	tàng	8	近	jìn	4	酸	suān	7	阔	kuò	9

阜 fù	阝	170	頁 yè	页	181	魚 yú	鱼	195
队	duì	2	页	yè	0	鱼	yú	0
防	fáng	4	顶	dǐng	2	鲜	xiān	6
阶	jiē	4	顺	shùn	3	鳥 niǎo	鸟	196
阳	yáng	4	项	xiàng	3	鸟	niǎo	0
阴	yīn	4	顿	dùn	4	鸡	jī	2
阵	zhèn	4	顾	gù	4	鸭	yā	5
阿	ā	5	顽	wán	4	麥 mài	麦	199
附	fù	5	预	yù	4	麦	mài	0
际	jì	5	领	lǐng	5	麻 má		200
陆	lù	5	频	pín	7	麻	má	0
阻	zǔ	5	颗	kē	8	黃 huáng		201
降	jiàng	6	额	é	9	黄	huáng	0
限	xiàn	6	题	tí	9	黑 hēi		203
除	chú	7	颜	yán	9	黑	hēi	0
险	xiǎn	7	風 fēng	风	182	默	mò	4
院	yuàn	7	风	fēng	0	鼓 gǔ		207
陪	péi	8	食 shí	饣食	184	鼓	gǔ	0
陷	xiàn	8	食	shí	0	鼠 shǔ		208
隐	yǐn	9	饭	fàn	4	鼠	shǔ	0
隔	gé	10	饮	yǐn	4	鼻 bí		209
随	suí	10	饱	bǎo	5	鼻	bí	0
障	zhàng	11	饰	shì	5	齊 qí	齐	210
隹 zhuī		172	饼	bǐng	6	齐	qí	0
集	jí	4	饺	jiǎo	6	齒 chǐ	齿	211
雄	xióng	4	餐	cān	7	龄	líng	5
雨 yǔ		173	饿	è	7	龍 lóng	龙	212
雨	yǔ	0	馆	guǎn	8	龙	lóng	0
雪	xuě	3	馒	mán	11			
雷	léi	5	首 shǒu		185			
零	líng	5	首	shǒu	0			
需	xū	6	香 xiāng		186			
震	zhèn	7	香	xiāng	0			
露	lù, lòu	12	馬 mǎ	马	187			
青 qīng	青	174	马	mǎ	0			
青	qīng	0	驾	jià	5			
静	jìng	6	驶	shǐ	5			
非 fēi		175	驻	zhù	5			
非	fēi	0	骄	jiāo	6			
辈	bèi	4	验	yàn	7			
靠	kào	7	骑	qí	8			
面 miàn	靣	176	骗	piàn	9			
面	miàn	0	骨 gǔ		188			
革 gé		177	骨	gǔ	0			
革	gé	0	高 gāo	高	189			
鞋	xié	6	高	gāo	0			
音 yīn		180	鬼 guǐ		194			
音	yīn	0	鬼	guǐ	0			

Main Entries

- Radicals in large **purple** type with radical number on right.
- Characters (子 zì): In **black** type. Duo Yin Zi shown by **red-brown** type and asterisk. Radical Code on right (e.g. 一 1.0) shows radical and extra strokes needed to write character.
- Words (词 cí): In smaller **dark blue**. Ordered by place of main character, number of characters in word, and pinyin. HSK level on far right side in **grey**.
- See introduction for more information about entries

Rad/子/词	Pinyin		English	Alt Rad	Rad Code	HSK
一	**yī**		one			1
一	yī		one, I, single		一 1.0	1
一	yī	num.	one, I, single, a (article), as soon as, entire, whole, all, throughout			1
一般	yībān	adj.	same, ordinary, so-so, common, general, generally, in general			2
一半	yībàn	num.	half			1
一边	yībiān	n.	one side, either side, on the one hand, on the other hand, doing while			1
一带	yīdài	n.	region, district			5
一代	yīdài	n.	generation			6
一旦	yīdàn	adv.	in case (sth happens), if, once (sth happens, then...), when, in a short time, in one day			5
一道	yīdào	adv.	together			6
一定	yīdìng	adv.	surely, certainly, necessarily, fixed, a certain (extent etc), given, particular, must			2
一番	yīfān	n.	one kind, one time, once			6
一共	yīgòng	adv.	altogether			2
一贯	yīguàn	adj.	consistent, constant, from start to finish, all along, persistent			6
一流	yīliú	adj.	top quality, front ranking			5
一路	yīlù	adv.	the whole journey, all the way, going the same way, going in the same direction, of the same kind			5
一律	yīlǜ	adj.	same, uniformly, all, without exception			4
一齐	yīqí	adv.	at the same time, simultaneously			6
一起	yīqǐ	adv.	in the same place, together, with, altogether (in total)			1
一切	• yīqiè	pro.	everything, every, all			3
一身	yīshēn	n.	whole body, from head to toe, single person, a suit of clothes			5
一生	yīshēng	n.	all one's life, throughout one's life			2
一时	yīshí	n.	a period of time, a while, for a short while, temporary, momentary, at the same time			6
一同	yītóng	adv.	along, together			6
一向	yīxiàng	adv.	always (previously), a period of time in the recent past			5
一些	yīxiē	m.w.	some, a few, a little, (following an adjective) slightly ...er			1
一行	yīxíng	n.	group travelling together, party, delegation			6
一样	yīyàng	adj.	same, like, equal to, the same as, just like			1
一再	yīzài	adv.	repeatedly			4

一直	yīzhí		adv.	straight (in a straight line), continuously, always, from the beginning of ... up to ..., all along	2
一致	yīzhì		adj.	unanimous, identical (views or opinions)	4
一句话	yī jù huà		phr.	in a word, in short	5
一辈子	yībèizi		n.	(for) a lifetime	5
一部分	- yībùfen		n.	portion, part of, subset	2
一次性	yīcìxìng		adj.	one-off (offer), one-time, single-use, disposable (goods)	6
一点点	yīdiǎndiǎn		n.	a little bit	2
一点儿	yīdiǎnr		n.	a bit, a few, a little, erhua variant of 一点 yīdiǎn	1
一方面	yīfāngmiàn		conj.	on the one hand..., on the other hand...	3
一会儿	yīhuìr	+	n.	a little while	1
一会儿	yīhuìr	+	adv.	in a moment, now...now...	2
一口气	yīkǒuqì		n.	one breath, in one breath, at a stretch	5
一块儿	yīkuàir		n.	the same place, in company, together, one, erhua variant of 一块 yīkuài	1
一路上	- yīlùshang	+	phr.	along the way, the whole way, (fig.) the whole time	6
一下儿	yīxiàr	+	n.	one time, once	1
一下儿	yīxiàr	+	adv.	in a while, all of a sudden, all at once	5
一下子	yīxiàzi		adv.	in a short while, all at once, all of a sudden	5
一般来说	yībānláishuō		phr.	generally speaking	4
一路平安	yīlùpíng'ān		vb.	to have a pleasant journey, Bon voyage!	2
一路顺风	yīlùshùnfēng		vb.	have a good trip (idiom)	2
一模一样	yīmóyīyàng		phr.	exactly the same (idiom), carbon copy	6
单一	dānyī		adj.	single, only, sole	5
如一	rúyī		vb.	to be consistent, to be the same	6
同一	tóngyī		adj.	identical, the same	6
统一	tǒngyī		vb.	to unify, to unite, to integrate	4
万一	wànyī		n.	just in case, if by any chance, contingency	4
唯一	wéiyī		adj.	only, sole	5
之一	zhī yī		n.	one of (sth), one out of a multitude, one (third, quarter, percent etc)	4
不一定	bù yīdìng		adv.	not necessarily, maybe	2
进一步	jìn yī bù		adv.	one step further, to move forward a step, further onwards	3
有一点	yǒuyīdiǎn		n.	a little, somewhat	2
不一会儿	bùyīhuìr		phr.	in no time at all	2
另一方面	lìngyīfāngmiàn		phr.	on the other hand, another aspect	3

七	**qī**		seven, 7	一 1.1	1
七	qī		num.	seven, 7	1
三	**sān**		three, 3	一 1.2	1
三	sān		num.	three, 3, surname San	1
三明治	sānmíngzhì		n.	sandwich (loanword)	6
再三	zàisān		adv.	over and over again, again and again	4
上	**shàng**		on top, upon, above	一 1.2	1
上	shàng		adj.	on top, upon, above, upper, to get on, to go up, to attend	1
上当	• shàng dàng		vb.	to be taken in (by sb's deceit), to be fooled, to be duped	6
上来	shàng lái		vb.	to come up, to approach, (verb complement indicating success)	3
上台	shàng tái		vb.	to rise to power (in politics), to go on stage (in the theatre)	6
上学	shàng xué		vb.	to go to school, to attend school	1

上班	shàngbān	vb.	to go to work, to be on duty, to start work, to go to the office	1
上边	- shàngbian	n.	the top, above, overhead, upwards, the top margin, above-mentioned, those higher up	1
上车	shàngchē	vb.	to get on or into (a bus, train, car etc)	1
上次	shàngcì	n.	last time	1
上帝	shàngdì	n.	the Lord on High (ancient China), God (Western)	6
上级	shàngjí	n.	higher authorities, superiors	5
上课	shàngkè	vb.	to go to class, to attend class, to go to teach a class	1
上楼	shànglóu	vb.	to go upstairs	4
上门	shàngmén	vb.	to drop in, to visit, to lock a door, (of a shop) to close, to go and live with one's wife's family, in effect becoming a member of her family	4
上面	- shàngmian	n.	on top of, above-mentioned	3
上去	- shàngqu	vb.	to go up	3
上升	shàngshēng	vb.	to rise, to go up, to ascend	3
上市	shàngshì	vb.	to hit the market (of a new product), to float (a company on the stock market)	6
上网	shàngwǎng	vb.	to go online, to connect to the Internet	1
上午	shàngwǔ	n.	morning	1
上下	shàngxià	n.	up and down, top and bottom, old and new, length, about	5
上演	shàngyǎn	vb.	to screen (a movie), to stage (a play), a screening, a staging	6
上衣	shàngyī	n.	jacket, upper outer garment	3
上涨	shàngzhǎng	vb.	to rise, to go up	5
上周	shàngzhōu	n.	last week	2
上个月	- shàng ge yuè	n.	last month	4
岸上	ànshàng	n.	ashore, on the riverbank	5
车上	chēshàng	n.	in the car	1
穿上	- chuānshang	vb.	to put on (clothes etc)	4
地上	• dìshang	n.	on the ground, on the floor	1
赶上	gǎnshàng	vb.	to keep up with, to catch up with, to overtake, to chance upon, in time for	6
关上	- guānshang	vb.	to close (a door), to turn off (light, electrical equipment etc)	1
加上	jiāshàng	vb.	to put in, to add, to add on, to add into, in addition, on top of that	5
楼上	lóushàng	n.	upstairs	1
路上	- lùshang	n.	on the road, on a journey, road surface	1
马上	mǎshàng	adv.	at once, right away, immediately, on horseback (i.e. by military force)	1
身上	- shēnshang	n.	on the body, at hand, among	1
台上	táishàng	n.	on stage, on the platform	4
天上	tiānshàng	n.	sky, heavens, celestial	2
晚上	- wǎnshang	n.	evening, night	1
网上	wǎngshàng	n.	online	1
向上	xiàngshàng	adv.	upward, up, to advance, to try to improve oneself, to make progress	5
以上	yǐshàng	n.	that level or higher, that amount or more, the above-mentioned, (used to indicate that one has completed one's remarks) that is all	2
早上	- zǎoshang	n.	early morning	1
看上去	- kànshangqu	adv.	it would appear, it seems (that)	3
表面上	- biǎomiàn shang	adv.	outwardly, superficially, on the face of it	6
赶不上	- gǎnbushàng	phr.	can't keep up with, can't catch up with, cannot overtake	6
基本上	- jīběnshang	adv.	basically, on the whole	3
实际上	- shíjì shang	adv.	in fact, in reality, as a matter of fact, in practice	3

事实上	shìshíshàng		adv.	in fact, in reality, actually, as a matter of fact, de facto, ipso facto	3
一路上	- yīlùshang		phr.	along the way, the whole way, (fig.) the whole time	6

万 wàn — ten thousand, innumerable — 1.2 · 2

万	wàn		num.	ten thousand, surname Wan	2
万一	wànyī		n.	just in case, if by any chance, contingency	4
千万	qiānwàn		num.	ten million, countless, many, one must by all means	3

下 xià — down, downwards, below — 1.2 · 1

下	xià	+	n.	down, downwards, below, lower, later, next (week etc), second (of two parts)	1
下	xià	+	m.w.	m.w. stroke, times	2
下班	xià bān		vb.	to finish work, to get off work	1
下课	xià kè		vb.	to finish class, to get out of class, (fig.) (esp. of a sports coach) to be dismissed, to be fired	1
下来	xià lái		vb.	to come down, (completed action marker)	3
下边	- xiàbian		n.	under, the underside, below	1
下车	xiàchē		vb.	to get off or out of (a bus, train, car etc)	1
下次	xiàcì		n.	next time	1
下降	xiàjiàng		vb.	to decline, to drop, to fall, to go down, to decrease	4
下楼	xiàlóu		vb.	to go downstairs	4
下面	- xiàmian		n.	below, next in order, lower level	3
下去	xiàqù		vb.	to go down, to descend, to go on, to continue, (of a servant) to withdraw	3
下午	xiàwǔ		n.	afternoon	1
下雪	xiàxuě		vb.	to snow	2
下雨	xiàyǔ		vb.	to rain	1
下载	xiàzài		vb.	to download	4
下周	xiàzhōu		n.	next week	2
下个月	- xià ge yuè		n.	next month	4
底下	- dǐxia		n.	the location below sth, afterwards	3
地下	• dìxià		n.	underground, subterranean, covert	4
放下	fàngxià		vb.	to lay down, to put down, to let go of, to relinquish, to set aside, to lower (the blinds etc)	2
零下	língxià		adj.	below zero	2
留下	liúxià		vb.	to leave behind, to stay behind, to remain, to keep, not to let (sb) go	2
楼下	lóuxià		n.	downstairs	1
如下	rú xià		vb.	as follows	5
上下	shàngxià		n.	up and down, top and bottom, old and new, length, about	5
剩下	- shèngxia		vb.	to be left over, to be remaining	5
天下	tiānxià		n.	land under heaven, the whole world, the whole of China, realm, rule	6
停下	tíngxià		vb.	to stop	4
以下	yǐxià		n.	that level or lower, that amount or less, the following	2
之下	zhī xià		n.	under, beneath, less than	5
坐下	- zuòxia		vb.	to sit down	1
地下室	• dìxiàshì		n.	basement, cellar	6
接下来	jiēxiàlái		vb.	to accept, to take, next, following	2
一下儿	yīxiàr	+	n.	one time, once	1
一下儿	yīxiàr	+	adv.	in a while, all of a sudden, all at once	5
一下子	yīxiàzi		adv.	in a short while, all at once, all of a sudden	5

丈	**zhàng**		to measure, husband	一 1.2 4
丈夫	- zhàngfu	*n.*	husband	4
不	**bù**		**(negative prefix), not, no**	**一 1.3 1**
不	bù	*adv.*	(negative prefix), not, no	1
不对	bù duì	*adj.*	incorrect, wrong, amiss, abnormal, queer	1
不安	bù'ān	*adj.*	unpeaceful, unstable, uneasy, disturbed, restless, worried	3
不必	bùbì	*adv.*	need not, does not have to, not necessarily	3
不便	bùbiàn	*adj.*	inconvenient, inappropriate, unsuitable, short of cash	6
不曾	bùcéng	*adv.*	hasn't yet, hasn't ever	5
不成	bùchéng	*vb.*	won't do, unable to, (at the end of a rhetorical question) can that be?	6
不错	bùcuò	*adj.*	correct, right, not bad, pretty good	2
不大	bùdà	*adv.*	not very, not too, not often	1
不但	bùdàn	*conj.*	not only (... but also...)	2
不断	bùduàn	*adv.*	unceasing, uninterrupted, continuous, constant	3
不够	bùgòu	*adv.*	not enough, insufficient, inadequate	2
不顾	bùgù	*vb.*	in spite of, regardless of	5
不管	bùguǎn	*conj.*	regardless of, no matter; not to be concerned	4
不光	bùguāng	*adv.*	not the only one, not only	3
不过	bùguò	*adv.*	only, merely, no more than, but, however, anyway (to get back to a previous topic), cannot be more (after adjectival)	2
不见	bùjiàn	*vb.*	not to see, not to meet, to have disappeared, to be missing	6
不禁	bùjìn	*vb.*	to be unable to stop doing sth (can't help doing sth, can't refrain from)	6
不仅	bùjǐn	*adv.*	not only (this one), not just (...) but also	3
不久	bùjiǔ	*adj.*	not long (after), before too long, soon, soon after	2
不利	bùlì	*adj.*	unfavourable, disadvantageous, harmful, detrimental	5
不良	bùliáng	*adj.*	bad, harmful, unhealthy	5
不料	bùliào	*conj.*	unexpectedly, to one's surprise	6
不论	bùlùn	*conj.*	whatever, no matter what (who, how), regardless of, not to discuss	3
不满	bùmǎn	*adj.*	resentful, discontented, dissatisfied	2
不免	bùmiǎn	*adv.*	inevitably	5
不然	bùrán	*conj.*	or else, otherwise, if not, how about ...?	4
不如	bùrú	*vb.*	not equal to, not as good as, inferior to, it would be better to	2
不少	bùshǎo	*adj.*	many, a lot, not few	2
不时	bùshí	*adv.*	from time to time, now and then, occasionally, frequently	5
不太	bùtài	*adj.*	not very ... , not too ...	2
不停	bùtíng	*adv.*	incessant	5
不通	bùtōng	*vb.*	to be obstructed, to be blocked up, to be impassable, to make no sense, to be illogical	6
不同	bùtóng	*adj.*	different, distinct, not the same, not alike	2
不行	bùxíng	*n.*	won't do, be out of the question, be no good, not work, not be capable	2
不幸	bùxìng	*n.*	misfortune, adversity, unfortunate, sad, unfortunately	5
不许	bùxǔ	*vb.*	not to allow, must not, can't	5
不要	bùyào	*adv.*	don't!, must not	2
不易	bùyì	*vb.*	not easy to do sth, difficult, unchanging	5
不用	bùyòng	*adv.*	need not	1
不再	bùzài	*adv.*	no more, no longer	6
不值	bùzhí	*vb.*	to be not worth	6

不止	bùzhǐ	vb.	to not stop; incessantly, without end, more than, not limited to	5
不足	bùzú	adj.	insufficient, lacking, deficiency, not enough, inadequate, not worth, cannot, should not	5
不得不 •	bù dé bù	phr.	have no choice or option but to, cannot but, have to, can't help it, can't avoid	3
不敢当	bù gǎndāng	phr.	(lit.) I dare not (accept the honour), (fig.) I don't deserve your praise, you flatter me	5
不要紧	bù yàojǐn	adj.	unimportant, not serious, it doesn't matter, never mind, it looks all right, but	4
不一定	bù yīdìng	adv.	not necessarily, maybe	2
不在乎 -	bù zàihu	vb.	not to care	4
不得了 •	bùdéliǎo	phr.	desperately serious, disastrous, extremely, exceedingly	5
不仅仅	bùjǐnjǐn	adv.	not only, not just	6
不客气 -	bùkèqi	phr.	you're welcome, don't mention it, impolite, rude, blunt	1
不耐烦	bùnàifán	adj.	impatient, to lose patience	5
不能不	bùnéngbù	adv.	have to, cannot but	5
不怎么	bùzěnme	adv.	not very, not particularly	6
不至于	bùzhìyú	vb.	unlikely to go so far as to, not as bad as	6
不好意思 -	bù hǎoyìsi	vb.	to feel embarrassed, to find it embarrassing, to be sorry (for inconveniencing sb)	2
不怎么样	bù zěnmeyàng	phr.	not up to much, very indifferent, nothing great about it, nothing good to be said about it	6
不一会儿	bùyīhuìr	phr.	in no time at all	2
从不	cóngbù	adv.	never	6
决不	jué bù	adv.	not at all, simply (can) not	5
差不多 -	chàbuduō	adj.	about the same, good enough, not bad, more or less, almost, nearly	2
对不起 -	duìbuqǐ	phr.	unworthy, to let down, I'm sorry, excuse me, pardon me, if you please, sorry? (please repeat)	1
赶不上 -	gǎnbushàng	phr.	can't keep up with, can't catch up with, cannot overtake	6
看不起 -	kànbuqǐ	vb.	to look down upon, to despise	4
来不及 -	láibují	phr.	there's not enough time (to do sth), it's too late (to do sth)	4
离不开 -	líbukāi	vb.	inseparable, inevitably linked to	4
了不起 •	liǎobuqǐ	adj.	amazing, terrific, extraordinary	4
能不能	néngbùnéng	phr.	can or cannot?, is it possible?, can we do it?	3
忍不住 -	rěnbuzhù	phr.	cannot help, unable to bear	5
舍不得	shěbude	vb.	to hate to do sth, to hate to part with, to begrudge	5
是不是 -	shìbushì	vb.	is or isn't, yes or no, whether or not	1
受不了 •	shòubuliǎo	phr.	unbearable, unable to endure, can't stand	4
说不定 -	shuōbudìng	vb.	can't say for sure, maybe	4
想不到 -	xiǎngbudào	vb.	to never expect, hard to imagine, it had not occurred to me	6
要不然 -	yàoburán	conj.	otherwise, or else, or	6
用不着 •	yòng bu zháo	n.	not need, have no use for (coll.)	5
只不过 -	zhǐbuguò	adv.	only, merely, nothing but, no more than, it's just that ...	5
好不容易	hǎobùróngyì	adv.	with great difficulty, very difficult	6
意想不到	yìxiǎngbùdào	phr.	unexpected, previously unimagined	6

丑 chǒu ugly, disgraceful — 1.3   5

丑	chǒu	adj.	ugly, (opp. 美 měi: beautiful), shameful, disgraceful	5

与	* yǔ, yù		and, to give; to take part in	一 1.3	4
与	yǔ	conj.	(formal) and, to give, together with		6
参与	• cānyù	vb.	to participate (in sth)		4
专	**zhuān**		focussed, special, expert	一 1.3	3
专辑	zhuānjí	n.	album, record (music), special collection of printed or broadcast material		5
专家	zhuānjiā	n.	expert, specialist		3
专利	zhuānlì	n.	patent, sth uniquely enjoyed (or possessed etc) by a certain group of people, monopoly		5
专门	zhuānmén	n.	specialist, specialized, customized		3
专题	zhuāntí	n.	specific topic (addressed by a book, lecture, TV program etc), article, report or program etc on a specific topic		3
专心	zhuānxīn	vb.	to concentrate, absorption, concentration, engrossed		4
专业	zhuānyè	n.	specialty, specialized field, main field of study (at university), major		3
专用	zhuānyòng	vb.	to be for a special purpose, to be dedicated		6
东	**dōng**		east, host	一 1.4	1
东	dōng	n.	east, master, owner, surname Dong		1
东北	dōngběi	n.	northeast, Northeast China, Manchuria		2
东边	- dōngbian	n.	east, east side, eastern part, to the east of		1
东部	dōngbù	n.	the east, eastern part		3
东方	dōngfāng	n.	the East, the Orient, two-character surname Dongfang		2
东南	dōngnán	n.	southeast		2
东西	- dōngxi	n.	east and west		1
房东	fángdōng	n.	landlord		3
股东	gǔdōng	n.	shareholder, stockholder		6
且	**qiě**		and, moreover	一 1.4	2
并且	bìngqiě	conj.	and, besides, moreover, furthermore, in addition		3
而且	érqiě	conj.	(not only ...) but also, moreover, in addition, furthermore		2
世	**shì**		life, age, generation	一 1.4	3
世纪	shìjì	n.	century		3
世界	shìjiè	n.	world		3
世界杯	shìjièbēi	n.	World Cup		3
去世	qùshì	vb.	to pass away, to die		3
全世界	quán shìjiè	n.	worldwide, entire world		5
业	**yè**		line of business, business	一 1.4	2
业务	yèwù	n.	business, professional work, service		5
业余	yèyú	adj.	in one's spare time, outside working hours, amateur (historian etc)		4
毕业	bìyè	n.	graduation, to graduate, to finish school		4
产业	chǎnyè	n.	industry, estate, property, industrial		5
创业	chuàngyè	vb.	to begin an undertaking, to start a major task, to initiate, to venture, venture, entrepreneurship		3
工业	gōngyè	n.	industry		3
行业	• hángyè	n.	industry, business		4
就业	jiùyè	vb.	to get a job, employment		3
开业	kāiyè	vb.	to open a business, to open a practice, open (for business)		3

农业	nóngyè	n.	agriculture, farming	3
企业	qǐyè	n.	company, firm, enterprise, corporation	4
商业	shāngyè	n.	business, trade, commerce	3
失业	shī yè	vb.	to have no job, to lose one's job	4
事业	shìyè	n.	undertaking, project, activity, (charitable, political or revolutionary) cause	3
物业	wùyè	n.	property, real estate	5
营业	yíngyè	vb.	to do business, to trade	4
职业	zhíyè	n.	occupation, profession, vocation, professional	3
专业	zhuānyè	n.	specialty, specialized field, main field of study (at university), major	3
作业	zuòyè	n.	school assignment, homework, work, task, operation	2
毕业生	bìyè shēng	n.	graduate	4

丢 **diū** — to lose, to put aside — ㇐ 1.5 — 5

丢	diū	vb.	to lose, to put aside, to throw	5

夹 **jiā** — to press from either side — ㇐ 1.5 — 5

夹	jiā	vb.	to squeeze, to pinch, to clamp	5

亚 **yà** — Asia, Asian — ㇐ 1.5 — 4

亚军	yàjūn	n.	second place (in a sports contest), runner-up	5
亚运会	yàyùnhuì	n.	Asian Games	4

两 **liǎng** — two, both — ㇐ 1.6 — 1

两	liǎng	+ num.	two, both, some, a few	1
两	liǎng	+ m.w.	m.w. tael, unit of weight equal to 50 grams (modern) or 1/16 of a catty 斤 jīn (old)	2
两岸	liǎng'àn	n.	bilateral, both shores, both sides, both coasts	5
两边	liǎngbiān	n.	either side, both sides	4
两侧	liǎngcè	n.	two sides, both sides	6
两手	liǎngshǒu	n.	one's two hands, two prongs (of a strategy), both aspects, eventualities etc, skills, expertise	6

严 **yán** — tight, stern — ㇐ 1.6 — 4

严	yán	adj.	strict, severe, serious, (air- or water-) tight, surname Yan	4
严格	yángé	adj.	strict, stringent, tight, rigorous	4
严厉	yánlì	adj.	severe, strict	5
严肃	yánsù	adj.	solemn, grave, serious, earnest, severe	5
严重	yánzhòng	adj.	grave, serious, severe, critical	4

丨 **gǔn** — line — 2

个 **gè** — general measure word, individual — 丨 2.2 — 1

个	gè	m.w.	general measure word, individual, this, that, size	1
个别	gèbié	adj.	individual, specific, respective, just one or two	4
个儿	gèr	n.	size, height, stature	5
个人	gèrén	n.	individual, personal, oneself	3
个体	gètǐ	n.	individual	4
个性	gèxìng	n.	individuality, personality	3
个子	gèzi	n.	height, stature, build, size	2

各个	gègè	pro.	every, various, separately, one by one	4
整个	zhěnggè	adj.	whole, entire, total	3
上个月	- shàng ge yuè	n.	last month	4
下个月	- xià ge yuè	n.	next month	4

丰 **fēng** — abundant, plentiful | 2.3 — 3

丰富	fēngfù	vb.	to enrich, rich, plentiful, abundant	3
丰收	fēngshōu	n.	bumper harvest	5

书 **shū** — book, letter | 2.3 — 1

书	shū	n.	book, letter, document, to write	1
书包	shūbāo	n.	schoolbag, satchel, bookbag	1
书店	shūdiàn	n.	bookstore	1
书法	shūfǎ	n.	calligraphy, handwriting, penmanship	5
书房	shūfáng	n.	study (room), studio	6
书柜	shūguì	n.	bookcase	5
书架	shūjià	n.	bookshelf	3
书桌	shūzhuō	n.	desk	5
读书	dú shū	vb.	to read a book, to study, to attend school	1
秘书	mìshū	n.	secretary	4
图书	túshū	n.	books (in a library or bookstore)	6
证书	zhèngshū	n.	credentials, certificate	5
图书馆	túshūguǎn	n.	library	1
说明书	shuōmíngshū	n.	(technical) manual, (book of) directions, synopsis (of a play or film), specification (patent)	6
通知书	tōngzhīshū	n.	written notice	4
协议书	xiéyìshū	n.	contract, protocol	5

中 * **zhōng, zhòng** — within, middle; to hit (target) | 2.3 — 1

中	zhōng	n.	within, among, in, centre, in the middle, in the midst of, medium, among, China	1
中部	zhōngbù	n.	middle part, central section	3
中餐	zhōngcān	n.	lunch, Chinese meal, Chinese food	2
中等	zhōngděng	adj.	medium	6
中断	zhōngduàn	vb.	to cut short, to break off, to discontinue, to interrupt	5
中国	zhōngguó	n.	China	1
中华	zhōnghuá	n.	the Chinese nation, China	6
中级	zhōngjí	adj.	middle level (in a hierarchy)	2
中间	zhōngjiān	n.	between, intermediate, mid, middle	1
中介	zhōngjiè	vb.	to act as intermediary, to link, intermediate, inter-, agency, agent	4
中年	zhōngnián	n.	middle age	2
中期	zhōngqī	n.	middle (of a period of time), medium-term (plan, forecast etc)	6
中外	zhōngwài	n.	China and foreign countries, home and abroad, foreign and domestic	6
中文	zhōngwén	n.	Chinese (language)	1
中午	zhōngwǔ	n.	noon, midday	1
中心	zhōngxīn	n.	centre, heart, core	2
中学	zhōngxué	n.	middle school	1
中央	zhōngyāng	n.	central, middle, centre, central authorities (of a state)	5
中药	zhōngyào	n.	traditional Chinese medicine	5

中医	zhōngyī	n.	traditional Chinese medical science, a doctor trained in Chinese medicine	2
中毒	• zhòngdú	vb.	to be poisoned, poisoning	5
中奖	• zhòngjiǎng	vb.	to win a prize, a successful gamble	4
中秋节	zhōngqiū jié	n.	the Mid-Autumn Festival on 15th of 8th lunar month	5
中小学	zhōngxiǎoxué	n.	middle and elementary school	2
中学生	zhōngxuéshēng	n.	middle-school student, high school student	1
中华民族	zhōnghuá mínzú	n.	the Chinese people	3
初中	chūzhōng	n.	junior middle school, junior high school	3
从中	cóngzhōng	adv.	from within, therefrom	5
当中	dāngzhōng	n.	among, in the middle, in the centre	3
高中	gāozhōng	n.	senior high school	2
集中	jízhōng	vb.	to concentrate, to centralize, to focus, centralized, concentrated, to put together	3
空中	kōngzhōng	n.	in the sky, in the air, air-bourne	5
期中	qīzhōng	n.	interim, midterm	4
其中	qízhōng	n.	among, in, included among these	2
途中	túzhōng	adv.	en route, on the way	4
心中	xīnzhōng	n.	central point, in one's thoughts, in one's heart	2
之中	zhī zhōng	n.	inside, among, in the midst of (doing sth), during	5

串 chuàn — to string together, to skewer | 2.6 6

串	chuàn	vb.	to string together, to skewer, to connect wrongly, to gang up, to rove, string, bunch, skewer	6

临 lín — to face, to overlook | 2.8 4

临时	línshí	adv.	as the time draws near, at the last moment, temporary, interim, ad hoc	4
光临	guānglín	vb.	(formal) to honour with one's presence, to attend	4
面临	miànlín	vb.	to face sth, to be confronted with	4

丶 zhǔ dot 3

为 * wèi, wéi — because of, for, to; to be, to become 丶 3.3 2

为	• wéi	vb.	to be, become	3
为	wèi	prep.	because of, for, to	2
为	wèi	+ prep.	in the interest of, for	3
为难	• wéinán	vb.	to feel embarrassed or awkward, to make things difficult (for someone), to find things difficult (to do or manage)	5
为期	• wéiqī	vb.	to be done by (a certain date), lasting (a certain time)	5
为止	• wéizhǐ	vb.	until, (used in combination with words like 到 dào or 至 zhì in constructs of the form 到...為止|到...为止)	5
为主	• wéizhǔ	vb.	to rely mainly on, to attach most importance to	5
为此	wèicǐ	conj.	for this reason, with regards to this, in this respect, in order to do this, to this end	6
为何	wèihé	adv.	why	6
为了	wèile	prep.	in order to, for the purpose of, so as to	3
为什么	wèishénme	adv.	why?, for what reason?	2
变为	• biànwéi	vb.	to change into	3
称为	• chēngwéi	vb.	called, to call sth (by a name), to name	3

成为	• chéngwéi	vb.	to become, to turn into		2
分为	• fēnwéi	vb.	to divide sth into (parts), to subdivide		4
列为	• lièwéi	vb.	to be classified as		4
认为	• rènwéi	vb.	to believe, to think, to consider, to feel		2
视为	• shìwéi	vb.	to view as, to see as, to consider to be, to deem		5
行为	• xíngwéi	n.	action, conduct, behaviour, activity		2
以为	• yǐwéi	vb.	to think (i.e. to take it to be true that ...)		2
因为	- yīnwei	conj.	because, owing to, on account of		2
作为	• zuòwéi	n.	one's conduct, deed, activity, accomplishment, achievement		4

主 zhǔ — owner, master ⟍ 3.4 2

主办	zhǔbàn	vb.	to organize, to host (a conference or sports event)	5
主持	zhǔchí	vb.	to take charge of, to manage or direct, to preside over, to uphold, to stand for (justice etc)	3
主导	zhǔdǎo	adj.	leading, dominant, prevailing, to lead, to direct, to dominate	5
主动	zhǔdòng	vb.	to take the initiative, to do sth of one's own accord, spontaneous, active	3
主观	zhǔguān	n.	subjective	5
主管	zhǔguǎn	vb.	to be in charge, to be responsible for, person in charge, manager	5
主角	• zhǔjué	n.	leading role, lead	6
主流	zhǔliú	n.	main stream (of a river), fig. the essential point, main viewpoint of a matter, mainstream (culture etc)	6
主人	zhǔrén	n.	master, host, owner	2
主任	zhǔrèn	n.	director, head	3
主题	zhǔtí	n.	theme, subject	4
主体	zhǔtǐ	n.	main part, bulk, body, subject, agent	5
主席	zhǔxí	n.	chairperson, premier, chairman	4
主要	zhǔyào	n.	main, principal, major, primary	2
主意	- zhǔyi	n.	plan, idea, decision	3
主张	zhǔzhāng	vb.	to advocate, to stand for, view, position, stand, proposition, viewpoint, assertion	3
主持人	zhǔchírén	n.	TV or radio presenter	6
车主	chēzhǔ	n.	vehicle owner	5
公主	gōngzhǔ	n.	princess	6
民主	mínzhǔ	n.	democracy	6
为主	• wéizhǔ	vb.	to rely mainly on, to attach most importance to	5
自主	zìzhǔ	vb.	to act for oneself, autonomous, independent	3

丽 lì — beautiful, magnificent ⟍ 3.7 3

美丽	měilì	adj.	beautiful	3

举 jǔ — to lift up, to hold up ⟍ 3.8 2

举	jǔ	vb.	to lift, to hold up, to cite, to enumerate, to act, to raise, to choose, to elect, act, move, deed	2
举办	jǔbàn	vb.	to conduct, to hold	3
举动	jǔdòng	n.	act, action, activity, move, movement	5
举手	jǔshǒu	vb.	to raise a hand, to put up one's hand (as signal)	2
举行	jǔxíng	vb.	to hold (a meeting, ceremony etc)	2
选举	xuǎnjǔ	vb.	to elect, election	6

丿 piě　slash　4

久　jiǔ　long time　丿 4.2　2

久	jiǔ	n.	(long) time, (long) duration of time	3
不久	bùjiǔ	adj.	not long (after), before too long, soon, soon after	2
长久	chángjiǔ	adv.	(for a) long time	6
多久	duōjiǔ	adv.	(of time) how long?, (not) a long time	2
好久	hǎojiǔ	adv.	quite a while	2

么　me　interrogative particle　丿 4.2　1

多么	duōme	adv.	how (wonderful etc), what (a great idea etc), however (difficult it may be etc), (in interrogative sentences) how (much etc), to what extent	2
那么	nàme	pro.	like that, in that way, or so, so, so very much, about, in that case	2
什么	shénme	pro.	what?, something, anything	1
要么	yàome	conj.	or, either one or the other	6
怎么	zěnme	pro.	how, however, what, why	1
这么	zhème	pro.	so much, this much, how much?, this way, like this	2
什么样	shénmeyàng	phr.	what kind?, what sort?, what appearance?	2
怎么办	zěnmebàn	phr.	what's to be done	2
怎么样	zěnmeyàng	pro.	how?, how about?, how was it?, how are things?	2
不怎么	bùzěnme	adv.	not very, not particularly	6
干什么	gàn shénme	vb.	what are you doing?, what's he up to?	1
没什么	méi shénme	vb.	nothing, it doesn't matter, it's nothing, never mind	1
为什么	wèishénme	adv.	why?, for what reason?	2
不怎么样	bù zěnmeyàng	phr.	not up to much, very indifferent, nothing great about it, nothing good to be said about it	6

义　yì　right conduct, righteousness　丿 4.2　3

义务	yìwù	n.	duty, obligation	4
含义	hányì	n.	meaning (implicit in a phrase), implied meaning, hidden meaning, hint, connotation	4
名义	míngyì	n.	name, titular, nominal, in name, ostensible purpose	6
意义	yìyì	n.	sense, meaning, significance, importance	3
正义	zhèngyì	n.	justice, righteousness, just, righteous	5

乌　wū　black, dark, crow, rook, raven　丿 4.3　6

乌云	wūyún	n.	black cloud, dark cloud	6

之　zhī　possessive particle (lit. equiv. of 的 de)　丿 4.3　4

之前	zhī qián	n.	before, prior to, ago, previously, beforehand	4
之下	zhī xià	n.	under, beneath, less than	5
之一	zhī yī	n.	one of (sth), one out of a multitude, one (third, quarter, percent etc)	4
之中	zhī zhōng	n.	inside, among, in the midst of (doing sth), during	5
之后	zhīhòu	n.	afterwards, following, later, after	4
之间	zhījiān	n.	between, among, inter-	4
之类	zhīlèi	phr.	and so on, and such	6
之内	zhīnèi	n.	inside, within	5
之外	zhīwài	n.	outside, excluding	5

分之	fēnzhī	adj.	(indicating a fraction) ... fēnzhī ... (e.g. 三分之二 sānfēn zhī'èr: two-thirds)		4
总之	zǒngzhī	conj.	in a word, in short, in brief		4
乏	**fá**		to lack, to be short of	丿 4.4	5
缺乏	quēfá	vb.	to lack, to be short of, lack, shortage		5
乎	**hū**		interrogative or excl. final particle	丿 4.4	4
几乎	jīhū	adv.	almost, nearly, practically		4
似乎	shìhū	adv.	apparently, to seem, to appear, as if, seemingly		4
在乎	- zàihu	vb.	to care about, equivalent of 在于 zài yú		4
不在乎	- bù zàihu	vb.	not to care		4
乐	*** lè, yuè**		happy, cheerful; enjoyable; music	丿 4.4	2
乐	lè	adj.	happy, cheerful, to laugh, surname Le		3
乐观	lèguān	adj.	optimistic, hopeful		3
乐趣	lèqù	n.	delight, pleasure, joy		4
乐队	• yuèduì	n.	band, pop group		3
乐曲	• yuèqǔ	n.	musical composition		6
欢乐	huānlè	n.	gaiety, gladness, glee, merriment, pleasure, happy, joyous, gay		3
可乐	kělè	adj.	amusing, entertaining, (loanword) cola		3
快乐	kuàilè	adj.	happy, merry		2
音乐	• yīnyuè	n.	music		2
娱乐	yúlè	vb.	to entertain, to amuse, entertainment, recreation, amusement, hobby, fun, joy		6
俱乐部	jùlèbù	n.	club (the organisation or its premises) (loanword)		5
音乐会	• yīnyuèhuì	n.	concert		2
乘	**chéng**		to ride, to mount	丿 4.9	5
乘	chéng	vb.	to ride, to mount, make use of, multiply		5
乘车	chéngchē	vb.	to ride (in a car or carriage), to drive, to motor		5
乘客	chéngkè	n.	passenger		5
乘坐	chéngzuò	vb.	to ride (in a vehicle)		5
乙	**yǐ**		second	乁乚	5
乙	yǐ		second, 2nd heavenly stem	乙 5.0	5
乙	yǐ	n.	second of the ten Heavenly Stems, second in order, letter B or Roman II in list A, B, C, or I, II, III		5
九	**jiǔ**		nine, 9	乙 5.1	1
九	jiǔ	num.	nine, 9		1
飞	**fēi**		to fly	乙 5.2	1
飞	fēi	vb.	to fly		1
飞船	fēichuán	n.	airship, spaceship		6
飞机	fēijī	n.	airplane		1
飞行	fēixíng	vb.	(of planes etc) to fly, flying, flight, aviation		3
飞行员	fēixíngyuán	n.	pilot, aviator		6
起飞	qǐfēi	vb.	(of an aircraft) to take off		2

卫	**wèi**		to guard, to protect, to defend	乙 5.2	3
卫生	wèishēng	n.	health, hygiene, sanitation		3
卫星	wèixīng	n.	satellite, moon		5
卫生间	wèishēngjiān	n.	bathroom, toilet, WC		3
保卫	bǎowèi	vb.	to defend, to safeguard		5
也	**yě**		also, class. final particle of affirmation	乙 5.2	1
也	yě	adv.	also, too, as well as, surname Ye		1
也好	yěhǎo	aux.	that's fine, may as well, (reduplicated) regardless of whether … or …		5
也许	yěxǔ	adv.	perhaps, maybe		2
再也	zàiyě	adv.	(not) any more		5
乱	**luàn**		disorder, upheaval	乙 5.6	
乱	luàn	n.	disorder, upheaval, riot, in confusion or disorder, in a confused state of mind,		3
混乱	hùnluàn	n.	confusion, chaos, disorder		6
乳	**rǔ**		breast, milk	乙 5.7	6
乳制品	rǔzhìpǐn	n.	dairy products		6

亅 jué   hook   6

了	* **le, liǎo**		particle of completed action; to finish	亅 6.1	1
了	le	aux.	[particle for a new situation or completed action]		1
了	• liǎo	vb.	to finish, to understand clearly		3
了解	• liǎojiě	vb.	to understand, to realize, to find out		4
了不起	• liǎobuqǐ	adj.	amazing, terrific, extraordinary		4
罢了	bàle	n.	a modal particle indicating (that's all, only, nothing much)		6
除了	chúle	prep.	besides, apart from (… also…), in addition to, except (for)		3
得了	• déle	vb.	all right!, that's enough!		5
极了	jíle	adv.	extremely, exceedingly; use: … 极了		3
算了	suàn le	vb.	let it be, let it pass, forget about it		6
完了	wánle	vb.	to be finished, to be done for, ruined, gone to the dogs, oh no		5
为了	wèile	prep.	in order to, for the purpose of, so as to		3
不得了	• bùdéliǎo	phr.	desperately serious, disastrous, extremely, exceedingly		5
受不了	• shòubuliǎo	phr.	unbearable, unable to endure, can't stand		4
予	**yǔ**		to give	亅 6.3	6
给予	• jǐyǔ	vb.	to accord, to give, to show (respect)		6
争	**zhēng**		to strive for, to vie for	亅 6.5	3
争	zhēng	vb.	to strive for, to vie for, to argue or debate, deficient or lacking (dialect), how or what (literary)		3
争夺	zhēngduó	vb.	to fight over, to contest, to vie over		6
争论	zhēnglùn	vb.	to argue, to debate, to contend, argument, contention, controversy, debate		4
争取	zhēngqǔ	vb.	to fight for, to strive for, to win over		3
争议	zhēngyì	n.	controversy, dispute, to dispute		5
斗争	dòuzhēng	n.	a struggle, fight, battle		6
竞争	jìngzhēng	vb.	to compete, competition		5

战争	zhànzhēng	n.	war, conflict	4
事	**shì**		**matter, thing**	」6.7 1
事	shì	n.	matter, thing, item, work, affair	1
事故	shìgù	n.	accident	3
事后	shìhòu	n.	after the event, in hindsight, in retrospect	6
事件	shìjiàn	n.	event, happening, incident	3
事情	- shìqing	n.	affair, matter, thing, business	2
事实	shìshí	n.	fact	3
事物	shìwù	n.	thing, object	4
事先	shìxiān	n.	in advance, before the event, beforehand, prior	4
事业	shìyè	n.	undertaking, project, activity, (charitable, political or revolutionary) cause	3
事实上	shìshíshàng	adv.	in fact, in reality, actually, as a matter of fact, de facto, ipso facto	3
办事	bànshì	vb.	to handle (affairs), to work	4
本事	- běnshi	n.	source material, original story	3
出事	chū shì	vb.	to have an accident, to meet with a mishap	6
此事	cǐshì	n.	this matter	6
从事	cóngshì	vb.	to go for, to engage in, to undertake, to deal with, to handle, to do	3
大事	dàshì	n.	major event, major political event (war or change of regime), major social event (wedding or funeral), (do sth) in a big way	5
故事	- gùshi	n.	old practice	2
好事	hǎoshì	n.	good action, deed, thing or work (also sarcastic, a fine thing indeed), charity, happy occasion, Daoist or Buddhist ceremony for souls of the dead	2
军事	jūnshì	n.	military affairs, military matters, military	6
没事	méishì	vb.	it's not important, it's nothing, never mind, to have nothing to do, to be free, to be all right (out of danger or trouble)	1
启事	qǐshì	n.	announcement (written, on billboard, letter, newspaper or website), to post information, a notice	5
时事	shíshì	n.	current trends, the present situation, how things are going	5
同事	tóngshì	n.	colleague, co-worker	2
有事	yǒushì	vb.	to be occupied with sth, to have sth on one's mind, there is something the matter	6
办事处	• bànshìchù	n.	office, agency	6

二	**èr**		**two**	**7**
二	**èr**		**two, 2**	二 7.0 1
二	èr	num.	two, 2, (Beijing dialect) stupid	1
二手	èrshǒu	adj.	indirectly acquired, second-hand (information, equipment etc), assistant	4
二维码	èrwéimǎ	n.	two-dimensional barcode, QR code	5
亏	**kuī**		**deficiency, deficit**	二 7.1 5
亏	kuī	n.	deficiency, deficit, luckily, it's lucky that..., (often ironically) fancy that...	5
于	**yú**		**in, at, to**	二 7.1 2
于	yú	prep.	in, at, to, from, by, than, out of	6

于是	yúshì	*conj.*	thereupon, as a result, consequently, thus, hence	4
便于	biànyú	*adj.*	easy to, convenient for	5
出于	chūyú	*prep.*	out of, from, due to, to stem from	5
处于	chǔyú	*vb.*	to be in (some state, position, or condition)	4
大于	dàyú	*adj.*	greater than, bigger than, more than, >	5
等于	děngyú	*vb.*	to equal, to be tantamount to	2
低于	dīyú	*vb.*	to be lower than	5
对于	duìyú	*prep.*	regarding, as far as sth is concerned, with regards to	4
敢于	gǎnyú	*vb.*	to have the courage to do sth, to dare to, bold in	6
高于	gāoyú	*adv.*	greater than, to exceed	5
关于	guānyú	*prep.*	pertaining to, concerning, with regard to, about, a matter of	4
过于	guòyú	*adv.*	too much, excessively	5
善于	shànyú	*vb.*	to be good at, to be adept at	4
属于	shǔyú	*vb.*	to be classified as, to belong to, to be part of	3
位于	wèiyú	*vb.*	to be located at, to be situated at, to lie	4
小于	xiǎoyú	*adj.*	less than, <	6
用于	yòngyú	*vb.*	use in, use on, use for	5
由于	yóuyú	*prep.*	due to, as a result of, thanks to, owing to, since, because	3
在于	zàiyú	*vb.*	to be in, to lie in, to consist in, to depend on, to rest with	4
至于	zhìyú	*prep.*	as for, as to, to go so far as to	6
终于	zhōngyú	*adv.*	at last, in the end, finally, eventually	3
不至于	bùzhìyú	*vb.*	unlikely to go so far as to, not as bad as	6
有利于	yǒulìyú	*vb.*	to be advantageous to, to be beneficial for	5

互 **hù** mutually, reciprocally 二 7.2 3

互动	hùdòng	*vb.*	to interact, interactive	6
互相	hùxiāng	*adv.*	each other, mutually, mutual	3
互联网	hùliánwǎng	*n.*	Internet	3
相互	xiānghù	*adj.*	each other, mutual	3

井 **jǐng** a well 二 7.2 6

井	jǐng	*n.*	a well	6

五 **wǔ** five, 5 二 7.2 1

五	wǔ	*num.*	five, 5	1
五颜六色	wǔyánliùsè	*phr.*	multi-coloured, every colour under the sun (idiom)	4

云 **yún** cloud 二 7.2 2

云	yún	*n.*	cloud, (classical) to say, Yunnan province, surname Yun	2
多云	duōyún	*adj.*	cloudy (meteorology)	2
乌云	wūyún	*n.*	black cloud, dark cloud	6

些 **xiē** m.w. indicating a small amount 二 7.5 1

些	xiē	*m.w.*	m.w. indicating a small amount, some, few	4
哪些	nǎxiē	*pro.*	which ones?, who?, what?	1
那些	nàxiē	*pro.*	those	1
一些	yīxiē	*m.w.*	some, a few, a little, (following an adjective) slightly ...er	1
有些	yǒuxiē	*pro.*	some, somewhat	1
这些	zhèxiē	*pro.*	these	1

亠 tóu lid 8

亡	**wáng**		to die, to lose	亠 8.1	6
伤亡	shāngwáng	n.	casualties, injuries and deaths		6
死亡	sǐwáng	vb.	to die, death		6
交	**jiāo**		to hand over, to deliver	亠 8.4	2
交	jiāo	vb.	to hand over, to deliver, to pay (money), to turn over, to make friends, to intersect (lines)		2
交代	jiāodài	vb.	to hand over, to explain, to make clear, to brief (sb), to account for, to justify oneself, to confess, (coll.) to finish		5
交费	jiāofèi	vb.	to pay a fee		3
交给	jiāogěi	vb.	to give, to deliver, to hand over		2
交换	jiāohuàn	vb.	to exchange, to swap, to switch (telecom), commutative (math), to commute		4
交际	jiāojì	n.	communication, social intercourse		4
交警	jiāojǐng	n.	traffic police		3
交流	jiāoliú	vb.	to exchange, exchange, communication, interaction, to have social contact (with sb)		3
交通	jiāotōng	vb.	to be connected, traffic, transportation, communications, liaison		2
交往	jiāowǎng	vb.	to associate (with), to have contact (with), to hang out (with), to date, (interpersonal) relationship, association, contact		3
交易	jiāoyì	n.	(business) transaction, business deal		3
交朋友	- jiāo péngyou	vb.	to make friends, (dialect) to start an affair with sb		2
成交	chéngjiāo	vb.	to complete a contract, to reach a deal		5
提交	tíjiāo	vb.	to submit (a report etc), to refer (a problem) to sb		6
外交	wàijiāo	n.	diplomacy, diplomatic, foreign affairs		3
公交车	gōngjiāochē	n.	public transport vehicle, town bus		2
外交官	wàijiāoguān	n.	diplomat		4
京	**jīng**		capital city	亠 8.6	1
京剧	jīngjù	n.	Beijing Opera		3
北京	běijīng	n.	Beijing		1
享	**xiǎng**		to enjoy	亠 8.6	5
享受	xiǎngshòu	vb.	to enjoy, to live it up, pleasure		5
分享	fēnxiǎng	vb.	to share (let others have some of sth good)		5
共享	gòngxiǎng	vb.	to share, to enjoy together		5
亮	**liàng**		bright, clear	亠 8.7	2
亮	liàng	adj.	bright, clear, resonant, to shine, to show, to reveal		2
明亮	míngliàng	adj.	bright, shining, glittering, to become clear		5
漂亮	- piàoliang	adj.	pretty, beautiful		2
月亮	- yuèliang	n.	the moon		2
赢	**yíng**		to beat, to win	亠 8.15	3
赢	yíng	vb.	to beat, to win, to profit		3
赢得	• yíngdé	vb.	to win, to gain		4

人 rén man 亻 9

人	rén		man, person	人 9.0 1
人	rén	n.	man, person, people	1
人才	réncái	n.	talent, talented person, looks, attractive looks	3
人工	réngōng	n.	artificial, manpower, manual work	3
人家	rénjiā	n.	household, dwelling, family, sb else's house, household business, house of woman's husband-to-be	4
人间	rénjiān	n.	the human world, the earth	5
人口	rénkǒu	n.	population, people	2
人类	rénlèi	n.	humanity, human race, mankind	3
人力	rénlì	n.	manpower, labour power	5
人们	rénmen	n.	people	2
人民	rénmín	n.	the people	3
人权	rénquán	n.	human rights	6
人群	rénqún	n.	crowd	3
人生	rénshēng	n.	life (one's time on earth)	3
人士	rénshì	n.	person, figure, public figure	5
人数	rénshù	n.	number of people	2
人物	rénwù	n.	person, character (in a play, novel etc), protagonist	5
人员	rényuán	n.	staff, crew, personnel	3
人民币	rénmínbì	n.	renminbi (RMB)	3
爱人	- àiren	n.	spouse (PRC), lover (non-PRC)	2
本人	běnrén	pro.	the person himself, I (humble form used in speeches), oneself, myself, in person, personal	5
别人	biérén	n.	other people, others, other person	1
病人	bìngrén	n.	sick person, patient, invalid	1
成人	chéngrén	n.	adult	4
大人	- dàren	n.	adult, grownup, title of respect toward superiors	2
敌人	dírén	n.	enemy	4
动人	dòngrén	adj.	touching, moving	3
恩人	ēnrén	n.	a benefactor, a person who has significantly helped sb else	6
夫人	- fūren	n.	lady, madam, Mrs.	4
富人	fùrén	n.	rich person, the rich	6
感人	gǎnrén	adj.	touching, moving	6
个人	gèrén	n.	individual, personal, oneself	3
工人	gōngrén	n.	worker	1
好人	hǎorén	n.	good person, healthy person, person who tries not to offend anyone, even at the expense of principle	2
华人	huárén	n.	ethnic Chinese person or people	3
坏人	huàirén	n.	bad person, villain	2
家人	jiārén	n.	household, (one's) family	1
惊人	jīngrén	adj.	astonishing	6
军人	jūnrén	n.	serviceman, soldier, military personnel	5
客人	kèrén	n.	visitor, guest, customer, client	2
老人	lǎorén	n.	old man or woman, the elderly, one's aged parents or grandparents	1
盲人	mángrén	n.	blind person	6

迷人	mírén	*adj.*	fascinating, enchanting, charming, tempting		5
名人	míngrén	*n.*	personage, celebrity		4
男人	nánrén	*n.*	a man, a male, men		1
女人	nǚrén	*n.*	woman		1
亲人	qīnrén	*n.*	one's close relatives		3
穷人	qióngrén	*n.*	poor people, the poor		4
商人	shāngrén	*n.*	merchant, businessman		2
诗人	shīrén	*n.*	bard, poet		4
熟人	shúrén	*n.*	acquaintance, friend		3
私人	sīrén	*adj.*	private, (opp. 公 gōng: public), personal, interpersonal, sb with whom one has a close personal relationship		5
新人	xīnrén	*n.*	newcomer, fresh talent, newlywed, esp. new bride, bride and groom, (paleoanthropology) Homo sapiens		6
行人	xíngrén	*n.*	pedestrian, traveller on foot, passer-by, official responsible for arranging audiences with the emperor		2
艺人	yìrén	*n.*	performing artist, actor		6
游人	yóurén	*n.*	a tourist		6
有人	yǒurén	*pro.*	someone, people, anyone, there is someone there, occupied (as in restroom)		2
主人	zhǔrén	*n.*	master, host, owner		2
残疾人	cánjírén	*n.*	disabled person		6
发言人	fāyánrén	*n.*	spokesperson		6
负责人	fùzérén	*n.*	person in charge		5
机器人	jīqìrén	*n.*	mechanical person, robot, android		5
主持人	zhǔchírén	*n.*	TV or radio presenter		6
亿	**yì**		hundred million	人 9.1	2
亿	yì	*num.*	hundred million		2
仓	**cāng**		barn, granary	人 9.2	6
仓库	cāngkù	*n.*	depot, storehouse, warehouse		6
从	**cóng**		from, through, via	人 9.2	1
从	cóng	*prep.*	from, through, via, to follow, to, obey, surname Cong		1
从没	cóng méi	*adv.*	never (in the past), never did		6
从而	cóng'ér	*conj.*	thus, thereby		5
从不	cóngbù	*adv.*	never		6
从此	cóngcǐ	*adv.*	from now on, since then, henceforth		4
从来	cónglái	*adv.*	always, at all times, never (if used in negative sentence)		3
从前	cóngqián	*n.*	previously, formerly, once upon a time		3
从事	cóngshì	*vb.*	to go for, to engage in, to undertake, to deal with, to handle, to do		3
从小	cóngxiǎo	*adv.*	from childhood, from a young age		2
从中	cóngzhōng	*adv.*	from within, therefrom		5
服从	fúcóng	*vb.*	to obey (an order), to comply, to defer		5
自从	zìcóng	*prep.*	since (a time), ever since		3
介	**jiè**		to introduce, to lie between	人 9.2	1
介绍	jièshào	*vb.*	to introduce (sb to sb), to give a presentation, to present (sb for a job etc), introduction		1
简介	jiǎnjiè	*n.*	summary, brief introduction		6
中介	zhōngjiè	*vb.*	to act as intermediary, to link, intermediate, inter-, agency, agent		4

仅	**jǐn**		barely, only	人 9.2	3
仅	jǐn	adv.	barely, only, merely		3
仅仅	jǐnjǐn	adv.	barely, only, merely, only (this and nothing more)		3
不仅	bùjǐn	adv.	not only (this one), not just (...) but also		3
不仅仅	bùjǐnjǐn	adv.	not only, not just		6
今	**jīn**		today, modern	人 9.2	1
今后	jīnhòu	n.	hereafter, henceforth, in the future, from now on		2
今年	jīnnián	n.	this year		1
今日	jīnrì	n.	today		5
今天	jīntiān	n.	today, at the present, now		1
如今	rújīn	n.	nowadays, now		4
至今	zhì jīn	adv.	so far, to this day, until now		3
仍	**réng**		still, yet	人 9.2	3
仍	réng	adv.	still, yet, to remain, keep -ing, continuing		3
仍旧	réngjiù	adv.	still (remaining), to remain (the same), yet		5
仍然	réngrán	adv.	still, yet		3
什	**shén**		what	人 9.2	1
什么	shénme	pro.	what, something, anything		1
什么样	shénmeyàng	phr.	what kind?, what sort?, what appearance?		2
干什么	gàn shénme	vb.	what are you doing?, what's he up to?		1
没什么	méi shénme	vb.	nothing, it doesn't matter, it's nothing, never mind		1
为什么	wèishénme	adv.	why?, for what reason?		2
代	**dài**		to substitute	人 9.3	3
代	dài	vb.	to substitute, to act on behalf of others, to replace, generation, dynasty, age, period, (historical) era		3
代表	dàibiǎo	n.	representative, delegate		3
代价	dàijià	n.	price, cost, consideration (in share dealing)		5
代理	dàilǐ	vb.	to act on behalf of sb in a responsible position, to act as an agent or proxy, surrogate, (computing) proxy		5
代替	dàitì	vb.	to replace, to take the place of		4
代表团	dàibiǎotuán	n.	delegation		3
当代	dāngdài	n.	the present age, the contemporary era		5
古代	gǔdài	n.	ancient times, olden times		3
交代	jiāodài	vb.	to hand over, to explain, to make clear, to brief (sb), to account for, to justify oneself, to confess, (coll.) to finish		5
近代	jìndài	n.	the not-very-distant past, modern times, excluding recent decades		4
年代	niándài	n.	a decade of a century (e.g. the Sixties), age, era, period		3
时代	shídài	n.	age, era, period		3
替代	tìdài	vb.	to substitute for, to replace, to supersede		4
现代	xiàndài	n.	modern times, modern age		3
一代	yīdài	n.	generation		6
付	**fù**		to pay	人 9.3	
付	fù	vb.	to pay, to hand over, surname Fu		3
付出	fùchū	vb.	to pay, to invest (energy or time in a friendship etc)		4
对付	- duìfu	vb.	to handle, to deal with, to cope, to get by with		4

支付	zhīfù	vb.	to pay (money)		3
令	**lìng**		**to order, to command**	人 9.3	5
令	lìng	vb.	to make or cause to be, to order, to command		5
命令	mìnglìng	n.	order, command		5
们	**men**		**plural marker for pronouns**	人 9.3	1
们	men	+ aff.	plural marker for pronouns, and nouns referring to individuals		1
你们	nǐmen	pro.	you (plural)		1
人们	rénmen	n.	people		2
他们	tāmen	pro.	they		1
她们	tāmen	pro.	they, them (for females)		1
它们	tāmen	pro.	they (for inanimate objects)		2
我们	wǒmen	pro.	we, us, ourselves, our		1
咱们	zánmen	pro.	we or us (including both the speaker and the person(s) spoken to), (dialect) I or me, (dialect) (in a coaxing or familiar way) you		2
他	**tā**		**he, him**	人 9.3	1
他	tā	pro.	he or him, (used for either sex when the sex is unknown or unimportant), (used before sb's name for emphasis)		1
他们	tāmen	pro.	they		1
其他	qítā	pro.	other, (sth or sb) else, the rest		2
仪	**yí**		**apparatus, rites**	人 9.3	6
仪器	yíqì	n.	instrument, apparatus		6
仪式	yíshì	n.	ceremony		6
以	**yǐ**		**by means of**	人 9.3	2
以便	yǐbiàn	conj.	so that, so as to, in order to		5
以后	yǐhòu	n.	after, later, afterwards, following, later on, in the future		2
以及	yǐjí	conj.	as well as, too, and		4
以来	yǐlái	n.	since (a previous event)		3
以内	yǐnèi	n.	within, less than		4
以前	yǐqián	n.	before, formerly, previous, ago		2
以上	yǐshàng	n.	that level or higher, that amount or more, the above-mentioned, (used to indicate that one has completed one's remarks) that is all		2
以外	yǐwài	n.	apart from, other than, except for, external, outside of, on the other side of, beyond		2
以往	yǐwǎng	n.	in the past, formerly		5
以为	• yǐwéi	vb.	to think (i.e. to take it to be true that…)		2
以下	yǐxià	n.	that level or lower, that amount or less, the following		2
得以	• déyǐ	vb.	to be able to, so that sb can, enabling, in order to, finally in a position to, with sth in view		5
加以	jiāyǐ	conj.	in addition, moreover, to apply (restrictions etc) to (sb)		5
可以	kěyǐ	vb.	to be possible, to be able to, not bad, pretty good		2
难以	nányǐ	adv.	hard to (predict, imagine etc)		5
所以	suǒyǐ	conj.	therefore, as a result, so, the reason why		2
足以	zúyǐ	vb.	to be sufficient to…, so much so that, so that		6
仔	**zǐ**		**young animal**	人 9.3	5
仔细	zǐxì	adj.	careful, attentive, cautious		5

牛仔裤	niúzǎikù	n.	jeans		5
传	**chuán**		**to pass on, to spread**	人 9.4	3
传	chuán	vb.	to pass on, to spread, to transmit, to infect, to transfer, to circulate, to conduct (electricity)		3
传播	chuánbō	vb.	to disseminate, to propagate, to spread		3
传出	chuánchū	vb.	to transmit outwards, to disseminate, efferent (nerve)		6
传达	chuándá	vb.	to pass on, to convey, to relay, to transmit, transmission		5
传递	chuándì	vb.	to transmit, to pass on to sb else, (math.) transitive		5
传来	chuánlái	vb.	(of a sound) to come through, to be heard, (of news) to arrive		3
传媒	chuánméi	n.	media		6
传输	chuánshū	vb.	to transmit, transmission		6
传说	chuánshuō	n.	legend, folklore, to repeat from mouth to mouth, they say that...		3
传统	chuántǒng	n.	tradition, traditional, convention, conventional		4
传言	chuányán	n.	rumour, hearsay		6
传真	chuánzhēn	n.	fax, facsimile		5
流传	liúchuán	vb.	to spread, to circulate, to hand down		4
宣传	xuānchuán	vb.	to disseminate, to give publicity to, propaganda		3
遗传	yíchuán	vb.	heredity, to inherit (a trait), to pass on (to one's offspring)		4
仿	**fǎng**		**to imitate, to copy**	人 9.4	5
仿佛	• fǎngfú	vb.	to seem, as if, alike, similar		6
模仿	mófǎng	vb.	to imitate, to copy, to emulate, to mimic, model		5
份	**fèn**		**part, share, ingredient, component**	人 9.4	2
份	fèn	m.w.	part, share, ingredient, component, m.w. for gifts, newspaper, magazine, papers, reports, contracts etc.		2
身份	shēnfèn	n.	identity, aspect of one's identity (i.e. sth that one is – mayor, father, permanent resident etc), role		4
月份	yuèfèn	n.	month		2
身份证	shēnfènzhèng	n.	identity card, ID		3
会	* **huì, kuài**		**meeting, conference; account**	人 9.4	1
会	huì	+ vb.	to be able to (can), to know how, be good at, be likely to, to assemble, to meet, to gather		1
会	huì	+ n.	meeting, conference		2
会见	huìjiàn	vb.	to meet with (sb who is paying a visit)		6
会谈	huìtán	n.	talks, discussions		5
会议	huìyì	n.	meeting, conference		3
会员	huìyuán	n.	member		3
会长	huìzhǎng	n.	president of a club, committee etc		6
会计	• kuàiji	n.	accountant, accountancy, accounting		4
大会	dàhuì	n.	general assembly, general meeting, convention		4
峰会	fēnghuì	n.	summit meeting		6
国会	guóhuì	n.	parliament, (in the U.S.) Congress, (in Japan) the Diet		6
机会	jīhuì	n.	opportunity, chance, occasion		2
聚会	jùhuì	n.	party, gathering, to meet, to get together		4
开会	kāi huì	vb.	to hold a meeting, to attend a meeting		1
社会	shèhuì	n.	society		3
体会	tǐhuì	vb.	to know from experience, to learn through experience, to realize, understanding, experience		3

晚会	wǎnhuì	n.	evening party	2
误会	wùhuì	vb.	to misunderstand, to mistake, misunderstanding	4
协会	xiéhuì	n.	an association, a society	6
学会	xuéhuì	vb.	to learn, to master, institute, learned society, (scholarly) association	6
宴会	yànhuì	n.	banquet, feast, dinner party	6
约会	yuēhuì	n.	appointment, engagement, date	4
待会儿	•dāihuìr	adv.	in a moment, later	6
那会儿	nàhuìr	n.	at that time (in the past or the future)	2
一会儿	yīhuìr	+n.	a little while	1
一会儿	yīhuìr	+adv.	in a moment, now…now…	2
博览会	bólǎnhuì	n.	exposition, international fair	5
亚运会	yàyùnhuì	n.	Asian Games	4
演唱会	yǎnchànghuì	n.	vocal recital or concert	3
音乐会	•yīnyuèhuì	n.	concert	2
运动会	yùndònghuì	n.	sports competition	4
座谈会	zuòtánhuì	n.	conference, symposium, rap session	6
不一会儿	bùyīhuìr	phr.	in no time at all	2

伙 huǒ companion, partner 人 9.4 4

伙	huǒ	n.	companion, partner, group, m.w. for groups of people, to combine, together	4
伙伴	huǒbàn	n.	partner, companion, comrade	4
大伙	dàhuǒ	n.	everybody, everyone, we all	5
小伙子	xiǎohuǒzi	n.	young man, young guy, lad, youngster	4

价 jià price, value 人 9.4 3

价	jià	n.	price, value, (chemistry) valence	5
价格	jiàgé	n.	price	3
价钱	jiàqián	n.	price	3
价值	jiàzhí	n.	value, worth, fig. values (ethical, cultural etc)	3
代价	dàijià	n.	price, cost, consideration (in share dealing)	5
定价	dìngjià	vb.	to set a price, to fix a price	6
房价	fángjià	n.	house price, cost of housing	6
高价	gāojià	n.	high price	4
降价	jiàngjià	vb.	to cut the price, to drive down the price, to get cheaper	4
票价	piàojià	n.	ticket price, fare, admission fee	3
评价	píngjià	vb.	to evaluate, to assess	3
特价	tèjià	n.	special price	4
物价	wùjià	n.	(commodity) prices	5
涨价	zhǎngjià	vb.	to appreciate (in value), to increase in price	5

件 jiàn item, component 人 9.4 2

件	jiàn	n.	item, component, m.w. for events, things, clothes etc	2
附件	fùjiàn	n.	enclosure, attachment (email), appendix	5
软件	ruǎnjiàn	n.	(computer) software	5
事件	shìjiàn	n.	event, happening, incident	3
条件	tiáojiàn	n.	condition, circumstances, term, factor, requirement, prerequisite, qualification	2
文件	wénjiàn	n.	document, file	3
硬件	yìngjiàn	n.	hardware	5

邮件	yóujiàn	n.	mail, post, email		3
证件	zhèngjiàn	n.	certificate, papers, credentials, document, ID		3
电子邮件 ·	diànzǐ yóujiàn	n.	email		3
企	**qǐ**		**to plan a project, to stand on tiptoe**	人 9.4	4
企图	qǐtú	vb.	to attempt, to try, attempt		6
企业	qǐyè	n.	company, firm, enterprise, corporation		4
任	**rèn**		**to appoint**	人 9.4	3
任	rèn	+ vb.	to appoint		3
任	rèn	+ conj.	no matter (what, how, etc.)		3
任何	rènhé	pro.	any, whatever, whichever, whatsoever		3
任务	- rènwu	n.	mission, assignment, task, duty, role		3
担任	dānrèn	vb.	to hold a governmental office or post, to assume office of, to take charge of, to serve as		4
信任	xìnrèn	vb.	to trust, to have confidence in		3
责任	zérèn	n.	responsibility, blame, duty		3
主任	zhǔrèn	n.	director, head		3
伞	**sǎn**		**umbrella**	人 9.4	4
伞	sǎn	n.	umbrella, parasol		4
伤	**shāng**		**to injure**	人 9.4	3
伤	shāng	vb.	to injure, injury, wound		3
伤害	shānghài	vb.	to injure, to harm		4
伤口	shāngkǒu	n.	wound, cut		6
伤亡	shāngwáng	n.	casualties, injuries and deaths		6
伤心	shāngxīn	vb.	to grieve, to be broken-hearted, to feel deeply hurt		3
伤员	shāngyuán	n.	wounded person		6
悲伤	bēishāng	adj.	sad, sorrowful		5
受伤	shòu shāng	vb.	to sustain injuries, wounded (in an accident etc), harmed		3
伟	**wěi**		**big, large, great**	人 9.4	3
伟大	wěidà	adj.	big, large, great, grand, worthy of the greatest admiration, important (contribution etc)		3
雄伟	xióngwěi	adj.	grand, imposing, magnificent, majestic		5
伍	**wǔ**		**five, company of five, troops**	人 9.4	6
队伍	- duìwu	n.	ranks, troops, queue, line, procession		6
休	**xiū**		**to rest, to stop**	人 9.4	1
休假	xiūjià	vb.	to take a vacation, to go on holiday		2
休息	- xiūxi	n.	rest, to rest		1
休闲	xiūxián	n.	leisure, relaxation, not working, idle, to enjoy leisure, to lie fallow		5
退休	tuìxiū	vb.	to retire, retirement (from work)		3
仰	**yǎng**		**to look upward**	人 9.4	6
仰	yǎng	vb.	to look upward, to look up to, to rely on, surname Yang		6
信仰	xìnyǎng	vb.	to believe in (a religion), firm belief, conviction		6
优	**yōu**		**superior, excellent**	人 9.4	3
优点	yōudiǎn	n.	merit, benefit, strong point, advantage		3

优惠	yōuhuì	adj.	favourable (terms), preferential (treatment), discount (price)		5
优良	yōuliáng	adj.	fine, good, first-rate		4
优美	yōuměi	adj.	graceful, fine, elegant		4
优势	yōushì	n.	superiority, dominance, advantage		3
优先	yōuxiān	vb.	to have priority, to take precedence		5
优秀	yōuxiù	adj.	outstanding, excellent		4
优质	yōuzhì	adj.	high quality		6
众	**zhòng**		many, numerous	人 9.4	3
众多	zhòngduō	adj.	numerous		5
大众	dàzhòng	n.	the masses, people, public		4
公众	gōngzhòng	n.	public		6
观众	guānzhòng	n.	spectators, audience, visitors (to an exhibition etc)		3
群众	qúnzhòng	n.	mass, multitude, the masses		5
听众	tīngzhòng	n.	audience, listeners		3
伴	**bàn**		partner, companion	人 9.5	4
伙伴	huǒbàn	n.	partner, companion, comrade		4
但	**dàn**		but, yet	人 9.5	2
但	dàn	conj.	but, yet, however, only, merely, still		2
但是	dànshì	conj.	but, however		2
不但	bùdàn	conj.	not only (... but also...)		2
低	**dī**		low, beneath	人 9.5	2
低	dī	adj.	low, (opp. 高 gāo: high), beneath, to lower (one's head), to let droop, to hang down, to incline		2
低头	dītóu	vb.	to bow the head, to yield, to give in		6
低温	dīwēn	n.	low temperature		6
低于	dīyú	vb.	to be lower than		5
降低	jiàngdī	vb.	to reduce, to lower, to bring down		4
佛	* **fó, fú**		Buddha, of Buddhism; similar	人 9.5	6
佛	fó	n.	Buddha; Buddhism		6
佛教	fójiào	n.	Buddhism, Buddhist		6
仿佛	• fǎngfú	vb.	to seem, as if, alike, similar		6
估	**gū**		to estimate, to guess	人 9.5	5
估计	gūjì	vb.	to estimate, to reckon		5
评估	pínggū	vb.	to evaluate, to assess, assessment, evaluation		5
何	**hé**		what, how	人 9.5	3
任何	rènhé	pro.	any, whatever, whichever, whatsoever		3
如何	rúhé	pro.	how, what way, what		3
为何	wèihé	adv.	why		6
你	**nǐ**		you	人 9.5	1
你	nǐ	pro.	you (informal, as opposed to courteous 您 nín)		1
你们	nǐmen	pro.	you (plural)		1
伸	**shēn**		to extend, to stretch out	人 9.5	5
伸	shēn	vb.	to stretch, to extend		5

延伸	yánshēn	vb.	to extend, to spread		5
似	**shì**		to seem, to appear	人 9.5	3
似的	shìde	aux.	seems as if, rather like		4
似乎	shìhū	adv.	apparently, to seem, to appear, as if, seemingly		4
好似	hǎoshì	vb.	to seem, to be like		6
类似	lèishì	vb.	to be similar to, to be analogous to		3
相似	xiāngshì	vb.	to resemble, similar, like, resemblance, similarity		3
体	**tǐ**		body, form	人 9.5	1
体操	tǐcāo	n.	gymnastics, gymnastic		4
体会	tǐhuì	vb.	to know from experience, to learn through experience, to realize, understanding, experience		3
体积	tǐjī	n.	volume, bulk		5
体检	tǐjiǎn	vb.	to have a check-up		4
体力	tǐlì	n.	physical strength, physical power		5
体现	tǐxiàn	vb.	to embody, to reflect, to incarnate		3
体验	tǐyàn	vb.	to experience for oneself		3
体育	tǐyù	n.	sports, physical education		2
体重	tǐzhòng	n.	body weight		4
体育场	tǐyùchǎng	n.	stadium		2
体育馆	tǐyùguǎn	n.	gym, gymnasium, stadium		2
个体	gètǐ	n.	individual		4
集体	jítǐ	n.	collective (decision), joint (effort), a group, a team, en masse, as a group		3
具体	jùtǐ	adj.	concrete, definite, specific		3
媒体	méitǐ	n.	media, esp. news media		3
气体	qìtǐ	n.	gas (i.e. gaseous substance)		5
全体	quántǐ	n.	all, entire		2
群体	qúntǐ	n.	community, colony		5
身体	shēntǐ	n.	the body, one's health		1
团体	tuántǐ	n.	group, organization, team		3
整体	zhěngtǐ	n.	whole entity, entire body, synthesis, as a whole (situation, construction, team etc), global, macrocosm, integral, holistic, whole		3
主体	zhǔtǐ	n.	main part, bulk, body, subject, agent		5
总体	zǒngtǐ	n.	total, entire, overall, population (statistics)		5
多媒体	duōméitǐ	n.	multimedia		6
位	**wèi**		position, location	人 9.5	2
位	wèi	n.	position, location, place, seat, m.w. for people (honourific)		2
位于	wèiyú	vb.	to be located at, to be situated at, to lie		4
位置	-wèizhi	n.	position, place, seat		4
部位	bùwèi	n.	position, place		5
单位	dānwèi	n.	unit (of measure), unit (group of people as a whole), work unit (place of employment, esp. in the PRC prior to economic reform)		2
地位	•dìwèi	n.	position, status, place		4
定位	dìngwèi	vb.	to orientate, to position, to categorize (as), to characterize (as), positioning, position, niche		6
岗位	gǎngwèi	n.	post, job		6
各位	gèwèi	pro.	everybody, all (guests, colleagues etc), all of you		3

学位	xuéwèi	n.	academic degree, place in school		5
职位	zhíwèi	n.	post, office, position		5
诸位	zhūwèi	pro.	(pro.) everyone, Ladies and Gentlemen, Sirs		6
座位	zuòwèi	n.	seat		2
余	**yú**		I, me (lit.)	人 9.5	4
其余	qíyú	pro.	the rest, the others, remaining, remainder, apart from them		4
业余	yèyú	adj.	in one's spare time, outside working hours, amateur (historian etc)		4
住	**zhù**		to live, to dwell	人 9.5	1
住	zhù	vb.	to live, to dwell, to stay, to reside, to stop, (suffix indicating firmness, steadiness, or coming to a halt)		1
住院	zhù yuàn	vb.	to be in hospital, to be hospitalized		2
住房	zhùfáng	n.	housing		2
住宅	zhùzhái	n.	residence, tenement		6
记住	- jìzhu	vb.	to remember, to bear in mind, to learn by heart		1
居住	jūzhù	vb.	to reside, to dwell, to live in a place, resident in		4
站住	zhànzhù	vb.	to stand		2
抓住	zhuāzhù	vb.	to grab, to capture		3
忍不住	- rěnbuzhù	phr.	cannot help, unable to bear		5
作	**zuò**		to do, to grow	人 9.5	1
作	zuò	vb.	to do, to grow, to write or compose, to pretend, to regard as, to feel, writings or works		6
作文	zuò wén	vb.	to write an essay, composition (student essay)		2
作战	zuò zhàn	vb.	to combat, to fight		6
作出	zuòchū	vb.	to put out, to come up with, to make (a choice, decision, proposal, response, comment etc)		4
作废	zuòfèi	vb.	to become invalid, to cancel, to delete, to nullify		6
作家	zuòjiā	n.	author		2
作品	zuòpǐn	n.	work (of art), opus		3
作为	• zuòwéi	n.	one's conduct, deed, activity, accomplishment, achievement		4
作业	zuòyè	n.	school assignment, homework, work, task, operation		2
作用	zuòyòng	vb.	to act on, to affect, action, use, effect, purpose		2
作者	zuòzhě	n.	author, writer		3
操作	cāozuò	vb.	to work, to operate, to manipulate		4
炒作	chǎozuò	vb.	to hype, to promote (in the media)		6
创作	chuàngzuò	vb.	to create, to produce, to write, creative work, creation		3
当作	• dàngzuò	vb.	to treat as, to regard as		6
动作	dòngzuò	n.	movement, motion, action		1
工作	gōngzuò	vb.	to work, (of a machine) to operate, job, work, task		1
合作	hézuò	vb.	to cooperate, to collaborate, to work together, cooperation		3
叫作	jiàozuò	vb.	to call, to be called		2
看作	kànzuò	vb.	to look upon as, to regard as		6
写作	xiězuò	vb.	to write, to compose, writing, written works		3
运作	yùnzuò	vb.	to operate, operations, workings, activities (usu. of an organization), thread (computing)		6
制作	zhìzuò	vb.	to make, to manufacture		3
著作	• zhùzuò	vb.	to write, literary work, book, article, writings		4
工作日	gōngzuò rì	n.	workday, working day, weekday		5

侧	cè		side, to incline towards	人 9.6	6
侧	cè	n.	side, to incline towards, to lean, inclined, lateral		6
两侧	liǎngcè	n.	two sides, both sides		6
供	gōng		to provide, to supply	人 9.6	4
供给	· gōngjǐ	vb.	to furnish, to provide, to supply (as in supply and demand)		6
供应	· gōngyìng	vb.	to supply, to provide, to offer		4
提供	tígōng	vb.	to offer, to supply, to provide, to furnish		4
佳	jiā		good, auspicious, beautiful, delightful	人 9.6	6
最佳	zuìjiā	adj.	optimum, optimal, peak, best (athlete, movie etc)		6
例	lì		precedent, example, regulation	人 9.6	2
例如	lìrú	vb.	to give an example		2
例外	lìwài	n.	exception, to be an exception		5
例子	lìzi	n.	case, (for) instance, example		2
比例	bǐlì	n.	proportion, scale		3
使	shǐ		to make, to cause	人 9.6	2
使	shǐ	vb.	to make, to cause, to enable, to use, to employ, to send, to instruct sb to do sth, envoy, messenger		3
使劲	shǐ jìn	vb.	to exert all one's strength		4
使得	shǐde	vb.	(to be) usable, workable, doable, to make, to cause		5
使用	shǐyòng	vb.	to use, to employ, to apply, to make use of		2
促使	cùshǐ	vb.	to induce, to promote, to urge, to impel, to bring about, to provoke		4
大使	dàshǐ	n.	ambassador, envoy		6
即使	jíshǐ	conj.	even if, even though		5
大使馆	dàshǐguǎn	n.	embassy		3
依	yī		to depend on	人 9.6	4
依次	yīcì	adv.	in order, in succession		6
依法	yīfǎ	adv.	according to law, legal (proceedings)		5
依旧	yījiù	adj.	as before, still		5
依据	yījù	n.	basis, foundation, according to		5
依靠	yīkào	vb.	to rely on sth (for support etc), to depend on		4
依赖	yīlài	vb.	to depend on, to be dependent on		6
依然	yīrán	adv.	still, as before		4
依照	yīzhào	prep.	according to, in light of		5
保	bǎo		to defend, to protect	人 9.7	3
保	bǎo	vb.	to defend, to protect, to care		3
保密	bǎo mì	vb.	to keep sth confidential, to maintain secrecy		4
保安	bǎo'ān	vb.	to ensure public security, to ensure safety (for workers engaged in production), public security, security guard		3
保持	bǎochí	vb.	to keep, to maintain, to hold, to preserve		3
保存	bǎocún	vb.	to conserve, to preserve, to keep, to save (a file etc) (computing)		3
保护	bǎohù	vb.	to protect, to defend, to safeguard, protection		3
保健	bǎojiàn	n.	health protection, health care, to maintain in good health		6
保留	bǎoliú	vb.	to keep, to retain, to have reservations (about sth), to hold back (from saying sth), to put aside for later		3
保守	bǎoshǒu	adj.	conservative, to guard, to keep		4

保卫	bǎowèi	vb.	to defend, to safeguard	5
保险	bǎoxiǎn	n.	insurance, to insure, safe, secure, be sure, be bound to	3
保养	bǎoyǎng	vb.	to take good care of (or conserve) one's health, to keep in good repair, to maintain, maintenance	5
保证	bǎozhèng	n.	guarantee, to guarantee, to ensure, to safeguard, to pledge	3
担保	dānbǎo	vb.	to guarantee, to vouch for	4
环保	huánbǎo	n.	environmental protection, environmentally friendly	3
确保	quèbǎo	vb.	to ensure, to guarantee	3

便 * **biàn, pián** plain; cheap 人 9.7 2

便	biàn	adj.	plain, informal, suitable, convenient, opportune	6
便利	biànlì	adj.	convenient, easy, to facilitate	5
便是	biànshì	adv.	emphasizes that sth is precisely or exactly as stated, even, if, just like, in the same way as	6
便条	biàntiáo	n.	(informal) note	5
便于	biànyú	adj.	easy to, convenient for	5
便宜	• piányi	adj.	cheap, inexpensive, small advantages	2
不便	bùbiàn	adj.	inconvenient, inappropriate, unsuitable, short of cash	6
方便	fāngbiàn	adj.	convenient, suitable, to facilitate, to make things easy, having money to spare, (euphemism) to relieve oneself	2
随便	suíbiàn	adj.	casual, random, as one wishes, as one pleases, anyhow	2
以便	yǐbiàn	conj.	so that, so as to, in order to	5
方便面	fāngbiànmiàn	n.	instant noodles	2

促 **cù** urgent, hurried 人 9.7 4

促进	cùjìn	vb.	to promote (an idea or cause), to advance, boost	4
促使	cùshǐ	vb.	to induce, to promote, to urge, to impel, to bring about, to provoke	4
促销	cùxiāo	vb.	to promote sales	4

俩 **liǎ** two, pair 人 9.7 4

俩	liǎ	num.	two, both, some	4

侵 **qīn** to invade, to encroach 人 9.7 6

侵犯	qīnfàn	vb.	to infringe on, to encroach on, to violate, to assault	6

俗 **sú** custom, convention 人 9.7 4

风俗	fēngsú	n.	social custom	4

信 **xìn** letter, mail 人 9.7 2

信	xìn	+ n.	letter, mail	2
信	xìn	+ vb.	to believe, to trust	3
信封	xìnfēng	n.	envelope	3
信号	xìnhào	n.	signal	2
信念	xìnniàn	n.	faith, belief, conviction	5
信任	xìnrèn	vb.	to trust, to have confidence in	3
信息	xìnxī	n.	information, news, message	2
信箱	xìnxiāng	n.	mailbox, post office box	5
信心	xìnxīn	n.	confidence, faith (in sb or sth)	2
信仰	xìnyǎng	vb.	to believe in (a religion), firm belief, conviction	6
信用	xìnyòng	vb.	to trust, credit (commerce), trustworthiness, creditworthiness	6
信用卡	xìnyòngkǎ	n.	credit card	2

诚信	chéngxìn	adj.	genuine, honest, in good faith, honesty, integrity	4
短信	duǎnxìn	n.	short message, text message	2
回信	huí xìn	vb.	to reply, to write back, letter written in reply	5
来信	láixìn	n.	incoming letter, to send us a letter	5
迷信	míxìn	n.	superstition, to have a superstitious belief (in sth)	5
通信	tōng xìn	vb.	to correspond (by letter etc), to communicate, communication	3
微信	wēixìn	n.	WeChat	4
相信	xiāngxìn	vb.	to be convinced (that sth is true), to believe, to accept sth as true	2
自信	zìxìn	vb.	to have confidence in oneself, self-confidence	4

倍 bèi — times, fold 人 9.8 4

倍	bèi	m.w.	(two, three, etc)-fold, times (multiplier)	4

倡 chàng — to lead, to initiate 人 9.8 5

倡导	chàngdǎo	vb.	to advocate, to initiate, to propose, to be a proponent of (an idea or school of thought)	5
提倡	tíchàng	vb.	to promote, to advocate	5

倒 * dào, dǎo — to place upside down; to fall 人 9.8 2

倒	• dǎo	vb.	to fall, to collapse, to lie horizontally, to overthrow, to fail, to go bankrupt, to change (trains or buses), to move around, to resell at a profit	2
倒	dào	vb.	to place upside down, to invert, to pour, to throw out, to move backwards, however, actually, as a matter of fact, contrary to expectation	2
倒闭	• dǎobì	vb.	to go bankrupt, to close down	4
倒车	• dǎo chē	vb.	to change buses, trains etc	4
倒车	dào chē	vb.	to reverse a car, to back a car	4
倒是	dàoshì	adv.	contrary to what one might expect, actually, contrariwise, why don't you	5
摔倒	• shuāidǎo	vb.	to fall down, to slip and fall, to throw sb to the ground	5

候 hòu — to wait, to inquire after 人 9.8 1

等候	děnghòu	vb.	to wait, to wait for	5
时候	- shíhou	n.	time, length of time, moment, period	1
问候	wènhòu	vb.	to give one's respects, to send a greeting, (fig.) (coll.) to make offensive reference to (somebody dear to the person to whom one is speaking)	4
那时候	- nàshíhou	n.	then, at that time, in those days (abbrev. 那时 nàshí: of course)	2
气候	qìhòu	n.	climate, atmosphere, situation	3
小时候	- xiǎoshíhou	n.	in one's childhood	2
有时候	- yǒu shíhou	adv.	sometimes	1

借 jiè — to lend, to borrow 人 9.8 2

借	jiè	vb.	to lend, to borrow, by means of, to take (an opportunity)	2
借鉴	jièjiàn	vb.	to draw on (others' experience), to learn from (how others do things), lesson to be learned (by observing others)	6

俱 jù — entirely, without exception 人 9.8 5

俱乐部	jùlèbù	n.	club (the organisation or its premises) (loanword)	5

倾	**qīng**		to overturn, to collapse	人9.8	6
倾向	qīngxiàng	n.	trend, tendency, orientation; to be inclined to, to prefer		6
修	**xiū**		to decorate, to embellish	人9.8	3
修	xiū	vb.	to decorate, to embellish, to repair, to write, to study		3
修车	xiūchē	vb.	to repair a bike (car etc)		6
修复	xiūfù	vb.	to restore, to renovate, restoration, (computing) to fix (a bug)		5
修改	xiūgǎi	vb.	to amend, to alter, to modify		3
修建	xiūjiàn	vb.	to build, to construct		5
修理	xiūlǐ	vb.	to repair, to fix, to prune, to trim, (coll.) to sort sb out, to fix sb		4
修养	xiūyǎng	n.	accomplishment, training, self-cultivation		5
必修	bìxiū	adj.	(of an academic course) required, compulsory		6
维修	wéixiū	n.	maintenance (of equipment), to protect and maintain		4
选修	xuǎnxiū	vb.	(at a school) to take as an elective, an elective, elective (subject)		5
装修	zhuāngxiū	vb.	to decorate, interior decoration, to fit up, to renovate		4
债	**zhài**		debt	人9.8	6
债	zhài	n.	debt		6
值	**zhí**		value, (to be) worth	人9.8	3
值	zhí	n.	value, (to be) worth, to happen to, to be on duty		3
值班	zhí bān	vb.	to work a shift, to be on duty		5
值得	zhíde	vb.	to be worth, to deserve		3
不值	bùzhí	vb.	to be not worth		6
价值	jiàzhí	n.	value, worth, fig. values (ethical, cultural etc)		3
升值	shēngzhí	vb.	to rise in value, to appreciate		6
增值	zēngzhí	vb.	to appreciate (financially), to increase in value, value-added (accountancy)		6
偿	**cháng**		to repay, to recompense	人9.9	5
补偿	bǔcháng	vb.	to compensate, to make up		5
赔偿	péicháng	vb.	to compensate		5
假	*** jià, jiǎ**		holiday; false	人9.9	1
假	• jiǎ	adj.	false, fake, (opp. 真 zhēn: true) if, in case, to borrow		2
假如	• jiǎrú	conj.	if		4
假期	jiàqī	n.	holiday, vacation		2
假日	jiàrì	n.	holiday, non-working day		6
长假	• chángjià	n.	long vacation		6
放假	fàng jià	vb.	to have a holiday or vacation		1
寒假	hánjià	n.	winter vacation		4
请假	qǐng jià	vb.	to request leave of absence		1
暑假	shǔjià	n.	summer vacation		4
休假	xiūjià	vb.	to take a vacation, to go on holiday		2
节假日	jiéjiàrì	n.	public holiday		6
健	**jiàn**		healthy, strong	人9.9	2
健康	jiànkāng	n.	health, healthy		2
健全	jiànquán	adj.	robust, sound		5
健身	jiànshēn	vb.	to exercise, to keep fit, to work out, physical exercise		4

保健	bǎojiàn	n.	health protection, health care, to maintain in good health		6
偶	**ǒu**		accidentally, coincidently, an idol	人 9.9	5
偶尔	ǒu'ěr	adv.	occasionally, once in a while, sometimes		5
偶然	ǒurán	adv.	incidentally, occasional, occasionally, by chance, randomly		5
偶像	ǒuxiàng	n.	idol		5
偏	**piān**		to be inclined to one side, slanting	人 9.9	6
偏	piān	vb.	to lean, to slant, oblique, prejudiced, to deviate from average, to stray from the intended line, stubbornly, contrary to expectations		6
停	**tíng**		to stop, to halt	人 9.9	2
停	tíng	vb.	to stop, to halt, to park (a car)		2
停车	tíngchē	vb.	to pull up (stop one's vehicle), to park, (of a machine) to stop working, to stall		2
停留	tíngliú	vb.	to stay somewhere temporarily, to stop over		5
停下	tíngxià	vb.	to stop		4
停止	tíngzhǐ	vb.	to stop, to halt, to cease		3
停车场	tíngchēchǎng	n.	car park, parking lot		2
不停	bùtíng	adv.	incessant		5
暂停	zàntíng	vb.	to suspend, time-out (e.g. in sports), stoppage, pause (media player)		5
偷	**tōu**		to steal, to pilfer	人 9.9	5
偷	tōu	vb.	to steal, to pilfer, to snatch, thief, stealthily		5
偷偷	tōutōu	adv.	stealthily, secretly, covertly, furtively, on the sly		5
小偷	xiǎotōu	n.	thief		5
做	**zuò**		to do, to make	人 9.9	1
做	zuò	vb.	to do, to make, to produce, to write, to compose, to act as, to engage in, to hold (a party), to be		1
做饭	zuò fàn	vb.	to prepare a meal, to cook		2
做客	zuò kè	vb.	to be a guest or visitor		3
做梦	zuò mèng	vb.	to dream, to have a dream, fig. illusion, fantasy, pipe dream		4
做到	zuòdào	vb.	to accomplish, to achieve		2
做法	zuòfǎ	n.	way of handling sth, method for making, work method, recipe, practice		2
傍	**bàng**		by side of, beside, near, close	人 9.10	6
傍晚	bàngwǎn	n.	in the evening, when night falls, towards evening, at night fall, at dusk		6
储	**chǔ**		to store, to save	人 9.10	6
储存	chǔcún	vb.	to stockpile, to store, to stockpile, storage		6
傅	**fù**		tutor, teacher	人 9.10	5
师傅	- shīfu	n.	master, qualified worker, respectful form of address for older men		5
傲	**ào**		proud, haughty, overbearing	人 9.11	6
骄傲	jiāo'ào	adj.	proud, arrogance, conceited, proud of sth		6
傻	**shǎ**		foolish	人 9.11	5
傻	shǎ	adj.	foolish		5

像	**xiàng**		to resemble, to be like	人 9.12	2
像	xiàng	+ vb.	to resemble, to be like, to look as if, such as, appearance, image		2
好像	hǎoxiàng	vb.	to seem like, to look like		2
录像	lùxiàng	vb.	to videotape, to videorecord, video recording		6
偶像	ǒuxiàng	n.	idol		5
摄像	shèxiàng	vb.	to videotape		5
音像	yīnxiàng	n.	audio and video, audio-visual		6
摄像机	shèxiàngjī	n.	video camera		5

儿 ér — son, legs — 10

儿	**ér**		son, child	儿 10.0	1
儿科	érkē	n.	paediatrics		6
儿女	érnǚ	n.	children, sons and daughters		5
儿童	értóng	n.	child		4
儿子	érzi	n.	son		1
个儿	gèr	n.	size, height, stature		5
画儿	huàr	n.	drawing, picture, painting		2
空儿	• kòngr	n.	empty space, free time		3
哪儿	nǎr	pro.	where?, wherever, anywhere		1
那儿	nàr	pro.	there		1
女儿	nǚ'ér	n.	daughter		1
少儿	• shào'ér	n.	(abbrev) children and early teenagers 少儿不宜 shào'érbùyí		6
这儿	zhèr	pro.	here (coll.)		1
幼儿园	yòu'éryuán	n.	kindergarten, nursery school		4
待会儿	• dāihuìr	adv.	in a moment, later		6
干活儿	gànhuór	vb.	to do manual labour, to work, erhua variant of 干活 gànhuó		2
模特儿	mótèr	n.	(fashion) model (loanword), mannequin		4
那会儿	nàhuìr	n.	at that time (in the past or the future)		2
笑话儿	xiàohuàr	n.	(spoken) joke		2
一点儿	yīdiǎnr	n.	a bit, a few, a little, erhua variant of 一点 yīdiǎn		1
一会儿	yīhuìr	+ n.	a little while		1
一会儿	yīhuìr	+ adv.	in a moment, now...now...		2
一块儿	yīkuàir	n.	the same place, in company, together, one, erhua variant of 一块 yīkuài		1
一下儿	yīxiàr	+ n.	one time, once		1
一下儿	yīxiàr	+ adv.	in a while, all of a sudden, all at once		5
不一会儿	bùyīhuìr	phr.	in no time at all		2
元	**yuán**		first, fundamental, origin	儿 10.2	1
元	yuán	adj.	first, principal, fundamental, origin, Chinese monetary unit, dollar, surname Yuan; the Yuan or Mongol dynasty (1279-1368)		1
元旦	yuándàn	n.	New Year's Day (Western calendar)		5
元素	yuánsù	n.	element, element of a set, chemical element		6
单元	dānyuán	n.	unit (forming an entity), element, (in a residential building) entrance or staircase		3
公元	gōngyuán	n.	CE (Common Era), AD		4
美元	měiyuán	n.	U.S. dollar		3

允	**yǔn**		to grant, to allow, to consent	儿 10.2	6
允许	yǔnxǔ	vb.	to permit, to allow		6
兄	**xiōng**		elder brother	儿 10.3	4
兄弟	xiōngdì	n.	brothers, younger brother		4
充	**chōng**		to fill, to be full, to supply	儿 10.4	3
充电	chōngdiàn	vb.	to recharge (a battery), (fig.) to recharge one's batteries (through leisure), to update one's skills and knowledge		4
充分	• chōngfèn	adj.	ample, sufficient, adequate, full, fully, to the full		4
充满	chōngmǎn	vb.	(to be) full of, brimming with, very full, permeated		3
充足	chōngzú	adj.	adequate, sufficient, abundant		5
充电器	chōngdiànqì	n.	battery charger		4
补充	bǔchōng	vb.	to replenish, to supplement, to complement, additional, supplementary		3
光	**guāng**		light, brilliant, to shine	儿 10.4	3
光	guāng	n.	light, ray		3
光辉	guānghuī	n.	radiance, glory, brilliant, magnificent		6
光临	guānglín	vb.	(formal) to honour with one's presence, to attend		4
光明	guāngmíng	n.	light, radiance, (fig.) bright (prospects etc), openhearted		3
光盘	guāngpán	n.	compact disc, CD or DVD, CD ROM		4
光荣	guāngróng	n.	honour and glory, glorious		5
光线	guāngxiàn	n.	light ray		5
不光	bùguāng	adv.	not the only one, not only		3
灯光	dēngguāng	n.	(stage) lighting, light		4
风光	fēngguāng	n.	scene, view, sight, landscape, to be well-regarded, to be well-off, grand (dialect), impressive (dialect)		5
观光	guānguāng	vb.	to tour, sightseeing, tourism		6
目光	mùguāng	n.	sight, vision, view, gaze, look		5
时光	shíguāng	n.	time, era, period of time		5
眼光	yǎnguāng	n.	gaze, insight, foresight, vision, way of looking at things		5
阳光	yángguāng	n.	sunshine		3
先	**xiān**		first, former, previous	儿 10.4	1
先	xiān	adv.	early, prior, former, in advance, first, (opp. 后 hòu: last)		1
先锋	xiānfēng	n.	vanguard, pioneer, avant-garde		6
先后	xiānhòu	n.	priority, in succession, one after another		5
先进	xiānjìn	adj.	advanced (technology), to advance		3
先前	xiānqián	n.	before, previously		5
先生	- xiānsheng	n.	teacher, husband, doctor (dialect)		1
领先	lǐngxiān	vb.	to lead, to be in front		3
事先	shìxiān	n.	in advance, before the event, beforehand, prior		4
首先	shǒuxiān	conj.	first (of all), in the first place		3
率先	lǜxiān	vb.	to take the lead, to show initiative		4
优先	yōuxiān	vb.	to have priority, to take precedence		5
原先	yuánxiān	adv.	originally, original, former		5
克	**kè**		to overcome, gram	儿 10.5	2
克	kè	vb.	to overcome, to restrain, gram		2

克服	kèfú	vb.	to (try to) overcome (hardships etc), to conquer, to put up with, to endure		3
千克	qiānkè	m.w.	kilogram		2
巧克力	qiǎokèlì	n.	chocolate (loanword)		4
免	**miǎn**		**to spare, to excuse from**	儿 10.5	4
免得	miǎnde	conj.	so as not to, so as to avoid		6
免费	miǎnfèi	vb.	(to be) free of charge		4
避免	bìmiǎn	vb.	to avert, to prevent, to avoid, to refrain from		4
不免	bùmiǎn	adv.	inevitably		5
难免	nánmiǎn	adj.	hard to avoid, difficult to escape from, will inevitably		4
兔	**tù**		**rabbit**	儿 10.6	5
兔	tù	n.	rabbit		5
党	**dǎng**		**party, club**	儿 10.8	6
党	dǎng	n.	party, club, association, surname Dang		6
政党	zhèngdǎng	n.	political party		6

入 rù enter   11

入	**rù**		**to enter, to go into**	入 11.0	2
入	rù	vb.	to enter, to go into, to join, to become a member of, to confirm or agree with		6
入学	rù xué	vb.	to enter a school or college, to go to school for the first time as a child		6
入口	rùkǒu	n.	entrance, to import		2
入门	rùmén	n.	entrance door, to enter a door, introduction (to a subject), to learn the basics of a subject		5
出入	chūrù	vb.	to go out and come in, entrance and exit, expenditure and income, discrepancy, inconsistent		6
加入	jiārù	vb.	to become a member, to join, to mix into, to participate in, to add in		4
进入	jìnrù	vb.	to enter, to join, to go into		2
列入	lièrù	vb.	to include on a list		4
融入	róngrù	vb.	to blend into, to integrate, to assimilate, to merge		6
深入	shēnrù	vb.	to penetrate deeply, thorough		3
收入	shōurù	vb.	to take in, income, revenue		2
输入	shūrù	vb.	to import, to input		3
投入	tóurù	vb.	to throw into, to put into, to throw oneself into, to participate in, to invest in, absorbed, engrossed		4
陷入	xiànrù	vb.	to sink into, to get caught up in, to land in (a predicament)		6
内	**nèi**		**inside**	入 11.2	3
内	nèi	n.	inside, inner, internal, within, interior		3
内部	nèibù	n.	interior, inside (part, section), internal		4
内地	• nèidì	n.	mainland China (PRC excluding Hong Kong and Macau, but including islands such as Hainan)		6
内科	nèikē	n.	internal medicine, general medicine		4
内容	nèiróng	n.	content, substance, details		3
内外	nèiwài	n.	inside and outside, domestic and foreign, approximately, about		6
内心	nèixīn	n.	heart, innermost being, (math.) incentre		3

内衣	nèiyī	n.	undergarment, underwear	6
内在	nèizài	adj.	inner, internal, intrinsic, innate	5
国内	guónèi	adj.	domestic, internal (to a country), civil	3
以内	yǐnèi	n.	within, less than	4
在内	zàinèi	vb.	(to be included) in it, among them	5
之内	zhīnèi	n.	inside, within	5

全 quán — all, whole, entire   入 11.4   2

全	quán	adj.	all, whole, entire, complete, surname Quan	2
全部	quánbù	adj.	whole, entire, complete	2
全场	quánchǎng	n.	everyone present, the whole audience, across-the-board, unanimously, whole duration (of a competition or match)	3
全都	quándōu	adv.	all, without exception	5
全国	quánguó	n.	whole nation, nationwide, countrywide, national	2
全家	quánjiā	n.	whole family	2
全力	quánlì	n.	full energy (strength), all-out (effort), fully (support)	6
全面	quánmiàn	adj.	all-around, comprehensive, total, overall	3
全年	quánnián	n.	the whole year, all year long	2
全球	quánqiú	n.	entire, total, global, the (whole) world, worldwide	3
全身	quánshēn	n.	whole body, em (typography)	2
全体	quántǐ	n.	all, entire	2
全新	quánxīn	adj.	all new, completely new	6
全世界	quán shìjiè	n.	worldwide, entire world	5
安全	ānquán	adj.	safe, secure, safety, security	2
健全	jiànquán	adj.	robust, sound	5
齐全	qíquán	adj.	complete, comprehensive	5
完全	wánquán	adj.	complete, whole, totally, entirely	2

八 bā — eight   12

八 bā — eight, 8   八 12.0   1

| 八 | bā | num. | eight, 8 | 1 |

公 gōng — public, collectively owned   八 12.2   2

公	gōng	adj.	public, collectively owned, (opp. 私 sī: private), common, international (e.g. high seas, metric system, calendar)	6
公安	gōng'ān	n.	(Ministry of) Public Security, public safety, public security	6
公布	gōngbù	vb.	to announce, to make public, to publish	3
公告	gōnggào	n.	post, announcement	5
公共	gōnggòng	adj.	public, common, communal	3
公鸡	gōngjī	n.	cock, rooster	6
公斤	gōngjīn	m.w.	kilogram (kg)	2
公开	gōngkāi	adj.	public, to publish, to make public	3
公里	gōnglǐ	m.w.	kilometre	2
公路	gōnglù	n.	highway, road	2
公民	gōngmín	n.	citizen	3
公平	gōngpíng	adj.	fair, impartial	2
公认	gōngrèn	vb.	publicly known (to be), accepted (as)	5
公式	gōngshì	n.	formula	5

公司	gōngsī	n.	(business) company, company, firm, corporation, incorporated	2
公园	gōngyuán	n.	park (for public recreation)	2
公元	gōngyuán	n.	CE (Common Era), AD	4
公正	gōngzhèng	adj.	just, fair, equitable	5
公众	gōngzhòng	n.	public	6
公主	gōngzhǔ	n.	princess	6
公交车	gōngjiāochē	n.	public transport vehicle, town bus	2
公务员	gōngwùyuán	n.	functionary, office-bearer	3
公共汽车	gōnggòng qìchē	n.	bus	2
办公	bàn gōng	vb.	to handle official business, to work (esp. in an office)	6
老公	lǎogōng	n.	(coll.) husband	4
办公室	bàngōngshì	n.	office, business premises, bureau	2
高速公路	gāosù gōnglù	n.	expressway, highway, freeway	3

六 liù — six, 6   八 12.2   1

六	liù	num.	six, 6	1
五颜六色	wǔyánliùsè	phr.	multi-coloured, every colour under the sun (idiom)	4

共 gòng — common, general   八 12.4   2

共	gòng	adj.	common, general, to share, together, total, altogether	4
共计	gòngjì	vb.	to sum up to, to total	5
共同	gòngtóng	adj.	common, joint, jointly, together, collaborative	3
共享	gòngxiǎng	vb.	to share, to enjoy together	5
共有	gòngyǒu	vb.	to have altogether, to have in all	3
公共	gōnggòng	adj.	public, common, communal	3
一共	yīgòng	adv.	altogether	2
总共	zǒnggòng	adv.	altogether, in sum, in all, in total	4
公共汽车	gōnggòng qìchē	n.	bus	2

关 guān — to close, relation, frontier pass   八 12.4   1

关	guān	+ vb.	to close, to shut, to turn off	1
关	guān	+ n.	mountain pass, check point, barrier, connection	4
关爱	guān'ài	vb.	to show concern and care for	6
关闭	guānbì	vb.	to close, to shut	4
关怀	guānhuái	n.	care, solicitude, to show care for, concerned about, attentive to	5
关机	guānjī	vb.	to turn off (a machine or device), to finish shooting a film	2
关键	guānjiàn	n.	crucial point, crux	5
关联	guānlián	n.	connection, related, linked, affiliated	6
关上	- guānshang	vb.	to close (a door), to turn off (light, electrical equipment etc)	1
关系	- guānxi	n.	relation, connection, relationship	3
关心	guānxīn	vb.	to be concerned about, to care about	2
关于	guānyú	prep.	pertaining to, concerning, with regard to, about, a matter of	4
关注	guānzhù	vb.	to pay attention to, to follow sth closely, to follow (on social media), concern, interest, attention	3
海关	hǎiguān	n.	customs (i.e. border crossing inspection)	3
机关	jīguān	n.	mechanism, gear, machine-operated, office, agency, organ, organization, establishment, institution, body, stratagem, scheme, intrigue, plot, trick	6
开关	kāiguān	n.	power switch, gas valve, to open the city (or frontier) gate, to open and close, to switch on and off	6

无关	wúguān	vb.	unrelated, having nothing to do (with sth else)	6
相关	xiāngguān	vb.	related, relevant, pertinent, to be interrelated, (statistics) correlation	3
有关	yǒuguān	vb.	to have sth to do with, to relate to, related to, to concern, concerning	6
没关系	- méi guānxi	vb.	it doesn't matter, that's all right, never mind	1

兴	**xìng**		to thrive, to prosper, to flourish	八 12.4 1
兴奋	xìngfèn	vb.	to be excited, excitement, (physiology) excitation	4
兴旺	xìngwàng	adj.	prosperous, thriving, to prosper, to flourish	6
兴趣	xìngqù	n.	interest (desire to know about sth), interest (thing in which one is interested), hobby	4
高兴	gāoxìng	adj.	happy, glad, willing (to do sth), in a cheerful mood	1
新兴	xīnxìng	adj.	rising, up and coming, newly developing	6
感兴趣	gǎn xìngqù	vb.	to be interested	4

兵	**bīng**		soldier, troops	八 12.5 4
兵	bīng	n.	soldiers, a force, an army, weapons, arms, military, warlike	4
士兵	shìbīng	n.	soldier	4

单	**dān**		single, odd (num.), simple	八 12.6 2
单	dān	adj.	single, odd (num.), (opp. 双 shuāng: two, odd), simple, only, sheet, list, surname Shàn	4
单纯	dānchún	adj.	simple, pure, unsophisticated, merely, purely	4
单打	dāndǎ	vb.	to compete one-to-one, singles (in sports)	6
单调	dāndiào	adj.	monotonous	4
单独	dāndú	adv.	alone, by oneself, on one's own	4
单位	dānwèi	n.	unit (of measure), unit (group of people as a whole), work unit (place of employment, esp. in the PRC prior to economic reform)	2
单一	dānyī	adj.	single, only, sole	5
单元	dānyuán	n.	unit (forming an entity), element, (in a residential building) entrance or staircase	3
菜单	càidān	n.	menu	2
简单	jiǎndān	adj.	simple, not complicated, (opp. 复杂 fùzá: complex)	3
名单	míngdān	n.	list of names	2

典	**diǎn**		law, canon	八 12.6 2
典礼	diǎnlǐ	n.	celebration, ceremony	5
典型	diǎnxíng	n.	model, typical case, archetype, typical, representative	4
词典	cídiǎn	n.	dictionary, also written 辞典 cídiǎn	2
辞典	cídiǎn	n.	dictionary, also written 词典 cídiǎn	5
古典	gǔdiǎn	adj.	classical	6
经典	jīngdiǎn	n.	the classics, scriptures, classical, classic (example, case etc), typical	4
字典	zìdiǎn	n.	character dictionary	2

具	**jù**		tool, device	八 12.6 3
具备	jùbèi	vb.	to possess, to have, equipped with, able to fulfil (conditions or requirements)	4
具体	jùtǐ	adj.	concrete, definite, specific	3
具有	jùyǒu	vb.	to have, to possess	3
工具	gōngjù	n.	tool, instrument, utensil, means (to achieve a goal etc)	3
家具	jiājù	n.	furniture	3
玩具	wánjù	n.	plaything, toy	3

其	**qí**		his, her, its	八 12.6	2
其	qí	pro.	his, her, its, their, that, such, it (refers to sth preceding it)		5
其次	qícì	conj.	next, secondly		3
其实	qíshí	adv.	actually, in fact, really		3
其他	qítā	pro.	other, (sth or sb) else, the rest		2
其余	qíyú	pro.	the rest, the others, remaining, remainder, apart from them		4
其中	qízhōng	n.	among, in, included among these		2
极其	jíqí	adv.	extremely		4
尤其	yóuqí	adv.	especially, particularly		5
养	**yǎng**		to raise, to bring up	八 12.7	2
养	yǎng	vb.	to raise (animals), to bring up (children), to keep (pets), to support, to give birth		2
养成	yǎngchéng	vb.	to cultivate, to raise, to form (a habit), to acquire		4
养老	yǎnglǎo	vb.	to provide for the elderly (family members), to enjoy a life in retirement		6
保养	bǎoyǎng	vb.	to take good care of (or conserve) one's health, to keep in good repair, to maintain, maintenance		5
疗养	liáoyǎng	vb.	to get well, to heal, to recuperate, to convalesce, convalescence, to nurse		4
培养	péiyǎng	vb.	to cultivate, to breed, to foster, to nurture, to educate, to groom (for a position), education, fostering, culture (biology)		4
收养	shōuyǎng	vb.	to take in and care for (an elderly person, a dog etc), to adopt (a child), adoption		6
修养	xiūyǎng	n.	accomplishment, training, self-cultivation		5
营养	yíngyǎng	n.	nutrition, nourishment		3
总	**zǒng**		always, to assemble	八 12.7	3
总	zǒng	adv.	always, to assemble, to gather, total, overall, head, chief, general, in every case		3
总部	zǒngbù	n.	general headquarters		6
总裁	zǒngcái	n.	chairman, director-general (of a company etc)		5
总共	zǒnggòng	adv.	altogether, in sum, in all, in total		4
总监	zǒngjiān	n.	head, director (of an organizational unit), (police) commissioner, inspector-general, rank of local governor in Tang dynasty administration		6
总结	zǒngjié	vb.	to sum up, to conclude, summary, résumé		3
总理	zǒnglǐ	n.	premier, prime minister		4
总量	zǒngliàng	n.	total, overall amount		6
总是	zǒngshì	adv.	always		3
总数	zǒngshù	n.	total, sum, aggregate		5
总算	zǒngsuàn	adv.	at long last, finally, on the whole		5
总体	zǒngtǐ	n.	total, entire, overall, population (statistics)		5
总统	zǒngtǒng	n.	president (of a country)		4
总之	zǒngzhī	conj.	in a word, in short, in brief		4
总经理	zǒngjīnglǐ	n.	general manager, CEO		6

	冂	jiōng		down box		13
册		cè		book, volume	冂 13.3	5
册		cè	n.	book, booklet, m.w. for books		5
注册		zhùcè	vb.	to register, to enrol		5
再		zài		again, once more	冂 13.4	1
再		zài	adv.	again, once more, re-, second, another, then (after sth, and not until then)		1
再次		zàicì	adv.	one more time, again, one more, once again		5
再见		zàijiàn	intj.	goodbye, see you again later		1
再三		zàisān	adv.	over and over again, again and again		4
再生		zàishēng	vb.	to be reborn, to regenerate, to be a second so-and-so (famous dead person), recycling, regeneration		6
再说		zàishuō	vb.	to say again, to put off a discussion until later, moreover, what's more, besides		6
再也		zàiyě	adv.	(not) any more		5
不再		bùzài	adv.	no more, no longer		6
一再		yīzài	adv.	repeatedly		4
冒		mào		to emit, to risk	冂 13.7	3
冒		mào	vb.	to emit, to send out, to cover, to risk, brave, bold, surname Mao		5
感冒		gǎnmào	vb.	to catch cold, (common) cold		3

	冖	mì		cover		14
写		xiě		to write	冖 14.3	1
写		xiě	vb.	to write		1
写作		xiězuò	vb.	to write, to compose, writing, written works		3
写字台		xiězì tái	n.	writing desk		6
写字楼		xiězìlóu	n.	office building		6
抄写		chāoxiě	vb.	to copy, to transcribe		4
描写		miáoxiě	vb.	to describe, to depict, to portray, description		4
听写		tīngxiě	vb.	(of a pupil) to write down (in a dictation exercise), dictation, (music) to transcribe by ear		1
农		nóng		agriculture, farming, farmer	冖 14.4	3
农村		nóngcūn	n.	rural area, village		3
农民		nóngmín	n.	peasant, farmer		3
农业		nóngyè	n.	agriculture, farming		3
农产品		nóngchǎnpǐn	n.	agricultural produce		5
冠		guān		cap, crown, hat	冖 14.7	5
冠军		guānjūn	n.	champion		5

	冫	bīng		ice		15
习		xí		practice, habit	冫 15.1	1
习惯		xíguàn	n.	habit, custom, usual practice, to be used to		2

补习	bǔxí	vb.	to take extra lessons in a cram school or with a private tutor	6
复习	fùxí	vb.	to revise, to review	2
练习	liànxí	vb.	to practice, exercise, drill, practice	2
实习	shíxí	vb.	to practice, field work, to intern, internship	2
学习	xuéxí	vb.	to learn, to study	1
预习	yùxí	vb.	to prepare a lesson	3

冬 dōng — winter ⟩ 15.3 — 2

冬季	dōngjì	n.	winter	4
冬天	dōngtiān	n.	winter	2

冰 bīng — ice ⟩ 15.4 — 4

冰	bīng	n.	ice	4
冰箱	bīngxiāng	n.	icebox, freezer cabinet, refrigerator	4
冰雪	bīngxuě	n.	ice and snow	4

冲 *chōng, chòng — to rush; powerful ⟩ 15.4 — 4

冲	chōng	vb.	to go straight ahead, to rush, to clash, thoroughfare	4
冲	• chòng	adj.	powerful, forceful, vigorous	6
冲动	chōngdòng	vb.	to have an urge, to be impetuous, impulse, urge	5
冲击	chōngjī	vb.	to attack, to batter, (of waves) to pound against, shock, impact	6
冲突	chōngtū	n.	conflict, to conflict, clash of opposing forces, collision (of interests), contention	5

决 jué — to decide, to determine ⟩ 15.4 — 3

决不	jué bù	adv.	not at all, simply (can) not	5
决策	juécè	n.	strategic decision, decision-making, policy decision, to determine policy	6
决定	juédìng	vb.	to decide (to do something), to resolve, decision	3
决赛	juésài	n.	finals (of a competition)	3
决心	juéxīn	n.	determination, resolution, determined, firm and resolute, to make up one's mind	3
坚决	jiānjué	adj.	firm, resolute, determined	3
解决	jiějué	vb.	to settle (a dispute), to resolve, to solve, to dispose of, to dispatch	3
半决赛	bànjuésài	n.	semi-finals	6

冻 dòng — to freeze, to congeal ⟩ 15.5 — 5

冻	dòng	vb.	to freeze, to feel very cold, aspic or jelly	5

况 kuàng — condition, situation ⟩ 15.5 — 3

情况	qíngkuàng	n.	circumstances, state of affairs, situation	3
状况	zhuàngkuàng	n.	condition, state, situation	3

冷 lěng — cold, cool ⟩ 15.5 — 1

冷	lěng	adj.	cold, cool, (opp. 热 rè: heat), surname Leng	1
冷静	lěngjìng	adj.	calm, cool-headed	4
冷气	lěngqì	n.	cold air, air conditioning	6
冷水	lěngshuǐ	n.	cold water, unboiled water, fig. not yet ready (of plans)	6
寒冷	hánlěng	adj.	cold (climate), frigid, very cold	4

净	**jìng**		clean, pure	冫 15.6	1
净	jìng	adj.	clean, completely, only, net (income, exports etc), (Chinese opera) painted face male role		6
干净	·gānjìng	adj.	clean, neat		1
纯净水	chúnjìngshuǐ	n.	purified water		4
凉	**liáng**		cool, cold	冫 15.8	2
凉	liáng	adj.	cool, cold		2
凉快	-liángkuai	adj.	nice and cold, pleasantly cool		2
凉水	liángshuǐ	n.	cool water, unboiled water		3
凉鞋	liángxié	n.	sandal		6
准	**zhǔn**		accurate, standard	冫 15.8	1
准	zhǔn	adj.	accurate, standard, definitely, certainly, about to become (bride, son-in-law etc), quasi-, para-		3
准备	zhǔnbèi	vb.	to prepare, to intend, preparation, to be about to		1
准确	zhǔnquè	adj.	accurate, exact, precise		2
准时	zhǔnshí	adj.	on time, punctual, on schedule		4
标准	biāozhǔn	n.	(an official) standard, norm, criterion		3
批准	pīzhǔn	vb.	to approve, to ratify		3
减	**jiǎn**		to lower, to decrease	冫 15.9	4
减	jiǎn	vb.	to lower, to decrease, to reduce, to subtract, to diminish		4
减肥	jiǎnféi	vb.	to lose weight		4
减轻	jiǎnqīng	vb.	to lighten, to ease, to alleviate		5
减少	jiǎnshǎo	vb.	to lessen, to decrease, to reduce, to lower		4
几	**jī**		**table**		**16**
几	**jǐ**		how much, how many	几 16.0	1
几	jǐ	num.	how much, how many		1
几乎	jīhū	adv.	almost, nearly, practically		4
凡	**fán**		ordinary, common	几 16.1	6
凡是	fánshì	adv.	each and every, every, all, any		6
平凡	píngfán	adj.	commonplace, ordinary, mediocre		6
凭	**píng**		to lean against, to rely on	几 16.6	5
凭	píng	prep.	to lean against, to rely on, on the basis of, no matter (how, what etc), proof		5
凵	**qū**		**open box**		**17**
凶	**xiōng**		terrible	凵 17.2	6
凶	xiōng	adj.	terrible, fearful		6
凶手	xiōngshǒu	n.	murderer, assassin		6
出	**chū**		to go out, to come out	凵 17.3	1
出	chū	vb.	to go out, to come out, to occur, to produce, to go beyond, to rise, to put forth		1

出门	chū mén		vb.	to go out, to leave home, to go on a journey, away from home, (of a woman) to get married	2
出面	chū miàn		vb.	to appear personally, to step in, to step forth, to show up	6
出名	chū míng		n.	well-known for sth, to become well known, to make one's mark	6
出事	chū shì		vb.	to have an accident, to meet with a mishap	6
出院	chū yuàn		vb.	to leave hospital, to be discharged from hospital	2
出版	chūbǎn		vb.	to publish	5
出差	• chūchāi		vb.	to go on an official or business trip	5
出场	chūchǎng		vb.	(of a performer) to come onto the stage to perform, (of an athlete) to enter the arena to compete	6
出动	chūdòng		vb.	to start out on a trip, to dispatch troops	6
出发	chūfā		vb.	to set off, to start (on a journey)	2
出访	chūfǎng		vb.	to go and visit in an official capacity or for investigation	6
出国	chūguó		vb.	to go abroad, to leave the country, emigration	2
出汗	chūhàn		vb.	to perspire, to sweat	5
出口	chūkǒu	+	n.	an export	2
出口	chūkǒu	+	n.	an exit	4
出来	chūlái		vb.	to come out, to appear, to arise	1
出路	chūlù		n.	a way out (lit. and fig.), opportunity for advancement, a way forward, outlet (for one's products)	6
出去	chūqù		vb.	to go out	1
出入	chūrù		vb.	to go out and come in, entrance and exit, expenditure and income, discrepancy, inconsistent	6
出色	chūsè		adj.	remarkable, outstanding	4
出生	chūshēng		vb.	to be born	2
出售	chūshòu		vb.	to sell, to offer for sale, to put on the market	4
出台	chūtái		vb.	to officially launch (a policy, program etc), to appear on stage, to appear publicly	6
出席	chūxí		vb.	to attend, to participate, present	4
出现	chūxiàn		vb.	to appear, to arise, to emerge, to show up	2
出行	chūxíng		vb.	to go out somewhere (relatively short trip), to set off on a journey (longer trip)	6
出于	chūyú		prep.	out of, from, due to, to stem from	5
出租	chūzū		vb.	to rent	2
出租车	chūzūchē		n.	taxi, cab, rental car	2
播出	bōchū		vb.	to broadcast, to air (a TV program etc)	3
查出	cháchū		vb.	to find out, to discover	6
超出	chāochū		vb.	to exceed, to overstep, to go too far, to encroach	6
传出	chuánchū		vb.	to transmit outwards, to disseminate, efferent (nerve)	6
得出	• déchū		vb.	to obtain (results), to arrive at (a conclusion)	2
发出	fāchū		vb.	to issue (an order, decree etc), to send out, to dispatch, to produce (a sound), to let out (a laugh)	3
付出	fùchū		vb.	to pay, to invest (energy or time in a friendship etc)	4
杰出	jiéchū		adj.	outstanding, distinguished, remarkable, prominent, illustrious	6
看出	kàn chū		vb.	to make out, to see	5
拿出	náchū		vb.	to take out, to put out, to provide, to put forward (a proposal), to come up with (evidence)	2
派出	pàichū		vb.	to send, to dispatch	6
认出	rènchū		n.	recognition, to recognize	3

输出	shūchū	vb.	to export, to output	5
提出	tíchū	vb.	to raise (an issue), to propose, to put forward, to suggest, to post (on a website), to withdraw (cash)	2
突出	tūchū	adj.	prominent, outstanding, to give prominence to, to project	3
推出	tuīchū	vb.	to push out, to release, to launch, to publish, to recommend	6
退出	tuìchū	vb.	to withdraw, to abort, to quit, to log out (computing)	3
外出	wàichū	vb.	to go out, to go away (on a trip etc)	6
显出	xiǎnchū	vb.	to express, to exhibit	6
演出	yǎnchū	vb.	to act (in a play), to perform, to put on (a performance), performance, concert, show	3
找出	zhǎochū	vb.	to find, to search out	2
支出	zhīchū	vb.	to spend, to pay out, expense	5
指出	zhǐchū	vb.	to indicate, to point out	3
作出	zuòchū	vb.	to put out, to come up with, to make (a choice, decision, proposal, response, comment etc)	4

击 jī — to strike, to hit   凵 17.3   5

冲击	chōngjī	vb.	to attack, to batter, (of waves) to pound against, shock, impact	6
打击	dǎjī	vb.	to hit, to strike, to attack, to crack down on sth, blow, (psychological) shock, percussion (music)	5
攻击	gōngjī	vb.	to attack, to accuse, to charge, an attack (terrorist or military)	6
射击	shèjī	vb.	to shoot, to fire (a gun)	5

刀 dāo — knife   刂 18

刀	dāo		knife, blade	刀 18.0 3
刀	dāo	n.	knife, blade, m.w. paper 100 sheets, surname Dao	3
剪刀	jiǎndāo	n.	scissors	5

分 * fēn, fèn — to divide; small unit of time   刀 18.2 1

分	fēn	+ vb.	to divide, to separate, to distribute, to allocate, to distinguish (good and bad)	1
分	fēn	+ m.w.	m.w. fraction, part, share, ingredient, part or subdivision	2
分工	fēn gōng	vb.	to divide up the work, division of labor	6
分别	fēnbié	vb.	to part or leave each other, to distinguish, difference, in different ways, differently, separately or individually	3
分布	fēnbù	vb.	to scatter, to distribute, to be distributed (over an area etc), (statistical, geographic) distribution	4
分成	fēnchéng	vb.	to divide (into), to split a bonus, to break into tenths, percentage allotment	5
分解	fēnjiě	vb.	to resolve, to decompose, to break down	5
分开	fēnkāi	vb.	to separate, to part	2
分类	fēnlèi	vb.	classify	5
分离	fēnlí	vb.	to separate	5
分裂	fēnliè	vb.	to split up, to divide, to break up, fission, schism	6
分配	fēnpèi	vb.	to distribute, to assign, to allocate, to partition (a hard drive)	3
分散	fēnsàn	vb.	to scatter, to disperse, to distribute	4
分手	fēnshǒu	vb.	to part company, to split up, to break up	4
分数	fēnshù	n.	(exam) grade, mark, score, fraction	2
分为	• fēnwéi	vb.	to divide sth into (parts), to subdivide	4

分析	fēnxī	vb.	to analyse, analysis	5
分享	fēnxiǎng	vb.	to share (let others have some of sth good)	5
分之	fēnzhī	adj.	(indicating a fraction) … fēnzhī … (e.g. 三分之二 sānfēn zhī'èr: two-thirds)	4
分钟	fēnzhōng	n.	minute	2
分组	fēnzǔ	vb.	to divide into groups, group (formed from a larger group), subgroup, (computer networking) packet	3
比分	bǐfēn	n.	score	4
部分	- bùfen	n.	part, share, section, piece	2
成分	• chéngfèn	n.	composition, make-up, ingredient, element, component, one's social status	6
充分	• chōngfèn	adj.	ample, sufficient, adequate, full, fully, to the full	4
处分	chǔfèn	vb.	to discipline sb, to punish, disciplinary action, to deal with (a matter)	5
得分	• défēn	vb.	to score	3
过分	• guòfèn	adj.	excessive, undue, overly	4
划分	huàfēn	vb.	to divide up, to partition, to differentiate	5
区分	qūfēn	vb.	to differentiate, to draw a distinction, to divide into categories	6
十分	shífēn	adv.	very, completely, utterly, extremely, absolutely, hundred percent, to divide into ten equal parts	2
水分	• shuǐfèn	n.	moisture content, (fig.) overstatement, padding	5
学分	xuéfēn	n.	academic credit, course credit	4
百分点	bǎifēndiǎn	n.	percentage point	6
大部分	- dàbùfen	n.	in large part, the greater part, the majority	2
一部分	- yībùfen	n.	portion, part of, subset	2
切	* qiē, qiè		**to cut, to slice; definitely**	刀 18.2 3
切	qiē	vb.	to cut, to slice, tangent (math)	4
切实	• qièshí	adj.	feasible, realistic, practical, earnestly, conscientiously	6
密切	• mìqiè	adj.	close, familiar, intimate, closely (related), to foster close ties, to pay close attention	4
迫切	• pòqiè	adj.	urgent, pressing	4
亲切	• qīnqiè	adj.	amiable, cordial, close and dear, familiar	3
一切	• yīqiè	pro.	everything, every, all	3
刊	**kān**		**to print, to carve**	刀 18.3 6
报刊	bàokān	n.	newspapers and periodicals, the press	6
创	**chuàng**		**to establish, to create**	刀 18.4 3
创办	chuàngbàn	vb.	to establish, to found, to launch	6
创建	chuàngjiàn	vb.	to found, to establish	6
创立	chuànglì	vb.	to establish, to set up, to found	5
创新	chuàngxīn	vb.	to bring forth new ideas, to blaze new trails, innovation	3
创业	chuàngyè	vb.	to begin an undertaking, to start a major task, to initiate, to venture, venture, entrepreneurship	3
创意	chuàngyì	n.	original idea, creative, creativity	6
创造	chuàngzào	vb.	to create, to bring about, to produce, innovation	3
创作	chuàngzuò	vb.	to create, to produce, to write, creative work, creation	3
开创	kāichuàng	vb.	to initiate, to start, to found	6

刚	gāng		hard, firm, strong	刀 18.4	2
刚	gāng	adj.	hard, firm, strong, just, barely, exactly		2
刚才	gāngcái	adv.	just now		2
刚刚	gānggāng	adv.	just recently, just a moment ago		2
刚好	gānghǎo	adv.	just, exactly, to happen to be		6

划	* huà, huá		to demarcate; to row boat	刀 18.4	2
划	• huá	vb.	to row, to paddle, to cut, to slash, to scratch		4
划	huà	vb.	to demarcate, to divide, to transfer		4
划船	• huáchuán	vb.	to row a boat, rowing boat, rowing (sport)		3
划分	huàfēn	vb.	to divide up, to partition, to differentiate		5
策划	cèhuà	vb.	to plot, to scheme, to bring about, to engineer, planning, producer, planner		6
规划	guīhuà	vb.	to plan (how to do sth), planning, plan, program		5
计划	jìhuà	n.	plan, project, program, to plan, to map out		2

列	liè		to line up, to arrange	刀 18.4	4
列	liè	vb.	to line up, to arrange, row, file, line, m.w. a row of things		4
列车	lièchē	n.	(railway) train		4
列入	lièrù	vb.	to include on a list		4
列为	• lièwéi	vb.	to be classified as		4
排列	páiliè	vb.	to arrange in order, (math.) permutation		4
系列	xìliè	n.	series, set		4

则	zé		rule, law	刀 18.4	4
否则	fǒuzé	conj.	if not, otherwise, else, or else		4
规则	guīzé	n.	rule, regulation, rules and regulations		4
原则	yuánzé	n.	principle, doctrine		4

别	bié		to leave, difference	刀 18.5	1
别	bié	+ adv.	(command/ advice) don't		1
别	bié	+ vb.	to leave, to part, to turn, to change		4
别的	biéde	n.	else, other		1
别人	biérén	n.	other people, others, other person		1
差别	• chābié	n.	difference, distinction, disparity		5
分别	fēnbié	vb.	to part or leave each other, to distinguish, difference, in different ways, differently, separately or individually		3
告别	gàobié	vb.	to leave, to bid farewell to, to say good-bye to		3
个别	gèbié	adj.	individual, specific, respective, just one or two		4
区别	qūbié	n.	difference, to distinguish, to discriminate, to make a distinction		3
特别	tèbié	adv.	especially, particularly, special, unusual		2
性别	xìngbié	n.	gender, sex		3

初	chū		beginning, initial	刀 18.5	3
初	chū	+ n.	at first, (at the) beginning, junior, basic		3
初	chū	+ adj.	first... (e.g first grade)		3
初步	chūbù	adj.	initial, preliminary, tentative		3
初等	chūděng	adj.	elementary (i.e. easy)		6
初级	chūjí	adj.	junior, primary		3
初期	chūqī	n.	initial stage, beginning period		5

初中	chūzhōng	n.	junior middle school, junior high school	3
当初	dāngchū	n.	at that time, originally	3
年初	niánchū	n.	beginning of the year	3
最初	zuìchū	n.	first, primary, initial, original, at first, initially, originally	4

利 lì — advantage, benefit   刀 18.5   2

利	lì	n.	advantage, benefit, profit, sharp, surname Li	6
利润	lìrùn	n.	profit	5
利息	lìxī	n.	interest (on a loan)	4
利益	lìyì	n.	benefit, (in sb's) interest	4
利用	lìyòng	vb.	to exploit, to make use of, to use, to take advantage of, to utilize	3
便利	biànlì	adj.	convenient, easy, to facilitate	5
不利	bùlì	adj.	unfavourable, disadvantageous, harmful, detrimental	5
福利	fúlì	n.	material benefit, benefit in kind, (social) welfare	5
吉利	jílì	adj.	lucky, auspicious, Geely (Chinese car manufacturer)	6
流利	liúlì	n.	fluent	2
权利	quánlì	n.	right (i.e. an entitlement to sth), (classical) power and wealth	4
胜利	shènglì	n.	victory	3
顺利	shùnlì	adv.	smoothly, without a hitch	2
有利	yǒulì	adj.	advantageous, to have advantages, favourable	3
专利	zhuānlì	n.	patent, sth uniquely enjoyed (or possessed etc) by a certain group of people, monopoly	5
有利于	yǒulìyú	vb.	to be advantageous to, to be beneficial for	5

判 pàn — to judge, to sentence   刀 18.5   3

判	pàn	vb.	to judge, to sentence, to discriminate, to discern, clearly distinguishable	6
判断	pànduàn	vb.	to judge, to determine, judgment	3
裁判	cáipàn	n.	judgment, to referee, umpire, judge, referee	5
谈判	tánpàn	vb.	to negotiate, negotiation, talks, conference	3

刺 cì — thorn, splinter   刀 18.6   4

| 刺 | cì | n. | thorn, splinter | 4 |
| 刺激 | cìjī | vb. | to provoke, to irritate, to upset, to stimulate, to excite, irritant | 4 |

到 dào — to arrive, to go   刀 18.6   1

到	dào	vb.	to arrive, to go, (verb complement denoting completion or result of an action); to (a place), until (a time), up to	1
到处	· dàochù	adv.	everywhere	2
到达	dàodá	vb.	to reach, to arrive	3
到底	dàodǐ	adv.	finally, in the end, when all is said and done, after all, to the end, to the last	3
到来	dàolái	vb.	to arrive, arrival, advent	5
到期	dàoqī	vb.	to fall due (loan etc), to expire (visa etc), to mature (investment bond etc)	6
报到	bàodào	vb.	to report for duty, to check in, to register	3
迟到	chídào	vb.	to arrive late	4
达到	dá dào	vb.	to reach, to achieve, to attain	3
得到	· dédào	vb.	to get, to obtain, to receive	1
等到	děngdào	vb.	to wait until, by the time when (sth is ready etc)	2
放到	fàngdào	vb.	to put to	3

感到	gǎndào	vb.	to feel, to sense, to have the feeling that, to think that, to move, to affect	2
赶到	gǎndào	vb.	to hurry (to some place)	3
回到	huídào	vb.	to return to	1
见到	jiàndào	vb.	to see	2
接到	jiē dào	vb.	to receive (letter etc)	2
看到	kàndào	vb.	to see	1
来到	láidào	vb.	to come, to arrive	1
拿到	nádào	vb.	to get, to obtain	2
碰到	pèngdào	vb.	to come across, to run into, to meet, to hit	2
起到	qǐdào	vb.	to have (a (motivating etc) effect), to play (a (stabilizing etc) role)	5
收到	shōudào	vb.	to receive	2
受到	shòudào	vb.	to receive (praise, an education, punishment etc), to be ...ed (praised, educated, punished etc)	2
送到	sòngdào	vb.	to send to, deliver to	2
提到	tídào	vb.	to mention, to raise (a subject), to refer to	2
听到	tīngdào	vb.	to hear	1
想到	xiǎngdào	vb.	to think of, to call to mind, to anticipate	2
遇到	yùdào	vb.	to meet, to run into, to come across	4
遭到	zāodào	vb.	to suffer, to meet with (sth unfortunate)	6
找到	zhǎodào	vb.	to find	1
直到	zhídào	adv.	until, up to now	3
做到	zuòdào	vb.	to accomplish, to achieve	2
没想到	méixiǎngdào	vb.	didn't expect	4
想不到	- xiǎngbudào	vb.	to never expect, hard to imagine, it had not occurred to me	6
意想不到	yìxiǎngbùdào	phr.	unexpected, previously unimagined	6

刮 guā — to shave, to scrape   刀 18.6   6

刮	guā	vb.	to scrape, to scrape, to smear, to blow (of the wind)	6

刻 kè — quarter (hour), short time interval   刀 18.6   2

刻	kè	+ n.	quarter (hour), short time interval, moment, oppressive	2
刻	kè	+ vb.	to carve, to engrave, to cut	5
此刻	cǐkè	n.	this moment, now, at present	5
立刻	lìkè	adv.	forthwith, immediate, prompt, promptly, straightway, thereupon, at once	3
深刻	shēnkè	adj.	profound, deep, deep-going	3
时刻	shíkè	n.	time, juncture, moment, period of time	3

券 quàn — deed, bond   刀 18.6   6

券	quàn	n.	deed, bond, contract, ticket, voucher	6

刷 shuā — to brush, to paint   刀 18.6   4

刷	shuā	vb.	to brush, to paint, to daub, to paste up, to skip class (of students), to fire from a job	4
刷牙	shuāyá	vb.	to brush one's teeth	4
刷子	shuāzi	n.	brush, scrub	4
牙刷	yáshuā	n.	toothbrush	4
印刷	yìnshuā	vb.	to print, printing	5

制	zhì		to make, to manufacture	刀 18.6	3
制成	zhìchéng	vb.	to manufacture, to turn out (a product)		5
制定	zhìdìng	vb.	to draw up, to formulate		3
制订	zhìdìng	vb.	to work out, to formulate		4
制度	zhìdù	n.	system (e.g. political, administrative etc), institution		3
制约	zhìyuē	vb.	to restrict, condition		5
制造	zhìzào	vb.	to manufacture, to make		3
制作	zhìzuò	vb.	to make, to manufacture		3
编制	biānzhì	vb.	to weave, to plait, to compile, to put together (a lesson plan, budget etc)		6
法制	fǎzhì	adj.	legal system, legality		5
复制	fùzhì	vb.	to duplicate, to make a copy of, to copy, to reproduce, to clone		4
机制	jīzhì	n.	machine processed, machine made, mechanism		5
控制	kòngzhì	vb.	to control, to exercise control over, to contain		5
限制	xiànzhì	vb.	to restrict, to limit, to confine, restriction, limit		4
研制	yánzhì	vb.	to manufacture, to develop		4
豆制品	dòuzhìpǐn	n.	legume-based product, soybean product		5
乳制品	rǔzhìpǐn	n.	dairy products		6
剑	jiàn		sword	刀 18.7	6
剑	jiàn	n.	sword		6
前	qián		front, forward	刀 18.7	1
前	qián	n.	front, forward, ahead, first, top (followed by a number), future, ago, before, BC, former, formerly		1
前边	- qiánbian	n.	front, the front side, in front of		1
前方	qiánfāng	n.	ahead, the front		6
前后	qiánhòu	n.	around, from beginning to end, all around, front and rear		3
前进	qiánjìn	vb.	to go forward, to forge ahead, to advance, onward		3
前景	qiánjǐng	n.	foreground, vista, (future) prospects, perspective		5
前来	qiánlái	vb.	to come (formal), before, previously		6
前面	- qiánmian	n.	ahead, in front, preceding, above		3
前年	- qiánnián	n.	the year before last		2
前提	qiántí	n.	premise, precondition, prerequisite		5
前天	qiántiān	n.	the day before yesterday		1
前头	- qiántou	n.	in front, at the head, ahead, above		4
前途	qiántú	n.	prospects, future outlook, journey		4
前往	qiánwǎng	vb.	to leave for, to proceed towards, to go		3
此前	cǐqián	n.	before this, before then, previously		6
从前	cóngqián	n.	previously, formerly, once upon a time		3
当前	dāngqián	n.	current, today's, modern, present, to be facing (us)		5
跟前	gēnqián	n.	the front (of), (in) front, (in) sb's presence, just before (a date)		5
面前	miànqián	n.	in front of, facing, (in the) presence (of)		2
目前	mùqián	n.	at the present time, currently		3
年前	niánqián	n.	before the end of the year, before the new year		5
提前	tíqián	vb.	to shift to an earlier date, to do sth ahead of time, in advance		3
先前	xiānqián	n.	before, previously		5
向前	xiàngqián	adv.	forward, onward		5
眼前	yǎnqián	n.	before one's eyes, now, at present		3

以前	yǐqián	n.	before, formerly, previous, ago		2
之前	zhī qián	n.	before, prior to, ago, previously, beforehand		4

剧 jù — theatrical work   刀 18.8   3

剧	jù	n.	theatrical work (play, opera, TV series etc), dramatic (change, increase etc), acute, severe		6
剧本	jùběn	n.	script for play, opera, movie etc, screenplay, scenario		5
剧场	jùchǎng	n.	theatre		3
悲剧	bēijù	n.	tragedy		5
话剧	huàjù	n.	stage play, modern drama		3
京剧	jīngjù	n.	Beijing Opera		3
喜剧	xǐjù	n.	comedy		5
戏剧	xìjù	n.	drama, play, theatre		5
电视剧	diànshìjù	n.	TV drama, soap opera		3
连续剧	liánxùjù	n.	serialized drama, dramatic series, show in parts		3

副 fù — secondary, auxiliary   刀 18.9   6

副	fù	+ adj.	secondary, auxiliary, deputy, assistant, vice-, (opp. 正 zhèng: principal, chief)		6
副	fù	+ m.w.	m.w. for a set of something e.g. pair of gloves, m.w. for a facial expression		6

剪 jiǎn — to cut, scissors   刀 18.9   5

剪	jiǎn	vb.	to cut (with scissors), scissors, surname Jian		5
剪刀	jiǎndāo	n.	scissors		5
剪子	jiǎnzi	n.	clippers, scissors, shears		5

剩 shèng — to remain, to be left   刀 18.10   5

剩	shèng	vb.	to remain, to be left, to have as remainder		5
剩下	- shèngxia	vb.	to be left over, to be remaining		5

力 lì — power   19

力 lì — power, force   力 19.0   2

力	lì	+ n.	power, force		3
力	lì	+ adj.	strong, capable		6
力量	- lìliang	n.	power, force, strength		3
力气	- lìqi	n.	strength		4
暴力	bàolì	n.	violence, force, violent		6
吃力	chīlì	vb.	to entail strenuous effort, to toil at a task, strenuous, laborious		5
大力	dàlì	adv.	energetically, vigorously		6
电力	diànlì	n.	electrical power, electricity		6
动力	dònglì	n.	motive power, force, (fig.) motivation, impetus		3
活力	huólì	n.	energy, vitality, vigour, vital force		5
尽力	jìnlì	vb.	to strive one's hardest, to spare no effort		4
精力	jīnglì	n.	energy, vigour		4
能力	nénglì	n.	capability, ability		3
努力	nǔlì	vb.	to make a great effort, to strive, to try hard		2
潜力	qiánlì	n.	potential, capacity		6
全力	quánlì	n.	full energy (strength), all-out (effort), fully (support)		6

权力	quánlì	n.	power, authority	6
人力	rénlì	n.	manpower, labour power	5
实力	shílì	n.	strength	3
势力	shìlì	n.	power, influence, a force (military, political etc)	5
体力	tǐlì	n.	physical strength, physical power	5
听力	tīnglì	n.	hearing, listening ability	3
压力	yālì	n.	pressure	3
有力	yǒulì	adj.	powerful, forceful, vigorous	5
智力	zhìlì	n.	intelligence, intellect	4
巧克力	qiǎokèlì	n.	chocolate (loanword)	4

办 bàn — to do, to manage　　力 19.2　2

办	bàn	vb.	to do, to manage, to handle, to go about, to run, to deal with	2
办公	bàn gōng	vb.	to handle official business, to work (esp. in an office)	6
办学	bàn xué	vb.	to run a school	6
办法	bànfǎ	n.	means, method, way (of doing sth)	2
办理	bànlǐ	vb.	to handle, to transact, to conduct	3
办事	bànshì	vb.	to handle (affairs), to work	4
办公室	bàngōngshì	n.	office, business premises, bureau	2
办事处	bànshìchù	n.	office, agency	6
承办	chéngbàn	vb.	to undertake, to accept a contract	5
创办	chuàngbàn	vb.	to establish, to found, to launch	6
举办	jǔbàn	vb.	to conduct, to hold	3
主办	zhǔbàn	vb.	to organize, to host (a conference or sports event)	5
怎么办	zěnmebàn	phr.	what's to be done	2

劝 quàn — to advise, to urge　　力 19.2　5

劝	quàn	vb.	to advise, to urge, to try to persuade, to exhort, to console, to soothe	5

功 gōng — result, merit　　力 19.3　3

功夫	gōngfu	n.	skill, art, kung fu, labour, effort	3
功课	gōngkè	n.	homework, assignment, task, classwork, lesson, study	3
功能	gōngnéng	n.	function, capability	3
成功	chénggōng	n.	success, succeed	3

加 jiā — to add, to increase　　力 19.3　2

加	jiā	vb.	to add, to increase, to plus	2
加班	jiā bān	vb.	to work overtime	4
加热	jiā rè	vb.	to heat	5
加油	jiā yóu	vb.	to add oil, to top up with gas, to refuel, to accelerate, to step on the gas, (fig.) to make an extra effort, to cheer sb on	2
加工	jiāgōng	vb.	to process, processing, working (of machinery)	3
加快	jiākuài	vb.	to accelerate, to speed up	3
加盟	jiāméng	vb.	to become a member of an alliance or union, to align, to join, participate	6
加强	jiāqiáng	vb.	to reinforce, to strengthen, to increase	3
加入	jiārù	vb.	to become a member, to join, to mix into, to participate in, to add in	4
加上	jiāshàng	vb.	to put in, to add, to add on, to add into, in addition, on top of that	5
加速	jiāsù	vb.	to speed up, to expedite	5
加以	jiāyǐ	conj.	in addition, moreover, to apply (restrictions etc) to (sb)	5

加油站	jiāyóuzhàn	n.	petrol (gas) station	4
参加	cānjiā	vb.	to participate, to take part, to join	2
更加	gèngjiā	adv.	more (than sth else), even more	3
增加	zēngjiā	vb.	to raise, to increase	3
动	**dòng**		**to move, to set in movement** 力 19.4	1
动	dòng	vb.	(of sth) to move, to set in movement, to displace, to touch, to make use of, to stir (emotions), to alter	1
动画	dònghuà	n.	animation, cartoon	6
动机	dòngjī	n.	motor, locomotive, motive, motivation, intention	5
动力	dònglì	n.	motive power, force, (fig.) motivation, impetus	3
动人	dòngrén	adj.	touching, moving	3
动手	dòngshǒu	vb.	to set about (a task), to hit, to punch, to touch	5
动态	dòngtài	n.	movement, motion, development, trend, dynamic (science)	5
动物	dòngwù	n.	animal	2
动摇	dòngyáo	vb.	to sway, to waver, to rock, to rattle, to destabilize, to pose a challenge	4
动员	dòngyuán	vb.	to mobilize, to arouse, mobilization	5
动作	dòngzuò	n.	movement, motion, action	1
动画片	dònghuàpiàn	n.	animated film	4
动物园	dòngwùyuán	n.	zoo	2
摆动	bǎidòng	vb.	to sway, to swing, to move back and forth, to oscillate	4
被动	bèidòng	adj.	passive	5
变动	biàndòng	vb.	to change, to fluctuate, change, fluctuation	5
波动	bōdòng	vb.	to undulate, to fluctuate, wave motion, rise and fall	6
冲动	chōngdòng	vb.	to have an urge, to be impetuous, impulse, urge	5
出动	chūdòng	vb.	to start out on a trip, to dispatch troops	6
打动	dǎdòng	vb.	to move (to pity), arousing (sympathy), touching	6
带动	dàidòng	vb.	to spur, to provide impetus, to drive	3
电动	diàndòng	n.	electric-powered	6
调动	diàodòng	vb.	to transfer, to manoeuvre (troops etc), movement of personnel, to mobilize, to bring into play	5
发动	fādòng	vb.	to start, to launch, to unleash, to mobilize, to arouse	3
感动	gǎndòng	vb.	to move (sb), to touch (sb emotionally), moving	2
互动	hùdòng	vb.	to interact, interactive	6
活动	huódòng	vb.	to exercise, to move about, to operate, to use connections (personal influence), loose, active, movable, activity, campaign, manoeuvre, behaviour	2
激动	jīdòng	vb.	to move emotionally, to stir up (emotions), to excite	4
举动	jǔdòng	n.	act, action, activity, move, movement	5
劳动	láodòng	n.	work, toil, physical labour	5
流动	liúdòng	vb.	to flow, to circulate, to go from place to place, to be mobile, (of assets) liquid	5
启动	qǐdòng	vb.	to start (a machine), (fig.) to set in motion, to launch (an operation), to activate (a plan)	5
生动	shēngdòng	adj.	vivid, lively	3
推动	tuīdòng	vb.	to push (for acceptance of a plan), to push forward, to promote, to actuate	3
行动	xíngdòng	n.	operation, action	2
移动	yídòng	vb.	to move, movement, migration, mobile, portable	4
运动	yùndòng	vb.	to move, to exercise, sports, exercise, motion, movement, campaign	2

振动	zhèndòng	vb.	to vibrate, to shake, vibration	5
主动	zhǔdòng	vb.	to take the initiative, to do sth of one's own accord, spontaneous, active	3
转动	zhuǎndòng	vb.	to turn, to move, to flex, to turn sth around, to swivel	4
转动	・zhuàndòng	vb.	to turn, to revolve, to rotate	6
自动	zìdòng	adj.	automatic, voluntarily	3
电动车	diàndòngchē	n.	electric car, electric bicycle, electric scooter	4
机动车	jīdòngchē	n.	motor vehicle	6
运动会	yùndònghuì	n.	sports competition	4
运动员	yùndòngyuán	n.	athlete	4

劲 jìn　strength, energy　力 19.5　4

使劲	shǐ jìn	vb.	to exert all one's strength	4
有劲	yǒujìn	adj.	vigorous, energetic, interesting, amusing	4

劳 láo　labour, toil　力 19.5　5

劳动	láodòng	n.	work, toil, physical labour	5

励 lì　to strive, to encourage　力 19.5　5

鼓励	gǔlì	vb.	to encourage	5
奖励	jiǎnglì	vb.	to reward, reward (as encouragement)	5

努 nǔ　to exert, to strive,　力 19.5　2

努力	nǔlì	vb.	to make a great effort, to strive, to try hard	2

助 zhù　to help, to aid　力 19.5　2

助理	zhùlǐ	n.	assistant	5
助手	zhùshǒu	n.	assistant, helper	5
帮助	bāngzhù	vb.	to help, to assist, assistance, aid,	2
补助	bǔzhù	vb.	to subsidize, subsidy, allowance	6
辅助	fǔzhù	vb.	to assist, to aid, supplementary, auxiliary, subsidiary	5
救助	jiùzhù	vb.	to help sb in trouble, aid, assistance	6
捐助	juānzhù	vb.	to donate, to offer (aid), contribution, donation	6
协助	xiézhù	vb.	to provide assistance, to aid	6
援助	yuánzhù	vb.	to help, to support, to aid, aid, assistance	6
赞助	zànzhù	vb.	to support, to assist, to sponsor	4
资助	zīzhù	vb.	to subsidize, to provide financial aid, subsidy	5

势 shì　power, force　力 19.6　3

势力	shìlì	n.	power, influence, a force (military, political etc)	5
强势	qiángshì	adj.	strong, powerful, (linguistics) emphatic, intensive	6
趋势	qūshì	n.	trend, tendency	4
形势	xíngshì	n.	circumstances, situation, terrain	4
优势	yōushì	n.	superiority, dominance, advantage	3

勇 yǒng　brave, courageous　力 19.7　4

勇敢	yǒnggǎn	adj.	brave, courageous	4
勇气	yǒngqì	n.	courage, valour	4
英勇	yīngyǒng	adj.	heroic, gallant, valiant	4

勤 qín　industrious, diligent　力 19.11　5

勤奋	qínfèn	adj.	hardworking, diligent	5

勹	**bāo**		**wrap**		**20**
勺	**sháo**		**spoon, ladle**	勹 20.1	6
勺	sháo	n.	spoon, ladle, m.w. unit of volume (trad) eqiv. to 10 ml		6
包	**bāo**		**to cover, to wrap**	勹 20.3	1
包	bāo	vb.	to cover, to wrap, to hold, bag, (m.w. for containers, packages), surname Bao		1
包裹	bāoguǒ	vb.	to wrap up, to bind up, bundle, parcel, package		4
包含	bāohán	vb.	to contain, to embody, to include		4
包括	bāokuò	vb.	to comprise, to include, to involve, to incorporate, to consist of		4
包围	bāowéi	vb.	to surround, to encircle, to hem in		5
包装	bāozhuāng	vb.	to pack, to package, to wrap, packaging		5
包子	bāozi	n.	steamed stuffed bun		1
背包	·bēibāo	n.	knapsack, rucksack, infantry pack, field pack, blanket roll		5
打包	dǎbāo	vb.	to wrap, to pack, to put leftovers in a doggy bag for take-out, to package (computing)		5
红包	hóngbāo	n.	money wrapped in red as a gift, bonus payment, kickback, bribe		4
面包	miànbāo	n.	bread		1
皮包	píbāo	n.	handbag, briefcase		3
钱包	qiánbāo	n.	purse, wallet		1
书包	shūbāo	n.	schoolbag, satchel, bookbag		1
匕	**bǐ**		**spoon**		**21**
化	**huà**		**to change, to convert**	匕 21.2	3
化	huà	+ aff.	suffix: -ize/ -ify (e.g. normalize, simplify), to change, to convert		3
化解	huàjiě	vb.	to dissolve, to resolve (contradictions), to dispel (doubts), to iron out (difficulties), to defuse (conflicts), to neutralize (fears)		6
化石	huàshí	n.	fossil		5
变化	biànhuà	n.	change, variation, to change, to vary		3
进化	jìnhuà	n.	evolution		5
绿化	lǜhuà	vb.	to make green with plants, to reforest		6
强化	qiánghuà	vb.	to strengthen, to intensify		6
深化	shēnhuà	vb.	to deepen, to intensify		6
文化	wénhuà	n.	culture, civilization, cultural		3
消化	xiāohuà	vb.	to digest, digestion, digestive		4
转化	zhuǎnhuà	vb.	to change, to transform, isomerization (chemistry)		5
北	**běi**		**north, northern**	匕 21.3	1
北	běi	n.	north, (classical) to be defeated		1
北边	-běibian	n.	north, north side, northern part, to the north of		1
北部	běibù	n.	northern part		3
北方	běifāng	n.	north, the northern part a country, China north of the Yellow River		2
北极	běijí	n.	the North Pole, the Arctic Pole, the north magnetic pole		5
北京	běijīng	n.	Beijing		1
东北	dōngběi	n.	northeast, Northeast China, Manchuria		2
南北	nánběi	n.	north and south, north to south		5

西北	xīběi	n.	northwest		2
ㄈ	**xǐ/xì**		**hiding enclosure**		**23**
匹	**pǐ**		m.w. bolt of cloth, horses	ㄈ 23.2	5
匹	pǐ	m.w.	m.w. for horses, m.w. for bolt of cloth, to be equal to, single		5
区	**qū**		region, area	ㄈ 23.2	3
区	qū	n.	region, area, district		3
区别	qūbié	n.	difference, to distinguish, to discriminate, to make a distinction		3
区分	qūfēn	vb.	to differentiate, to draw a distinction, to divide into categories		6
区域	qūyù	n.	area, region, district		5
城区	chéngqū	n.	city district, urban area		6
地区	·dìqū	n.	local, regional, district (not necessarily formal administrative unit), region, area, as suffix to city name		3
郊区	jiāoqū	n.	suburban district, outskirts, suburbs		5
山区	shānqū	n.	mountain area		5
社区	shèqū	n.	community, neighbourhood		5
市区	shìqū	n.	urban district, downtown, city centre		4
灾区	zāiqū	n.	disaster area, stricken region		5
医	**yī**		to cure, to heal	ㄈ 23.5	1
医疗	yīliáo	n.	medical treatment		4
医生	yīshēng	n.	doctor		1
医学	yīxué	n.	medicine, medical science, study of medicine		4
医药	yīyào	n.	medical care and medicines, medicine (drug), medical, pharmaceutical		6
医院	yīyuàn	n.	hospital		1
西医	xīyī	n.	Western medicine, a doctor trained in Western medicine		2
中医	zhōngyī	n.	traditional Chinese medical science, a doctor trained in Chinese medicine		2
十	**shí**		**ten**		**24**
十	**shí**		ten, 10	十 24.0	1
十	shí	num.	ten, 10		1
十分	shífēn	adv.	very, completely, utterly, extremely, absolutely, hundred percent, to divide into ten equal parts		2
十足	shízú	adj.	ample, complete, hundred percent, a pure shade (of some colour)		5
千	**qiān**		thousand	十 24.1	2
千	qiān	num.	thousand		2
千克	qiānkè	m.w.	kilogram		2
千万	qiānwàn	num.	ten million, countless, many, one must by all means		3
升	**shēng**		to rise, to hoist	十 24.2	3
升	shēng	vb.	to rise, to hoist, to promote, m.w. unit of volume trad eqiv. to 1 litre		3
升学	shēng xué	vb.	to enter the next grade school		6
升高	shēnggāo	vb.	to raise, to ascend		5

升级	shēngjí	vb.	to escalate (in intensity), to go up by one grade, to be promoted, to upgrade (computing)		6
升值	shēngzhí	vb.	to rise in value, to appreciate		6
毫升	háoshēng	m.w.	millilitre		4
上升	shàngshēng	vb.	to rise, to go up, to ascend		3
提升	tíshēng	vb.	to promote, to upgrade		6
直升机	zhíshēngjī	n.	helicopter		6
午	**wǔ**		noon	＋24.2	1
午餐	wǔcān	n.	lunch, luncheon		2
午饭	wǔfàn	n.	lunch		1
午睡	wǔshuì	vb.	to take a nap, siesta		2
上午	shàngwǔ	n.	morning		1
下午	xiàwǔ	n.	afternoon		1
中午	zhōngwǔ	n.	noon, midday		1
端午节	duānwǔ jié	n.	Dragon Boat Festival		6
半	**bàn**		half	＋24.3	1
半	bàn	num.	half, semi-, incomplete, (after a number) and a half		1
半年	bànnián	n.	half a year		1
半天	bàntiān	n.	half of the day, a long time, quite a while, mid-air		1
半夜	bànyè	n.	midnight, in the middle of the night		2
半决赛	bànjuésài	n.	semi-finals		6
多半	duōbàn	n.	most, greater part, mostly, most likely		6
一半	yībàn	num.	half		1
华	**huá**		flowery, illustrious, Chinese	＋24.4	3
华人	huárén	n.	ethnic Chinese person or people		3
华语	huáyǔ	n.	Chinese (language)		5
中华	zhōnghuá	n.	the Chinese nation, China		6
中华民族	zhōnghuá mínzú	n.	the Chinese people		3
协	**xié**		to be united, to cooperate	＋24.4	5
协会	xiéhuì	n.	an association, a society		6
协商	xiéshāng	vb.	to consult with, to talk things over, agreement		6
协调	• xiétiáo	vb.	to coordinate, to harmonize, to fit together, to match (colours etc), harmonious, concerted		6
协议	xiéyì	n.	agreement, pact, protocol		5
协助	xiézhù	vb.	to provide assistance, to aid		6
协议书	xiéyìshū	n.	contract, protocol		5
卖	**mài**		to sell, to betray	＋24.6	2
卖	mài	vb.	to sell, to betray, to spare no effort, to show off or flaunt		2
买卖	- mǎimai	n.	buying and selling, business, business transactions		5
外卖	wàimài	n.	take away (meal), takeout (meal), takeout (business),		2
丧	**sàng**		to mourn	＋24.6	6
丧失	sàngshī	vb.	to lose, to forfeit		6
南	**nán**		south	＋24.7	1
南	nán	n.	South, surname Nan		1

南北	nánběi	n.	north and south, north to south		5
南边	nánbian	n.	south, south side, southern part, to the south of		1
南部	nánbù	n.	southern part		3
南方	nánfāng	n.	south, the southern part of the country, the South		2
南极	nánjí	n.	south pole		5
东南	dōngnán	n.	southeast		2
西南	xīnán	n.	southwest		2

博 bó — to gamble   十 24.10   5

博客	bókè	n.	blog (loanword), blogger		5
博士	bóshì	n.	doctor, court academician (in feudal China), Ph.D.		5
博览会	bólǎnhuì	n.	exposition, international fair		5
博物馆	bówùguǎn	n.	museum		5
赌博	dǔbó	vb.	to gamble		6
微博	wēibó	n.	microblogging, microblog		5

卜 bǔ — divination   25

卡 kǎ — calorie, card   卜 25.3   2

卡	kǎ	m.w.	m.w. calorie, (coll.) slow, (loanword) card		2
贺卡	hèkǎ	n.	greeting card, congratulation card		5
信用卡	xìnyòngkǎ	n.	credit card		2
银行卡	yínhángkǎ	n.	bank card, ATM card		2

占 zhàn — to observe, to divine   卜 25.3   2

占	zhàn	vb.	to observe, to divine		2
占据	zhànjù	vb.	to occupy, to hold		6
占领	zhànlǐng	vb.	to occupy (a territory), to hold		5
占有	zhànyǒu	vb.	to have, to own, to hold, to occupy, to possess, to account for (a high proportion etc)		5

卩 jié — seal   卩 26

危 wēi — dangerous, precarious   卩 26.4   3

危害	wēihài	vb.	to jeopardize, to harm, to endanger, harmful effect, damage		3
危机	wēijī	n.	crisis		6
危险	wēixiǎn	n.	danger, dangerous		3

印 yìn — to print, to stamp   卩 26.4   2

印	yìn	vb.	to print, to stamp, to engrave, to mark, surname Yin		6
印刷	yìnshuā	vb.	to print, printing		5
印象	yìnxiàng	n.	impression		3
打印	dǎyìn	vb.	to affix a seal, to stamp, to print out (with a printer)		2
复印	fùyìn	vb.	to photocopy, to duplicate a document		3
脚印	jiǎoyìn	n.	footprint		6
打印机	dǎyìnjī	n.	printer		6

即 jí — promptly, quickly   卩 26.5   4

即将	jíjiāng	adv.	on the eve of, to be about to, to be on the verge of		4

即使	jíshǐ	conj.	even if, even though	5
立即	lìjí	adv.	immediately	4

却 què — but, yet ⼙ 26.5 4

却	què	adv.	but, yet, however, while, to go back, to decline, to retreat, nevertheless, even though	4
却是	quèshì	conj.	nevertheless, actually, the fact is ...	6

卷 * juǎn, juàn — to roll; book, file ⼙ 26.6 4

卷	juǎn	vb.	to roll (up), to sweep up, to carry on, roll	4
卷	• juàn	n.	book, file, m.w. chapter/ section	4
试卷	• shìjuàn	n.	examination paper, test paper	4

厂 hàn — cliff 27

厂 chǎng — factory, workshop ⼚ 27.0 3

厂	chǎng	n.	factory, yard, depot, workhouse, works, (industrial) plant	3
厂商	chǎngshāng	n.	manufacturer, producer	6
厂长	chǎngzhǎng	n.	factory director	5
工厂	gōngchǎng	n.	factory	3

历 lì — history ⼚ 27.2 3

历史	lìshǐ	n.	history	4
简历	jiǎnlì	n.	curriculum vitae (CV), résumé, biographical notes	4
经历	jīnglì	n.	experience	3
日历	rìlì	n.	calendar	4

厅 tīng — hall, central room ⼚ 27.2 5

厅	tīng	n.	(reception) hall, living room, office, provincial government department	5
餐厅	cāntīng	n.	dining hall, dining room, restaurant	5
大厅	dàtīng	n.	hall, lounge	5
客厅	kètīng	n.	drawing room (room for arriving guests), living room	5

厉 lì — strict, stern ⼚ 27.3 5

厉害	- lìhai	adj.	(used to describe sb or sth that makes a very strong impression, whether favourable or unfavourable) terrible, intense	5
严厉	yánlì	adj.	severe, strict	5

压 yā — to press, to crush ⼚ 27.4 3

压	yā	vb.	to press, to push down, to keep under (control), pressure	3
压力	yālì	n.	pressure	3
压迫	yāpò	vb.	to oppress, to repress, to constrict, oppression, stress (physics)	6

厌 yàn — to dislike, to detest ⼚ 27.4 5

讨厌	tǎoyàn	vb.	to dislike, to loathe, disagreeable, troublesome, annoying	5

质 zhì — matter, material ⼚ 27.4 4

质量	zhìliàng	n.	quality, (physics) mass	4
本质	běnzhì	n.	essence, nature, innate character, intrinsic quality	6
品质	pǐnzhì	n.	character, intrinsic quality (of a person), quality (of a product or service, or as in quality of life, air quality etc)	4

素质	sùzhì	n.	inner quality, basic essence		6
物质	wùzhì	n.	matter, substance, material, materialistic		5
性质	xìngzhì	n.	nature, characteristic		4
优质	yōuzhì	adj.	high quality		6

厕 cè — toilet, lavatory ⌈ 27.6   6

厕所	cèsuǒ	n.	toilet, lavatory	6

厚 hòu — thick, substantial ⌈ 27.7   4

厚	hòu	adj.	thick, (opp. 薄 báo: thin), deep or profound, kind, generous, rich or strong in flavour, to favour, to stress	4
深厚	shēnhòu	adj.	deep, profound	4

厘 lí — m.w. of small length, weight ⌈ 27.7   4

厘米	límǐ	m.w.	centimetre	4

原 yuán — source, origin ⌈ 27.8   2

原	yuán	n.	source, origin, cause, beginning, raw, level, surname Yuan	6
原地	• yuándì	n.	the original place, the place where one currently is, place of origin, local (product)	6
原告	yuángào	n.	complainant, plaintiff	6
原来	yuánlái	adj.	original, former, originally, formerly, at first, so, actually, as it turns out	2
原理	yuánlǐ	n.	principle, theory	5
原谅	yuánliàng	vb.	to excuse, to forgive, to pardon	6
原料	yuánliào	n.	raw material	4
原始	yuánshǐ	adj.	first, original, primitive, original (document etc)	5
原先	yuánxiān	adv.	originally, original, former	5
原因	yuányīn	n.	cause, origin, root cause, reason	2
原有	yuányǒu	adj.	original, former	5
原则	yuánzé	n.	principle, doctrine	4
草原	cǎoyuán	n.	grassland, prairie	5
高原	gāoyuán	n.	plateau	5
平原	píngyuán	n.	field, plain	5

厨 chú — kitchen ⌈ 27.10   5

厨房	chúfáng	n.	kitchen	5
厨师	chúshī	n.	cook, chef	6

厶 sī — private   28

去 qù — to go, to leave, to depart ∠ 28.3   1

去	qù	vb.	to go, to go to (a place), (of a time etc) last, just passed, to send, to remove, to get rid of, to reduce	1
去掉	qùdiào	vb.	to get rid of, to exclude, to eliminate, to remove, to delete, to strip out, to extract	6
去年	qùnián	n.	last year	1
去世	qùshì	vb.	to pass away, to die	3
出去	chūqù	vb.	to go out	1
过去	guòqù	+ vb.	to go over, to pass by	2
过去	guòqù	+ n.	(the) past, former times	3

回去	huí qù	vb.	to return, to go back	1
进去	- jìnqu	vb.	to go in	1
上去	- shàngqu	vb.	to go up	3
失去	shīqù	vb.	to lose	3
下去	xiàqù	vb.	to go down, to descend, to go on, to continue, (of a servant) to withdraw	3
看上去	- kànshangqu	adv.	it would appear, it seems (that)	3

县 **xiàn** county △ 28.5   4

县	xiàn	n.	county	4

参 **cān** to take part in, to intervene △ 28.6   2

参观	cānguān	vb.	to look around, to tour, to visit	2
参加	cānjiā	vb.	to participate, to take part, to join	2
参考	cānkǎo	n.	consultation, reference, to consult, to refer	4
参赛	cānsài	vb.	to compete, to take part in a competition	6
参与	• cānyù	vb.	to participate (in sth)	4
参展	cānzhǎn	vb.	to exhibit at or take part in a trade show etc	6

又 yòu again   29

又	yòu		again, in addition	又 29.0 2
又	yòu	adv.	(once) again, also, both... and..., and yet, (used for emphasis) anyway	2

叉 **chā** fork, prong 又 29.1   5

叉	chā	n.	fork, pitchfork, prong, pick, cross, intersect, "X"	5
叉子	chāzi	n.	fork	5

反 **fǎn** to reverse, opposite 又 29.2   3

反	fǎn	vb.	to reverse, to return, to oppose, opposite, against, anti-, instead, contrary, in reverse, (opp. 正 zhèng: right, obverse) inside out or upside down	4
反而	fǎn'ér	adv.	instead, on the contrary, contrary (to expectations)	4
反对	fǎnduì	vb.	to fight against, to oppose, to be opposed to, opposition	3
反复	fǎnfù	adv.	repeatedly, over and over, to upend, unstable, to come and go, (of an illness) to return	3
反抗	fǎnkàng	vb.	to resist, to rebel	6
反问	fǎnwèn	vb.	to ask (a question) in reply, to answer a question with a question, rhetorical question	6
反响	fǎnxiǎng	n.	repercussions, reaction, echo	6
反应	• fǎnyìng	vb.	to react, to respond, reaction, response, reply, chemical reaction	3
反映	fǎnyìng	vb.	to mirror, to reflect, mirror image, reflection, (fig.) to report, to make known, to render	4
反正	fǎnzhèng	adv.	anyway, in any case, to come over from the enemy's side	3
违反	wéifǎn	vb.	to violate (a law)	5
相反	xiāngfǎn	adj.	opposite, contrary	4

及 **jí** to extend, to reach 又 29.2   3

及格	jígé	vb.	to pass an exam or a test, to meet a minimum standard	4
及时	jíshí	adj.	in time, promptly, without delay, timely	3

普及	pǔjí	vb.	to spread extensively, to generalize, widespread, popular, universal, ubiquitous, pervasive	3
涉及	shèjí	vb.	to involve, to touch upon (a topic)	6
以及	yǐjí	conj.	as well as, too, and	4
来不及	- láibují	phr.	there's not enough time (to do sth), it's too late (to do sth)	4
来得及	láidejí	phr.	there's still time, able to do sth in time	4

双 shuāng — set of two, pair   又 29.2   3

双	shuāng	adj.	set of two, double, (opp. 单 dān: single, odd), m.w. for pairs, surname Shuang	3
双打	shuāngdǎ	n.	doubles (in sports)	6
双方	shuāngfāng	n.	bilateral, both sides, both parties involved	3
双手	shuāngshǒu	n.	both hands	5

友 yǒu — friend, companion   又 29.2   1

友好	yǒuhǎo	adj.	friendly (relations), close friends	2
友谊	yǒuyì	n.	companionship, fellowship, friendship	5
好友	hǎoyǒu	n.	close friend, pal, (social networking website) friend	4
朋友	- péngyou	n.	friend, boyfriend or girlfriend	1
网友	wǎngyǒu	n.	online friend, Internet user	1
战友	zhànyǒu	n.	comrade-in-arms, battle companion	6
交朋友	- jiāo péngyou	vb.	to make friends, (dialect) to start an affair with sb	2
老朋友	- lǎopéngyou	n.	old friend, (slang) period, menstruation	2
男朋友	- nánpéngyou	n.	boyfriend	1
女朋友	- nǚpéngyou	n.	girlfriend	1
小朋友	- xiǎopéngyou	n.	child	1

发 * fā, fà — to issue, to send out; hair   又 29.3   2

发	fā	vb.	to send out, to issue, to show feelings	2
发病	fā bìng	n.	onset, outbreak (of a disease)	6
发电	fā diàn	vb.	to generate electricity, to send a telegram	6
发表	fābiǎo	vb.	to issue, to publish	3
发布	fābù	vb.	to release, to issue, to announce, to distribute	5
发出	fāchū	vb.	to issue (an order, decree etc), to send out, to dispatch, to produce (a sound), to let out (a laugh)	3
发达	fādá	adj.	developed (country etc), flourishing, to develop	3
发动	fādòng	vb.	to start, to launch, to unleash, to mobilize, to arouse	3
发放	fāfàng	vb.	to provide, to give, to grant	6
发挥	fāhuī	vb.	to display, to exhibit, to bring out implicit or innate qualities, to express (a thought or moral), to develop (an idea), to elaborate (on a theme)	4
发觉	fājué	vb.	to become aware, to detect, to realize, to perceive	5
发明	fāmíng	vb.	to invent, an invention	3
发怒	fānù	vb.	to get angry	6
发票	fāpiào	n.	invoice, receipt or bill for purchase	4
发起	fāqǐ	vb.	to originate, to initiate, to launch (an attack, an initiative etc), to start, to propose sth (for the first time)	6
发烧	fāshāo	vb.	to have a high temperature (from illness), to have a fever	4
发射	fāshè	vb.	to shoot (a projectile), to fire (a rocket), to launch, to emit (a particle), to discharge, emanation, emission	5

发生	fāshēng	vb.	to happen, to occur, to take place, to break out	3
发送	fāsòng	vb.	to transmit, to dispatch, to issue (an official document or credential)	3
发现	fāxiàn	vb.	to find, to discover	2
发行	fāxíng	vb.	to publish, to issue (stocks, currency etc), to release, to distribute (a film)	5
发言	fāyán	vb.	to make a speech, statement, utterance	3
发炎	fāyán	vb.	to become inflamed, inflammation	6
发展	fāzhǎn	n.	development, growth, to develop, to grow, to expand	3
发言人	fāyánrén	n.	spokesperson	6
爆发	bàofā	vb.	to break out, to erupt, to explode, to burst out	6
出发	chūfā	vb.	to set off, to start (on a journey)	2
打发	- dǎfa	vb.	to dispatch sb to do sth, to make sb leave, to pass (the time), (old) to make arrangements, (old) to bestow (alms etc)	6
开发	kāifā	vb.	to exploit (a resource), to open up (for development), to develop	3
理发	• lǐfà	n.	a barber, hairdressing	3
启发	qǐfā	vb.	to enlighten, to explain (a text etc), to stimulate (a mental attitude), enlightenment, revelation, motivation	5
沙发	shāfā	n.	sofa (loanword)	3
头发	- tóufa	n.	hair (on the head)	2
研发	yánfā	n.	research and development, to develop	6

变 **biàn**   to change, to transform   又 29.6   2

变	biàn	vb.	to change, to become different, to transform, to vary, rebellion	2
变成	biàn chéng	vb.	to change into, to turn into, to become	2
变形	biàn xíng	vb.	to become deformed, to change shape, to morph, deformation	6
变动	biàndòng	vb.	to change, to fluctuate, change, fluctuation	5
变更	biàngèng	vb.	to change, to alter, to modify	6
变化	biànhuà	n.	change, variation, to change, to vary	3
变换	biànhuàn	vb.	to transform, to convert, to vary, to alternate, a transformation	6
变为	• biànwéi	vb.	to change into	3
改变	gǎibiàn	vb.	to change, to alter, to transform	2
转变	zhuǎnbiàn	vb.	to change, to transform, shift, transformation	3

艰 **jiān**   difficult, hard   又 29.6   5

艰苦	jiānkǔ	adj.	difficult, hard, arduous	5
艰难	jiānnán	adj.	difficult, hard, challenging	5

取 **qǔ**   to take, to get, to choose   又 29.6   2

取	qǔ	vb.	to take, to get, to choose, to fetch	2
取得	• qǔdé	vb.	to acquire, to get, to obtain	2
取款	qǔkuǎn	vb.	to withdraw money from a bank	6
取消	qǔxiāo	vb.	to cancel, cancellation	3
取款机	qǔkuǎn jī	n.	ATM, cash dispenser	6
采取	cǎiqǔ	vb.	to adopt or carry out (measures, policies, course of action), to take	3
夺取	duóqǔ	vb.	to seize, to capture, to wrest control of	6
获取	huòqǔ	vb.	to gain, to get, to acquire	4
领取	lǐngqǔ	vb.	to receive, to draw, to get	6
录取	lùqǔ	vb.	to accept an applicant (prospective student, employee etc) who passes an entrance exam, to admit (a student), to hire (a job candidate)	4
收取	shōuqǔ	vb.	to receive, to collect	6

听取	tīngqǔ	*vb.*	to hear (news), to listen to		6
争取	zhēngqǔ	*vb.*	to fight for, to strive for, to win over		3
受	**shòu**		to receive, to accept, to suffer	又 29.6	2
受	shòu	*vb.*	to receive, to accept, to suffer, to be subjected to, to bear, to stand, pleasant, (passive marker)		3
受伤	shòu shāng	*vb.*	to sustain injuries, wounded (in an accident etc), harmed		3
受到	shòudào	*vb.*	to receive (praise, an education, punishment etc), to be ...ed (praised, educated, punished etc)		2
受灾	shòuzāi	*vb.*	to be hit by a natural calamity, disaster-stricken		5
受不了	• shòubuliǎo	*phr.*	unbearable, unable to endure, can't stand		4
承受	chéngshòu	*vb.*	to bear, to support, to inherit		4
感受	gǎnshòu	*vb.*	to sense, perception, to feel (through the senses), to experience, a feeling, an impression, an experience		3
接受	jiēshòu	*vb.*	to accept, to receive		2
难受	nánshòu	*vb.*	to feel unwell, to suffer pain, to be difficult to bear		2
忍受	rěnshòu	*vb.*	to bear, to endure		5
享受	xiǎngshòu	*vb.*	to enjoy, to live it up, pleasure		5
遭受	zāoshòu	*vb.*	to suffer, to sustain (loss, misfortune)		6
叔	**shū**		uncle, father's younger brother	又 29.6	4
叔叔	- shūshu	*n.*	father's younger brother, uncle		4
难	* **nán, nàn**		difficult, hard; unable	又 29.8	1
难	nán	*adj.*	difficult (to...), problem, (opp. 易 yì: easy), difficulty, difficult, not good		1
难道	nándào	*adv.*	don't tell me ..., could it be that...?		3
难得	• nándé	*adj.*	seldom, rare, hard to come by		5
难度	nándù	*n.*	degree of difficulty		3
难过	nánguò	*vb.*	to feel sad, to feel unwell, (of life) to be difficult		2
难看	nánkàn	*adj.*	ugly, unsightly		2
难免	nánmiǎn	*adj.*	hard to avoid, difficult to escape from, will inevitably		4
难受	nánshòu	*vb.*	to feel unwell, to suffer pain, to be difficult to bear		2
难题	nántí	*n.*	difficult problem		2
难听	nántīng	*adj.*	unpleasant to hear, coarse, vulgar, offensive, shameful		2
难忘	nánwàng	*adj.*	unforgettable		6
难以	nányǐ	*adv.*	hard to (predict, imagine etc)		5
艰难	jiānnán	*adj.*	difficult, hard, challenging		5
困难	- kùnnan	*adj.*	difficult, challenging, straitened circumstances, difficult situation		3
为难	• wéinán	*vb.*	to feel embarrassed or awkward, to make things difficult (for someone), to find things difficult (to do or manage)		5
灾难	• zāinàn	*n.*	disaster, catastrophe		5
很难说	hěnnánshuō	*phr.*	it's hard to say		6

口 kǒu   mouth   30

口	kǒu		mouth, entrance	口 30.0	1
口	kǒu	*n.*	mouth, m.w. for things with mouths (people, domestic animals, cannons, wells etc), m.w. for bites or mouthfuls		1
口袋	- kǒudai	*n.*	pocket, bag, sack		4

口号	kǒuhào		n.	slogan, catchphrase	5
口试	kǒushì		n.	oral examination, oral test	6
口语	kǒuyǔ		n.	colloquial speech, spoken language, vernacular language, slander, gossip	4
出口	chūkǒu	+	n.	an export	2
出口	chūkǒu	+	n.	an exit	4
窗口	chuāngkǒu		n.	window, opening providing restricted access (e.g. customer service window), computer operating system window	6
港口	gǎngkǒu		n.	port, harbour, airport	6
进口	jìnkǒu		vb.	to import, imported, entrance, inlet (for the intake of air, water etc)	4
路口	lùkǒu		n.	crossing, intersection (of roads)	1
门口	ménkǒu		n.	doorway, gate	1
人口	rénkǒu		n.	population, people	2
入口	rùkǒu		n.	entrance, to import	2
伤口	shāngkǒu		n.	wound, cut	6
一口气	yīkǒuqì		n.	one breath, in one breath, at a stretch	5
古	**gǔ**			ancient, old	☐ 30.2 3
古	gǔ		adj.	ancient, old, surname Gu	3
古代	gǔdài		n.	ancient times, olden times	3
古典	gǔdiǎn		adj.	classical	6
古老	gǔlǎo		adj.	ancient, old, age-old	5
号	**hào**			name, size, number	☐ 30.2 1
号	hào		n.	name, mark, size, number, date	1
号码	hàomǎ		n.	number	4
号召	hàozhào		vb.	to call, to appeal	5
车号	chēhào		n.	vehicle number (license plate number, taxi number, bus number, train car number)	6
称号	chēnghào		n.	name, term of address, title	5
符号	fúhào		n.	symbol, mark, sign	4
口号	kǒuhào		n.	slogan, catchphrase	5
括号	kuòhào		n.	parentheses, brackets	4
信号	xìnhào		n.	signal	2
型号	xínghào		n.	model (particular version of a manufactured article), type (product specification in terms of colour, size etc)	4
叫	**jiào**			to call, to cry, to shout	☐ 30.2 1
叫	jiào	+	vb.	to call, to cry, to shout, to name, be called, to greet, to hire, to order	1
叫	jiào	+	prep.	preposition that introduces to doer of the action	3
叫作	jiàozuò		vb.	to call, to be called	2
句	**jù**			sentence	☐ 30.2 2
句	jù		n.	sentence, clause, phrase, m.w. for sentences or lines	2
句子	jùzi		n.	sentence	2
一句话	yī jù huà		phr.	in a word, in short	5
可	**kě**			can, may	☐ 30.2 2
可	kě		adv.	can, may, able to, to approve, to permit, to suit, (particle used for emphasis) certainly, very	5
可爱	kě'ài		adj.	adorable, cute, lovely	2

可见	kějiàn	conj.	it can clearly be seen (that this is the case), it is (thus) clear, clear, visible	4
可靠	kěkào	adj.	reliable	3
可乐	kělè	adj.	amusing, entertaining, (loanword) cola	3
可怜	kělián	adj.	pitiful, pathetic, to have pity on	5
可能	kěnéng	n.	possibility, probability; might (happen), possible, probable, maybe, perhaps	2
可怕	kěpà	adj.	awful, dreadful, fearful, formidable, frightful, scary, hideous, horrible, terrible, terribly	2
可是	kěshì	conj.	but, however, (used for emphasis) indeed	2
可惜	kěxī	adv.	it is a pity, what a pity, unfortunately	5
可以	kěyǐ	vb.	to be possible, to be able to, not bad, pretty good	2
认可	rènkě	vb.	to approve, approval, acknowledgment, OK	3
许可	xǔkě	vb.	to allow, to permit	5
尽可能	jǐnkěnéng	adv.	as far as possible, to do one's utmost	5

另 **lìng**   separately, other   ☐ 30.2   3

另	lìng	adv.	separately, other, another, separate	6
另外	lìngwài	adv.	additional, in addition, besides, separate, other, moreover, furthermore	3
另一方面	lìngyīfāngmiàn	phr.	on the other hand, another aspect	3

史 **shǐ**   history, chronicle   ☐ 30.2   4

历史	lìshǐ	n.	history	4

司 **sī**   to take charge of   ☐ 30.2   2

司机	sījī	n.	chauffeur, driver	2
司长	sīzhǎng	n.	bureau chief	6
公司	gōngsī	n.	(business) company, company, firm, corporation, incorporated	2
官司	-guānsi	n.	lawsuit	6
寿司	shòusī	n.	sushi	5
打官司	-dǎ guānsi	vb.	to file a lawsuit, to sue, to dispute	6

台 **tái**   platform, stage   ☐ 30.2   3

台	tái	n.	platform, stage, m.w. for machines or vehicles, (classical) you (in letters)	3
台灯	táidēng	n.	desk lamp, table lamp	6
台风	táifēng	n.	hurricane, typhoon	5
台阶	táijiē	n.	steps, flight of steps, step (over obstacle), fig. way out of an embarrassing situation	4
台上	táishàng	n.	on stage, on the platform	4
出台	chūtái	vb.	to officially launch (a policy, program etc), to appear on stage, to appear publicly	6
窗台	chuāngtái	n.	windowsill, window ledge	4
电台	diàntái	n.	transmitter-receiver, broadcasting station, radio station	3
平台	píngtái	n.	platform, terrace, flat-roofed building	6
上台	shàng tái	vb.	to rise to power (in politics), to go on stage (in the theatre)	6
舞台	wǔtái	n.	stage, arena, fig. in the limelight	3
阳台	yángtái	n.	balcony, porch	4
站台	zhàntái	n.	platform (at a railway station)	6
电视台	diànshìtái	n.	television station	3

写字台	xiězì tái	n.	writing desk	6
叹	**tàn**		to sigh	▢ 30.2 6
叹气	tàn qì	vb.	to sigh, to heave a sigh	6
叶	**yè**		leaf, blade, page	▢ 30.2 4
叶子	yèzi	n.	foliage, leaf, leaf like thing, blade	4
茶叶	cháyè	n.	tea, tea leaves	4
树叶	shùyè	n.	tree leaves	4
右	**yòu**		right	▢ 30.2 1
右	yòu	n.	right (-hand), the Right (politics), west (old)	1
右边	- yòubian	n.	right side, right, to the right	1
左右	zuǒyòu	n.	left and right, nearby, approximately, attendant, to control, to influence	3
召	**zhào**		to summon	▢ 30.2 4
召开	zhàokāi	vb.	to convene (a conference or meeting), to convoke, to call together	4
号召	hàozhào	vb.	to call, to appeal	5
只	* **zhǐ, zhī**		only, just; single, m.w. for birds	▢ 30.2 2
只	• zhī	adj.	single, one only, m.w. for birds and certain animals, one of a pair, some utensils, vessels etc	3
只	zhǐ	adv.	only, just, merely	2
只见	zhǐ jiàn	vb.	to see (the same thing) over and over again, to see, to one's surprise, (sth happen suddenly)	5
只得	• zhǐdé	vb.	to have no alternative but to, to be obliged to	6
只顾	zhǐgù	adv.	solely preoccupied (with one thing), engrossed, focusing (on sth), to look after only one aspect	6
只管	zhǐguǎn	adv.	solely engrossed in one thing, just (one thing, no need to worry about the rest), simply, by all means, please feel free, do not hesitate (to ask for sth)	6
只好	zhǐhǎo	adv.	without any better option, to have to, to be forced to	3
只能	zhǐnéng	vb.	to have no other choice (can only), to be obliged to do sth	2
只是	zhǐshì	adv.	merely, simply, only, but	3
只要	zhǐyào	conj.	if only, so long as	2
只有	zhǐyǒu	conj.	only have ..., there is only ..., (used in combination with 才 cái) it is only if one ... (that one can ...)	3
只不过	- zhǐbuguò	adv.	only, merely, nothing but, no more than, it's just that ...	5
船只	• chuánzhī	n.	shipping, vessels	6
吃	**chī**		to eat	▢ 30.3 1
吃	chī	vb.	to eat	1
吃惊	chī jīng	vb.	to be startled, to be shocked, to be amazed	4
吃饭	chīfàn	vb.	to have a meal, to eat, to make a living	1
吃力	chīlì	vb.	to entail strenuous effort, to toil at a task, strenuous, laborious	5
好吃	hǎochī	adj.	tasty, delicious	1
小吃	xiǎochī	n.	snack, refreshments	4
吊	**diào**		to hang, to suspend	▢ 30.3 6
吊	diào	vb.	to hang, to suspend, tower crane, a string of 1000 coins (arch.),	6

各	gè		each, every	📖 30.3	3
各	gè	pro.	each, every		3
各地	• gèdì	n.	in all parts of (a country), various regions		3
各个	gègè	pro.	every, various, separately, one by one		4
各位	gèwèi	pro.	everybody, all (guests, colleagues etc), all of you		3
各种	gèzhǒng	n.	all kinds of, various kinds, every kind of,		3
各自	gèzì	pro.	each, respective, apiece		3

合	hé		to close, to join, to unite	📖 30.3	2
合	hé	vb.	to close, to join, to unite, to suit, to be equal to, whole, together		3
合并	hébìng	vb.	to merge, to annex		5
合成	héchéng	vb.	to compose, to constitute, compound, synthesis, mixture, synthetic		5
合法	héfǎ	adj.	lawful, legitimate, legal		3
合格	hégé	vb.	to meet the standard required, qualified, eligible (voter etc)		3
合理	hélǐ	adj.	rational, reasonable, fair		3
合适	héshì	adj.	suitable, fitting, appropriate		2
合同	- hétong	n.	(business) contract		4
合约	héyuē	n.	treaty, contract		6
合作	hézuò	vb.	to cooperate, to collaborate, to work together, cooperation		3
场合	chǎnghé	n.	situation, occasion, context, setting, location, venue		3
符合	fúhé	vb.	in keeping with, in accordance with, tallying with, in line with, to agree with, to conform to, to correspond with, to manage, to handle		4
混合	hùnhé	vb.	to mix, to blend, hybrid, composite		6
集合	jíhé	vb.	to gather, to assemble, set (math.)		4
结合	jiéhé	vb.	to combine, to link, to integrate, binding		3
联合	liánhé	vb.	to combine, to join, unite, alliance		3
配合	pèihé	adj.	matching, fitting in with, compatible with, to correspond, to fit, to conform to, rapport, to coordinate with		3
融合	rónghé	n.	a mixture, an amalgam, fusion, welding together, to be in harmony with (nature), to harmonize with, to fit in		6
适合	shìhé	vb.	to fit, to suit		3
综合	zōnghé	adj.	comprehensive, composite, synthesized, mixed, to sum up, to integrate, to synthesize		4
组合	zǔhé	vb.	to assemble, to combine, to compose, combination, association, set, compilation, (math.) combinatorial		3
联合国	liánhéguó	n.	United Nations		3

后	hòu		back, behind	📖 30.3	1
后	hòu	n.	back, behind, rear, afterwards, after, later, post-, (opp. 前 qián: front, 先 xiān: earlier, first)		1
后边	- hòubian	n.	back, rear, behind		1
后果	hòuguǒ	n.	consequences, aftermath		3
后悔	hòuhuǐ	vb.	to regret, to repent		5
后来	hòulái	n.	afterwards, later		2
后面	- hòumian	n.	rear, back, behind, later, afterwards		3
后年	hòunián	n.	the year after next		3
后天	hòutiān	n.	the day after tomorrow, acquired (not innate), a posteriori		1
后头	- hòutou	n.	behind, the back, the rear, later, afterwards, (in) the future		4
背后	bèihòu	n.	behind, at the back, in the rear, behind sb's back		3

此后	cǐhòu	n.	after this, afterwards, hereafter	5
过后	guòhòu	n.	after the event	6
今后	jīnhòu	n.	hereafter, henceforth, in the future, from now on	2
落后	luòhòu	vb.	to fall behind, to lag (in technology etc), backward, to retrogress	3
前后	qiánhòu	n.	around, from beginning to end, all around, front and rear	3
然后	ránhòu	conj.	then (afterwards), after that, afterwards	2
事后	shìhòu	n.	after the event, in hindsight, in retrospect	6
随后	suíhòu	adv.	soon after	5
王后	wánghòu	n.	queen	6
往后	wǎnghòu	n.	from now on, in the future, time to come	6
先后	xiānhòu	n.	priority, in succession, one after another	5
以后	yǐhòu	n.	after, later, afterwards, following, later on, in the future	2
之后	zhīhòu	n.	afterwards, following, later, after	4
最后	zuìhòu	n.	final, last, finally, ultimate	1

吉 jí — lucky, auspicious □ 30.3 · 6

吉利	jílì	adj.	lucky, auspicious, Geely (Chinese car manufacturer)	6
吉祥	jíxiáng	adj.	lucky, auspicious, propitious	6

吗 ma — final interrogative particle □ 30.3 · 1

吗	ma	aux.	[final interrogative particle (particle for yes/no questions)]	1
干吗	gànma	adv.	why?, whatever for?, what's going on?, what are you doing?,	3

名 míng — name, noun □ 30.3 · 1

名	míng	n.	name, noun (part of speech), place (e.g. among winners), famous, m.w. for people	2
名额	míng'é	n.	quota, number of places, place (in an institution, a group etc)	6
名称	míngchēng	n.	name (of a thing), name (of an organization)	2
名单	míngdān	n.	list of names	2
名牌	míngpái	n.	famous brand, nameplate, name tag	4
名片	míngpiàn	n.	(business) card	4
名人	míngrén	n.	personage, celebrity	4
名胜	míngshèng	n.	a place famous for its scenery or historical relics, scenic spot	6
名义	míngyì	n.	name, titular, nominal, in name, ostensible purpose	6
名誉	míngyù	n.	fame, reputation, honour, honourary, emeritus (of retired professor)	6
名字	míngzi	n.	name (of a person or thing)	1
报名	bào míng	vb.	to sign up, to enter one's name, to apply, to register, to enrol, to enlist	2
出名	chū míng	n.	well-known for sth, to become well known, to make one's mark	6
地名	· dìmíng	n.	place name, toponym	6
点名	diǎnmíng	n.	to roll call, to mention sb by name, (to call or praise or criticize sb) by name	4
排名	páimíng	vb.	to rank (1st, 2nd etc), ranking	3
签名	qiānmíng	vb.	to sign (one's name with a pen etc), to autograph, signature	5
姓名	xìngmíng	n.	surname and given name, full name	2
有名	yǒumíng	adj.	famous, well-known	1
知名	zhīmíng	adj.	well-known, famous	6
著名	· zhùmíng	n.	famous, noted, well-known, celebrated	4

同	**tóng**		**same, similar**	📖 30.3	1
同	tóng	adj.	same, similar, together, with		6
同胞	tóngbāo	n.	born of the same parents, sibling, fellow citizen, compatriot		6
同行	tóngxíng	n.	person of the same profession, of the same trade, occupation or industry		6
同期	tóngqī	n.	the corresponding time period (in a different year etc), concurrent, synchronous		6
同情	tóngqíng	vb.	to sympathize with, sympathy		4
同时	tóngshí	adv.	at the same time, simultaneously		2
同事	tóngshì	n.	colleague, co-worker		2
同学	tóngxué	vb.	to study at the same school, fellow student, classmate		1
同样	tóngyàng	adj.	same, equal, equivalent		2
同一	tóngyī	adj.	identical, the same		6
同意	tóngyì	vb.	to agree, to consent, to approve		3
不同	bùtóng	adj.	different, distinct, not the same, not alike		2
共同	gòngtóng	adj.	common, joint, jointly, together, collaborative		3
合同	- hétong	n.	(business) contract		4
胡同	hútóng	n.	lane, alley (also with a neutral tone on the second syllable)		5
陪同	péitóng	vb.	to accompany		6
认同	rèntóng	vb.	to approve of, to endorse, to acknowledge, to recognize, to identify oneself with		6
如同	rútóng	vb.	to be like, to be similar		5
相同	xiāngtóng	adj.	identical, same		2
一同	yītóng	adv.	along, together		6
吐	* **tǔ, tù**		**to spit, to say; to vomit**	📖 30.3	5
吐	tǔ	vb.	to spit, to send out (silk from a silkworm, bolls from cotton flowers etc), to say, to pour out (one's grievances)		5
吐	• tù	vb.	to vomit, to give up unwillingly		5
吓	**xià**		**to scare, to frighten**	📖 30.3	5
吓	xià	vb.	to scare, to intimidate, to threaten, (interjection showing disapproval) tut-tut, (interjection showing astonishment)		5
向	**xiàng**		**direction, towards**	📖 30.3	2
向	xiàng	n.	direction, towards, to turn, to face		2
向导	xiàngdǎo	n.	guide		5
向前	xiàngqián	adv.	forward, onward		5
向上	xiàngshàng	adv.	upward, up, to advance, to try to improve oneself, to make progress		5
方向	fāngxiàng	n.	direction, orientation, path to follow		2
面向	miànxiàng	vb.	to face, to turn towards, to incline to, geared towards, catering for, -oriented, facial feature, appearance, aspect, facet		6
倾向	qīngxiàng	n.	trend, tendency, orientation		6
一向	yīxiàng	adv.	always (previously), a period of time in the recent past		5
转向	zhuǎnxiàng	vb.	to change direction, fig. to change one's stance		5
吧	* **ba, bā**		**emphatic final particle; bar**	📖 30.4	1
吧	ba	aux.	[indicates suggestion, request, consent or approval, doubt]		1
酒吧	• jiǔbā	n.	bar, pub, saloon		4
网吧	• wǎngbā	n.	Internet café		6

吵	chǎo		to quarrel, to make a noise	☐ 30.4	3
吵	chǎo	vb.	to quarrel, to make a noise, noisy, to disturb by making a noise		3
吵架	chǎojià	vb.	to quarrel, to have a row, quarrel		3
吹	**chuī**		to blow, to blast	☐ 30.4	2
吹	chuī	vb.	to blow, to play a wind instrument, to blast, to puff, to boast, to brag, to end in failure, to fall through		2
呆	**dāi**		foolish, stupid	☐ 30.4	5
呆	dāi	adj.	foolish, stupid, expressionless, blank, to stay		5
吨	**dūn**		ton	☐ 30.4	5
吨	dūn	m.w.	ton (loanword)		5
否	**fǒu**		to negate, to deny	☐ 30.4	3
否定	fǒudìng	vb.	to negate, to deny, to reject, negative (answer), negation		3
否认	fǒurèn	vb.	to declare to be untrue, to deny		3
否则	fǒuzé	conj.	if not, otherwise, else, or else		4
能否	néngfǒu	phr.	whether or not, can it or can't it, is it possible?		6
是否	shìfǒu	adv.	whether (or not), if, is or isn't		4
告	**gào**		to leave	☐ 30.4	1
告别	gàobié	vb.	to leave, to bid farewell to, to say good-bye to		3
告诉	-gàosu	vb.	to press charges, to file a complaint		1
报告	bàogào	vb.	to inform, to report, to make known, report, speech, talk, lecture		3
被告	bèigào	n.	defendant		6
公告	gōnggào	n.	post, announcement		5
广告	guǎnggào	vb.	to advertise, a commercial, advertisement		2
警告	jǐnggào	vb.	to warn, to admonish		5
原告	yuángào	n.	complainant, plaintiff		6
转告	zhuǎngào	vb.	to pass on, to communicate, to transmit		4
含	**hán**		to keep, to contain	☐ 30.4	4
含	hán	vb.	to keep, to contain, to suck (keep in your mouth without chewing)		4
含量	hánliàng	n.	content, quantity contained		4
含义	hányì	n.	meaning (implicit in a phrase), implied meaning, hidden meaning, hint, connotation		4
含有	hányǒu	vb.	to contain, to have including		4
包含	bāohán	vb.	to contain, to embody, to include		4
启	**qǐ**		to open, to begin	☐ 30.4	5
启动	qǐdòng	vb.	to start (a machine), (fig.) to set in motion, to launch (an operation), to activate (a plan)		5
启发	qǐfā	vb.	to enlighten, to explain (a text etc), to stimulate (a mental attitude), enlightenment, revelation, motivation		5
启事	qǐshì	n.	announcement (written, on billboard, letter, newspaper or website), to post information, a notice		5
听	**tīng**		to listen, to hear, to obey	☐ 30.4	1
听	tīng	vb.	to listen, to hear, to obey, a can (loanword from English tin), m.w. for canned beverages		1
听讲	tīng jiǎng	vb.	to attend a lecture, to listen to a talk		2

听到	tīngdào	vb.	to hear	1
听见	tīngjiàn	vb.	to hear	1
听力	tīnglì	n.	hearing, listening ability	3
听取	tīngqǔ	vb.	to hear (news), to listen to	6
听说	tīngshuō	vb.	to hear (sth said), one hears (that), hearsay, listening and speaking	2
听写	tīngxiě	vb.	(of a pupil) to write down (in a dictation exercise), dictation, (music) to transcribe by ear	1
听众	tīngzhòng	n.	audience, listeners	3
打听	- dǎting	vb.	to ask about, to make some inquiries, to ask around	3
好听	hǎotīng	adj.	pleasant to hear	1
难听	nántīng	adj.	unpleasant to hear, coarse, vulgar, offensive, shameful	2
收听	shōutīng	vb.	to listen to (a radio broadcast)	3

吞 tūn — to swallow □ 30.4 6

吞	tūn	vb.	to swallow, to take	6

吸 xī — to breathe, to suck in □ 30.4 4

吸	xī	vb.	to breathe, to suck in, to absorb, to inhale	4
吸毒	xī dú	vb.	to take (addictive) drugs	6
吸管	xīguǎn	n.	(drinking) straw, pipette, eyedropper, snorkel	4
吸收	xīshōu	vb.	to absorb, to assimilate, to ingest, to recruit	4
吸烟	xīyān	vb.	to smoke	4
吸引	xīyǐn	vb.	to attract (interest, investment etc)	4
呼吸	hūxī	vb.	to breathe	4

呀 ya — particle used to express surprise □ 30.4 4

呀	ya	aux.	[particle equivalent to 啊 after a vowel, expressing surprise or doubt]	4

员 yuán — person, employee □ 30.4 3

员	yuán	+ aff.	person, employee, member (e.g. 服务员 fúwùyuán)	3
员工	yuángōng	n.	staff, personnel, employee	3
成员	chéngyuán	n.	member	3
船员	chuányuán	n.	sailor, crew member	6
动员	dòngyuán	vb.	to mobilize, to arouse, mobilization	5
队员	duìyuán	n.	team member	3
会员	huìyuán	n.	member	3
球员	qiúyuán	n.	sports club member, footballer, golfer etc	6
人员	rényuán	n.	staff, crew, personnel	3
伤员	shāngyuán	n.	wounded person	6
学员	xuéyuán	n.	student, member of an institution of learning, officer cadet	6
演员	yǎnyuán	n.	actor or actress, performer	3
飞行员	fēixíngyuán	n.	pilot, aviator	6
公务员	gōngwùyuán	n.	functionary, office-bearer	3
售货员	shòuhuòyuán	n.	salesperson	4
宇航员	yǔhángyuán	n.	astronaut or cosmonaut	6
运动员	yùndòngyuán	n.	athlete	4

和 * hé, huo — harmony, peace; to blend □ 30.5 1

和	hé	conj.	and, with, harmony, peace	1
和平	hépíng	adj.	peaceful	3
和谐	héxié	adj.	harmonious, harmony, melodious	6

暖和	• nuǎnhuo	*adj.*	warm, nice and warm, to warm up		3
温和	wēnhé	*adj.*	mild, gentle, moderate		5

呼 hū   to breathe   ☐ 30.5   4

呼吸	hūxī	*vb.*	to breathe		4
招呼	- zhāohu	*vb.*	to call out to, to greet, to say hello to, to inform, to take care of, to take care that one does not		4

咖 kā   coffee, a phonetic   ☐ 30.5   3

咖啡	kāfēi	*n.*	coffee (loanword)		3

命 mìng   life, destiny, fate   ☐ 30.5   3

命	mìng	+ *n.*	life, destiny, fate, order or command, to assign a name, title etc		6
命令	mìnglìng	*n.*	order, command		5
命运	mìngyùn	*n.*	fate, destiny		3
救命	jiùmìng	*vb.*	to save sb's life, (intj.) help!, save me!		6
生命	shēngmìng	*n.*	life (as the characteristic of living beings), living being, creature		3

呢 ne   interrogative or emphatic final   ☐ 30.5   1

呢	ne	*aux.*	[particle indicating that a previously asked question is to be applied to the preceding word ("What about ...?", And ...?)]		1

味 wèi   taste, smell   ☐ 30.5   2

味	wèi	*n.*	taste, smell, (fig.) (noun suffix) feel, quality, sense, m.w. for ingredients of a Chinese medicine prescription		4
味道	- wèidao	*n.*	flavour, smell, hint of		2
意味着	- yìwèizhe	*vb.*	to signify, to mean, to imply		5

周 zhōu   week, circumference   ☐ 30.5   2

周	zhōu	*n.*	week, weekly, m.w. circle, circuit		2
周末	zhōumò	*n.*	weekend		2
周年	zhōunián	*n.*	anniversary, annual		2
周期	zhōuqī	*n.*	period, cycle		5
周围	zhōuwéi	*n.*	surroundings, environment, to encompass		3
上周	shàngzhōu	*n.*	last week		2
四周	sìzhōu	*n.*	all around		5
下周	xiàzhōu	*n.*	next week		2

哈 hā   sound of laughter   ☐ 30.6   3

哈哈	hāhā	*n.*	joke, (onom.) laughing out loud		3

咳 ké   to cough   ☐ 30.6   5

咳	ké	*vb.*	to cough		5

骂 mà   to scold, to curse   ☐ 30.6   5

骂	mà	*vb.*	to scold, to curse, to condemn, to verbally abuse		5

品 pǐn   article, product   ☐ 30.6   3

品	pǐn	+ *n.*	article, commodity, product, goods, kind, grade, rank, character, disposition, nature		5
品	pǐn	+ *vb.*	to taste (with discrimination), to sample		5
品牌	pǐnpái	*n.*	brand name, trademark		6

品质	pǐnzhì	n.	character, intrinsic quality (of a person), quality (of a product or service, or as in quality of life, air quality etc)		4
品种	pǐnzhǒng	n.	breed, variety		5
产品	chǎnpǐn	n.	goods, merchandise, product		4
成品	chéngpǐn	n.	finished goods, a finished product		6
毒品	dúpǐn	n.	drugs, narcotics, poison		6
精品	jīngpǐn	n.	quality goods, premium product, fine work (of art)		6
商品	shāngpǐn	n.	commodity, goods, merchandise		3
食品	shípǐn	n.	foodstuff, food, provisions		3
物品	wùpǐn	n.	articles, goods, materials		6
药品	yàopǐn	n.	medicaments, medicine, drug		6
用品	yòngpǐn	n.	articles for use, products, goods		6
作品	zuòpǐn	n.	work (of art), opus		3
豆制品	dòuzhìpǐn	n.	legume-based product, soybean product		5
农产品	nóngchǎnpǐn	n.	agricultural produce		5
乳制品	rǔzhìpǐn	n.	dairy products		6
水产品	shuǐchǎnpǐn	n.	aquatic products (including fish, crabs, seaweed etc)		5
哇	**wā**		sound of crying or vomiting	☐ 30.6	6
哇	wā	intj.	wow (coll.), sound of crying or vomiting		6
咸	**xián**		salted, salty	☐ 30.6	4
咸	xián	adj.	salted, salty, stingy, miserly		4
响	**xiǎng**		to make a sound, to sound	☐ 30.6	2
响	xiǎng	vb.	to make a sound, to sound, to ring, loud, echo, sound, noise, m.w. for noises		2
响声	xiǎngshēng	n.	noise		6
反响	fǎnxiǎng	n.	repercussions, reaction, echo		6
影响	yǐngxiǎng	n.	influence, effect, to influence, to affect (usually adversely), to disturb		2
咬	**yǎo**		to bite, to nip	☐ 30.6	5
咬	yǎo	vb.	to bite, to nip, to nibble gently		5
咱	**zán**		we, us	☐ 30.6	2
咱	zán	pro.	we, us, our		2
咱们	zánmen	pro.	we or us (including both the speaker and the person(s) spoken to), (dialect) I or me, (dialect) (in a coaxing or familiar way) you		2
咨	**zī**		to inquire, to consult	☐ 30.6	6
咨询	zīxún	vb.	to consult, to seek advice, consultation, (sales) inquiry (formal)		6
哥	**gē**		elder brother	☐ 30.7	1
哥哥	- gēge	n.	older brother		1
大哥	dàgē	n.	eldest brother, big brother (polite address for a man of about the same age as oneself), gang leader, boss		4
帅哥	shuàigē	n.	handsome guy, handsome (form of address)		4
哭	**kū**		to cry, to weep	☐ 30.7	2
哭	kū	vb.	to cry, to weep		2

哪	**nǎ**		which	□ 30.7	1
哪	nǎ	+ *pro.*	which (pronoun, in questions), whichever, any that		1
哪	nǎ	+ *adv.*	[grammar: used to express negation in rhetorical questions]		4
哪里	- nǎli	*pro.*	where?, somewhere, anywhere, wherever, nowhere (negative answer to question), humble expression denying compliment		1
哪怕	nǎpà	*conj.*	even, even if, even though, no matter how		4
哪儿	nǎr	*pro.*	where?, wherever, anywhere		1
哪些	nǎxiē	*pro.*	which ones?, who?, what?		1
哲	**zhé**		wise	□ 30.7	6
哲学	zhéxué	*n.*	philosophy		6
啊	**a**		exclamatory particle	□ 30.8	2
啊	a	*aux.*	[auxiliary word at end of sentence expressing enthusiasm, what is obvious, a warning, questioning]		2
啊	a	*intj.*	interjection of surprise, Ah!, Oh!		4
唱	**chàng**		to sing, to call loudly	□ 30.8	1
唱	chàng	*vb.*	to sing, to call loudly, to chant		1
唱歌	chàng gē	*vb.*	to sing a song		1
唱片	chàngpiàn	*n.*	gramophone record, LP, music CD, musical album		4
歌唱	gēchàng	*vb.*	to sing		6
演唱	yǎnchàng	*n.*	sung performance, to sing for an audience		3
演唱会	yǎnchànghuì	*n.*	vocal recital or concert		3
啡	**fēi**		morphine, coffee	□ 30.8	3
咖啡	kāfēi	*n.*	coffee (loanword)		3
啦	**la**		final particle of assertion	□ 30.8	6
啦	la	*aux.*	[final particle of assertion], (onom.) sound of singing, cheering etc, (dialect) to chat		6
啤	**pí**		beer	□ 30.8	3
啤酒	píjiǔ	*n.*	beer (loanword)		3
商	**shāng**		commerce, business	□ 30.8	1
商标	shāngbiāo	*n.*	trademark, logo		5
商场	shāngchǎng	*n.*	shopping mall, shopping centre, department store, emporium		1
商城	shāngchéng	*n.*	shopping centre		6
商店	shāngdiàn	*n.*	store, shop		1
商量	- shāngliang	*vb.*	to consult, to talk over, to discuss		2
商品	shāngpǐn	*n.*	commodity, goods, merchandise		3
商人	shāngrén	*n.*	merchant, businessman		2
商务	shāngwù	*n.*	commercial affairs, commercial, commerce, business		4
商业	shāngyè	*n.*	business, trade, commerce		3
厂商	chǎngshāng	*n.*	manufacturer, producer		6
工商	gōngshāng	*n.*	industry and commerce		6
协商	xiéshāng	*vb.*	to consult with, to talk things over, agreement		6
售	**shòu**		to sell	□ 30.8	4
售货员	shòuhuòyuán	*n.*	salesperson		4

出售	chūshòu	vb.	to sell, to offer for sale, to put on the market		4
销售	xiāoshòu	vb.	to sell, to market, sales (representative, agreement etc)		4
唯	**wéi**		only	☐ 30.8	5
唯一	wéiyī	adj.	only, sole		5
喊	**hǎn**		to yell, to shout	☐ 30.9	2
喊	hǎn	vb.	to yell, to shout, to call out for (a person)		2
喝	**hē**		to drink	☐ 30.9	1
喝	hē	vb.	to drink		1
喷	**pēn**		to puff	☐ 30.9	5
喷	pēn	vb.	to puff, to spout, to spray, to spurt		5
善	**shàn**		good, virtuous	☐ 30.9	3
善良	shànliáng	adj.	good and honest, kind-hearted		4
善于	shànyú	vb.	to be good at, to be adept at		4
改善	gǎishàn	vb.	to make better, to improve		4
完善	wánshàn	adj.	(of systems, facilities etc) comprehensive, well-developed, excellent, to refine, to improve		3
喂	**wèi**		interjection to call attention	☐ 30.9	2
喂	wèi	+ intj.	hello (on the phone also pron. wéi)		2
喂	wèi	+ vb.	to feed		4
喜	**xǐ**		to like, to love, to enjoy	☐ 30.9	1
喜爱	xǐ'ài	vb.	to like, to love, to be fond of, favourite		4
喜欢	- xǐhuan	vb.	to like, to be fond of		1
喜剧	xǐjù	n.	comedy		5
惊喜	jīngxǐ	n.	nice surprise, to be pleasantly surprised		6
嘉	**jiā**		excellent, joyful	☐ 30.11	6
嘉宾	jiābīn	n.	esteemed guest, honoured guest, guest (on a show)		6
嘛	**ma**		final exclamatory particle	☐ 30.11	6
嘛	ma	aux.	[modal particle indicating that sth is obvious, particle indicating a pause for emphasis]		6
嘴	**zuǐ**		mouth	☐ 30.12	2
嘴	zuǐ	n.	mouth, beak, nozzle, spout (of teapot etc)		2
嘴巴	- zuǐba	n.	mouth		4
器	**qì**		vessel, instrument	☐ 30.13	3
器官	qìguān	n.	organ (part of body tissue), apparatus		4
电器	diànqì	n.	(electrical) appliance, device		6
机器	jīqì	n.	machine		3
武器	wǔqì	n.	weapon, arms		3
仪器	yíqì	n.	instrument, apparatus		6
机器人	jīqìrén	n.	mechanical person, robot, android		5
充电器	chōngdiànqì	n.	battery charger		4
热水器	rèshuǐqì	n.	water heater		6

口 wéi   enclosure   31

四	**sì**		four, 4	口 31.2 1
四	sì	*num.*	four, 4	1
四处	• sìchù	*n.*	all over the place, everywhere and all directions	6
四周	sìzhōu	*n.*	all around	5
回	**huí**		to return, to turn around	口 31.3 1
回	huí	+ *vb.*	to return, to go back, to turn around, to reply	1
回	huí	+ *m.w.*	m.w. for matters or actions	2
回去	huí qù	*vb.*	to return, to go back	1
回信	huí xìn	*vb.*	to reply, to write back, letter written in reply	5
回报	huíbào	*vb.*	to report back, to reciprocate, (in) return, reciprocation, payback, retaliation	5
回避	huíbì	*vb.*	to shun, to avoid (sb), to skirt, to evade (an issue), to step back, to withdraw, to recuse (a judge etc)	5
回答	huídá	*vb.*	to reply, to answer, the answer	1
回到	huídào	*vb.*	to return to	1
回复	huífù	*vb.*	to reply, to recover, to return (to a previous condition), Re: in reply to (email)	4
回顾	huígù	*vb.*	to look back, to review	5
回国	huíguó	*vb.*	to return to one's home country	2
回家	huíjiā	*vb.*	to return home	1
回来	huílái	*vb.*	to return, to come back	1
回收	huíshōu	*vb.*	to recycle, to reclaim, to retrieve, to recover, to recall (a defective product)	5
回头	huítóu	*vb.*	to turn round, to turn one's head, later, by and by	5
回忆	huíyì	*vb.*	to recall, memories	5
回应	• huíyìng	*vb.*	to respond, response	6
返回	fǎnhuí	*vb.*	to return to, to come (or go) back	5
收回	shōuhuí	*vb.*	to regain, to retake, to take back, to withdraw, to revoke	4
团	**tuán**		lump, ball	口 31.3 3
团	tuán	*n.*	lump, ball, to roll into a ball, to gather, group, society, round, m.w. for a lump or a soft mass	3
团队	tuánduì	*n.*	team	6
团结	tuánjié	*vb.*	to unite, unity, solidarity, united	3
团体	tuántǐ	*n.*	group, organization, team	3
团长	tuánzhǎng	*n.*	regimental command, head of a delegation	5
集团	jítuán	*n.*	group, bloc, corporation, conglomerate	5
代表团	dàibiǎotuán	*n.*	delegation	3
因	**yīn**		cause, reason	口 31.3 2
因	yīn	*n.*	cause, reason, because	6
因而	yīn'ér	*conj.*	therefore, as a result, thus, and as a result, ...	5
因此	yīncǐ	*conj.*	thus, consequently, as a result	3
因素	yīnsù	*n.*	element, factor	6
因为	- yīnwei	*conj.*	because, owing to, on account of	2
原因	yuányīn	*n.*	cause, origin, root cause, reason	2

困	kùn		to surround, to besiege	☐ 31.4	3
困	kùn	adj.	sleepy, tired		3
困难	- kùnnan	adj.	difficult, challenging, straitened circumstances, difficult situation		3
困扰	kùnrǎo	vb.	to perplex, to disturb, to cause complications		5
贫困	pínkùn	adj.	impoverished, poverty		6
围	wéi		to encircle, to surround	☐ 31.4	3
围	wéi	vb.	to encircle, to surround, to enclose, surname Wei		3
围巾	wéijīn	n.	scarf, shawl		4
围绕	wéirào	vb.	to revolve around, to centre on (an issue)		5
包围	bāowéi	vb.	to surround, to encircle, to hem in		5
范围	fànwéi	n.	range, scope, limit, extent		3
周围	zhōuwéi	n.	surroundings, environment, to encompass		3
园	yuán		garden, park	☐ 31.4	2
园	yuán	n.	garden, park, surname Yuan		6
园林	yuánlín	n.	gardens, park, landscape garden		5
公园	gōngyuán	n.	park (for public recreation)		2
花园	huāyuán	n.	garden		2
家园	jiāyuán	n.	home, homeland		6
校园	xiàoyuán	n.	campus		2
动物园	dòngwùyuán	n.	zoo		2
幼儿园	yòu'éryuán	n.	kindergarten, nursery school		4
固	gù		to become solid	☐ 31.5	4
固定	gùdìng	vb.	to fix, to fasten, to set rigidly in place, fixed, set, regular		4
巩固	gǒnggù	vb.	to consolidate, consolidation, to strengthen		6
坚固	jiāngù	adj.	firm, firmly, hard, stable		4
国	guó		country, state	☐ 31.5	1
国	guó	n.	country, state, nation, surname Guo		1
国产	guóchǎn	adj.	domestically produced		6
国歌	guógē	n.	national anthem		6
国会	guóhuì	n.	parliament, (in the U.S.) Congress, (in Japan) the Diet		6
国籍	guójí	n.	nationality		5
国际	guójì	adj.	international		2
国家	guójiā	n.	country, nation, state		1
国民	guómín	n.	nationals, citizens, people of a nation		5
国内	guónèi	adj.	domestic, internal (to a country), civil		3
国旗	guóqí	n.	flag (of a country)		6
国庆	guóqìng	n.	National Day		3
国外	guówài	n.	abroad, external (affairs), overseas, foreign		1
国王	guówáng	n.	king		6
爱国	àiguó	vb.	to love one's country, patriotic		4
出国	chūguó	vb.	to go abroad, to leave the country, emigration		2
回国	huíguó	vb.	to return to one's home country		2
全国	quánguó	n.	whole nation, nationwide, countrywide, national		2
外国	wàiguó	n.	foreign (country)		1
中国	zhōngguó	n.	China		1

祖国	zǔguó	n.	one's country, native land		6
联合国	liánhéguó	n.	United Nations		3
图	**tú**		diagram, picture	□ 31.5	1
图	tú	n.	diagram, picture, drawing, chart, map		3
图案	tú'àn	n.	design, pattern		4
图画	túhuà	n.	drawing, picture		3
图片	túpiàn	n.	image, picture, photograph		2
图书	túshū	n.	books (in a library or bookstore)		6
图书馆	túshūguǎn	n.	library		1
地图	• dìtú	n.	map		1
企图	qǐtú	vb.	to attempt, to try, attempt		6
试图	shìtú	vb.	to attempt, to try		5
圆	**yuán**		circle, round, circular	□ 31.7	4
圆	yuán	n.	circle, round, circular, spherical, (of the moon) full, unit of Chinese currency (yuan)		4
圆满	yuánmǎn	adj.	satisfactory, consummate, perfect		4
圆珠笔	yuánzhūbǐ	n.	ballpoint pen		6
圈	**quān**		to circle	□ 31.8	4
圈	quān	vb.	to circle, to surround, circle, ring, m.w. for loops, orbits		4

土 tǔ earth 32

土	**tǔ**		earth, soil	土 32.0	3
土	tǔ	+ n.	earth, soil, land, ground		3
土	tǔ	+ adj.	local, native, homemade, crude		6
土地	• tǔdì	n.	land, soil, territory		4
土豆	tǔdòu	n.	potato		5
本土	běntǔ	n.	one's native country, native, local, metropolitan territory		6
圣	**shèng**		sage, emperor, master	土 32.2	6
圣诞节	shèngdàn jié	n.	Christmas season, Christmas Day		6
场	**chǎng**		courtyard, place	土 32.3	1
场	chǎng	n.	courtyard, place, field, m.w. for games, performances, etc.		2
场地	• chǎngdì	n.	space, site, place, sports pitch		6
场馆	chǎngguǎn	n.	sporting venue, arena		6
场合	chǎnghé	n.	situation, occasion, context, setting, location, venue		3
场景	chǎngjǐng	n.	scene, scenario, setting		6
场面	chǎngmiàn	n.	scene, spectacle, occasion, situation		5
场所	chǎngsuǒ	n.	location, place		3
操场	cāochǎng	n.	playground, sports field, drill ground		4
出场	chūchǎng	vb.	(of a performer) to come onto the stage to perform, (of an athlete) to enter the arena to compete		6
当场	dāngchǎng	n.	at the scene, on the spot		5
广场	guǎngchǎng	n.	public square, plaza		2
机场	jīchǎng	n.	airport, airfield		1
剧场	jùchǎng	n.	theatre		3

考场	kǎochǎng	n.	exam room		6
立场	lìchǎng	n.	position, standpoint		5
球场	qiúchǎng	n.	stadium, sports ground, court, pitch, field, golf course		2
全场	quánchǎng	n.	everyone present, the whole audience, across-the-board, unanimously, whole duration (of a competition or match)		3
赛场	sàichǎng	n.	racetrack, field (for athletics competition)		6
商场	shāngchǎng	n.	shopping mall, shopping centre, department store, emporium		1
市场	shìchǎng	n.	marketplace, market (also in abstract)		3
现场	xiànchǎng	n.	the scene (of a crime, accident etc), (on) the spot, (at) the site		3
在场	zàichǎng	vb.	to be present, to be on the scene		5
战场	zhànchǎng	n.	battlefield		6
体育场	tǐyùchǎng	n.	stadium		2
停车场	tíngchēchǎng	n.	car park, parking lot		2
地	* **de, dì**		**structural particle; earth, region**	土 32.3	1
地	de	aux.	-ly, structural particle: used before a verb or adjective, linking it to preceding modifying adverbial adjunct, ground		1
地	• dì	n.	the earth, ground, field, place, land		1
地板	• dìbǎn	n.	floor		6
地带	• dìdài	n.	zone		5
地点	• dìdiǎn	n.	place, site, location, venue		1
地方	• dìfāng	n.	region, regional (away from the central administration), local		4
地方	• dìfang	n.	place, space, room, part (respect)		1
地面	• dìmiàn	n.	floor, ground, surface		4
地名	• dìmíng	n.	place name, toponym		6
地球	• dìqiú	n.	the earth		2
地区	• dìqū	n.	local, regional, district (not necessarily formal administrative unit), region, area, as suffix to city name		3
地上	• dìshang	n.	on the ground, on the floor		1
地铁	• dìtiě	n.	subway, metro		2
地图	• dìtú	n.	map		1
地位	• dìwèi	n.	position, status, place		4
地下	• dìxià	n.	underground, subterranean, covert		4
地形	• dìxíng	n.	topography, terrain, landform		5
地震	• dìzhèn	n.	earthquake		5
地址	• dìzhǐ	n.	address		4
地铁站	• dìtiězhàn	n.	subway station		2
地下室	• dìxiàshì	n.	basement, cellar		6
本地	• běndì	n.	local, this locality		6
遍地	• biàndì	adv.	everywhere, all over		6
草地	• cǎodì	n.	lawn, meadow, sod, turf		2
场地	• chǎngdì	n.	space, site, place, sports pitch		6
当地	• dāngdì	adj.	local		3
各地	• gèdì	n.	in all parts of (a country), various regions		3
基地	• jīdì	n.	base (of operations), industrial or military base		5
陆地	• lùdì	n.	dry land (as opposed to the sea)		4
内地	• nèidì	n.	mainland China (PRC excluding Hong Kong and Macau, but including islands such as Hainan)		6
特地	• tèdì	adv.	specially, for a special purpose		6

土地	• tǔdì	n.	land, soil, territory	4
外地	• wàidì	n.	parts of the country other than where one is	2
原地	• yuándì	n.	the original place, the place where one currently is, place of origin, local (product)	6

在 zài — to be at, to be in, to be on 土 32.3 1

在	zài	vb.	(to be located) at, (to be) in, to exist, in the middle of doing sth, (indicating an action in progress)	1
在场	zàichǎng	vb.	to be present, to be on the scene	5
在乎	- zàihu	vb.	to care about, equivalent of 在于 zài yú	4
在家	zàijiā	vb.	to be at home, (at a workplace) to be in (as opposed to being away on official business 出差 chū chāi)	1
在内	zàinèi	vb.	(to be included) in it, among them	5
在于	zàiyú	vb.	to be in, to lie in, to consist in, to depend on, to rest with	4
处在	chǔzài	vb.	to be situated at, to find oneself at	5
存在	cúnzài	vb.	to exist, to be, existence	3
内在	nèizài	adj.	inner, internal, intrinsic, innate	5
实在	shízài	adv.	really, actually, indeed, true, real, honest, (philosophy) reality	2
实在	- shízai	adj.	(coll.) done well, done dependably	2
所在	suǒzài	n.	place, location, (after a noun) place where it is located	5
现在	xiànzài	n.	now, at present, at the moment, modern, current, nowadays	1
正在	zhèngzài	adv.	just at (that time), right in (that place), right in the middle of (doing sth)	1
自在	- zìzai	adj.	free, unrestrained, comfortable, at ease	6
不在乎	- bù zàihu	vb.	not to care	4

坏 huài — bad, spoiled 土 32.4 1

坏	huài	adj.	bad, (opp. 好 hǎo: good), spoiled, broken, to break down, (suffix) to the utmost	1
坏处	- huàichu	n.	harm, troubles	2
坏人	huàirén	n.	bad person, villain	2
破坏	pòhuài	n.	destruction, damage, to wreck, to break, to destroy	3

圾 jī — garbage, rubbish 土 32.4 4

垃圾	lājī	n.	rubbish, refuse, garbage, (coll.) of poor quality	4

坚 jiān — hard, strong 土 32.4 3

坚持	jiānchí	vb.	to persevere with, to persist in, to insist on	3
坚定	jiāndìng	adj.	firm, steady, staunch, resolute	5
坚固	jiāngù	adj.	firm, firmly, hard, stable	4
坚决	jiānjué	adj.	firm, resolute, determined	3
坚强	jiānqiáng	adj.	staunch, strong	3

均 jūn — equal, even 土 32.4 4

平均	píngjūn	n.	average, on average, evenly, in equal proportions	4

块 kuài — lump, piece, m.w. currency 土 32.4 1

块	kuài	n.	lump (of earth), chunk, piece, m.w. for pieces of cloth, cake, soap etc, (coll.) m.w. for money and currency units	1
一块儿	yīkuàir	n.	the same place, in company, together, one, erhua variant of 一块 yīkuài	1

址	zhǐ		site, location	土 32.4	4
地址	• dìzhǐ	n.	address		4
网址	wǎngzhǐ	n.	website, web address, URL		4

坐	zuò		to sit, to travel by	土 32.4	1
坐	zuò	vb.	to sit, to travel by, to take, surname Zuo		1
坐下	- zuòxia	vb.	to sit down		1
乘坐	chéngzuò	vb.	to ride (in a vehicle)		5
请坐	qǐngzuò	vb.	please sit down		1

垃	lā		rubbish, refuse	土 32.5	4
垃圾	lājī	n.	rubbish, refuse, garbage, (coll.) of poor quality		4

坡	pō		slope	土 32.5	6
坡	pō	n.	slope		6
山坡	shānpō	n.	hillside		6

坦	tǎn		flat, smooth,	土 32.5	5
平坦	píngtǎn	adj.	level, even, smooth, flat		5

型	xíng		mould, type	土 32.6	4
型	xíng	n.	mould, type, style, model		4
型号	xínghào	n.	model (particular version of a manufactured article), type (product specification in terms of colour, size etc)		4
大型	dàxíng	adj.	large, large-scale		4
典型	diǎnxíng	n.	model, typical case, archetype, typical, representative		4
类型	lèixíng	n.	type, category, genre, form, style		4
模型	móxíng	n.	model, mould, matrix, pattern		4
小型	xiǎoxíng	n.	small scale, small size		4
新型	xīnxíng	adj.	new type, new kind		4
造型	zàoxíng	vb.	to model, to shape, appearance, style, design, form, pose		4

城	chéng		city, town	土 32.7	3
城	chéng	n.	city walls, city, town		3
城里	chénglǐ	n.	inside the city, downtown		5
城区	chéngqū	n.	city district, urban area		6
城市	chéngshì	n.	city, town		3
城乡	chéngxiāng	n.	city and countryside		6
城镇	chéngzhèn	n.	town, cities and towns		6
长城	• chángchéng	n.	the Great Wall		3
商城	shāngchéng	n.	shopping centre		6

埋	mái		to bury	土 32.7	6
埋	mái	vb.	to bury, to cover up		6

堆	duī		to heap, to pile	土 32.8	5
堆	duī	vb.	to pile up, to heap up, a mass, pile, heap, stack, large amount		5

基	jī		foundation, base	土 32.8	3
基本	jīběn	adj.	basic, fundamental, main, elementary		3
基础	jīchǔ	n.	base, foundation, basis, underlying		3
基地	• jīdì	n.	base (of operations), industrial or military base		5

基金	jījīn	n.	fund	5
基本上	- jīběnshang	adv.	basically, on the whole	3
基督教	jīdūjiào	n.	Christianity	6

培 **péi** — to bank up with soil, to cultivate — 土 32.8 4

培训	péixùn	vb.	to cultivate, to train, to groom, training	4
培养	péiyǎng	vb.	to cultivate, to breed, to foster, to nurture, to educate, to groom (for a position), education, fostering, culture (biology)	4
培育	péiyù	vb.	to train, to breed	4
培训班	péixùnbān	n.	training class	4

堂 **táng** — hall, main room — 土 32.8 2

教堂	jiàotáng	n.	church, chapel	6
课堂	kètáng	n.	classroom	2
礼堂	lǐtáng	n.	assembly hall, auditorium	6
食堂	shítáng	n.	dining hall	4
天堂	tiāntáng	n.	paradise, heaven	6

域 **yù** — district, region — 土 32.8 5

区域	qūyù	n.	area, region, district	5

堵 **dǔ** — to block up, to stop up — 土 32.9 4

堵	dǔ	vb.	to block up (a road, pipe etc), to stop up (a hole), (fig.) (of a person) choked up with anxiety or stress, wall (literary), m.w. for walls	4
堵车	dǔchē	n.	traffic jam, (of traffic) to get congested	4

塞 **sāi** — to stop up, to stuff — 土 32.10 6

塞	sāi	vb.	to stop up, to stuff	6

塑 **sù** — to sculpt — 土 32.10 4

塑料	sùliào	n.	plastics	4
塑料袋	sùliàodài	n.	plastic bag	4

塔 **tǎ** — pagoda, tower — 土 32.10 6

塔	tǎ	n.	pagoda, tower, minaret, stupa (abbr. loanword from Sanskrit tapo), spire, tall building	6

填 **tián** — to fill — 土 32.10 4

填	tián	vb.	to fill or stuff, (of a form etc) to fill in	4
填空	• tiánkòng	vb.	to fill a job vacancy, to fill in a blank (e.g. on questionnaire or exam paper)	4

境 **jìng** — boundary, frontier — 土 32.11 3

边境	biānjìng	n.	frontier, border	5
环境	huánjìng	n.	environment, circumstances, surroundings	3

墓 **mù** — grave, tomb — 土 32.11 6

墓	mù	n.	grave, tomb, mausoleum	6

墙 **qiáng** — wall — 土 32.11 2

墙	qiáng	n.	wall	2
墙壁	qiángbì	n.	wall, city wall	5

墨	**mò**		ink, writing	土 32.12	6
墨水	mòshuǐ	n.	ink		6
增	**zēng**		to increase, to add to	土 32.12	3
增	zēng	vb.	to increase, to expand, to add		5
增产	zēng chǎn	vb.	to increase production		5
增大	zēngdà	vb.	to enlarge, to amplify, to magnify		5
增多	zēngduō	vb.	to increase, to grow in number		5
增加	zēngjiā	vb.	to raise, to increase		3
增进	zēngjìn	vb.	to promote, to enhance, to further, to advance (a cause etc)		6
增强	zēngqiáng	vb.	to increase, to strengthen		5
增长	zēngzhǎng	vb.	to grow, to increase		3
增值	zēngzhí	vb.	to appreciate (financially), to increase in value, value-added (accountancy)		6
壁	**bì**		wall	土 32.13	5
隔壁	gébì	n.	next door, neighbour		5
墙壁	qiángbì	n.	wall, city wall		5

士 shì scholar 33

士	**shì**		scholar	土 33.0	4
士兵	shìbīng	n.	soldier		4
巴士	bāshì	n.	bus (loanword), motor coach		4
博士	bóshì	n.	doctor, court academician (in feudal China), Ph.D.		5
护士	- hùshi	n.	nurse		4
男士	nánshì	n.	man, gentleman		4
女士	nǚshì	n.	lady, madam		4
人士	rénshì	n.	person, figure, public figure		5
硕士	shuòshì	n.	master's degree, person who has a master's degree, learned person		5
战士	zhànshì	n.	fighter, soldier, warrior		4
壮	**zhuàng**		big, large	土 33.3	6
壮观	zhuàngguān	adj.	spectacular, magnificent sight		6
强壮	qiángzhuàng	adj.	strong, sturdy, robust		6
声	**shēng**		sound, voice	土 33.4	2
声	shēng	n.	sound, voice, tone, noise, reputation, m.w. for sounds		5
声明	shēngmíng	vb.	to state, to declare, statement, declaration		3
声音	shēngyīn	n.	voice, sound		2
大声	dà shēng	n.	loud voice, in a loud voice, loudly		2
歌声	gēshēng	n.	singing voice, fig. original voice of a poet		3
铃声	língshēng	n.	ring, ringtone, bell stroke, tintinnabulation		5
响声	xiǎngshēng	n.	noise		6
相声	· xiàngshēng	n.	comic dialogue, sketch, crosstalk		5
小声	xiǎoshēng	adv.	in a low voice, (speak) in whispers		2
笑声	xiàoshēng	n.	laughter		6
掌声	zhǎngshēng	n.	applause		6

壶	hú		jar, pot	士 33.7	6
壶	hú	n.	jar, pot, m.w. for bottled liquid		6
夂	**zhǐ**		**go**		**34**
处	* chǔ, chù		to dwell; place	夂 34.2	2
处	chǔ	vb.	to reside, to live, to dwell, to be in, to be situated at, to stay, to get along with, to be in a position of, to deal with, to punish		4
处罚	chǔfá	vb.	to penalize, to punish		5
处分	chǔfèn	vb.	to discipline sb, to punish, disciplinary action, to deal with (a matter)		5
处理	chǔlǐ	vb.	to handle, to treat, to deal with, to process, to deal with a criminal case, to mete out punishment, to offer for sale at a reduced price, to punish		3
处于	chǔyú	vb.	to be in (some state, position, or condition)		4
处在	chǔzài	vb.	to be situated at, to find oneself at		5
处处	• chùchù	n.	everywhere, in all respects		6
处长	• chùzhǎng	n.	department head, section chief		6
长处	• chángchù	n.	good aspects, strong points		3
此处	• cǐchù	n.	this place, here (literary)		6
到处	• dàochù	adv.	everywhere		2
短处	• duǎnchù	n.	shortcoming, defect, fault, one's weak points		3
好处	- hǎochu	adj.	easy to get along with		2
坏处	- huàichu	n.	harm, troubles		2
深处	• shēnchù	n.	abyss, depths, deepest or most distant part		5
四处	• sìchù	n.	all over the place, everywhere and all directions		6
相处	xiāngchǔ	vb.	to be in contact (with sb), to associate, to interact, to get along (well, poorly)		4
用处	- yòngchu	n.	usefulness		6
远处	• yuǎnchù	n.	distant place		5
办事处	• bànshìchù	n.	office, agency		6
务	wù		affairs, business	夂 34.2	2
服务	fúwù	vb.	to serve, service		2
家务	jiāwù	n.	household duties, housework		4
任务	- rènwu	n.	mission, assignment, task, duty, role		3
商务	shāngwù	n.	commercial affairs, commercial, commerce, business		4
业务	yèwù	n.	business, professional work, service		5
义务	yìwù	n.	duty, obligation		4
职务	zhíwù	n.	post, position, job, duties		5
公务员	gōngwùyuán	n.	functionary, office-bearer		3
备	bèi		to prepare, to be ready	夂 34.5	1
具备	jùbèi	vb.	to possess, to have, equipped with, able to fulfil (conditions or requirements)		4
配备	pèibèi	vb.	to allocate, to provide, to outfit with		5
设备	shèbèi	n.	equipment, facilities, installations		3
预备	yùbèi	vb.	to prepare, to make ready, preparation, preparatory		5
装备	zhuāngbèi	n.	equipment, to equip, to outfit		6

准备	zhǔnbèi	vb.	to prepare, to intend, preparation, to be about to		1

夊 suī   go slowly   35

复	fù		to return, to duplicate	夊 35.6	2
复苏	fùsū	vb.	to recover, to resuscitate		6
复习	fùxí	vb.	to revise, to review		2
复印	fùyìn	vb.	to photocopy, to duplicate a document		3
复杂	fùzá	adj.	complex, complicated, (opp. 简单 jiǎndān: simple)		3
复制	fùzhì	vb.	to duplicate, to make a copy of, to copy, to reproduce, to clone		4
重复	• chóngfù	vb.	to repeat, to duplicate		2
答复	dáfù	vb.	to answer, to reply, Reply to: (in email header)		5
反复	fǎnfù	adv.	repeatedly, over and over, to upend, unstable, to come and go, (of an illness) to return		3
恢复	huīfù	vb.	to reinstate, to resume, to restore, to recover, to regain, to rehabilitate		5
回复	huífù	vb.	to reply, to recover, to return (to a previous condition), Re: in reply to (email)		4
康复	kāngfù	vb.	to recuperate, to recover (health), to convalesce		6
修复	xiūfù	vb.	to restore, to renovate, restoration, (computing) to fix (a bug)		5
夏	xià		summer, great	夊 35.7	2
夏季	xiàjì	n.	summer		4
夏天	xiàtiān	n.	summer		2

夕 xī   evening   36

夕	xī		evening, night	夕 36.0	5
除夕	chúxī	n.	lunar New Year's Eve		5
外	wài		outside, exterior	夕 36.2	1
外	wài	n.	outside, exterior, in addition, foreign, external		1
外币	wàibì	n.	foreign currency		6
外边	- wàibian	n.	outside, outer surface, abroad, place other than one's home		1
外部	wàibù	n.	external part, external		6
外出	wàichū	vb.	to go out, to go away (on a trip etc)		6
外地	• wàidì	n.	parts of the country other than where one is		2
外观	wàiguān	n.	exterior appearance, to view sth from the outside, exterior condition		6
外国	wàiguó	n.	foreign (country)		1
外汇	wàihuì	n.	foreign (currency) exchange		4
外交	wàijiāo	n.	diplomacy, diplomatic, foreign affairs		3
外界	wàijiè	n.	the outside world, external		5
外科	wàikē	n.	surgery (branch of medicine)		6
外来	wàilái	adj.	external, foreign, outside		6
外卖	wàimài	n.	take away (meal), takeout (meal), takeout (business),		2
外面	- wàimian	n.	outside, surface, exterior, external appearance		3
外套	wàitào	n.	coat, jacket		4
外头	- wàitou	n.	outside, out		6
外文	wàiwén	n.	foreign language (written)		3
外衣	wàiyī	n.	outer clothing, semblance, appearance		6

外语	wàiyǔ		n.	foreign language	1
外资	wàizī		n.	foreign investment	6
外交官	wàijiāoguān		n.	diplomat	4
此外	cǐwài		conj.	besides, in addition, moreover, furthermore	4
对外	duìwài		n.	external, foreign, pertaining to external or foreign (affairs)	6
格外	géwài		adv.	especially, particularly	4
国外	guówài		n.	abroad, external (affairs), overseas, foreign	1
海外	hǎiwài		n.	overseas, abroad	6
户外	hùwài		n.	outdoor	6
例外	lìwài		n.	exception, to be an exception	5
另外	lìngwài		adv.	additional, in addition, besides, separate, other, moreover, furthermore	3
内外	nèiwài		n.	inside and outside, domestic and foreign, approximately, about	6
以外	yǐwài		n.	apart from, other than, except for, external, outside of, on the other side of, beyond	2
意外	yìwài		n.	unexpected, accident, mishap	3
之外	zhīwài		n.	outside, excluding	5
中外	zhōngwài		n.	China and foreign countries, home and abroad, foreign and domestic	6

多 duō — much, many, more than, over 夕 36.3 1

多	duō	+	adj.	many, (opp. 少 shǎo: short of), much, excessive	1
多	duō	+	adv.	over a specified amount, much more	2
多半	duōbàn		n.	most, greater part, mostly, most likely	6
多次	duōcì		adv.	many times, repeatedly	4
多久	duōjiǔ		adv.	(of time) how long?, (not) a long time	2
多么	duōme		adv.	how (wonderful etc), what (a great idea etc), however (difficult it may be etc), (in interrogative sentences) how (much etc), to what extent	2
多年	duōnián		n.	many years, for many years, longstanding	4
多少	- duōshao		pro.	how many, number, amount, somewhat	1
多数	duōshù		n.	majority, most	2
多样	duōyàng		adj.	diverse, diversity, manifold	4
多云	duōyún		adj.	cloudy (meteorology)	2
多种	duōzhǒng		adj.	many kinds of, multiple, diverse, multi-	4
多方面	duōfāngmiàn		adj.	many-sided, in many aspects	6
多媒体	duōméitǐ		n.	multimedia	6
大多	dàduō		adv.	for the most part, many, most, the greater part, mostly	4
好多	hǎoduō		num.	many, quite a lot, much better	2
许多	xǔduō		num.	many, a lot of, much	2
增多	zēngduō		vb.	to increase, to grow in number	5
众多	zhòngduō		adj.	numerous	5
大多数	dàduōshù		n.	(great) majority	2
差不多	- chàbuduō		adj.	about the same, good enough, not bad, more or less, almost, nearly	2
绝大多数	juédàduōshù		n.	absolute majority, overwhelming majority	6

夜 yè — night 夕 36.5 2

夜	yè		n.	night	2
夜间	yèjiān		n.	night-time, evening or night (e.g. classes)	5
夜里	- yèli		n.	during the night, at night, nighttime	2
半夜	bànyè		n.	midnight, in the middle of the night	2

黑夜	hēiyè	n.	night	6
日夜	rìyè	n.	day and night, around the clock	6
开夜车	kāi yèchē	vb.	to burn the midnight oil, to work late into the night	6

够 gòu — enough, adequate 夕 36.8 2

够	gòu	adj.	enough (sufficient), enough (too much), (coll.) (before adj.) really, (coll.) to reach by stretching out	2
不够	bùgòu	adv.	not enough, insufficient, inadequate	2
能够	nénggòu	vb.	to be capable of, to be able to, can	2
足够	zúgòu	vb.	to be enough, to be sufficient	3

大 dà — big 37

大 dà — big, great, large 大 37.0 1

大	dà	adj.	big, great, huge, large, major, (opp. 小 xiǎo: little), wide, deep, older (than), oldest, eldest, greatly, very much, (dialect) father, father's elder or younger brother	1
大声	dà shēng	n.	loud voice, in a loud voice, loudly	2
大巴	dàbā	n.	(coll.) large bus, coach	4
大大	dàdà	adv.	greatly, enormously, (dialect) dad, uncle	2
大胆	dàdǎn	adj.	brazen, audacious, outrageous, bold, daring, fearless	5
大道	dàdào	n.	main street, avenue	6
大都	· dàdū	adv.	almost all, for the most part, mostly (also -dōu), metropolitan, Dadu (capital of China during the Yuan Dynasty, 1280-1368, modern day Beijing	5
大多	dàduō	adv.	for the most part, many, most, the greater part, mostly	4
大方	- dàfang	n.	expert, scholar, mother earth, a type of green tea	4
大概	dàgài	adv.	roughly, probably, rough, approximate, about, general idea	3
大纲	dàgāng	n.	synopsis, outline, program, leading principles	5
大哥	dàgē	n.	eldest brother, big brother (polite address for a man of about the same age as oneself), gang leader, boss	4
大海	dàhǎi	n.	sea, ocean	2
大会	dàhuì	n.	general assembly, general meeting, convention	4
大伙	dàhuǒ	n.	everybody, everyone, we all	5
大家	dàjiā	n.	everyone, influential family, great expert	2
大街	dàjiē	n.	street, main street	6
大姐	dàjiě	n.	big sister, elder sister, older sister (also polite term of address for a girl or woman slightly older than the speaker)	4
大力	dàlì	adv.	energetically, vigorously	6
大量	dàliàng	n.	great amount, large quantity, bulk, numerous, generous, magnanimous	2
大楼	dàlóu	n.	building (a relatively large, multi-storey one)	4
大陆	dàlù	n.	mainland China (reference to the PRC)	4
大妈	dàmā	n.	father's elder brother's wife, aunt (affectionate term for an elderly woman)	4
大门	dàmén	n.	entrance, door, gate, large and influential family	2
大米	dàmǐ	n.	(husked) rice	6
大脑	dànǎo	n.	brain, cerebrum	5
大批	dàpī	n.	large quantities of	6
大人	- dàren	n.	adult, grownup, title of respect toward superiors	2

大赛	dàsài	n.	grand contest	6
大师	dàshī	n.	great master, master	6
大使	dàshǐ	n.	ambassador, envoy	6
大事	dàshì	n.	major event, major political event (war or change of regime), major social event (wedding or funeral), (do sth) in a big way	5
大厅	dàtīng	n.	hall, lounge	5
大象	dàxiàng	n.	elephant	5
大小	dàxiǎo	n.	dimension, magnitude, size, measurement, large and small, at any rate, adults and children, consideration of seniority	2
大型	dàxíng	adj.	large, large-scale	4
大学	dàxué	n.	the Great Learning, one of the Four Books 四书 Sì shū in Confucianism	1
大爷	- dàye	n.	arrogant idler, self-centred show-off	4
大衣	dàyī	n.	overcoat, topcoat, cloak	2
大于	dàyú	adj.	greater than, bigger than, more than, >	5
大约	dàyuē	adv.	approximately, probably	3
大致	dàzhì	adv.	more or less, roughly, approximately	5
大众	dàzhòng	n.	the masses, people, public	4
大夫	- dàfu	n.	senior official (in imperial China)	3
大规模	dà guīmó	adj.	large scale, extensive, wide scale, broad scale	4
大部分	- dàbùfen	n.	in large part, the greater part, the majority	2
大多数	dàduōshù	n.	(great) majority	2
大奖赛	dàjiǎngsài	n.	grand prix	5
大使馆	dàshǐguǎn	n.	embassy	3
大熊猫	dàxióngmāo	n.	giant panda (Ailuropoda melanoleuca)	5
大学生	dàxuéshēng	n.	university student, college student	1
大自然	dàzìrán	n.	nature (the natural world)	2
不大	bùdà	adv.	not very, not too, not often	1
放大	fàngdà	vb.	to enlarge, to magnify	5
高大	gāodà	adj.	tall, lofty	5
广大	guǎngdà	adj.	(of an area) vast or extensive, large-scale, widespread, (of people) numerous	3
宏大	hóngdà	adj.	great, grand	6
巨大	jùdà	adj.	huge, immense, very large, tremendous, gigantic, enormous	4
扩大	kuòdà	vb.	to expand, to enlarge, to broaden one's scope	4
强大	qiángdà	adj.	large, formidable, powerful, strong	3
特大	tèdà	adj.	exceptionally big	6
伟大	wěidà	adj.	huge, great, grand, worthy of the greatest admiration, important (contribution etc)	3
增大	zēngdà	vb.	to enlarge, to amplify, to magnify	5
长大	zhǎngdà	vb.	to grow up	2
重大	zhòngdà	adj.	great, important, major, significant	3
绝大多数	juédàduōshù	n.	absolute majority, overwhelming majority	6
夫	**fū**		**man, male adult**	大 37.1 3
夫妇	fūfù	n.	a (married) couple, husband and wife	4
夫妻	fūqī	n.	husband and wife, married couple	4
夫人	- fūren	n.	lady, madam, Mrs.	4
大夫	- dàfu	n.	senior official (in imperial China)	3

功夫	- gōngfu	n.	skill, art, kung fu, labour, effort		3
工夫	- gōngfu	n.	(old) labourer		3
丈夫	- zhàngfu	n.	husband		4
太	**tài**		highest, greatest	大 37.1	1
太	tài	adj.	highest, greatest, too (much), very, extremely		1
太空	tàikōng	n.	outer space		5
太太	- tàitai	n.	married woman, Mrs., Madam, wife		2
太阳	tàiyáng	n.	sun		2
太阳能	tàiyángnéng	n.	solar energy		6
不太	bùtài	adj.	not very … , not too …		2
老太太	- lǎotàitai	n.	elderly lady (respectful), esteemed mother		3
天	**tiān**		day, sky, heaven	大 37.1	1
天	tiān	n.	day, sky, heaven, celestial		1
天才	tiāncái	n.	talent, gift, genius, talented, gifted		5
天空	tiānkōng	n.	sky		3
天气	tiānqì	n.	weather		1
天然	tiānrán	adj.	natural		6
天上	tiānshàng	n.	sky, heavens, celestial		2
天堂	tiāntáng	n.	paradise, heaven		6
天文	tiānwén	n.	astronomy		5
天下	tiānxià	n.	land under heaven, the whole world, the whole of China, realm, rule		6
天真	tiānzhēn	adj.	naive, innocent, artless		4
天然气	tiānránqì	n.	natural gas		5
白天	báitiān	n.	daytime, during the day, day		1
半天	bàntiān	n.	half of the day, a long time, quite a while, mid-air		1
春天	chūntiān	n.	spring (season)		2
当天	• dàngtiān	n.	on that day		6
冬天	dōngtiān	n.	winter		2
后天	hòutiān	n.	the day after tomorrow, acquired (not innate), a posteriori		1
今天	jīntiān	n.	today, at the present, now		1
蓝天	lántiān	n.	blue sky		6
聊天	liáotiān	vb.	to chat, to gossip		6
明天	míngtiān	n.	tomorrow		1
前天	qiántiān	n.	the day before yesterday		1
晴天	qíngtiān	n.	clear sky, sunny day		2
秋天	qiūtiān	n.	autumn		2
夏天	xiàtiān	n.	summer		2
阴天	yīntiān	n.	cloudy day, overcast sky		2
整天	zhěngtiān	n.	all day long, whole day		3
昨天	zuótiān	n.	yesterday		1
星期天	xīngqītiān	n.	Sunday		1
失	**shī**		to lose, to make mistake	大 37.2	3
失业	shī yè	vb.	to have no job, to lose one's job		4
失败	shībài	vb.	to be defeated, to lose, to fail (e.g. experiments), failure, defeat		4
失去	shīqù	vb.	to lose		3
失望	shīwàng	adj.	disappointed, to lose hope, to despair		4

失误	shīwù	n.	lapse, mistake, to make a mistake, fault, service fault (in volleyball, tennis etc)	5
丧失	sàngshī	vb.	to lose, to forfeit	6
损失	sǔnshī	n.	loss, damage	5
消失	xiāoshī	vb.	to disappear, to fade away	3

头 tóu — head, top 大 37.2 **2**

头	tóu	+ m.w.	m.w. for certain domestic animals, livestock	2
头	tóu	+ aff.	top, end, remnant	2
头	tóu	+ adj.	first, leading	3
头发	- tóufa	n.	hair (on the head)	2
头脑	tóunǎo	n.	brains, mind, skull, (fig.) gist (of a matter), leader, boss	3
头疼	tóuténg	n.	headache	6
低头	dītóu	vb.	to bow the head, to yield, to give in	6
点头	diǎntóu	vb.	to nod	2
骨头	- gǔtou	n.	bone	4
后头	- hòutou	n.	behind, the back, the rear, later, afterwards, (in) the future	4
回头	huítóu	vb.	to turn round, to turn one's head, later, by and by	5
街头	jiētóu	n.	street	6
镜头	jìngtóu	n.	camera lens, camera shot (in a movie etc), scene	4
开头	kāitóu	n.	beginning, to start	6
老头	lǎotóu	n.	old fellow, old man, father, husband	3
里头	- lǐtou	n.	inside, interior	2
码头	- mǎtou	n.	dock, pier, wharf	5
馒头	- mántou	n.	steamed roll, steamed bun, steamed bread	6
木头	- mùtou	n.	slow-witted, blockhead, log (of wood, timber etc)	3
前头	- qiántou	n.	in front, at the head, ahead, above	4
舌头	- shétou	n.	tongue	6
石头	- shítou	n.	stone	3
抬头	táitóu	vb.	to raise one's head, to gain ground, account name, or space for writing the name on checks, bills etc	5
外头	- wàitou	n.	outside, out	6
摇头	yáotóu	vb.	to shake one's head	5
指头	- zhǐtou	n.	finger, toe	6
钟头	zhōngtóu	n.	hour	6

央 yāng — centre, middle 大 37.2 **5**

中央	zhōngyāng	n.	central, middle, centre, central authorities (of a state)	5

夺 duó — to take by force 大 37.3 **6**

夺	duó	vb.	to seize, to take away forcibly, to wrest control of, to compete or strive for, to force one's way through, to leave out, to lose	6
夺取	duóqǔ	vb.	to seize, to capture, to wrest control of	6
争夺	zhēngduó	vb.	to fight over, to contest, to vie over	6

买 mǎi — to buy, to purchase 大 37.3 **1**

买	mǎi	vb.	to buy, to purchase	1
买卖	- mǎimai	n.	buying and selling, business, business transactions	5
购买	gòumǎi	vb.	to purchase, to buy	4

奋	fèn		to strive	大 37.5	4
奋斗	fèndòu	vb.	to strive, to struggle		4
勤奋	qínfèn	adj.	hardworking, diligent		5
兴奋	xìngfèn	adj.	be excited, excitement, (physiology) excitation		4
奉	fèng		to offer	大 37.5	6
奉献	fèngxiàn	vb.	to offer respectfully, to consecrate, to dedicate, to devote		6
奈	nài		to bear	大 37.5	5
无奈	wúnài	vb.	to have no alternative, frustrated, exasperated, helpless, (conjunction) but unfortunately		5
奇	qí		strange, unusual	大 37.5	3
奇怪	qíguài	adj.	strange, odd, to marvel, to be baffled		3
奇妙	qímiào	adj.	fantastic, wonderful		6
好奇	• hàoqí	adj.	inquisitive, curious, inquisitiveness, curiosity		3
神奇	shénqí	adj.	magical, mystical, miraculous		5
奔	bēn		to run fast, to flee, to rush about	大 37.6	6
奔跑	bēnpǎo	vb.	to run		6
奖	jiǎng		prize, award	大 37.6	4
奖	jiǎng	n.	prize, award, encouragement		4
奖金	jiǎngjīn	n.	premium, award money, bonus		4
奖励	jiǎnglì	vb.	to reward, reward (as encouragement)		5
奖学金	jiǎngxuéjīn	n.	scholarship		4
抽奖	chōujiǎng	vb.	to draw a prize, a lottery, a raffle		4
获奖	huòjiǎng	vb.	to win an award		4
中奖	• zhòngjiǎng	vb.	to win a prize, a successful gamble		4
大奖赛	dàjiǎngsài	n.	grand prix		5
类	lèi		kind, type, class	大 37.6	3
类	lèi	n.	kind, type, class, category, similar, like, to resemble		3
类似	lèishì	vb.	to be similar to, to be analogous to		3
类型	lèixíng	n.	type, category, genre, form, style		4
分类	fēnlèi	vb.	classify		5
人类	rénlèi	n.	humanity, human race, mankind		3
之类	zhīlèi	phr.	and so on, and such		6
种类	zhǒnglèi	n.	kind, genus, type, category, variety, species, sort, class		4
牵	qiān		to lead along	大 37.6	6
牵	qiān	vb.	to lead along, to pull (an animal on a tether), (bound form) to involve, to draw in		6
奏	zòu		to play music	大 37.6	6
奏	zòu	vb.	to play music, to achieve, to present a memorial to the emperor (old)		6
节奏	jiézòu	n.	rhythm, tempo, musical pulse, cadence, beat		6
演奏	yǎnzòu	vb.	to perform on a musical instrument		6
套	tào		to cover, to encase	大 37.7	2
套	tào	vb.	to cover, to encase, cover, sheath, m.w. for book sets, m.w. for suite of rooms		2

套餐	tàocān	n.	set meal, product or service package (e.g. for a cell phone subscription)		4
配套	pèi tào	vb.	to form a complete set, compatible, matching, complementary		5
手套	shǒutào	n.	glove, mitten		4
外套	wàitào	n.	coat, jacket		4

女 nǚ woman 38

女 nǚ female, woman, girl 女 38.0 1

女	nǚ	adj.	female, (opp. 男 nán: male), woman, girl, daughter		1
女儿	nǚ'ér	n.	daughter		1
女孩	nǚhái	n.	girl, lass		1
女人	nǚrén	n.	woman		1
女生	nǚshēng	n.	schoolgirl, female student, girl		1
女士	nǚshì	n.	lady, madam		4
女性	nǚxìng	n.	woman, the female sex		5
女子	• nǚzǐ	n.	woman, female		3
女朋友	- nǚpéngyou	n.	girlfriend		1
儿女	érnǚ	n.	children, sons and daughters		5
妇女	fùnǚ	n.	woman		6
父女	fùnǚ	n.	father and daughter		6
美女	měinǚ	n.	beautiful woman		4
母女	mǔnǚ	n.	mother-daughter		6
男女	nánnǚ	n.	men and women, male and female		4
孙女	sūnnǚ	n.	son's daughter, granddaughter		4
子女	• zǐnǚ	n.	children, sons and daughters		3

奶 nǎi milk 女 38.2 1

奶	nǎi	n.	milk		1
奶茶	nǎichá	n.	milk tea		3
奶粉	nǎifěn	n.	powdered milk		6
奶奶	- nǎinai	n.	(informal) grandma (paternal grandmother), (respectful) mistress of the house		1
奶牛	nǎiniú	n.	milk cow, dairy cow		6
牛奶	niúnǎi	n.	cow's milk		1
酸奶	suānnǎi	n.	yogurt		4

妇 fù woman, wife 女 38.3 4

妇女	fùnǚ	n.	woman		6
夫妇	fūfù	n.	a (married) couple, husband and wife		4

好 * hǎo, hào good, excellent; to like 女 38.3 1

好	hǎo	+ adj.	good, fine, nice, well, (opp. 坏 huài: bad, harmful), proper, good to, easy to (suffix indicating completion or readiness), (of two people) close		1
好	hǎo	+ adv.	very, so		2
好	• hào	vb.	to like, to love, to be fond of		4
好吃	hǎochī	adj.	tasty, delicious		1
好处	- hǎochu	adj.	easy to get along with		2
好多	hǎoduō	num.	many, quite a lot, much better		2

好好	hǎohǎo	adv.	well, carefully, nicely, properly	3
好久	hǎojiǔ	adv.	quite a while	2
好看	hǎokàn	adj.	good-looking, nice-looking, good (of a movie, book, TV show etc), embarrassed, humiliated	1
好人	hǎorén	n.	good person, healthy person, person who tries not to offend anyone, even at the expense of principle	2
好事	hǎoshì	n.	good action, deed, thing or work (also sarcastic, a fine thing indeed), charity, happy occasion, Daoist or Buddhist ceremony for souls of the dead	2
好似	hǎoshì	vb.	to seem, to be like	6
好听	hǎotīng	adj.	pleasant to hear	1
好玩	hǎowán	adj.	amusing, fun, interesting	1
好像	hǎoxiàng	vb.	to seem like, to look like	2
好友	hǎoyǒu	n.	close friend, pal, (social networking website) friend	4
好运	hǎoyùn	n.	good luck	5
好转	hǎozhuǎn	vb.	to improve, to take a turn for the better, improvement	6
好奇 •	hàoqí	adj.	inquisitive, curious, inquisitiveness, curiosity	3
好学 •	hàoxué	adj.	eager to study, studious, erudite	6
好不容易	hǎobùróngyì	adv.	with great difficulty, very difficult	6
爱好 •	àihào	vb.	to like, to take pleasure in, keen on, fond of, interest, hobby, appetite for	1
刚好	gānghǎo	adv.	just, exactly, to happen to be	6
搞好	gǎohǎo	vb.	to do well at, to do a good job	5
看好	kànhǎo	vb.	to keep an eye on	6
良好	liánghǎo	adj.	good, favourable, well, fine	4
美好	měihǎo	adj.	beautiful, fine	3
恰好	qiàhǎo	adj.	as it turns out, by lucky coincidence, (of number, time, size etc) just right	6
挺好	tǐnghǎo	adj.	very good	2
要好	yàohǎo	vb.	to be on good terms, to be close friends, striving for self-improvement	6
也好	yěhǎo	aux.	that's fine, may as well, (reduplicated) regardless of whether ... or ...	5
友好	yǒuhǎo	adj.	friendly (relations), close friends	2
正好	zhènghǎo	adv.	just (in time), just right, just enough, to happen to, to chance to, by chance, it just so happens that	2
只好	zhǐhǎo	adv.	without any better option, to have to, to be forced to	3
最好	zuìhǎo	adj.	best, (you) had better (do what we suggest)	1
不好意思 -	bù hǎoyìsi	vb.	to feel embarrassed, to find it embarrassing, to be sorry (for inconveniencing sb)	2

妈 mā   mother, mama   女 38.3   1

| 妈妈 - | māma | n. | mama, mummy, mommy, mother | 1 |
| 大妈 | dàmā | n. | father's elder brother's wife, aunt (affectionate term for an elderly woman) | 4 |

如 rú   if, as if   女 38.3   2

如	rú	conj.	if, as if, such as	6
如下	rú xià	vb.	as follows	5
如此	rúcǐ	adv.	in this way, so	5
如果	rúguǒ	conj.	if, in case, in the event that	2

如何	rúhé	*pro.*	how, what way, what		3
如今	rújīn	*n.*	nowadays, now		4
如同	rútóng	*vb.*	to be like, to be similar		5
如一	rúyī	*vb.*	to be consistent, to be the same		6
比如	bǐrú	*conj.*	for example, for instance, such as		2
不如	bùrú	*vb.*	not equal to, not as good as, inferior to, it would be better to		2
假如	• jiǎrú	*conj.*	if		4
例如	lìrú	*vb.*	to give an example		2
正如	zhèngrú	*adv.*	just as, precisely as		5
比如说	bǐrúshuō	*conj.*	for example		2

她 tā — she, her   女 38.3

她	tā	*pro.*	she	1
她们	tāmen	*pro.*	they, them (for females)	1

妙 miào — clever, wonderful   女 38.4

妙	miào	*adj.*	clever, wonderful, excellent, ingenious, subtle	6
奇妙	qímiào	*adj.*	fantastic, wonderful	6
巧妙	qiǎomiào	*adj.*	ingenious, clever, ingenuity, artifice	6

姑 gū — paternal aunt, husband's sister   女 38.5

姑姑	- gūgu	*n.*	paternal aunt	6
姑娘	- gūniang	*n.*	girl, young woman, young lady, daughter, paternal aunt (old)	3

姐 jiě — elder sister, young lady   女 38.5

姐姐	- jiějie	*n.*	older sister	1
姐妹	jiěmèi	*n.*	sisters, siblings, sister (school, city etc)	4
大姐	dàjiě	*n.*	big sister, elder sister, older sister (also polite term of address for a girl or woman slightly older than the speaker)	4
小姐	xiǎojiě	*n.*	young lady, miss, (slang) prostitute	1

妹 mèi — younger sister   女 38.5

妹妹	- mèimei	*n.*	younger sister, young woman	1
姐妹	jiěmèi	*n.*	sisters, siblings, sister (school, city etc)	4

妻 qī — wife   女 38.5

妻子	qīzi	*n.*	wife and children	4
夫妻	fūqī	*n.*	husband and wife, married couple	4

始 shǐ — to begin, to start   女 38.5

始终	shǐzhōng	*adv.*	from beginning to end, all along	3
开始	kāishǐ	*vb.*	to begin, beginning, to start, initial	3
原始	yuánshǐ	*adj.*	first, original, primitive, original (document etc)	5

委 wěi — to appoint, to send   女 38.5

委托	wěituō	*vb.*	to entrust, to trust, to commission	5

姓 xìng — to be surnamed, family name   女 38.5

姓	xìng	*vb.*	to be surnamed, family name, surname	2
姓名	xìngmíng	*n.*	surname and given name, full name	2
老百姓	lǎobǎixìng	*n.*	ordinary people, the person in the street	3

娃	**wá**		baby, doll, pretty girl	女 38.6	6
娃娃	- wáwa	n.	baby, small child, doll		6
威	**wēi**		power, might	女 38.6	6
威胁	wēixié	vb.	to threaten, to menace		6
姨	**yí**		mother's sister, aunt	女 38.6	4
阿姨	āyí	n.	maternal aunt, stepmother, childcare worker, nursemaid, woman of similar age to one's parents (term of address used by child)		4
娘	**niáng**		mother, young girl, woman, wife	女 38.7	3
姑娘	- gūniang	n.	girl, young woman, young lady, daughter, paternal aunt (old)		3
新娘	xīnniáng	n.	bride		4
娱	**yú**		to amuse, joy	女 38.7	6
娱乐	yúlè	vb.	to entertain, to amuse, entertainment, recreation, amusement, hobby, fun, joy		6
文娱	wényú	n.	cultural recreation, entertainment		6
婚	**hūn**		marriage	女 38.8	3
婚礼	hūnlǐ	n.	wedding ceremony, wedding		4
结婚	jiéhūn	vb.	to marry, to get married		3
离婚	lí hūn	vb.	to divorce, divorced from (one's spouse)		3
婆	**pó**		old woman, grandmother	女 38.8	4
老婆	- lǎopo	n.	(coll.) wife		4
媒	**méi**		go-between, matchmaker, medium	女 38.9	3
媒体	méitǐ	n.	media, esp. news media		3
传媒	chuánméi	n.	media		6
多媒体	duōméitǐ	n.	multimedia		6
嫌	**xián**		to dislike	女 38.10	6
嫌	xián	vb.	to dislike, suspicion, resentment, enmity		6

子 zǐ child   39

子	* **zi, zǐ**		offspring, child; fruit, seed of	子 39.0	1
子	zi	+ aff.	noun suffix, son, child, seed, egg, small thing, 1st earthly branch: 11 p.m.-1 a.m.		1
子弹	• zǐdàn	n.	bullet		5
子女	• zǐnǚ	n.	children, sons and daughters		3
包子	bāozi	n.	steamed stuffed bun		1
杯子	bēizi	n.	cup, glass		1
被子	bèizi	n.	quilt		3
本子	běnzi	n.	book, notebook		1
鼻子	bízi	n.	nose		5
叉子	chāzi	n.	fork		5
池子	chízi	n.	pond, bathhouse pool, dance floor of a ballroom, (old) stalls (front rows in a theatre)		5
尺子	chǐzi	n.	rule, ruler (measuring instrument)		4

虫子	chóngzi	n.	insect, bug, worm	4
窗子	chuāngzi	n.	window	4
肚子	dùzi	n.	belly, abdomen, stomach	4
儿子	érzi	n.	son	1
房子	fángzi	n.	house, building (single- or two-story), apartment, room	1
父子	• fùzǐ	n.	father and son	6
稿子	gǎozi	n.	draft of a document, script, manuscript, mental plan, precedent	6
个子	gèzi	n.	height, stature, build, size	2
柜子	guìzi	n.	cupboard, cabinet	5
孩子	háizi	n.	child, son or daughter, children	1
盒子	hézi	n.	box, case	5
胡子	húzi	n.	beard, moustache or whiskers, facial hair	5
剪子	jiǎnzi	n.	clippers, scissors, shears	5
饺子	jiǎozi	n.	dumpling, pot-sticker (type of dumpling)	2
镜子	jìngzi	n.	mirror	4
句子	jùzi	n.	sentence	2
裤子	kùzi	n.	trousers, pants	3
筷子	kuàizi	n.	chopsticks	2
例子	lìzi	n.	case, (for) instance, example	2
轮子	lúnzi	n.	wheel	4
帽子	màozi	n.	hat, cap, (fig.) label, bad name	4
面子	miànzi	n.	outer surface, outside, honour, reputation, face (as in losing face), self-respect, feelings, (medicinal) powder	5
母子	• mǔzǐ	n.	mother and child, parent and subsidiary (companies), principal and interest	6
男子	• nánzǐ	n.	a man, a male	3
脑子	nǎozi	n.	brains, mind	5
女子	• nǚzǐ	n.	woman, female	3
牌子	páizi	n.	sign, trademark, brand	3
盘子	pánzi	n.	tray, plate, dish	4
胖子	pàngzi	n.	fat person	4
骗子	piànzi	n.	swindler, a cheat	5
瓶子	píngzi	n.	bottle	2
妻子	qīzi	n.	wife and children	4
茄子	qiézi	n.	eggplant (Solanum melongena L.), aubergine, brinjal, Guinea squash, phonetic cheese (when being photographed)	6
裙子	qúnzi	n.	skirt	3
日子	rìzi	n.	day, a (calendar) date, days of one's life	2
沙子	shāzi	n.	sand, grit	3
扇子	• shànzi	n.	fan	5
刷子	shuāzi	n.	brush, scrub	4
孙子	sūnzi	n.	grandson, Sun Zi (Chinese philosopher - Sūn zǐ)	4
袜子	wàzi	n.	socks, stockings	4
王子	• wángzǐ	n.	prince, son of a king	6
屋子	wūzi	n.	house, room	3
箱子	xiāngzi	n.	suitcase, chest, box, case, trunk	4
鸭子	yāzi	n.	duck	5
样子	yàngzi	n.	appearance, manner, pattern, model	2
叶子	yèzi	n.	foliage, leaf	4

椅子	yǐzi	n.	chair	2
影子	yǐngzi	n.	shadow, reflection, (fig.) hint, indication, influence	4
院子	yuànzi	n.	courtyard, garden, yard, patio	2
种子	zhǒngzi	n.	seed	3
竹子	zhúzi	n.	bamboo	5
柱子	zhùzi	n.	pillar	6
桌子	zhuōzi	n.	table, desk	1
电子版 ·	diànzǐbǎn	n.	electronic edition, digital version	5
电子邮件 ·	diànzǐ yóujiàn	n.	email	3
小伙子	xiǎohuǒzi	n.	young man, young guy, lad, youngster	4
一辈子	yībèizi	n.	(for) a lifetime	5
一下子	yīxiàzi	adv.	in a short while, all at once, all of a sudden	5

存 cún — to exist, to deposit, to store   子 39.3   3

存	cún	vb.	to exist, to deposit, to store, to keep, to survive	3
存款	cún kuǎn	vb.	to deposit money (in a bank etc), bank savings, bank deposit	5
存在	cúnzài	vb.	to exist, to be, existence	3
保存	bǎocún	vb.	to conserve, to preserve, to keep, to save (a file etc) (computing)	3
储存	chǔcún	vb.	to stockpile, to store, to stockpile, storage	6
生存	shēngcún	vb.	to exist, to survive	3

孙 sūn — grandchild, descendent   子 39.3   4

孙女	sūnnǚ	n.	son's daughter, granddaughter	4
孙子	sūnzi	n.	grandson, Sun Zi (Chinese philosopher - Sūn zǐ)	4

字 zì — letter, character, word   子 39.3   1

字	zì	n.	letter, symbol, character, word	1
字典	zìdiǎn	n.	character dictionary	2
字母	zìmǔ	n.	letter (of the alphabet)	4
汉字	hànzì	n.	Chinese character	1
名字	míngzi	n.	name (of a person or thing)	1
签字	qiān zì	vb.	to sign (one's name), signature	5
识字	shízì	vb.	to learn to read	6
数字	shùzì	n.	numeral, digit, number, figure, amount, digital (electronics etc)	2
文字	wénzì	n.	characters, script, writing, written language, writing (form or style), phraseology	3
写字台	xiězì tái	n.	writing desk	6
写字楼	xiězìlóu	n.	office building	6

孤 gū — orphaned, fatherless, solitary   子 39.5   6

孤	gū	adj.	lone, lonely	6
孤独	gūdú	adj.	lonely, solitary	6

季 jì — quarter of year, season   子 39.5   4

季	jì	n.	season, period, surname Ji	4
季度	jìdù	n.	quarter of a year, season (sports)	4
季节	jìjié	n.	time, season, period	4
春季	chūnjì	n.	springtime	4
冬季	dōngjì	n.	winter	4
秋季	qiūjì	n.	autumn, fall, year	4
夏季	xiàjì	n.	summer	4

学	**xué**		**to learn, to study, learning, school**	子 39.5	1
学	xué	vb.	to learn, to study, to imitate, science, -ology		1
学费	xuéfèi	n.	tuition fee, tuition		3
学分	xuéfēn	n.	academic credit, course credit		4
学会	xuéhuì	vb.	to learn, to master, institute, learned society, (scholarly) association		6
学科	xuékē	n.	subject, branch of learning, course, academic discipline		5
学年	xuénián	n.	academic year		4
学期	xuéqī	n.	term, semester		2
学生	- xuésheng	n.	student, schoolchild		1
学时	xuéshí	n.	class hour, period		4
学术	xuéshù	n.	learning, science, academic		4
学位	xuéwèi	n.	academic degree, place in school		5
学问	- xuéwen	n.	learning, knowledge		4
学习	xuéxí	vb.	to learn, to study		1
学校	xuéxiào	n.	school		1
学员	xuéyuán	n.	student, member of an institution of learning, officer cadet		6
学院	xuéyuàn	n.	college, educational institute, school, faculty		1
学者	xuézhě	n.	scholar		5
办学	bàn xué	vb.	to run a school		6
大学	dàxué	n.	the Great Learning, one of the Four Books 四书 Sì shū in Confucianism		1
放学	fàngxué	vb.	to dismiss students at the end of the school day		1
好学	• hàoxué	adj.	eager to study, studious, erudite		6
教学	jiàoxué	vb.	to teach (as a professor)		2
开学	kāixué	n.	foundation of a university or college, school opening, the start of a new term		2
科学	kēxué	n.	science, scientific knowledge, scientific, rational		2
留学	liúxué	vb.	to study abroad		3
入学	rù xué	vb.	to enter a school or college, to go to school for the first time as a child		6
上学	shàng xué	vb.	to go to school, to attend school		1
升学	shēng xué	vb.	to enter the next grade school		6
同学	tóngxué	vb.	to study at the same school, fellow student, classmate		1
文学	wénxué	n.	literature		3
小学	xiǎoxué	n.	elementary school, primary school		1
医学	yīxué	n.	medicine, medical science, study of medicine		4
哲学	zhéxué	n.	philosophy		6
中学	zhōngxué	n.	middle school		1
自学	zìxué	n.	self-study, to study on one's own		6
大学生	dàxuéshēng	n.	university student, college student		1
奖学金	jiǎngxuéjīn	n.	scholarship		4
教学楼	jiàoxuélóu	n.	teaching block, school building		1
留学生	liúxuéshēng	n.	student studying abroad, (foreign) exchange student		2
小学生	xiǎoxuéshēng	n.	primary school student, schoolchild		1
中学生	zhōngxuéshēng	n.	middle-school student, high school student		1
中小学	zhōngxiǎoxué	n.	middle and elementary school		2
孩	**hái**		**baby, child, children**	子 39.6	1
孩子	háizi	n.	child, son or daughter, children		1

男孩	nánhái	n.	boy	1
女孩	nǚhái	n.	girl, lass	1
小孩	xiǎohái	n.	child	1

宀 mián roof 40

宁 níng — calm, peaceful, serene, healthy — 宀 40.2 4

宁静	níngjìng	adj.	tranquil, tranquillity, serenity, calm	4

它 tā — it — 宀 40.2 2

它	tā	pro.	it	2
它们	tāmen	pro.	they (for inanimate objects)	2

安 ān — peaceful, calm, safe — 宀 40.3 2

安	ān	adj.	peaceful, calm, safe, (opp. 危 wēi: dangerous), content, settle, stabilize, surname An	4
安检	ānjiǎn	n.	security check, to undergo a security check	6
安静	ānjìng	adj.	quiet, peaceful, calm	2
安排	ānpái	vb.	to arrange, to plan, to set up, arrangements, plans	3
安全	ānquán	adj.	safe, secure, safety, security	2
安慰	ānwèi	vb.	to comfort, to console	5
安置	ānzhì	vb.	to find a place for, to help settle down, to arrange for, to get into bed, placement	4
安装	ānzhuāng	vb.	to install, to erect, to fix, to mount, installation	3
保安	bǎo'ān	vb.	to ensure public security, to ensure safety (for workers engaged in production), public security, security guard	3
不安	bù'ān	adj.	unpeaceful, unstable, uneasy, disturbed, restless, worried	3
公安	gōng'ān	n.	(Ministry of) Public Security, public safety, public security	6
平安	píng'ān	adj.	safe and sound, well, without mishap, quiet and safe, at peace	2
晚安	wǎn'ān	phr.	good night, good evening	2
治安	zhì'ān	n.	law and order, public security	5
一路平安	yīlùpíng'ān	vb.	to have a pleasant journey, Bon voyage!	2

守 shǒu — to guard, to defend — 宀 40.3 4

守	shǒu	vb.	to guard, to defend, to keep watch, to abide by the law, to observe (rules or ritual), nearby, adjoining	4
保守	bǎoshǒu	adj.	conservative, to guard, to keep	4
防守	fángshǒu	vb.	to defend, to protect (against)	6
遵守	zūnshǒu	vb.	to comply with, to abide by, to respect (an agreement)	5

宇 yǔ — house, building — 宀 40.3 6

宇航员	yǔhángyuán	n.	astronaut or cosmonaut	6

宅 zhái — residence, dwelling — 宀 40.3 6

住宅	zhùzhái	n.	residence, tenement	6

宏 hóng — great, vast — 宀 40.4 6

宏大	hóngdà	adj.	great, grand	6

完 wán — to finish, to be over — 宀 40.4 2

完	wán	vb.	to finish, to be over, whole, complete, entire	2

完成	wánchéng	vb.	to complete, to accomplish	2
完了	wánle	vb.	to be finished, to be done for, ruined, gone to the dogs, oh no	5
完美	wánměi	adj.	perfect, perfection, perfectly	3
完全	wánquán	adj.	complete, whole, totally, entirely	2
完善	wánshàn	adj.	(of systems, facilities etc) comprehensive, well-developed, excellent, to refine, to improve	3
完整	wánzhěng	adj.	complete, intact	3
宝	**bǎo**		**jewel, gem** ⼧ 40.5	4
宝	bǎo	n.	jewel, gem, treasure, precious	4
宝宝	-bǎobao	n.	darling, baby	4
宝贝	bǎobèi	n.	treasured object, treasure, darling, baby, cowry, good-for-nothing or queer character	4
宝贵	bǎoguì	adj.	valuable, precious, to value, to treasure, to set store by	4
宝石	bǎoshí	n.	precious stone, gem	4
珠宝	zhūbǎo	n.	pearls, jewels, precious stones	6
宠	**chǒng**		**to favour, to dote on** ⼧ 40.5	6
宠物	chǒngwù	n.	house pet	6
定	**dìng**		**to set, to fix** ⼧ 40.5	2
定	dìng	vb.	to set, to fix, to determine, to decide, to order	4
定价	dìngjià	vb.	to set a price, to fix a price	6
定期	dìngqī	adj.	at set dates, at regular intervals, periodic, limited to a fixed period of time, fixed term	3
定时	dìngshí	vb.	to fix a time, fixed time, timed (of explosive etc)	6
定位	dìngwèi	vb.	to orientate, to position, to categorize (as), to characterize (as), positioning, position, niche	6
测定	cèdìng	vb.	to determine (by measuring or surveying)	6
否定	fǒudìng	vb.	to negate, to deny, to reject, negative (answer), negation	3
固定	gùdìng	vb.	to fix, to fasten, to set rigidly in place, fixed, set, regular	4
规定	guīdìng	n.	provision, to fix, to set, to formulate, to stipulate, to provide, regulation, rule	3
坚定	jiāndìng	adj.	firm, steady, staunch, resolute	5
鉴定	jiàndìng	vb.	to appraise, to identify, to evaluate	6
决定	juédìng	vb.	to decide (to do something), to resolve, decision	3
肯定	kěndìng	vb.	to be certain, to be positive, assuredly, definitely, to give recognition, to affirm, affirmative (answer)	5
确定	quèdìng	vb.	to fix (on sth), to determine, to be sure, to ensure, to make certain, to ascertain, definite, certain, fixed	3
认定	rèndìng	vb.	to maintain (that sth is true), to determine (a fact), determination (of an amount), of the firm opinion, to believe firmly	5
特定	tèdìng	adj.	special, specific, designated, particular	5
稳定	wěndìng	adj.	steady, stable, stability, to stabilize, to pacify	4
一定	yīdìng	adv.	surely, certainly, necessarily, fixed, a certain (extent etc), given, particular, must	2
约定	yuēdìng	vb.	to agree on sth (after discussion), to conclude a bargain, to arrange, to promise, to stipulate, to make an appointment	6
指定	zhǐdìng	vb.	to appoint, to assign, to indicate clearly and with certainty, designated	6
制定	zhìdìng	vb.	to draw up, to formulate	3

不一定	bù yīdìng	adv.	not necessarily, maybe		2
说不定	- shuōbudìng	vb.	can't say for sure, maybe		4

官 guān — official, public servant ⼧ 40.5   4

官	guān	n.	an official, governmental, organ (of the body), surname Guan		4
官方	guānfāng	n.	government, official (approved or issued by an authority)		4
官司	- guānsi	n.	lawsuit		6
法官	fǎguān	n.	judge (in court)		4
器官	qìguān	n.	organ (part of body tissue), apparatus		4
打官司	- dǎ guānsi	vb.	to file a lawsuit, to sue, to dispute		6
外交官	wàijiāoguān	n.	diplomat		4

审 shěn — to examine, to investigate ⼧ 40.5   6

审查	shěnchá	vb.	to examine, to investigate, to censor out, censorship		6

实 shí — real, true, solid, full ⼧ 40.5   2

实惠	shíhuì	n.	tangible benefit, material advantages, cheap, economical, advantageous (deal), substantial (discount)		5
实际	shíjì	n.	reality, practice, practical, realistic, real, actual		2
实践	shíjiàn	vb.	to put into practice, to live up to (a promise), to carry out (a project), practice		6
实力	shílì	n.	strength		3
实施	shíshī	vb.	to implement, to carry out		4
实习	shíxí	vb.	to practice, field work, to intern, internship		2
实现	shíxiàn	vb.	to achieve, to implement, to realize, to bring about		2
实行	shíxíng	vb.	to implement, to carry out, to put into practice		3
实验	shíyàn	n.	experiment, test		3
实用	shíyòng	adj.	practical, functional, pragmatic, applied (science)		4
实在	shízài	adv.	really, actually, indeed, true, real, honest, (philosophy) reality		2
实在	- shízai	adj.	(coll.) done well, done dependably		2
实际上	- shíjì shang	adv.	in fact, in reality, as a matter of fact, in practice		3
实验室	shíyànshì	n.	laboratory		3
诚实	chéngshí	adj.	honest, honesty, honourable, truthful		4
果实	guǒshí	n.	fruit (produced by a plant), (fig.) fruits (of success etc), results, gains		4
结实	• jiēshi	vb.	to bear fruit, to form seed		3
老实	- lǎoshi	adj.	honest, sincere, well-behaved, open and guileless, naive		4
落实	luòshí	adj.	practical, workable, to implement, to carry out, to decide		5
其实	qíshí	adv.	actually, in fact, really		3
切实	• qièshí	adj.	feasible, realistic, practical, earnestly, conscientiously		6
确实	quèshí	adv.	indeed, really, reliable, real, true		3
事实	shìshí	n.	fact		3
踏实	- tàshi	adj.	firmly-based, steady, steadfast, to have peace of mind, free from anxiety		6
现实	xiànshí	n.	reality, actuality, real, actual, realistic, pragmatic, materialistic, self-interested		3
扎实	- zhāshi	adj.	strong, sturdy, practical		6
真实	zhēnshí	adj.	true, real		3
证实	zhèngshí	vb.	to confirm (sth to be true), to verify		5
事实上	shìshíshàng	adv.	in fact, in reality, actually, as a matter of fact, de facto, ipso facto		3
说实话	shuōshíhuà	vb.	to speak the truth, truth to tell, frankly		6

宜	yí		suitable, right, fitting	⼧ 40.5	2
便宜	• piányi	adj.	cheap, inexpensive, small advantages		2
宗	**zōng**		lineage, ancestry, clan	⼧ 40.5	6
宗教	zōngjiào	n.	religion		6
宫	**gōng**		palace	⼧ 40.6	6
宫	gōng	n.	palace, surname Gong		6
客	**kè**		guest, traveller, customer	⼧ 40.6	1
客车	kèchē	n.	coach, bus, passenger train		6
客观	kèguān	adj.	objective, impartial		3
客户	kèhù	n.	client, customer		5
客气	- kèqi	adj.	polite, courteous, formal, modest		5
客人	kèrén	n.	visitor, guest, customer, client		2
客厅	kètīng	n.	drawing room (room for arriving guests), living room		5
博客	bókè	n.	blog (loanword), blogger		5
乘客	chéngkè	n.	passenger		5
顾客	gùkè	n.	client, customer		2
旅客	lǚkè	n.	traveller, tourist		2
请客	qǐng kè	vb.	to give a dinner party, to entertain guests, to invite to dinner		2
游客	yóukè	n.	traveller, tourist, (online gaming) guest player		2
做客	zuò kè	vb.	to be a guest or visitor		3
不客气	- bùkèqi	phr.	you're welcome, don't mention it, impolite, rude, blunt		1
室	**shì**		room, home	⼧ 40.6	2
室	shì	n.	room, surname Shi		3
教室	jiàoshì	n.	classroom		2
卧室	wòshì	n.	bedroom		5
办公室	bàngōngshì	n.	office, business premises, bureau		2
地下室	• dìxiàshì	n.	basement, cellar		6
实验室	shíyànshì	n.	laboratory		3
阅览室	yuèlǎnshì	n.	reading room		5
宣	**xuān**		to declare, to announce	⼧ 40.6	3
宣布	xuānbù	vb.	to declare, to announce, to proclaim		3
宣传	xuānchuán	vb.	to disseminate, to give publicity to, propaganda		3
宾	**bīn**		guest, visitor	⼧ 40.7	5
宾馆	bīnguǎn	n.	guesthouse, lodge, hotel		5
嘉宾	jiābīn	n.	esteemed guest, honoured guest, guest (on a show)		6
害	**hài**		to do harm to	⼧ 40.7	3
害	hài	vb.	to do harm to, to cause trouble, to destroy, to kill, to harm, evil, calamity		5
害怕	hàipà	vb.	to be afraid, to be scared		3
厉害	- lìhai	adj.	(used to describe sb or sth that makes a very strong impression, whether favourable or unfavourable) terrible, intense		5
伤害	shānghài	vb.	to injure, to harm		4
损害	sǔnhài	n.	harm, to damage, to impair		5
危害	wēihài	vb.	to jeopardize, to harm, to endanger, harmful effect, damage		3

| 有害 | yǒu hài | adj. | destructive, harmful, damaging | 5 |
| 灾害 | zāihài | n. | calamity, disaster | 5 |

家 jiā — house, home, family   宀 40.7   1

家	jiā	+ n.	family, home, household, residence, m.w. for families or business establishments, domesticated, tamed (opp. 野 yě: untamed, wild)	1
家	jiā	+ aff.	noun suffix e.g. scientist 科学家 kēxuéjiā	2
家电	jiādiàn	n.	household electric appliance	6
家具	jiājù	n.	furniture	3
家里	jiālǐ	n.	home	1
家人	jiārén	n.	household, (one's) family	1
家属	jiāshǔ	n.	family member, (family) dependent	3
家庭	jiātíng	n.	family, household	2
家务	jiāwù	n.	household duties, housework	4
家乡	jiāxiāng	n.	hometown, native place	3
家园	jiāyuán	n.	home, homeland	6
家长	jiāzhǎng	n.	head of a household, family head, patriarch, parent or guardian of a child	2
搬家	bānjiā	vb.	to move house, removal	3
大家	dàjiā	n.	everyone, influential family, great expert	2
国家	guójiā	n.	country, nation, state	1
画家	huàjiā	n.	painter	2
回家	huíjiā	vb.	to return home	1
老家	lǎojiā	n.	native place, place of origin, home state or region	4
全家	quánjiā	n.	whole family	2
人家	rénjiā	n.	household, dwelling, family, sb else's house, household business, house of woman's husband-to-be	4
在家	zàijiā	vb.	to be at home, (at a workplace) to be in (as opposed to being away on official business 出差 chū chāi)	1
专家	zhuānjiā	n.	expert, specialist	3
作家	zuòjiā	n.	author	2

宽 kuān — wide, broad, relaxed   宀 40.7   4

宽	kuān	adj.	wide, broad, relaxed, lenient, surname Kuan	4
宽度	kuāndù	n.	width	5
宽广	kuānguǎng	adj.	wide, broad, extensive, vast	4
宽阔	kuānkuò	adj.	expansive, wide, width, thickness	6

容 róng — to hold, to contain   宀 40.7   3

容易	róngyì	adj.	easy, likely, liable (to)	3
美容	měiróng	vb.	to improve one's appearance (using cosmetics or cosmetic surgery), to make oneself more attractive, to beautify	6
内容	nèiróng	n.	content, substance, details	3
笑容	xiàoróng	n.	smile, smiling expression	6
形容	xíngróng	vb.	to describe, description, appearance, look	4
好不容易	hǎobùróngyì	adv.	with great difficulty, very difficult	6

宴 yàn — to entertain, to feast   宀 40.7   6

| 宴会 | yànhuì | n. | banquet, feast, dinner party | 6 |

寄	jì		to send, to transmit	宀 40.8	4
寄	jì	vb.	to send, to mail, to entrust, to depend on, to attach oneself to, to live (in a house), to lodge		4
密	**mì**		**dense, close, intimate**	宀 40.8	4
密	mì	adj.	dense, close, intimate, secret, surname Mi		4
密码	mìmǎ	n.	secret code, ciphertext, password, PIN		4
密切	mìqiè	adj.	close, familiar, intimate, closely (related), to foster close ties, to pay close attention		4
保密	bǎo mì	vb.	to keep sth confidential, to maintain secrecy		4
紧密	jǐnmì	adj.	inseparably close		4
秘密	mìmì	n.	secret		4
亲密	qīnmì	adj.	intimate, close		4
宿	**sù**		**to stop, to rest**	宀 40.8	5
宿舍	sùshě	n.	dormitory, dorm room, living quarters, hostel		5
富	**fù**		**abundant, wealthy**	宀 40.9	3
富	fù	adj.	abundant, rich, (opp. 穷 qióng: poor), wealthy, surname Fu		3
富人	fùrén	n.	rich person, the rich		6
富有	fùyǒu	adj.	rich, to be full of		6
财富	cáifù	n.	wealth, riches		4
丰富	fēngfù	vb.	to enrich, rich, plentiful, abundant		3
寒	**hán**		**cold, wintry, chilly**	宀 40.9	4
寒假	hánjià	n.	winter vacation		4
寒冷	hánlěng	adj.	cold (climate), frigid, very cold		4
察	**chá**		**to examine, to notice**	宀 40.11	3
观察	guānchá	vb.	to observe, to watch, to survey, to examine, observation, view, perspective		3
警察	jǐngchá	n.	police, police officer		3
考察	kǎochá	vb.	to inspect, to observe and study, on-the-spot investigation		4
赛	**sài**		**to compete, to contend, match**	宀 40.11	3
赛	sài	vb.	to compete, competition, match, to surpass, better than, superior to, to excel		6
赛场	sàichǎng	n.	racetrack, field (for athletics competition)		6
比赛	bǐsài	n.	competition (sports etc), match		3
参赛	cānsài	vb.	to compete, to take part in a competition		6
大赛	dàsài	n.	grand contest		6
竞赛	jìngsài	n.	race, competition		5
决赛	juésài	n.	finals (of a competition)		3
联赛	liánsài	n.	(sports) league, league tournament		6
半决赛	bànjuésài	n.	semi-finals		6
大奖赛	dàjiǎngsài	n.	grand prix		5

寸 cùn inch 41

					寸 41.0	4
寸	**cùn**			**inch**		
寸	cùn		n.	a unit of length, inch, thumb		5
尺寸	- chǐcun		n.	size, dimension, measurement		4

对 duì right, correct 寸 41.2 1

对	duì	+ adj.	right, correct, opposite, towards; couple, pair		1
对	duì	+ prep.	(with regard to) at, for, on; to answer, to treat (sb a certain way), to match together, to fit		2
对比	duìbǐ	vb.	to contrast, contrast, ratio		4
对待	duìdài	vb.	to treat, treatment		3
对方	duìfāng	n.	counterpart, other person involved, opposite side, other side, receiving party		3
对付	- duìfu	vb.	to handle, to deal with, to cope, to get by with		4
对话	duìhuà	n.	dialogue		2
对抗	duìkàng	vb.	to withstand, to resist, to stand off, antagonism, confrontation		6
对立	duìlì	vb.	to oppose, to set sth against, to be antagonistic to, antithetical, relative opposite, opposing, diametrical		5
对面	duìmiàn	n.	(sitting) opposite, across (the street), directly in front, to be face to face		2
对手	duìshǒu	n.	opponent, rival, competitor, (well-matched) adversary, match		3
对外	duìwài	n.	external, foreign, pertaining to external or foreign (affairs)		6
对象	duìxiàng	n.	target, object, partner, boyfriend, girlfriend		3
对应	• duìyìng	vb.	to correspond, a correspondence, corresponding, homologous, matching with sth, counterpart		5
对于	duìyú	prep.	regarding, as far as sth is concerned, with regards to		4
对不起	- duìbuqǐ	phr.	unworthy, to let down, I'm sorry, excuse me, pardon me, if you please, sorry? (please repeat)		1
不对	bù duì	adj.	incorrect, wrong, amiss, abnormal, queer		1
反对	fǎnduì	vb.	to fight against, to oppose, to be opposed to, opposition		3
绝对	juéduì	adj.	absolute, unconditional		3
面对	miànduì	vb.	to confront, to face		3
应对	• yìngduì	vb.	to answer, to reply, to handle, to deal with, response		6
针对	zhēnduì	vb.	to target, to focus on, to be aimed at or against, in response to		4
面对面	miànduìmiàn	phr.	face to face		6

导 dǎo to direct, to guide 寸 41.3 3

导演	dǎoyǎn	vb.	to direct, director (film etc)	3
导游	dǎoyóu	n.	tour guide, guidebook, to conduct a tour	4
导致	dǎozhì	vb.	to lead to, to create, to cause, to bring about	4
倡导	chàngdǎo	vb.	to advocate, to initiate, to propose, to be a proponent of (an idea or school of thought)	5
领导	lǐngdǎo	n.	lead, leading, to lead, leadership, leader	3
向导	xiàngdǎo	n.	guide	5
引导	yǐndǎo	vb.	to guide, to lead (around), to conduct, to boot, introduction, primer	4
指导	zhǐdǎo	vb.	to guide, to give directions, to direct, to coach, guidance, tuition	3
主导	zhǔdǎo	adj.	leading, dominant, prevailing, to lead, to direct, to dominate	5

寺	sì		temple	寸 41.3	6
寺	sì	n.	Buddhist temple, mosque, government bureau or office (in ancient China)		6
寿	**shòu**		old age, long life	寸 41.4	5
寿司	shòusī	n.	sushi		5
长寿	• chángshòu	adj.	longevity, live a long time		5
封	**fēng**		to confer, to seal, letter	寸 41.6	2
封	fēng	+ m.w.	m.w. for letters, something sealed		2
封	fēng	+ vb.	to confer, to seal, to bestow, letter, envelope		5
封闭	fēngbì	vb.	to seal, to close, to confine, to seal off, to close down, sealed, confined, closed, unreceptive		4
信封	xìnfēng	n.	envelope		3
射	**shè**		to shoot	寸 41.7	5
射	shè	vb.	to shoot, to launch, to allude to, radio- (chemistry)		5
射击	shèjī	vb.	to shoot, to fire (a gun)		5
发射	fāshè	vb.	to shoot (a projectile), to fire (a rocket), to launch, to emit (a particle), to discharge, emanation, emission		5
注射	zhùshè	n.	injection, to inject		5
尊	**zūn**		to respect	寸 41.9	5
尊敬	zūnjìng	vb.	to respect, to revere		5
尊重	zūnzhòng	vb.	to esteem, to respect, to honour, to value, eminent, serious, proper		5

小 xiǎo small ⺌ ⺍ 42

小	xiǎo		small, little, children	小 42.0	1
小	xiǎo	+ n.	little ones, children, small, little, (opp. 大 dà: big)		1
小	xiǎo	+ aff.	noun prefix e.g. 小王 before family name		2
小吃	xiǎochī	n.	snack, refreshments		4
小费	xiǎofèi	n.	tip, gratuity		6
小孩	xiǎohái	n.	child		1
小姐	xiǎojiě	n.	young lady, miss, (slang) prostitute		1
小麦	xiǎomài	n.	wheat		6
小声	xiǎoshēng	adv.	in a low voice, (speak) in whispers		2
小时	xiǎoshí	n.	hour		1
小说	xiǎoshuō	n.	novel, fiction		2
小偷	xiǎotōu	n.	thief		5
小心	xiǎoxīn	vb.	to be careful, to take care		2
小型	xiǎoxíng	n.	small scale, small size		4
小学	xiǎoxué	n.	elementary school, primary school		1
小于	xiǎoyú	adj.	less than, <		6
小组	xiǎozǔ	n.	group		2
小伙子	xiǎohuǒzi	n.	young man, young guy, lad, youngster		4
小朋友	- xiǎopéngyou	n.	child		1
小时候	- xiǎoshíhou	n.	in one's childhood		2
小学生	xiǎoxuéshēng	n.	primary school student, schoolchild		1

矮小	ǎixiǎo	*adj.*	short and small, low and small, undersized		4
从小	cóngxiǎo	*adv.*	from childhood, from a young age		2
大小	dàxiǎo	*n.*	dimension, magnitude, size, measurement, large and small, at any rate, adults and children, consideration of seniority		2
胆小	dǎnxiǎo	*adj.*	cowardly, timid		5
缩小	suōxiǎo	*vb.*	to reduce, to decrease, to shrink		4
中小学	zhōngxiǎoxué	*n.*	middle and elementary school		2
少	* **shǎo, shào**		**few, less, inadequate; young**	小 42.1	1
少	shǎo	*adj.*	few, (opp. 多 duō: many), less, to lack, to be missing, to stop (doing sth), seldom		1
少数	shǎoshù	*n.*	small number, few, minority		2
少儿	• shào'ér	*n.*	(abbrev) children and early teenagers 少儿不宜 shào'érbùyí		6
少年	• shàonián	*n.*	early youth, youngster, (literary) youth, young man		2
不少	bùshǎo	*adj.*	many, a lot, not few		2
多少	- duōshao	*pro.*	how many, number, amount, somewhat		1
减少	jiǎnshǎo	*vb.*	to lessen, to decrease, to reduce, to lower		4
缺少	quēshǎo	*n.*	lack, shortage of, shortfall, to be short (of), to lack		3
至少	zhìshǎo	*adv.*	at least, (to say the) least		3
青少年	• qīngshàonián	*n.*	adolescent, youth, teenager		2
尔	**ěr**		**you, thou**	小 42.2	5
偶尔	ǒu'ěr	*adv.*	occasionally, once in a while, sometimes		5
当	* **dāng, dàng**		**to be, to act as; right**	小 42.3	2
当	dāng	*vb.*	to be, to act as, manage, withstand, when, during, ought, should, match equally		2
当	• dàng	*adj.*	proper, right, at on in the very same…		6
当场	dāngchǎng	*n.*	at the scene, on the spot		5
当初	dāngchū	*n.*	at that time, originally		3
当代	dāngdài	*n.*	the present age, the contemporary era		5
当地	• dāngdì	*adj.*	local		3
当年	dāngnián	*n.*	in those days, then, in those years, during that time		5
当前	dāngqián	*n.*	current, today's, modern, present, to be facing (us)		5
当然	dāngrán	*adv.*	only natural, as it should be, certainly, of course, without doubt		3
当时	dāngshí	*n.*	then, at that time, while		2
当选	dāngxuǎn	*vb.*	to be elected, to be selected		5
当中	dāngzhōng	*n.*	among, in the middle, in the centre		3
当成	• dàngchéng	*vb.*	to consider as, to take to be		6
当天	• dàngtiān	*n.*	on that day		6
当作	• dàngzuò	*vb.*	to treat as, to regard as		6
恰当	• qiàdàng	*adj.*	appropriate, suitable		6
上当	• shàng dàng	*vb.*	to be taken in (by sb's deceit), to be fooled, to be duped		6
适当	• shìdàng	*adj.*	suitable, appropriate		6
相当	xiāngdāng	*vb.*	to match, to be equivalent to, appropriate, considerably, to a certain extent, fairly, quite		3
应当	yīngdāng	*vb.*	[as aux] should, ought to		3
正当	zhèngdāng	*n.*	timely, just (when needed)		6
不敢当	bù gǎndāng	*phr.*	(lit.) I dare not (accept the honour), (fig.) I don't deserve your praise, you flatter me		5

尖	**jiān**		sharp, pointed	小 42.3	6
尖	jiān	*adj.*	point (of needle), sharp, shrewd, pointed		6
尚	**shàng**		still, yet, even	小 42.5	4
高尚	gāoshàng	*adj.*	noble, lofty, refined, exquisite		4
尝	**cháng**		to taste	小 42.6	5
尝	cháng	*vb.*	to taste, try flavour of, (past tense marker)		5
尝试	chángshì	*vb.*	to try, to attempt		5
辉	**huī**		brightness, lustre	小 42.9	6
光辉	guānghuī	*n.*	radiance, glory, brilliant, magnificent		6

尢 wāng — lame — 尢 43

尤	**yóu**		especially, particularly	尢 43.1	5
尤其	yóuqí	*adv.*	especially, particularly		5
就	**jiù**		at once, right away	尢 43.9	1
就	jiù	*adv.*	at once, right away, only, just (emphasis), as early as, already, as soon as, then		1
就是	jiùshì	*adv.*	precisely, exactly, even, if, just like, in the same way as		3
就算	jiùsuàn	*conj.*	granted that, even if		6
就要	jiùyào	*adv.*	will, shall, to be going to		2
就业	jiùyè	*vb.*	to get a job, employment		3
就是说	jiùshìshuō	*conj.*	in other words, that is		6
成就	chéngjiù	*n.*	accomplishment, success, achievement		3
早就	zǎojiù	*adj.*	already at an earlier time		2
这就是说	zhèjiùshìshuō	*phr.*	in other words, that is to say		6

尸 shī — corpse — 44

尺	**chǐ**		a ruler, a Chinese foot	尸 44.1	4
尺	chǐ	*n.*	a ruler, a Chinese foot, one third of a metre		4
尺寸	- chǐcun	*n.*	size, dimension, measurement		4
尺子	chǐzi	*n.*	rule, ruler (measuring instrument)		4
尽	**jǐn**		to exhaust, to use up	尸 44.3	3
尽	jǐn	*vb.*	to use up, to exhaust, to end, to finish, to the utmost, exhausted, finished, to the limit (of sth), all, entirely		6
尽管	jǐnguǎn	*conj.*	despite, although, in spite of, unhesitatingly, do not hesitate (to ask, complain etc), (go ahead and do it) without hesitating		5
尽快	jǐnkuài	*adv.*	as quickly as possible		4
尽量	jǐnliàng	*adv.*	as much as possible, to the greatest extent		3
尽力	jǐnlì	*vb.*	to strive one's hardest, to spare no effort		4
尽可能	jǐnkěnéng	*adv.*	as far as possible, to do one's utmost		5
层	**céng**		storey, floor	尸 44.4	2
层	céng	*m.w.*	storey, floor (of a building), layer, laminated		2
层次	céngcì	*n.*	layer, level, gradation, arrangement of ideas, (a person's) standing		5

层面	céngmiàn		n.	aspect, facet, level (political, psychological, spiritual etc), (geology) bedding plane	6
高层	gāocéng		adj.	high level, high class	6
局	**jú**			office	尸 44.4 4
局	jú	+	n.	office, situation	4
局	jú	+	m.w.	m.w. for games: match, set, round etc	6
局面	júmiàn		n.	aspect, phase, situation	5
局长	júzhǎng		n.	bureau chief	5
邮局	yóujú		n.	post office	4
尾	**wěi**			tail, end	尸 44.4 4
尾巴	- wěiba		n.	tail, tail like part	4
届	**jiè**			to become due, period	尸 44.5 5
届	jiè		vb.	to arrive at (place or time), to become due, period, m.w. for events, meetings, elections, sporting fixtures, years (of graduation)	5
居	**jū**			to live, to dwell	尸 44.5 4
居民	jūmín		n.	resident, inhabitant	4
居然	jūrán		n.	unexpectedly, to one's surprise, go so far as to	5
居住	jūzhù		vb.	to reside, to dwell, to live in a place, resident in	4
邻居	línjū		n.	neighbour, next door	5
屏	**píng**			folding screen, shield	尸 44.6 6
屏幕	píngmù		n.	screen (TV, computer or movie)	6
屋	**wū**			house, room	尸 44.6 3
屋	wū		n.	house, room, building, shelter	5
屋子	wūzi		n.	house, room	3
房屋	fángwū		n.	house, building	3
展	**zhǎn**			to open up, to unfold, to stretch	尸 44.7 3
展开	zhǎn kāi		vb.	to unfold, to carry out, to be in full swing, to launch	3
展览	zhǎnlǎn		vb.	to put on display, to exhibit, exhibition, show	5
展示	zhǎnshì		vb.	to reveal, to display, to show, to exhibit sth	5
展现	zhǎnxiàn		vb.	to come out, to emerge, to reveal, to display	5
参展	cānzhǎn		vb.	to exhibit at or take part in a trade show etc	6
车展	chēzhǎn		n.	motor show	6
发展	fāzhǎn		n.	development, growth, to develop, to grow, to expand	3
进展	jìnzhǎn		vb.	to make headway, to make progress	3
开展	kāizhǎn		vb.	to launch, to develop, to unfold, (of an exhibition etc) to open	3
扩展	kuòzhǎn		vb.	to extend, to expand, extension, expansion	4
属	**shǔ**			class, category, type	尸 44.9 3
属	shǔ		n.	class, category, type, genus (taxonomy), family members, dependents, to belong to, subordinate to, affiliated with	3
属于	shǔyú		vb.	to be classified as, to belong to, to be part of	3
家属	jiāshǔ		n.	family member, (family) dependent	3
亲属	qīnshǔ		n.	kin, kindred, relatives	6

山 shān mountain — 46

山	**shān**		mountain, hill, peak	山 46.0 1
山	shān	n	mountain, hill, peak, surname Shan	1
山峰	shānfēng	n	(mountain) peak	6
山谷	shāngǔ	n	valley, ravine	6
山坡	shānpō	n	hillside	6
山区	shānqū	n	mountain area	5
登山	dēngshān	vb.	to climb a mountain, climbing, mountaineering	4
爬山	páshān	vb.	to climb a mountain, to mountaineer, hiking, mountaineering	2
岁	**suì**		year, age, harvest	山 46.3 1
岁	suì	n	year, year (of crop harvests), m.w. for years (of age),	1
岁数	-suìshu	n	age (number of years old)	6
岁月	suìyuè	n	years, time	5
岛	**dǎo**		island	山 46.4 6
岛	dǎo	n	island	6
岗	**gǎng**		post, position	山 46.4 6
岗位	gǎngwèi	n	post, job	6
岸	**àn**		bank, shore, coast	山 46.5 5
岸	àn	n	bank, shore, beach, coast	5
岸上	ànshàng	n	ashore, on the riverbank	5
两岸	liǎng'àn	n	bilateral, both shores, both sides, both coasts	5
峰	**fēng**		peak, summit, hump	山 46.7 6
峰会	fēnghuì	n	summit meeting	6
高峰	gāofēng	n	peak, summit, height	6
山峰	shānfēng	n	(mountain) peak	6
崇	**chóng**		to esteem, to honour	山 46.8 6
崇拜	chóngbài	vb.	to worship, to adore	6

工 gōng work — 48

工	**gōng**		labour, work, worker	工 48.0 1
工厂	gōngchǎng	n	factory	3
工程	gōngchéng	n	engineering, an engineering project, project, undertaking	4
工夫	-gōngfu	n	(old) labourer	3
工具	gōngjù	n	tool, instrument, utensil, means (to achieve a goal etc)	3
工人	gōngrén	n	worker	1
工商	gōngshāng	n	industry and commerce	6
工业	gōngyè	n	industry	3
工艺	gōngyì	n	arts and crafts, industrial arts	5
工资	gōngzī	n	wages, pay	3
工作	gōngzuò	vb.	to work, (of a machine) to operate, job, work, task	1
工程师	gōngchéngshī	n	engineer	3

工作日	gōngzuò rì	n.	workday, working day, weekday		5
罢工	bà gōng	n.	a strike, to go on strike		6
打工	dǎ gōng	vb.	to work a temporary or casual job, (of students) to have a job outside of class time, or during vacation		2
分工	fēn gōng	vb.	to divide up the work, division of labor		6
加工	jiāgōng	vb.	to process, processing, working (of machinery)		3
民工	míngōng	n.	migrant worker (who moved from a rural area of China to a city to find work), temporary worker enlisted on a public project		6
人工	réngōng	n.	artificial, manpower, manual work		3
手工	shǒugōng	n.	handwork, manual		4
员工	yuángōng	n.	staff, personnel, employee		3
职工	zhígōng	n.	workers, staff		3
清洁工	qīngjiégōng	n.	cleaner, janitor, garbage collector		6
巨	**jù**		**large, great, enormous**	工 48.2	4
巨大	jùdà	adj.	huge, immense, very large, tremendous, gigantic, enormous		4
巧	**qiǎo**		**skilful, timely**	工 48.2	3
巧	qiǎo	adj.	skilful, timely, opportunely, coincidentally, as it happens		3
巧妙	qiǎomiào	adj.	ingenious, clever, ingenuity, artifice		6
巧克力	qiǎokèlì	n.	chocolate (loanword)		4
技巧	jìqiǎo	n.	skill, technique		4
左	**zuǒ**		**left**	工 48.2	1
左	zuǒ	n.	the left side, left, east, surname Zuo		1
左边	- zuǒbian	n.	left, the left side, to the left of		1
左右	zuǒyòu	n.	left and right, nearby, approximately, attendant, to control, to influence		3
巩	**gǒng**		**to bind, to consolidate**	工 48.3	6
巩固	gǒnggù	vb.	to consolidate, consolidation, to strengthen		6
差	*** chà, chā, chāi**		**to fall short of; difference; to send**	工 48.7	1
差	chà	vb.	to differ from, to fall short of		1
差别	• chābié	n.	difference, distinction, disparity		5
差距	• chājù	n.	disparity, gap		5
差异	• chāyì	n.	difference, discrepancy		6
差点	chàdiǎn	adv.	almost, nearly		5
差不多	- chàbuduō	adj.	about the same, good enough, not bad, more or less, almost, nearly		2
出差	• chūchāi	vb.	to go on an official or business trip		5

己 jǐ oneself 49

己	**jǐ**		**self, oneself, personal**	己 49.0	2
自己	zìjǐ	pro.	oneself, one's own		2
已	**yǐ**		**already, to stop**	己 49.0	2
已	yǐ	adv.	already, to stop, then, afterwards		3
已经	yǐjīng	adv.	already		2
早已	zǎoyǐ	adv.	long ago, for a long time		3

巴	**bā**		bus, coach	己 49.1	4
巴士	bāshì	n.	bus (loanword), motor coach		4
大巴	dàbā	n.	(coll.) large bus, coach		4
尾巴	- wěiba	n.	tail, tail like part		4
嘴巴	- zuǐba	n.	mouth		4

巾 jīn turban 50

巾	**jīn**		towel, turban	巾 50.0	4
毛巾	máojīn	n.	towel		4
围巾	wéijīn	n.	scarf, shawl		4
币	**bì**		currency, coins, legal tender	巾 50.1	3
外币	wàibì	n.	foreign currency		6
人民币	rénmínbì	n.	renminbi (RMB)		3
布	**bù**		to declare, to announce, to spread	巾 50.2	3
布	bù	vb.	to declare, to announce, to spread, to make known		3
布满	bùmǎn	vb.	to be covered with, to be filled with		6
布置	bùzhì	vb.	to put in order, to arrange, to decorate, to fix up, to deploy		4
发布	fābù	vb.	to release, to issue, to announce, to distribute		5
分布	fēnbù	vb.	to scatter, to distribute, to be distributed (over an area etc), (statistical, geographic) distribution		4
公布	gōngbù	vb.	to announce, to make public, to publish		3
宣布	xuānbù	vb.	to declare, to announce, to proclaim		3
市	**shì**		market, city	巾 50.2	2
市	shì	n.	market, city		2
市场	shìchǎng	n.	marketplace, market (also in abstract)		3
市民	shìmín	n.	city resident		6
市区	shìqū	n.	urban district, downtown, city centre		4
市长	shìzhǎng	n.	mayor		2
超市	chāoshì	n.	supermarket		2
城市	chéngshì	n.	city, town		3
都市	• dūshì	n.	city, metropolis		6
上市	shàngshì	vb.	to hit the market (of a new product), to float (a company on the stock market)		6
帅	**shuài**		handsome, graceful, commander	巾 50.2	4
帅	shuài	adj.	handsome, graceful, commander, commander-in-chief, surname Shuai		4
帅哥	shuàigē	n.	handsome guy, handsome (form of address)		4
师	**shī**		teacher, master, specialist	巾 50.3	1
师傅	- shīfu	n.	master, qualified worker, respectful form of address for older men		5
师父	- shīfu	n.	master, teacher		6
师生	shīshēng	n.	teachers and students		6
厨师	chúshī	n.	cook, chef		6
大师	dàshī	n.	great master, master		6
教师	jiàoshī	n.	teacher		2

老师	lǎoshī	n.	teacher	1
律师	lǜshī	n.	lawyer	4
工程师	gōngchéngshī	n.	engineer	3
设计师	shèjìshī	n.	designer, architect	6
摄影师	shèyǐngshī	n.	photographer, cameraman	5

希 xī — to hope, to expect, to strive for 巾 50.4 3

希望	xīwàng	vb.	to wish for, to desire, to hope	3

帘 lián — screen, curtain, flag as shop sign 巾 50.5 5

窗帘	chuānglián	n.	window curtains	5

带 dài — band, belt, girdle 巾 50.6 2

带	dài	n.	band, belt, girdle, ribbon, tire, area, zone, region	2
带动	dàidòng	vb.	to spur, to provide impetus, to drive	3
带来	dàilái	vb.	to bring, to bring about, to produce	2
带领	dàilǐng	vb.	to guide, to lead	3
带有	dàiyǒu	vb.	to have, to involve	5
地带	dìdài	n.	zone	5
胶带	jiāodài	n.	adhesive tape, rubber belt, recording tape	5
领带	lǐngdài	n.	necktie	5
一带	yīdài	n.	region, district	5

帝 dì — supreme ruler, emperor, God 巾 50.6 6

皇帝	huángdì	n.	emperor	6
上帝	shàngdì	n.	the Lord on High (ancient China), God (Western)	6

帮 bāng — to help, to defend 巾 50.7 1

帮	bāng	vb.	to help, to assist, to support, for sb (i.e. as a help), hired (as worker), side (of pail, boat etc), outer layer	1
帮忙	bāngmáng	vb.	to help, to lend a hand, to do a favour, to do a good turn	1
帮助	bāngzhù	vb.	to help, to assist, assistance, aid	2

席 xí — to be present, to attend 巾 50.7 4

出席	chūxí	vb.	to attend, to participate, present	4
首席	shǒuxí	n.	chief (representative, correspondent etc)	6
主席	zhǔxí	n.	chairperson, premier, chairman	4

常 cháng — common, normal 巾 50.8 1

常	cháng	adj.	common, normal, ordinary, constant, always, often, frequently, surname Chang	1
常常	chángcháng	adv.	frequently, often	1
常规	chángguī	n.	code of conduct, conventions, common practice, routine (medical procedure etc)	6
常见	chángjiàn	n.	commonly seen, common, to see sth frequently	2
常年	chángnián	n.	all year round, for years on end, average year	6
常识	chángshí	n.	common sense, general knowledge	4
常用	chángyòng	adj.	in common usage	2
非常	fēicháng	adv.	very, very much, unusual, extraordinary	1
经常	jīngcháng	adv.	frequently, constantly, regularly, often, day-to-day, everyday, daily	2
平常	píngcháng	adj.	ordinary, common, usually, ordinarily	2
日常	rìcháng	adj.	daily, everyday	3

时常	shícháng	adv.	often, frequently	5
通常	tōngcháng	adj.	regular, usual, normal, usually, normally	3
异常	yìcháng	adj.	exceptional, abnormal, an anomaly	6
正常	zhèngcháng	adj.	regular, normal, ordinary	2

幅 fú — width, roll   巾 50.9   5

幅	fú	n.	width, roll, m.w. for textiles or pictures	5
幅度	fúdù	n.	width, extent, range, scope	5

帽 mào — hat, cap   巾 50.9   4

帽子	màozi	n.	hat, cap, (fig.) label, bad name	4

幕 mù — curtain, screen   巾 50.11   5

闭幕	bìmù	vb.	the curtain falls, lower the curtain, to come to an end (of a meeting)	5
开幕	kāimù	vb.	to open (a conference), to inaugurate	5
屏幕	píngmù	n.	screen (TV, computer or movie)	6
闭幕式	bìmùshì	n.	closing ceremony	5
开幕式	kāimùshì	n.	opening ceremony	5

干 gān — dry   51

干	* gàn, gān		to do, to work, to act; dry, empty	干 51.0 1
干	• gān	adj.	dry, (opp. 湿 shī: moist) empty, hollow	1
干	gàn	vb.	to do, to act, to manage, to work, trunk, stem, main part	1
干杯	• gānbēi	vb.	to drink a toast, cheers! (proposing a toast), here's to you!, bottoms up!, (lit.) dry cup	2
干脆	• gāncuì	adj.	straightforward, clear-cut, blunt (e.g. statement), you might as well, simply	5
干净	• gānjìng	adj.	clean, neat	1
干扰	• gānrǎo	vb.	to disturb, to interfere, perturbation, interference (physics)	5
干涉	• gānshè	vb.	to interfere, to meddle, interference	6
干预	• gānyù	vb.	to meddle, to intervene, intervention	5
干吗	gànma	adv.	why?, whatever for?, what's going on?, what are you doing?,	3
干什么	gàn shénme	vb.	what are you doing?, what's he up to?	1
干活儿	gànhuór	vb.	to do manual labour, to work, erhua variant of 干活 gànhuó	2
饼干	• bǐnggān	n.	biscuit, cracker, cookie	5
能干	nénggàn	adj.	capable, competent	4

平 píng — flat, even, peaceful   干 51.2   2

平	píng	adj.	flat, level, equal, even, peaceful, ordinary, surname Ping	2
平安	píng'ān	adj.	safe and sound, well, without mishap, quiet and safe, at peace	2
平常	píngcháng	adj.	ordinary, common, usually, ordinarily	2
平等	píngděng	adj.	equal, equality	2
平凡	píngfán	adj.	commonplace, ordinary, mediocre	6
平方	píngfāng	m.w.	square (as in square foot, square mile, square root)	4
平衡	pínghéng	n.	balance, equilibrium	6
平静	píngjìng	adj.	tranquil, undisturbed, serene	4
平均	píngjūn	n.	average, on average, evenly, in equal proportions	4
平时	píngshí	n.	ordinarily, in normal times, in peacetime	2
平台	píngtái	n.	platform, terrace, flat-roofed building	6

平坦	píngtǎn	*adj.*	level, even, smooth, flat	5
平稳	píngwěn	*adj.*	smooth, steady	4
平原	píngyuán	*n.*	field, plain	5
平方米	píngfāngmǐ	*m.w.*	square meter	6
公平	gōngpíng	*adj.*	fair, impartial	2
和平	hépíng	*adj.*	peaceful	3
水平	shuǐpíng	*n.*	level (of achievement etc), standard, horizontal	2
一路平安	yīlùpíng'ān	*vb.*	to have a pleasant journey, Bon voyage!	2

年 nián — year   干 51.3   1

年	nián	*n.*	year, yearly harvest (old)	1
年初	niánchū	*n.*	beginning of the year	3
年代	niándài	*n.*	a decade of a century (e.g. the Sixties), age, era, period	3
年底	niándǐ	*n.*	the end of the year, year-end	3
年度	niándù	*n.*	year (e.g. school year, fiscal year), annual	5
年级	niánjí	*n.*	grade, year (in school, college etc)	2
年纪	niánjì	*n.*	age	3
年龄	niánlíng	*n.*	(a person's) age	5
年前	niánqián	*n.*	before the end of the year, before the new year	5
年轻	niánqīng	*adj.*	young	2
半年	bànnián	*n.*	half a year	1
常年	chángnián	*n.*	all year round, for years on end, average year	6
当年	dāngnián	*n.*	in those days, then, in those years, during that time	5
多年	duōnián	*n.*	many years, for many years, longstanding	4
过年	guònián	*vb.*	to celebrate the Chinese New Year	2
后年	hòunián	*n.*	the year after next	3
今年	jīnnián	*n.*	this year	1
老年	lǎonián	*n.*	elderly, old age, autumn of one's years	2
明年	míngnián	*n.*	next year	1
前年	qiánnián	*n.*	the year before last	2
青年	qīngnián	*n.*	youth, youthful years, young person, the young	2
去年	qùnián	*n.*	last year	1
全年	quánnián	*n.*	the whole year, all year long	2
少年	• shàonián	*n.*	early youth, youngster, (literary) youth, young man	2
童年	tóngnián	*n.*	childhood	4
往年	wǎngnián	*n.*	in former years, in previous years	6
新年	xīnnián	*n.*	New Year	1
学年	xuénián	*n.*	academic year	4
中年	zhōngnián	*n.*	middle age	2
周年	zhōunián	*n.*	anniversary, annual	2
青少年	• qīngshàonián	*n.*	adolescent, youth, teenager	2

并 bìng — and, furthermore, also   干 51.5   3

并	bìng	+	*conj.*	and, also, really, together with	3
并	bìng	+	*vb.*	to combine, to merge, to stand side by side	4
并且	bìngqiě		*conj.*	and, besides, moreover, furthermore, in addition	3
合并	hébìng		*vb.*	to merge, to annex	5

幸 xìng — luck, good luck   干 51.5   3

幸福	xìngfú	*n.*	happiness, happy, blessed	3

幸运	xìngyùn	n	fortunate, lucky, fortune, luck	3
不幸	bùxìng	n	misfortune, adversity, unfortunate, sad, unfortunately	5

幺 yāo　short thread　52

乡	**xiāng**		**country, village**	幺 52.0　3
乡	xiāng	n	country, countryside, rural area, native place, home village or town, township (PRC administrative unit)	5
乡村	xiāngcūn	n	village, countryside	5
城乡	chéngxiāng	n	city and countryside	6
故乡	gùxiāng	n	home, homeland, native place	3
家乡	jiāxiāng	n	hometown, native place	3
老乡	lǎoxiāng	n	fellow townsman, fellow villager, sb from the same hometown	6
幻	**huàn**		**illusion, mirage**	幺 52.1　6
幻想	huànxiǎng	n	delusion, fantasy	6
幼	**yòu**		**infant, young child**	幺 52.2　4
幼儿园	yòu'éryuán	n	kindergarten, nursery school	4
幽	**yōu**		**quiet, secluded, tranquil**	幺 52.6　5
幽默	yōumò	n	(loanword) humour, humorous	5

广 guǎng　dotted cliff　53

广	**guǎng**		**wide, extensive, broad**	广 53.0　2
广	guǎng	adj.	wide, extensive, broad, to spread, surname Guang	5
广播	guǎngbō	n	broadcast	3
广场	guǎngchǎng	n	public square, plaza	2
广大	guǎngdà	adj.	(of an area) vast or extensive, large-scale, widespread, (of people) numerous	3
广泛	guǎngfàn	adj.	extensive, wide range	5
广告	guǎnggào	vb.	to advertise, a commercial, advertisement	2
广阔	guǎngkuò	adj.	wide, vast	6
宽广	kuānguǎng	adj.	wide, broad, extensive, vast	4
推广	tuīguǎng	vb.	to extend, to spread, to popularize, generalization, promotion (of a product etc)	3
庆	**qìng**		**to congratulate, to celebrate**	广 53.3　3
庆祝	qìngzhù	vb.	to celebrate	3
国庆	guóqìng	n	National Day	3
庄	**zhuāng**		**village, hamlet**	广 53.3　6
村庄	cūnzhuāng	n	village, hamlet	6
床	**chuáng**		**bed, couch**	广 53.4　1
床	chuáng	n	bed, couch, framework, chassis, m.w. bedding	1
起床	qǐchuáng	vb.	to get out of bed, to get up	1
库	**kù**		**depot, treasury, storehouse**	广 53.4　5
库	kù	n	depot, treasury, warehouse, storehouse, (file) library	5

仓库	cāngkù	n.	depot, storehouse, warehouse		6
水库	shuǐkù	n.	reservoir		5
序	**xù**		series, sequence	广 53.4	4
程序	chéngxù	n.	procedures, sequence, order, computer program		4
顺序	shùnxù	n.	sequence, order		4
应	* **yīng, yìng**		to agree, should; to answer	广 53.4	2
应	yīng	vb.	to agree, must, should, ought to, surname Ying		4
应	• yìng	vb.	to answer, to comply, to cope with, to respond, to agree, to deal with		5
应当	yīngdāng	vb.	[as aux] should, ought to		3
应该	yīnggāi	n.	[as aux] ought to, should, must		2
应对	• yìngduì	vb.	to answer, to reply, to handle, to deal with, response		6
应急	• yìngjí	vb.	to respond to an emergency, to meet a contingency, (attributive) emergency		6
应用	• yìngyòng	vb.	to put to use, to apply, practical, applied (science, linguistics etc), application, practical use, (computing) app		3
答应	- dāying	vb.	to answer, to respond, to answer positively, to agree, to accept, to promise		2
对应	• duìyìng	vb.	to correspond, a correspondence, corresponding, homologous, matching with sth, counterpart		5
反应	• fǎnyìng	vb.	to react, to respond, reaction, response, reply, chemical reaction		3
供应	• gōngyìng	vb.	to supply, to provide, to offer		4
回应	• huíyìng	vb.	to respond, response		6
适应	• shìyìng	vb.	to adapt, to fit, to suit		3
相应	• xiāngyìng	vb.	to correspond, answering (one another), to agree (among the part), corresponding, relevant, appropriate, (modify) accordingly		5
底	**dǐ**		bottom, base	广 53.5	3
底	dǐ	n.	bottom, base, heart of the matter		4
底下	- dǐxia	n.	the location below sth, afterwards		3
彻底	chèdǐ	adj.	thorough, thoroughly, complete		4
到底	dàodǐ	adv.	finally, in the end, when all is said and done, after all, to the end, to the last		3
海底	hǎidǐ	n.	seabed, seafloor, bottom of the ocean		6
年底	niándǐ	n.	the end of the year, year-end		3
月底	yuèdǐ	n.	end of the month		4
店	**diàn**		shop, store	广 53.5	1
店	diàn	n.	shop, store, inn		2
饭店	fàndiàn	n.	restaurant, hotel		1
酒店	jiǔdiàn	n.	wine shop, pub (public house), hotel, restaurant		2
旅店	lǚdiàn	n.	inn, small hotel		6
商店	shāngdiàn	n.	store, shop		1
书店	shūdiàn	n.	bookstore		1
药店	yàodiàn	n.	pharmacy		2
废	**fèi**		to give up, to discard	广 53.5	6
作废	zuòfèi	vb.	to become invalid, to cancel, to delete, to nullify		6
府	**fǔ**		prefecture, prefect, government	广 53.5	4
政府	zhèngfǔ	n.	government		4

度	**dù**		**degree, system, linear measure**	广 53.6	2
度	dù	n.	degree, system, linear measure, limit, extent, degree of intensity, m.w. degree (angles, temperature etc), kilowatt-hour		2
度过	dùguò	vb.	to pass, to spend (time), to survive, to get through		4
长度	• chángdù	n.	length		5
程度	chéngdù	n.	degree (level or extent), level		3
风度	fēngdù	n.	elegance (for men), elegant demeanour, grace, poise		5
幅度	fúdù	n.	width, extent, range, scope		5
高度	gāodù	n.	height, altitude, elevation, high degree, highly		5
过度	guòdù	adj.	excessive, over-, excess, going too far, extravagant, intemperate, overdue		5
季度	jìdù	n.	quarter of a year, season (sports)		4
角度	jiǎodù	n.	angle, point of view		2
宽度	kuāndù	n.	width		5
难度	nándù	n.	degree of difficulty		3
年度	niándù	n.	year (e.g. school year, fiscal year), annual		5
强度	qiángdù	n.	strength, intensity		5
深度	shēndù	n.	depth, (of a speech etc) profundity, advanced stage of development		5
速度	sùdù	n.	speed, rate, velocity, (music) tempo		3
态度	- tàidu	n.	manner, bearing, attitude, approach		2
温度	wēndù	n.	temperature		2
制度	zhìdù	n.	system (e.g. political, administrative etc), institution		3
庭	**tíng**		**courtyard, spacious hall or yard**	广 53.7	2
法庭	fǎtíng	n.	court of law		6
家庭	jiātíng	n.	family, household		2
座	**zuò**		**seat, base**	广 53.7	2
座	zuò	n.	seat, base		2
座位	zuòwèi	n.	seat		2
座谈会	zuòtánhuì	n.	conference, symposium, rap session		6
讲座	jiǎngzuò	n.	a course of lectures		4
让座	ràngzuò	vb.	to give up one's seat for sb		6
康	**kāng**		**healthy, abundant**	广 53.8	2
康复	kāngfù	vb.	to recuperate, to recover (health), to convalesce		6
健康	jiànkāng	n.	health, healthy		2
廴	**yǐn**		**long stride**		**54**
延	**yán**		**to delay**	廴 54.4	4
延期	yán qī	vb.	to delay, to extend, to postpone, to defer		4
延长	• yáncháng	vb.	to extend, to prolong, to lengthen		4
延伸	yánshēn	vb.	to extend, to spread		5
延续	yánxù	vb.	to continue, to go on, to last		4
建	**jiàn**		**to establish, to found**	廴 54.6	3
建	jiàn	vb.	to establish, to found, to set up, to build, to construct		3
建成	jiànchéng	vb.	to establish, to build		3

建立	jiànlì	vb.	to establish, to set up, to found	3
建设	jiànshè	vb.	to build, to construct, construction, constructive	3
建议	jiànyì	vb.	to propose, to suggest, to recommend, proposal, suggestion, recommendation	3
建造	jiànzào	vb.	to construct, to build	5
建筑	jiànzhù	vb.	to construct, building	5
重建	chóngjiàn	vb.	to rebuild, to re-establish, reconstruction, rebuilding	6
创建	chuàngjiàn	vb.	to found, to establish	6
构建	gòujiàn	vb.	to construct (sth abstract)	6
修建	xiūjiàn	vb.	to build, to construct	5

廾 gǒng   two hands   55

开 kāi   to open, to start   廾 55.1   1

开	kāi	vb.	to open, to start, to turn on, to boil, to write out (a prescription, check, invoice etc), to operate (a vehicle), carat (gold)	1
开会	kāi huì	vb.	to hold a meeting, to attend a meeting	1
开车	kāichē	vb.	to drive a car	1
开创	kāichuàng	vb.	to initiate, to start, to found	6
开发	kāifā	vb.	to exploit (a resource), to open up (for development), to develop	3
开放	kāifàng	vb.	to bloom, to open, to be open (to the public), to open up (to the outside), to be open-minded	3
开关	kāiguān	n.	power switch, gas valve, to open the city (or frontier) gate, to open and close, to switch on and off	6
开花	kāihuā	vb.	to bloom, to blossom, to flower, fig. to burst open, to feel happy or elated, new development grows out	4
开机	kāijī	vb.	to start an engine, to boot up (a computer), to press Ctrl-Alt-Delete, to begin shooting a film or TV show	2
开幕	kāimù	vb.	to open (a conference), to inaugurate	5
开设	kāishè	vb.	to offer (goods or services), to open (for business etc)	6
开始	kāishǐ	vb.	to begin, beginning, to start, initial	3
开水	kāishuǐ	n.	boiled water, boiling water	4
开通	kāitong	vb.	to open up (windows for air, ideas for discussion, transportation routes etc)	6
开头	kāitóu	n.	beginning, to start	6
开心	kāixīn	vb.	to feel happy, to rejoice, to have a great time, to make fun of sb	2
开学	kāixué	n.	foundation of a university or college, school opening, the start of a new term	2
开业	kāiyè	vb.	to open a business, to open a practice, open (for business)	3
开展	kāizhǎn	vb.	to launch, to develop, to unfold, (of an exhibition etc) to open	3
开玩笑	kāi wánxiào	vb.	to play a joke, to make fun of, to joke	1
开夜车	kāi yèchē	vb.	to burn the midnight oil, to work late into the night	6
开幕式	kāimùshì	n.	opening ceremony	5
打开	dǎkāi	vb.	to open, to show (a ticket), to turn on, to switch on	1
分开	fēnkāi	vb.	to separate, to part	2
隔开	gékāi	vb.	to separate	4
公开	gōngkāi	adj.	public, to publish, to make public	3
解开	jiěkāi	vb.	to untie, to undo, to solve (a mystery)	3
拉开	lākāi	vb.	to pull open, to pull apart, to space out, to increase	4

离开	líkāi	vb.	to depart, to leave		2
推开	tuīkāi	vb.	to push open (a gate etc), to push away, to reject, to decline		3
展开	zhǎn kāi	vb.	to unfold, to carry out, to be in full swing, to launch		3
召开	zhàokāi	vb.	to convene (a conference or meeting), to convoke, to call together		4
走开	zǒukāi	vb.	to leave, to walk away, to beat it, to move aside		2
离不开	líbukāi	vb.	inseparable, inevitably linked to		4

异 yì — different   廾 55.3   6

异常	yìcháng	adj.	exceptional, abnormal, an anomaly	6
差异	chāyì	n.	difference, discrepancy	6

弄 nòng — to do, to play or fiddle with   廾 55.4   2

弄	nòng	vb.	to do, to play or fiddle with, to manage, to handle, to make	2

弃 qì — to abandon   廾 55.4   5

放弃	fàngqì	vb.	to renounce, to abandon, to give up	5

弋 yì — shoot   56

式 shì — type, style   弋 56.3   3

式	shì	n.	type, form, pattern, style	5
方式	fāngshì	n.	way, manner, style, mode, pattern	3
公式	gōngshì	n.	formula	5
模式	móshì	n.	mode, method, pattern	5
形式	xíngshì	n.	outer appearance, form, shape, formality	3
仪式	yíshì	n.	ceremony	6
正式	zhèngshì	adj.	formal, official	3
闭幕式	bìmùshì	n.	closing ceremony	5
开幕式	kāimùshì	n.	opening ceremony	5

弓 gōng — bow   57

引 yǐn — to draw (e.g. a bow), to pull   弓 57.1   4

引	yǐn	vb.	to draw (e.g. a bow), to pull, to stretch sth, to extend, to lengthen, to involve or implicate in, to attract, to lead	4
引导	yǐndǎo	vb.	to guide, to lead (around), to conduct, to boot, introduction, primer	4
引进	yǐnjìn	vb.	to recommend, to introduce (from outside)	4
引起	yǐnqǐ	vb.	to give rise to, to lead to, to cause, to arouse	4
吸引	xīyǐn	vb.	to attract (interest, investment etc)	4

弟 dì — young brother, junior   弓 57.4   1

弟弟 | 弟	dì di | dì	n.	younger brother, brother, junior male, I (modest word in letter)	1
徒弟	túdì	n.	apprentice, disciple	6
兄弟	xiōngdì	n.	brothers, younger brother	4

张 zhāng — to stretch, to extend   弓 57.4   3

张	zhāng	vb.	to stretch, to extend, to expand, m.w. for flat objects, surname Zhang	3
紧张	jǐnzhāng	n.	nervous, keyed up, intense, tense, strained, in short supply, scarce	3
主张	zhǔzhāng	vb.	to advocate, to stand for, view, position, stand, proposition, viewpoint, assertion	3

弯	**wān**		to bend	弓 57.6	4
弯	wān	vb.	to bend, curved (opp. 直 zhí: vertical), a bend, a turn (in the road etc), m.w. for sth curved		4
弯曲	wānqū	vb.	to bend, to curve around, curved, crooked, to wind, to warp		6
转弯	zhuǎn wān	vb.	to turn, to go around a corner		4
弱	**ruò**		weak	弓 57.7	4
弱	ruò	adj.	weak, (opp. 强 qiáng: strong), feeble, young, inferior, (following a decimal or fraction) slightly less than		4
薄弱	bóruò	adj.	weak, frail		5
弹	* **dàn, tán**		to shoot; ball	弓 57.8	5
弹	• tán	vb.	to shoot, to flick, to pluck (stringed musical instrument)		5
炸弹	zhàdàn	n.	bomb		6
子弹	zǐdàn	n.	bullet		5
强	* **qiáng, qiǎng**		strong, powerful; to make an effort	弓 57.9	3
强	qiáng	adj.	strong, powerful, energetic, (opp. 弱 ruò: weak)		3
强大	qiángdà	adj.	large, formidable, powerful, strong		3
强盗	qiángdào	vb.	to rob (with force), bandit, robber		6
强调	qiángdiào	vb.	to emphasize (a statement), to stress		3
强度	qiángdù	n.	strength, intensity		5
强化	qiánghuà	vb.	to strengthen, to intensify		6
强烈	qiángliè	adj.	intense, (violently) strong		3
强势	qiángshì	adj.	strong, powerful, (linguistics) emphatic, intensive		6
强壮	qiángzhuàng	adj.	strong, sturdy, robust		6
强迫	• qiǎngpò	vb.	to compel, to force		5
加强	jiāqiáng	vb.	to reinforce, to strengthen, to increase		3
坚强	jiānqiáng	adj.	staunch, strong		3
顽强	wánqiáng	adj.	tenacious, hard to defeat		6
增强	zēngqiáng	vb.	to increase, to strengthen		5
彐	**jì**		snout	彐 58	
归	**guī**		to go back to, to return	彐 58.2	4
归	guī	vb.	to go back to, to return, to converge, surname Gui		4
寻	**xún**		to seek	彐 58.3	4
寻求	xúnqiú	vb.	to seek, to look for		5
寻找	xúnzhǎo	vb.	to seek, to look for		4
灵	**líng**		spirit, soul, intelligence, mind	彐 58.4	6
灵活	línghuó	adj.	flexible, nimble, agile		6
心灵	xīnlíng	adj.	bright, smart, quick-witted, heart, thoughts, spirit		6
录	**lù**		to record, to copy	彐 58.5	3
录	lù	vb.	to record, to copy		3
录取	lùqǔ	vb.	to accept an applicant (prospective student, employee etc) who passes an entrance exam, to admit (a student), to hire (a job candidate)		4
录像	lùxiàng	vb.	to videotape, to videorecord, video recording		6

录音	lùyīn	vb.	to record (sound), sound recording	3
录音机	lùyīnjī	n.	(tape) recording machine, tape recorder	6
登录	dēnglù	vb.	to register, to log in	4
纪录	jìlù	vb.	to record or document, take notes, record (as in world record)	3
记录	jìlù	vb.	to record, record (written account), note-taker, record (in sports etc)	3

三 shān bristle 59

形 xíng to appear, to look ≡ 59.4 3

形	xíng	vb.	to appear, to look, form, shape	6
形成	xíngchéng	vb.	to form, to take shape	3
形容	xíngróng	vb.	to describe, description, appearance, look	4
形式	xíngshì	n.	outer appearance, form, shape, formality	3
形势	xíngshì	n.	circumstances, situation, terrain	4
形态	xíngtài	n.	shape, form, pattern, morphology	5
形象	xíngxiàng	n.	image, form, figure	3
形状	xíngzhuàng	n.	form, shape	3
变形	biàn xíng	vb.	to become deformed, to change shape, to morph, deformation	6
地形	· dìxíng	n.	topography, terrain, landform	5
情形	- qíngxing	n.	circumstances, situation	5

须 xū must, to have to ≡ 59.6 2

必须	bìxū	vb.	to have to, must, compulsory, necessarily	2

彩 cǎi hue, colour, variegated colours ≡ 59.8 3

彩票	cǎipiào	n.	lottery ticket	5
彩色	cǎisè	n.	colour, multi-coloured	3
精彩	jīngcǎi	adj.	wonderful, marvellous, brilliant	3
色彩	sècǎi	n.	tint, colouring, colouration, (fig.) flavour, character	4

影 yǐng shadow, image ≡ 59.12 1

影迷	yǐngmí	n.	film enthusiast, movie fan	6
影片	yǐngpiàn	n.	film, movie	2
影视	yǐngshì	n.	movies and television	3
影响	yǐngxiǎng	n.	influence, effect, to influence, to affect (usually adversely), to disturb	2
影星	yǐngxīng	n.	film star	6
影子	yǐngzi	n.	shadow, reflection, (fig.) hint, indication, influence	4
电影	diànyǐng	n.	movie, film	1
摄影	shè yǐng	vb.	to take a photograph, photography, to shoot (a movie)	5
阴影	yīnyǐng	n.	(lit. and fig.) shadow	6
电影院	diànyǐngyuàn	n.	cinema, movie theatre	1
摄影师	shèyǐngshī	n.	photographer, cameraman	5

彳 chì step 60

彻 chè thorough, penetrating 彳 60.4 4

彻底	chèdǐ	adj.	thorough, thoroughly, complete	4

彼	bǐ		that, there, those	彳 60.5	5
	彼此	bǐcǐ	pro. each other, one another		5
径	jìng		narrow path, diameter	彳 60.5	6
	田径	tiánjìng	n. track and field (athletics)		6
	途径	tújìng	n. way, channel		6
往	wǎng		to go (in a direction)	彳 60.5	2
	往	wǎng	vb. to go (in a direction), toward, in the past		2
	往后	wǎnghòu	n. from now on, in the future, time to come		6
	往来	wǎnglái	n. dealings, contacts, to go back and forth		6
	往年	wǎngnián	n. in former years, in previous years		6
	往往	wǎngwǎng	adv. usually, in many cases, more often than not		3
	交往	jiāowǎng	vb. to associate (with), to have contact (with), to hang out (with), to date, (interpersonal) relationship, association, contact		3
	来往	láiwǎng	vb. to come and go, to have dealings with, to be in relation with		6
	前往	qiánwǎng	vb. to leave for, to proceed towards, to go		3
	以往	yǐwǎng	n. in the past, formerly		5
征	zhēng		to invade, to attack	彳 60.5	4
	征服	zhēngfú	vb. to conquer, to subdue, to vanquish		4
	征求	zhēngqiú	vb. to solicit, to seek, to request (opinions, feedback etc), to petition		4
	特征	tèzhēng	n. characteristic, diagnostic property, distinctive feature, trait		4
	象征	xiàngzhēng	n. emblem, symbol, token, badge, to symbolize, to signify, to stand for		5
待	* dài, dāi		to wait, to treat; to go beyond	彳 60.6	3
	待	• dāi	vb. to go beyond (a span of time)		5
	待遇	dàiyù	n. treatment, pay, salary, status, rank		4
	待会儿	• dāihuìr	adv. in a moment, later		6
	等待	děngdài	vb. to wait, to wait for		3
	对待	duìdài	vb. to treat, treatment		3
	接待	jiēdài	vb. to receive (a visitor), to admit (allow sb to enter)		3
	看待	kàndài	vb. to look upon, to regard		5
	期待	qīdài	vb. to look forward to, to await, expectation		4
很	hěn		very, quite	彳 60.6	1
	很	hěn	adv. (adverb of degree), very, quite		1
	很难说	hěnnánshuō	phr. it's hard to say		6
律	lǜ		statute	彳 60.6	4
	律师	lǜshī	n. lawyer		4
	法律	fǎlǜ	n. law		4
	规律	guīlǜ	n. rule (e.g. of science), law of behaviour, regular pattern, rhythm, discipline		4
	纪律	jìlǜ	n. discipline		4
	一律	yīlǜ	adj. same, uniformly, all, without exception		4
徒	tú		disciple, follower	彳 60.7	6
	徒弟	túdì	n. apprentice, disciple		6

汉字	拼音	词类	释义	参考
得	* de, dé, děi		aux. for possibility; to get; to need to	彳 60.8　1
得	• dé	vb.	to obtain, to get, to gain, to catch (a disease), proper, suitable, proud, contented, to allow, to permit, ready, finished; need, must, have to, be sure to	2
得	de	aux.	[after a verb or adjective to express possibility]	2
得	• děi	vb.	to need, to have to	4
得出	• déchū	vb.	to obtain (results), to arrive at (a conclusion)	2
得到	• dédào	vb.	to get, to obtain, to receive	1
得分	• défēn	vb.	to score	3
得了	• déle	vb.	all right!, that's enough!	5
得以	• déyǐ	vb.	to be able to, so that sb can, enabling, in order to, finally in a position to, with sth in view	5
得意	• déyì	adj.	proud of oneself, pleased with oneself, complacent	4
懂得	dǒngde	vb.	to understand, to know, to grasp	2
获得	• huòdé	vb.	to obtain, to receive, to get	4
记得	jìde	vb.	to remember	1
觉得	juéde	vb.	to think, to feel	1
免得	miǎnde	conj.	so as not to, so as to avoid	6
难得	• nándé	adj.	seldom, rare, hard to come by	5
取得	• qǔdé	vb.	to acquire, to get, to obtain	2
认得	rènde	vb.	to recognize, to remember sth (or sb) on seeing it, to know	3
舍得	shěde	vb.	to be willing to part with sth	5
使得	shǐde	vb.	(to be) usable, workable, doable, to make, to cause	5
显得	xiǎnde	vb.	to seem, to look, to appear	3
晓得	xiǎode	vb.	to know	6
赢得	• yíngdé	vb.	to win, to gain	4
值得	zhíde	vb.	to be worth, to deserve	3
只得	• zhǐdé	vb.	to have no alternative but to, to be obliged to	6
不得不	• bù dé bù	phr.	have no choice or option but to, cannot but, have to, can't help it, can't avoid	3
不得了	• bùdéliǎo	phr.	desperately serious, disastrous, extremely, exceedingly	5
看得见	kàndejiàn	vb.	can see, visible	6
看得起	kàndeqǐ	vb.	to show respect for, to think highly of	6
来得及	láidejí	phr.	there's still time, able to do sth in time	4
用得着	• yòngdezháo	vb.	to be able to use, useable, to have a use for sth, (in interrogative sentence) to be necessary to	6
舍不得	shěbude	vb.	to hate to do sth, to hate to part with, to begrudge	5
循	xún		to follow	彳 60.9　6
循环	xúnhuán	vb.	to cycle, to circulate, circle, loop	6
微	wēi		small, prefix micro-, trifling	彳 60.10　4
微博	wēibó	n.	microblogging, microblog	5
微笑	wēixiào	n.	smile	4
微信	wēixìn	n.	WeChat	4
微波炉	wēibōlú	n.	microwave oven	6
稍微	shāowēi	adv.	a little bit	5
德	dé		ethics, morality, virtue	彳 60.12　5
道德	dàodé	n.	virtue, morality, ethics	5

 xīn   heart   忄 小 61

心   xīn   heart, mind   心 61.0 2

心	xīn	n.	heart, mind, intention, centre, core	3
心理	xīnlǐ	n.	psychology, mentality	4
心里	-xīnli	n.	chest, heart, mind	2
心灵	xīnlíng	adj.	bright, smart, quick-witted, heart, thoughts, spirit	6
心情	xīnqíng	n.	mood, frame of mind	2
心态	xīntài	n.	attitude (of the heart), state of one's psyche, way of thinking, mentality	5
心疼	xīnténg	vb.	to love dearly, to feel sorry for sb, to regret, to grudge, to be distressed	5
心愿	xīnyuàn	n.	cherished desire, dream, craving, wish, aspiration	6
心脏	xīnzàng	n.	heart	6
心中	xīnzhōng	n.	central point, in one's thoughts, in one's heart	2
心脏病	xīnzàngbìng	n.	heart disease	6
爱心	àixīn	n.	compassion, kindness, care for others, love	3
背心	bèixīn	n.	sleeveless garment (vest, waistcoat, singlet, tank top etc)	6
粗心	cūxīn	adj.	careless, thoughtless	4
担心	dānxīn	adj.	anxious, worried, uneasy, to worry, to be anxious	4
恶心	-èxin	vb.	to feel sick, disgust, nauseating, to embarrass (deliberately)	4
放心	fàngxīn	vb.	to feel relieved, to feel reassured, to be at ease	2
关心	guānxīn	vb.	to be concerned about, to care about	2
核心	héxīn	n.	core, nucleus	6
决心	juéxīn	n.	determination, resolution, determined, firm and resolute, to make up one's mind	3
开心	kāixīn	vb.	to feel happy, to rejoice, to have a great time, to make fun of sb	2
耐心	nàixīn	vb.	to be patient, patience	5
内心	nèixīn	n.	heart, innermost being, (math.) incentre	3
热心	rèxīn	n.	enthusiasm, zeal, zealous, zest, enthusiastic, ardent, warm-hearted	4
伤心	shāngxīn	vb.	to grieve, to be broken-hearted, to feel deeply hurt	3
小心	xiǎoxīn	vb.	to be careful, to take care	2
信心	xìnxīn	n.	confidence, faith (in sb or sth)	2
虚心	xūxīn	adj.	open-minded, humble	5
用心	yòngxīn	n.	motive, intention, to be diligent or attentive, careful	6
中心	zhōngxīn	n.	centre, heart, core	2
忠心	zhōngxīn	n.	good faith, devotion, loyalty, dedication	6
专心	zhuānxīn	vb.	to concentrate, absorption, concentration, engrossed	4

必   bì   certainly, must   心 61.1 2

必	bì	adv.	certainly, must, will, necessarily	5
必将	bìjiāng	adv.	inevitably	6
必然	bìrán	adj.	inevitable, certain, necessity	3
必修	bìxiū	adj.	(of an academic course) required, compulsory	6
必须	bìxū	vb.	to have to, must, compulsory, necessarily	2
必需	bìxū	vb.	to need, to require, essential, indispensable	5
必要	bìyào	adj.	necessary, essential, indispensable, required	3
不必	bùbì	adv.	need not, does not have to, not necessarily	3
未必	wèibì	adv.	not necessarily, maybe not	4

忆	**yì**		to remember	心 61.1	5
回忆	huíyì	vb.	to recall, memories		5
记忆	jìyì	vb.	to remember, to recall, memory		5
忙	**máng**		busy	心 61.3	1
忙	máng	adj.	busy, (opp. 闲 xián: idle), hurriedly, to hurry, to rush		1
帮忙	bāngmáng	vb.	to help, to lend a hand, to do a favour, to do a good turn		1
赶忙	gǎnmáng	vb.	to hurry, to hasten, to make haste		6
慌忙	huāngmáng	adj.	in a great rush, in a flurry		5
急忙	jímáng	adv.	hastily		4
连忙	liánmáng	adv.	promptly, at once		3
忍	**rěn**		to bear	心 61.3	5
忍	rěn	vb.	to bear, to endure, to tolerate, to restrain oneself		5
忍受	rěnshòu	vb.	to bear, to endure		5
忍不住	- rěnbuzhù	phr.	cannot help, unable to bear		5
忘	**wàng**		to forget	心 61.3	1
忘	wàng	vb.	to forget, to overlook, to neglect		1
忘记	wàngjì	vb.	to forget		1
难忘	nánwàng	adj.	unforgettable		6
志	**zhì**		purpose	心 61.3	3
志愿	zhìyuàn	n.	aspiration, ambition, to volunteer		3
志愿者	zhìyuànzhě	n.	volunteer		3
标志	biāozhì	n.	sign, mark, symbol, logo, to symbolize, to indicate, to mark		4
意志	yìzhì	n.	will, willpower, determination		5
杂志	zázhì	n.	magazine		3
忽	**hū**		to neglect, suddenly	心 61.4	2
忽略	hūlüè	vb.	to neglect, to overlook, to ignore		6
忽然	hūrán	adv.	suddenly, all of a sudden		2
忽视	hūshì	vb.	to neglect, to ignore		4
怀	**huái**		to cherish	心 61.4	4
怀念	huáiniàn	vb.	to cherish the memory of, to think of, to reminisce		4
怀疑	huáiyí	vb.	to doubt (sth), to be sceptical of, to have one's doubts, to harbour suspicions, to suspect that		4
关怀	guānhuái	n.	care, solicitude, to show care for, concerned about, attentive to		5
快	**kuài**		rapid, quick	心 61.4	1
快	kuài	adj.	rapid, quick, (opp. 慢 màn: slow), speed, rate, soon, almost, to make haste, clever, sharp (of knives or wits), forthright, plainspoken, gratified, pleased, pleasant		1
快车	kuài chē	n.	express (train, bus etc)		6
快餐	kuàicān	n.	fast food, snack, quick meal		2
快递	kuàidì	n.	express delivery		4
快点	kuàidiǎn	vb.	to do sth more quickly, Hurry up!, Get a move on!		2
快活	- kuàihuo	adj.	happy, cheerful		5
快乐	kuàilè	adj.	happy, merry		2
快速	kuàisù	adj.	fast, high-speed, rapid		3

快要	kuàiyào	*adv.*	almost, nearly, almost all	2
赶快	gǎnkuài	*adv.*	at once, immediately	3
加快	jiākuài	*vb.*	to accelerate, to speed up	3
尽快	jǐnkuài	*adv.*	as quickly as possible	4
凉快	- liángkuai	*adj.*	nice and cold, pleasantly cool	2
特快	tèkuài	*adj.*	express (train, delivery etc)	6
痛快	- tòngkuai	*adj.*	delighted, to one's heart's content, straightforward	4
愉快	yúkuài	*adj.*	cheerful, cheerily, delightful, pleasant, pleasantly, pleasing, happy, delighted	6
念	**niàn**		to read, to study	心 61.4 3
念	niàn	*vb.*	to read, to study (a subject), to attend (a school), to read aloud, to give (sb) a tongue-lashing	3
概念	gàiniàn	*n.*	concept, idea	3
观念	guānniàn	*n.*	notion, thought, concept, sense, views, ideology, general impressions	3
怀念	huáiniàn	*vb.*	to cherish the memory of, to think of, to reminisce	4
纪念	jìniàn	*vb.*	to commemorate, to remember	3
想念	xiǎngniàn	*vb.*	to miss, to remember with longing, to long to see again	4
信念	xìnniàn	*n.*	faith, belief, conviction	5
态	**tài**		manner, bearing	心 61.4 2
态度	- tàidu	*n.*	manner, bearing, attitude, approach	2
动态	dòngtài	*n.*	movement, motion, development, trend, dynamic (science)	5
心态	xīntài	*n.*	attitude (of the heart), state of one's psyche, way of thinking, mentality	5
形态	xíngtài	*n.*	shape, form, pattern, morphology	5
状态	zhuàngtài	*n.*	state of affairs, state, mode, situation	3
忧	**yōu**		sorrow, to worry	心 61.4 6
担忧	dānyōu	*vb.*	to worry, to be concerned	6
忠	**zhōng**		loyal, devoted, honest	心 61.4 6
忠心	zhōngxīn	*n.*	good faith, devotion, loyalty, dedication	6
怪	**guài**		strange, odd	心 61.5 3
怪	guài	+ *adj.*	strange, odd, monster	4
怪	guài	+ *vb.*	to blame	5
奇怪	qíguài	*adj.*	strange, odd, to marvel, to be baffled	3
急	**jí**		urgent, pressing	心 61.5 2
急	jí	*adj.*	urgent, pressing, rapid, hurried, worried, to make (sb) anxious	2
急救	jíjiù	*n.*	first aid, emergency treatment	6
急忙	jímáng	*adv.*	hastily	4
紧急	jǐnjí	*adj.*	urgent, emergency	3
应急	• yìngjí	*vb.*	to respond to an emergency, to meet a contingency, (attributive) emergency	6
着急	• zháojí	*vb.*	to worry, to feel anxious	4
怜	**lián**		to pity, to sympathize	心 61.5 5
可怜	kělián	*adj.*	pitiful, pathetic, to have pity on	5

怒	nù		anger, rage	心 61.5	6
发怒	fānù	vb.	to get angry		6
愤怒	fènnù	adj.	angry, indignant, wrath, ire		6
怕	pà		to be afraid	心 61.5	2
怕	pà	+ vb.	to be afraid, cannot withstand		2
怕	pà	+ adv.	I am afraid (that), I suppose, perhaps		3
害怕	hàipà	vb.	to be afraid, to be scared		3
可怕	kěpà	adj.	awful, dreadful, fearful, formidable, frightful, scary, hideous, horrible, terrible, terribly		2
恐怕	kǒngpà	vb.	to fear, to dread, I'm afraid that..., perhaps, maybe		3
哪怕	nǎpà	conj.	even, even if, even though, no matter how		4
思	sī		to think	心 61.5	2
思考	sīkǎo	vb.	to think, to consider, to reflect on, to ponder over		4
思维	sīwéi	n.	(line of) thought, thinking		5
思想	sīxiǎng	n.	thought, thinking, idea, ideology		3
意思	- yìsi	n.	idea, opinion, meaning, wish, desire, interest, fun, token of appreciation, affection etc		2
有意思	- yǒuyìsi	adj.	interesting, meaningful, enjoyable, fun		2
不好意思	- bù hǎoyìsi	vb.	to feel embarrassed, to find it embarrassing, to be sorry (for inconveniencing sb)		2
性	xìng		nature, character	心 61.5	3
性	xìng	+ aff.	noun suffix designating a specified quantity e.g. 科学性 kēxuéxìng scientific; nature, character, quality, gender		3
性别	xìngbié	n.	gender, sex		3
性格	xìnggé	n.	nature, disposition, temperament, character		3
性能	xìngnéng	n.	function, performance		5
性质	xìngzhì	n.	nature, characteristic		4
个性	gèxìng	n.	individuality, personality		3
男性	nánxìng	n.	the male sex, a male		5
女性	nǚxìng	n.	woman, the female sex		5
特性	tèxìng	n.	property, characteristic		5
一次性	yīcìxìng	adj.	one-off (offer), one-time, single-use, disposable (goods)		6
怨	yuàn		to blame, to complain	心 61.5	5
怨	yuàn	vb.	to blame, to complain, hatred, enmity, resentment		5
抱怨	bàoyuàn	vb.	to complain, to grumble, to harbour a complaint, to feel dissatisfied		5
怎	zěn		what, why, how	心 61.5	1
怎么	zěnme	pro.	how, however, what, why		1
怎样	zěnyàng	pro.	how, what kind		2
怎么办	zěnmebàn	phr.	what's to be done		2
怎么样	zěnmeyàng	pro.	how?, how about?, how was it?, how are things?		2
不怎么	bùzěnme	adv.	not very, not particularly		6
不怎么样	bù zěnmeyàng	phr.	not up to much, very indifferent, nothing great about it, nothing good to be said about it		6

恶	è		evil, wicked	心 61.6	4
恶心	- èxin	vb.	to feel sick, disgust, nauseating, to embarrass (deliberately)		4
罪恶	zuì'è	n.	crime, evil, sin		6
恩	ēn		kindness, mercy	心 61.6	6
恩人	ēnrén	n.	a benefactor, a person who has significantly helped sb else		6
恨	hèn		to hate, to regret	心 61.6	5
恨	hèn	vb.	to hate, to regret, hatred, dislike		5
恢	huī		to restore	心 61.6	5
恢复	huīfù	vb.	to reinstate, to resume, to restore, to recover, to regain, to rehabilitate		5
恐	kǒng		to fear, fearful	心 61.6	3
恐怕	kǒngpà	vb.	to fear, to dread, I'm afraid that..., perhaps, maybe		3
恋	liàn		to love, to long for	心 61.6	5
恋爱	liàn'ài	vb.	to love, (romantic) love		5
虑	lǜ		to be concerned, to worry about	心 61.6	4
考虑	kǎolǜ	vb.	to think over, to consider, consideration		4
恰	qià		just, exactly, proper	心 61.6	6
恰当	• qiàdàng	adj.	appropriate, suitable		6
恰好	qiàhǎo	adj.	as it turns out, by lucky coincidence, (of number, time, size etc) just right		6
恰恰	qiàqià	adj.	exactly, just, precisely		6
息	xī		to rest, to put stop to, breath	心 61.6	1
利息	lìxī	n.	interest (on a loan)		4
消息	- xiāoxi	n.	news, information		3
信息	xìnxī	n.	information, news, message		2
休息	- xiūxi	n.	rest, to rest		1
患	huàn		to suffer, to worry about	心 61.7	6
患者	huànzhě	n.	patient, sufferer		6
悔	huǐ		to repent, to show remorse	心 61.7	5
后悔	hòuhuǐ	vb.	to regret, to repent		5
您	nín		you (courteous)	心 61.7	1
您	nín	pro.	you (courteous, as opposed to informal 你 nǐ)		1
悄	qiāo		silent (bound form)	心 61.7	5
悄悄	qiāoqiāo	adv.	quietly, secretly, stealthily, quiet, worried		5
悟	wù		to realize, to become aware	心 61.7	6
觉悟	juéwù	vb.	to come to understand, to realize, consciousness, awareness, Buddhist enlightenment (Sanskrit: cittotpāda)		6
悉	xī		to know, to learn about	心 61.7	5
熟悉	- shúxi	vb.	to be familiar with, to know well		5

悬	**xuán**		to hang, to feel anxious	心 61.7	6
悬	xuán	vb.	to hang or suspend, to worry, public announcement, unresolved, baseless, without foundation		6
悲	**bēi**		sorrow, sad	心 61.8	5
悲惨	bēicǎn	adj.	miserable, tragic		6
悲剧	bēijù	n.	tragedy		5
悲伤	bēishāng	adj.	sad, sorrowful		5
惨	**cǎn**		sad, wretched	心 61.8	6
惨	cǎn	adj.	miserable, wretched, cruel, inhuman, disastrous, tragic, dim, gloomy		6
悲惨	bēicǎn	adj.	miserable, tragic		6
惯	**guàn**		to be used to, habit	心 61.8	2
习惯	xíguàn	n.	habit, custom, usual practice, to be used to		2
惠	**huì**		favour, benefit	心 61.8	5
实惠	shíhuì	n.	tangible benefit, material advantages, cheap, economical, advantageous (deal), substantial (discount)		5
优惠	yōuhuì	adj.	favourable (terms), preferential (treatment), discount (price)		5
惊	**jīng**		to frighten, to surprise	心 61.8	4
惊人	jīngrén	adj.	astonishing		6
惊喜	jīngxǐ	n.	nice surprise, to be pleasantly surprised		6
吃惊	chī jīng	vb.	to be startled, to be shocked, to be amazed		4
震惊	zhènjīng	vb.	to shock, to astonish		5
情	**qíng**		feeling, emotion	心 61.8	2
情感	qínggǎn	n.	feeling, emotion, to move (emotionally)		3
情节	qíngjié	n.	plot, circumstances		5
情景	qíngjǐng	n.	scene, spectacle, circumstances, situation		4
情况	qíngkuàng	n.	circumstances, state of affairs, situation		3
情形	- qíngxing	n.	circumstances, situation		5
情绪	qíngxù	n.	mood, state of mind, moodiness		6
爱情	àiqíng	n.	romance, love (romantic)		2
表情	biǎoqíng	n.	(facial) expression, to express one's feelings		4
病情	bìngqíng	n.	state of an illness, patient's condition		6
感情	gǎnqíng	n.	emotion, sentiment, affection, feelings between two persons		3
激情	jīqíng	n.	passion, fervor, enthusiasm, strong emotion		6
热情	rèqíng	adj.	cordial, enthusiastic, passion, passionate, passionately		2
神情	shénqíng	n.	look, expression		5
事情	- shìqing	n.	affair, matter, thing, business		2
同情	tóngqíng	vb.	to sympathize with, sympathy		4
心情	xīnqíng	n.	mood, frame of mind		2
惜	**xī**		to pity, to regret	心 61.8	5
可惜	kěxī	adv.	it is a pity, what a pity, unfortunately		5
珍惜	zhēnxī	vb.	to treasure, to value, to cherish		5

愁	**chóu**		to worry about	心 61.9	5
愁	chóu	vb.	to worry about, be anxious, anxiety, sorrow, sadness, grief		5
愤	**fèn**		to resent, to hate	心 61.9	6
愤怒	fènnù	adj.	angry, indignant, wrath, ire		6
感	**gǎn**		to feel, to perceive	心 61.9	2
感到	gǎndào	vb.	to feel, to sense, to have the feeling that, to think that, to move, to affect		2
感动	gǎndòng	vb.	to move (sb), to touch (sb emotionally), moving		2
感觉	gǎnjué	vb.	to feel, to become aware of, feeling, sense, perception		2
感冒	gǎnmào	vb.	to catch cold, (common) cold		3
感情	gǎnqíng	n.	emotion, sentiment, affection, feelings between two persons		3
感人	gǎnrén	adj.	touching, moving		6
感受	gǎnshòu	vb.	to sense, perception, to feel (through the senses), to experience, a feeling, an impression, an experience		3
感想	gǎnxiǎng	n.	impressions, reflections, thoughts		5
感谢	gǎnxiè	n.	thanks, gratitude, to thank		2
感兴趣	gǎn xìngqù	vb.	to be interested		4
流感	liúgǎn	n.	flu, influenza		6
敏感	mǐngǎn	adj.	sensitive, susceptible		5
情感	qínggǎn	n.	feeling, emotion, to move (emotionally)		3
想	**xiǎng**		to think, to wish	心 61.9	1
想	xiǎng	vb.	to think, to believe, to suppose, to wish, to want, to miss (feel wistful about the absence of sb or sth)		1
想到	xiǎngdào	vb.	to think of, to call to mind, to anticipate		2
想法	xiǎngfǎ	n.	way of thinking, opinion, notion, to think of a way (to do sth)		2
想念	xiǎngniàn	vb.	to miss, to remember with longing, to long to see again		4
想起	xiǎngqǐ	vb.	to recall, to think of, to call to mind		2
想象	xiǎngxiàng	vb.	to imagine, to fancy		4
想不到	- xiǎngbudào	vb.	to never expect, unexpected, hard to imagine, it had not occurred to me		6
感想	gǎnxiǎng	n.	impressions, reflections, thoughts		5
幻想	huànxiǎng	n.	delusion, fantasy		6
理想	lǐxiǎng	n.	an ideal, a dream, ideal, perfect		2
联想	liánxiǎng	vb.	to associate (cognitively), to make an associative connection, mental association		5
梦想	mèngxiǎng	vb.	(fig.) to dream of, dream		4
设想	shèxiǎng	vb.	to imagine, to assume, to envisage, tentative plan, to have consideration for		5
思想	sīxiǎng	n.	thought, thinking, idea, ideology		3
没想到	méixiǎngdào	vb.	didn't expect		4
意想不到	yìxiǎngbùdào	phr.	unexpected, previously unimagined		6
意	**yì**		thought, idea	心 61.9	2
意见	yìjiàn	n.	idea, opinion, suggestion, objection, complaint		2
意识	- yìshi	n.	consciousness, awareness, to be aware, to realize		5
意思	- yìsi	n.	idea, opinion, meaning, wish, desire, interest, fun, token of appreciation, affection etc		2

意外	yìwài	n.	unexpected, accident, mishap		3
意义	yìyì	n.	sense, meaning, significance, importance		3
意愿	yìyuàn	n.	aspiration, wish (for), desire		6
意志	yìzhì	n.	will, willpower, determination		5
意味着	- yìwèizhe	vb.	to signify, to mean, to imply		5
意想不到	yìxiǎngbùdào	phr.	unexpected, previously unimagined		6
创意	chuàngyì	n.	original idea, creative, creativity		6
得意	• déyì	adj.	proud of oneself, pleased with oneself, complacent		4
故意	gùyì	adv.	deliberately, on purpose		2
满意	mǎnyì	vb.	to be satisfied, to be pleased, to one's satisfaction		2
民意	mínyì	n.	public opinion, popular will, public will		6
生意	- shēngyi	n.	life force, vitality		3
随意	suíyì	adv.	as one wishes, according to one's wishes, voluntary, conscious		5
特意	tèyì	adv.	specially, intentionally		6
同意	tóngyì	vb.	to agree, to consent, to approve		3
愿意	yuànyì	vb.	to wish, to want, ready, willing (to do sth)		2
主意	- zhǔyi	n.	plan, idea, decision		3
注意	zhùyì	vb.	to take note of, to pay attention to		3
有意思	- yǒuyìsi	adj.	interesting, meaningful, enjoyable, fun		2
不好意思	- bù hǎoyìsi	vb.	to feel embarrassed, to find it embarrassing, to be sorry (for inconveniencing sb)		2

愉 yú — pleasant, delightful 心 61.9 6

愉快	yúkuài	adj.	cheerful, cheerily, delightful, pleasant, pleasantly, pleasing, happy, delighted	6

慌 huāng — to get panicky, to lose one's head 心 61.10 5

慌	huāng	vb.	to get panicky, to lose one's head, in a hurry, flustered	5
慌忙	huāngmáng	adj.	in a great rush, in a flurry	5

愿 yuàn — hope, wish, desire 心 61.10 2

愿	yuàn	n.	hope, wish, desire, vow, to be ready, to be willing	5
愿望	yuànwàng	n.	desire, wish	3
愿意	yuànyì	vb.	to wish, to want, ready, willing (to do sth)	2
心愿	xīnyuàn	n.	cherished desire, dream, craving, wish, aspiration	6
意愿	yìyuàn	n.	aspiration, wish (for), desire	6
志愿	zhìyuàn	n.	aspiration, ambition, to volunteer	3
祝愿	zhùyuàn	vb.	to wish	6
自愿	zìyuàn	vb.	voluntary	5
志愿者	zhìyuànzhě	n.	volunteer	3

慧 huì — bright, intelligent 心 61.11 6

智慧	zhìhuì	n.	wisdom, knowledge, intelligent, intelligence	6

慢 màn — slow, leisurely 心 61.11 1

慢	màn	adj.	slow, (opp. 快 kuài: quick), leisurely, sluggish, to postpone	1
慢车	mànchē	n.	local bus or train, slow train with many stops	6
慢慢	mànmàn	adv.	slowly	3

慰 wèi — to comfort, to console 心 61.11 5

慰问	wèiwèn	vb.	to express sympathy, greetings, consolation etc	5

安慰	ānwèi	vb.	to comfort, to console		5
懂	**dǒng**		**to understand, to comprehend**	心 61.13	2
懂	dǒng	vb.	to understand, to comprehend, to know		2
懂得	dǒngde	vb.	to understand, to know, to grasp		2
憾	**hàn**		**to regret, remorse**	心 61.13	6
遗憾	yíhàn	n.	regret, to regret, to be sorry that		6
懒	**lǎn**		**lazy, languid**	心 61.13	6
懒	lǎn	adj.	lazy, slothful, sluggish, languid, listless		6

戈 gē — halberd — 62

戏	**xì**		**theatrical play, show**	戈 62.2	3
戏	xì	n.	trick, drama, play, show, to play		5
戏剧	xìjù	n.	drama, play, theatre		5
戏曲	• xìqǔ	n.	Chinese opera, traditional opera, singing parts in 传奇 chuánqí and 杂剧 zájù		6
游戏	yóuxì	n.	game		3
游戏机	yóuxìjī	n.	video game, game machine		6
成	**chéng**		**to accomplish, to become**	戈 62.3	2
成	chéng	+ vb.	to finish, to complete, to accomplish, to turn into, to become		2
成	chéng	+ m.w.	one tenth, 1/10, 10%		6
成本	chéngběn	n.	(manufacturing, production etc) costs		5
成分	• chéngfèn	n.	composition, make-up, ingredient, element, component, one's social status		6
成功	chénggōng	n.	success, succeed		3
成果	chéngguǒ	n.	result, achievement, gain, profit		3
成绩	chéngjī	n.	achievement, performance records, grades		2
成交	chéngjiāo	vb.	to complete a contract, to reach a deal		5
成就	chéngjiù	n.	accomplishment, success, achievement		3
成立	chénglì	vb.	to establish, to set up, to be tenable, to hold water		3
成品	chéngpǐn	n.	finished goods, a finished product		6
成人	chéngrén	n.	adult		4
成熟	chéngshú	adj.	mature, ripe, to mature, to ripen		3
成为	• chéngwéi	vb.	to become, to turn into		2
成效	chéngxiào	n.	effect, result		5
成语	chéngyǔ	n.	idiom, proverb		5
成员	chéngyuán	n.	member		3
成长	chéngzhǎng	vb.	to mature, to grow, growth		3
变成	biàn chéng	vb.	to change into, to turn into, to become		2
不成	bùchéng	vb.	won't do, unable to, (at the end of a rhetorical question) can that be?		6
达成	dá chéng	vb.	to reach (an agreement), to accomplish		5
当成	• dàngchéng	vb.	to consider as, to take to be		6
分成	fēnchéng	vb.	to divide (into), to split a bonus, to break into tenths, percentage allotment		5
构成	gòuchéng	vb.	to constitute, to form, to compose, to make up, to configure (computing)		4

合成	héchéng	vb.	to compose, to constitute, compound, synthesis, mixture, synthetic	5
建成	jiànchéng	vb.	to establish, to build	3
看成	kànchéng	vb.	to regard as	5
生成	shēngchéng	vb.	to generate, to produce, generated, produced	5
完成	wánchéng	vb.	to complete, to accomplish	2
形成	xíngchéng	vb.	to form, to take shape	3
养成	yǎngchéng	vb.	to cultivate, to raise, to form (a habit), to acquire	4
赞成	zànchéng	vb.	to approve, to endorse, (literary) to assist	4
造成	zàochéng	vb.	to bring about, to create, to cause	3
制成	zhìchéng	vb.	to manufacture, to turn out (a product)	5
组成	zǔchéng	vb.	to form, to make up, to constitute	2

戒 jiè — to warn, to caution   戈 62.3 5

| 戒 | jiè | vb. | to guard against, to exhort, to admonish or warn, to give up or stop doing sth, Buddhist monastic discipline, ring (for a finger) | 5 |

我 wǒ — I, me, my   戈 62.3 1

我	wǒ	pro.	I, me, my	1
我们	wǒmen	pro.	we, us, ourselves, our	1
自我	zìwǒ	n.	self-, ego (psychology)	6

或 huò — or, either, else   戈 62.4 2

或	huò	conj.	or, either, else, perhaps, maybe	2
或是	huòshì	conj.	or, either one or the other, even if	5
或许	huòxǔ	adv.	perhaps, maybe	4
或者	huòzhě	conj.	or, possibly, maybe, perhaps	2

战 zhàn — war, fighting   戈 62.5 4

战场	zhànchǎng	n.	battlefield	6
战斗	zhàndòu	vb.	to fight, to engage in combat, struggle, battle	4
战略	zhànlüè	n.	strategy	6
战胜	zhànshèng	vb.	to prevail over, to defeat, to surmount	4
战士	zhànshì	n.	fighter, soldier, warrior	4
战术	zhànshù	n.	tactics	6
战友	zhànyǒu	n.	comrade-in-arms, battle companion	6
战争	zhànzhēng	n.	war, conflict	4
• 挑战	tiǎozhàn	vb.	to challenge, challenge	4
作战	zuò zhàn	vb.	to combat, to fight	6

载 zài — to load with, to carry   戈 62.6 4

| 记载 | jìzài | vb. | to write down, to record, written account | 4 |
| 下载 | xiàzài | vb. | to download | 4 |

截 jié — to cut off, to stop   戈 62.10 6

| 截止 | jiézhǐ | vb. | to close, to stop, to put a stop to sth, cut-off point, stopping point, deadline | 6 |
| 截至 | jiézhì | vb. | up to (a time), by (a time) | 6 |

戴 dài — to wear on top, to support   戈 62.14 4

| 戴 | dài | vb. | to wear on top, to support, to put on, to wear (accessories), to respect, surname Dai | 4 |

戶 hù door 户戶 63

户	**hù**			door, family	戶 63.0 4
户	hù	n.		a household, door, family	4
户外	hùwài	n.		outdoor	6
窗户	- chuānghu	n.		window	4
客户	kèhù	n.		client, customer	5
用户	yònghù	n.		user, consumer, subscriber, customer	5
账户	zhànghù	n.		bank account, online account	6
房	**fáng**			house, building	戶 63.4 1
房东	fángdōng	n.		landlord	3
房价	fángjià	n.		house price, cost of housing	6
房间	fángjiān	n.		room	1
房屋	fángwū	n.		house, building	3
房子	fángzi	n.		house, building (single- or two-story), apartment, room	1
房租	fángzū	n.		rent for a room or house	3
病房	bìngfáng	n.		ward (of a hospital), sickroom	6
厨房	chúfáng	n.		kitchen	5
楼房	lóufáng	n.		a building of two or more stories	6
书房	shūfáng	n.		study (room), studio	6
住房	zhùfáng	n.		housing	2
所	**suǒ**			place, location	戶 63.4 2
所	suǒ	+ n.		place, office, m.w. for houses, small buildings, institutions etc	3
所	suǒ	+ n.		that which, particle introducing a relative clause or passive	6
所以	suǒyǐ	conj.		therefore, as a result, so, the reason why	2
所有	suǒyǒu	adj.		all, to have, to possess, to own	2
所在	suǒzài	n.		place, location, (after a noun) place where it is located	5
所长	suǒzhǎng	n.		what one is good at	3
厕所	cèsuǒ	n.		toilet, lavatory	6
场所	chǎngsuǒ	n.		location, place	3
无所谓	wúsuǒwèi	vb.		to be indifferent, not to matter, cannot be said to be	4
研究所	yánjiūsuǒ	n.		research institute, graduate studies, graduate school	5
扁	**biǎn**			flat, tablet, signboard	戶 63.5 6
扁	biǎn	adj.		flat, tablet, signboard, surname Pian	6
扇	*** shān, shàn**			to fan, to slap; fan, leaf	戶 63.6 5
扇	shān	vb.		to fan, to slap sb on the face	5
扇	• shàn	n.		fan, leaf, m.w. doors, windows	5
扇子	• shànzi	n.		fan	5

手 shǒu hand 扌手 64

才	**cái**			just now, only, talent	手 64.0 2
才	cái	+ adv.		just now, (before an expression of quantity) only	2
才	cái	+ n.		ability, talent, gift	4

才能	cáinéng	n.	talent, ability, capacity		3
刚才	gāngcái	adv.	just now		2
人才	réncái	n.	talent, talented person, looks, attractive looks		3
天才	tiāncái	n.	talent, gift, genius, talented, gifted		5

手 **shǒu** hand 手 64.0 1

手	shǒu	n.	hand, (formal) to hold, person engaged in certain types of work, person skilled in certain types of work, personal(ly), convenient, m.w. for skill		1
手表	shǒubiǎo	n.	wristwatch		2
手段	shǒuduàn	n.	method, means (of doing sth), strategy, trick		5
手法	shǒufǎ	n.	technique, trick, skill		5
手工	shǒugōng	n.	handwork, manual		4
手机	shǒujī	n.	cell phone, mobile phone		1
手里	shǒulǐ	adj.	in hand, (a situation is) in sb's hands		4
手术	shǒushù	n.	(surgical) operation, surgery		4
手套	shǒutào	n.	glove, mitten		4
手续	shǒuxù	n.	procedure		3
手指	shǒuzhǐ	n.	finger		3
手续费	shǒuxùfèi	n.	service charge, processing fee, commission		6
动手	dòngshǒu	vb.	to set about (a task), to hit, to punch, to touch		5
对手	duìshǒu	n.	opponent, rival, competitor, (well-matched) adversary, match		3
二手	èrshǒu	adj.	indirectly acquired, second-hand (information, equipment etc), assistant		4
分手	fēnshǒu	vb.	to part company, to split up, to break up		4
高手	gāoshǒu	n.	expert, past master, dab hand		6
歌手	gēshǒu	n.	singer		3
举手	jǔshǒu	vb.	to raise a hand, to put up one's hand (as signal)		2
联手	liánshǒu	n.	(lit.) to join hands, to act together		6
两手	liǎngshǒu	n.	one's two hands, two prongs (of a strategy), both aspects, eventualities etc, skills, expertise		6
双手	shuāngshǒu	n.	both hands		5
随手	suíshǒu	adv.	conveniently, without extra trouble, while doing it, in passing		4
握手	wòshǒu	vb.	to shake hands		3
凶手	xiōngshǒu	n.	murderer, assassin		6
选手	xuǎnshǒu	n.	athlete, contestant		3
招手	zhāo shǒu	vb.	to wave, to beckon		5
助手	zhùshǒu	n.	assistant, helper		5
洗手间	xǐshǒujiān	n.	toilet, lavatory, washroom		1

扎 **zhā** to prick, to stab 手 64.1 6

扎	zhā	vb.	to prick, to stab, to plunge, to get into sth		6
扎实	- zhāshi	adj.	strong, sturdy, practical		6

打 * **dǎ, dá** to strike, to hit; dozen 手 64.2 1

打	• dá	m.w.	m.w. dozen (loanword)		4
打	dǎ	+ vb.	to hit, to beat, to play, to type		1
打	dǎ	+ prep.	from, since		5
打工	dǎ gōng	vb.	to work a temporary or casual job, (of students) to have a job outside of class time, or during vacation		2

打破	dǎ pò	vb.	to break, to smash	3
打败	dǎbài	vb.	to defeat, to overpower, to beat, to be defeated	4
打扮	- dǎban	vb.	to decorate, to dress, to make up, to adorn, manner of dressing, style of dress	5
打包	dǎbāo	vb.	to wrap, to pack, to put leftovers in a doggy bag for take-out, to package (computing)	5
打车	dǎchē	vb.	to take a taxi (in town), to hitch a lift	1
打动	dǎdòng	vb.	to move (to pity), arousing (sympathy), touching	6
打断	dǎduàn	vb.	to interrupt, to break off, to break (a bone)	6
打发	- dǎfa	vb.	to dispatch sb to do sth, to make sb leave, to pass (the time), (old) to make arrangements, (old) to bestow (alms etc)	6
打击	dǎjī	vb.	to hit, to strike, to attack, to crack down on sth, blow, (psychological) shock, percussion (music)	5
打架	dǎjià	vb.	to fight, to scuffle, to come to blows	5
打开	dǎkāi	vb.	to open, to show (a ticket), to turn on, to switch on	1
打雷	dǎléi	vb.	to rumble with thunder, clap of thunder	4
打牌	dǎpái	vb.	to play mah-jong or cards	6
打球	dǎqiú	vb.	to play ball, to play with a ball	1
打扰	dǎrǎo	vb.	to disturb, to bother, to trouble	5
打扫	dǎsǎo	vb.	to clean, to sweep	4
打算	dǎsuàn	vb.	to plan, to intend, to calculate, plan, intention, calculation	2
打听	- dǎting	vb.	to ask about, to make some inquiries, to ask around	3
打印	dǎyìn	vb.	to affix a seal, to stamp, to print out (with a printer)	2
打造	dǎzào	vb.	to create, to build, to develop, to forge (of metal)	6
打折	dǎzhé	vb.	to give a discount	4
打针	dǎzhēn	vb.	to give or have an injection	4
打电话	dǎ diànhuà	vb.	to make a telephone call	1
打官司	- dǎ guānsi	vb.	to file a lawsuit, to sue, to dispute	6
打印机	dǎyìnjī	n.	printer	6
挨打	• áidǎ	vb.	to take a beating, to get thrashed, to come under attack	6
拨打	bōdǎ	vb.	to call, to dial	6
单打	dāndǎ	vb.	to compete one-to-one, singles (in sports)	6
双打	shuāngdǎ	n.	doubles (in sports)	6

扑	**pū**		to pounce on, to rush at	手 64.2 6
扑	pū	vb.	to throw oneself at, to pounce on, to devote one's energies, to flap, to flutter, to dab, to pat, to bend over	6

扔	**rēng**		to throw, to hurl	手 64.2 5
扔	rēng	vb.	to throw, to hurl, to throw away, to cast	5

扣	**kòu**		to button up, to knock	手 64.3 6
扣	kòu	vb.	to button up, to knock, to strike, to deduct, knot, button	6

扩	**kuò**		to expand, to enlarge, to stretch	手 64.3 4
扩大	kuòdà	vb.	to expand, to enlarge, to broaden one's scope	4
扩展	kuòzhǎn	vb.	to extend, to expand, extension, expansion	4

扫	**sǎo**		to sweep, to clear away	手 64.3 4
扫	sǎo	vb.	to sweep, to clear away, to eliminate	4
打扫	dǎsǎo	vb.	to clean, to sweep	4

托	**tuō**		to support, to trust	手 64.3	5
托	tuō	vb.	to support, to trust, to entrust, to be entrusted with, to act as trustee		6
摩托	mótuō	n.	motor (loanword), motorbike		5
委托	wěituō	vb.	to entrust, to trust, to commission		5
扬	**yáng**		to raise, to scatter	手 64.3	4
表扬	biǎoyáng	vb.	to praise, to commend		4
执	**zhí**		to hold in hand, to carry out	手 64.3	5
执行	zhíxíng	vb.	to implement, to carry out, to execute, to run		5
把	**bǎ**		to hold, to contain, to grasp	手 64.4	3
把	bǎ	+ vb.	to hold, to contain, to grasp, to take hold of, handle, particle marking the following noun as a direct object		3
把	bǎ	+ m.w.	m.w. for objects with handle		3
把握	bǎwò	vb.	to grasp (also fig.), to seize, to hold, assurance, certainty, sure (of the outcome)		3
扮	**bàn**		to dress up, to dress up as	手 64.4	5
扮演	bànyǎn	vb.	to play the role of, to act		5
打扮	- dǎban	vb.	to decorate, to dress, to make up, to adorn, manner of dressing, style of dress		5
报	**bào**		newspaper, periodical	手 64.4	2
报	bào	+ n.	newspaper, periodical, bulletin, telegram, judgement, to report, to tell, to announce		3
报名	bào míng	vb.	to sign up, to enter one's name, to apply, to register, to enrol, to enlist		2
报答	bàodá	vb.	to repay, to requite		5
报道	bàodào	vb.	to report (news), report		3
报到	bàodào	vb.	to report for duty, to check in, to register		3
报告	bàogào	vb.	to inform, to report, to make known, report, speech, talk, lecture		3
报警	bàojǐng	vb.	to sound an alarm, to report sth to the police		5
报刊	bàokān	n.	newspapers and periodicals, the press		6
报考	bàokǎo	vb.	to enter oneself for an examination		6
报纸	bàozhǐ	n.	newspaper, newsprint		2
海报	hǎibào	n.	poster, playbill, notice		6
回报	huíbào	vb.	to report back, to reciprocate, (in) return, reciprocation, payback, retaliation		5
汇报	huìbào	vb.	to report, to give an account of, report		4
日报	rìbào	n.	daily newspaper		2
通报	tōngbào	vb.	to inform, to notify, to announce, circular, bulletin, scientific journal		6
晚报	wǎnbào	n.	evening newspaper, (in a newspaper's name) Evening News		2
预报	yùbào	n.	forecast		3
抄	**chāo**		to copy, to seize	手 64.4	4
抄	chāo	vb.	to make a copy, to plagiarize, to search and seize, to raid, to grab, to go off with, to take a shortcut, to make a turning move, to fold one's arms		4
抄写	chāoxiě	vb.	to copy, to transcribe		4

承	chéng		to bear, to undertake	手 64.4	4
承办	chéngbàn	vb.	to undertake, to accept a contract		5
承担	chéngdān	vb.	to undertake, to assume (responsibility etc)		4
承诺	chéngnuò	vb.	to promise, to undertake to do something, commitment		6
承认	chéngrèn	vb.	to admit, to concede, to recognize, recognition (diplomatic, artistic etc), to acknowledge		4
承受	chéngshòu	vb.	to bear, to support, to inherit		4
继承	jìchéng	vb.	to inherit, to succeed to (the throne etc), to carry on (a tradition etc)		5

扶	fú		to support, to help	手 64.4	5
扶	fú	vb.	to support with the hand, to help sb up, to support oneself by holding onto something, to help		5

护	hù		to protect, to guard, to defend	手 64.4	2
护	hù	vb.	to protect		6
护士	- hùshi	n.	nurse		4
护照	hùzhào	n.	passport		2
爱护	àihù	vb.	to cherish, to treasure, to take care of, to love and protect		4
保护	bǎohù	vb.	to protect, to defend, to safeguard, protection		3
维护	wéihù	vb.	to defend, to safeguard, to protect, to uphold, to maintain		4

技	jì		skill, talent	手 64.4	3
技能	jìnéng	n.	technical ability, skill		5
技巧	jìqiǎo	n.	skill, technique		4
技术	jìshù	n.	technology, technique, skill		3
科技	kējì	n.	science and technology		3
高科技	gāokējì	n.	high tech, high technology		6

抗	kàng		to resist, to defy	手 64.4	6
抗议	kàngyì	vb.	to protest, protest		6
抵抗	dǐkàng	vb.	to resist, resistance		6
对抗	duìkàng	vb.	to withstand, to resist, to stand off, antagonism, confrontation		6
反抗	fǎnkàng	vb.	to resist, to rebel		6

扭	niǔ		to turn, to twist	手 64.4	6
扭	niǔ	vb.	to turn, to twist, to wring, to sprain, to swing one's hips		6

批	pī		to ascertain, to criticize	手 64.4	3
批	pī	+ vb.	to ascertain, to criticize, to scrape, to slice		4
批	pī	+ m.w.	batch, lot, group		4
批评	pīpíng	vb.	to criticize, criticism		3
批准	pīzhǔn	vb.	to approve, to ratify		3
大批	dàpī	n.	large quantities of		6

抢	qiǎng		to plunder, to rob	手 64.4	5
抢	qiǎng	vb.	to rob, to snatch, to fight/compete over, to scrape		5
抢救	qiǎngjiù	vb.	to rescue		5

扰	rǎo		to disturb, to annoy	手 64.4	5
打扰	dǎrǎo	vb.	to disturb, to bother, to trouble		5
干扰	• gānrǎo	vb.	to disturb, to interfere, perturbation, interference (physics)		5

困扰	kùnrǎo	vb.	to perplex, to disturb, to cause complications		5
投	**tóu**		**to throw, to cast**	手 64.4	4
投	tóu	vb.	to cast, to send, to throw oneself (into the river etc), to seek refuge, to place oneself into the hands of		4
投票	tóupiào	vb.	to vote, vote		6
投入	tóurù	vb.	to throw into, to put into, to throw oneself into, to participate in, to invest in, absorbed, engrossed		4
投诉	tóusù	n.	complaint, to complain, to register a complaint (esp. as a customer)		4
投资	tóuzī	n.	investment, to invest		4
找	**zhǎo**		**to search, to find**	手 64.4	1
找	zhǎo	vb.	to try to find, to look for, to call on sb, to find, to seek, to return, to give change		1
找出	zhǎochū	vb.	to find, to search out		2
找到	zhǎodào	vb.	to find		1
寻找	xúnzhǎo	vb.	to seek, to look for		4
折	**zhé**		**to break off, to snap**	手 64.4	4
折	zhé	vb.	to break, to fracture, to convert into, to fold, discount, turning stroke in Chinese characters, folder		4
打折	dǎzhé	vb.	to give a discount		4
抓	**zhuā**		**to grab, to clutch**	手 64.4	3
抓	zhuā	vb.	to grab, to catch, to arrest, to snatch, to scratch		3
抓紧	zhuā jǐn	vb.	to grasp firmly, to pay special attention to, to rush in, to make the most of		4
抓住	zhuāzhù	vb.	to grab, to capture		3
拔	**bá**		**to uproot, to pull out**	手 64.5	5
拔	bá	vb.	to pull up, to pull out, to draw out by suction, to select, to pick, to stand out (above level), to surpass, to seize		5
选拔	xuǎnbá	vb.	to select the best		6
拜	**bài**		**to do obeisance, to bow**	手 64.5	5
拜访	bàifǎng	vb.	to pay a visit, to call on		5
崇拜	chóngbài	vb.	to worship, to adore		6
礼拜	lǐbài	n.	week, religious service, worship		5
抱	**bào**		**to embrace, to hold in arms**	手 64.5	4
抱	bào	vb.	to hold, to carry (in one's arms), to hug, to embrace, to surround, to cherish, (coll.) (of clothes) to fit nicely		4
抱歉	bàoqiàn	vb.	to be sorry, to feel apologetic, sorry!		6
抱怨	bàoyuàn	vb.	to complain, to grumble, to harbour a complaint, to feel dissatisfied		5
拥抱	yōngbào	vb.	to embrace, to hug		5
拨	**bō**		**to move, to dispel**	手 64.5	6
拨打	bōdǎ	vb.	to call, to dial		6
拆	**chāi**		**to break up, to split apart**	手 64.5	5
拆	chāi	vb.	to tear open, to tear down, to tear apart, to open		5
拆除	chāichú	vb.	to tear down, to demolish, to dismantle, to remove		5
拆迁	chāiqiān	vb.	to demolish a building and relocate the inhabitants		6

抽	**chōu**		**to draw out, to pull out**	手 64.5	4
抽	chōu	vb.	to draw out, to pull out from in between, to remove part of the whole, (of certain plants) to sprout or bud, to whip or thrash		4
抽奖	chōujiǎng	vb.	to draw a prize, a lottery, a raffle		4
抽烟	chōuyān	vb.	to smoke (a cigarette, tobacco)		4
担	**dān**		**to carry, to bear**	手 64.5	4
担保	dānbǎo	vb.	to guarantee, to vouch for		4
担任	dānrèn	vb.	to hold a governmental office or post, to assume office of, to take charge of, to serve as		4
担心	dānxīn	adj.	anxious, worried, uneasy, to worry, to be anxious		4
担忧	dānyōu	vb.	to worry, to be concerned		6
承担	chéngdān	vb.	to undertake, to assume (responsibility etc)		4
负担	fùdān	n.	burden, to bear a burden		4
抵	**dǐ**		**to resist, to oppose**	手 64.5	6
抵达	dǐdá	vb.	to arrive, to reach (a destination)		6
抵抗	dǐkàng	vb.	to resist, resistance		6
拐	**guǎi**		**to turn, to abduct**	手 64.5	6
拐	guǎi	vb.	to turn to, kidnap, to limp, corner		6
拒	**jù**		**to ward off with hand, to defend**	手 64.5	5
拒绝	jùjué	vb.	to refuse, to decline, to reject		5
拉	**lā**		**to pull, to drag**	手 64.5	2
拉	lā	vb.	to pull, to play (a bowed instrument), to drag, to draw, to chat, (coll.) to empty one's bowels		2
拉开	lākāi	vb.	to pull open, to pull apart, to space out, to increase		4
拍	**pāi**		**to clap, to tap**	手 64.5	3
拍	pāi	vb.	to pat, to clap, to slap, to swat, to take (a photo), to shoot (a film), racket (sports), beat (music)		3
拍摄	pāishè	vb.	to film, to shoot (a picture)		5
拍照	pāizhào	vb.	to take a picture		4
球拍	qiúpāi	n.	racket		6
披	**pī**		**to wear, to split**	手 64.5	5
披	pī	vb.	to drape over one's shoulders, to open, to unroll, to split open, to spread out		5
抬	**tái**		**to lift, to carry**	手 64.5	5
抬	tái	vb.	to lift, to raise, (of two or more persons) to carry		5
抬头	táitóu	vb.	to raise one's head, to gain ground, account name, or space for writing the name on checks, bills etc		5
拖	**tuō**		**to drag, to delay**	手 64.5	6
拖	tuō	vb.	to drag, to tow, to trail, to hang down, to mop (the floor), to delay, to drag on		6
拖鞋	tuōxié	n.	slippers, sandals, flip-flops		6
押	**yā**		**to pledge, to deposit**	手 64.5	5
押金	yājīn	n.	deposit, down payment		5

拥	**yōng**		to embrace, to hug	手 64.5	5
拥抱	yōngbào	vb.	to embrace, to hug		5
拥有	yōngyǒu	vb.	to have, to possess		5
择	**zé**		to select, to choose	手 64.5	4
选择	xuǎnzé	vb.	to select, to pick, choice, option, alternative		4
招	**zhāo**		to beckon, to summon	手 64.5	4
招	zhāo	vb.	to recruit, to provoke, to beckon, to incur, to infect, contagious, a move (chess), a manoeuvre, device, trick, to confess		6
招生	zhāo shēng	vb.	to enrol new students, to get students		5
招手	zhāo shǒu	vb.	to wave, to beckon		5
招呼	- zhāohu	vb.	to call out to, to greet, to say hello to, to inform, to take care of, to take care that one does not		4
招聘	zhāopìn	vb.	to invite applications for a job, to recruit		6
按	**àn**		to put hand on, to press with hand	手 64.6	3
按	àn	vb.	to press, to push, to leave aside or shelve, to control, to restrain, to keep one's hand on, to check or refer to, according to		3
按摩	ànmó	n.	massage, to massage		5
按时	ànshí	adv.	on time, before deadline, on schedule		4
按照	ànzhào	prep.	according to, in accordance with, in the light of, on the basis of		3
持	**chí**		to sustain, to support	手 64.6	3
持续	chíxù	vb.	to continue, to persist, to last, sustainable, preservation		3
持有	chíyǒu	vb.	to hold (passport, views etc)		6
保持	bǎochí	vb.	to keep, to maintain, to hold, to preserve		3
坚持	jiānchí	vb.	to persevere with, to persist in, to insist on		3
维持	wéichí	vb.	to keep, to maintain, to preserve		4
支持	zhīchí	vb.	to be in favour of, to support, to back, support, backing, to stand by		3
主持	zhǔchí	vb.	to take charge of, to manage or direct, to preside over, to uphold, to stand for (justice etc)		3
主持人	zhǔchírén	n.	TV or radio presenter		6
挡	**dǎng**		to obstruct, to impede	手 64.6	5
挡	dǎng	vb.	to block, to hinder, gear, equipment		5
挂	**guà**		to hang, to suspend	手 64.6	3
挂	guà	vb.	to hang or suspend (from a hook etc), to hang up (the phone), (of a line) to be dead, to be worried or concerned, to register or record, m.w. for set or line of objects		3
挥	**huī**		to direct, to wipe away	手 64.6	4
发挥	fāhuī	vb.	to display, to exhibit, to bring out implicit or innate qualities, to express (a thought or moral), to develop (an idea), to elaborate (on a theme)		4
指挥	zhǐhuī	vb.	to conduct, to command, to direct, conductor (of an orchestra)		4
挤	**jǐ**		to crowd, to squeeze	手 64.6	5
挤	jǐ	vb.	to crowd in, to cram in, to force others aside, to press, to squeeze, to find (time in one's busy schedule)		5

括	**kuò**		to include, to enclose	手 64.6	4
括号	kuòhào	n.	parentheses, brackets		4
包括	bāokuò	vb.	to comprise, to include, to involve, to incorporate, to consist of		4
概括	gàikuò	vb.	to summarize, to generalize, briefly		4
拿	**ná**		to take, to hold	手 64.6	1
拿	ná	vb.	to hold, to seize, to catch, to apprehend, to take, by means of, (used in the same way as 把 bǎ: to mark the following noun as a direct object)		1
拿出	náchū	vb.	to take out, to put out, to provide, to put forward (a proposal), to come up with (evidence)		2
拿到	nádào	vb.	to get, to obtain		2
拿走	názǒu	vb.	to take away		6
拼	**pīn**		to join together, to link	手 64.6	5
拼	pīn	vb.	to piece together, to join together, to stake all, adventurous, at the risk of one's life, to spell		5
拾	**shí**		to pick up, to collect	手 64.6	5
拾	shí	vb.	to pick up (from ground), to collect, to tidy up, num. ten (on banknotes)		5
收拾	- shōushi	vb.	to put in order, to tidy up, to pack, to repair, (coll.) to sort sb out, to fix sb		5
挑	* **tiāo, tiǎo**		to carry, to choose; to prop up	手 64.6	4
挑	tiāo	vb.	to carry on a shoulder pole, to choose, to pick, to nit-pick		4
挑	• tiǎo	vb.	to prop up, to support, rising stroke in Chinese characters		4
挑选	tiāoxuǎn	vb.	to choose, to select		4
挑战	• tiǎozhàn	vb.	to challenge, challenge		4
挖	**wā**		to dig, to dig out	手 64.6	6
挖	wā	vb.	to dig, to excavate, to scoop out		6
挣	**zhèng**		to strive, to endeavor	手 64.6	5
挣	zhèng	vb.	(coll.) to earn or make, to strive, to endeavor, to struggle		5
挣钱	zhèngqián	vb.	to make money		5
指	**zhǐ**		finger, to point	手 64.6	3
指	zhǐ	n.	finger, toe, to point at or to, to indicate or refer to, to depend on, to count on, (of hair) to stand on end		3
指标	zhǐbiāo	n.	(production) target, quota, index, indicator, sign, signpost, (computing) pointer		5
指出	zhǐchū	vb.	to indicate, to point out		3
指导	zhǐdǎo	vb.	to guide, to give directions, to direct, to coach, guidance, tuition		3
指定	zhǐdìng	vb.	to appoint, to assign, to indicate clearly and with certainty, designated		6
指挥	zhǐhuī	vb.	to conduct, to command, to direct, conductor (of an orchestra)		4
指甲	- zhǐjia	n.	fingernail		5
指示	zhǐshì	vb.	to point out, to indicate, to instruct, directives, instructions		5
指数	zhǐshù	n.	(numerical, statistical) index, (math.) exponent, index, exponential (function, growth)		6
指头	- zhǐtou	n.	finger, toe		6

指责	zhǐzé	vb.	to criticize, to find fault with, to denounce		5
指着	zhǐzhe	vb.	to point		6
手指	shǒuzhǐ	n.	finger		3

挨 * āi, ái — to be (or get) close to; to suffer 手 64.7 6

挨	āi	vb.	to be (or get) close to, to be next to, to press		6
挨着	āizhe	adv.	near		6
挨打	• áidǎ	vb.	to take a beating, to get thrashed, to come under attack		6

捕 bǔ — to arrest, to catch 手 64.7 6

捕	bǔ	vb.	to catch, to seize, to capture, to hunt		6

换 huàn — to change 手 64.7 2

换	huàn	vb.	to exchange, to change (clothes etc), to substitute, to switch, to convert (currency)		2
变换	biànhuàn	vb.	to transform, to convert, to vary, to alternate, a transformation		6
更换	• gēnghuàn	vb.	to replace (a worn-out tire etc), to change (one's address etc)		5
交换	jiāohuàn	vb.	to exchange, to swap, to switch (telecom), commutative (math), to commute		4
转换	zhuǎnhuàn	vb.	to change, to switch, to convert, to transform		5

捡 jiǎn — to pick up 手 64.7 6

捡	jiǎn	vb.	to pick up, to collect, to gather		6

捐 juān — to tax, to contribute 手 64.7 6

捐	juān	n.	tax, contribution, to contribute, to donate, to abandon, to renounce		6
捐款	juānkuǎn	vb.	to donate money, to contribute funds, donation, contribution (of money)		6
捐赠	juānzèng	vb.	to contribute (as a gift), to donate, benefaction		6
捐助	juānzhù	vb.	to donate, to offer (aid), contribution, donation		6

损 sǔn — to diminish, to impair 手 64.7 5

损害	sǔnhài	n.	harm, to damage, to impair		5
损失	sǔnshī	n.	loss, damage		5

挺 tǐng — to stand upright, to straighten 手 64.7 2

挺	tǐng	+ vb.	to stick out (a part of the body), to (physically) straighten up, to support, to withstand, outstanding		2
挺	tǐng	+ adv.	straight, erect, (coll.) quite, very		4
挺好	tǐnghǎo	adj.	very good		2

振 zhèn — to raise, to excite 手 64.7 5

振动	zhèndòng	vb.	to vibrate, to shake, vibration		5

捉 zhuō — to grasp, to clutch, 手 64.7 6

捉	zhuō	vb.	to clutch, to grab, to capture, to seize		6

措 cuò — to place, to collect 手 64.8 4

措施	cuòshī	n.	measure, step		4

掉 diào — to turn, to move 手 64.8 2

掉	diào	vb.	to fall, to drop, to lag behind, to lose, to go missing, to reduce, fall (in prices), to lose (value, weight etc), to wag, to swing		2

| 去掉 | qùdiào | vb. | to get rid of, to exclude, to eliminate, to remove, to delete, to strip out, to extract | | 6 |

接 jiē — to receive, to continue, to catch — 手 64.8 — 2

接	jiē	vb.	to receive, to answer (the phone), to meet or welcome sb, to connect, to catch, to join, to extend, to take one's turn on duty		2
接到	jiē dào	vb.	to receive (letter etc)		2
接触	jiēchù	vb.	to touch, to contact, access, in touch with		5
接待	jiēdài	vb.	to receive (a visitor), to admit (allow sb to enter)		3
接近	jiējìn	vb.	to approach, to get close to		3
接连	jiēlián	adv.	on end, in a row, in succession		5
接收	jiēshōu	vb.	to receive, to accept, to admit, to take over (e.g. a factory), to expropriate, reception (of transmitted signal)		6
接受	jiēshòu	vb.	to accept, to receive		2
接着	jiēzhe	vb.	to catch and hold on, to continue, to go on to do sth, to follow, to carry on, then, after that, subsequently, to proceed, to ensue, in turn, in one's turn		2
接下来	jiēxiàlái	vb.	to accept, to take, next, following		2
间接	• jiànjiē	adj.	indirect, second-hand (opp. 直接 zhíjiē: direct, immediate)		5
连接	liánjiē	vb.	to link, to join, to attach, connection, a link (on web page)		5
迎接	yíngjiē	vb.	to meet, to welcome, to greet		3
直接	zhíjiē	adj.	direct (opp. 间接 jiànjiē: indirect), immediate, straightforward		2

据 jù — to occupy, to take possession of — 手 64.8 — 3

据	jù	n.	evidence, according to, to act in accordance with, to depend on, to seize, to occupy		6
据说	jùshuō	vb.	it is said that, reportedly		3
根据	gēnjù	n.	according to, based on, basis, foundation		4
数据	shùjù	n.	data, numbers, digital		4
依据	yījù	n.	basis, foundation, according to		5
占据	zhànjù	vb.	to occupy, to hold		6
证据	zhèngjù	n.	evidence, proof, testimony		3

控 kòng — to accuse, to charge, to control — 手 64.8 — 5

| 控制 | kòngzhì | vb. | to control, to exercise control over, to contain | | 5 |

排 pái — row, rank, line — 手 64.8 — 2

排	pái	+ n.	a row, a line, platoon, raft, m.w. for lines, rows etc		2
排	pái	+ vb.	to set in order, to arrange, to line up, to eliminate, to drain		3
排队	pái duì	vb.	to line up		2
排除	páichú	vb.	to eliminate, to remove, to exclude, to rule out		5
排列	páiliè	vb.	to arrange in order, (math.) permutation		4
排名	páimíng	vb.	to rank (1st, 2nd etc), ranking		3
排球	páiqiú	n.	volleyball		2
排行榜	páixíngbǎng	n.	the charts (of best-sellers), table of ranking		6
安排	ānpái	vb.	to arrange, to plan, to set up, arrangements, plans		3

授 shòu — to give to, to transmit, to confer — 手 64.8 — 4

| 教授 | jiàoshòu | n. | professor, to instruct, to lecture on | | 4 |

探 tàn — to find, to search for — 手 64.8 — 6

| 探索 | tànsuǒ | vb. | to explore, to probe | | 6 |

探讨	tàntǎo	vb.	to investigate, to probe		6
掏	**tāo**		**to take out, to pull out, to clean out**	手 64.8	6
掏	tāo	vb.	to take out, to dig out, to fish out, to pull out, to clean out		6
推	**tuī**		**to push, to expel, to push forward**	手 64.8	2
推	tuī	vb.	to push, to cut, to refuse, to reject, to decline, to shirk (responsibility), to put off, to delay, to push forward, to nominate, to elect, massage		2
推迟	tuīchí	vb.	to postpone, to put off, to defer		4
推出	tuīchū	vb.	to push out, to release, to launch, to publish, to recommend		6
推动	tuīdòng	vb.	to push (for acceptance of a plan), to push forward, to promote, to actuate		3
推广	tuīguǎng	vb.	to extend, to spread, to popularize, generalization, promotion (of a product etc)		3
推进	tuījìn	vb.	to impel, to carry forward, to push on, to advance, to drive forward		3
推开	tuīkāi	vb.	to push open (a gate etc), to push away, to reject, to decline		3
推销	tuīxiāo	vb.	to market, to sell		4
推行	tuīxíng	vb.	to put into effect, to carry out		5
掌	**zhǎng**		**palm of hand, sole of foot, paw**	手 64.8	5
掌声	zhǎngshēng	n.	applause		6
掌握	zhǎngwò	vb.	to grasp (often fig.), to control, to seize (initiative, opportunity, destiny), to master, to know well, to understand something well and know how to use it, fluency		5
鼓掌	gǔ zhǎng	vb.	to applaud, to clap		5
插	**chā**		**to insert, to stick into, to plant**	手 64.9	5
插	chā	vb.	to insert, to stick in, to pierce		5
揭	**jiē**		**to divulge, to uncover**	手 64.9	6
揭	jiē	vb.	to divulge, to uncover, to lift (the lid), to expose, surname Jie		6
描	**miáo**		**to copy, to trace, to sketch**	手 64.9	4
描述	miáoshù	vb.	to describe, description		4
描写	miáoxiě	vb.	to describe, to depict, to portray, description		4
搜	**sōu**		**to search, to seek, to investigate**	手 64.9	5
搜	sōu	vb.	to search		5
搜索	sōusuǒ	vb.	to search (a place), to search (a database), to search for (sth)		5
提	**tí**		**to hold in hand, to carry**	手 64.9	2
提	tí	vb.	to carry, to lift, to raise (an issue)		2
提倡	tíchàng	vb.	to promote, to advocate		5
提出	tíchū	vb.	to raise (an issue), to propose, to put forward, to suggest, to post (on a website), to withdraw (cash)		2
提到	tídào	vb.	to mention, to raise (a subject), to refer to		2
提高	tígāo	vb.	to raise, to increase, to improve		2
提供	tígōng	vb.	to offer, to supply, to provide, to furnish		4
提交	tíjiāo	vb.	to submit (a report etc), to refer (a problem) to sb		6
提起	tíqǐ	vb.	to mention, to speak of, to lift, to pick up, to arouse, to raise (a topic, a heavy weight, one's fist, one's spirits etc)		5
提前	tíqián	vb.	to shift to an earlier date, to do sth ahead of time, in advance		3

提升	tíshēng	vb.	to promote, to upgrade		6
提示	tíshì	vb.	to point out, to remind (sb of sth), to suggest, suggestion, tip, reminder, notice		5
提问	tíwèn	vb.	to question, to quiz, to grill		3
提醒	tíxǐng	vb.	to remind, to call attention to, to warn of		4
前提	qiántí	n.	premise, precondition, prerequisite		5
握	**wò**		**to grasp, to hold fast**	手 64.9	3
握	wò	vb.	to hold, to grasp, to clench (one's fist), to master, m.w: a handful		5
握手	wòshǒu	vb.	to shake hands		3
把握	bǎwò	vb.	to grasp (also fig.), to seize, to hold, assurance, certainty, sure (of the outcome)		3
掌握	zhǎngwò	vb.	to grasp (often fig.), to control, to seize (initiative, opportunity, destiny), to master, to know well, to understand something well and know how to use it, fluency		5
援	**yuán**		**to aid, to assist, to lead, to cite**	手 64.9	6
援助	yuánzhù	vb.	to help, to support, to aid, aid, assistance		6
救援	jiùyuán	vb.	to save, to support, to help, to assist		6
支援	zhīyuán	vb.	to provide assistance, to support, to back		6
摆	**bǎi**		**to put, to display, to swing**	手 64.10	4
摆	bǎi	vb.	to arrange, to place, to exhibit, to move to and fro, a pendulum		4
摆动	bǎidòng	vb.	to sway, to swing, to move back and forth, to oscillate		4
摆脱	bǎituō	vb.	to break away from, to cast off (old ideas etc), to get rid of, to break away (from), to break out (of), to free oneself from		4
搬	**bān**		**to transfer, to move, to remove**	手 64.10	3
搬	bān	vb.	to move (i.e. relocate oneself), to move (sth relatively heavy or bulky), to shift, to copy indiscriminately		3
搬家	bānjiā	vb.	to move house, removal		3
搭	**dā**		**to join together, to attach to**	手 64.10	6
搭	dā	vb.	to put up, to build (scaffolding), to hang (clothes on a pole), to connect, to join, to arrange in pairs, to match		6
搭档	dādàng	vb.	to cooperate, partner		6
搭配	dāpèi	vb.	to pair up, to match, to arrange in pairs, to add sth into a group		6
搞	**gǎo**		**to clear, to clarify**	手 64.10	5
搞	gǎo	vb.	to do, to make, to go in for, to set up, to get hold of, to take care of		5
搞好	gǎohǎo	vb.	to do well at, to do a good job		5
摄	**shè**		**to take in, to absorb, to act as deputy**	手 64.10	5
摄影	shè yǐng	vb.	to take a photograph, photography, to shoot (a movie)		5
摄像	shèxiàng	vb.	to videotape		5
摄像机	shèxiàngjī	n.	video camera		5
摄影师	shèyǐngshī	n.	photographer, cameraman		5
拍摄	pāishè	vb.	to film, to shoot (a picture)		5
摇	**yáo**		**to shake, to wave, to sweep**	手 64.10	4
摇	yáo	vb.	to shake, to wave, to rock, to wag, to swing, to wave, to sweep, surname Yao		4
摇头	yáotóu	vb.	to shake one's head		5

动摇	dòngyáo	vb.	to sway, to waver, to rock, to rattle, to destabilize, to pose a challenge		4

摩 mó — to rub, to scour, to grind, friction 手 64.11 5

摩擦	mócā	n.	friction, rubbing, chafing, fig. disharmony, conflict		5
摩托	mótuō	n.	motor (loanword), motorbike		5
按摩	ànmó	n.	massage, to massage		5

摸 mō — to gently touch with hand, to caress 手 64.11 4

摸	mō	vb.	to feel with the hand, to touch, to stroke, to grope, to steal, to abstract		4

摔 shuāi — to fall to the ground, to stumble 手 64.11 5

摔	shuāi	vb.	to throw down, to fall, to drop and break		5
摔倒	·shuāidǎo	vb.	to fall down, to slip and fall, to throw sb to the ground		5

摘 zhāi — to take, to borrow, to pick 手 64.11 5

摘	zhāi	vb.	to take, to borrow, to pick (flowers, fruit etc), to pluck, to select, to remove, to take off (glasses, hat etc)		5

播 bō — to sow, to spread 手 64.12 3

播	bō	vb.	to sow, to scatter, to spread, to broadcast		6
播出	bōchū	vb.	to broadcast, to air (a TV program etc)		3
播放	bōfàng	vb.	to broadcast, to transmit		3
传播	chuánbō	vb.	to disseminate, to propagate, to spread		3
广播	guǎngbō	n.	broadcast		3
直播	zhíbō	adj.	(TV, radio) to broadcast live, live broadcast, (Internet) to livestream, (agriculture) direct seeding		3

撤 chè — to omit, to remove, to withdraw 手 64.12 6

撤离	chèlí	vb.	to withdraw from, to evacuate		6
撤销	chèxiāo	vb.	to repeal, to revoke, (computing) to undo		6

撑 chēng — to prop up, to support 手 64.12 6

撑	chēng	vb.	to support, to prop up, to push or move with a pole, to maintain, to open or unfurl, to fill to bursting point, brace, stay, support		6
支撑	zhīchēng	vb.	to prop up, to support, strut, brace		6

撞 zhuàng — to knock against, to bump into 手 64.12 5

撞	zhuàng	vb.	to knock against, to bump into, to run into, to meet by accident		5

操 cāo — to conduct, to run, to control 手 64.13 4

操场	cāochǎng	n.	playground, sports field, drill ground		4
操纵	cāozòng	vb.	to operate, to control, to rig, to manipulate		6
操作	cāozuò	vb.	to work, to operate, to manipulate		4
体操	tǐcāo	n.	gymnastics, gymnastic		4

擦 cā — to wipe, to erase, to polish 手 64.14 4

擦	cā	vb.	to wipe, to erase, rubbing (a brush stroke in painting), to clean, to polish		4
摩擦	mócā	n.	friction, rubbing, chafing, fig. disharmony, conflict		5

支	**zhī**		**branch**	**65**
支	**zhī**		to disperse, to pay, to support	支 65.0 3
支	zhī	+ *m.w.*	m.w. for long, narrow objects, branch	3
支	zhī	+ *vb.*	to support, to put up, to pay	4
支撑	zhīchēng	*vb.*	to prop up, to support, strut, brace	6
支持	zhīchí	*vb.*	to be in favour of, to support, to back, support, backing, to stand by	3
支出	zhīchū	*vb.*	to spend, to pay out, expense	5
支付	zhīfù	*vb.*	to pay (money)	3
支配	zhīpèi	*vb.*	to control, to dominate, to allocate	5
支援	zhīyuán	*vb.*	to provide assistance, to support, to back	6

攴	**pū**		**rap**	**攵 66**
收	**shōu**		to gather together, to collect	攴 66.2 2
收	shōu	*vb.*	to receive, to accept, to collect, to put away, to restrain, to stop, in care of (used on address line after name)	2
收藏	shōucáng	*vb.*	to hoard, to collect, collection, to bookmark (Internet)	6
收到	shōudào	*vb.*	to receive	2
收费	shōufèi	*vb.*	to charge a fee	3
收购	shōugòu	*vb.*	to purchase (from various places), to acquire (a company)	5
收回	shōuhuí	*vb.*	to regain, to retake, to take back, to withdraw, to revoke	4
收获	shōuhuò	*vb.*	to harvest, to reap, to gain, crop, harvest, profit, gain, bonus, reward	4
收集	shōují	*vb.*	to gather, to collect	5
收看	shōukàn	*vb.*	to watch (a TV program)	3
收取	shōuqǔ	*vb.*	to receive, to collect	6
收入	shōurù	*vb.*	to take in, income, revenue	2
收拾	- shōushi	*vb.*	to put in order, to tidy up, to pack, to repair, (coll.) to sort sb out, to fix sb	5
收听	shōutīng	*vb.*	to listen to (a radio broadcast)	3
收养	shōuyǎng	*vb.*	to take in and care for (an elderly person, a dog etc), to adopt (a child), adoption	6
收益	shōuyì	*n.*	earnings, profit	4
收音机	shōuyīnjī	*n.*	radio	3
丰收	fēngshōu	*n.*	bumper harvest	5
回收	huíshōu	*vb.*	to recycle, to reclaim, to retrieve, to recover, to recall (a defective product)	5
接收	jiēshōu	*vb.*	to receive, to accept, to admit, to take over (e.g. a factory), to expropriate, reception (of transmitted signal)	6
没收	• mòshōu	*vb.*	to confiscate, to seize	6
吸收	xīshōu	*vb.*	to absorb, to assimilate, to ingest, to recruit	4

改	**gǎi**		to change, to improve	攴 66.3 2
改	gǎi	*vb.*	to change, to alter, to transform, to correct	2
改变	gǎibiàn	*vb.*	to change, to alter, to transform	2
改革	gǎigé	*n.*	reform	5
改进	gǎijìn	*n.*	improvement, to improve, to make better	3
改善	gǎishàn	*vb.*	to make better, to improve	4

改造	gǎizào	vb.	to transform, to reform, to remodel, to remould	3
改正	gǎizhèng	vb.	to correct, to amend, to put right, correction	4
改装	gǎizhuāng	vb.	to change one's costume, to repackage, to remodel, to refit, to modify, to convert	6
修改	xiūgǎi	vb.	to amend, to alter, to modify	3

攻 gōng — to attack, to assault, to criticize   攴 66.3   6

| 攻击 | gōngjī | vb. | to attack, to accuse, to charge, an attack (terrorist or military) | 6 |
| 进攻 | jìngōng | vb. | to attack, to assault, to go on the offensive, attack, assault, offense (sports) | 6 |

放 fàng — to put, to release   攴 66.4   1

放	fàng	vb.	to put, to place, to release, to free, to let go, to let out, to set off (fireworks)	1
放假	fàng jià	vb.	to have a holiday or vacation	1
放大	fàngdà	vb.	to enlarge, to magnify	5
放到	fàngdào	vb.	to put to	3
放弃	fàngqì	vb.	to renounce, to abandon, to give up	5
放松	fàngsōng	vb.	to loosen, to relax	4
放下	fàngxià	vb.	to lay down, to put down, to let go of, to relinquish, to set aside, to lower (the blinds etc)	2
放心	fàngxīn	vb.	to feel relieved, to feel reassured, to be at ease	2
放学	fàngxué	vb.	to dismiss students at the end of the school day	1
播放	bōfàng	vb.	to broadcast, to transmit	3
发放	fāfàng	vb.	to provide, to give, to grant	6
解放	jiěfàng	vb.	to liberate, to emancipate, liberation, refers to the Communists' victory over the Nationalists in 1949	5
开放	kāifàng	vb.	to bloom, to open, to be open (to the public), to open up (to the outside), to be open-minded	3

政 zhèng — government, political affairs   攴 66.4   4

政策	zhèngcè	n.	policy	6
政党	zhèngdǎng	n.	political party	6
政府	zhèngfǔ	n.	government	4
政权	zhèngquán	n.	regime, political power	6
政治	zhèngzhì	n.	politics, political	4

故 gù — happening, reason, former   攴 66.5   2

故事	gùshi	n.	old practice	2
故乡	gùxiāng	n.	home, homeland, native place	3
故意	gùyì	adv.	deliberately, on purpose	2
故障	gùzhàng	n.	malfunction, breakdown, defect, shortcoming, fault, failure, impediment, error, bug (in software)	6
事故	shìgù	n.	accident	3
缘故	yuángù	n.	reason, cause	6

效 xiào — result, effect   攴 66.6   3

效果	xiàoguǒ	n.	result, effect, efficacy, (theatre) sound or visual effects	3
效率	xiàolǜ	n.	efficiency	4
成效	chéngxiào	n.	effect, result	5
无效	wúxiào	vb.	not valid, ineffective, in vain	6

有效	yǒuxiào	adj.	effective, in effect, valid		3
教	* **jiào, jiāo**		**teaching, religion; to teach**	攴 66.7	1
教	• jiāo	vb.	to teach, to instruct		1
教材	jiàocái	n.	teaching material		3
教练	jiàoliàn	n.	instructor, sports coach, trainer		3
教师	jiàoshī	n.	teacher		2
教室	jiàoshì	n.	classroom		2
教授	jiàoshòu	n.	professor, to instruct, to lecture on		4
教堂	jiàotáng	n.	church, chapel		6
教学	jiàoxué	vb.	to teach (as a professor)		2
教训	jiàoxùn	vb.	to provide guidance, to lecture sb, to upbraid, a talking-to, a bitter lesson		4
教育	jiàoyù	vb.	to educate, to teach, education		2
教学楼	jiàoxuélóu	n.	teaching block, school building		1
教育部	jiàoyùbù	n.	Ministry of Education		6
道教	dàojiào	n.	Taoism, Daoism		6
佛教	fójiào	n.	Buddhism, Buddhist		6
请教	qǐngjiào	vb.	to ask for guidance, to consult		3
宗教	zōngjiào	n.	religion		6
基督教	jīdūjiào	n.	Christianity		6
救	**jiù**		**to save, to rescue, to help**	攴 66.7	3
救	jiù	vb.	to save, to assist, to rescue, to aid, to help		3
救灾	jiù zāi	vb.	to relieve disaster, to help disaster victims		5
救命	jiùmìng	vb.	to save sb's life, (intj.) help!, save me!		6
救援	jiùyuán	vb.	to save, to support, to help, to assist		6
救助	jiùzhù	vb.	to help sb in trouble, aid, assistance		6
急救	jíjiù	n.	first aid, emergency treatment		6
抢救	qiǎngjiù	vb.	to rescue		5
敏	**mǐn**		**fast, quick, clever, smart**	攴 66.7	5
敏感	mǐngǎn	adj.	sensitive, susceptible		5
过敏	guòmǐn	vb.	oversensitive, allergic, allergy		5
敢	**gǎn**		**to dare, to venture, bold, brave**	攴 66.8	3
敢	gǎn	vb.	to dare, daring, (polite) may I venture		3
敢于	gǎnyú	vb.	to have the courage to do sth, to dare to, bold in		6
勇敢	yǒnggǎn	adj.	brave, courageous		4
不敢当	bù gǎndāng	phr.	(lit.) I dare not (accept the honour), (fig.) I don't deserve your praise, you flatter me		5
散	* **sàn, sǎn**		**to scatter, to disperse; scattered**	攴 66.8	3
散	• sǎn	adj.	scattered, loose, to come loose, to fall apart, leisurely, powdered medicine		4
散	sàn	vb.	to break up, to disperse, to scatter		5
散文	• sǎnwén	n.	prose, essay		5
散步	sàn bù	vb.	to take a walk, to go for a walk		3
分散	fēnsàn	vb.	to scatter, to disperse, to distribute		4

敬	**jìng**		to respect, to honour, respectfully	攴 66.9	5
尊敬	zūnjìng	vb.	to respect, to revere		5
数	**shù**		number, several	攴 66.9	2
数	shù	n.	number, amount, several, a few, fate, destiny		2
数据	shùjù	n.	data, numbers, digital		4
数量	shùliàng	n.	amount, quantity		3
数码	shùmǎ	n.	number, numerals, figures, digital, amount, numerical code		4
数目	shùmù	n.	amount, number		5
数字	shùzì	n.	numeral, digit, number, figure, amount, digital (electronics etc)		2
次数	cìshù	n.	number of times, frequency, order number (in a series), power (math.), degree of a polynomial (math.)		6
多数	duōshù	n.	majority, most		2
分数	fēnshù	n.	(exam) grade, mark, score, fraction		2
人数	rénshù	n.	number of people		2
少数	shǎoshù	n.	small number, few, minority		2
岁数	- suìshu	n.	age (number of years old)		6
无数	wúshù	adj.	countless, numberless, innumerable		4
指数	zhǐshù	n.	(numerical, statistical) index, (math.) exponent, index, exponential (function, growth)		6
总数	zǒngshù	n.	total, sum, aggregate		5
大多数	dàduōshù	n.	(great) majority		2
绝大多数	juédàduōshù	n.	absolute majority, overwhelming majority		6
敲	**qiāo**		to strike, to beat, to pound	攴 66.10	5
敲	qiāo	vb.	to hit, to strike, to hammer, to tap, to rap, to knock, to rip sb off, to overcharge		5
敲门	qiāomén	vb.	to knock on a door		5
整	**zhěng**		orderly, neat, tidy, whole	攴 66.11	3
整	zhěng	adj.	in good order, whole (opp. 零 líng: fragmentary), complete, entire, in order, orderly, to repair, to mend, to renovate, (coll.) to fix sb, to give sb a hard time, to mess with sb		3
整顿	zhěngdùn	vb.	to tidy up, to reorganize, to consolidate, to rectify		6
整个	zhěnggè	adj.	whole, entire, total		3
整理	zhěnglǐ	vb.	to arrange, to tidy up, to sort out, to straighten out, to list systematically, to collate (data, files), to pack (luggage)		3
整齐	zhěngqí	adj.	orderly, neat, even, tidy		3
整体	zhěngtǐ	n.	whole entity, entire body, synthesis, as a whole (situation, construction, team etc), global, macrocosm, integral, holistic, whole		3
整天	zhěngtiān	n.	all day long, whole day		3
整整	zhěngzhěng	adj.	whole, full		3
整治	zhěngzhì	vb.	to bring under control, to regulate, to restore to good condition, (coll.) to fix (a person), to prepare (a meal etc)		6
调整	• tiáozhěng	vb.	to adjust, adjustment, revision		3
完整	wánzhěng	adj.	complete, intact		3

文	**wén**		**script**		**67**
文	wén		literature, culture, writing	文 67.0	1
文化	wénhuà	n.	culture, civilization, cultural		3
文件	wénjiàn	n.	document, file		3
文明	wénmíng	n.	civilized, civilization, culture		3
文学	wénxué	n.	literature		3
文艺	wényì	n.	literature and art		5
文娱	wényú	n.	cultural recreation, entertainment		6
文章	wénzhāng	n.	article, essay, literary works, writings, hidden meaning		3
文字	wénzì	n.	characters, script, writing, written language, writing (form or style), phraseology		3
课文	kèwén	n.	text		1
论文	lùnwén	n.	paper, treatise, thesis		4
散文	• sǎnwén	n.	prose, essay		5
天文	tiānwén	n.	astronomy		5
外文	wàiwén	n.	foreign language (written)		3
英文	yīngwén	n.	English (language)		2
中文	zhōngwén	n.	Chinese (language)		1
作文	zuò wén	vb.	to write an essay, composition (student essay)		2
斗	**dǒu**		**dipper**		**68**
斗	dòu		Chinese peck, liquid measure	斗 68.0	4
斗争	dòuzhēng	n.	a struggle, fight, battle		6
奋斗	fèndòu	vb.	to strive, to struggle		4
战斗	zhàndòu	vb.	to fight, to engage in combat, struggle, battle		4
料	**liào**		**material, ingredients**	斗 68.6	4
料	liào	+ n.	material, stuff, grain		6
料	liào	+ vb.	to expect, to anticipate, to guess		6
不料	bùliào	conj.	unexpectedly, to one's surprise		6
材料	cáiliào	n.	material, data, makings, stuff		4
燃料	ránliào	n.	fuel		4
塑料	sùliào	n.	plastics		4
饮料	yǐnliào	n.	drink, beverage		5
原料	yuánliào	n.	raw material		4
资料	zīliào	n.	material, resources, data, information, profile (Internet)		4
塑料袋	sùliàodài	n.	plastic bag		4
斜	**xié**		**slanting, sloping**	斗 68.7	5
斜	xié	adj.	inclined, slanting, oblique, tilting		5

斤 jīn axe 69

斤	**jīn**		a catty: weight equal to 500 g	斤 69.0	2
斤	jīn	n.	catty, (PRC) weight equal to 500 g, (Tw) weight equal to 600 g, (HK, Malaysia, Singapore) slightly over 604 g		2
公斤	gōngjīn	m.w.	kilogram (kg)		2
断	**duàn**		**to sever, to cut off**	斤 69.7	3
断	duàn	vb.	to break, to snap, to cut off, to give up or abstain from sth, to judge, (usu. used in the negative) absolutely, definitely, decidedly		3
不断	búduàn	adv.	unceasing, uninterrupted, continuous, constant		3
打断	dǎduàn	vb.	to interrupt, to break off, to break (a bone)		6
判断	pànduàn	vb.	to judge, to determine, judgment		3
诊断	zhěnduàn	n.	diagnosis, to diagnose		5
中断	zhōngduàn	vb.	to cut short, to break off, to discontinue, to interrupt		5
新	**xīn**		**new, recent, fresh**	斤 69.9	1
新	xīn	adj.	new, (opp. 老 lǎo: old, 旧 jiù: past), fresh, newly, recently		1
新郎	xīnláng	n.	bridegroom, groom		4
新年	xīnnián	n.	New Year		1
新娘	xīnniáng	n.	bride		4
新人	xīnrén	n.	newcomer, fresh talent, newlywed, esp. new bride, bride and groom, (palaeoanthropology) Homo sapiens		6
新闻	xīnwén	n.	news		2
新鲜	xīnxiān	adj.	fresh (experience, food etc), freshness, novel, uncommon		4
新兴	xīnxìng	adj.	rising, up and coming, newly developing		6
新型	xīnxíng	adj.	new type, new kind		4
重新	• chóngxīn	adv.	again, once more, re-		2
创新	chuàngxīn	vb.	to bring forth new ideas, to blaze new trails, innovation		3
革新	géxīn	vb.	to innovate, innovation		6
更新	• gēngxīn	vb.	to replace the old with new, to renew, to renovate, to upgrade, to update, to regenerate		5
全新	quánxīn	adj.	all new, completely new		6

方 fāng square 70

方	**fāng**		a square, rectangle, a region	方 70.0	1
方	fāng	n.	square, direction, side, method, surname Fang		4
方案	fāng'àn	n.	plan, program (for action etc), proposal, proposed bill		4
方便	fāngbiàn	adj.	convenient, suitable, to facilitate, to make things easy, having money to spare, (euphemism) to relieve oneself		2
方法	fāngfǎ	n.	method, way, means		2
方面	fāngmiàn	n.	respect, aspect, field, side		2
方式	fāngshì	n.	way, manner, style, mode, pattern		3
方向	fāngxiàng	n.	direction, orientation, path to follow		2
方针	fāngzhēn	n.	policy, guidelines		4
方便面	fāngbiànmiàn	n.	instant noodles		2
北方	běifāng	n.	north, the northern part a country, China north of the Yellow River		2

比方	- bǐfang	n.	analogy, instance, for instance		5
大方	- dàfang	n.	expert, scholar, mother earth, a type of green tea		4
地方	• dìfāng	n.	region, regional (away from the central administration), local		4
地方	• dìfang	n.	place, space, room, part (respect)		1
东方	dōngfāng	n.	the East, the Orient, two-character surname Dongfang		2
对方	duìfāng	n.	counterpart, other person involved, opposite side, other side, receiving party		3
官方	guānfāng	n.	government, official (approved or issued by an authority)		4
南方	nánfāng	n.	south, the southern part of the country, the South		2
平方	píngfāng	m.w.	square (as in square foot, square mile, square root)		4
前方	qiánfāng	n.	ahead, the front		6
双方	shuāngfāng	n.	bilateral, both sides, both parties involved		3
西方	xīfāng	n.	the West, the Occident, Western countries		2
远方	yuǎnfāng	n.	far away, a distant location		6
多方面	duōfāngmiàn	adj.	many-sided, in many aspects		6
平方米	píngfāngmǐ	m.w.	square meter		6
一方面	yīfāngmiàn	conj.	on the one hand…, on the other hand…		3
另一方面	lìngyīfāngmiàn	phr.	on the other hand, another aspect		3

施 shī — to grant, to bestow — 方 70.5 — 4

措施	cuòshī	n.	measure, step	4
设施	shèshī	n.	facilities, installation	4
实施	shíshī	vb.	to implement, to carry out	4

旅 lǚ — trip, journey — 方 70.6 — 2

旅店	lǚdiàn	n.	inn, small hotel	6
旅馆	lǚguǎn	n.	hotel	3
旅客	lǚkè	n.	traveller, tourist	2
旅行	lǚxíng	vb.	to travel, journey, trip	2
旅游	lǚyóu	n.	trip, journey, tourism, travel, tour, to travel	2
旅行社	lǚxíngshè	n.	travel agency	3

旁 páng — side, by side, close by — 方 70.6 — 1

旁	páng	n.	one side, other, different, lateral component of a Chinese character (such as 刂 dāo, 亻 rén etc)	5
旁边	pángbiān	n.	lateral, side, to the side, beside	1

旋 xuán — to revolve, to move in orbit — 方 70.7 — 6

旋转	xuánzhuǎn	vb.	to rotate, to revolve, to spin, to whirl	6

族 zú — a family clan, ethnic group, tribe — 方 70.7 — 3

族	zú	+ n.	clan, race, nationality, ethnicity, tribe	6
族	zú	+ n.	a group of things (or people) with common features, a social group (e.g. 上班族 shàngbānzú: group of office workers)	6
民族	mínzú	n.	nationality, ethnic group	3
中华民族	zhōnghuá mínzú	n.	the Chinese people	3

旗 qí — banner, flag, streamer — 方 70.10 — 6

国旗	guóqí	n.	flag (of a country)	6

无 wú not 无 71

无 wú not to have, negative 无 71.0 4

无	wú	vb.	not to have, no, none, not, to lack, un-, -less	4
无法	wú fǎ	vb.	unable, incapable	4
无边	wúbiān	vb.	without boundary, not bordered	6
无关	wúguān	vb.	unrelated, having nothing to do (with sth else)	6
无聊	wúliáo	adj.	bored, boring, senseless	4
无论	wúlùn	conj.	no matter what or how, regardless of whether...	4
无奈	wúnài	vb.	to have no alternative, frustrated, exasperated, helpless, (conjunction) but unfortunately	5
无数	wúshù	adj.	countless, numberless, innumerable	4
无限	wúxiàn	adj.	unlimited, unbounded	4
无效	wúxiào	vb.	not valid, ineffective, in vain	6
无疑	wúyí	vb.	no doubt, undoubtedly	5
无所谓	wúsuǒwèi	vb.	to be indifferent, not to matter, cannot be said to be	4

既 jì already, de facto, since 无 71.5 4

| 既 | jì | adv. | already, since, both... (and...) | 4 |
| 既然 | jìrán | conj. | since, as, this being the case | 4 |

日 rì sun 72

日 rì sun, day, daytime 日 72.0 1

日	rì	n.	sun, solar, day, date, time	1
日报	rìbào	n.	daily newspaper	2
日常	rìcháng	adj.	daily, everyday	3
日记	rìjì	n.	diary	4
日历	rìlì	n.	calendar	4
日期	rìqī	n.	date	1
日夜	rìyè	n.	day and night, around the clock	6
日语	rìyǔ	n.	Japanese (language)	6
日子	rìzi	n.	day, a (calendar) date, days of one's life	2
假日	jiàrì	n.	holiday, non-working day	6
节日	jiérì	n.	holiday, festival	2
今日	jīnrì	n.	today	5
近日	jìnrì	n.	(in) the past few days, recently, (within) the next few days	6
明日	míngrì	n.	tomorrow	6
生日	shēngrì	n.	birthday	1
工作日	gōngzuò rì	n.	workday, working day, weekday	5
节假日	jiéjiàrì	n.	public holiday	6
星期日	xīngqīrì	n.	Sunday	1

旦 dàn dawn, morning, day 日 72.1 5

| 一旦 | yīdàn | adv. | in case (sth happens), if, once (sth happens, then...), when, in a short time, in one day | 5 |
| 元旦 | yuándàn | n. | New Year's Day (Western calendar) | 5 |

旧	**jiù**		**old, ancient**	日 72.1	3
旧	jiù	adj.	old, (opp. 新 xīn: new), former, worn (with age)		3
仍旧	réngjiù	adv.	still (remaining), to remain (the same), yet		5
依旧	yījiù	adj.	as before, still		5
早	**zǎo**		**early, soon, morning**	日 72.2	1
早	zǎo	adj.	early, morning, good morning!, long ago, prematurely		1
早餐	zǎocān	n.	breakfast		2
早晨	- zǎochen	n.	early morning		2
早饭	zǎofàn	n.	breakfast		1
早就	zǎojiù	adj.	already at an earlier time		2
早期	zǎoqī	n.	early period, early phase, early stage		5
早上	- zǎoshang	n.	early morning		1
早晚	zǎowǎn	n.	morning and evening, sooner or later		6
早已	zǎoyǐ	adv.	long ago, for a long time		3
时	**shí**		**time, season, era**	日 72.3	1
时	shí	n.	time, season, current, o'clock, when, surname Shi		3
时而	shí'ér	adv.	occasionally, from time to time		6
时常	shícháng	adv.	often, frequently		5
时代	shídài	n.	age, era, period		3
时光	shíguāng	n.	time, era, period of time		5
时候	- shíhou	n.	time, length of time, moment, period		1
时机	shíjī	n.	fortunate timing, occasion, opportunity		5
时间	shíjiān	n.	time, period		1
时节	shíjié	n.	season, time, particular time		6
时刻	shíkè	n.	time, juncture, moment, period of time		3
时期	shíqī	n.	period, phase		6
时时	shíshí	adv.	often, constantly		6
时事	shíshì	n.	current trends, the present situation, how things are going		5
时装	shízhuāng	n.	fashion, fashionable clothes		6
按时	ànshí	adv.	on time, before deadline, on schedule		4
不时	bùshí	adv.	from time to time, now and then, occasionally, frequently		5
此时	cǐshí	n.	now, this moment		5
当时	dāngshí	n.	then, at that time, while		2
定时	dìngshí	vb.	to fix a time, fixed time, timed (of explosive etc)		6
过时	guòshí	vb.	old-fashioned, out of date, to be later than the time stipulated or agreed upon		6
及时	jíshí	adj.	in time, promptly, without delay, timely		3
临时	línshí	adv.	as the time draws near, at the last moment, temporary, interim, ad hoc		4
平时	píngshí	n.	ordinarily, in normal times, in peacetime		2
随时	suíshí	adv.	at any time, at all times, at the right time		2
同时	tóngshí	adv.	at the same time, simultaneously		2
小时	xiǎoshí	n.	hour		1
学时	xuéshí	n.	class hour, period		4
一时	yīshí	n.	a period of time, a while, for a short while, temporary, momentary, at the same time		6
暂时	zànshí	adj.	temporary, provisional, for the time being		5

这时	zhèshí	phr.	at this time, at this moment, (abbrev. of 这时候 zhè shíhou)		2
准时	zhǔnshí	adj.	on time, punctual, on schedule		4
那时候	- nàshíhou	n.	then, at that time, in those days (abbrev. 那时 nàshí: of course)		2
小时候	- xiǎoshíhou	n.	in one's childhood		2
有时候	- yǒu shíhou	adv.	sometimes		1
畅	**chàng**		smoothly, freely	日 72.4	6
畅通	chàngtōng	adj.	unimpeded, free-flowing, straight path, unclogged, move without obstruction		6
昌	**chāng**		prosperous, good	日 72.4	6
昌盛	chāngshèng	adj.	prosperous		6
昏	**hūn**		faint, dark, nightfall	日 72.4	6
昏	hūn	adj.	faint, dark, dim, confused, muddled, dusk, to loose consciousness		6
明	**míng**		bright, light, brilliant	日 72.4	1
明白	- míngbai	adj.	clear, obvious, unequivocal, to understand, to realize		1
明亮	míngliàng	adj.	bright, shining, glittering, to become clear		5
明明	míngmíng	adv.	obviously, plainly, undoubtedly, definitely		5
明年	míngnián	n.	next year		1
明确	míngquè	adj.	clear-cut, definite, explicit, to clarify, to specify, to make definite		3
明日	míngrì	n.	tomorrow		6
明天	míngtiān	n.	tomorrow		1
明显	míngxiǎn	adj.	clear, distinct, obvious		3
明星	míngxīng	n.	star, celebrity		2
表明	biǎomíng	vb.	to make clear, to make known, to state clearly, to indicate, known		3
聪明	- cōngming	adj.	intelligent, clever, bright, smart, acute (of sight and hearing)		5
发明	fāmíng	vb.	to invent, an invention		3
光明	guāngmíng	n.	light, radiance, (fig.) bright (prospects etc), openhearted		3
声明	shēngmíng	vb.	to state, to declare, statement, declaration		3
说明	shuōmíng	vb.	to explain, to illustrate, to indicate, to show, to prove, explanation, directions, caption		2
透明	tòumíng	adj.	transparent, open (non-secretive)		4
文明	wénmíng	n.	civilized, civilization, culture		3
鲜明	xiānmíng	adj.	bright, clear-cut, distinct		4
证明	zhèngmíng	n.	proof, certificate, identification, testimonial		3
清明节	qīngmíngjié	n.	Qingming or Pure Brightness Festival or Tomb Sweeping Day, celebration for the dead (in early April)		6
三明治	sānmíngzhì	n.	sandwich (loanword)		6
说明书	shuōmíngshū	n.	(technical) manual, (book of) directions, synopsis (of a play or film), specification (patent)		6
旺	**wàng**		prosperous, flourishing	日 72.4	6
兴旺	xìngwàng	adj.	prosperous, thriving, to prosper, to flourish		6
易	**yì**		easy, to change	日 72.4	3
不易	bùyì	vb.	not easy to do sth, difficult, unchanging		5
交易	jiāoyì	n.	(business) transaction, business deal		3
贸易	màoyì	n.	(commercial) trade		5
轻易	qīngyì	adv.	easily, lightly, rashly		4

容易	róngyì	*adj.*	easy, likely, liable (to)	3
好不容易	hǎobùróngyì	*adv.*	with great difficulty, very difficult	6

春 chūn — spring, love, vitality   日 72.5   2

春节	chūn jié	*n.*	Spring Festival (Chinese New Year)	2
春季	chūnjì	*n.*	springtime	4
春天	chūntiān	*n.*	spring (season)	2
青春	qīngchūn	*n.*	youth, youthfulness	4

是 shì — indeed, yes, to be   日 72.5   1

是	shì	*vb.*	indeed, yes, to be, (is, am, are), right, this, that,	1
是否	shìfǒu	*adv.*	whether (or not), if, is or isn't	4
是不是	- shìbushì	*vb.*	is or isn't, yes or no, whether or not	1
便是	biànshì	*adv.*	emphasizes that sth is precisely or exactly as stated, even, if, just like, in the same way as	6
但是	dànshì	*conj.*	but, however	2
倒是	dàoshì	*adv.*	contrary to what one might expect, actually, contrariwise, why don't you	5
而是	érshì	*conj.*	rather	4
凡是	fánshì	*adv.*	each and every, every, all, any	6
更是	gèngshì	*adv.*	even more (so)	6
还是	- háishi	*adv.*	or, still, nevertheless, had better	1
或是	huòshì	*conj.*	or, either one or the other, even if	5
就是	jiùshì	*adv.*	precisely, exactly, even, if, just like, in the same way as	3
可是	kěshì	*conj.*	but, however, (used for emphasis) indeed	2
老是	lǎoshì	*adv.*	always	2
却是	quèshì	*conj.*	nevertheless, actually, the fact is ...	6
算是	suànshì	*adv.*	considered to be, at last	6
要是	- yàoshi	*conj.*	(coll.) if	3
于是	yúshì	*conj.*	thereupon, as a result, consequently, thus, hence	4
正是	zhèngshì	*adv.*	just right, exactly, precisely	2
只是	zhǐshì	*adv.*	merely, simply, only, but	3
总是	zǒngshì	*adv.*	always	3
就是说	jiùshìshuō	*conj.*	in other words, that is	6
有的是	yǒudeshì	*phr.*	have plenty of, there's no lack of	3
这就是说	zhèjiùshìshuō	*phr.*	in other words, that is to say	6

显 xiǎn — manifest, display, evident   日 72.5   3

显	xiǎn	*vb.*	to make visible, to reveal, prominent, conspicuous	5
显出	xiǎnchū	*vb.*	to express, to exhibit	6
显得	xiǎnde	*vb.*	to seem, to look, to appear	3
显然	xiǎnrán	*adj.*	clear, evident, obvious(ly)	3
显示	xiǎnshì	*vb.*	to show, to illustrate, to display, to demonstrate	3
显著	xiǎnzhù	*adj.*	outstanding, notable, remarkable, statistically significant	4
明显	míngxiǎn	*adj.*	clear, distinct, obvious	3

星 xīng — a star, planet, any point of light   日 72.5   1

星期	xīngqī	*n.*	week	1
星星	- xīngxing	*n.*	star in the sky	2
星期日	xīngqīrì	*n.*	Sunday	1

星期天	xīngqītiān	n.	Sunday		1
歌星	gēxīng	n.	singing star, famous singer		6
明星	míngxīng	n.	star, celebrity		2
球星	qiúxīng	n.	sports star (ball sport)		6
卫星	wèixīng	n.	satellite, moon		5
影星	yǐngxīng	n.	film star		6
映	**yìng**		to reflect light, to project	日 72.5	4
反映	fǎnyìng	vb.	to mirror, to reflect, mirror image, reflection, (fig.) to report, to make known, to render		4
昨	**zuó**		yesterday, in former times, past	日 72.5	1
昨天	zuótiān	n.	yesterday		1
晒	**shài**		to dry in sun, to expose to sun	日 72.6	4
晒	shài	vb.	(of the sun) to shine on, to bask in (the sunshine), to dry (clothes, grain etc) in the sun, (fig.)		4
晓	**xiǎo**		dawn, daybreak, clear	日 72.6	6
晓得	xiǎode	vb.	to know		6
晕	* **yūn, yùn**		dizzy, faint; halo in sky, fog	日 72.6	6
晕	yūn	adj.	confused, dizzy, giddy, to faint, to swoon, to lose consciousness, to pass out		6
晕车	• yùnchē	vb.	to be dizzy, to be giddy, halo in sky		6
晨	**chén**		early morning, daybreak	日 72.7	2
清晨	qīngchén	n.	early morning		5
早晨	- zǎochen	n.	early morning		2
晚	**wǎn**		night, evening, late	日 72.7	1
晚	wǎn	n.	evening, night, late		1
晚安	wǎn'ān	phr.	good night, good evening		2
晚报	wǎnbào	n.	evening newspaper, (in a newspaper's name) Evening News		2
晚餐	wǎncān	n.	evening meal, dinner		2
晚点	wǎndiǎn	vb.	(of trains etc) to be late, delayed, behind schedule, light dinner		4
晚饭	wǎnfàn	n.	evening meal, dinner, supper		1
晚会	wǎnhuì	n.	evening party		2
晚上	- wǎnshang	n.	evening, night		1
傍晚	bàngwǎn	n.	in the evening, when night falls, towards evening, at night fall, at dusk		6
早晚	zǎowǎn	n.	morning and evening, sooner or later		6
景	**jǐng**		scenery, view, conditions	日 72.8	3
景	jǐng	n.	scenery, view, conditions, surname Jing		6
景点	jǐngdiǎn	n.	scenic spot, place of interest (tourism)		6
景色	jǐngsè	n.	scenery, scene, landscape, view		3
景象	jǐngxiàng	n.	scene, sight (to behold)		5
背景	bèijǐng	n.	background, backdrop, context, (fig.) powerful backer		4
场景	chǎngjǐng	n.	scene, scenario, setting		6
风景	fēngjǐng	n.	scenery, landscape		4
前景	qiánjǐng	n.	foreground, vista, (future) prospects, perspective		5

情景	qíngjǐng	n.	scene, spectacle, circumstances, situation		4
普	**pǔ**		universal, general, widespread	日 72.8	2
普遍	pǔbiàn	adj.	universal, general, widespread, common		3
普及	pǔjí	vb.	to spread extensively, to generalize, widespread, popular, universal, ubiquitous, pervasive		3
普通	pǔtōng	adj.	common, ordinary, general, average		2
普通话	pǔtōnghuà	n.	Mandarin (common language)		2
晴	**qíng**		fine, clear, fine weather	日 72.8	2
晴	qíng	adj.	fine, clear, fine (weather)		2
晴朗	qínglǎng	adj.	sunny and cloudless		5
晴天	qíngtiān	n.	clear sky, sunny day		2
暑	**shǔ**		hot	日 72.8	4
暑假	shǔjià	n.	summer vacation		4
暂	**zàn**		temporary	日 72.8	5
暂时	zànshí	adj.	temporary, provisional, for the time being		5
暂停	zàntíng	vb.	to suspend, time-out (e.g. in sports), stoppage, pause (media player)		5
智	**zhì**		wisdom, knowledge, intelligence	日 72.8	4
智慧	zhìhuì	n.	wisdom, knowledge, intelligent, intelligence		6
智力	zhìlì	n.	intelligence, intellect		4
智能	zhìnéng	n.	intellectual power, intelligent, able, smart (phone, system, bomb etc)		4
理智	lǐzhì	n.	reason, intellect, rationality, rational		6
暗	**àn**		dark, obscure, in secret	日 72.9	4
暗	àn	adj.	dark, obscure, in secret, covert		4
暗示	ànshì	vb.	to hint, to suggest, suggestion, hint		4
黑暗	hēi'àn	adj.	dark, darkly, darkness		4
暖	**nuǎn**		warm, genial	日 72.9	3
暖	nuǎn	adj.	warm		5
暖和	• nuǎnhuo	adj.	warm, nice and warm, to warm up		3
暖气	nuǎnqì	n.	central heating, heater, warm air		4
温暖	wēnnuǎn	adj.	warm, to make warm		3
暴	**bào**		violent, brutal	日 72.11	6
暴力	bàolì	n.	violence, force, violent		6
暴露	bàolù	vb.	to expose, to reveal, to lay bare		6
暴雨	bàoyǔ	n.	torrential rain, rainstorm		6
暴风雨	bàofēngyǔ	n.	rainstorm, storm, tempest		6
风暴	fēngbào	n.	storm, violent commotion, fig. crisis (e.g. revolution, uprising, financial crisis etc)		6

曰 yuē say 73

电	**diàn**		electricity, electric, lightning	日 73.1	1
电	diàn	n.	lightning, electricity, electric, to get (or give) an electric shock, phone call or telegram etc, to send via telephone or telegram etc		1
电车	diànchē	n.	trolleybus		6

电池	diànchí	n.	battery	5
电灯	diàndēng	n.	electric light	4
电动	diàndòng	n.	electric-powered	6
电话	diànhuà	n.	telephone	1
电力	diànlì	n.	electrical power, electricity	6
电脑	diànnǎo	n.	computer	1
电器	diànqì	n.	(electrical) appliance, device	6
电视	diànshì	n.	television, TV	1
电台	diàntái	n.	transmitter-receiver, broadcasting station, radio station	3
电梯	diàntī	n.	elevator, escalator	4
电影	diànyǐng	n.	movie, film	1
电源	diànyuán	n.	electric power source	4
电动车	diàndòngchē	n.	electric car, electric bicycle, electric scooter	4
电饭锅	diànfànguō	n.	electric rice cooker	5
电视机	diànshìjī	n.	television set	1
电视剧	diànshìjù	n.	TV drama, soap opera	3
电视台	diànshìtái	n.	television station	3
电影院	diànyǐngyuàn	n.	cinema, movie theatre	1
电子版 •	diànzǐbǎn	n.	electronic edition, digital version	5
电子邮件 •	diànzǐ yóujiàn	n.	email	3
充电	chōngdiàn	vb.	to recharge (a battery), (fig.) to recharge one's batteries (through leisure), to update one's skills and knowledge	4
发电	fā diàn	vb.	to generate electricity, to send a telegram	6
家电	jiādiàn	n.	household electric appliance	6
闪电	shǎndiàn	n.	lightning	4
充电器	chōngdiànqì	n.	battery charger	4
打电话	dǎ diànhuà	vb.	to make a telephone call	1

曲 * qū, qǔ   crooked, bent; tune   日 73.2   5

歌曲 •	gēqǔ	n.	song	5
弯曲	wānqū	vb.	to bend, to curve around, curved, crooked, to wind, to warp	6
戏曲 •	xìqǔ	n.	Chinese opera, traditional opera, singing parts in 传奇 chuánqí and 杂剧 zájù	6
乐曲 •	yuèqǔ	n.	musical composition	6

更 * gèng, gēng   more, still further; to replace   日 73.3   2

更	gèng	adv.	more, even more, further, still, still more	2
更换 •	gēnghuàn	vb.	to replace (a worn-out tire etc), to change (one's address etc)	5
更新 •	gēngxīn	vb.	to replace the old with new, to renew, to renovate, to upgrade, to update, to regenerate	5
更加	gèngjiā	adv.	more (than sth else), even more	3
更是	gèngshì	adv.	even more (so)	6
变更	biàngèng	vb.	to change, to alter, to modify	6

曾 céng   already, sign of past   日 73.8   3

曾	céng	adv.	once, in the past, surname Zeng	4
曾经	céngjīng	adv.	once, already, former, previously, ever, (past tense marker used before verb or clause)	3
不曾	bùcéng	adv.	hasn't yet, hasn't ever	5

替	tì		to change, to replace	曰 73.8	4
替	tì	vb.	to substitute for, to take the place of, to replace, for, on behalf of, to stand in for		4
替代	tìdài	vb.	to substitute for, to replace, to supersede		4
代替	dàitì	vb.	to replace, to take the place of		4

最	zuì		most, extremely, exceedingly	曰 73.8	1
最	zuì	adv.	most, the most, -est (superlative suffix)		1
最初	zuìchū	n.	first, primary, initial, original, at first, initially, originally		4
最好	zuìhǎo	adj.	best, (you) had better (do what we suggest)		1
最后	zuìhòu	n.	final, last, finally, ultimate		1
最佳	zuìjiā	adj.	optimum, optimal, peak, best (athlete, movie etc)		6
最近	zuìjìn	n.	recently, soon, nearest		2
最终	zuìzhōng	n.	final, ultimate		6

月 yuè moon 74

月	yuè		moon, month	月 74.0	1
月	yuè	n.	moon, month, monthly		1
月饼	yuèbǐng	n.	mooncake (esp. for the Mid-Autumn Festival)		5
月底	yuèdǐ	n.	end of the month		4
月份	yuèfèn	n.	month		2
月亮	- yuèliang	n.	the moon		2
月球	yuèqiú	n.	the moon		5
岁月	suìyuè	n.	years, time		5
上个月	- shàng ge yuè	n.	last month		4
下个月	- xià ge yuè	n.	next month		4

有	yǒu		to have, to own, to exist	月 74.2	1
有	yǒu	vb.	to have, to own, there is, there are, to exist, to be		1
有害	yǒu hài	adj.	destructive, harmful, damaging		5
有空	• yǒu kòng	vb.	to have time (to do sth)		2
有的	yǒude	pro.	(there are) some (who are…), some (exist)		1
有毒	yǒudú	adj.	poisonous		5
有关	yǒuguān	vb.	to have sth to do with, to relate to, related to, to concern, concerning		6
有劲	yǒujìn	adj.	vigorous, energetic, interesting, amusing		4
有利	yǒulì	adj.	advantageous, to have advantages, favourable		3
有力	yǒulì	adj.	powerful, forceful, vigorous		5
有名	yǒumíng	adj.	famous, well-known		1
有趣	yǒuqù	adj.	interesting, fascinating, amusing		4
有人	yǒurén	pro.	someone, people, anyone, there is someone there, occupied (as in restroom)		2
有事	yǒushì	vb.	to be occupied with sth, to have sth on one's mind, there is something the matter		6
有限	yǒuxiàn	adj.	limited, finite		4
有效	yǒuxiào	adj.	effective, in effect, valid		3
有些	yǒuxiē	pro.	some, somewhat		1
有用	yǒuyòng	adj.	useful		1
有着	yǒuzhe	vb.	to have, to possess		5

有时候 -	yǒu shíhou	adv.	sometimes	1
有的是	yǒudeshì	phr.	have plenty of, there's no lack of	3
有利于	yǒulìyú	vb.	to be advantageous to, to be beneficial for	5
有没有	yǒuméiyǒu	phr.	(before a noun) Do (you, they etc) have ...?, Is there a ...?, (before a verb) Did (you, they etc) (verb, infinitive)?	6
有一点	yǒuyīdiǎn	n.	a little, somewhat	2
有意思 -	yǒuyìsi	adj.	interesting, meaningful, enjoyable, fun	2
持有	chíyǒu	vb.	to hold (passport, views etc)	6
带有	dàiyǒu	vb.	to have, to involve	5
富有	fùyǒu	adj.	rich, to be full of	6
共有	gòngyǒu	vb.	to have altogether, to have in all	3
还有	háiyǒu	adv.	furthermore, in addition, still, also	1
含有	hányǒu	vb.	to contain, to have including	4
具有	jùyǒu	vb.	to have, to possess	3
没有	méiyǒu	vb.	haven't, hasn't, doesn't exist, to not have, to not be	1
所有	suǒyǒu	adj.	all, to have, to possess, to own	2
特有	tèyǒu	adj.	specific (to), characteristic (of), distinctive	5
现有	xiànyǒu	n.	currently existing, currently available	5
拥有	yōngyǒu	vb.	to have, to possess	5
原有	yuányǒu	adj.	original, former	5
占有	zhànyǒu	vb.	to have, to own, to hold, to occupy, to possess, to account for (a high proportion etc)	5
只有	zhǐyǒu	conj.	only have ..., there is only ..., (used in combination with 才 cái) it is only if one ... (that one can ...)	3

服	**fú**		**clothes, wear, dress**	月 74.4
服	fú	n.	clothes, dress, garment, to serve (in the military, a prison sentence etc), to obey, to be convinced (by an argument)	6
服从	fúcóng	vb.	to obey (an order), to comply, to defer	5
服务	fúwù	vb.	to serve, service	2
服装	fúzhuāng	n.	dress, clothing, costume, clothes	3
克服	kèfú	vb.	to (try to) overcome (hardships etc), to conquer, to put up with, to endure	3
舒服 -	shūfu	adj.	comfortable, feeling well	2
说服	shuōfú	vb.	to persuade, to convince, to talk sb over	4
衣服 -	yīfu	n.	clothes	1
征服	zhēngfú	vb.	to conquer, to subdue, to vanquish	4
羽绒服	yǔróngfú	n.	down-filled garment	5

朋	**péng**		**friend, pal, acquaintance**	月 74.4 1
朋友 -	péngyou	n.	friend, boyfriend or girlfriend	1
交朋友 -	jiāo péngyou	vb.	to make friends, (dialect) to start an affair with sb	2
老朋友 -	lǎopéngyou	n.	old friend, (slang) period, menstruation	2
男朋友 -	nánpéngyou	n.	boyfriend	1
女朋友 -	nǚpéngyou	n.	girlfriend	1
小朋友 -	xiǎopéngyou	n.	child	1

朗	**lǎng**		**clear, bright, distinct**	月 74.7 5
朗读	lǎngdú	vb.	to read aloud	5
晴朗	qínglǎng	adj.	sunny and cloudless	5

望	**wàng**		to look at, look forward, to hope	月 74.7	3
望见	wàngjiàn	vb.	to espy, to spot		6
绝望	juéwàng	vb.	to despair, to give up all hope, desperate, desperation		5
看望	kànwàng	vb.	to visit, to pay a call to		4
渴望	kěwàng	vb.	to thirst for, to long for		5
盼望	pànwàng	vb.	to hope for, to look forward to		6
期望	qīwàng	vb.	to have expectations, to earnestly hope, expectation, hope		5
失望	shīwàng	adj.	disappointed, to lose hope, to despair		4
希望	xīwàng	vb.	to wish for, to desire, to hope		3
愿望	yuànwàng	n.	desire, wish		3
朝	**cháo**		dynasty, imperial court	月 74.8	3
朝	cháo	n.	dynasty, imperial court, facing, towards		3
期	**qī**		period of time, date	月 74.8	1
期	qī	n.	a period of time, phase, stage, m.w. for issues of a periodical, courses of study, time, term, period, to hope		3
期待	qīdài	vb.	to look forward to, to await, expectation		4
期间	qījiān	n.	period of time, time, time period, period		4
期末	qīmò	n.	end of term		4
期望	qīwàng	vb.	to have expectations, to earnestly hope, expectation, hope		5
期限	qīxiàn	n.	time limit, deadline, allotted time		4
期中	qīzhōng	n.	interim, midterm		4
本期	běnqī	n.	the current period, this term (usually in finance)		6
长期	• chángqī	n.	long term, long time, long range (of a forecast)		3
初期	chūqī	n.	initial stage, beginning period		5
到期	dàoqī	vb.	to fall due (loan etc), to expire (visa etc), to mature (investment bond etc)		6
定期	dìngqī	adj.	at set dates, at regular intervals, periodic, limited to a fixed period of time, fixed term		3
短期	duǎnqī	n.	short term, short-term		3
假期	jiàqī	n.	holiday, vacation		2
近期	jìnqī	n.	near in time, in the near future, very soon, recent		3
日期	rìqī	n.	date		1
时期	shíqī	n.	period, phase		6
同期	tóngqī	n.	the corresponding time period (in a different year etc), concurrent, synchronous		6
为期	• wéiqī	vb.	to be done by (a certain date), lasting (a certain time)		5
星期	xīngqī	n.	week		1
学期	xuéqī	n.	term, semester		2
延期	yán qī	vb.	to delay, to extend, to postpone, to defer		4
预期	yùqī	vb.	to expect, to anticipate		5
早期	zǎoqī	n.	early period, early phase, early stage		5
中期	zhōngqī	n.	middle (of a period of time), medium-term (plan, forecast etc)		6
周期	zhōuqī	n.	period, cycle		5
星期日	xīngqīrì	n.	Sunday		1
星期天	xīngqītiān	n.	Sunday		1

木	mù	tree	75
木	**mù**	tree, wood, lumber, wooden	木 75.0 3
木头	- mùtou	n. slow-witted, blockhead, log (of wood, timber etc)	3
本	**běn**	**root, origin, source; oneself**	木 75.1 1
本	běn	+ m.w. m.w. for books, periodicals, files etc., root, stem, origin, source, basis, the current, original, inherent	1
本	běn	+ pro. oneself, this, originally, at first	6
本地	• běndì	n. local, this locality	6
本科	běnkē	n. undergraduate course, undergraduate (attributive)	4
本来	běnlái	adj. original, originally, at first, it goes without saying, of course	3
本领	běnlǐng	n. skill, ability, capability	3
本期	běnqī	n. the current period, this term (usually in finance)	6
本人	běnrén	pro. the person himself, I (humble form used in speeches), oneself, myself, in person, personal	5
本身	běnshēn	pro. itself, in itself, per se	6
本事	- běnshi	n. source material, original story	3
本土	běntǔ	n. one's native country, native, local, metropolitan territory	6
本质	běnzhì	n. essence, nature, innate character, intrinsic quality	6
本子	běnzi	n. book, notebook	1
成本	chéngběn	n. (manufacturing, production etc) costs	5
根本	gēnběn	n. foundation, base, root; fundamental, basic; simply, absolutely (not), (not) at all	3
基本	jīběn	adj. basic, fundamental, main, elementary	3
剧本	jùběn	n. script for play, opera, movie etc, screenplay, scenario	5
课本	kèběn	n. textbook	1
资本	zīběn	n. capital (economics)	5
基本上	- jīběnshang	adv. basically, on the whole	3
笔记本	bǐjìběn	n. notebook (stationery)	2
末	**mò**	**final, last, end**	木 75.1 2
末	mò	n. tip, end, final stage, latter part, inessential detail, powder, dust, opera role of old man	4
期末	qīmò	n. end of term	4
周末	zhōumò	n. weekend	2
术	**shù**	**art, skill, method**	木 75.1 3
技术	jìshù	n. technology, technique, skill	3
美术	měishù	n. art, fine arts, painting	3
手术	shǒushù	n. (surgical) operation, surgery	4
武术	wǔshù	n. military skill or technique (in former times), all kinds of martial art sports (some claiming spiritual development), self-defence	3
学术	xuéshù	n. learning, science, academic	4
艺术	yìshù	n. art	3
战术	zhànshù	n. tactics	6
未	**wèi**	**not yet**	木 75.1 4
未必	wèibì	adv. not necessarily, maybe not	4

未来	wèilái	n.	future, tomorrow		4
朵	**duǒ**		**m.w. for flowers and clouds**	木 75.2	5
朵	duǒ	m.w.	m.w. for flowers and clouds		5
耳朵	- ěrduo	n.	ear		5
机	**jī**		**desk, machine, moment**	木 75.2	1
机场	jīchǎng	n.	airport, airfield		1
机构	jīgòu	n.	mechanism, structure, organization, agency, institution		4
机关	jīguān	n.	mechanism, gear, machine-operated, office, agency, organ, organization, establishment, institution, body, stratagem, scheme, intrigue, plot, trick		6
机会	jīhuì	n.	opportunity, chance, occasion		2
机票	jīpiào	n.	air ticket, passenger ticket		1
机器	jīqì	n.	machine		3
机械	jīxiè	n.	machine, machinery, mechanical, (old) cunning, scheming		6
机遇	jīyù	n.	opportunity, favourable circumstance, stroke of luck		4
机制	jīzhì	n.	machine processed, machine made, mechanism		5
机动车	jīdòngchē	n.	motor vehicle		6
机器人	jīqìrén	n.	mechanical person, robot, android		5
动机	dòngjī	n.	motor, locomotive, motive, motivation, intention		5
耳机	ěrjī	n.	headphones, earphones, telephone receiver		4
飞机	fēijī	n.	airplane		1
关机	guānjī	vb.	to turn off (a machine or device), to finish shooting a film		2
开机	kāijī	vb.	to start an engine, to boot up (a computer), to press Ctrl-Alt-Delete, to begin shooting a film or TV show		2
时机	shíjī	n.	fortunate timing, occasion, opportunity		5
手机	shǒujī	n.	cell phone, mobile phone		1
司机	sījī	n.	chauffeur, driver		2
危机	wēijī	n.	crisis		6
相机	• xiàngjī	vb.	camera (abbr. for 照相机 zhàoxiàngjī), to wait for the opportune moment, as the circumstances allow		2
打印机	dǎyìnjī	n.	printer		6
电视机	diànshìjī	n.	television set		1
计算机	jìsuànjī	n.	computer, calculator		2
录音机	lùyīnjī	n.	(tape) recording machine, tape recorder		6
取款机	qǔkuǎn jī	n.	ATM, cash dispenser		6
摄像机	shèxiàngjī	n.	video camera		5
收音机	shōuyīnjī	n.	radio		3
洗衣机	xǐyījī	n.	washer, washing machine		2
游戏机	yóuxìjī	n.	video game, game machine		6
直升机	zhíshēngjī	n.	helicopter		6
权	**quán**		**power, right, authority**	木 75.2	4
权	quán	n.	right, authority, power, surname Quan		6
权利	quánlì	n.	right (i.e. an entitlement to sth), (classical) power and wealth		4
权力	quánlì	n.	power, authority		6
人权	rénquán	n.	human rights		6
政权	zhèngquán	n.	regime, political power		6

杀	**shā**		to kill, to slaughter	木 75.2	5
杀	shā	vb.	to kill, to murder, to attack, to weaken or reduce, to smart (dialect), (used after a verb) extremely		5
杀毒	shādú	vb.	to disinfect, (computing) to destroy a computer virus		5
自杀	zìshā	vb.	to kill oneself, to commit suicide		5
杂	**zá**		mixed, blended, to mix	木 75.2	3
杂	zá	adj.	mixed, miscellaneous, various, to mix		6
杂志	zázhì	n.	magazine		3
复杂	fùzá	adj.	complex, complicated, (opp. 简单 jiǎndān: simple)		3
材	**cái**		material, stuff, timber	木 75.3	3
材料	cáiliào	n.	material, data, makings, stuff		4
教材	jiàocái	n.	teaching material		3
身材	shēncái	n.	stature, build (height and weight), figure		4
题材	tícái	n.	subject matter		5
村	**cūn**		village, hamlet	木 75.3	3
村	cūn	n.	village, hamlet, rustic, boorish		3
村庄	cūnzhuāng	n.	village, hamlet		6
农村	nóngcūn	n.	rural area, village		3
乡村	xiāngcūn	n.	village, countryside		5
杆	**gān**		pole, shaft of spear	木 75.3	6
杆	gān	n.	stick, pole, lever, m.w. for long objects such as guns		6
极	**jí**		utmost, pole, extreme	木 75.3	3
极	jí	n.	utmost, extremity, pole (geography, physics), top, extreme, final,		4
极端	jíduān	adj.	extreme		6
极了	jíle	adv.	extremely, exceedingly; use: … 极了		3
极其	jíqí	adv.	extremely		4
北极	běijí	n.	the North Pole, the Arctic Pole, the north magnetic pole		5
积极	jījí	adj.	active, energetic, vigorous, positive (outlook), proactive		3
南极	nánjí	n.	south pole		5
消极	xiāojí	adj.	negative, passive, inactive		5
来	**lái**		to come, coming, to return	木 75.3	1
来	lái	vb.	to come, to arrive, to come round, ever since, next		1
来到	láidào	vb.	to come, to arrive		1
来往	láiwǎng	vb.	to come and go, to have dealings with, to be in relation with		6
来信	láixìn	n.	incoming letter, to send us a letter		5
来源	láiyuán	n.	source (of information etc), origin		4
来自	láizì	vb.	to come from (a place), From: (in email header)		2
来不及	- láibují	phr.	there's not enough time (to do sth), it's too late (to do sth)		4
来得及	láidejí	phr.	there's still time, able to do sth in time		4
本来	běnlái	adj.	original, originally, at first, it goes without saying, of course		3
出来	chūlái	vb.	to come out, to appear, to arise		1
传来	chuánlái	vb.	(of a sound) to come through, to be heard, (of news) to arrive		3
从来	cónglái	adv.	always, at all times, never (if used in negative sentence)		3
带来	dàilái	vb.	to bring, to bring about, to produce		2

到来	dàolái	vb.	to arrive, arrival, advent		5
过来	- guò lai	vb.	to come over, to manage, to handle, to be able to take care of		2
后来	hòulái	n.	afterwards, later		2
回来	huílái	vb.	to return, to come back		1
将来	jiānglái	n.	in the future, future, the future		3
进来	jìnlái	vb.	to come in		1
近来	jìnlái	n.	recently, lately		5
看来	kànlái	adv.	apparently, it seems that		4
起来	- qǐ lai	vb.	to stand up, to get up		1
前来	qiánlái	vb.	to come (formal), before, previously		6
上来	shàng lái	vb.	to come up, to approach, (verb complement indicating success)		3
外来	wàilái	adj.	external, foreign, outside		6
往来	wǎnglái	n.	dealings, contacts, to go back and forth		6
未来	wèilái	n.	future, tomorrow		4
下来	xià lái	vb.	to come down, (completed action marker)		3
以来	yǐlái	n.	since (a previous event)		3
迎来	yínglái	vb.	to welcome (a visitor or newcomer), (fig.) to usher in		6
用来	yònglái	vb.	to be used for		5
原来	yuánlái	adj.	original, former, originally, formerly, at first, so, actually, as it turns out		2
越来越	yuèláiyuè	adv.	more and more		2
自来水	zìláishuǐ	n.	running water, tap water		6
接下来	jiēxiàlái	vb.	to accept, to take, next, following		2
看起来	- kànqilai	adv.	seemingly, apparently, looks as if, appear to be, gives the impression that, seems on the face of it to be		3
一般来说	yībānláishuō	phr.	generally speaking		4
李	**lǐ**		plum, plum tree	木 75.3	3
行李	- xíngli	n.	luggage		3
束	**shù**		to bind, to control, to bale	木 75.3	3
束	shù	vb.	to tie, to bind, to control, to restrain, to bale (m.w. for bunches, bundles, bouquets, etc.), surname Shu		3
结束	jiéshù	vb.	to finish, to end, to conclude, to close		3
约束	yuēshù	vb.	to restrict, to limit to, to constrain, restriction, constraint		5
条	**tiáo**		strip, string, clause	木 75.3	1
条	tiáo	n.	strip, item, article, clause (of law or treaty), m.w. for long thin things (ribbon, river, road, trousers etc)		2
条件	tiáojiàn	n.	condition, circumstances, term, factor, requirement, prerequisite, qualification		2
便条	biàntiáo	n.	(informal) note		5
面条	miàntiáo	n.	noodles		1
薯条	shǔtiáo	n.	chips (French fries), French fried potatoes		6
板	**bǎn**		plank, board, iron or tin plate	木 75.4	2
板	bǎn	n.	board, plank, plate, shutter, tempo in music		3
地板	• dìbǎn	n.	floor		6
黑板	hēibǎn	n.	blackboard		2
老板	lǎobǎn	n.	boss, proprietor, shopkeeper		3

杯	**bēi**		cup, glass	木 75.4	1
杯	bēi	n.	cup, glass, trophy, (m.w. for cups, classes, drinks)		1
杯子	bēizi	n.	cup, glass		1
干杯	• gānbēi	vb.	to drink a toast, cheers! (proposing a toast), here's to you!, bottoms up!, (lit.) dry cup		2
世界杯	shìjièbēi	n.	World Cup		3
构	**gòu**		frame, building, structure	木 75.4	4
构成	gòuchéng	vb.	to constitute, to form, to compose, to make up, to configure (computing)		4
构建	gòujiàn	vb.	to construct (sth abstract)		6
构造	gòuzào	n.	structure, composition, tectonic (geology)		4
机构	jīgòu	n.	mechanism, structure, organization, agency, institution		4
结构	jiégòu	n.	structure, composition, makeup, architecture		4
果	**guǒ**		fruit, result	木 75.4	1
果酱	guǒjiàng	n.	jam		6
果然	guǒrán	adv.	really, sure enough, as expected, if indeed		3
果实	guǒshí	n.	fruit (produced by a plant), (fig.) fruits (of success etc), results, gains		4
果树	guǒshù	n.	fruit tree		6
果汁	guǒzhī	n.	fruit juice		3
成果	chéngguǒ	n.	result, achievement, gain, profit		3
后果	hòuguǒ	n.	consequences, aftermath		3
结果	jiéguǒ	vb.	to bear fruit		2
苹果	píngguǒ	n.	apple (tree and fruit)		3
如果	rúguǒ	conj.	if, in case, in the event that		2
水果	shuǐguǒ	n.	fruit		1
效果	xiàoguǒ	n.	result, effect, efficacy, (theatre) sound or visual effects		3
杰	**jié**		hero, heroic, outstanding	木 75.4	6
杰出	jiéchū	adj.	outstanding, distinguished, remarkable, prominent, illustrious		6
林	**lín**		forest, grove, woods	木 75.4	4
森林	sēnlín	n.	forest		4
树林	shùlín	n.	forest, woods, grove		4
园林	yuánlín	n.	gardens, park, landscape garden		5
枪	**qiāng**		spear, gun, rifle	木 75.4	5
枪	qiāng	n.	spear, lance, gun, rifle, sth shaped or working like a gun, m.w. rifle shot		5
松	**sōng**		loose, to loosen, pine tree	木 75.4	4
松	sōng	adj.	loose, soft, to loosen, to relax, pine tree (pinus), dried minced meat, surname Song		4
松树	sōngshù	n.	pine, pine tree		4
放松	fàngsōng	vb.	to loosen, to relax		4
轻松	qīngsōng	adj.	light, gentle, relaxed, effortless, uncomplicated, to relax, to take things less seriously		4
析	**xī**		to break apart, to divide, to split wood	木 75.4	5
分析	fēnxī	vb.	to analyse, analysis		5

枝	zhī		branch, twig, branch off	木 75.4	6
枝	zhī	n.	branch, twig, m.w. for sticks, rods, pencils etc		6
标	**biāo**		**mark, symbol, label**	木 75.5	3
标题	biāotí	n.	title, heading, headline, caption, subject		3
标志	biāozhì	n.	sign, mark, symbol, logo, to symbolize, to indicate, to mark		4
标准	biāozhǔn	n.	(an official) standard, norm, criterion		3
目标	mùbiāo	n.	target, goal, objective		3
商标	shāngbiāo	n.	trademark, logo		5
鼠标	shǔbiāo	n.	mouse (computing)		5
指标	zhǐbiāo	n.	(production) target, quota, index, indicator, sign, signpost, (computing) pointer		5
查	**chá**		**to investigate, to examine**	木 75.5	2
查	chá	vb.	to examine, to investigate, to check, surname Zha		2
查出	cháchū	vb.	to find out, to discover		6
查看	chákàn	vb.	to look over, to examine, to check up, to ferret out		6
查询	cháxún	vb.	to check, to inquire, to consult (a document etc), inquiry, query		5
调查	diàochá	n.	investigation, inquiry, to investigate, to survey, survey, (opinion) poll		3
检查	jiǎnchá	n.	inspection, to examine, to inspect		2
审查	shěnchá	vb.	to examine, to investigate, to censor out, censorship		6
柴	**chái**		**firewood, fuel**	木 75.5	5
火柴	huǒchái	n.	match (for lighting fire)		5
柜	**guì**		**cabinet, cupboard, shop counter**	木 75.5	5
柜子	guìzi	n.	cupboard, cabinet		5
书柜	shūguì	n.	bookcase		5
架	**jià**		**rack, stand, to prop up**	木 75.5	3
架	jià	n.	frame, rack, framework, to support, m.w. for planes, large vehicles, radios etc		3
吵架	chǎojià	vb.	to quarrel, to have a row, quarrel		3
打架	dǎjià	vb.	to fight, to scuffle, to come to blows		5
书架	shūjià	n.	bookshelf		3
衣架	yījià	n.	clothes hanger, clothes rack		3
栏	**lán**		**railing, balustrade, animal pen**	木 75.5	6
栏目	lánmù	n.	regular column or segment (in a publication or broadcast program), program (TV or radio)		6
某	**mǒu**		**certain thing or person**	木 75.5	3
某	mǒu	pro.	some, a certain, sb or sth indefinite, such-and-such		3
染	**rǎn**		**to dye, to be contagious**	木 75.5	5
染	rǎn	vb.	to dye, to catch (a disease), to acquire (bad habits etc), to contaminate, to add colour washes to a painting		5
污染	wūrǎn	n.	pollution, contamination		5
柿	**shì**		**persimmon**	木 75.5	5
西红柿	xīhóngshì	n.	tomato		5

树	shù		tree, to plant, to set up	木 75.5	1
树	shù	n.	tree, to plant, to cultivate, to set up		1
树林	shùlín	n.	forest, woods, grove		4
树叶	shùyè	n.	tree leaves		4
果树	guǒshù	n.	fruit tree		6
松树	sōngshù	n.	pine, pine tree		4
桃树	táoshù	n.	peach tree		5
柱	**zhù**		**pillar, post, to support**	木 75.5	6
柱子	zhùzi	n.	pillar		6
案	**àn**		**table, bench, legal case**	木 75.6	4
答案	dá'àn	n.	answer, solution		4
档案	dàng'àn	n.	file, record, archive		6
方案	fāng'àn	n.	plan, program (for action etc), proposal, proposed bill		4
图案	tú'àn	n.	design, pattern		4
档	**dàng**		**shelf, frame, crosspiece**	木 75.6	6
档	dàng	n.	variant of 挡 dǎng, gear		6
档案	dàng'àn	n.	file, record, archive		6
搭档	dādàng	vb.	to cooperate, partner		6
高档	gāodàng	adj.	superior quality, high grade, top grade		6
格	**gé**		**pattern, standard, form**	木 75.6	3
格外	géwài	adv.	especially, particularly		4
表格	biǎogé	n.	form, table		3
风格	fēnggé	n.	style		4
合格	hégé	vb.	to meet the standard required, qualified, eligible (voter etc)		3
及格	jígé	vb.	to pass an exam or a test, to meet a minimum standard		4
价格	jiàgé	n.	price		3
性格	xìnggé	n.	nature, disposition, temperament, character		3
严格	yángé	adj.	strict, stringent, tight, rigorous		4
资格	zīgé	n.	qualifications, seniority		3
根	**gēn**		**root, basis, foundation**	木 75.6	3
根	gēn	n.	root, basis, m.w. for long slender objects, e.g. cigarettes, guitar strings		4
根本	gēnběn	n.	foundation, base, root; fundamental, basic; simply, absolutely (not), (not) at all		3
根据	gēnjù	n.	according to, based on, basis, foundation		4
核	**hé**		**seed, core, nut, atom**	木 75.6	5
核心	héxīn	n.	core, nucleus		6
考核	kǎohé	vb.	to examine, to check up on, to assess, to review, appraisal, review, evaluation		5
桥	**qiáo**		**bridge, beam, crosspiece**	木 75.6	3
桥	qiáo	n.	bridge, surname Qiao		3
桥梁	qiáoliáng	n.	bridge (lit. and fig.)		6

					木 75.6	5
桃	**táo**		peach, peach shaped			
桃	táo	n.	peach, peach shaped thing, walnut			5
桃花	táohuā	n.	peach blossom, (fig.) love affair			5
桃树	táoshù	n.	peach tree			5
校	**xiào**		school, military field officer		木 75.6	1
校园	xiàoyuán	n.	campus			2
校长	xiàozhǎng	n.	(college, university) president, headmaster			2
学校	xuéxiào	n.	school			1
样	**yàng**		shape, form, pattern		木 75.6	1
样	yàng	n.	manner, pattern, way, appearance, shape, m.w. kind, type			6
样子	yàngzi	n.	appearance, manner, pattern, model			2
多样	duōyàng	adj.	diverse, diversity, manifold			4
模样	móyàng	n.	look, style, appearance, approximation, about			5
那样	nàyàng	pro.	that kind, that sort			2
同样	tóngyàng	adj.	same, equal, equivalent			2
一样	yīyàng	adj.	same, like, equal to, the same as, just like			1
怎样	zěnyàng	pro.	how, what kind			2
照样	zhàoyàng	adv.	as before, (same) as usual, in the same manner, still, nevertheless			6
这样	zhèyàng	pro.	this kind of, so, this way, like this, such			2
什么样	shénmeyàng	phr.	what kind?, what sort?, what appearance?			2
怎么样	zěnmeyàng	pro.	how?, how about?, how was it?, how are things?			2
不怎么样	bù zěnmeyàng	phr.	not up to much, very indifferent, nothing great about it, nothing good to be said about it			6
一模一样	yīmóyīyàng	phr.	exactly the same (idiom), carbon copy			6
桌	**zhuō**		table, desk, stand		木 75.6	1
桌子	zhuōzi	n.	table, desk			1
书桌	shūzhuō	n.	desk			5
检	**jiǎn**		to check, to examine		木 75.7	2
检测	jiǎncè	vb.	to detect, to test, detection, sensing			4
检查	jiǎnchá	n.	inspection, to examine, to inspect			2
检验	jiǎnyàn	vb.	to inspect, to examine, to test			5
安检	ānjiǎn	n.	security check, to undergo a security check			6
体检	tǐjiǎn	vb.	to have a check-up			4
梨	**lí**		pear		木 75.7	5
梨	lí	n.	pear, surname Li			5
梁	**liáng**		bridge, beam, handle		木 75.7	6
桥梁	qiáoliáng	n.	bridge (lit. and fig.)			6
梅	**méi**		plums, prunes		木 75.7	6
梅花	méihuā	n.	plum blossom, clubs (a suit in card games), wintersweet (dialect)			6
梦	**mèng**		dream, illusion		木 75.7	4
梦	mèng	n.	dream, illusion			4
梦见	mèngjiàn	vb.	to dream about (sth or sb), to see in a dream			4
梦想	mèngxiǎng	vb.	(fig.) to dream of, dream			4

做梦	zuò mèng	vb.	to dream, to have a dream, fig. illusion, fantasy, pipe dream		4
梯	**tī**		ladder, steps, stairs	木 75.7	4
电梯	diàntī	n.	elevator, escalator		4
楼梯	lóutī	n.	stair, staircase		4
械	**xiè**		weapons, implements, instruments	木 75.7	6
机械	jīxiè	n.	machine, machinery, mechanical, (old) cunning, scheming		6
棒	**bàng**		stick, club, strong, fine	木 75.8	5
棒	bàng	n.	stick, club, cudgel, smart, capable, strong, wonderful, m.w. for legs of a relay race		5
棵	**kē**		m.w. for trees, cabbages	木 75.8	4
棵	kē	m.w.	m.w. for trees, cabbages, plants etc		4
棉	**mián**		cotton, cotton padded	木 75.8	6
棉	mián	n.	generic term for cotton or kapok, cotton, padded or quilted with cotton		6
森	**sēn**		forest, luxuriant vegetation	木 75.8	4
森林	sēnlín	n.	forest		4
椅	**yǐ**		chair, seat	木 75.8	2
椅子	yǐzi	n.	chair		2
轮椅	lúnyǐ	n.	wheelchair		4
植	**zhí**		to plant, to grow, plants,	木 75.8	4
植物	zhíwù	n.	plant, vegetation		4
种植	• zhòngzhí	vb.	to plant, to grow (a crop), to cultivate		4
楚	**chǔ**		clear, name of feudal state	木 75.9	2
清楚	- qīngchu	adj.	clear, distinct, to understand thoroughly, to be clear about		2
概	**gài**		general idea, approximately	木 75.9	3
概括	gàikuò	vb.	to summarize, to generalize, briefly		4
概念	gàiniàn	n.	concept, idea		3
大概	dàgài	adv.	roughly, probably, rough, approximate, about, general idea		3
楼	**lóu**		building of two or more stories	木 75.9	1
楼	lóu	n.	floor, storied building, surname Lou		1
楼道	lóudào	n.	corridor, passageway (in storied building)		6
楼房	lóufáng	n.	a building of two or more stories		6
楼上	lóushàng	n.	upstairs		1
楼梯	lóutī	n.	stair, staircase		4
楼下	lóuxià	n.	downstairs		1
大楼	dàlóu	n.	building (a relatively large, multi-storey one)		4
上楼	shànglóu	vb.	to go upstairs		4
下楼	xiàlóu	vb.	to go downstairs		4
教学楼	jiàoxuélóu	n.	teaching block, school building		1
写字楼	xiězìlóu	n.	office building		6

榜	**bǎng**		placard, list of names	木 75.10	6
排行榜	páixíngbǎng	n.	the charts (of best-sellers), table of ranking		6
横	**héng**		horizontal, across	木 75.11	6
横	héng	adj.	horizontal (opp. 直 zhí: vertical), across, horizontal stroke (in Chinese characters), to place (sth) flat (on a surface)		6
模	**mó**		model, standard, pattern	木 75.11	4
模范	mófàn	n.	model, fine example		5
模仿	mófǎng	vb.	to imitate, to copy, to emulate, to mimic, model		5
模糊	-móhu	adj.	vague, indistinct, fuzzy		5
模式	móshì	n.	mode, method, pattern		5
模型	móxíng	n.	model, mould, matrix, pattern		4
模样	móyàng	n.	look, style, appearance, approximation, about		5
模特儿	mótèr	n.	(fashion) model (loanword), mannequin		4
规模	guīmó	n.	scale, scope, extent		4
一模一样	yīmóyīyàng	phr.	exactly the same (idiom), carbon copy		6
大规模	dà guīmó	adj.	large scale, extensive, wide scale, broad scale		4

欠 qiàn lack 76

欠	**qiàn**		to owe, to lack	欠 76.0	5
欠	qiàn	vb.	to owe, to lack, to deficient, to yawn, to raise slightly a part of the body		5
次	**cì**		order, sequence, next	欠 76.2	1
次	cì	+ m.w.	m.w. for enumerated events: time; next in sequence, second, the second (day, time etc), order, sequence		1
次	cì	+ adj.	secondary, vice-, sub-, infra-, inferior quality, substandard, hypo- (chemistry)		4
次数	cìshù	n.	number of times, frequency, order number (in a series), power (math.), degree of a polynomial (math.)		6
层次	céngcì	n.	layer, level, gradation, arrangement of ideas, (a person's) standing		5
此次	cǐcì	n.	this time		6
多次	duōcì	adv.	many times, repeatedly		4
其次	qícì	conj.	next, secondly		3
上次	shàngcì	n.	last time		1
首次	shǒucì	n.	first, first time, for the first time		6
下次	xiàcì	n.	next time		1
依次	yīcì	adv.	in order, in succession		6
再次	zàicì	adv.	one more time, again, one more, once again		5
一次性	yīcìxìng	adj.	one-off (offer), one-time, single-use, disposable (goods)		6
欢	**huān**		happy, glad, joy	欠 76.2	1
欢乐	huānlè	n.	gaiety, gladness, glee, merriment, pleasure, happy, joyous, gay		3
欢迎	huānyíng	vb.	to welcome, welcome		2
喜欢	-xǐhuan	vb.	to like, to be fond of		1
欣	**xīn**		happy, joyous, delighted	欠 76.4	5
欣赏	xīnshǎng	vb.	to appreciate, to enjoy, to admire		5

欲	yù		to want, to need	欠 76.7	6
食欲	shíyù	n.	appetite		6
款	**kuǎn**		**item, article, clause**	欠 76.8	5
存款	cún kuǎn	vb.	to deposit money (in a bank etc), bank savings, bank deposit		5
贷款	dàikuǎn	n.	a loan		5
罚款	fákuǎn	vb.	to fine, penalty, fine (monetary)		5
汇款	huì kuǎn	vb.	to remit money, remittance		5
捐款	juānkuǎn	vb.	to donate money, to contribute funds, donation, contribution (of money)		6
取款	qǔkuǎn	vb.	to withdraw money from a bank		6
取款机	qǔkuǎn jī	n.	ATM, cash dispenser		6
欺	**qī**		**to cheat, to double-cross**	欠 76.8	6
欺负	- qīfu	vb.	to bully		6
歇	**xiē**		**to rest, to stop, to lodge**	欠 76.9	5
歇	xiē	vb.	to rest, to take a break, to stop, to halt, (dialect) to sleep, a moment, a short while		5
歌	**gē**		**song, lyrics, to sing**	欠 76.10	1
歌	gē	n.	song, lyrics, to sing, to chant		1
歌唱	gēchàng	vb.	to sing		6
歌词	gēcí	n.	song lyric, lyrics		6
歌迷	gēmí	n.	fan of a singer		3
歌曲	• gēqǔ	n.	song		5
歌声	gēshēng	n.	singing voice, fig. original voice of a poet		3
歌手	gēshǒu	n.	singer		3
歌星	gēxīng	n.	singing star, famous singer		6
唱歌	chàng gē	vb.	to sing a song		1
国歌	guógē	n.	national anthem		6
民歌	míngē	n.	folk song		6
诗歌	shīgē	n.	poem		5
歉	**qiàn**		**to apologise, to regret**	欠 76.10	6
抱歉	bàoqiàn	vb.	to be sorry, to feel apologetic, sorry!		6
道歉	dàoqiàn	vb.	to apologize		6

止 zhǐ stop — 77

止	zhǐ		to stop, to desist, to detain	止 77.0	3
止	zhǐ	vb.	to stop, to prohibit, until, only		6
不止	bùzhǐ	vb.	to not stop; incessantly, without end, more than, not limited to		5
防止	fángzhǐ	vb.	to prevent, to guard against, to take precautions		3
截止	jiézhǐ	vb.	to close, to stop, to put a stop to sth, cut-off point, stopping point, deadline		6
禁止	jìnzhǐ	vb.	to prohibit, to forbid, to ban		4
停止	tíngzhǐ	vb.	to stop, to halt, to cease		3
为止	• wéizhǐ	vb.	until, (used in combination with words like 到 dào or 至 zhì in constructs of the form 到...為止|到...为止)		5

终止	zhōngzhǐ	*vb.*	to stop, to terminate (law)		5
阻止	zǔzhǐ	*vb.*	to prevent, to block		4

正 zhèng — right, proper, correct 止 77.1 1

正	zhèng	+ *adv.*	straight, upright, punctual, just, just now		1
正	zhèng	+ *adj.*	right, obverse, (opp. 反 fǎn: reverse), in the middle, main (opp. 偏 piān: leaning) honest, upright, pure (of colour), principal, chief (opp. 副 fù: deputy, assistant)		3
正版	zhèngbǎn	*adj.*	genuine, legal		5
正常	zhèngcháng	*adj.*	regular, normal, ordinary		2
正当	zhèngdāng	*vb.*	timely, just (when needed)		6
正规	zhèngguī	*adj.*	regular, according to standards		5
正好	zhènghǎo	*adv.*	just (in time), just right, just enough, to happen to, to chance to, by chance, it just so happens that		2
正确	zhèngquè	*adj.*	correct, proper		2
正如	zhèngrú	*adv.*	just as, precisely as		5
正是	zhèngshì	*adv.*	just right, exactly, precisely		2
正式	zhèngshì	*adj.*	formal, official		3
正义	zhèngyì	*n.*	justice, righteousness, just, righteous		5
正在	zhèngzài	*adv.*	just at (that time), right in (that place), right in the middle of (doing sth)		1
反正	fǎnzhèng	*adv.*	anyway, in any case, to come over from the enemy's side		3
改正	gǎizhèng	*vb.*	to correct, to amend, to put right, correction		4
公正	gōngzhèng	*adj.*	just, fair, equitable		5
纠正	jiūzhèng	*vb.*	to correct, to make right		6
真正	zhēnzhèng	*adj.*	genuine, real, true, genuinely		2

此 cǐ — this, these 止 77.2 3

此	cǐ	*pro.*	this, these, in this case, then		4
此处	• cǐchù	*n.*	this place, here (literary)		6
此次	cǐcì	*n.*	this time		6
此后	cǐhòu	*n.*	after this, afterwards, hereafter		5
此刻	cǐkè	*n.*	this moment, now, at present		5
此前	cǐqián	*n.*	before this, before then, previously		6
此时	cǐshí	*n.*	now, this moment		5
此事	cǐshì	*n.*	this matter		6
此外	cǐwài	*conj.*	besides, in addition, moreover, furthermore		4
此致	cǐzhì	*vb.*	I hereby express (used at the end of a letter to introduce a polite salutation)		6
彼此	bǐcǐ	*pro.*	each other, one another		5
从此	cóngcǐ	*adv.*	from now on, since then, henceforth		4
如此	rúcǐ	*adv.*	in this way, so		5
为此	wèicǐ	*conj.*	for this reason, with regards to this, in this respect, in order to do this, to this end		6
因此	yīncǐ	*conj.*	thus, consequently, as a result		3
由此	yóucǐ	*adv.*	hereby, from this		5

步 bù — step, pace, to walk, to stroll 止 77.3 3

步	bù	*n.*	a step, to walk, to stroll, to march, surname Bu		3
步行	bùxíng	*vb.*	to go on foot, to walk		4

初步	chūbù	*adj.*	initial, preliminary, tentative		3
脚步	jiǎobù	*n.*	footstep, step		5
进步	jìnbù	*n.*	progress, improvement, to improve, to progress		3
跑步	pǎo bù	*vb.*	to run, to jog, (military) to march at the double		3
散步	sàn bù	*vb.*	to take a walk, to go for a walk		3
逐步	zhúbù	*adv.*	progressively, step by step		4
进一步	jìn yī bù	*adv.*	one step further, to move forward a step, further onwards		3

武 wǔ — military, martial — 止 77.4 — 3

武器	wǔqì	*n.*	weapon, arms		3
武术	wǔshù	*n.*	military skill or technique (in former times), all kinds of martial art sports (some claiming spiritual development), self-defence		3

歹 dǎi — death — 歹 78

死 sǐ — to die, to be dead, lifeless — 歹 78.2 — 3

死	sǐ	*vb.*	to die, to be dead, (opp. 生 shēng, 活 huó) lifeless, impassable, uncrossable, inflexible, rigid, extremely, damned		3
死亡	sǐwáng	*vb.*	to die, death		6

残 cán — to injure, to spoil, broken — 歹 78.5 — 6

残疾	cánjí	*n.*	deformity on a person or animal, disabled, handicapped		6
残酷	cánkù	*adj.*	cruel, cruelty		6
残疾人	cánjírén	*n.*	disabled person		6

殊 shū — different, special, unusual — 歹 78.6 — 4

特殊	tèshū	*adj.*	special, particular, unusual, extraordinary		4

殖 zhí — to breed, to spawn, to increase — 歹 78.8 — 6

繁殖	fánzhí	*vb.*	to breed, to reproduce, to propagate		6

殳 shū — weapon — 79

段 duàn — section, piece, division — 殳 79.5 — 2

段	duàn	*m.w.*	m.w. for paragraph, segment, section, period of time, surname Duan		2
阶段	jiēduàn	*n.*	stage, section, phase, period		4
手段	shǒuduàn	*n.*	method, means (of doing sth), strategy, trick		5

毁 huǐ — to destroy — 殳 79.9 — 6

毁	huǐ	*vb.*	destroy, to damage, to ruin, to slander		6

毋 wú — do not — 母 母 80

母 mǔ — mother, female elders, female — 毋 80.1 — 3

母	mǔ	*n.*	mother, elderly female relative, origin, source, (of animals) female		6
母鸡	mǔjī	*n.*	hen, don't know (humorous slang mimicking Cantonese 唔知)		6
母女	mǔnǚ	*n.*	mother-daughter		6
母亲	- mǔqin	*n.*	mother		3

母子	· mǔzǐ	n.	mother and child, parent and subsidiary (companies), principal and interest	6
父母	fùmǔ	n.	father and mother, parents	3
字母	zìmǔ	n.	letter (of the alphabet)	4
祖母	zǔmǔ	n.	father's mother, paternal grandmother	6

每 měi — every, each   毋 80.3

| 每 | měi | pro. | each, every, per | 3 |

毒 dú — poison, venom, poisonous   毋 80.4 5

毒	dú	n.	poison, to poison, poisonous, malicious, cruel, fierce, narcotics	5
毒品	dúpǐn	n.	drugs, narcotics, poison	6
病毒	bìngdú	n.	virus	5
杀毒	shādú	vb.	to disinfect, (computing) to destroy a computer virus	5
吸毒	xī dú	vb.	to take (addictive) drugs	6
消毒	xiāo dú	vb.	to disinfect, to sterilize	5
有毒	yǒudú	adj.	poisonous	5
中毒	· zhòngdú	vb.	to be poisoned, poisoning	5

比 bǐ — compare   81

比 bǐ — to compare, comparison, than   比 81.0 1

比	bǐ	vb.	to compare, (indicates comparison), to gesticulate, ratio	1
比方	- bǐfang	n.	analogy, instance, for instance	5
比分	bǐfēn	n.	score	4
比较	bǐjiào	vb.	to compare, to contrast, comparatively, relatively, quite, comparison	3
比例	bǐlì	n.	proportion, scale	3
比如	bǐrú	conj.	for example, for instance, such as	2
比赛	bǐsài	n.	competition (sports etc), match	3
比重	bǐzhòng	n.	proportion, specific gravity	5
比如说	bǐrúshuō	conj.	for example	2
对比	duìbǐ	vb.	to contrast, contrast, ratio	4
相比	xiāngbǐ	vb.	to compare	3

毕 bì — to end, to finish, to conclude   比 81.2 4

毕竟	bìjìng	adv.	after all, all in all, when all is said and done, in the final analysis	5
毕业	bìyè	n.	graduation, to graduate, to finish school	4
毕业生	bìyè shēng	n.	graduate	4

毛 máo — fur   82

毛 máo — hair, fur, feathers, coarse   毛 82.0 1

毛	máo	+ m.w.	Chinese unit of money equal to 1/10 yuan	1
毛	máo	+ n.	hair, fur, feather, surname Mao	3
毛笔	máobǐ	n.	writing brush	5
毛病	máobìng	n.	fault, defect, shortcomings, ailment	3
毛巾	máojīn	n.	towel	4
毛衣	máoyī	n.	(wool) sweater	4
羽毛球	yǔmáoqiú	n.	shuttlecock, badminton	5

毫	háo		fine hair, measure of length	毛 82.7	4
毫米	háomǐ	m.w.	millimetre		4
毫升	háoshēng	m.w.	millilitre		4

氏 shì clan 83

民	mín		people, subjects, citizens	氏 83.1	3
民歌	míngē	n.	folk song		6
民工	míngōng	n.	migrant worker (who moved from a rural area of China to a city to find work), temporary worker enlisted on a public project		6
民间	mínjiān	n.	among the people, popular, folk, non-governmental, involving people rather than governments		3
民警	mínjǐng	n.	civil police, PRC police		6
民意	mínyì	n.	public opinion, popular will, public will		6
民主	mínzhǔ	n.	democracy		6
民族	mínzú	n.	nationality, ethnic group		3
公民	gōngmín	n.	citizen		3
国民	guómín	n.	nationals, citizens, people of a nation		5
居民	jūmín	n.	resident, inhabitant		4
农民	nóngmín	n.	peasant, farmer		3
人民	rénmín	n.	the people		3
市民	shìmín	n.	city resident		6
移民	yímín	vb.	to immigrate, to migrate, emigrant, immigrant		4
人民币	rénmínbì	n.	renminbi (RMB)		3
中华民族	zhōnghuá mínzú	n.	the Chinese people		3

气 qì steam 84

气	qì		steam, vapor, breath	气 84.0	1
气	qì	n.	gas, air, smell, weather, to make angry, to annoy, to get angry, vital energy		2
气氛	qìfēn	n.	atmosphere, mood		6
气候	qìhòu	n.	climate, atmosphere, situation		3
气球	qìqiú	n.	balloon		4
气体	qìtǐ	n.	gas (i.e. gaseous substance)		5
气温	qìwēn	n.	air temperature		2
气象	qìxiàng	n.	meteorological feature		5
客气	- kèqi	adj.	polite, courteous, formal, modest		5
空气	kōngqì	n.	air, atmosphere		2
冷气	lěngqì	n.	cold air, air conditioning		6
力气	- lìqi	n.	strength		4
煤气	méiqì	n.	coal gas, gas (fuel)		5
暖气	nuǎnqì	n.	central heating, heater, warm air		4
脾气	- píqi	n.	character, temperament, disposition, bad temper		5
生气	shēngqì	vb.	to get angry, to take offense, angry, vitality, liveliness		1
叹气	tànqì	vb.	to sigh, to heave a sigh		6
天气	tiānqì	n.	weather		1
氧气	yǎngqì	n.	oxygen		6

勇气	yǒngqì	n.	courage, valour		4
运气	- yùnqi	n.	luck (good or bad)		4
不客气	- bùkèqi	phr.	you're welcome, don't mention it, impolite, rude, blunt		1
天然气	tiānránqì	n.	natural gas		5
一口气	yīkǒuqì	n.	one breath, in one breath, at a stretch		5

氛 **fēn** — gas, vapor, air — 气 84.4 — 6

气氛	qìfēn	n.	atmosphere, mood		6

氧 **yǎng** — oxygen — 气 84.6 — 6

氧气	yǎngqì	n.	oxygen		6

水 shuǐ water 氵 85

水 **shuǐ** — water, liquid — 水 85.0 — 1

水	shuǐ	n.	water, river, liquid, juice, surname Shui		1
水分	• shuǐfèn	n.	moisture content, (fig.) overstatement, padding		5
水果	shuǐguǒ	n.	fruit		1
水库	shuǐkù	n.	reservoir		5
水泥	shuǐní	n.	cement		6
水平	shuǐpíng	n.	level (of achievement etc), standard, horizontal		2
水灾	shuǐzāi	n.	flood, flood damage		5
水产品	shuǐchǎnpǐn	n.	aquatic products (including fish, crabs, seaweed etc)		5
海水	hǎishuǐ	n.	seawater		4
洪水	hóngshuǐ	n.	flood, deluge		6
胶水	jiāoshuǐ	n.	glue		5
酒水	jiǔshuǐ	n.	beverage, a drink		6
开水	kāishuǐ	n.	boiled water, boiling water		4
泪水	lèishuǐ	n.	teardrop, tears		4
冷水	lěngshuǐ	n.	cold water, unboiled water, fig. not yet ready (of plans)		6
凉水	liángshuǐ	n.	cool water, unboiled water		3
墨水	mòshuǐ	n.	ink		6
汽水	qìshuǐ	n.	soft drink, soda, pop		4
热水	rèshuǐ	n.	hot water		6
跳水	tiàoshuǐ	vb.	to dive (into water), (sports) diving, to commit suicide by jumping into water, (fig.) (of stock prices etc) to fall dramatically		6
污水	wūshuǐ	n.	sewage		5
薪水	xīnshuǐ	n.	salary, wage		6
药水	yàoshuǐ	n.	liquid medicine		2
雨水	yǔshuǐ	n.	rainwater, Rainwater (one of 24 solar terms)		5
热水器	rèshuǐqì	n.	water heater		6
纯净水	chúnjìngshuǐ	n.	purified water		4
矿泉水	kuàngquánshuǐ	n.	mineral spring water		4
自来水	zìláishuǐ	n.	running water, tap water		6

永 **yǒng** — long, forever — 水 85.1 — 2

永远	yǒngyuǎn	adv.	always, forever, eternal		2

汉	**hàn**		Chinese people, Chinese language	水 85.2	1
汉语	hànyǔ	n.	Chinese (language)		1
汉字	hànzì	n.	Chinese character		1
汇	**huì**		to flow together, to gather	水 85.2	4
汇	huì	vb.	to converge, to gather, to transfer, collection		4
汇款	huì kuǎn	vb.	to remit money, remittance		5
汇报	huìbào	vb.	to report, to give an account of, report		4
汇率	huìlǜ	n.	exchange rate		4
词汇	cíhuì	n.	vocabulary, list of words (e.g. for language teaching purposes), word		4
外汇	wàihuì	n.	foreign (currency) exchange		4
求	**qiú**		to seek, to demand, to request	水 85.2	2
求	qiú	vb.	to seek, to look for, to request, to demand, to beseech		2
求职	qiúzhí	vb.	to seek employment		6
请求	qǐngqiú	vb.	to request, to ask, request		2
需求	xūqiú	n.	requirement, to require, (economics) demand		3
寻求	xúnqiú	vb.	to seek, to look for		5
要求	·yāoqiú	vb.	to demand, to request, to require, requirement, to stake a claim, to ask		2
征求	zhēngqiú	vb.	to solicit, to seek, to request (opinions, feedback etc), to petition		4
追求	zhuīqiú	vb.	to pursue (a goal etc) stubbornly, to seek after, to woo		4
汁	**zhī**		juice, fluid, sap	水 85.2	3
果汁	guǒzhī	n.	fruit juice		3
池	**chí**		pool, pond, moat	水 85.3	5
池子	chízi	n.	pond, bathhouse pool, dance floor of a ballroom, (old) stalls (front rows in a theatre)		5
电池	diànchí	n.	battery		5
游泳池	yóuyǒngchí	n.	swimming pool		5
汗	**hàn**		perspiration, sweat	水 85.3	5
汗	hàn	n.	perspiration, sweat		5
出汗	chūhàn	vb.	to perspire, to sweat		5
江	**jiāng**		large river, yangzi	水 85.3	4
江	jiāng	n.	large river, Yangtze (abbrev.), surname Jiang		4
汤	**tāng**		soup, broth	水 85.3	3
汤	tāng	n.	hot water, soup, broth, Chinese medicine liquid preparation, surname Tang		3
污	**wū**		filthy, dirty, impure	水 85.3	5
污染	wūrǎn	n.	pollution, contamination		5
污水	wūshuǐ	n.	sewage		5
沉	**chén**		to sink, heavy, deep	水 85.4	4
沉	chén	vb.	to sink, (opp. 浮 fú: to float), to keep down, to submerge, heavy, deep, profound		4
沉默	chénmò	adj.	taciturn, uncommunicative, silent		4
沉重	chénzhòng	adj.	heavy, hard, serious, critical		4

沟	gōu		ditch, drain	水 85.4	5
沟	gōu	n.	ditch, gutter, groove, gully, ravine		5
沟通	gōutōng	vb.	to join, to connect, to link up, to communicate		5
没	* méi, mò		not, have not; to drown, to sink	水 85.4	1
没	méi	vb.	(negative prefix for verbs), have not, not, none		1
没错	méi cuò	vb.	that's right, sure!, rest assured!, that's good, can't go wrong		4
没用	méi yòng	adj.	useless		3
没法	méifǎ	vb.	at a loss, unable to do anything about it, to have no choice		4
没事	méishì	vb.	it's not important, it's nothing, never mind, to have nothing to do, to be free, to be all right (out of danger or trouble)		1
没有	méiyǒu	vb.	haven't, hasn't, doesn't exist, to not have, to not be		1
没收	• mòshōu	vb.	to confiscate, to seize		6
没关系	méi guānxi	vb.	it doesn't matter, that's all right, never mind		1
没什么	méi shénme	vb.	nothing, it doesn't matter, it's nothing, never mind, don't mention it, you're welcome		1
没想到	méixiǎngdào	vb.	didn't expect		4
从没	cóng méi	adv.	never (in the past), never did		6
有没有	yǒuméiyǒu	phr.	(before a noun) Do (you, they etc) have ...?, Is there a ...?, (before a verb) Did (you, they etc) (verb, infinitive)?		6
汽	qì		steam, vapor, gas	水 85.4	1
汽车	qìchē	n.	car, automobile, bus		1
汽水	qìshuǐ	n.	soft drink, soda, pop		4
汽油	qìyóu	n.	petrol, gasoline		4
公共汽车	gōnggòng qìchē	n.	bus		2
沙	shā		sand, gravel, pebbles	水 85.4	3
沙发	shāfā	n.	sofa (loanword)		3
沙漠	shāmò	n.	desert		5
沙子	shāzi	n.	sand, grit		3
波	bō		waves, ripples, storm	水 85.5	6
波动	bōdòng	vb.	to undulate, to fluctuate, wave motion, rise and fall		6
波浪	bōlàng	n.	wave		6
微波炉	wēibōlú	n.	microwave oven		6
法	fǎ		law, rule, method	水 85.5	2
法	fǎ	n.	law, method, way, statute, standard, (Buddhism) dharma, France, French		4
法官	fǎguān	n.	judge (in court)		4
法规	fǎguī	n.	legislation, statute		5
法律	fǎlǜ	n.	law		4
法庭	fǎtíng	n.	court of law		6
法语	fǎyǔ	n.	French (language)		6
法院	fǎyuàn	n.	court of law, court		4
法制	fǎzhì	adj.	legal system, legality		5
办法	bànfǎ	n.	means, method, way (of doing sth)		2
方法	fāngfǎ	n.	method, way, means		2
合法	héfǎ	adj.	lawful, legitimate, legal		3

看法	kànfǎ	n.	way of looking at a thing, view, opinion	2
没法	méifǎ	vb.	at a loss, unable to do anything about it, to have no choice	4
手法	shǒufǎ	n.	technique, trick, skill	5
书法	shūfǎ	n.	calligraphy, handwriting, penmanship	5
说法	- shuōfa	vb.	to expound Buddhist teachings	5
违法	wéifǎ	vb.	illegal, to break the law	5
无法	wúfǎ	vb.	unable, incapable	4
想法	xiǎngfǎ	n.	way of thinking, opinion, notion, to think of a way (to do sth)	2
依法	yīfǎ	adv.	according to law, legal (proceedings)	5
用法	yòngfǎ	n.	usage	6
语法	yǔfǎ	n.	grammar	4
做法	zuòfǎ	n.	way of handling sth, method for making, work method, recipe, practice	2

泛 fàn — extensive, general, to drift 水 85.5 5

广泛	guǎngfàn	adj.	extensive, wide range	5

河 hé — river, stream 水 85.5 2

河	hé	n.	river, stream, Milky Way (galaxy), (Hé) Huang He River or Yellow River, surname He	2

泪 lèi — tears, to shed tears 水 85.5 4

泪	lèi	n.	tears, sth. tear-like, to shed tears, to weep	4
泪水	lèishuǐ	n.	teardrop, tears	4
眼泪	yǎnlèi	n.	tears, crying	4

泥 ní — mud, mire, paste 水 85.5 6

泥	ní	n.	mud, mire, earth, clay, paste, pulp	6
水泥	shuǐní	n.	cement	6

泡 pào — bubbles, to soak 水 85.5 6

泡	pào	n.	bubble, bubbles, bubble like, to soak, to pour boiling water into, to dawdle	6

泼 pō — to splash, to sprinkle 水 85.5 5

泼	pō	vb.	to splash, to spill, to spill, rough and coarse, brutish	5
活泼	- huópo	adj.	lively, vivacious, brisk, active, (chemistry) reactive	5

浅 qiǎn — shallow, simple, superficial 水 85.5 4

浅	qiǎn	adj.	shallow, (opp. 深 shēn: deep), simple, easy, superficial, pale	4

泉 quán — spring, mouth of spring 水 85.5 4

泉	quán	n.	spring (small stream), mouth of a spring, coin (archaic)	5
矿泉水	kuàngquánshuǐ	n.	mineral spring water	4

沿 yán — along, to follow a course, to go along 水 85.5 6

沿	yán	prep.	along, to follow (a line, tradition etc), to carry on, to trim (a border with braid, tape etc), border, edge	6
沿海	yánhǎi	adj.	coastal	6
沿着	yánzhe	vb.	to go along, to follow	6

泳 yǒng — to swim 水 85.5 3

游泳	yóuyǒng	n.	swimming, to swim	3

游泳池	yóuyǒngchí	n.	swimming pool		5
油	**yóu**		oil, fat, grease	水 85.5	2
油	yóu	n.	oil, fat, grease, petroleum, to apply tung oil, paint or varnish, oily, greasy, glib, cunning		2
加油	jiā yóu	vb.	to add oil, to top up with gas, to refuel, to accelerate, to step on the gas, (fig.) to make an extra effort, to cheer sb on		2
酱油	jiàngyóu	n.	soy sauce		6
汽油	qìyóu	n.	petrol, gasoline		4
石油	shíyóu	n.	oil, petroleum		3
加油站	jiāyóuzhàn	n.	petrol (gas) station		4
治	**zhì**		to rule, to manage	水 85.5	4
治	zhì	vb.	to rule, to govern, to manage, to control, to harness (a river), to treat (a disease), to wipe out (a pest), to punish, to research		4
治安	zhì'ān	n.	law and order, public security		5
治病	zhìbìng	vb.	to treat an illness		6
治理	zhìlǐ	vb.	to govern, to administer, to manage, to control, governance		5
治疗	zhìliáo	vb.	to treat (an illness), medical treatment, therapy		4
防治	fángzhì	vb.	to prevent and cure, prevention and cure		5
整治	zhěngzhì	vb.	to bring under control, to regulate, to restore to good condition, (coll.) to fix (a person), to prepare (a meal etc)		6
政治	zhèngzhì	n.	politics, political		4
三明治	sānmíngzhì	n.	sandwich (loanword)		6
注	**zhù**		to pour, to fill, to concentrate	水 85.5	3
注册	zhùcè	vb.	to register, to enrol		5
注射	zhùshè	n.	injection, to inject		5
注视	zhùshì	vb.	to watch attentively, to gaze at		5
注意	zhùyì	vb.	to take note of, to pay attention to		3
注重	zhùzhòng	vb.	to pay attention to, to emphasize		5
关注	guānzhù	vb.	to pay attention to, to follow sth closely, to follow (on social media), concern, interest, attention		3
测	**cè**		to measure, to estimate	水 85.6	4
测	cè	vb.	to survey, to measure, to estimate, to infer		4
测定	cèdìng	vb.	to determine (by measuring or surveying)		6
测量	cèliáng	vb.	to survey, to measure, to gauge, to determine		4
测试	cèshì	vb.	to test (machinery etc), to test (students), test, quiz, exam, beta (software)		4
猜测	cāicè	vb.	to guess, to conjecture, to surmise		5
监测	jiāncè	vb.	to monitor		6
检测	jiǎncè	vb.	to detect, to test, detection, sensing		4
预测	yùcè	vb.	to forecast, to predict		4
洞	**dòng**		cave, hole	水 85.6	5
洞	dòng	n.	cave, hole, zero (unambiguous spoken form when spelling out numbers)		5
漏洞	lòudòng	n.	leak, hole, gap, loophole		5
洪	**hóng**		vast, flood	水 85.6	6
洪水	hóngshuǐ	n.	flood, deluge		6

活	**huó**		to live, alive	水 85.6	2
活	huó	vb.	to live, (opp. 死 sǐ: to die), alive, living, work, workmanship		3
活动	huódòng	vb.	to exercise, to move about, to operate, to use connections (personal influence), loose, active, movable, activity, campaign, manoeuvre, behaviour		2
活力	huólì	n.	energy, vitality, vigour, vital force		5
活泼	- huópo	adj.	lively, vivacious, brisk, active, (chemistry) reactive		5
活跃	huóyuè	adj.	active, lively, excited, to enliven, to brighten up		6
快活	- kuàihuo	adj.	happy, cheerful		5
灵活	línghuó	adj.	flexible, nimble, agile		6
生活	shēnghuó	n.	life, activity, to live, livelihood		2
干活儿	gànhuór	vb.	to do manual labour, to work, erhua variant of 干活 gànhuó		2
生活费	shēnghuófèi	n.	cost of living, living expenses, alimony		6

济	**jì**		to help, to relieve, to ferry	水 85.6	3
经济	jīngjì	n.	economy, economic		3

洁	**jié**		clean, pure	水 85.6	6
清洁	qīngjié	adj.	clean, to clean		6
清洁工	qīngjiégōng	n.	cleaner, janitor, garbage collector		6

流	**liú**		to flow, to drift, stream	水 85.6	2
流	liú	vb.	to flow, to disseminate, to circulate or spread, to move or drift, stream, stream like, class		2
流传	liúchuán	vb.	to spread, to circulate, to hand down		4
流动	liúdòng	vb.	to flow, to circulate, to go from place to place, to be mobile, (of assets) liquid		5
流感	liúgǎn	n.	flu, influenza		6
流利	liúlì	n.	fluent		2
流通	liútōng	vb.	to circulate, to distribute, circulation, distribution		5
流行	liúxíng	vb.	(of a contagious disease etc) to spread, to propagate, (of a style of clothing, song etc) popular, fashionable		2
潮流	cháoliú	n.	tide, current, trend		4
交流	jiāoliú	vb.	to exchange, exchange, communication, interaction, to have social contact (with sb)		3
一流	yīliú	adj.	top quality, front ranking		5
主流	zhǔliú	n.	main stream (of a river), fig. the essential point, main viewpoint of a matter, mainstream (culture etc)		6

浓	**nóng**		thick, strong, concentrated	水 85.6	4
浓	nóng	adj.	thick, concentrated, dense, strong (smell etc), (opp. 淡 dàn: bland)		4

派	**pài**		school, group, branch	水 85.6	3
派	pài	n.	school, group, faction, branch (river), tributary, to dispatch, to send, to assign, to appoint		3
派出	pàichū	vb.	to send, to dispatch		6

洒	**sǎ**		to sprinkle, to spray, to spill	水 85.6	5
洒	sǎ	vb.	to sprinkle, to spray, to spill, to shed, to wipe away		5

洗	**xǐ**		to wash, to rinse, to clean	水 85.6	1
洗	xǐ	vb.	to wash, to bathe, to develop (photo)		1

洗澡	xǐzǎo	vb.	to bathe, to take a shower		2
洗手间	xǐshǒujiān	n.	toilet, lavatory, washroom		1
洗衣粉	xǐyīfěn	n.	laundry detergent, washing powder		6
洗衣机	xǐyījī	n.	washer, washing machine		2
清洗	qīngxǐ	vb.	to wash, to clean, to purge		6

洋 yáng — ocean, vast, foreign 水 85.6   6

洋	yáng	n.	ocean, vast, foreign, silver dollar or coin	6
海洋	hǎiyáng	n.	ocean	6

浮 fú — to float, superficial 水 85.7   6

浮	fú	vb.	to float (opp. 沉 chén: to sink) superficial, floating, unstable, movable, provisional, temporary, transient, impetuous, hollow, inflated, to exceed, superfluous, excessive, surplus	6

海 hǎi — sea, ocean, maritime 水 85.7   2

海	hǎi	n.	ocean, sea, surname Hai	2
海报	hǎibào	n.	poster, playbill, notice	6
海边	hǎibiān	n.	coast, seaside, seashore, beach	2
海底	hǎidǐ	n.	seabed, seafloor, bottom of the ocean	6
海关	hǎiguān	n.	customs (i.e. border crossing inspection)	3
海军	hǎijūn	n.	navy	6
海浪	hǎilàng	n.	sea wave	6
海水	hǎishuǐ	n.	seawater	4
海外	hǎiwài	n.	overseas, abroad	6
海湾	hǎiwān	n.	bay, gulf	6
海鲜	hǎixiān	n.	seafood	4
海洋	hǎiyáng	n.	ocean	6
大海	dàhǎi	n.	sea, ocean	2
沿海	yánhǎi	adj.	coastal	6

浪 làng — wave, to waste 水 85.7   3

浪费	làngfèi	vb.	to waste, to squander	3
浪漫	làngmàn	adj.	romantic, unconventional	5
波浪	bōlàng	n.	wave	6
海浪	hǎilàng	n.	sea wave	6

润 rùn — moist, smooth, freshen 水 85.7   5

利润	lìrùn	n.	profit	5

涉 shè — to wade across, to go through 水 85.7   6

涉及	shèjí	vb.	to involve, to touch upon (a topic)	6
干涉	gānshè	vb.	to interfere, to meddle, interference	6

消 xiāo — to vanish, to cause to disappear 水 85.7   3

消毒	xiāo dú	vb.	to disinfect, to sterilize	5
消除	xiāochú	vb.	to eliminate, to remove	5
消防	xiāofáng	adj.	firefighting, fire control	5
消费	xiāofèi	vb.	to consume, to spend	3
消耗	xiāohào	vb.	to use up, to consume	6
消化	xiāohuà	vb.	to digest, digestion, digestive	4

消极	xiāojí	adj.	negative, passive, inactive	5
消灭	xiāomiè	vb.	to put an end to, to annihilate, to cause to perish, to perish, annihilation (in quantum field theory)	6
消失	xiāoshī	vb.	to disappear, to fade away	3
消息	- xiāoxi	n.	news, information	3
消费者	xiāofèi zhě	n.	consumer	5
取消	qǔxiāo	vb.	to cancel, cancellation	3

涨 * zhǎng, zhàng — to rise in price; to distend 水 85.7 5

涨	zhǎng	vb.	to rise (of prices, rivers)	5
涨	• zhàng	vb.	to swell, to distend, to have a rush of blood to the head	6
涨价	zhǎng jià	vb.	to appreciate (in value), to increase in price	5
上涨	shàngzhǎng	vb.	to rise, to go up	5

淡 dàn — bland, insipid, diluted, weak 水 85.8 4

| 淡 | dàn | adj. | bland, insipid, diluted, weak, mild, light in colour, tasteless, indifferent, (opp. 浓 nóng: concentrated) | 4 |

混 hùn — to mix, to confuse 水 85.8 6

混	hùn	vb.	to mix, to confuse, to disguise, to muddle along	6
混合	hùnhé	vb.	to mix, to blend, hybrid, composite	6
混乱	hùnluàn	n.	confusion, chaos, disorder	6

渐 jiàn — gradually 水 85.8 4

| 渐渐 | jiànjiàn | adv. | gradually | 4 |
| 逐渐 | zhújiàn | adv. | gradually | 4 |

清 qīng — clear, pure, to clear up 水 85.8 2

清	qīng	adj.	clear, pure, to settle, to clear up, Qing Dynasty (1644-1911)	6
清晨	qīngchén	n.	early morning	5
清楚	- qīngchu	adj.	clear, distinct, to understand thoroughly, to be clear about	2
清洁	qīngjié	adj.	clean, to clean	6
清理	qīnglǐ	vb.	to clear up, to tidy up, to dispose of	5
清洗	qīngxǐ	vb.	to wash, to clean, to purge	6
清醒	qīngxǐng	adj.	clear-headed, sober, awake	4
清洁工	qīngjiégōng	n.	cleaner, janitor, garbage collector	6
清明节	qīngmíngjié	n.	Qingming or Pure Brightness Festival or Tomb Sweeping Day, celebration for the dead (in early April)	6

深 shēn — deep, depth, deeply 水 85.8 3

深	shēn	adj.	deep, (opp. 浅 qiǎn: shallow), depth, deeply, (of a colour) dark, deep, rich	3
深处	• shēnchù	n.	abyss, depths, deepest or most distant part	5
深度	shēndù	n.	depth, (of a speech etc) profundity, advanced stage of development	5
深厚	shēnhòu	adj.	deep, profound	4
深化	shēnhuà	vb.	to deepen, to intensify	6
深刻	shēnkè	adj.	profound, deep, deep-going	3
深入	shēnrù	vb.	to penetrate deeply, thorough	3
深深	shēnshēn	adj.	deep, profound	6

添 tiān — to add to, to increase 水 85.8 6

| 添 | tiān | vb. | to add, to increase, to replenish | 6 |

214

液	yè		liquid, juice, fluid	水 85.8	6
血液	xuèyè	n.	blood		6
渡	**dù**		**to cross, to ferry**	水 85.9	6
渡	dù	vb.	to cross, to pass through, to ferry across, (used in place names) ferry crossing		6
过渡	guòdù	vb.	to cross over (by ferry), to pass from one form to another, transition, interim, caretaker (administration)		6
港	**gǎng**		**port, harbour**	水 85.9	6
港口	gǎngkǒu	n.	port, harbour, airport		6
湖	**hú**		**lake**	水 85.9	2
湖	hú	n.	lake, Hubei, Hunan, bluish green		2
渴	**kě**		**thirsty, yearn, pine**	水 85.9	1
渴	kě	adj.	thirsty, yearningly		1
渴望	kěwàng	vb.	to thirst for, to long for		5
渠	**qú**		**ditch, canal, channel**	水 85.9	6
渠道	qúdào	n.	irrigation ditch, (fig.) channel, means		6
湿	**shī**		**moist, wet**	水 85.9	4
湿	shī	adj.	moist, (opp. 干 gān: dry), wet, humid, damp, illness		4
潮湿	cháoshī	adj.	damp, moist		4
湾	**wān**		**bay, inlet, bend of stream**	水 85.9	6
海湾	hǎiwān	n.	bay, gulf		6
温	**wēn**		**warm, mild**	水 85.9	2
温度	wēndù	n.	temperature		2
温和	wēnhé	adj.	mild, gentle, moderate		5
温暖	wēnnuǎn	adj.	warm, to make warm		3
低温	dīwēn	n.	low temperature		6
高温	gāowēn	n.	high temperature		5
降温	jiàngwēn	vb.	to become cooler, to lower the temperature, cooling, (of interest, activity etc) to decline		4
气温	qìwēn	n.	air temperature		2
游	**yóu**		**to swim, to travel**	水 85.9	2
游	yóu	vb.	to swim, to travel, to drift, to wander		3
游客	yóukè	n.	traveller, tourist, (online gaming) guest player		2
游人	yóurén	n.	a tourist		6
游玩	yóuwán	vb.	to amuse oneself, to have fun, to go sightseeing, to take a stroll		6
游戏	yóuxì	n.	game		3
游行	yóuxíng	n.	march, parade, demonstration		6
游泳	yóuyǒng	n.	swimming, to swim		3
游戏机	yóuxìjī	n.	video game, game machine		6
游泳池	yóuyǒngchí	n.	swimming pool		5
导游	dǎoyóu	n.	tour guide, guidebook, to conduct a tour		4
旅游	lǚyóu	n.	trip, journey, tourism, travel, tour, to travel		2

滑	**huá**		to slip, to slide, slippery, polished	水 85.10	5
滑	huá	vb.	to slip, to slide, slippery, cunning, crafty, surname Hua		5
满	**mǎn**		full, filled, satisfied	水 85.10	2
满	mǎn	adj.	full, orig. plentiful, abundant, to fill, completely		2
满意	mǎnyì	vb.	to be satisfied, to be pleased, to one's satisfaction		2
满足	mǎnzú	vb.	to satisfy, to meet (the needs of), to be satisfied		3
不满	bùmǎn	adj.	resentful, discontented, dissatisfied		2
布满	bùmǎn	vb.	to be covered with, to be filled with		6
充满	chōngmǎn	vb.	(to be) full of, brimming with, very full, permeated		3
圆满	yuánmǎn	adj.	satisfactory, consummate, perfect		4
源	**yuán**		spring, source, head	水 85.10	4
电源	diànyuán	n.	electric power source		4
来源	láiyuán	n.	source (of information etc), origin		4
资源	zīyuán	n.	natural resource, resource		4
滴	**dī**		to drip, a drop	水 85.11	6
滴	dī	vb.	to drip, a drop, bead, m.w. drop		6
滚	**gǔn**		to boil, to roll	水 85.11	5
滚	gǔn	vb.	to boil, to roll, to take a hike, Get lost!		5
漏	**lòu**		to leak, to drip, funnel, hour glass	水 85.11	5
漏	lòu	vb.	to leak, to divulge, to leave out by mistake, water clock or hourglass (old)		5
漏洞	lòudòng	n.	leak, hole, gap, loophole		5
漫	**màn**		to overflow, spreading	水 85.11	5
漫长	· màncháng	adj.	very long, endless		5
漫画	mànhuà	n.	caricature, cartoon, Japanese manga		5
浪漫	làngmàn	adj.	romantic, unconventional		5
漠	**mò**		desert, aloof, indifferent, cool	水 85.11	5
沙漠	shāmò	n.	desert		5
漂	**piào**		elegant, polished	水 85.11	2
漂亮	- piàoliang	adj.	pretty, beautiful		2
演	**yǎn**		to perform, to put on	水 85.11	3
演	yǎn	vb.	to perform, to put on, to develop, to evolve, to practice		3
演唱	yǎnchàng	n.	sung performance, to sing for an audience		3
演出	yǎnchū	vb.	to act (in a play), to perform, to put on (a performance), performance, concert, show		3
演讲	yǎnjiǎng	n.	lecture, to make a speech		4
演员	yǎnyuán	n.	actor or actress, performer		3
演奏	yǎnzòu	vb.	to perform on a musical instrument		6
演唱会	yǎnchànghuì	n.	vocal recital or concert		3
扮演	bànyǎn	vb.	to play the role of, to act		5
表演	biǎoyǎn	n.	play, show, performance, exhibition, to perform, to act, to demonstrate		3
导演	dǎoyǎn	vb.	to direct, director (film etc)		3

上演	shàngyǎn	vb.	to screen (a movie), to stage (a play), a screening, a staging		6
潮	**cháo**		**tide, damp**	水 85.12	4
潮	cháo	n.	tide, current, damp, moist, humid		4
潮流	cháoliú	n.	tide, current, trend		4
潮湿	cháoshī	adj.	damp, moist		4
高潮	gāocháo	n.	high tide, high water, upsurge, climax, orgasm, chorus		4
潜	**qián**		**hidden, secret, latent**	水 85.12	6
潜力	qiánlì	n.	potential, capacity		6
激	**jī**		**to arouse, to excite, to incite**	水 85.13	4
激动	jīdòng	vb.	to move emotionally, to stir up (emotions), to excite		4
激烈	jīliè	adj.	(of competition or fighting) intense, fierce, (of pain) acute, (of an expression of opinion) impassioned, vehement, (of a course of action) drastic, extreme		4
激情	jīqíng	n.	passion, fervor, enthusiasm, strong emotion		6
刺激	cìjī	vb.	to provoke, to irritate, to upset, to stimulate, to excite, irritant		4
澡	**zǎo**		**bath**	水 85.13	2
洗澡	xǐzǎo	vb.	to bathe, to take a shower		2

火 huǒ fire ⺣ 86

火	**huǒ**		**fire, flame, to burn**	火 86.0	1
火	huǒ	+ n.	fire, flame, to burn, to be angry, (Chinese Med. internal fire)		3
火	huǒ	+ adj.	urgent, hot (popular), fiery		4
火柴	huǒchái	n.	match (for lighting fire)		5
火车	huǒchē	n.	train		1
火箭	huǒjiàn	n.	rocket		6
火腿	huǒtuǐ	n.	ham		5
火灾	huǒzāi	n.	serious fire (in a city or a forest etc)		5
着火	·zháohuǒ	vb.	to ignite, to burn		4
灭	**miè**		**to extinguish, to wipe out**	火 86.1	6
灭	miè	vb.	to extinguish or put out, to go out (of a fire etc), to exterminate or wipe out, to drown		6
消灭	xiāomiè	vb.	to put an end to, to annihilate, to cause to perish, to perish, annihilation (in quantum field theory)		6
灯	**dēng**		**lantern, lamp**	火 86.2	2
灯	dēng	n.	lamp, light, lantern, burner		2
灯光	dēngguāng	n.	(stage) lighting, light		4
电灯	diàndēng	n.	electric light		4
台灯	táidēng	n.	desk lamp, table lamp		6
灰	**huī**		**ashes, dust, lime**	火 86.2	5
灰色	huīsè	adj.	gray, ash gray, grizzly, pessimistic, gloomy, dispirited, ambiguous		5
灾	**zāi**		**calamity, disaster**	火 86.3	5
灾	zāi	n.	calamity, disaster, catastrophe, adversity		5
灾害	zāihài	n.	calamity, disaster		5

灾难	• zāinàn	n.	disaster, catastrophe		5
灾区	zāiqū	n.	disaster area, stricken region		5
火灾	huǒzāi	n.	serious fire (in a city or a forest etc)		5
救灾	jiù zāi	vb.	to relieve disaster, to help disaster victims		5
受灾	shòuzāi	vb.	to be hit by a natural calamity, disaster-stricken		5
水灾	shuǐzāi	n.	flood, flood damage		5
炒	**chǎo**		**to sauté, to stir-fry, to roast**	火 86.4	6
炒	chǎo	vb.	to sauté, to stir-fry, to speculate, to hype, to fire/sack (sb)		6
炒股	chǎogǔ	vb.	(coll.) to speculate in shares/stocks		6
炒作	chǎozuò	vb.	to hype, to promote (in the media)		6
炉	**lú**		**fireplace, oven, furnace**	火 86.4	6
微波炉	wēibōlú	n.	microwave oven		6
炎	**yán**		**flame, blaze, hot**	火 86.4	6
发炎	fāyán	vb.	to become inflamed, inflammation		6
点	**diǎn**		**dot, speck, spot**	火 86.5	1
点	diǎn	n.	point, dot, drop, speck, o'clock, point (in space or time), to draw a dot, to check on a list, to touch briefly, to hint, to pour a liquid drop by drop, dot stroke in Chinese characters, m.w. for items		1
点名	diǎnmíng	n.	to roll call, to mention sb by name, (to call or praise or criticize sb) by name		4
点燃	diǎnrán	vb.	to ignite, to set on fire, aflame		5
点头	diǎntóu	vb.	to nod		2
差点	chàdiǎn	adv.	almost, nearly		5
地点	• dìdiǎn	n.	place, site, location, venue		1
观点	guāndiǎn	n.	point of view, viewpoint, standpoint		2
焦点	jiāodiǎn	n.	focus, focal point		6
景点	jǐngdiǎn	n.	scenic spot, place of interest (tourism)		6
快点	kuàidiǎn	vb.	to do sth more quickly, Hurry up!, Get a move on!		2
起点	qǐdiǎn	n.	starting point		6
缺点	quēdiǎn	n.	weak point, fault, shortcoming, disadvantage		3
热点	rèdiǎn	n.	hot spot, point of special interest		6
试点	shìdiǎn	n.	test point, to carry out trial, pilot scheme		6
特点	tèdiǎn	n.	characteristic (feature), trait, feature		2
晚点	wǎndiǎn	vb.	(of trains etc) to be late, delayed, behind schedule, light dinner		4
优点	yōudiǎn	n.	merit, benefit, strong point, advantage		3
终点	zhōngdiǎn	n.	the end, end point, finishing line (in a race), destination, terminus		5
重点	zhòngdiǎn	vb.	to recount (e.g. results of election), to re-evaluate		2
一点点	yīdiǎndiǎn	n.	a little bit		2
一点儿	yīdiǎnr	n.	a bit, a few, a little, erhua variant of 一点 yīdiǎn		1
百分点	bǎifēndiǎn	n.	percentage point		6
有一点	yǒuyīdiǎn	n.	a little, somewhat		2
烂	**làn**		**rotten, spoiled, decayed**	火 86.5	5
烂	làn	adj.	soft, mushy, well-cooked and soft, rotten, worn out, chaotic, messy, to rot, to decompose, utterly, thoroughly, bad		5

炼	**liàn**		**to smelt, to refine, to distil**	火 86.5	4
锻炼	duànliàn	*vb.*	to toughen, to temper, to engage in physical exercise, to work out, (fig.) to develop one's skills, to train oneself		4
炮	**pào**		**cannon, large gun, artillery**	火 86.5	6
炮	pào	*n.*	cannon, large gun, firecracker, cannon (Chinese chess piece)		6
炸	**zhà**		**to explode**	火 86.5	6
炸	zhà	*vb.*	to explode, to blow up		6
炸弹	zhàdàn	*n.*	bomb		6
炸药	zhàyào	*adj.*	explosive (material)		6
爆炸	bàozhà	*n.*	explosion, to explode, to blow up, to detonate		6
烦	**fán**		**to feel vexed, to trouble**	火 86.6	3
烦	fán	*vb.*	to feel vexed, (polite) to trouble, superfluous and confusing, edgy		4
麻烦	- máfan	*adj.*	inconvenient, troublesome, annoying, to trouble or bother sb, to put sb to trouble		3
不耐烦	bùnàifán	*adj.*	impatient, to lose patience		5
烤	**kǎo**		**to bake, to roast, to toast**	火 86.6	5
烤肉	kǎoròu	*n.*	barbecue (lit. roast meat)		5
烤鸭	kǎoyā	*n.*	roast duck		5
烈	**liè**		**fiery, violent, ardent**	火 86.6	3
激烈	jīliè	*adj.*	(of competition or fighting) intense, fierce, (of pain) acute, (of an expression of opinion) impassioned, vehement, (of a course of action) drastic, extreme		4
强烈	qiángliè	*adj.*	intense, (violently) strong		3
热烈	rèliè	*adj.*	enthusiastic, ardent, warm		3
热	**rè**		**heat, fever**	火 86.6	1
热	rè	*n.*	heat, fever, to warm up, to heat up, hot (of weather) (opp. 冷 lěng: cold, chilly)		1
热爱	rè'ài	*vb.*	to love ardently, to adore		3
热点	rèdiǎn	*n.*	hot spot, point of special interest		6
热量	rèliàng	*n.*	heat, quantity of heat, calorific value		5
热烈	rèliè	*adj.*	enthusiastic, ardent, warm		3
热门	rèmén	*adj.*	popular, hot, in vogue		5
热闹	- rènao	*adj.*	bustling with noise and excitement, lively		4
热情	rèqíng	*adj.*	cordial, enthusiastic, passion, passionate, passionately		2
热水	rèshuǐ	*n.*	hot water		6
热线	rèxiàn	*n.*	hotline (communications link)		6
热心	rèxīn	*n.*	enthusiasm, zeal, zealous, zest, enthusiastic, ardent, warm-hearted		4
热水器	rèshuǐqì	*n.*	water heater		6
加热	jiā rè	*vb.*	to heat		5
烧	**shāo**		**to burn, to bake, to roast**	火 86.6	4
烧	shāo	*vb.*	to burn, to cook, to stew, to bake, to roast, to heat, to boil (tea, water etc), fever, to run a temperature, (coll.) to let things go to one's head		4
发烧	fāshāo	*vb.*	to have a high temperature (from illness), to have a fever		4
燃烧	ránshāo	*vb.*	to ignite, to combust, to burn, combustion, flaming		4

烟	yān		smoke, soot	火 86.6	3
烟	yān	n.	smoke, soot, opium, tobacco, cigarettes		3
烟花	yānhuā	n.	fireworks, prostitute (esp. in Yuan theatre)		6
抽烟	chōuyān	vb.	to smoke (a cigarette, tobacco)		4
吸烟	xīyān	vb.	to smoke		4
焦	**jiāo**		burned, scorched, anxious	火 86.8	6
焦点	jiāodiǎn	n.	focus, focal point		6
然	**rán**		correct, certainly	火 86.8	2
然而	rán'ér	conj.	however, yet, but		4
然后	ránhòu	conj.	then (afterwards), after that, afterwards		2
必然	bìrán	adj.	inevitable, certain, necessity		3
不然	bùrán	conj.	or else, otherwise, if not, how about …?		4
当然	dāngrán	adv.	only natural, as it should be, certainly, of course, without doubt		3
果然	guǒrán	adv.	really, sure enough, as expected, if indeed		3
忽然	hūrán	adv.	suddenly, all of a sudden		2
既然	jìrán	conj.	since, as, this being the case		4
竟然	jìngrán	adv.	unexpectedly, to one's surprise, in spite of everything, in that crazy way, actually, to go as far as to		4
居然	jūrán	n.	unexpectedly, to one's surprise, go so far as to		5
偶然	ǒurán	adv.	incidentally, occasional, occasionally, by chance, randomly		5
仍然	réngrán	adv.	still, yet		3
虽然	suīrán	conj.	although, even though, even if		2
天然	tiānrán	adj.	natural		6
突然	tūrán	adj.	sudden, abrupt, unexpected		3
显然	xiǎnrán	adj.	clear, evident, obvious(ly)		3
依然	yīrán	adv.	still, as before		4
自然	zìrán	n.	nature, natural, naturally		3
天然气	tiānránqì	n.	natural gas		5
大自然	dàzìrán	n.	nature (the natural world)		2
要不然	- yàoburán	conj.	otherwise, or else, or		6
煮	**zhǔ**		to cook	火 86.8	6
煮	zhǔ	vb.	to cook, to boil		6
煤	**méi**		coal	火 86.9	5
煤	méi	n.	coal, coke, charcoal, carbon		5
煤气	méiqì	n.	coal gas, gas (fuel)		5
照	**zhào**		to shine, to illumine, to reflect	火 86.9	2
照	zhào	vb.	to shine, to illuminate, to reflect, to look at (one's reflection), to take (a photo), according to, in accordance with, as requested, photo, licence		3
照相	• zhào xiàng	vb.	to take a photograph		2
照顾	- zhàogu	vb.	to take care of, to show consideration, to attend to, to look after		2
照片	zhàopiàn	n.	photograph, picture		2
照样	zhàoyàng	adv.	as before, (same) as usual, in the same manner, still, nevertheless		6
照耀	zhàoyào	vb.	to shine, to illuminate		6
按照	ànzhào	prep.	according to, in accordance with, in the light of, on the basis of		3

护照	hùzhào	n.	passport		2
驾照	jiàzhào	n.	driver's license		5
拍照	pāizhào	vb.	to take a picture		4
依照	yīzhào	prep.	according to, in light of		5

熊 **xióng** — a bear — 火 86.10 — 5

熊	xióng	n.	a bear, blazing, surname Xiong		5
大熊猫	dàxióngmāo	n.	giant panda (Ailuropoda melanoleuca)		5

熟 **shú** — well-cooked, ripe, familiar with — 火 86.11 — 2

熟	shú	adj.	cooked (of food), ripe (of fruit), mature (of seeds), familiar, skilled, (opp. 生 shēng: unripe, raw), deep (sleep), (also pron.: shóu)		2
熟练	shúliàn	adj.	practiced, proficient, skilled, skilful		4
熟人	shúrén	n.	acquaintance, friend		3
熟悉	- shúxi	vb.	to be familiar with, to know well		5
成熟	chéngshú	adj.	mature, ripe, to mature, to ripen		3

燃 **rán** — to burn, to light fire, to ignite — 火 86.12 — 4

燃料	ránliào	n.	fuel		4
燃烧	ránshāo	vb.	to ignite, to combust, to burn, combustion, flaming		4
点燃	diǎnrán	vb.	to ignite, to set on fire, aflame		5

爆 **bào** — to burst, to explode — 火 86.15 — 6

爆	bào	vb.	to explode or burst, to quick fry or quick boil		6
爆发	bàofā	vb.	to break out, to erupt, to explode, to burst out		6
爆炸	bàozhà	n.	explosion, to explode, to blow up, to detonate		6

爪 **zhǎo** — claw — 爫 87

爬 **pá** — to crawl, to creep, to climb — 爪 87.4 — 2

爬	pá	vb.	to crawl, to climb, to get up or sit up		2
爬山	páshān	vb.	to climb a mountain, to mountaineer, hiking, mountaineering		2

爱 **ài** — to love, to be fond of, to like — 爪 87.6 — 1

爱	ài	vb.	to love, to be fond of, to like, affection, to be inclined (to do sth), to tend to (happen)		1
爱国	àiguó	vb.	to love one's country, patriotic		4
爱好	• àihào	vb.	to like, to take pleasure in, keen on, fond of, interest, hobby, appetite for		1
爱护	àihù	vb.	to cherish, to treasure, to take care of, to love and protect		4
爱情	àiqíng	n.	romance, love (romantic)		2
爱人	- àiren	n.	spouse (PRC), lover (non-PRC)		2
爱心	àixīn	n.	compassion, kindness, care for others, love		3
关爱	guān'ài	vb.	to show concern and care for		6
可爱	kě'ài	adj.	adorable, cute, lovely		2
恋爱	liàn'ài	vb.	to love, (romantic) love		5
亲爱	qīn'ài	adj.	dear, beloved, darling		4
热爱	rè'ài	vb.	to love ardently, to adore		3
喜爱	xǐ'ài	vb.	to like, to love, to be fond of, favourite		4

父	**fù**		**father**		**88**
父	fù		father	父 88.0	3
父母	fùmǔ	n	father and mother, parents		3
父女	fùnǚ	n	father and daughter		6
父亲	- fùqin	n	father		3
父子	• fùzǐ	n	father and son		6
师父	- shīfu	n	master, teacher		6
祖父	zǔfù	n	father's father, paternal grandfather		6
爷	yé		father, grandfather	父 88.2	1
爷爷	- yéye	n	(coll.) father's father, paternal grandfather		1
大爷	- dàye	n	arrogant idler, self-centreed show-off		4
爸	bà		father, papa	父 88.4	1
爸爸	- bàba	n	(informal) father		1
爻	**yáo**		**double x**		**89**
爽	shuǎng		happy, cheerful, refreshing	爻 89.7	6
爽	shuǎng	adj.	bright, clear, crisp, open, frank, straightforward, to feel well, fine, pleasurable, invigorating, to deviate		6
爿	**qiáng**		**half tree trunk**		**90**
将	jiāng		will, going to, future	爿 90.6	3
将	jiāng	adv.	will, shall, to use, to take, to checkmate, just a short while ago, (introduces object of main verb, used in the same way as 把 bǎ)		5
将近	jiāngjìn	adv.	almost, nearly, close to		3
将军	jiāngjūn	n	a general (military officer)		6
将来	jiānglái	n	in the future, future, the future		3
将要	jiāngyào	adv.	will, shall, to be going to		5
必将	bìjiāng	adv.	inevitably		6
即将	jíjiāng	adv.	on the eve of, to be about to, to be on the verge of		4
片	**piàn**		**slice**		**91**
片	piàn		slice, splinter, strip	片 91.0	2
片	piàn	n	disk, sheet, slice, to slice, fragmentary		2
片面	piànmiàn	adj.	unilateral, one-sided		4
唱片	chàngpiàn	n	gramophone record, LP, music CD, musical album		4
短片	duǎnpiàn	n	short film, video clip		6
名片	míngpiàn	n	(business) card		4
薯片	shǔpiàn	n	fried potato chips		6
图片	túpiàn	n	image, picture, photograph		2
相片	• xiàngpiàn	n	image, photograph		4
药片	yàopiàn	n	a (medicine) pill or tablet		2

影片	yǐngpiàn	n.	film, movie		2
照片	zhàopiàn	n.	photograph, picture		2
动画片	dònghuàpiàn	n.	animated film		4

版 bǎn — printing blocks, edition 片 91.4 — 5

版	bǎn	n.	a register, block of printing, edition, version, page	5
出版	chūbǎn	vb.	to publish	5
盗版	dàobǎn	vb.	to illegally copy, to pirate	6
正版	zhèngbǎn	adj.	genuine, legal	5
电子版	diànzǐbǎn	n.	electronic edition, digital version	5

牌 pái — signboard, placard 片 91.8 — 3

牌	pái	n.	mah-jong tile, playing card, game pieces, signboard, plate, tablet, medal	4
牌子	páizi	n.	sign, trademark, brand	3
车牌	chēpái	n.	license plate	6
打牌	dǎpái	vb.	to play mah-jong or cards	6
金牌	jīnpái	n.	gold medal	3
名牌	míngpái	n.	famous brand, nameplate, name tag	4
品牌	pǐnpái	n.	brand name, trademark	6
铜牌	tóngpái	n.	bronze medal, bronze plaque bearing a business name or logo etc	6
银牌	yínpái	n.	silver medal	3

牙 yá fang 92

牙 yá — tooth 牙 92.0 — 4

牙	yá	n.	tooth, ivory, tooth like thing	4
牙刷	yáshuā	n.	toothbrush	4
刷牙	shuāyá	vb.	to brush one's teeth	4
西班牙语	xībānyáyǔ	n.	Spanish (language)	6

牛 niú cow 牜 牛 93

牛 niú — cow, ox, bull 牛 93.0 — 1

牛	niú	+ n.	ox, cow, bull, surname Niu	3
牛	niú	+ adj.	brave, stubborn, awesome (slang)	5
牛奶	niúnǎi	n.	cow's milk	1
牛仔裤	niúzǎikù	n.	jeans	5
奶牛	nǎiniú	n.	milk cow, dairy cow	6

牢 láo — prison, stable, pen 牛 93.3 — 6

| 牢 | láo | n. | prison, old (for animals), sacrificial animal, firm, sturdy | 6 |

物 wù — thing, substance, creature 牛 93.4 — 2

物价	wùjià	n.	(commodity) prices	5
物品	wùpǐn	n.	articles, goods, materials	6
物业	wùyè	n.	property, real estate	5
物质	wùzhì	n.	matter, substance, material, materialistic	5
宠物	chǒngwù	n.	house pet	6

动物	dòngwù	n.	animal		2
购物	gòuwù	n.	shopping		4
礼物	lǐwù	n.	gift, present		2
人物	rénwù	n.	person, character (in a play, novel etc), protagonist		5
食物	shíwù	n.	food		2
事物	shìwù	n.	thing, object		4
药物	yàowù	n.	medicaments, pharmaceuticals, medication, medicine, drug		4
植物	zhíwù	n.	plant, vegetation		4
博物馆	bówùguǎn	n.	museum		5
动物园	dòngwùyuán	n.	zoo		2

牲 shēng — sacrificial animal, animal — 牛 93.5 — 6

牺牲	xīshēng	vb.	to sacrifice one's life, to sacrifice (sth valued), beast slaughtered as a sacrifice		6

特 tè — special, unique, distinguished — 牛 93.6 — 2

特	tè	adj.	special, unique, distinguished, especially, unusual, very		6
特别	tèbié	adv.	especially, particularly, special, unusual		2
特大	tèdà	adj.	exceptionally big		6
特地	tèdì	adv.	specially, for a special purpose		6
特点	tèdiǎn	n.	characteristic (feature), trait, feature		2
特定	tèdìng	adj.	special, specific, designated, particular		5
特价	tèjià	n.	special price		4
特快	tèkuài	adj.	express (train, delivery etc)		6
特色	tèsè	n.	characteristic, distinguishing feature or quality		3
特殊	tèshū	adj.	special, particular, unusual, extraordinary		4
特性	tèxìng	n.	property, characteristic		5
特意	tèyì	adv.	specially, intentionally		6
特有	tèyǒu	adj.	specific (to), characteristic (of), distinctive		5
特征	tèzhēng	n.	characteristic, diagnostic property, distinctive feature, trait		4
独特	dútè	adj.	unique, distinct, having special characteristics		4
模特儿	mótèr	n.	(fashion) model (loanword), mannequin		4

牺 xī — sacrifice — 牛 93.6 — 6

牺牲	xīshēng	vb.	to sacrifice one's life, to sacrifice (sth valued), beast slaughtered as a sacrifice		6

犬 quǎn — dog — 犭 94

犯 fàn — to commit crime, to violate — 犬 94.2 — 6

犯	fàn	vb.	to violate, to offend, to assault, criminal, crime, to make a mistake, recurrence (of mistake or sth bad)		6
犯规	fànguī	vb.	to break the rules, an illegality, a foul		6
犯罪	fànzuì	vb.	to commit a crime, crime, offense		6
侵犯	qīnfàn	vb.	to infringe on, to encroach on, to violate, to assault		6

状 zhuàng — form, appearance, shape — 犬 94.3 — 3

状况	zhuàngkuàng	n.	condition, state, situation		3
状态	zhuàngtài	n.	state of affairs, state, mode, situation		3
现状	xiànzhuàng	n.	current situation		5

形状	xíngzhuàng	n.	form, shape		3
症状	zhèngzhuàng	n.	symptom (of an illness)		6
狂	**kuáng**		**mad, violent**	犬 94.4	5
狂	kuáng	adj.	mad, wild, violent, insane, extremely		5
疯狂	fēngkuáng	adj.	crazy, frantic, extreme popularity		5
犹	**yóu**		**to be similar to, to be just like**	犬 94.4	5
犹豫	yóuyù	vb.	to hesitate		5
狗	**gǒu**		**dog**	犬 94.5	2
狗	gǒu	n.	dog, canis familiaris, cursed		2
独	**dú**		**alone, solely, solitary, only**	犬 94.6	4
独立	dúlì	adj.	independent, independence, to stand alone		4
独特	dútè	adj.	unique, distinct, having special characteristics		4
独自	dúzì	adv.	alone		4
单独	dāndú	adv.	alone, by oneself, on one's own		4
孤独	gūdú	adj.	lonely, solitary		6
狠	**hěn**		**vicious, cruel, extreme**	犬 94.6	6
狠	hěn	adj.	ruthless, fierce, ferocious, determined, to harden (one's heart)		6
猜	**cāi**		**to guess**	犬 94.8	5
猜	cāi	vb.	to guess, to suppose, to suspect		5
猜测	cāicè	vb.	to guess, to conjecture, to surmise		5
猛	**měng**		**violent, bold**	犬 94.8	6
猛	měng	adj.	ferocious, fierce, violent, brave, suddenly, abrupt, (coll.) heartily		6
猴	**hóu**		**monkey, ape, monkey-like**	犬 94.9	5
猴	hóu	n.	monkey, ape, monkey-like, to squat on the heels like a monkey		5
猫	**māo**		**cat**	犬 94.9	2
猫	māo	n.	cat, feline		2
大熊猫	dàxióngmāo	n.	giant panda (Ailuropoda melanoleuca)		5
献	**xiàn**		**to offer, to present**	犬 94.9	5
献	xiàn	vb.	to offer, to present, to dedicate, to donate, to show, to put on display, worthy person (old)		5
奉献	fèngxiàn	vb.	to offer respectfully, to consecrate, to dedicate, to devote		6
贡献	gòngxiàn	vb.	to contribute, to dedicate, to devote, contribution		6
猪	**zhū**		**pig, hog**	犬 94.9	3
猪	zhū	n.	hog, pig, swine, wild boar		3

玄 xuán profound 95

率	**lǜ**		**ratio, rate, limit**	玄 95.6	4
率领	lǜlǐng	vb.	to lead, to command, to head		5
率先	lǜxiān	vb.	to take the lead, to show initiative		4
汇率	huìlǜ	n.	exchange rate		4
效率	xiàolǜ	n.	efficiency		4

225

玉 yù jade 玉 王 96

王 wáng — king, ruler   玉 96.0 2
王	wáng	n.	king, ruler, emperor, surname Wang	4
王后	wánghòu	n.	queen	6
王子	• wángzǐ	n.	prince, son of a king	6
国王	guówáng	n.	king	6

玉 yù — jade   玉 96.0 4
| 玉 | yù | n. | jade, precious stone, gem | 4 |
| 玉米 | yùmǐ | n. | corn, maize | 4 |

环 huán — jade ring or bracelet, ring   玉 96.4 3
环	huán	n.	ring, circle, hoop, link, to surround, surname Huan	3
环保	huánbǎo	n.	environmental protection, environmentally friendly	3
环节	huánjié	n.	(zoology) segment (of the body of a worm, centipede etc), (fig.) a part of an integrated whole: aspect (of a project)	5
环境	huánjìng	n.	environment, circumstances, surroundings	3
循环	xúnhuán	vb.	to cycle, to circulate, circle, loop	6

玩 wán — to play with, to enjoy   玉 96.4 1
玩	wán	vb.	to play, have a good time, visit, enjoy	1
玩具	wánjù	n.	plaything, toy	3
好玩	hǎowán	adj.	amusing, fun, interesting	1
游玩	yóuwán	vb.	to amuse oneself, to have fun, to go sightseeing, to take a stroll	6
开玩笑	kāi wánxiào	vb.	to play a joke, to make fun of, to joke	1

现 xiàn — to appear, to manifest   玉 96.4 1
现场	xiànchǎng	n.	the scene (of a crime, accident etc), (on) the spot, (at) the site	3
现代	xiàndài	n.	modern times, modern age	3
现金	xiànjīn	n.	cash	3
现实	xiànshí	n.	reality, actuality, real, actual, realistic, pragmatic, materialistic, self-interested	3
现象	xiànxiàng	n.	phenomenon	3
现有	xiànyǒu	n.	currently existing, currently available	5
现在	xiànzài	n.	now, at present, at the moment, modern, current, nowadays	1
现状	xiànzhuàng	n.	current situation	5
表现	biǎoxiàn	vb.	to show, to show off, to display, to manifest, expression, manifestation, show, display, performance (at work etc), behaviour	3
出现	chūxiàn	vb.	to appear, to arise, to emerge, to show up	2
发现	fāxiàn	vb.	to find, to discover	2
实现	shíxiàn	vb.	to achieve, to implement, to realize, to bring about	2
体现	tǐxiàn	vb.	to embody, to reflect, to incarnate	3
展现	zhǎnxiàn	vb.	to come out, to emerge, to reveal, to display	5

玻 bō — glass   玉 96.5 5
| 玻璃 | - bōli | n. | glass | 5 |

珍 zhēn — precious, valuable, rare   玉 96.5 5
| 珍贵 | zhēnguì | adj. | precious | 5 |

珍惜	zhēnxī	vb.	to treasure, to value, to cherish	5
珍珠	zhēnzhū	n.	pearl	5
袖珍	xiùzhēn	adj.	pocket-sized, pocket (book etc)	6

班 bān — team, class, shift 玉 96.6 1

班	bān	n.	team, class, squad, shift, surname Ban	1
班级	bānjí	n.	class (group of students), grade (in school)	3
班长	bānzhǎng	n.	class monitor, squad leader, team leader	2
航班	hángbān	n.	scheduled flight, flight number, plane, scheduled sailing, sailing number, passenger ship	4
加班	jiā bān	vb.	to work overtime	4
上班	shàngbān	vb.	to go to work, to be on duty, to start work, to go to the office	1
下班	xià bān	vb.	to finish work, to get off work	1
值班	zhí bān	vb.	to work a shift, to be on duty	5
西班牙语	xībānyáyǔ	n.	Spanish (language)	6
培训班	péixùnbān	n.	training class	4

珠 zhū — gem, jewel, pearl 玉 96.6 5

珠宝	zhūbǎo	n.	pearls, jewels, precious stones	6
珍珠	zhēnzhū	n.	pearl	5
圆珠笔	yuánzhūbǐ	n.	ballpoint pen	6

理 lǐ — reason, logic, manage 玉 96.7 2

理	lǐ	n.	texture, grain (of wood), inner essence, intrinsic order, reason, logic, truth, science	6
理财	lǐcái	n.	financial management, finance	6
理发	·lǐfà	n.	a barber, hairdressing	3
理解	lǐjiě	vb.	to comprehend, to understand, comprehension, understanding	3
理论	lǐlùn	n.	theory	3
理想	lǐxiǎng	n.	an ideal, a dream, ideal, perfect	2
理由	lǐyóu	n.	reason, grounds, justification	3
理智	lǐzhì	n.	reason, intellect, rationality, rational	6
办理	bànlǐ	vb.	to handle, to transact, to conduct	3
处理	chǔlǐ	vb.	to handle, to treat, to deal with, to process, to deal with a criminal case, to mete out punishment, to offer for sale at a reduced price, to punish	3
代理	dàilǐ	vb.	to act on behalf of sb in a responsible position, to act as an agent or proxy, surrogate, (computing) proxy	5
道理	-dàoli	n.	reason, argument, sense, principle, basis, justification	2
管理	guǎnlǐ	vb.	to supervise, to manage, to administer, management, administration	3
合理	hélǐ	adj.	rational, reasonable, fair	3
经理	jīnglǐ	n.	manager, director	2
清理	qīnglǐ	vb.	to clear up, to tidy up, to dispose of	5
心理	xīnlǐ	n.	psychology, mentality	4
修理	xiūlǐ	vb.	to repair, to fix, to prune, to trim, (coll.) to sort sb out, to fix sb	4
原理	yuánlǐ	n.	principle, theory	5
真理	zhēnlǐ	n.	truth	5
整理	zhěnglǐ	vb.	to arrange, to tidy up, to sort out, to straighten out, to list systematically, to collate (data, files), to pack (luggage)	3

治理	zhìlǐ	vb.	to govern, to administer, to manage, to control, governance		5
助理	zhùlǐ	n.	assistant		5
总理	zǒnglǐ	n.	premier, prime minister		4
总经理	zǒngjīnglǐ	n.	general manager, CEO		6

球 qiú — ball, sphere, globe — 玉 96.7

球	qiú	n.	ball, sphere, globe, round	1
球场	qiúchǎng	n.	stadium, sports ground, court, pitch, field, golf course	2
球队	qiúduì	n.	sports team (basketball, soccer, football etc)	2
球迷	qiúmí	n.	fan (ball sports)	3
球拍	qiúpāi	n.	racket	6
球鞋	qiúxié	n.	athletic shoes	2
球星	qiúxīng	n.	sports star (ball sport)	6
球员	qiúyuán	n.	sports club member, footballer, golfer etc	6
打球	dǎqiú	vb.	to play ball, to play with a ball	1
地球	· dìqiú	n.	the earth	2
篮球	lánqiú	n.	basketball	2
排球	páiqiú	n.	volleyball	2
皮球	píqiú	n.	ball (made of rubber, leather etc)	6
气球	qìqiú	n.	balloon	4
全球	quánqiú	n.	entire, total, global, the (whole) world, worldwide	3
网球	wǎngqiú	n.	tennis, tennis ball	2
月球	yuèqiú	n.	the moon	5
足球	zúqiú	n.	soccer ball, a football	3
羽毛球	yǔmáoqiú	n.	shuttlecock, badminton	5

琴 qín — Chinese lute or guitar — 玉 96.8 5

琴	qín	n.	(general name for certain musical instruments e.g. 钢琴 gāngqín: piano), Chinese lute or guitar (like Zither)	5
钢琴	gāngqín	n.	piano	5

璃 lí — glass — 玉 96.11 5

玻璃	- bōli	n.	glass	5

瓜 guā — melon — 97

瓜 guā — melon, gourd — 瓜 97.0 4

瓜	guā	n.	melon, gourd, cucumber, squash	4
黄瓜	huángguā	n.	cucumber	4
西瓜	xīguā	n.	watermelon	4

瓦 wǎ — tile — 98

瓶 píng — jug, vase, jar — 瓦 98.6 2

瓶	píng	n.	bottle, (m.w. for bottles)	2
瓶子	píngzi	n.	bottle	2
花瓶	huāpíng	n.	flower vase, fig. just a pretty face	6

甘	**gān**		sweet		**99**
甚	**shèn**		great extent, considerably	甘 99.4	4
甚至	shènzhì	*adv.*	even, so much so that		4
甜	**tián**		sweet	甘 99.6	3
甜	tián	*adj.*	sweet, sweetness, (opp. 苦 kǔ: bitter), sound (sleep)		3
酸甜苦辣	suāntiánkǔlà	*phr.*	sour, sweet, bitter and spicy hot, fig. the joys and sorrows of life		5
生	**shēng**		life		**100**
生	**shēng**		to be born, life, raw	生 100.0	1
生	shēng	+ *vb.*	to be born, (opp 死 sǐ: to die) to give birth, to grow, to light (a fire), to get or have sth (be afflicted with)		2
生	shēng	+ *adj.*	raw, (opp. 熟 shú: ripe, cooked), living, fresh, unripe, unfamiliar, life, lifetime		3
生病	shēngbìng	*vb.*	to fall ill		1
生产	shēngchǎn	*vb.*	to produce, to manufacture, to give birth to a child		3
生成	shēngchéng	*vb.*	to generate, to produce, generated, produced		5
生词	shēngcí	*n.*	new word (in textbook), word that is unfamiliar or not yet studied		2
生存	shēngcún	*vb.*	to exist, to survive		3
生动	shēngdòng	*adj.*	vivid, lively		3
生活	shēnghuó	*n.*	life, activity, to live, livelihood		2
生命	shēngmìng	*n.*	life (as the characteristic of living beings), living being, creature		3
生气	shēngqì	*vb.*	to get angry, to take offense, angry, vitality, liveliness		1
生日	shēngrì	*n.*	birthday		1
生意	- shēngyi	*n.*	life force, vitality		3
生长	shēngzhǎng	*vb.*	to grow		3
生活费	shēnghuófèi	*n.*	cost of living, living expenses, alimony		6
产生	chǎnshēng	*vb.*	to arise, to come into being, to come about, to give rise to, to bring into being, to bring about, to produce		3
出生	chūshēng	*vb.*	to be born		2
诞生	dànshēng	*vb.*	to be born		6
发生	fāshēng	*vb.*	to happen, to occur, to take place, to break out		3
花生	huāshēng	*n.*	peanut, groundnut		6
考生	kǎoshēng	*n.*	exam candidate, student whose name has been put forward for an exam		2
男生	nánshēng	*n.*	schoolboy, male student, boy, guy (young adult male)		1
女生	nǚshēng	*n.*	schoolgirl, female student, girl		1
人生	rénshēng	*n.*	life (one's time on earth)		3
师生	shīshēng	*n.*	teachers and students		6
卫生	wèishēng	*n.*	health, hygiene, sanitation		3
先生	- xiānsheng	*n.*	teacher, husband, doctor (dialect)		1
学生	- xuésheng	*n.*	student, schoolchild		1
野生	yěshēng	*adj.*	wild, undomesticated		6
医生	yīshēng	*n.*	doctor		1
一生	yīshēng	*n.*	all one's life, throughout one's life		2

再生	zàishēng	vb.	to be reborn, to regenerate, to be a second so-and-so (famous dead person), recycling, regeneration	6
招生	zhāo shēng	vb.	to enrol new students, to get students	5
维生素	wéishēngsù	n.	vitamin	6
卫生间	wèishēngjiān	n.	bathroom, toilet, WC	3
毕业生	bìyè shēng	n.	graduate	4
大学生	dàxuéshēng	n.	university student, college student	1
留学生	liúxuéshēng	n.	student studying abroad, (foreign) exchange student	2
小学生	xiǎoxuéshēng	n.	primary school student, schoolchild	1
研究生	yánjiūshēng	n.	graduate student, postgraduate student, research student	4
中学生	zhōngxuéshēng	n.	middle-school student, high school student	1

用 yòng use 101

用	yòng		to use, to employ, to apply	用 101.0 1
用	yòng	vb.	to use, to employ, to have to, to eat or drink, expense or outlay, usefulness, hence, therefore	1
用处	- yòngchu	n.	usefulness	6
用法	yòngfǎ	n.	usage	6
用户	yònghù	n.	user, consumer, subscriber, customer	5
用来	yònglái	vb.	to be used for	5
用品	yòngpǐn	n.	articles for use, products, goods	6
用途	yòngtú	n.	use, application	4
用心	yòngxīn	n.	motive, intention, to be diligent or attentive, careful	6
用于	yòngyú	vb.	use in, use on, use for	5
用不着	• yòng bu zháo	n.	not need, have no use for (coll.)	5
用得着	• yòngdezháo	vb.	to be able to use, useable, to have a use for sth, (in interrogative sentence) to be necessary to	6
不用	bùyòng	adv.	need not	1
采用	cǎiyòng	vb.	to adopt, to employ, to use	3
常用	chángyòng	adj.	in common usage	2
费用	fèiyòng	n.	cost, expenditure, expense	3
利用	lìyòng	vb.	to exploit, to make use of, to use, to take advantage of, to utilize	3
没用	méi yòng	adj.	useless	3
实用	shíyòng	adj.	practical, functional, pragmatic, applied (science)	4
使用	shǐyòng	vb.	to use, to employ, to apply, to make use of	2
适用	shìyòng	vb.	to be applicable	3
通用	tōngyòng	vb.	to use anywhere, anytime (card, ticket etc), to be used by everyone (language, textbook etc), (of two or more things) interchangeable	5
信用	xìnyòng	vb.	to trust, credit (commerce), trustworthiness, creditworthiness	6
应用	• yìngyòng	vb.	to put to use, to apply, practical, applied (science, linguistics etc), application, practical use, (computing) app	3
有用	yǒuyòng	adj.	useful	1
运用	yùnyòng	vb.	to use, to put to use	4
专用	zhuānyòng	vb.	to be for a special purpose, to be dedicated	6
作用	zuòyòng	vb.	to act on, to affect, action, use, effect, purpose	2
信用卡	xìnyòngkǎ	n.	credit card	2

田	**tián**	**field**			**102**
甲	**jiǎ**	**armour, shell, 1st heavenly stem**		田 102.0	5
甲	jiǎ	n.	armour, shell, nail, first of the ten Heavenly Stems, (used for an unspecified person or thing), first item in a list, letter A or roman I in list A, B, C, or I, II, III		5
指甲	- zhǐjia	n.	fingernail		5
申	**shēn**	**to state to a superior**		田 102.0	4
申请	shēnqǐng	vb.	to apply for sth, application (form etc)		4
田	**tián**	**field, arable land, cultivated**		田 102.0	6
田	tián	n.	field, surname, surname Tian		6
田径	tiánjìng	n.	track and field (athletics)		6
由	**yóu**	**cause, reason, from**		田 102.0	2
由	yóu	n.	cause, reason, to follow, from, because of, due to, by, via, through, (before a noun and a verb) it is for ... to ...		3
由此	yóucǐ	adv.	hereby, from this		5
由于	yóuyú	prep.	due to, as a result of, thanks to, owing to, since, because		3
理由	lǐyóu	n.	reason, grounds, justification		3
自由	zìyóu	n.	freedom, free, liberty		2
男	**nán**	**male, man, son**		田 102.2	1
男	nán	adj.	male, (opp. 女 nǚ: female), man, son, baron, lowest of five orders of nobility		1
男孩	nánhái	n.	boy		1
男女	nánnǚ	n.	men and women, male and female		4
男人	nánrén	n.	a man, a male, men		1
男生	nánshēng	n.	schoolboy, male student, boy, guy (young adult male)		1
男士	nánshì	n.	man, gentleman		4
男性	nánxìng	n.	the male sex, a male		5
男子	• nánzǐ	n.	a man, a male		3
男朋友	- nánpéngyou	n.	boyfriend		1
画	**huà**	**a painting, picture, to draw**		田 102.3	2
画	huà	n.	picture, painting, to draw, to paint		2
画儿	huàr	n.	drawing, picture, painting		2
画家	huàjiā	n.	painter		2
画面	huàmiàn	n.	scene, tableau, picture, image, screen (displayed by a computer), (motion picture) frame, field of view		5
动画	dònghuà	n.	animation, cartoon		6
绘画	huìhuà	n.	drawing, painting		6
漫画	mànhuà	n.	caricature, cartoon, Japanese manga		5
图画	túhuà	n.	drawing, picture		3
动画片	dònghuàpiàn	n.	animated film		4
界	**jiè**	**boundary, limit, domain**		田 102.4	3
界	jiè	+ n.	boundary, scope, extent, group, kingdom (taxonomy), , society, the world		6

界	jiè	+ n.	circles e.g. literary and art circle		6
世界	shìjiè	n.	world		3
外界	wàijiè	n.	the outside world, external		5
世界杯	shìjièbēi	n.	World Cup		3
全世界	quán shìjiè	n.	worldwide, entire world		5

留 liú — to stay, to keep, to detain — 田 102.5 — 2

留	liú	vb.	to stay, to stop, to halt, to keep, to leave (behind, a message), to retain		2
留下	liúxià	vb.	to leave behind, to stay behind, to remain, to keep, not to let (sb) go		2
留学	liúxué	vb.	to study abroad		3
留言	liúyán	vb.	to leave a message, to leave one's comments, message		6
留学生	liúxuéshēng	n.	student studying abroad, (foreign) exchange student		2
保留	bǎoliú	vb.	to keep, to retain, to have reservations (about sth), to hold back (from saying sth), to put aside for later		3
停留	tíngliú	vb.	to stay somewhere temporarily, to stop over		5

略 lüè — approximately, roughly — 田 102.6 — 6

策略	cèlüè	n.	strategy, tactics, crafty, adroit		6
忽略	hūlüè	vb.	to neglect, to overlook, to ignore		6
战略	zhànlüè	n.	strategy		6

番 fān — m.w. for acts or deeds — 田 102.7 — 6

番	fān	m.w.	m.w. for acts or deeds, m.w. for iterations or times: -fold, foreign, surname Pan		6
番茄	fānqié	n.	tomato		6
一番	yīfān	n.	one kind, one time, once		6

疋 pǐ — bolt of cloth — 疋 103

疑 yí — to doubt, to question — 疋 103.9 — 4

疑问	yíwèn	n.	question, interrogation, doubt		4
怀疑	huáiyí	vb.	to doubt (sth), to be sceptical of, to have one's doubts, to harbour suspicions, to suspect that		4
无疑	wúyí	vb.	no doubt, undoubtedly		5

疒 nè — sickness — 104

疗 liáo — to treat, to cure — 疒 104.2 — 4

疗养	liáoyǎng	vb.	to get well, to heal, to recuperate, to convalesce, convalescence, to nurse		4
医疗	yīliáo	n.	medical treatment		4
治疗	zhìliáo	vb.	to treat (an illness), medical treatment, therapy		4

疯 fēng — insane, mad — 疒 104.4 — 5

疯	fēng	adj.	insane, mad, mentally ill, foolish, wild		5
疯狂	fēngkuáng	adj.	crazy, frantic, extreme popularity		5

病 bìng — illness — 疒 104.5 — 1

病	bìng	n.	illness, sickness, disease		1
病毒	bìngdú	n.	virus		5

病房	bìngfáng	n.	ward (of a hospital), sickroom		6
病情	bìngqíng	n.	state of an illness, patient's condition		6
病人	bìngrén	n.	sick person, patient, invalid		1
发病	fā bìng	n.	onset, outbreak (of a disease)		6
疾病	jíbìng	n.	disease, sickness, ailment		6
看病	kàn bìng	vb.	to visit a doctor, to see a patient		1
毛病	máobìng	n.	fault, defect, shortcomings, ailment		3
生病	shēngbìng	vb.	to fall ill		1
治病	zhìbìng	vb.	to treat an illness		6
心脏病	xīnzàngbìng	n.	heart disease		6

疾 jí — disease, sickness, to hate — 疒 104.5 6

疾病	jíbìng	n.	disease, sickness, ailment	6
残疾	cánjí	n.	deformity on a person or animal, disabled, handicapped	6
残疾人	cánjírén	n.	disabled person	6

疼 téng — aching, ache — 疒 104.5 2

疼	téng	adj.	aching, ache, pain, (it) hurts, sore, to love dearly	2
疼痛	téngtòng	n.	pain, ache, sore	6
头疼	tóuténg	n.	headache	6
心疼	xīnténg	vb.	to love dearly, to feel sorry for sb, to regret, to grudge, to be distressed	5

症 zhèng — disease, illness — 疒 104.5 6

症状	zhèngzhuàng	n.	symptom (of an illness)	6

痛 tòng — to have a pain or ache — 疒 104.7 3

痛	tòng	+ adv.	deeply, thoroughly, bitterly	3
痛苦	tòngkǔ	n.	pain, suffering, painful	3
痛快	- tòngkuai	adj.	delighted, to one's heart's content, straightforward	4
疼痛	téngtòng	n.	pain, ache, sore	6

瘦 shòu — thin, lean, meagre — 疒 104.10 5

瘦	shòu	adj.	thin, (opp. 胖 pàng: fat, 肥 féi: fat) emaciated, to lose weight, (of clothing) tight, (of meat) lean, (of land) unproductive,	5

癶 bō — dotted tent, legs — 105

登 dēng — to rise, to board, to climb — 癶 105.7 4

登	dēng	vb.	to rise, to scale (a height), to ascend, to mount, to publish or record, to enter (e.g. in a register), to press down with the foot	4
登记	dēngjì	vb.	to register (one's name)	4
登录	dēnglù	vb.	to register, to log in	4
登山	dēngshān	vb.	to climb a mountain, climbing, mountaineering	4

白 bái — white — 106

白 bái — white, pure, bright — 白 106.0 1

白	bái	+ adj.	white, snowy, pure, bright, surname Bai	1
白	bái	+ adv.	in vain, to no purpose, free of charge	3
白菜	báicài	n.	Chinese cabbage, bok choi, pak choi	3

白酒	báijiǔ	n.	baijiu, a spirit usually distilled from sorghum	5
白领	báilǐng	n.	white-collar, white-collar worker	6
白色	báisè	adj.	white, fig. reactionary, anti-communist	2
白天	báitiān	n.	daytime, during the day, day	1
明白	- míngbai	adj.	clear, obvious, unequivocal, to understand, to realize	1

百 bǎi — hundred, numerous, many 白 106.1

百	bǎi	num.	hundred, numerous, many, surname Bai	1
百货	bǎihuò	n.	general merchandise	4
百分点	bǎifēndiǎn	n.	percentage point	6
老百姓	lǎobǎixìng	n.	ordinary people, the person in the street	3

的 * de, dí, dì — possessive, adjectival suffix 白 106.3

的	de	aux.	of, ~'s (possessive particle), (used after an attribute), (used to form nominal expression), (used at the end of a declarative sentence for emphasis)	1
的话	dehuà	aux.	if (coming after a conditional clause)	2
的确	• díquè	adv.	really, indeed	4
别的	biéde	n.	else, other	1
目的	• mùdì	n.	purpose, aim, goal, target, objective	2
似的	shìde	aux.	seems as if, rather like	4
有的	yǒude	pro.	(there are) some (who are...), some (exist)	1
真的	zhēnde	adv.	really, real, truly, true	1
有的是	yǒudeshì	phr.	have plenty of, there's no lack of	3

皇 huáng — emperor 白 106.4

皇帝	huángdì	n.	emperor	6

皮 pí — skin 107

皮 pí — skin, leather 皮 107.0

皮	pí	n.	skin, leather, fur, surname Pi	3
皮包	píbāo	n.	handbag, briefcase	3
皮肤	pífū	n.	skin	5
皮球	píqiú	n.	ball (made of rubber, leather etc)	6
皮鞋	píxié	n.	leather shoes	5
调皮	• tiáopí	adj.	naughty, mischievous, unruly	4
顽皮	wánpí	adj.	naughty	6

皿 mǐn — dish 108

盆 pén — basin, pot 皿 108.4

盆	pén	n.	basin, flower pot, unit of volume equal to 12 斗 dòu and 8 升 shēng, approx. 128 litres	5
脸盆	liǎnpén	n.	washbowl, basin for washing hands and face	5

监 jiān — to supervise, to control 皿 108.5

监测	jiāncè	vb.	to monitor	6
监督	jiāndū	vb.	to control, to supervise, to inspect	6

总监	zǒngjiān	n.	head, director (of an organizational unit), (police) commissioner, inspector-general, rank of local governor in Tang dynasty administration		6
盐	**yán**		**salt**	皿 108.5	4
盐	yán	n.	salt		4
益	**yì**		**profit, benefit, advantage**	皿 108.5	4
利益	lìyì	n.	benefit, (in sb's) interest		4
收益	shōuyì	n.	earnings, profit		4
盗	**dào**		**to rob, thief**	皿 108.6	6
盗版	dàobǎn	vb.	to illegally copy, to pirate		6
强盗	qiángdào	vb.	to rob (with force), bandit, robber		6
盖	**gài**		**lid, cover, to cover**	皿 108.6	4
盖	gài	n.	lid, top, cover, to cover, to build, surname Ge		4
盒	**hé**		**small box**	皿 108.6	5
盒	hé	n.	small box, case e.g. for matches, jewels, shoes		5
盒饭	héfàn	n.	meal in a partitioned box		5
盒子	hézi	n.	box, case		5
盘	**pán**		**tray, plate, dish**	皿 108.6	4
盘	pán	+ n.	plate, dish, tray, board, hard drive (computing), to coil up or twist, to check, m.w. for food: dish, helping, m.w. for coils of wire, m.w. for games of chess		4
盘子	pánzi	n.	tray, plate, dish		4
光盘	guāngpán	n.	compact disc, CD or DVD, CD ROM		4
键盘	jiànpán	n.	keyboard		5
盛	**shèng**		**abundant, flourishing**	皿 108.7	6
盛行	shèngxíng	vb.	to be in vogue, to be prevalent		6
昌盛	chāngshèng	adj.	prosperous		6
盟	**méng**		**to swear, to ally with**	皿 108.8	6
加盟	jiāméng	vb.	to become a member of an alliance or union, to align, to join, participate		6
联盟	liánméng	n.	alliance, union, coalition		6
目	**mù**		**eye**		**109**
目	mù		eye, item, to look	目 109.0	2
目标	mùbiāo	n.	target, goal, objective		3
目的	• mùdì	n.	purpose, aim, goal, target, objective		2
目光	mùguāng	n.	sight, vision, view, gaze, look		5
目前	mùqián	n.	at the present time, currently		3
节目	jiémù	n.	program, item (on a program)		2
栏目	lánmù	n.	regular column or segment (in a publication or broadcast program), program (TV or radio)		6
数目	shùmù	n.	amount, number		5
题目	tímù	n.	subject, title, topic		3

项目	xiàngmù	n.	item, project, (sports) event		4
盲	**máng**		blind, unperceptive	目 109.3	6
盲人	mángrén	n.	blind person		6
直	**zhí**		straight, erect, vertical	目 109.3	2
直	zhí	adj.	straight (opp. 弯 wān: curved, 曲 qū: crooked), vertical (opp. 横 héng: horizontal), frank, directly, continuously, surname Zhi		3
直播	zhíbō	adj.	(TV, radio) to broadcast live, live broadcast, (Internet) to livestream, (agriculture) direct seeding		3
直到	zhídào	adv.	until, up to now		3
直接	zhíjiē	adj.	direct (opp. 间接 jiànjiē: indirect), immediate, straightforward		2
直线	zhíxiàn	n.	straight line, sharply (rise or fall)		5
直升机	zhíshēngjī	n.	helicopter		6
简直	jiǎnzhí	adv.	simply, at all, practically		3
一直	yīzhí	adv.	straight (in a straight line), continuously, always, from the beginning of ... up to ..., all along		2
盾	**dùn**		shield, shield-shaped object	目 109.4	5
矛盾	máodùn	n.	contradiction, conflict, problem		5
看	* **kàn, kān**		to look, to see; to look after	目 109.4	1
看	• kān	vb.	to look after, to take care of, to guard		6
看	kàn	vb.	to see, to look at, to read, to watch		1
看管	• kānguǎn	vb.	to look after		6
看病	kàn bìng	vb.	to visit a doctor, to see a patient		1
看出	kàn chū	vb.	to make out, to see		5
看成	kànchéng	vb.	to regard as		5
看待	kàndài	vb.	to look upon, to regard		5
看到	kàndào	vb.	to see		1
看法	kànfǎ	n.	way of looking at a thing, view, opinion		2
看好	kànhǎo	vb.	to keep an eye on		6
看见	kànjiàn	vb.	to see, to catch sight of		1
看来	kànlái	adv.	apparently, it seems that		4
看望	kànwàng	vb.	to visit, to pay a call to		4
看作	kànzuò	vb.	to look upon as, to regard as		6
看不起	- kànbuqǐ	vb.	to look down upon, to despise		4
看得见	kàndejiàn	vb.	can see, visible		6
看得起	kàndeqǐ	vb.	to show respect for, to think highly of		6
看起来	- kànqilai	adv.	seemingly, apparently, looks as if, appear to be, gives the impression that, seems on the face of it to be		3
看上去	- kànshangqu	adv.	it would appear, it seems (that)		3
查看	chákàn	vb.	to look over, to examine, to check up, to ferret out		6
观看	guānkàn	vb.	to watch, to view		3
好看	hǎokàn	adj.	good-looking, nice-looking, good (of a movie, book, TV show etc), embarrassed, humiliated		1
难看	nánkàn	adj.	ugly, unsightly		2
收看	shōukàn	vb.	to watch (a TV program)		3
眼看	yǎnkàn	adv.	soon, in a moment, to look on as sth happens		6

盼	**pàn**		to look, to gaze, to expect	目 109.4	6
盼望	pànwàng	vb.	to hope for, to look forward to		6
省	**shěng**		province, to save	目 109.4	2
省	shěng	+ n.	province, provincial capital		2
省	shěng	+ vb.	to save, to economize, to do without, to omit, to leave out		2
省钱	shěngqián	vb.	to save money		6
节省	jiéshěng	n.	saving, to save, to use sparingly, to cut down on		4
相	* **xiāng, xiàng**		mutual, each other; appearance	目 109.4	2
相比	xiāngbǐ	vb.	to compare		3
相处	xiāngchù	vb.	to be in contact (with sb), to associate, to interact, to get along (well, poorly)		4
相当	xiāngdāng	vb.	to match, to be equivalent to, appropriate, considerably, to a certain extent, fairly, quite		3
相等	xiāngděng	vb.	to be equal, equally, equivalent		5
相反	xiāngfǎn	adj.	opposite, contrary		4
相关	xiāngguān	vb.	related, relevant, pertinent, to be interrelated, (statistics) correlation		3
相互	xiānghù	adj.	each other, mutual		3
相似	xiāngshì	vb.	to resemble, similar, like, resemblance, similarity		3
相同	xiāngtóng	adj.	identical, same		2
相信	xiāngxìn	vb.	to be convinced (that sth is true), to believe, to accept sth as true		2
相应	• xiāngyìng	vb.	to correspond, answering (one another), to agree (among the part), corresponding, relevant, appropriate, (modify) accordingly		5
相机	• xiàngjī	vb.	camera (abbr. for 照相机 zhàoxiàngjī), to wait for the opportune moment, as the circumstances allow		2
相片	• xiàngpiàn	n.	image, photograph		4
相声	• xiàngshēng	n.	comic dialogue, sketch, crosstalk		5
互相	hùxiāng	adv.	each other, mutually, mutual		3
首相	• shǒuxiàng	n.	prime minister (of Japan or UK etc)		6
照相	• zhào xiàng	vb.	to take a photograph		2
真相	• zhēnxiàng	adj.	the truth about sth, the actual facts		5
眠	**mián**		to close eyes, to sleep, to hibernate	目 109.5	5
睡眠	shuìmián	n.	sleep, to sleep, (computing) to enter sleep mode		5
真	**zhēn**		real, actual, true	目 109.5	1
真	zhēn	adj.	real, true, genuine, (opp. 真 jiǎ: false) really, truly, indeed		1
真诚	zhēnchéng	adj.	true, sincere, genuine		5
真的	zhēnde	adv.	really, real, truly, true		1
真理	zhēnlǐ	n.	truth		5
真实	zhēnshí	adj.	true, real		3
真相	• zhēnxiàng	adj.	the truth about sth, the actual facts		5
真正	zhēnzhèng	adj.	genuine, real, true, genuinely		2
传真	chuánzhēn	n.	fax, facsimile		5
认真	rènzhēn	adj.	conscientious, earnest, serious, to take seriously, to take to heart		1
天真	tiānzhēn	adj.	naive, innocent, artless		4

					目 109.6	2
眼	**yǎn**		**eye, hole**			
眼	yǎn	n.	eye, eyelet, small hole, crux or key point (of a matter), opening, m.w. well, etc.			2
眼光	yǎnguāng	n.	gaze, insight, foresight, vision, way of looking at things			5
眼镜	yǎnjìng	n.	spectacles, eyeglasses			4
眼睛	- yǎnjing	n.	eye			2
眼看	yǎnkàn	adv.	soon, in a moment, to look on as sth happens			6
眼泪	yǎnlèi	n.	tears, crying			4
眼里	yǎnlǐ	n.	in one's eyes, in one's view			4
眼前	yǎnqián	n.	before one's eyes, now, at present			3
亲眼	qīnyǎn	adv.	with one's own eyes, personally			6
着	*** zhe, zháo**		**-ing, affix for action in progress**		目 109.6	1
着	• zháo	vb.	to touch, to come into contact with, to be troubled by something, to ignite			4
着	zhe	aux.	-ing, aspect particle indicating action in progress			1
着火	• zháohuǒ	vb.	to ignite, to burn			4
着急	• zháojí	vb.	to worry, to feel anxious			4
挨着	āizhe	adv.	near			6
背着	• bēizhe	vb.	carrying on one's back			6
接着	jiēzhe	vb.	to catch and hold on, to continue, to go on to do sth, to follow, to carry on, then, after that, subsequently, to proceed, to ensue, in turn, in one's turn			2
睡着	• shuìzháo	vb.	to fall asleep			4
随着	suízhe	prep.	along with, in the wake of, following			5
沿着	yánzhe	vb.	to go along, to follow			6
有着	yǒuzhe	vb.	to have, to possess			5
指着	zhǐzhe	vb.	to point			6
意味着	yìwèizhe	vb.	to signify, to mean, to imply			5
用不着	• yòng bu zháo	n.	not need, have no use for (coll.)			5
用得着	• yòngdezháo	vb.	to be able to use, useable, to have a use for sth, (in interrogative sentence) to be necessary to			6
督	**dū**		**to supervise, to oversee**		目 109.8	6
监督	jiāndū	vb.	to control, to supervise, to inspect			6
基督教	jīdūjiào	n.	Christianity			6
睛	**jīng**		**eyeball, pupil of eye**		目 109.8	2
眼睛	- yǎnjing	n.	eye			2
睡	**shuì**		**to sleep, to doze**		目 109.8	1
睡	shuì	vb.	to sleep, to doze, to lie down			1
睡觉	• shuìjiào	vb.	to go to bed, to sleep			1
睡眠	shuìmián	n.	sleep, to sleep, (computing) to enter sleep mode			5
睡着	• shuìzháo	vb.	to fall asleep			4
午睡	wǔshuì	vb.	to take a nap, siesta			2
瞧	**qiáo**		**to look at, to see**		目 109.12	5
瞧	qiáo	vb.	to look at, to see, to see (a doctor), to visit			5

矛 máo spear 110

矛	**máo**		spear, lance	矛 110.0 5
矛盾	máodùn	n.	contradiction, conflict, problem	5

矢 shǐ arrow 111

知	**zhī**		to know, to comprehend	矢 111.3 1
知道	- zhīdao	vb.	to know, to become aware of	1
知名	zhīmíng	adj.	well-known, famous	6
知识	- zhīshi	n.	knowledge	1
通知	tōngzhī	vb.	to notify, to inform, notice, notification	2
通知书	tōngzhīshū	n.	written notice	4
短	**duǎn**		short, brief	矢 111.7 2
短	duǎn	adj.	short, brief, (opp. 长 cháng: long), to lack, weak point, fault	2
短处	• duǎnchù	n.	shortcoming, defect, fault, one's weak points	3
短裤	duǎnkù	n.	shorts	3
短片	duǎnpiàn	n.	short film, video clip	6
短期	duǎnqī	n.	short term, short-term	3
短信	duǎnxìn	n.	short message, text message	2
长短	• chángduǎn	n.	length, duration, accident, right and wrong, good and bad, long and short	6
缩短	suōduǎn	vb.	to curtail, to cut down	4
矮	**ǎi**		low, short	矢 111.8 4
矮	ǎi	adj.	low, short (in height)	4
矮小	ǎixiǎo	adj.	short and small, low and small, undersized	4

石 shí stone 112

石	**shí**		stone, rock, mineral	石 112.0 3
石头	- shítou	n.	stone	3
石油	shíyóu	n.	oil, petroleum	3
宝石	bǎoshí	n.	precious stone, gem	4
化石	huàshí	n.	fossil	5
矿	**kuàng**		ore, mine	石 112.3 4
矿	kuàng	n.	ore (or mineral), mine	6
矿泉水	kuàngquánshuǐ	n.	mineral spring water	4
码	**mǎ**		number, counter, code	石 112.3 4
码头	- mǎtou	n.	dock, pier, wharf	5
号码	hàomǎ	n.	number	4
密码	mìmǎ	n.	secret code, ciphertext, password, PIN	4
起码	qǐmǎ	adv.	at the minimum, at the very least	5
数码	shùmǎ	n.	number, numerals, figures, digital, amount, numerical code	4
二维码	èrwéimǎ	n.	two-dimensional barcode, QR code	5

础	**chǔ**		foundation stone, plinth	石 112.5	3
基础	jīchǔ	n.	base, foundation, basis, underlying		3
破	**pò**		to break, to split	石 112.5	3
破	pò	vb.	to break, split or cleave, to get rid of, to destroy, broken, damaged, worn out, lousy, rotten,		3
破产	pòchǎn	vb.	to go bankrupt, to become impoverished, bankruptcy		4
破坏	pòhuài	n.	destruction, damage, to wreck, to break, to destroy		3
打破	dǎ pò	vb.	to break, to smash		3
突破	tūpò	vb.	to break through, to make a breakthrough, to surmount (an obstacle), (sports) to break through the opponent's defence		5
硕	**shuò**		great, eminent, large, big	石 112.6	5
硕士	shuòshì	n.	master's degree, person who has a master's degree, learned person		5
研	**yán**		to grind, to rub, to research	石 112.6	4
研发	yánfā	n.	research and development, to develop		6
研究	yánjiū	n.	research, a study		4
研制	yánzhì	vb.	to manufacture, to develop		4
研究生	yánjiūshēng	n.	graduate student, postgraduate student, research student		4
研究所	yánjiūsuǒ	n.	research institute, graduate studies, graduate school		5
调研	diàoyán	vb.	to investigate and research, research, investigation		6
科研	kēyán	n.	(scientific) research		6
确	**què**		sure, certain, real	石 112.7	2
确保	quèbǎo	vb.	to ensure, to guarantee		3
确定	quèdìng	vb.	to fix (on sth), to determine, to be sure, to ensure, to make certain, to ascertain, definite, certain, fixed		3
确立	quèlì	vb.	to establish, to institute		5
确认	quèrèn	vb.	to confirm, to verify, confirmation		4
确实	quèshí	adv.	indeed, really, reliable, real, true		3
的确	· díquè	adv.	really, indeed		4
明确	míngquè	adj.	clear-cut, definite, explicit, to clarify, to specify, to make definite		3
正确	zhèngquè	adj.	correct, proper		2
准确	zhǔnquè	adj.	accurate, exact, precise		2
硬	**yìng**		hard, firm, strong	石 112.7	5
硬	yìng	adj.	hard, (opp. 软 ruǎn: soft, flexible), stiff, strong, firm, resolutely, doggedly, good (quality), able (person), (of food) filling, substantial		5
硬件	yìngjiàn	n.	hardware		5
碍	**ài**		to obstruct, to block, to deter	石 112.8	5
障碍	zhàng'ài	n.	barrier, obstruction, hindrance, impediment, obstacle		6
阻碍	zǔ'ài	vb.	to obstruct, to hinder, to block, obstruction, hindrance		5
碰	**pèng**		to collide, to bump into	石 112.8	2
碰	pèng	vb.	to touch, to bump, to encounter		2
碰见	pèng jiàn	vb.	to run into, to meet (unexpectedly), to bump into		2
碰到	pèngdào	vb.	to come across, to run into, to meet, to hit		2
碎	**suì**		to break, to smash	石 112.8	5
碎	suì	vb.	to break down, to break into pieces, fragmentary		5

碗	**wǎn**		bowl, small dish	石 112.8	2
碗	wǎn	*n.*	bowl, small dish, cup, m.w. for food and drink: bowl		2
磨	**mó**		to grind, to polish	石 112.11	6
磨	mó	*vb.*	to rub, to grind, to polish, to sharpen, to wear down, to die out, to waste time, to pester, to insist		6

示 shì — spirit — 礻 113

示	**shì**		to show, to demonstrate	示 113.0	2
示范	shìfàn	*vb.*	to demonstrate, to show how to do sth, demonstration, a model example		5
暗示	ànshì	*vb.*	to hint, to suggest, suggestion, hint		4
表示	biǎoshì	*vb.*	to express, to show, to say, to state, to indicate, to mean		2
提示	tíshì	*vb.*	to point out, to remind (sb of sth), to suggest, suggestion, tip, reminder, notice		5
显示	xiǎnshì	*vb.*	to show, to illustrate, to display, to demonstrate		3
展示	zhǎnshì	*vb.*	to reveal, to display, to show, to exhibit sth		5
指示	zhǐshì	*vb.*	to point out, to indicate, to instruct, directives, instructions		5
礼	**lǐ**		social custom, manners, courtesy	示 113.1	2
礼	lǐ	*n.*	ceremony, courtesy, gift, rite, surname Li		5
礼拜	lǐbài	*n.*	week, religious service, worship		5
礼貌	lǐmào	*n.*	courtesy, manners		5
礼堂	lǐtáng	*n.*	assembly hall, auditorium		6
礼物	lǐwù	*n.*	gift, present		2
典礼	diǎnlǐ	*n.*	celebration, ceremony		5
婚礼	hūnlǐ	*n.*	wedding ceremony, wedding		4
送礼	sòng lǐ	*vb.*	to give a present		6
社	**shè**		group of families, company, society	示 113.3	3
社	shè	*n.*	society, group, club, agency, (old) god of the land		5
社会	shèhuì	*n.*	society		3
社区	shèqū	*n.*	community, neighbourhood		5
旅行社	lǚxíngshè	*n.*	travel agency		3
神	**shén**		spirit, deity, supernatural being	示 113.5	3
神	shén	*n.*	deity, unusual, mysterious, spirit		5
神话	shénhuà	*n.*	legend, fairy tale, myth, mythology		4
神经	shénjīng	*n.*	nerve, mental state, (coll.) unhinged		5
神秘	shénmì	*adj.*	mysterious, mystery		4
神奇	shénqí	*adj.*	magical, mystical, miraculous		5
神情	shénqíng	*n.*	look, expression		5
精神	jīngshén	*n.*	spirit, mind, consciousness, thought, mental, psychological, essence, gist		3
精神	- jīngshen	*n.*	vigour, vitality, drive; lively		3
祝	**zhù**		to wish	示 113.5	3
祝	zhù	*vb.*	to wish, bless, surname Zhu		3
祝福	zhùfú	*n.*	blessings, to wish sb well		4

祝贺	zhùhè	vb.	to congratulate, congratulations		5
祝愿	zhùyuàn	vb.	to wish		6
庆祝	qìngzhù	vb.	to celebrate		3

祖 zǔ — ancestor, forefather, grandfather — 示 113.5 — 6

祖父	zǔfù	n.	father's father, paternal grandfather		6
祖国	zǔguó	n.	one's country, native land		6
祖母	zǔmǔ	n.	father's mother, paternal grandmother		6

票 piào — ticket — 示 113.6 — 1

票	piào	n.	ticket, ballot, banknote		1
票价	piàojià	n.	ticket price, fare, admission fee		3
彩票	cǎipiào	n.	lottery ticket		5
车票	chēpiào	n.	ticket (for a bus or train)		1
发票	fāpiào	n.	invoice, receipt or bill for purchase		4
股票	gǔpiào	n.	share certificate, stock (finance)		6
机票	jīpiào	n.	air ticket, passenger ticket		1
门票	ménpiào	n.	ticket (for theatre, cinema etc)		1
投票	tóupiào	vb.	to vote, vote		6
退票	tuìpiào	vb.	to bounce (a check), to return a ticket, ticket refund		6
邮票	yóupiào	n.	(postage) stamp		3

祥 xiáng — lucky, auspicious, good omen — 示 113.6 — 6

吉祥	jíxiáng	adj.	lucky, auspicious, propitious		6

禁 jìn — to prohibit, to forbid — 示 113.8 — 4

禁止	jìnzhǐ	vb.	to prohibit, to forbid, to ban		4
不禁	bùjìn	vb.	to be unable to stop doing sth (can't help doing sth, can't refrain from)		6

福 fú — happiness, good fortune — 示 113.9 — 3

福	fú	n.	happiness, good fortune, luck, surname Fu; abbr. for Fujian province 福建省 Fújiàn shěng		3
福利	fúlì	n.	material benefit, benefit in kind, (social) welfare		5
幸福	xìngfú	n.	happiness, happy, blessed		3
祝福	zhùfú	n.	blessings, to wish sb well		4

肉 róu — track — 114

离 lí — to leave, to depart — 肉 114.6 — 2

离	lí	vb.	to leave, to depart, to go away, to part from, surname Li		2
离婚	lí hūn	vb.	to divorce, divorced from (one's spouse)		3
离开	líkāi	vb.	to depart, to leave		2
离不开	- líbukāi	vb.	inseparable, inevitably linked to		4
撤离	chèlí	vb.	to withdraw from, to evacuate		6
分离	fēnlí	vb.	to separate		5
距离	jùlí	n.	distance		4
脱离	tuōlí	vb.	to separate oneself from, to break away from, to be divorced from		5
远离	yuǎnlí	vb.	to be far from, to keep away from		6

禾 hé grain 115

私	sī		private, personal, secret	禾 115.2	5
私人	sīrén	adj.	private, (opp. 公 gōng: public), personal, interpersonal, sb with whom one has a close personal relationship		5
隐私	yǐnsī	n.	secrets, private business, privacy		6
走私	zǒusī	vb.	to smuggle, to have an illicit affair		6
秀	xiù		excellent, elegant	禾 115.2	4
优秀	yōuxiù	adj.	outstanding, excellent		4
科	kē		section, department	禾 115.4	2
科	kē	n.	branch of study, administrative section, division, field, branch, stage directions, family (taxonomy), rules		2
科技	kējì	n.	science and technology		3
科学	kēxué	n.	science, scientific knowledge, scientific, rational		2
科研	kēyán	n.	(scientific) research		6
本科	běnkē	n.	undergraduate course, undergraduate (attributive)		4
儿科	érkē	n.	paediatrics		6
内科	nèikē	n.	internal medicine, general medicine		4
外科	wàikē	n.	surgery (branch of medicine)		6
学科	xuékē	n.	subject, branch of learning, course, academic discipline		5
高科技	gāokējì	n.	high tech, high technology		6
秒	miǎo		a second	禾 115.4	5
秒	miǎo	m.w.	second (unit of time), arc second (angular measurement unit), (coll.) instantly		5
秋	qiū		autumn, fall	禾 115.4	2
秋季	qiūjì	n.	autumn, fall, year		4
秋天	qiūtiān	n.	autumn		2
中秋节	zhōngqiū jié	n.	the Mid-Autumn Festival on 15th of 8th lunar month		5
种	* zhǒng, zhòng		seed, race, breed; to plant	禾 115.4	3
种	zhǒng	n.	seed, species, kind, type, m.w. for types, kinds, sorts		3
种	• zhòng	vb.	to grow, to plant, to cultivate		4
种类	zhǒnglèi	n.	kind, genus, type, category, variety, species, sort, class		4
种种	zhǒngzhǒng	adj.	all kinds of		6
种子	zhǒngzi	n.	seed		3
种植	• zhòngzhí	vb.	to plant, to grow (a crop), to cultivate		4
多种	duōzhǒng	adj.	many kinds of, multiple, diverse, multi-		4
各种	gèzhǒng	n.	all kinds of, various kinds, every kind of,		3
品种	pǐnzhǒng	n.	breed, variety		5
称	chēng		to call, to say	禾 115.5	2
称	chēng	+ vb.	to call, to say, to commend		2
称	chēng	+ vb.	to weigh		5
称号	chēnghào	n.	name, term of address, title		5
称为	• chēngwéi	vb.	called, to call sth (by a name), to name		3
称赞	chēngzàn	vb.	to praise, to acclaim, to commend, to compliment		4

名称	míngchēng	n.	name (of a thing), name (of an organization)		2
积	**jī**		to accumulate, to store up	禾 115.5	3
积极	jījí	adj.	active, energetic, vigorous, positive (outlook), proactive		3
积累	jīlèi	vb.	to accumulate, accumulation, cumulative, cumulatively		4
面积	miànjī	n.	area (of a floor, piece of land etc), surface area, tract of land		3
体积	tǐjī	n.	volume, bulk		5
秘	**mì**		secret, mysterious	禾 115.5	4
秘密	mìmì	n.	secret		4
秘书	mìshū	n.	secretary		4
神秘	shénmì	adj.	mysterious, mystery		4
租	**zū**		to rent, to lease	禾 115.5	2
租	zū	vb.	to hire, to rent, to charter, to rent out, to lease out, rent, land tax		2
租金	zūjīn	n.	rent		6
出租	chūzū	vb.	to rent		2
房租	fángzū	n.	rent for a room or house		3
出租车	chūzūchē	n.	taxi, cab, rental car		2
移	**yí**		to move, to shift	禾 115.6	4
移	yí	vb.	to move, to shift, to change, to alter, to remove		4
移动	yídòng	vb.	to move, movement, migration, mobile, portable		4
移民	yímín	vb.	to immigrate, to migrate, emigrant, immigrant		4
转移	zhuǎnyí	vb.	to shift, to divert or distract (attention etc), to change, to transform, metastasis (medicine), to evacuate (people)		4
程	**chéng**		journey, rule, distance	禾 115.7	3
程度	chéngdù	n.	degree (level or extent), level		3
程序	chéngxù	n.	procedures, sequence, order, computer program		4
工程	gōngchéng	n.	engineering, an engineering project, project, undertaking		4
过程	guòchéng	n.	course of events, process		3
课程	kèchéng	n.	course, academic program		3
行程	xíngchéng	n.	journey, course of a journey, distance travelled, trajectory, itinerary, route, course (of history), stroke (of a piston)		6
工程师	gōngchéngshī	n.	engineer		3
稍	**shāo**		a little	禾 115.7	5
稍	shāo	adv.	a little, rather, somewhat		5
稍微	shāowēi	adv.	a little bit		5
税	**shuì**		tax	禾 115.7	6
税	shuì	n.	tax, duties, tariff		6
稳	**wěn**		steady, stable	禾 115.9	4
稳	wěn	adj.	steady, stable, firm, solid, sure		4
稳定	wěndìng	adj.	steady, stable, stability, to stabilize, to pacify		4
平稳	píngwěn	adj.	smooth, steady		4
稿	**gǎo**		draft, manuscript	禾 115.10	6
稿子	gǎozi	n.	draft of a document, script, manuscript, mental plan, precedent		6

穴 xué cave 116

究	**jiū**		to examine, to investigate	穴 116.2	4
究竟	jiūjìng	vb.	to go to the bottom of a matter, after all, when all is said and done, (in an interrogative sentence) finally, outcome, result		4
讲究	- jiǎngjiu	vb.	to pay particular attention to, carefully selected for quality, tastefully chosen		4
研究	yánjiū	n.	research, a study		4
追究	zhuījiū	vb.	to investigate, to look into		6
研究生	yánjiūshēng	n.	graduate student, postgraduate student, research student		4
研究所	yánjiūsuǒ	n.	research institute, graduate studies, graduate school		5
穷	**qióng**		poor, destitute, impoverished	穴 116.2	4
穷	qióng	adj.	poor, (opp. 富 fù: rich), destitute, to use up, to exhaust, thoroughly, extremely, (coll.) persistently and pointlessly		4
穷人	qióngrén	n.	poor people, the poor		4
空	* **kōng, kòng**		empty; empty space, free time	穴 116.3	2
空	kōng	adj.	empty, hollow, void, sky, air, in vain		3
空	• kòng	n.	empty space, empty room, free time, to vacate to empty		4
空间	kōngjiān	n.	space, room, (fig.) scope, leeway, (astronomy) outer space, (physics, math.) space		4
空军	kōngjūn	n.	air force		6
空气	kōngqì	n.	air, atmosphere		2
空调	kōngtiáo	n.	air conditioning, air conditioner (including units that have a heating mode)		3
空中	kōngzhōng	n.	in the sky, in the air, air-bourne		5
空儿	• kòngr	n.	empty space, free time		3
航空	hángkōng	n.	aviation		4
太空	tàikōng	n.	outer space		5
天空	tiānkōng	n.	sky		3
填空	• tiánkòng	vb.	to fill a job vacancy, to fill in a blank (e.g. on questionnaire or exam paper)		4
有空	• yǒu kòng	vb.	to have time (to do sth)		2
穿	**chuān**		to wear, to penetrate, to pierce	穴 116.4	1
穿	chuān	vb.	to wear, to put on, to dress, to bore through, to pierce, to perforate, to penetrate, to pass through, to thread		1
穿上	- chuānshang	vb.	to put on (clothes etc)		4
突	**tū**		suddenly, abruptly, unexpectedly	穴 116.4	3
突出	tūchū	adj.	prominent, outstanding, to give prominence to, to project		3
突破	tūpò	vb.	to break through, to make a breakthrough, to surmount (an obstacle), (sports) to break through the opponent's defence		5
突然	tūrán	adj.	sudden, abrupt, unexpected		3
冲突	chōngtū	n.	conflict, to conflict, clash of opposing forces, collision (of interests), contention		5
窗	**chuāng**		window	穴 116.7	4
窗户	- chuānghu	n.	window		4

窗口	chuāngkǒu	n.	window, opening providing restricted access (e.g. customer service window), computer operating system window	6
窗帘	chuānglián	n.	window curtains	5
窗台	chuāngtái	n.	windowsill, window ledge	4
窗子	chuāngzi	n.	window	4

立 lì stand 117

立	**lì**		**to stand, to set up**	立 117.0 3
立	lì	vb.	to stand, to set up, to establish, to appoint, surname Li	5
立场	lìchǎng	n.	position, standpoint	5
立即	lìjí	adv.	immediately	4
立刻	lìkè	adv.	forthwith, immediate, prompt, promptly, straightway, thereupon, at once	3
成立	chénglì	vb.	to establish, to set up, to be tenable, to hold water	3
创立	chuànglì	vb.	to establish, to set up, to found	5
独立	dúlì	adj.	independent, independence, to stand alone	4
对立	duìlì	vb.	to oppose, to set sth against, to be antagonistic to, antithetical, relative opposite, opposing, diametrical	5
建立	jiànlì	vb.	to establish, to set up, to found	3
确立	quèlì	vb.	to establish, to institute	5
设立	shèlì	vb.	to set up, to establish	3
产	**chǎn**		**to give birth to, to produce**	立 117.1 3
产量	chǎnliàng	n.	output	6
产品	chǎnpǐn	n.	goods, merchandise, product	4
产生	chǎnshēng	vb.	to arise, to come into being, to come about, to give rise to, to bring into being, to bring about, to produce	3
产业	chǎnyè	n.	industry, estate, property, industrial	5
财产	cáichǎn	n.	property, assets, estate	4
国产	guóchǎn	adj.	domestically produced	6
破产	pòchǎn	vb.	to go bankrupt, to become impoverished, bankruptcy	4
生产	shēngchǎn	vb.	to produce, to manufacture, to give birth to a child	3
遗产	yíchǎn	n.	heritage, legacy, inheritance, bequest	4
增产	zēng chǎn	vb.	to increase production	5
资产	zīchǎn	n.	property, assets	5
农产品	nóngchǎnpǐn	n.	agricultural produce	5
水产品	shuǐchǎnpǐn	n.	aquatic products (including fish, crabs, seaweed etc)	5
亲	**qīn**		**relatives, parents**	立 117.4 3
亲	qīn	n.	parent, one's own (flesh and blood), relative, related, marriage, bride, close, intimate, in person, first-hand, to kiss, to be in favour of	3
亲爱	qīn'ài	adj.	dear, beloved, darling	4
亲密	qīnmì	adj.	intimate, close	4
亲切	• qīnqiè	adj.	amiable, cordial, close and dear, familiar	3
亲人	qīnrén	n.	one's close relatives	3
亲属	qīnshǔ	n.	kin, kindred, relatives	6
亲眼	qīnyǎn	adv.	with one's own eyes, personally	6
亲自	qīnzì	adv.	personally, in person, oneself	3
父亲	- fùqin	n.	father	3

母亲	- mǔqin	n.	mother		3
竞	**jìng**		to contend, to compete	立 117.5	5
竞赛	jìngsài	n.	race, competition		5
竞争	jìngzhēng	vb.	to compete, competition		5
站	**zhàn**		station, to stand up, a stand	立 117.5	1
站	zhàn	+ n.	station, branch of a company or organization, website		1
站	zhàn	+ vb.	to stand, to halt, to stop		2
站台	zhàntái	n.	platform (at a railway station)		6
站住	zhànzhù	vb.	to stand		2
车站	chēzhàn	n.	rail station, bus stop		1
网站	wǎngzhàn	n.	website, network station, node		2
地铁站	· dìtiězhàn	n.	subway station		2
加油站	jiāyóuzhàn	n.	petrol (gas) station		4
竟	**jìng**		finally, after all, at last	立 117.6	4
竟然	jìngrán	adv.	unexpectedly, to one's surprise, in spite of everything, in that crazy way, actually, to go as far as to		4
毕竟	bìjìng	adv.	after all, all in all, when all is said and done, in the final analysis		5
究竟	jiūjìng	vb.	to go to the bottom of a matter, after all, when all is said and done, (in an interrogative sentence) finally, outcome, result		4
章	**zhāng**		composition, chapter, section	立 117.6	3
章	zhāng	n.	chapter, section, literary work, seal, surname Zhang		6
文章	wénzhāng	n.	article, essay, literary works, writings, hidden meaning		3
童	**tóng**		child, boy, servant boy	立 117.7	4
童话	tónghuà	n.	children's fairy tales		4
童年	tóngnián	n.	childhood		4
儿童	értóng	n.	child		4
端	**duān**		end, extremity	立 117.9	6
端	duān	n.	end, extremity, item, port, to hold sth level with both hands, to carry, upright, proper		6
端午节	duānwǔ jié	n.	Dragon Boat Festival		6
极端	jíduān	adj.	extreme		6

竹 zhú bamboo ⺮ 118

竹	**zhú**		bamboo	竹 118.0	5
竹子	zhúzi	n.	bamboo		5
笔	**bǐ**		pen, writing brush	竹 118.4	2
笔	bǐ	n.	pen, pencil, writing brush, to write or compose, the strokes of Chinese characters, m.w. for sums of money, deals		2
笔记	bǐjì	vb.	to take down (in writing), notes, a type of literature consisting mainly of short sketches		2
笔试	bǐshì	n.	written examination, paper test (for an applicant)		6
笔记本	bǐjìběn	n.	notebook (stationery)		2
钢笔	gāngbǐ	n.	fountain pen		5
毛笔	máobǐ	n.	writing brush		5

铅笔	qiānbǐ	n.	(lead) pencil		6
圆珠笔	yuánzhūbǐ	n.	ballpoint pen		6

笑 **xiào** — to smile, to laugh — 竹 118.4 — 1

笑	xiào	vb.	to smile, to laugh	1
笑话	- xiàohua	n.	joke, jest	2
笑脸	xiàoliǎn	n.	smiling face, smiley :)	6
笑容	xiàoróng	n.	smile, smiling expression	6
笑声	xiàoshēng	n.	laughter	6
笑话儿	xiàohuàr	n.	(spoken) joke	2
微笑	wēixiào	n.	smile	4
开玩笑	kāi wánxiào	vb.	to play a joke, to make fun of, to joke	1

笨 **bèn** — stupid, foolish — 竹 118.5 — 4

笨	bèn	adj.	stupid, foolish, silly, slow-witted, clumsy	4

第 **dì** — number affix, sequence — 竹 118.5 — 1

第	dì	+ aff.	(prefix indicating ordinal number, e.g. first, second 第二 dì èr), order, (old) rank in the imperial examinations, (literary) but, just	1

符 **fú** — tally, symbol, charm — 竹 118.5 — 4

符号	fúhào	n.	symbol, mark, sign	4
符合	fúhé	vb.	in keeping with, in accordance with, tallying with, in line with, to agree with, to conform to, to correspond with, to manage, to handle	4

策 **cè** — scheme, plan — 竹 118.6 — 6

策划	cèhuà	vb.	to plot, to scheme, to bring about, to engineer, planning, producer, planner	6
策略	cèlüè	n.	strategy, tactics, crafty, adroit	6
决策	juécè	n.	strategic decision, decision-making, policy decision, to determine policy	6
政策	zhèngcè	n.	policy	6

答 ** dá, dā* — to answer, to return; to assent to — 竹 118.6 — 1

答	dá	vb.	to answer, to return	5
答应	- dāying	vb.	to answer, to respond, to answer positively, to agree, to accept, to promise	2
答案	dá'àn	n.	answer, solution	4
答复	dáfù	vb.	to answer, to reply, Reply to: (in email header)	5
报答	bàodá	vb.	to repay, to requite	5
回答	huídá	vb.	to reply, to answer, the answer	1

等 **děng** — to wait for, class — 竹 118.6 — 1

等	děng	+ vb.	to wait for, to await	1
等	děng	+ n.	class, rank, grade, equal to, same as, et cetera, and so on	2
等待	děngdài	vb.	to wait, to wait for	3
等到	děngdào	vb.	to wait until, by the time when (sth is ready etc)	2
等候	děnghòu	vb.	to wait, to wait for	5
等级	děngjí	n.	grade, rank, status	5
等于	děngyú	vb.	to equal, to be tantamount to	2
初等	chūděng	adj.	elementary (i.e. easy)	6
高等	gāoděng	adj.	high-level, higher (animals, education etc), advanced (math etc)	6

平等	píngděng	*adj.*	equal, equality		2
相等	xiāngděng	*vb.*	to be equal, equally, equivalent		5
中等	zhōngděng	*adj.*	medium		6
筑	**zhù**		to build	竹 118.6	5
建筑	jiànzhù	*vb.*	to construct, building		5
简	**jiǎn**		simple, brief	竹 118.7	3
简单	jiǎndān	*adj.*	simple, not complicated, (opp. 复杂 fùzá: complex)		3
简介	jiǎnjiè	*n.*	summary, brief introduction		6
简历	jiǎnlì	*n.*	curriculum vitae (CV), résumé, biographical notes		4
简直	jiǎnzhí	*adv.*	simply, at all, practically		3
筷	**kuài**		chopsticks	竹 118.7	2
筷子	kuàizi	*n.*	chopsticks		2
签	**qiān**		to sign, to endorse	竹 118.7	5
签	qiān	+ *vb.*	to sign, to autograph, to make brief comments		5
签字	qiān zì	*vb.*	to sign (one's name), signature		5
签订	qiāndìng	*vb.*	to agree to and sign (a treaty etc)		5
签名	qiānmíng	*vb.*	to sign (one's name with a pen etc), to autograph, signature		5
签约	qiānyuē	*vb.*	to sign a contract or agreement		5
签证	qiānzhèng	*n.*	visa, certificate, to certify		5
管	**guǎn**		pipe, tube	竹 118.8	3
管	guǎn	*n.*	pipe, tube, to take care (of), to control, to manage, m.w. for long thin objects, surname Guan		3
管道	guǎndào	*n.*	tubing, pipeline, (fig.) channel, means		6
管理	guǎnlǐ	*vb.*	to supervise, to manage, to administer, management, administration		3
不管	bùguǎn	*conj.*	regardless of, no matter; not to be concerned		4
尽管	jǐnguǎn	*conj.*	despite, although, in spite of, unhesitatingly, do not hesitate (to ask, complain etc), (go ahead and do it) without hesitating		5
看管	• kānguǎn	*vb.*	to look after		6
吸管	xīguǎn	*n.*	(drinking) straw, pipette, eyedropper, snorkel		4
血管	xuèguǎn	*n.*	vein, artery		6
只管	zhǐguǎn	*adv.*	solely engrossed in one thing, just (one thing, no need to worry about the rest), simply, by all means, please feel free, do not hesitate (to ask for sth)		6
主管	zhǔguǎn	*vb.*	to be in charge, to be responsible for, person in charge, manager		5
算	**suàn**		to count, to calculate	竹 118.8	2
算	suàn	*vb.*	to regard as, to figure, to calculate, to compute		2
算了	suàn le	*vb.*	let it be, let it pass, forget about it		6
算是	suànshì	*adv.*	considered to be, at last		6
打算	dǎsuàn	*vb.*	to plan, to intend, to calculate, plan, intention, calculation		2
计算	jìsuàn	*vb.*	to count, to calculate, to compute		3
就算	jiùsuàn	*conj.*	granted that, even if		6
总算	zǒngsuàn	*adv.*	at long last, finally, on the whole		5
计算机	jìsuànjī	*n.*	computer, calculator		2

箭	**jiàn**		arrow	竹 118.9	6
箭	jiàn	n.	arrow, distance of one arrow flight		6
火箭	huǒjiàn	n.	rocket		6
篇	**piān**		sheet, piece of writing	竹 118.9	2
篇	piān	n.	sheet, piece of writing, bound set of bamboo slips used for record keeping (old), m.w. for written items: chapter, article		2
箱	**xiāng**		case, box	竹 118.9	3
箱	xiāng	n.	case, box, trunk, chest		4
箱子	xiāngzi	n.	suitcase, chest, box, case, trunk		4
冰箱	bīngxiāng	n.	icebox, freezer cabinet, refrigerator		4
信箱	xìnxiāng	n.	mailbox, post office box		5
邮箱	yóuxiāng	n.	mailbox, post office box, email, email inbox		3
篮	**lán**		basket	竹 118.10	2
篮球	lánqiú	n.	basketball		2
籍	**jí**		record, register	竹 118.14	5
国籍	guójí	n.	nationality		5

米 mǐ rice 119

米	**mǐ**		rice	米 119.0	1
米	mǐ	+ m.w.	metre		2
米	mǐ	+ n.	rice (husked - uncooked), sth resembling rice		3
米饭	mǐfàn	n.	(cooked) rice		1
大米	dàmǐ	n.	(husked) rice		6
毫米	háomǐ	m.w.	millimetre		4
厘米	límǐ	m.w.	centimetre		4
玉米	yùmǐ	n.	corn, maize		4
平方米	píngfāngmǐ	m.w.	square meter		6
粉	**fěn**		powder	米 119.4	6
奶粉	nǎifěn	n.	powdered milk		6
洗衣粉	xǐyīfěn	n.	laundry detergent, washing powder		6
粗	**cū**		coarse, rough	米 119.5	4
粗	cū	adj.	coarse, rough, thick, (opp. 细 xì: thin), careless		4
粗心	cūxīn	adj.	careless, thoughtless		4
粥	**zhōu**		congee, porridge	米 119.6	6
粥	zhōu	n.	congee, porridge, gruel		6
粮	**liáng**		food, grain, provisions	米 119.7	4
粮食	- liángshi	n.	foodstuff, cereals		4
精	**jīng**		energy, spirit, essence	米 119.8	3
精	jīng	n.	energy, spirit, vitality, essence, extract, semen, seed, (Chinese medicine) fundamental essence maintaining body function, highly perfected		6

精彩	jīngcǎi	adj.	wonderful, marvellous, brilliant		3
精力	jīnglì	n.	energy, vigour		4
精美	jīngměi	adj.	delicate, fine, refinement		6
精品	jīngpǐn	n.	quality goods, premium product, fine work (of art)		6
精神	jīngshén	n.	spirit, mind, consciousness, thought, mental, psychological, essence, gist		3
精神	- jīngshen	n.	vigour, vitality, drive; lively		3

| **糊** | **hú** | | to paste | 米 119.9 | 5 |
| 模糊 | - móhu | adj. | vague, indistinct, fuzzy | | 5 |

糕	**gāo**		cake, pastry	米 119.10	5
蛋糕	dàngāo	n.	cake		5
糟糕	zāogāo	adj.	too bad, how terrible, what bad luck, terrible, bad		5

| **糖** | **táng** | | sugar | 米 119.10 | 3 |
| 糖 | táng | n. | sugar, sweets, candy | | 3 |

糟	**zāo**		sediment, dregs, to pickle	米 119.11	5
糟	zāo	n.	sediment, dregs, pickled in wine, rotten, messy, ruined		5
糟糕	zāogāo	adj.	too bad, how terrible, what bad luck, terrible, bad		5

糸 mì silk 糹糸 120

系	* **xì, jì**		system, line, link; to tie	糸 120.1	1
系	• jì	vb.	to tie, to fasten, to button up		6
系	xì	n.	system, line, link, (literary) to bind, to fasten		3
系列	xìliè	n.	series, set		4
系统	xìtǒng	n.	system		4
关系	- guānxi	n.	relation, connection, relationship		3
联系	liánxì	n.	connection, contact, relation, to get in touch with, to integrate, to link, to touch		3
没关系	- méi guānxi	vb.	it doesn't matter, that's all right, never mind		1

纠	**jiū**		to investigate, to entangle	糸 120.2	6
纠纷	jiūfēn	n.	dispute		6
纠正	jiūzhèng	vb.	to correct, to make right		6

红	**hóng**		red, popular	糸 120.3	2
红	hóng	adj.	red, symbol of success, bonus, popular, surname Hong		2
红包	hóngbāo	n.	money wrapped in red as a gift, bonus payment, kickback, bribe		4
红茶	hóngchá	n.	black tea		3
红酒	hóngjiǔ	n.	red wine		3
红色	hóngsè	adj.	red (colour), revolutionary		2
通红	tōnghóng	adj.	very red, red through and through, to blush (deep red)		6
西红柿	xīhóngshì	n.	tomato		5

级	**jí**		level, rank	糸 120.3	2
级	jí	n.	level, grade, rank, step (of stairs)		2
班级	bānjí	n.	class (group of students), grade (in school)		3
超级	chāojí	adj.	super-, ultra-, hyper-		3

初级	chūjí	*adj.*	junior, primary	3
等级	děngjí	*n.*	grade, rank, status	5
高级	gāojí	*adj.*	high level, high grade, advanced, high-ranking	2
年级	niánjí	*n.*	grade, year (in school, college etc)	2
上级	shàngjí	*n.*	higher authorities, superiors	5
升级	shēngjí	*vb.*	to escalate (in intensity), to go up by one grade, to be promoted, to upgrade (computing)	6
中级	zhōngjí	*adj.*	middle level (in a hierarchy)	2

纪 jì — discipline, period, age   糸 120.3 — 3

纪录	jìlù	*vb.*	to record or document, take notes, record (as in world record)	3
纪律	jìlǜ	*n.*	discipline	4
纪念	jìniàn	*vb.*	to commemorate, to remember	3
年纪	niánjì	*n.*	age	3
世纪	shìjì	*n.*	century	3

约 yuē — agreement, covenant   糸 120.3 — 3

约	yuē	*vb.*	agreement, covenant, treaty, to arrange, economical	3
约定	yuēdìng	*vb.*	to agree on sth (after discussion), to conclude a bargain, to arrange, to promise, to stipulate, to make an appointment	6
约会	yuēhuì	*n.*	appointment, engagement, date	4
约束	yuēshù	*vb.*	to restrict, to limit to, to constrain, restriction, constraint	5
大约	dàyuē	*adv.*	approximately, probably	3
合约	héyuē	*n.*	treaty, contract	6
节约	jiéyuē	*vb.*	to economize, to conserve (resources), economy, frugal	3
签约	qiānyuē	*vb.*	to sign a contract or agreement	5
预约	yùyuē	*n.*	booking, reservation, to book, to make an appointment	6
制约	zhìyuē	*vb.*	to restrict, condition	5

纯 chún — pure, clean, simple   糸 120.4 — 4

纯	chún	*adj.*	pure, clean, simple, unmixed, genuine	4
纯净水	chúnjìngshuǐ	*n.*	purified water	4
单纯	dānchún	*adj.*	simple, pure, unsophisticated, merely, purely	4

纷 fēn — in disorder, scattered, tangled   糸 120.4 — 4

纷纷	fēnfēn	*adv.*	one after another, in succession, one by one, continuously, diverse, in profusion, numerous and confused, pell-mell	4
纠纷	jiūfēn	*n.*	dispute	6

纲 gāng — heavy rope, hawser, main points   糸 120.4 — 5

大纲	dàgāng	*n.*	synopsis, outline, program, leading principles	5

紧 jǐn — tight, urgent   糸 120.4 — 3

紧	jǐn	*adj.*	tight, strict, close at hand, near, urgent, tense, hard up, short of money, to tighten	3
紧急	jǐnjí	*adj.*	urgent, emergency	3
紧紧	jǐnjǐn	*vb.*	closely, tightly	5
紧密	jǐnmì	*adj.*	inseparably close	4
紧张	jǐnzhāng	*n.*	nervous, keyed up, intense, tense, strained, in short supply, scarce	3
赶紧	gǎnjǐn	*adv.*	hurriedly, without delay	3

抓紧	zhuā jǐn	vb.	to grasp firmly, to pay special attention to, to rush in, to make the most of		4
不要紧	bù yàojǐn	adj.	unimportant, not serious, it doesn't matter, never mind, it looks all right, but		4
纳	**nà**		to admit, to accept	糸 120.4	6
采纳	cǎinà	vb.	to accept, to adopt		6
素	**sù**		white, plain, basic	糸 120.4	6
素质	sùzhì	n.	inner quality, basic essence		6
要素	yàosù	n.	essential factor, key constituent		6
因素	yīnsù	n.	element, factor		6
元素	yuánsù	n.	element, element of a set, chemical element		6
维生素	wéishēngsù	n.	vitamin		6
索	**suǒ**		rope, cable	糸 120.4	5
搜索	sōusuǒ	vb.	to search (a place), to search (a database), to search for (sth)		5
探索	tànsuǒ	vb.	to explore, to probe		6
线索	xiànsuǒ	n.	trail, clues, thread (of a story)		5
纸	**zhǐ**		paper	糸 120.4	2
纸	zhǐ	n.	paper		2
报纸	bàozhǐ	n.	newspaper, newsprint		2
纵	**zòng**		vertical, lengthwise	糸 120.4	6
操纵	cāozòng	vb.	to operate, to control, to rig, to manipulate		6
经	**jīng**		classic works, to pass through	糸 120.5	2
经常	jīngcháng	adv.	frequently, constantly, regularly, often, day-to-day, everyday, daily		2
经典	jīngdiǎn	n.	the classics, scriptures, classical, classic (example, case etc), typical		4
经费	jīngfèi	n.	funds, expenditure		5
经过	jīngguò	vb.	to pass, to go through, process, course		2
经济	jīngjì	n.	economy, economic		3
经理	jīnglǐ	n.	manager, director		2
经历	jīnglì	n.	experience		3
经验	jīngyàn	n.	experience, to experience		3
经营	jīngyíng	vb.	to engage in (business etc), to run, to operate		3
曾经	céngjīng	adv.	once, already, former, previously, ever, (past tense marker used before verb or clause)		3
神经	shénjīng	n.	nerve, mental state, (coll.) unhinged		5
已经	yǐjīng	adv.	already		2
总经理	zǒngjīnglǐ	n.	general manager, CEO		6
累	**lèi**		tired, to tire	糸 120.5	1
累	lèi	adj.	tired, to tire, to work hard		1
积累	jīlèi	vb.	to accumulate, accumulation, cumulative, cumulatively		4
练	**liàn**		to practise, to exercise	糸 120.5	2
练	liàn	vb.	to practise, to train, to drill, to perfect (one's skill), to exercise, (literary) white silk, to boil and scour raw silk		2
练习	liànxí	vb.	to practice, exercise, drill, practice		2
教练	jiàoliàn	n.	instructor, sports coach, trainer		3

熟练	shúliàn	adj.	practiced, proficient, skilled, skilful		4
训练	xùnliàn	vb.	to train, to drill, training		3

绍 shào — to continue, to carry on,   糸 120.5 1

介绍	jièshào	vb.	to introduce (sb to sb), to give a presentation, to present (sb for a job etc), introduction		1

细 xì — fine, slender, thin   糸 120.5 4

细	xì	adj.	thin or slender, (opp. 粗 xū: coarse), finely particulate, thin and soft, fine, delicate, trifling, (of a sound) quiet, frugal		4
细胞	xìbāo	n.	cell (biology)		6
细节	xìjié	n.	details, particulars		4
细菌	xìjūn	n.	bacterium, germ		6
细致	xìzhì	adj.	delicate, fine, careful, meticulous, painstaking		4
详细	xiángxì	adj.	detailed, in detail, minute		5
仔细	zǐxì	adj.	careful, attentive, cautious		5

线 xiàn — thread, wire   糸 120.5 3

线	xiàn	n.	thread, string, wire, line		3
线路	xiànlù	n.	line, circuit, wire, road, railway track, bus route		6
线索	xiànsuǒ	n.	trail, clues, thread (of a story)		5
光线	guāngxiàn	n.	light ray		5
路线	lùxiàn	n.	itinerary, route, political line		3
热线	rèxiàn	n.	hotline (communications link)		6
直线	zhíxiàn	n.	straight line, sharply (rise or fall)		5

织 zhī — to weave, to knit   糸 120.5 5

织	zhī	vb.	to weave, to knit, to organize, to unite		6
组织	zǔzhī	vb.	to organize, organization, (biology) tissue, (textiles) weave		5

终 zhōng — end, finish   糸 120.5 3

终点	zhōngdiǎn	n.	the end, end point, finishing line (in a race), destination, terminus		5
终身	zhōngshēn	n.	lifelong, all one's life, marriage		5
终于	zhōngyú	adv.	at last, in the end, finally, eventually		3
终止	zhōngzhǐ	vb.	to stop, to terminate (law)		5
始终	shǐzhōng	adv.	from beginning to end, all along		3
最终	zuìzhōng	n.	final, ultimate		6

紫 zǐ — purple, violet   糸 120.5 5

紫	zǐ	adj.	purple, violet, amethyst		5

组 zǔ — set, group   糸 120.5 2

组	zǔ	m.w.	m.w. for sets, set, group, to organize, to team up, compose, surname Zu		2
组成	zǔchéng	vb.	to form, to make up, to constitute		2
组合	zǔhé	vb.	to assemble, to combine, to compose, combination, association, set, compilation, (math.) combinatorial		3
组长	zǔzhǎng	n.	group leader		2
组织	zǔzhī	vb.	to organize, organization, (biology) tissue, (textiles) weave		5
重组	• chóngzǔ	vb.	to reorganize, to recombine, recombination		6
分组	fēnzǔ	vb.	to divide into groups, group (formed from a larger group), subgroup, (computer networking) packet		3

小组	xiǎozǔ		n.	group	2
给	* **gěi, jǐ**			to, for, to give; to supply	糸 120.6 1
给	gěi		prep.	to, for, for the benefit of, to give, to allow, to do sth (for sb), (grammatical equivalent of 被 bèi)	1
给予	• jǐyǔ		vb.	to accord, to give, to show (respect)	6
递给	dìgěi		vb.	to hand it (i.e. the aforementioned item) to (sb)	5
供给	• gōngjǐ		vb.	to furnish, to provide, supply (as in supply and demand)	6
交给	jiāogěi		vb.	to give, to deliver, to hand over	2
送给	sònggěi		vb.	to send, to give as a present	2
绘	**huì**			to draw, to sketch, to paint	糸 120.6 6
绘画	huìhuà		n.	drawing, painting	6
结	* **jié, jiē**			knot, tie; join, connect	糸 120.6 2
结	jié		vb.	to tie, knot	4
结实	• jiēshi		vb.	to bear fruit, to form seed	3
结构	jiégòu		n.	structure, composition, makeup, architecture	4
结果	jiéguǒ		vb.	to bear fruit	2
结合	jiéhé		vb.	to combine, to link, to integrate, binding	3
结婚	jiéhūn		vb.	to marry, to get married	3
结论	jiélùn		n.	conclusion, verdict	4
结束	jiéshù		vb.	to finish, to end, to conclude, to close	3
团结	tuánjié		vb.	to unite, unity, solidarity, united	3
总结	zǒngjié		vb.	to sum up, to conclude, summary, résumé	3
绝	**jué**			to cut, to sever	糸 120.6 3
绝	jué		vb.	to cut short, to exhaust, to die, hopeless, absolutely	6
绝对	juéduì		adj.	absolute, unconditional	3
绝望	juéwàng		vb.	to despair, to give up all hope, desperate, desperation	5
绝大多数	juédàduōshù		n.	absolute majority, overwhelming majority	6
拒绝	jùjué		vb.	to refuse, to decline, to reject	5
络	**luò**			to wrap around, web, net	糸 120.6 4
联络	liánluò		vb.	to get in touch with, to contact, to stay in contact (with), liaison, (math.) connection	5
网络	wǎngluò		n.	network, Internet	4
绕	**rào**			to wind	糸 120.6 5
绕	rào		vb.	to wind, to coil, move round	5
围绕	wéirào		vb.	to revolve around, to centre on (an issue)	5
绒	**róng**			silk, cotton, or woollen fabric	糸 120.6 5
羽绒服	yǔróngfú		n.	down-filled garment	5
统	**tǒng**			interrelated	糸 120.6 4
统计	tǒngjì		n.	statistics, to count, to add up	4
统一	tǒngyī		vb.	to unify, to unite, to integrate	4
传统	chuántǒng		n.	tradition, traditional, convention, conventional	4
系统	xìtǒng		n.	system	4
总统	zǒngtǒng		n.	president (of a country)	4

继	jì		to continue, to follow	糸 120.7	3
继承	jìchéng	vb.	to inherit, to succeed to (the throne etc), to carry on (a tradition etc)		5
继续	jìxù	vb.	to continue, to proceed with, to go on with		3
绩	jī		achievement, merit	糸 120.8	2
成绩	chéngjī	n.	achievement, performance records, grades		2
绿	lǜ		green	糸 120.8	2
绿	lǜ	adj.	green, (slang) to cheat on (one's spouse or boyfriend or girlfriend)		2
绿茶	lǜchá	n.	green tea, (slang) (of a girl) seemingly innocent and charming but actually calculating and manipulative, a girl who has these qualities		3
绿化	lǜhuà	vb.	to make green with plants, to reforest		6
绿色	lǜsè	n.	green (colour), eco-friendly		2
维	wéi		to maintain, to tie up	糸 120.8	4
维持	wéichí	vb.	to keep, to maintain, to preserve		4
维护	wéihù	vb.	to defend, to safeguard, to protect, to uphold, to maintain		4
维修	wéixiū	n.	maintenance (of equipment), to protect and maintain		4
维生素	wéishēngsù	n.	vitamin		6
思维	sīwéi	n.	(line of) thought, thinking		5
二维码	èrwéimǎ	n.	two-dimensional barcode, QR code		5
绪	xù		end of thread, threads	糸 120.8	6
情绪	qíngxù	n.	mood, state of mind, moodiness		6
续	xù		to continue, to add	糸 120.8	3
持续	chíxù	vb.	to continue, to persist, to last, sustainable, preservation		3
继续	jìxù	vb.	to continue, to proceed with, to go on with		3
连续	liánxù	adj.	continuous, in a row, serial, consecutive		3
陆续	lùxù	adv.	in turn, successively, one after the other, bit by bit		4
手续	shǒuxù	n.	procedure		3
延续	yánxù	vb.	to continue, to go on, to last		4
连续剧	liánxùjù	n.	serialized drama, dramatic series, show in parts		3
手续费	shǒuxùfèi	n.	service charge, processing fee, commission		6
综	zōng		to sum up	糸 120.8	4
综合	zōnghé	adj.	comprehensive, composite, synthesized, mixed, to sum up, to integrate, to synthesize		4
编	biān		to weave, to arrange	糸 120.9	4
编	biān	vb.	to weave, to plait, to organize, to group, to arrange, to edit, to compile, to write, to compose, to fabricate, to make up		4
编辑	biānjí	vb.	to edit, to compile		5
编辑	biānjí	n.	editor, compiler		5
编制	biānzhì	vb.	to weave, to plait, to compile, to put together (a lesson plan, budget etc)		6
缓	huǎn		slow, leisurely	糸 120.9	4
缓解	huǎnjiě	vb.	to bring relief, to alleviate (a crisis), to dull (a pain)		4

缘	yuán		edge, reason, fate	糸 120.9	6
缘故	yuángù	n.	reason, cause		6
边缘	biānyuán	n.	edge, fringe, verge, brink, periphery, marginal, borderline		6
繁	fán		complicated, in great numbers	糸 120.11	5
繁荣	fánróng	adj.	prosperous, booming (economy)		5
繁殖	fánzhí	vb.	to breed, to reproduce, to propagate		6
频繁	pínfán	adv.	frequently, often		5
缩	suō		to contract, to draw in	糸 120.11	4
缩短	suōduǎn	vb.	to curtail, to cut down		4
缩小	suōxiǎo	vb.	to reduce, to decrease, to shrink		4

缶 fǒu jar 121

缺	quē		to be short of, lack, gap	缶 121.4	3
缺	quē	vb.	to be short of, deficiency, lack, scarce, vacant post		3
缺点	quēdiǎn	n.	weak point, fault, shortcoming, disadvantage		3
缺乏	quēfá	vb.	to lack, to be short of, lack, shortage		5
缺少	quēshǎo	n.	lack, shortage of, shortfall, to be short (of), to lack		3
缺陷	quēxiàn	n.	defect, flaw, physical defect		6

网 wǎng net 罒 网 冈 122

网	wǎng		net, network	网 122.0	1
网	wǎng	n.	net, network		2
网吧	• wǎngbā	n.	Internet café		6
网络	wǎngluò	n.	network, Internet		4
网球	wǎngqiú	n.	tennis, tennis ball		2
网上	wǎngshàng	n.	online		1
网页	wǎngyè	n.	web page		6
网友	wǎngyǒu	n.	online friend, Internet user		1
网站	wǎngzhàn	n.	website, network station, node		2
网址	wǎngzhǐ	n.	website, web address, URL		4
上网	shàngwǎng	vb.	to go online, to connect to the Internet		1
互联网	hùliánwǎng	n.	Internet		3
罚	fá		to punish, to penalize	网 122.4	5
罚	fá	vb.	to punish, to discipline, to penalize		5
罚款	fákuǎn	vb.	to fine, penalty, fine (monetary)		5
处罚	chǔfá	vb.	to penalize, to punish		5
罢	bà		to cease, to finish, to stop	网 122.5	6
罢工	bà gōng	n.	a strike, to go on strike		6
罢了	bàle	n.	a modal particle indicating (that's all, only, nothing much)		6
置	zhì		to place, to lay out, to set aside	网 122.8	4
安置	ānzhì	vb.	to find a place for, to help settle down, to arrange for, to get into bed, placement		4

布置	bùzhì	vb.	to put in order, to arrange, to decorate, to fix up, to deploy	4
配置	pèizhì	vb.	to deploy, to allocate, configuration, allocation	6
设置	shèzhì	vb.	to set up, to install	4
位置	- wèizhi	n.	position, place, seat	4
装置	zhuāngzhì	vb.	to install, installation, equipment, system, unit, device	4

罪 zuì — crime, sin — 网 122.8 — 6

罪	zuì	n.	crime, sin, hardship, fault, blame	6
罪恶	zuì'è	n.	crime, evil, sin	6
犯罪	fànzuì	vb.	to commit a crime, crime, offense	6

羊 yáng — sheep — 羋 羊 123

羊 yáng — sheep, goat — 羊 123.0 — 3

羊	yáng	n.	sheep, goat, surname Yang	3

美 měi — beautiful, pretty, pleasing — 羊 123.3 — 3

美	měi	adj.	beautiful, (opp. 丑 chǒu: ugly), pretty, pleasing, the Americas	3
美好	měihǎo	adj.	beautiful, fine	3
美金	měijīn	n.	US dollar ($)	4
美丽	měilì	adj.	beautiful	3
美女	měinǚ	n.	beautiful woman	4
美容	měiróng	vb.	to improve one's appearance (using cosmetics or cosmetic surgery), to make oneself more attractive, to beautify	6
美食	měishí	n.	culinary delicacy, fine food, gourmet food	3
美术	měishù	n.	art, fine arts, painting	3
美元	měiyuán	n.	U.S. dollar	3
精美	jīngměi	adj.	delicate, fine, refinement	6
完美	wánměi	adj.	perfect, perfection, perfectly	3
优美	yōuměi	adj.	graceful, fine, elegant	4

群 qún — group, crowd — 羊 123.7 — 3

群	qún	n.	group, crowd, flock, herd, pack etc, surname Qún	3
群体	qúntǐ	n.	community, colony	5
群众	qúnzhòng	n.	mass, multitude, the masses	5
人群	rénqún	n.	crowd	3

羽 yǔ — feather — 124

羽 yǔ — feather, plume, wings — 羽 124.0 — 5

羽毛球	yǔmáoqiú	n.	shuttlecock, badminton	5
羽绒服	yǔróngfú	n.	down-filled garment	5

翻 fān — to turn over, to climb over — 羽 124.12 — 4

翻	fān	vb.	to turn over, to climb over, to translate	4
翻译	fānyì	vb.	to translate, to interpret, translator, interpreter, translation, interpretation	4

耀 yào — to shine, to dazzle, glory — 羽 124.14 — 6

照耀	zhàoyào	vb.	to shine, to illuminate	6

老 lǎo old 耂 125

考	**kǎo**		to examine, to test	老 125.0 1
考	kǎo	vb.	to check, to verify, to test, to examine, to take an exam, to take an entrance exam for, deceased father	1
考察	kǎochá	vb.	to inspect, to observe and study, on-the-spot investigation	4
考场	kǎochǎng	n.	exam room	6
考核	kǎohé	vb.	to examine, to check up on, to assess, to review, appraisal, review, evaluation	5
考虑	kǎolǜ	vb.	to think over, to consider, consideration	4
考生	kǎoshēng	n.	exam candidate, student whose name has been put forward for an exam	2
考试	kǎoshì	vb.	to take an exam, exam	1
考题	kǎotí	n.	exam question	6
考验	kǎoyàn	vb.	to test, to put to the test, trial, ordeal	3
报考	bàokǎo	vb.	to enter oneself for an examination	6
补考	bǔkǎo	vb.	to sit for a makeup exam, to resit an exam, makeup exam, resit	6
参考	cānkǎo	n.	consultation, reference, to consult, to refer	4
高考	gāokǎo	n.	college entrance exam	6
思考	sīkǎo	vb.	to think, to consider, to reflect on, to ponder over	4
老	**lǎo**		old, aged, experienced	老 125.0 1
老	lǎo	+ adv.	for a long time, always, very	1
老	lǎo	+ adj.	old - not young, aged (opp. 幼 yòu: young, 少 shào: young), old - not new (opp. 新 xīn: new), tough, original	2
老	lǎo	+ aff.	prefix used before the surname of a person to indicate affection or familiarity, e.g lǎo wáng 老王	2
老板	lǎobǎn	n.	boss, proprietor, shopkeeper	3
老公	lǎogōng	n.	(coll.) husband	4
老家	lǎojiā	n.	native place, place of origin, home state or region	4
老年	lǎonián	n.	elderly, old age, autumn of one's years	2
老婆	- lǎopo	n.	(coll.) wife	4
老人	lǎorén	n.	old man or woman, the elderly, one's aged parents or grandparents	1
老师	lǎoshī	n.	teacher	1
老是	lǎoshì	adv.	always	2
老实	- lǎoshi	adj.	honest, sincere, well-behaved, open and guileless, naive	4
老头	lǎotóu	n.	old fellow, old man, father, husband	3
老乡	lǎoxiāng	n.	fellow townsman, fellow villager, sb from the same hometown	6
老百姓	lǎobǎixìng	n.	ordinary people, the person in the street	3
老朋友	- lǎopéngyou	n.	old friend, (slang) period, menstruation	2
老太太	- lǎotàitai	n.	elderly lady (respectful), esteemed mother	3
古老	gǔlǎo	adj.	ancient, old, age-old	5
养老	yǎnglǎo	vb.	to provide for the elderly (family members), to enjoy a life in retirement	6
者	**zhě**		that which, he who, those who	老 125.4 2
者	zhě	+ aff.	(after a verb or adjective) one who (is) ..., (after a noun) person involved in ..., -er, -ist	3
读者	dúzhě	n.	reader	3

患者	huànzhě	n.	patient, sufferer		6
或者	huòzhě	conj.	or, possibly, maybe, perhaps		2
记者	jìzhě	n.	reporter, journalist		3
学者	xuézhě	n.	scholar		5
作者	zuòzhě	n.	author, writer		3
消费者	xiāofèi zhě	n.	consumer		5
志愿者	zhìyuànzhě	n.	volunteer		3

而 ér and 126

而	ér		and, and then, and yet, but	而 126.0	2
而	ér	conj.	and, as well as, and so, but (not), yet (not), (indicates causal relation), (indicates change of state), (indicates contrast)		4
而且	érqiě	conj.	(not only ...) but also, moreover, in addition, furthermore		2
而是	érshì	conj.	rather		4
从而	cóng'ér	conj.	thus, thereby		5
反而	fǎn'ér	adv.	instead, on the contrary, contrary (to expectations)		4
然而	rán'ér	conj.	however, yet, but		4
时而	shí'ér	adv.	occasionally, from time to time		6
因而	yīn'ér	conj.	therefore, as a result, thus, and as a result, ...		5
耐	nài		to endure, to bear	而 126.3	5
耐心	nàixīn	vb.	to be patient, patience		5
不耐烦	bùnàifán	adj.	impatient, to lose patience		5

耒 lěi plow 127

耗	hào		to use up, to waste	耒 127.4	6
消耗	xiāohào	vb.	to use up, to consume		6

耳 ěr ear 128

耳	ěr		ear	耳 128.0	4
耳朵	-ěrduo	n.	ear		5
耳机	ěrjī	n.	headphones, earphones, telephone receiver		4
聊	liáo		to chat	耳 128.5	4
聊	liáo	vb.	to chat, to depend upon (literary), temporarily, just, slightly		6
聊天	liáotiān	vb.	to chat, to gossip		6
无聊	wúliáo	adj.	bored, boring, senseless		4
职	zhí		duty, profession	耳 128.5	3
职工	zhígōng	n.	workers, staff		3
职能	zhínéng	n.	function, role		5
职位	zhíwèi	n.	post, office, position		5
职务	zhíwù	n.	post, position, job, duties		5
职业	zhíyè	n.	occupation, profession, vocation, professional		3
职责	zhízé	n.	duty, responsibility, obligation		6
辞职	cízhí	vb.	to resign		5

求职	qiúzhí	vb.	to seek employment		6
联	**lián**		**to connect, to join, to ally**	耳 128.6	3
联合	liánhé	vb.	to combine, to join, unite, alliance		3
联络	liánluò	vb.	to get in touch with, to contact, to stay in contact (with), liaison, (math.) connection		5
联盟	liánméng	n.	alliance, union, coalition		6
联赛	liánsài	n.	(sports) league, league tournament		6
联手	liánshǒu	n.	(lit.) to join hands, to act together		6
联系	liánxì	n.	connection, contact, relation, to get in touch with, to integrate, to link, to touch		3
联想	liánxiǎng	vb.	to associate (cognitively), to make an associative connection, mental association		5
联合国	liánhéguó	n.	United Nations		3
关联	guānlián	n.	connection, related, linked, affiliated		6
互联网	hùliánwǎng	n.	Internet		3
聘	**pìn**		**to engage, to employ, to betroth**	耳 128.7	6
聘请	pìnqǐng	vb.	to engage, to hire (a lawyer etc)		6
招聘	zhāopìn	vb.	to invite applications for a job, to recruit		6
聚	**jù**		**to assemble, to meet together**	耳 128.8	4
聚	jù	vb.	to congregate, to assemble, to mass, to gather together, to amass, to polymerize		4
聚会	jùhuì	n.	party, gathering, to meet, to get together		4
聪	**cōng**		**intelligent, clever, acute hearing**	耳 128.9	5
聪明	- cōngming	adj.	intelligent, clever, bright, smart, acute (of sight and hearing)		5

聿 yù brush 聿 129

肃	**sù**		**respectful, solemn**	聿 129.4	5
严肃	yánsù	adj.	solemn, grave, serious, earnest, severe		5

肉 ròu meat 月 130

肉	**ròu**		**flesh, meat**	肉 130.0	1
肉	ròu	n.	meat, flesh, pulp (of a fruit), (coll.) (of a fruit) squashy, (of a person) flabby, irresolute		1
肌肉	jīròu	n.	muscle, flesh		5
烤肉	kǎoròu	n.	barbecue (lit. roast meat)		5
肌	**jī**		**muscle tissue, meat on bones**	肉 130.2	5
肌肉	jīròu	n.	muscle, flesh		5
肠	**cháng**		**intestines, sausage**	肉 130.3	5
肠	cháng	n.	intestine, sausage, emotion		5
香肠	xiāngcháng	n.	sausage		5
肚	**dù**		**belly, abdomen**	肉 130.3	4
肚子	dùzi	n.	belly, abdomen, stomach		4

肝	**gān**		liver		肉 130.3	6
肝	gān	n.	liver			6
肥	**féi**		fat, fertile		肉 130.4	4
肥	féi	adj.	fat, (opp. 瘦 shòu: thin), fertile, loose-fitting or large, to fertilize, to become rich by illegal means, fertilizer, manure			4
减肥	jiǎnféi	vb.	to lose weight			4
肺	**fèi**		lung		肉 130.4	6
肺	fèi	n.	lung			6
肤	**fū**		skin, superficial, shallow		肉 130.4	5
皮肤	pífū	n.	skin			5
股	**gǔ**		thigh, share		肉 130.4	6
股	gǔ	n.	thigh, part of a whole, portion of a sum, m.w. for long winding things like ropes, rivers etc, m.w. for smoke, smells etc: thread, puff, whiff, m.w. for bands of people, gangs etc, m.w. for sudden actions			6
股东	gǔdōng	n.	shareholder, stockholder			6
股票	gǔpiào	n.	share certificate, stock (finance)			6
炒股	chǎogǔ	vb.	(coll.) to speculate in shares/stocks			6
肩	**jiān**		shoulder, to shoulder		肉 130.4	5
肩	jiān	n.	shoulder, to shoulder (responsibilities etc)			5
肯	**kěn**		to agree		肉 130.4	5
肯	kěn	vb.	to agree, to consent, to be ready (to do sth), willing			6
肯定	kěndìng	vb.	to be certain, to be positive, assuredly, definitely, to give recognition, to affirm, affirmative (answer)			5
胁	**xié**		flank, ribs		肉 130.4	6
威胁	wēixié	vb.	to threaten, to menace			6
育	**yù**		to rear, to give birth to, to educate		肉 130.4	2
教育	jiàoyù	vb.	to educate, to teach, education			2
培育	péiyù	vb.	to train, to breed			4
体育	tǐyù	n.	sports, physical education			2
教育部	jiàoyùbù	n.	Ministry of Education			6
体育场	tǐyùchǎng	n.	stadium			2
体育馆	tǐyùguǎn	n.	gym, gymnasium, stadium			2
肿	**zhǒng**		to swell, swelling		肉 130.4	6
肿	zhǒng	vb.	to swell, swelling, swollen			6
胞	**bāo**		womb, placenta		肉 130.5	6
同胞	tóngbāo	n.	born of the same parents, sibling, fellow citizen, compatriot			6
细胞	xìbāo	n.	cell (biology)			6
背	* **bèi, bēi**		back, back side, behind; to bear		肉 130.5	2
背	• bēi	vb.	to carry on the back or shoulder, to bear			3
背	bèi	+ n.	the back of the body or object, to turn away			2
背	bèi	+ adj.	out of the way, off the beaten track			3
背包	• bēibāo	n.	knapsack, rucksack, infantry pack, field pack, blanket roll			5

背着	• bēizhe	vb.	carrying on one's back		6
背后	bèihòu	n.	behind, at the back, in the rear, behind sb's back		3
背景	bèijǐng	n.	background, backdrop, context, (fig.) powerful backer		4
背心	bèixīn	n.	sleeveless garment (vest, waistcoat, singlet, tank top etc)		6

胆 dǎn — gall bladder, courage 肉 130.5 5

胆	dǎn	n.	gall bladder, courage, guts, gall, inner container (e.g. bladder of a football, inner container of a thermos)	5
胆小	dǎnxiǎo	adj.	cowardly, timid	5
大胆	dàdǎn	adj.	brazen, audacious, outrageous, bold, daring, fearless	5

胡 hú — recklessly, wildly 肉 130.5 5

胡同	hútóng	n.	lane, alley (also with a neutral tone on the second syllable)	5
胡子	húzi	n.	beard, moustache or whiskers, facial hair	5

胖 pàng — fat, plump 肉 130.5 3

胖	pàng	adj.	fat, plump, (opp. 瘦 shòu: thin), healthy, at ease	3
胖子	pàngzi	n.	fat person	4

胜 shèng — victory, to win 肉 130.5 3

胜	shèng	n.	victory, success, to beat, to defeat, to surpass, victorious, superior to, to get the better of	3
胜负	shèngfù	n.	victory or defeat, the outcome of a battle	5
胜利	shènglì	n.	victory	3
名胜	míngshèng	n.	a place famous for its scenery or historical relics, scenic spot	6
战胜	zhànshèng	vb.	to prevail over, to defeat, to surmount	4

胃 wèi — stomach 肉 130.5 5

胃	wèi	n.	stomach	5

脆 cuì — brittle, fragile 肉 130.6 5

脆	cuì	adj.	brittle, fragile, crisp, crunchy, clear and loud voice, neat	5
干脆	• gāncuì	adj.	straightforward, clear-cut, blunt (e.g. statement), you might as well, simply	5

胶 jiāo — glue, gum, resin, rubber 肉 130.6 5

胶带	jiāodài	n.	adhesive tape, rubber belt, recording tape	5
胶水	jiāoshuǐ	n.	glue	5

脑 nǎo — brain 肉 130.6 1

脑袋	- nǎodai	n.	head, skull, brains, mental capability	4
脑子	nǎozi	n.	brains, mind	5
大脑	dànǎo	n.	brain, cerebrum	5
电脑	diànnǎo	n.	computer	1
首脑	shǒunǎo	n.	head (of state), summit (meeting), leader	6
头脑	tóunǎo	n.	brains, mind, skull, (fig.) gist (of a matter), leader, boss	3

能 néng — to be able, can, permitted to, ability 肉 130.6 1

能	néng	vb.	to be able, can, to be capable, energy, ability, surname Neng	1
能否	néngfǒu	phr.	whether or not, can it or can't it, is it possible?	6
能干	nénggàn	adj.	capable, competent	4
能够	nénggòu	vb.	to be capable of, to be able to, can	2

能力	nénglì	n.	capability, ability	3
能量	néngliàng	n.	energy, capabilities	5
能不能	néngbùnéng	phr.	can or cannot?, is it possible?, can we do it?	3
才能	cáinéng	n.	talent, ability, capacity	3
功能	gōngnéng	n.	function, capability	3
技能	jìnéng	n.	technical ability, skill	5
节能	jié néng	vb.	to save energy, energy-saving	6
可能	kěnéng	n.	possibility, probability; might (happen), possible, probable, maybe, perhaps	2
性能	xìngnéng	n.	function, performance	5
职能	zhínéng	n.	function, role	5
只能	zhǐnéng	vb.	to have no other choice (can only), to be obliged to do sth	2
智能	zhìnéng	n.	intellectual power, intelligent, able, smart (phone, system, bomb etc)	4
不能不	bùnéngbù	adv.	have to, cannot but	5
尽可能	jìnkěnéng	adv.	as far as possible, to do one's utmost	5
太阳能	tàiyángnéng	n.	solar energy	6

胸 xiōng — thorax, bosom, chest, mind   肉 130.6   4

| 胸部 | xiōngbù | n. | chest | 4 |

脏 zàng — internal organs, viscera   肉 130.6   2

脏	zàng	n.	internal organs (usually heart, lung, spleen, liver, kidney), viscera	2
心脏	xīnzàng	n.	heart	6
心脏病	xīnzàngbìng	n.	heart disease	6

脚 jiǎo — foot, base   肉 130.7   2

脚	jiǎo	n.	foot, leg (of an animal or an object), base (of an object), dregs	2
脚步	jiǎobù	n.	footstep, step	5
脚印	jiǎoyìn	n.	footprint	6

脸 liǎn — face, reputation   肉 130.7   2

脸	liǎn	n.	face, front part, reputation, facial expression	2
脸盆	liǎnpén	n.	washbowl, basin for washing hands and face	5
脸色	liǎnsè	n.	complexion, look	5
笑脸	xiàoliǎn	n.	smiling face, smiley :)	6

脱 tuō — to shed, to take off   肉 130.7   4

脱	tuō	vb.	to shed, to take off, to escape, to get away from	4
脱离	tuōlí	vb.	to separate oneself from, to break away from, to be divorced from	5
摆脱	bǎituō	vb.	to break away from, to cast off (old ideas etc), to get rid of, to break away (from), to break out (of), to free oneself from	4

腐 fǔ — to rot, rotten   肉 130.8   4

| 豆腐 | - dòufu | n. | tofu, bean curd | 4 |

脾 pí — spleen, pancreas, disposition   肉 130.8   5

| 脾气 | - píqi | n. | character, temperament, disposition, bad temper | 5 |

腰 yāo — waist, lower back   肉 130.9   4

| 腰 | yāo | n. | waist, lower back, pocket, middle, loins | 4 |

腿	**tuǐ**		leg, thigh	肉 130.10	2
腿	tuǐ	*n.*	leg, thigh, ham		2
火腿	huǒtuǐ	*n.*	ham		5
膜	**mó**		membrane, film	肉 130.11	6
膜	mó	*n.*	membrane, film		6

臣 chén minister 131

卧	**wò**		to lie down, to crouch	臣 131.2	5
卧铺	wòpù	*n.*	a bed (on a train), a couchette		6
卧室	wòshì	*n.*	bedroom		5

自 zì self 132

自	**zì**		self, private, personal, from	自 132.0	2
自	zì	*pro.*	self, oneself, from, since, naturally, surely		4
自从	zìcóng	*prep.*	since (a time), ever since		3
自动	zìdòng	*adj.*	automatic, voluntarily		3
自豪	zìháo	*adj.*	proud (of one's achievements etc)		5
自己	zìjǐ	*pro.*	oneself, one's own		2
自觉	zìjué	*vb.*	conscious, aware, on one's own initiative, conscientious		3
自然	zìrán	*n.*	nature, natural, naturally		3
自杀	zìshā	*vb.*	to kill oneself, to commit suicide		5
自身	zìshēn	*n.*	itself, oneself, one's own		3
自我	zìwǒ	*n.*	self-, ego (psychology)		6
自信	zìxìn	*vb.*	to have confidence in oneself, self-confidence		4
自学	zìxué	*n.*	self-study, to study on one's own		6
自由	zìyóu	*n.*	freedom, free, liberty		2
自愿	zìyuàn	*vb.*	voluntary		5
自在	- zìzai	*adj.*	free, unrestrained, comfortable, at ease		6
自主	zìzhǔ	*vb.*	to act for oneself, autonomous, independent		3
自来水	zìláishuǐ	*n.*	running water, tap water		6
自行车	zìxíngchē	*n.*	bicycle, bike		2
自言自语	zì yán zì yǔ	*phr.*	to talk to oneself, to think aloud, to soliloquize		6
独自	dúzì	*adv.*	alone		4
各自	gèzì	*pro.*	each, respective, apiece		3
来自	láizì	*vb.*	to come from (a place), From: (in email header)		2
亲自	qīnzì	*adv.*	personally, in person, oneself		3
大自然	dàzìrán	*n.*	nature (the natural world)		2
臭	**chòu**		smelly, disgusting	自 132.4	5
臭	chòu	*adj.*	smelly, (opp. 香 xiāng: fragrant) to smell (bad), disgusting, loathsome, terrible		5

至 zhì arrive 133

至	**zhì**		to reach, to arrive	至 133.0	3
至	zhì	vb.	to arrive, most, to, until		5
至今	zhìjīn	adv.	so far, to this day, until now		3
至少	zhìshǎo	adv.	at least, (to say the) least		3
至于	zhìyú	prep.	as for, as to, to go so far as to		6
截至	jiézhì	vb.	up to (a time), by (a time)		6
甚至	shènzhì	adv.	even, so much so that		4
不至于	bùzhìyú	vb.	unlikely to go so far as to, not as bad as		6
致	**zhì**		to send, to deliver, to cause	至 133.3	4
此致	cǐzhì	vb.	I hereby express (used at the end of a letter to introduce a polite salutation)		6
大致	dàzhì	adv.	more or less, roughly, approximately		5
导致	dǎozhì	vb.	to lead to, to create, to cause, to bring about		4
细致	xìzhì	adj.	delicate, fine, careful, meticulous, painstaking		4
一致	yīzhì	adj.	unanimous, identical (views or opinions)		4

舌 shé tongue 135

舌	**shé**		tongue, clapper of bell	舌 135.0	6
舌头	- shétou	n.	tongue		6
舍	**shě**		house, dwelling	舌 135.2	5
舍得	shěde	vb.	to be willing to part with sth		5
舍不得	shěbude	vb.	to hate to do sth, to hate to part with, to begrudge		5
宿舍	sùshě	n.	dormitory, dorm room, living quarters, hostel		5
敌	**dí**		enemy, foe	舌 135.4	4
敌人	dírén	n.	enemy		4
舒	**shū**		to stretch, to unfold, easy	舌 135.6	2
舒服	- shūfu	adj.	comfortable, feeling well		2
舒适	shūshì	adj.	cosy, snug		4
辞	**cí**		words, speech	舌 135.7	5
辞典	cídiǎn	n.	dictionary, also written 词典 cídiǎn		5
辞职	cízhí	vb.	to resign		5

舛 chuǎn oppose 136

舞	**wǔ**		to dance	舛 136.8	3
舞	wǔ	vb.	to dance, to wield, to brandish		5
舞蹈	wǔdǎo	n.	dance (performance art), dancing		6
舞台	wǔtái	n.	stage, arena, fig. in the limelight		3
跳舞	tiào wǔ	vb.	to dance		3

舟 zhōu　boat　137

般	bān		sort, kind, category	舟 137.4　2
一般	yībān	adj.	same, ordinary, so-so, common, general, generally, in general	2
一般来说	yībānláishuō	phr.	generally speaking	4
航	háng		boat, to navigate	舟 137.4　4
航班	hángbān	n.	scheduled flight, flight number, plane, scheduled sailing, sailing number, passenger ship	4
航空	hángkōng	n.	aviation	4
宇航员	yǔhángyuán	n.	astronaut or cosmonaut	6
舰	jiàn		warship	舟 137.4　6
军舰	jūnjiàn	n.	warship, military naval vessel	6
船	chuán		boat, vessel	舟 137.5　2
船	chuán	n.	boat, vessel, ship	2
船长	chuán zhǎng	n.	captain (of a boat), skipper	6
船员	chuányuán	n.	sailor, crew member	6
船只	• chuánzhī	n.	shipping, vessels	6
飞船	fēichuán	n.	airship, spaceship	6
划船	• huáchuán	vb.	to row a boat, rowing boat, rowing (sport)	3
轮船	lúnchuán	n.	steamship, steamer, ocean liner, ship	4

艮 gēn　stopping　138

良	liáng		good, virtuous, respectable	艮 138.1　4
良好	liánghǎo	adj.	good, favourable, well, fine	4
不良	bùliáng	adj.	bad, harmful, unhealthy	5
善良	shànliáng	adj.	good and honest, kind-hearted	4
优良	yōuliáng	adj.	fine, good, first-rate	4

色 sè　colour　139

色	sè		colour, form, body, beauty	色 139.0　2
色	sè	n.	colour, tint, hue, shade, form, body, beauty, kind, (Buddhism) appearance of things	4
色彩	sècǎi	n.	tint, colouring, colouration, (fig.) flavour, character	4
白色	báisè	adj.	white, fig. reactionary, anti-communist	2
彩色	cǎisè	n.	colour, multi-coloured	3
出色	chūsè	adj.	remarkable, outstanding	4
黑色	hēisè	n.	black (colour)	2
红色	hóngsè	adj.	red (colour), revolutionary	2
黄色	huángsè	n.	yellow (colour), decadent	2
灰色	huīsè	adj.	gray, ash gray, grizzly, pessimistic, gloomy, dispirited, ambiguous	5
景色	jǐngsè	n.	scenery, scene, landscape, view	3
角色	• juésè	n.	role, character in a novel, persona	4
蓝色	lánsè	n.	blue (colour)	2

脸色	liǎnsè	n.	complexion, look		5
绿色	lǜsè	n.	green, (colour), eco-friendly		2
特色	tèsè	n.	characteristic, distinguishing feature or quality		3
颜色	yánsè	n.	colour, countenance, appearance, facial expression, pigment		2
五颜六色	wǔyánliùsè	phr.	multi-coloured, every colour under the sun (idiom)		4

艳 yàn — colourful, gaudy — 色 139.4 — 5

鲜艳	xiānyàn	adj.	bright-coloured, gaily coloured		5

艹 cǎo — grass — 艹 140

艺 yì — skill, art, craft — 艹 140.1 — 3

艺人	yìrén	n.	performing artist, actor		6
艺术	yìshù	n.	art		3
工艺	gōngyì	n.	arts and crafts, industrial arts		5
文艺	wényì	n.	literature and art		5

节 jié — joint, node, knot — 艹 140.2 — 2

节	jié	+ n.	joint, node, knot, division, festival, (m.w. for segments)		2
节	jié	+ vb.	to save, to economise, to abridge		6
节能	jié néng	vb.	to save energy, energy-saving		6
节目	jiémù	n.	program, item (on a program)		2
节日	jiérì	n.	holiday, festival		2
节省	jiéshěng	n.	saving, to save, to use sparingly, to cut down on		4
节约	jiéyuē	vb.	to economize, to conserve (resources), economy, frugal		3
节奏	jiézòu	n.	rhythm, tempo, musical pulse, cadence, beat		6
节假日	jiéjiàrì	n.	public holiday		6
春节	chūn jié	n.	Spring Festival (Chinese New Year)		2
环节	huánjié	n.	(zoology) segment (of the body of a worm, centipede etc), (fig.) a part of an integrated whole: aspect (of a project)		5
季节	jìjié	n.	time, season, period		4
情节	qíngjié	n.	plot, circumstances		5
时节	shíjié	n.	season, time, particular time		6
调节	diàojié	vb.	to adjust, to regulate, to harmonize, to reconcile (accountancy etc)		5
细节	xìjié	n.	details, particulars		4
音节	yīnjié	n.	syllable		2
端午节	duānwǔ jié	n.	Dragon Boat Festival		6
清明节	qīngmíngjié	n.	Qingming or Pure Brightness Festival or Tomb Sweeping Day, celebration for the dead (in early April)		6
圣诞节	shèngdàn jié	n.	Christmas season, Christmas Day		6
中秋节	zhōngqiū jié	n.	the Mid-Autumn Festival on 15th of 8th lunar month		5

花 huā — flower, to spend, blurred — 艹 140.4 — 1

花	huā	+ n.	flower, blossoms, pattern		1
花	huā	+ vb.	to spend (money or time)		2
花	huā	+ adj.	blurred, fancy, multicoloured		4
花费	huāfèi	n.	expense, cost, to spend (time or money), expenditure		6
花瓶	huāpíng	n.	flower vase, fig. just a pretty face		6
花生	huāshēng	n.	peanut, groundnut		6
花园	huāyuán	n.	garden		2

开花	kāihuā	vb.	to bloom, to blossom, to flower, fig. to burst open, to feel happy or elated, new development grows out		4
梅花	méihuā	n.	plum blossom, clubs (a suit in card games), wintersweet (dialect)		6
桃花	táohuā	n.	peach blossom, (fig.) love affair		5
鲜花	xiānhuā	n.	flower, fresh flowers		4
烟花	yānhuā	n.	fireworks, prostitute (esp. in Yuan theatre)		6
苏	**sū**		to revive, wild red basil	艹 140.4	6
复苏	fùsū	vb.	to recover, to resuscitate		6
范	**fàn**		pattern, model	艹 140.5	3
范围	fànwéi	n.	range, scope, limit, extent		3
防范	fángfàn	vb.	to be on guard, wariness, to guard against, preventive		6
规范	guīfàn	n.	norm, standard, specification, regulation, rule, within the rules, to fix rules, to regulate, to specify		3
模范	mófàn	n.	model, fine example		5
示范	shìfàn	vb.	to demonstrate, to show how to do sth, demonstration, a model example		5
茄	**qié**		aubergine, eggplant	艹 140.5	6
茄子	qiézi	n.	eggplant (Solanum melongena L.), aubergine, brinjal, Guinea squash, phonetic cheese (when being photographed)		6
番茄	fānqié	n.	tomato		6
苦	**kǔ**		bitter, hardship, suffering	艹 140.5	3
苦	kǔ	adj.	bitter, (opp. 甘 gān: sweet, 甜 tián: sweet) hardship, pain, to suffer, to bring suffering to, painstakingly		4
艰苦	jiānkǔ	adj.	difficult, hard, arduous		5
痛苦	tòngkǔ	n.	pain, suffering, painful		3
辛苦	xīnkǔ	adj.	exhausting, hard, tough, arduous, to work hard, to go to a lot of trouble, hardship(s)		5
酸甜苦辣	suāntiánkǔlà	phr.	sour, sweet, bitter and spicy hot, fig. the joys and sorrows of life		5
苹	**píng**		artemisia, apple	艹 140.5	3
苹果	píngguǒ	n.	apple (tree and fruit)		3
若	**ruò**		if	艹 140.5	6
若	ruò	conj.	if, to seem		6
英	**yīng**		hero, England	艹 140.5	2
英文	yīngwén	n.	English (language)		2
英雄	yīngxióng	n.	hero		6
英勇	yīngyǒng	adj.	heroic, gallant, valiant		4
英语	yīngyǔ	n.	English (language)		2
草	**cǎo**		grass, straw, herbs	艹 140.6	2
草	cǎo	n.	grass, straw, herbs, manuscript, draft of a document, careless, rough		2
草地	cǎodì	n.	lawn, meadow, sod, turf		2
草原	cǎoyuán	n.	grassland, prairie		5
茶	**chá**		tea	艹 140.6	1
茶	chá	n.	tea, tea plant		1
茶叶	cháyè	n.	tea, tea leaves		4

红茶	hóngchá	n.	black tea		3
绿茶	lǜchá	n.	green tea, (slang) (of a girl) seemingly innocent and charming but actually calculating and manipulative, a girl who has these qualities		3
奶茶	nǎichá	n.	milk tea		3
荣	**róng**		glory, honour, prosper	艹 140.6	5
繁荣	fánróng	adj.	prosperous, booming (economy)		5
光荣	guāngróng	n.	honour and glory, glorious		5
药	**yào**		medicine	艹 140.6	2
药	yào	n.	medicine (e.g. 草药 cǎoyào: herbal medicine), drug, substance used for a specific purpose (e.g. poisoning, explosion, fermenting)		2
药店	yàodiàn	n.	pharmacy		2
药片	yàopiàn	n.	a (medicine) pill or tablet		2
药品	yàopǐn	n.	medicaments, medicine, drug		6
药水	yàoshuǐ	n.	liquid medicine		2
药物	yàowù	n.	medicaments, pharmaceuticals, medication, medicine, drug		4
医药	yīyào	n.	medical care and medicines, medicine (drug), medical, pharmaceutical		6
炸药	zhàyào	adj.	explosive (material)		6
中药	zhōngyào	n.	(traditional) Chinese medicine		5
获	**huò**		to capture, to obtain	艹 140.7	4
获	huò	vb.	to reap, to harvest		4
获得	• huòdé	vb.	to obtain, to receive, to get		4
获奖	huòjiǎng	vb.	to win an award		4
获取	huòqǔ	vb.	to gain, to get, to acquire		4
收获	shōuhuò	vb.	to harvest, to reap, to gain, crop, harvest, profit, gain, bonus, reward		4
菜	**cài**		dish, vegetable	艹 140.8	1
菜	cài	n.	dish (type of food), vegetable, cuisine		1
菜单	càidān	n.	menu		2
白菜	báicài	n.	Chinese cabbage, bok choi, pak choi		3
蔬菜	shūcài	n.	vegetables		5
菌	**jūn**		germ, fungus	艹 140.8	6
细菌	xìjūn	n.	bacterium, germ		6
萄	**táo**		grape	艹 140.8	5
葡萄	- pútao	n.	grape		5
葡萄酒	- pútaojiǔ	n.	(grape) wine		5
营	**yíng**		camp, barracks, to build	艹 140.8	3
营养	yíngyǎng	n.	nutrition, nourishment		3
营业	yíngyè	vb.	to do business, to trade		4
经营	jīngyíng	vb.	to engage in (business etc), to run, to operate		3
著	* **zhe, zhù**		aspect part. ind. action in progress	艹 140.8	4
著名	• zhùmíng	n.	famous, noted, well-known, celebrated		4
著作	• zhùzuò	vb.	to write, literary work, book, article, writings		4
显著	xiǎnzhù	adj.	outstanding, notable, remarkable, statistically significant		4

落	* luò, là		to fall; to leave out	艹 140.9	3
落	• là	vb.	(coll.) to leave out, to be missing, to leave behind, to lag behind		5
落	luò	vb.	to fall, to drop, to lower		4
落后	luòhòu	vb.	to fall behind, to lag (in technology etc), backward, to retrogress		3
落实	luòshí	adj.	practical, workable, to implement, to carry out, to decide		5
降落	jiàngluò	vb.	to descend, to land		4
葡	pú		grape	艹 140.9	5
葡萄	- pútao	n.	grape		5
葡萄酒	- pútaojiǔ	n.	(grape) wine		5
蓝	lán		blue, indigo (plant)	艹 140.10	2
蓝	lán	adj.	blue, indigo (plant), surname Lan		2
蓝领	lánlǐng	n.	blue-collar, blue-collar worker		6
蓝色	lánsè	n.	blue (colour)		2
蓝天	lántiān	n.	blue sky		6
蒙	* méng, mēng		to cover; to cheat	艹 140.10	6
蒙	• mēng	vb.	to cheat, to make a wild guess, unconscious		6
蒙	méng	vb.	to cover, to receive, to encounter		6
蔬	shū		vegetables, greens	艹 140.11	5
蔬菜	shūcài	n.	vegetables		5
蕉	jiāo		banana, plantain	艹 140.12	3
香蕉	xiāngjiāo	n.	banana		3
薄	* báo, bó		thin, weak; meagre, slight	艹 140.13	4
薄	báo	adj.	thin, (opp. 厚 hòu: thick), weak, light, cold in manner, indifferent, infertile		4
薄弱	bóruò	adj.	weak, frail		5
薪	xīn		fuel, salary	艹 140.13	6
薪水	xīnshuǐ	n.	salary, wage		6
藏	cáng		to hide, to store	艹 140.14	6
藏	cáng	vb.	to hide, to conceal, to store		6
收藏	shōucáng	vb.	to hoard, to collect, collection, to bookmark (Internet)		6
隐藏	yǐncáng	vb.	to hide, to conceal, to mask, to shelter, to harbour (i.e. keep sth hidden), to hide oneself, to lie low, to nestle, hidden		6
薯	shǔ		potato, yam	艹 140.14	6
薯片	shǔpiàn	n.	fried potato chips		6
薯条	shǔtiáo	n.	chips (French fries), French fried potatoes		6
虍	hū		tiger	141	
虎	hǔ		tiger, brave, fierce	虍 141.2	5
虎	hǔ	n.	tiger, brave, fierce, hero		5
虚	xū		empty, false, weak	虍 141.5	5
虚心	xūxīn	adj.	open-minded, humble		5

| 谦虚 | qiānxū | adj. | modest, self-effacing, to make modest remarks | | 6 |

虫 huǐ insect 142

虫	chóng		insects, worms	虫 142.0	4
虫子	chóngzi	n.	insect, bug, worm		4
虽	**suī**		**although**	虫 142.3	2
虽	suī	conj.	although, even though		6
虽然	suīrán	conj.	although, even though, even if		2
蛋	**dàn**		**egg**	虫 142.5	1
蛋	dàn	n.	egg, oval-shaped thing		2
蛋糕	dàngāo	n.	cake		5
鸡蛋	jīdàn	n.	(chicken) egg, hen's egg		1
蛇	**shé**		**snake**	虫 142.5	5
蛇	shé	n.	snake, serpent		5
融	**róng**		**to melt, to blend**	虫 142.10	6
融合	rónghé	n.	a mixture, an amalgam, fusion, welding together, to be in harmony with (nature), to harmonize with, to fit in		6
融入	róngrù	vb.	to blend into, to integrate, to assimilate, to merge		6
金融	jīnróng	n.	banking, finance, financial		6

血 xuè blood 143

血	xuè		blood	血 143.0	3
血	xuè	n.	blood, related by blood		3
血管	xuèguǎn	n.	vein, artery		6
血液	xuèyè	n.	blood		6

行 xíng walk enclosure 144

行	* xíng, háng		to go, okay; row, line of business	行 144.0	1
行	• háng	n.	row, line, commercial firm, line of business, profession, to rank m.w. line, row		3
行	xíng	vb.	to go, to walk, to be current, to do, will do, okay!		1
行业	• hángyè	n.	industry, business		4
行程	xíngchéng	n.	journey, course of a journey, distance travelled, trajectory, itinerary, route, course (of history), stroke (of a piston)		6
行动	xíngdòng	n.	operation, action		2
行李	- xíngli	n.	luggage		3
行人	xíngrén	n.	pedestrian, traveller on foot, passer-by, official responsible for arranging audiences with the emperor		2
行驶	xíngshǐ	vb.	to travel along a route (of vehicles etc)		5
行为	• xíngwéi	n.	action, conduct, behaviour, activity		2
不行	bùxíng	n.	won't do, be out of the question, be no good, not work, not be capable		2
步行	bùxíng	vb.	to go on foot, to walk		4

出行	chūxíng	vb.	to go out somewhere (relatively short trip), to set off on a journey (longer trip)	6
发行	fāxíng	vb.	to publish, to issue (stocks, currency etc), to release, to distribute (a film)	5
飞行	fēixíng	vb.	(of planes etc) to fly, flying, flight, aviation	3
进行	jìnxíng	vb.	to advance, to conduct, underway, in progress, to do, to carry out, to carry on, to execute	2
举行	jǔxíng	vb.	to hold (a meeting, ceremony etc)	2
流行	liúxíng	vb.	(of a contagious disease etc) to spread, to propagate, (of a style of clothing, song etc) popular, fashionable	2
旅行	lǚxíng	vb.	to travel, journey, trip	2
盛行	shèngxíng	vb.	to be in vogue, to be prevalent	6
实行	shíxíng	vb.	to implement, to carry out, to put into practice	3
送行	sòngxíng	vb.	to see someone off, to throw someone a send-off party	6
通行	tōngxíng	vb.	to go through, to pass through, to be in general use	6
同行	tóngxíng	n.	person of the same profession, of the same trade, occupation or industry	6
推行	tuīxíng	vb.	to put into effect, to carry out	5
一行	yīxíng	n.	group travelling together, party, delegation	6
银行	• yínháng	n.	bank	2
游行	yóuxíng	n.	march, parade, demonstration	6
运行	yùnxíng	vb.	to move along one's course (of celestial bodies etc), (fig.) to function, to be in operation, (of a train service etc) to operate, to run, (of a computer) to run	5
执行	zhíxíng	vb.	to implement, to carry out, to execute, to run	5
飞行员	fēixíngyuán	n.	pilot, aviator	6
旅行社	lǚxíngshè	n.	travel agency	3
排行榜	páixíngbǎng	n.	the charts (of best-sellers), table of ranking	6
银行卡	• yínhángkǎ	n.	bank card, ATM card	2
自行车	zìxíngchē	n.	bicycle, bike	2

街 jiē   street, road, thoroughfare   行 144.6   2

街	jiē	n.	street	2
街道	jiēdào	n.	street	4
街头	jiētóu	n.	street	6
大街	dàjiē	n.	street, main street	6

衡 héng   to weigh, weight   行 144.10   6

衡量	• héngliáng	vb.	to weigh, to examine, to consider	6
平衡	pínghéng	n.	balance, equilibrium	6

衣 yī   clothes   衤 145

衣	yī		clothes, clothing	衣 145.0 1
衣服	- yīfu	n.	clothes	1
衣架	yījià	n.	clothes hanger, clothes rack	3
衬衣	chènyī	n.	shirt	3
大衣	dàyī	n.	overcoat, topcoat, cloak	2
毛衣	máoyī	n.	(wool) sweater	4
内衣	nèiyī	n.	undergarment, underwear	6

上衣	shàngyī	n.	jacket, upper outer garment	3
外衣	wàiyī	n.	outer clothing, semblance, appearance	6
雨衣	yǔyī	n.	raincoat	6
洗衣粉	xǐyīfěn	n.	laundry detergent, washing powder	6
洗衣机	xǐyījī	n.	washer, washing machine	2

补 bǔ — to repair, to patch 衣 145.2

补	bǔ	vb.	to repair, to patch, to mend, to make up for, to fill (a vacancy), to supplement	3
补课	bǔ kè	vb.	to make up missed lesson, to reschedule a class	6
补偿	bǔcháng	vb.	to compensate, to make up	5
补充	bǔchōng	vb.	to replenish, to supplement, to complement, additional, supplementary	3
补考	bǔkǎo	vb.	to sit for a makeup exam, to resit an exam, makeup exam, resit	6
补贴	bǔtiē	vb.	to subsidize, subsidy, allowance, to supplement (one's salary etc), benefit	5
补习	bǔxí	vb.	to take extra lessons in a cram school or with a private tutor	6
补助	bǔzhù	vb.	to subsidize, subsidy, allowance	6

表 biǎo — exterior surface, to show 衣 145.3

表	biǎo	n.	exterior surface, a model, a form, a meter, to show	2
表达	biǎodá	vb.	to express, to convey	3
表格	biǎogé	n.	form, table	3
表面	biǎomiàn	n.	surface, face, outside, appearance	3
表明	biǎomíng	vb.	to make clear, to make known, to state clearly, to indicate, known	3
表情	biǎoqíng	n.	(facial) expression, to express one's feelings	4
表示	biǎoshì	vb.	to express, to show, to say, to state, to indicate, to mean	2
表现	biǎoxiàn	vb.	to show, to show off, to display, to manifest, expression, manifestation, show, display, performance (at work etc), behaviour	3
表演	biǎoyǎn	n.	play, show, performance, exhibition, to perform, to act, to demonstrate	3
表扬	biǎoyáng	vb.	to praise, to commend	4
表面上	- biǎomiàn shang	adv.	outwardly, superficially, on the face of it	6
代表	dàibiǎo	n.	representative, delegate	3
发表	fābiǎo	vb.	to issue, to publish	3
手表	shǒubiǎo	n.	wristwatch	2
代表团	dàibiǎotuán	n.	delegation	3

衬 chèn — to line, lining, inner garments 衣 145.3

衬衫	chènshān	n.	shirt, blouse	3
衬衣	chènyī	n.	shirt	3

衫 shān — garment, jacket 衣 145.3

衬衫	chènshān	n.	shirt, blouse	3

被 bèi — by 衣 145.5

被	bèi	prep.	by, (indicates passive-voice clauses), (literary) to cover, to meet with, (coll.), quilt	3
被迫	bèi pò	vb.	to be compelled, to be forced	4
被动	bèidòng	adj.	passive	5
被告	bèigào	n.	defendant	6

被子	bèizi		n.	quilt	3
袋	**dài**			**bag, sack, pouch**	衣 145.5 4
袋	dài		n.	bag, sack, pouch, pocket, m.w. bagful	4
口袋	- kǒudai		n.	pocket, bag, sack	4
脑袋	- nǎodai		n.	head, skull, brains, mental capability	4
塑料袋	sùliàodài		n.	plastic bag	4
袜	**wà**			**socks, stockings**	衣 145.5 4
袜子	wàzi		n.	socks, stockings	4
袖	**xiù**			**sleeve, to put something in a sleeve**	衣 145.5 6
袖珍	xiùzhēn		adj.	pocket-sized, pocket (book etc)	6
领袖	lǐngxiù		n.	leader	6
裁	**cái**			**to cut out, to decrease**	衣 145.6 5
裁判	cáipàn		n.	judgment, to referee, umpire, judge, referee	5
总裁	zǒngcái		n.	chairman, director-general (of a company etc)	5
裂	**liè**			**to split, to crack**	衣 145.6 6
裂	liè		vb.	to split, to crack, to break open, to rend	6
分裂	fēnliè		vb.	to split up, to divide, to break up, fission, schism	6
装	**zhuāng**			**adornment**	衣 145.6 2
装	zhuāng		n.	adornment, to adorn, dress, clothing, costume (of an actor in a play), to play a role	2
装备	zhuāngbèi		n.	equipment, to equip, to outfit	6
装饰	zhuāngshì		vb.	to decorate, decoration, decorative, ornamental	5
装修	zhuāngxiū		vb.	to decorate, interior decoration, to fit up, to renovate	4
装置	zhuāngzhì		vb.	to install, installation, equipment, system, unit, device	4
安装	ānzhuāng		vb.	to install, to erect, to fix, to mount, installation	3
包装	bāozhuāng		vb.	to pack, to package, to wrap, packaging	5
服装	fúzhuāng		n.	dress, clothing, costume, clothes	3
改装	gǎizhuāng		vb.	to change one's costume, to repackage, to remodel, to refit, to modify, to convert	6
时装	shízhuāng		n.	fashion, fashionable clothes	6
西装	xīzhuāng		n.	suit, Western-style clothes	5
裤	**kù**			**trousers, pants**	衣 145.7 3
裤子	kùzi		n.	trousers, pants	3
短裤	duǎnkù		n.	shorts	3
牛仔裤	niúzǐkù		n.	jeans	5
裙	**qún**			**skirt, apron**	衣 145.7 3
裙子	qúnzi		n.	skirt	3
裹	**guǒ**			**to wrap, to bind**	衣 145.8 4
包裹	bāoguǒ		vb.	to wrap up, to bind up, bundle, parcel, package	4

西 xī west   西西 146

西 xī — west, the West   西 146.0 1

西	xī	n.	west, Western, the West, Spanish	1
西北	xīběi	n.	northwest	2
西边	- xībian	n.	west, west side, western part, to the west of	1
西部	xībù	n.	western part	3
西餐	xīcān	n.	Western-style food	2
西方	xīfāng	n.	the West, the Occident, Western countries	2
西瓜	xīguā	n.	watermelon	4
西南	xīnán	n.	southwest	2
西医	xīyī	n.	Western medicine, a doctor trained in Western medicine	2
西装	xīzhuāng	n.	suit, Western-style clothes	5
西红柿	xīhóngshì	n.	tomato	5
西班牙语	xībānyáyǔ	n.	Spanish (language)	6
东西	- dōngxi	n.	east and west	1

要 * yào, yāo — to want, to ask for; to demand   西 146.3 1

要	yào	+ vb.	to want, to ask (for), to wish, to need, must, shall	1
要	yào	+ conj.	if, suppose, or/either	4
要求	• yāoqiú	vb.	to demand, to request, to require, requirement, to stake a claim, to ask	2
要好	yàohǎo	vb.	to be on good terms, to be close friends, striving for self-improvement	6
要么	yàome	conj.	or, either one or the other	6
要是	- yàoshi	conj.	(coll.) if	3
要素	yàosù	n.	essential factor, key constituent	6
要不然	- yàoburán	conj.	otherwise, or else, or	6
必要	bìyào	adj.	necessary, essential, indispensable, required	3
不要	bùyào	adv.	don't!, must not	2
将要	jiāngyào	adv.	will, shall, to be going to	5
就要	jiùyào	adv.	will, shall, to be going to	2
快要	kuàiyào	adv.	almost, nearly, almost all	2
需要	xūyào	vb.	to need, to want, to demand, to require, requirement, need	3
只要	zhǐyào	conj.	if only, so long as	2
重要	zhòngyào	adj.	important, significant, major	1
主要	zhǔyào	n.	main, principal, major, primary	2
不要紧	bù yàojǐn	adj.	unimportant, not serious, it doesn't matter, never mind, it looks all right, but	4

见 jiàn see   见 147

见 jiàn — to see, to meet   见 147.0 1

见	jiàn	vb.	to see, to meet, to appear (to be sth), to interview	1
见到	jiàndào	vb.	to see	2
见过	jiànguò	vb.	have seen	2
见面	jiànmiàn	vb.	to meet, to see each other	1
不见	bùjiàn	vb.	not to see, not to meet, to have disappeared, to be missing	6

常见	chángjiàn	n.	commonly seen, common, to see sth frequently	2
会见	huìjiàn	vb.	to meet with (sb who is paying a visit)	6
看见	kànjiàn	vb.	to see, to catch sight of	1
可见	kějiàn	conj.	it can clearly be seen (that this is the case), it is (thus) clear, clear, visible	4
梦见	mèngjiàn	vb.	to dream about (sth or sb), to see in a dream	4
碰见	pèngjiàn	vb.	to run into, to meet (unexpectedly), to bump into	2
听见	tīngjiàn	vb.	to hear	1
望见	wàngjiàn	vb.	to espy, to spot	6
意见	yìjiàn	n.	idea, opinion, suggestion, objection, complaint	2
遇见	yùjiàn	vb.	to meet	4
再见	zàijiàn	intj.	goodbye, see you again later	1
只见	zhǐjiàn	vb.	to see (the same thing) over and over again, to see, to one's surprise, (sth happen suddenly)	5
看得见	kàndejiàn	vb.	can see, visible	6

观 guān — to observe, view 见 147.2 2

观察	guānchá	vb.	to observe, to watch, to survey, to examine, observation, view, perspective	3
观点	guāndiǎn	n.	point of view, viewpoint, standpoint	2
观光	guānguāng	vb.	to tour, sightseeing, tourism	6
观看	guānkàn	vb.	to watch, to view	3
观念	guānniàn	n.	notion, thought, concept, sense, views, ideology, general impressions	3
观众	guānzhòng	n.	spectators, audience, visitors (to an exhibition etc)	3
参观	cānguān	vb.	to look around, to tour, to visit	2
客观	kèguān	adj.	objective, impartial	3
乐观	lèguān	adj.	optimistic, hopeful	3
外观	wàiguān	n.	exterior appearance, to view sth from the outside, exterior condition	6
主观	zhǔguān	n.	subjective	5
壮观	zhuàngguān	adj.	spectacular, magnificent sight	6

规 guī — rule, regulation 见 147.4 3

规定	guīdìng	n.	provision, to fix, to set, to formulate, to stipulate, to provide, regulation, rule	3
规范	guīfàn	n.	norm, standard, specification, regulation, rule, within the rules, to fix rules, to regulate, to specify	3
规划	guīhuà	vb.	to plan (how to do sth), planning, plan, program	5
规律	guīlǜ	n.	rule (e.g. of science), law of behaviour, regular pattern, rhythm, discipline	4
规模	guīmó	n.	scale, scope, extent	4
规则	guīzé	n.	rule, regulation, rules and regulations	4
常规	chángguī	n.	code of conduct, conventions, common practice, routine (medical procedure etc)	6
法规	fǎguī	n.	legislation, statute	5
犯规	fànguī	vb.	to break the rules, an illegality, a foul	6
违规	wéiguī	vb.	to violate (rules), irregular, illegal, corrupt	5
正规	zhèngguī	adj.	regular, according to standards	5
大规模	dà guīmó	adj.	large scale, extensive, wide scale, broad scale	4

视	shì		to look at, to inspect	見 147.4	1
视频	shìpín	n	video		5
视为	• shìwéi	vb.	to view as, to see as, to consider to be, to deem		5
电视	diànshì	n	television, TV		1
忽视	hūshì	vb.	to neglect, to ignore		4
近视	jìnshì	n	short-sighted, near-sighted, myopia		6
影视	yǐngshì	n	movies and television		3
重视	zhòngshì	vb.	to attach importance to sth, to value		2
注视	zhùshì	vb.	to watch attentively, to gaze at		5
电视机	diànshìjī	n	television set		1
电视剧	diànshìjù	n	TV drama, soap opera		3
电视台	diànshìtái	n	television station		3

觉	* jué, jiào		to sense, to feel; a sleep	見 147.5	1
觉	• jiào	n	a sleep, a nap		6
觉得	juéde	vb.	to think, to feel		1
觉悟	juéwù	vb.	to come to understand, to realize, consciousness, awareness, Buddhist enlightenment (Sanskrit: cittotpāda)		6
发觉	fājué	vb.	to become aware, to detect, to realize, to perceive		5
感觉	gǎnjué	vb.	to feel, to become aware of, feeling, sense, perception		2
睡觉	• shuìjiào	vb.	to go to bed, to sleep		1
自觉	zìjué	vb.	conscious, aware, on one's own initiative, conscientious		3

览	lǎn		to look at, to read	見 147.5	5
展览	zhǎnlǎn	vb.	to put on display, to exhibit, exhibition, show		5
博览会	bólǎnhuì	n	exposition, international fair		5
阅览室	yuèlǎnshì	n	reading room		5

角 jiǎo   horn   148

角	* jiǎo, jué		horn, angle, corner; role	角 148.0	2
角	jiǎo	n	horn, angle, unit of money (1/10 yuan), corner, m.w. quarter		2
角度	jiǎodù	n	angle, point of view		2
角色	• juésè	n	role, character in a novel, persona		4
主角	• zhǔjué	n	leading role, lead		6

触	chù		to touch	角 148.6	5
接触	jiēchù	vb.	to touch, to contact, access, in touch with		5

解	jiě		to separate, to divide	角 148.6	3
解	jiě	vb.	to separate, to divide, to understand, to solve		6
解除	jiěchú	vb.	to remove, to sack, to get rid of, to relieve (sb of their duties), to free, to lift (an embargo), to rescind (an agreement)		5
解放	jiěfàng	vb.	to liberate, to emancipate, liberation, refers to the Communists' victory over the Nationalists in 1949		5
解决	jiějué	vb.	to settle (a dispute), to resolve, to solve, to dispose of, to dispatch		3
解开	jiěkāi	vb.	to untie, to undo, to solve (a mystery)		3
解释	jiěshì	n	explanation, to explain, to interpret, to resolve		4
解说	jiěshuō	vb.	to explain, to comment		6

分解	fēnjiě	vb.	to resolve, to decompose, to break down	5
化解	huàjiě	vb.	to dissolve, to resolve (contradictions), to dispel (doubts), to iron out (difficulties), to defuse (conflicts), to neutralize (fears)	6
缓解	huǎnjiě	vb.	to bring relief, to alleviate (a crisis), to dull (a pain)	4
理解	lǐjiě	vb.	to comprehend, to understand, comprehension, understanding	3
了解	• liǎojiě	vb.	to understand, to realize, to find out	4
调解	• tiáojiě	vb.	to mediate, to bring parties to an agreement	5
误解	wùjiě	vb.	to misunderstand, to misread, misunderstanding	5

言 yán speech   讠言 149

言	**yán**		words, speech, to speak, to say 言 149.0	2
言语	yányǔ	n.	words, speech, (spoken) language	5
传言	chuányán	n.	rumour, hearsay	6
发言	fāyán	vb.	to make a speech, statement, utterance	3
留言	liúyán	vb.	to leave a message, to leave one's comments, message	6
语言	yǔyán	n.	language	2
发言人	fāyánrén	n.	spokesperson	6
自言自语	zì yán zì yǔ	phr.	to talk to oneself, to think aloud, to soliloquize	6
订	**dìng**		to agree, to conclude 言 149.2	3
订	dìng	vb.	to agree, to conclude, to draw up, to subscribe to (a newspaper etc), to order	3
签订	qiāndìng	vb.	to agree to and sign (a treaty etc)	5
预订	yùdìng	vb.	to place an order, to book ahead	4
制订	zhìdìng	vb.	to work out, to formulate	4
计	**jì**		to count, to calculate 言 149.2	2
计划	jìhuà	n.	plan, project, program, to plan, to map out	2
计算	jìsuàn	vb.	to count, to calculate, to compute	3
计算机	jìsuànjī	n.	computer, calculator	2
共计	gòngjì	vb.	to sum up to, to total	5
估计	gūjì	vb.	to estimate, to reckon	5
会计	• kuàiji	n.	accountant, accountancy, accounting	4
设计	shèjì	n.	plan, design, to design, to plan	3
统计	tǒngjì	n.	statistics, to count, to add up	4
预计	yùjì	vb.	to forecast, to predict, to estimate	3
设计师	shèjìshī	n.	designer, architect	6
认	**rèn**		to recognize, to know 言 149.2	1
认	rèn	vb.	to recognize, to know, to admit	5
认出	rènchū	n.	recognition, to recognize	3
认得	rènde	vb.	to recognize, to remember sth (or sb) on seeing it, to know	3
认定	rèndìng	vb.	to maintain (that sth is true), to determine (a fact), determination (of an amount), of the firm opinion, to believe firmly	5
认可	rènkě	vb.	to approve, approval, acknowledgment, OK	3
认识	- rènshi	vb.	to know, to recognize, to be familiar with, to get acquainted with sb, knowledge, understanding, awareness, cognition	1
认同	rèntóng	vb.	to approve of, to endorse, to acknowledge, to recognize, to identify oneself with	6

认为	· rènwéi	vb.	to believe, to think, to consider, to feel		2
认真	rènzhēn	adj.	conscientious, earnest, serious, to take seriously, to take to heart		1
承认	chéngrèn	vb.	to admit, to concede, to recognize, recognition (diplomatic, artistic etc), to acknowledge		4
否认	fǒurèn	vb.	to declare to be untrue, to deny		3
公认	gōngrèn	vb.	publicly known (to be), accepted (as)		5
确认	quèrèn	vb.	to confirm, to verify, confirmation		4
记	**jì**		**to record, to note**	言 149.3	1
记	jì	vb.	to record, to note, to memorize, to remember, mark, sign, m.w. for blows, kicks, shots		1
记得	jìde	vb.	to remember		1
记录	jìlù	vb.	to record, record (written account), note-taker, record (in sports etc)		3
记忆	jìyì	vb.	to remember, to recall, memory		5
记载	jìzài	vb.	to write down, to record, written account		4
记者	jìzhě	n.	reporter, journalist		3
记住	- jìzhu	vb.	to remember, to bear in mind, to learn by heart		1
笔记	bǐjì	vb.	to take down (in writing), notes, a type of literature consisting mainly of short sketches		2
登记	dēngjì	vb.	to register (one's name)		4
日记	rìjì	n.	diary		4
忘记	wàngjì	vb.	to forget		1
笔记本	bǐjìběn	n.	notebook (stationery)		2
让	**ràng**		**to yield, to permit**	言 149.3	2
让	ràng	vb.	to yield, to permit, to let sb do sth, to have sb do sth, to make sb (feel sad etc), by (indicates the agent in a passive clause)		2
让座	ràngzuò	vb.	to give up one's seat for sb		6
转让	zhuǎnràng	vb.	to transfer (ownership, rights etc)		5
讨	**tǎo**		**to invite, to provoke**	言 149.3	2
讨论	tǎolùn	vb.	to discuss, to talk over		2
讨厌	tǎoyàn	vb.	to dislike, to loathe, disagreeable, troublesome, annoying		5
探讨	tàntǎo	vb.	to investigate, to probe		6
训	**xùn**		**to teach, to train**	言 149.3	3
训练	xùnliàn	vb.	to train, to drill, training		3
教训	jiàoxùn	vb.	to provide guidance, to lecture sb, to upbraid, a talking-to, a bitter lesson		4
培训	péixùn	vb.	to cultivate, to train, to groom, training		4
培训班	péixùnbān	n.	training class		4
讯	**xùn**		**to question, to ask**	言 149.3	6
通讯	tōngxùn	n.	communications, news story, dispatch		6
议	**yì**		**to comment on, to discuss**	言 149.3	3
议论	yìlùn	vb.	to comment, to talk about, to discuss, discussion		4
议题	yìtí	n.	topic of discussion, topic, subject, issue (under discussion)		6
会议	huìyì	n.	meeting, conference		3
建议	jiànyì	vb.	to propose, to suggest, to recommend, proposal, suggestion, recommendation		3
抗议	kàngyì	vb.	to protest, protest		6

协议	xiéyì	n.	agreement, pact, protocol		5
争议	zhēngyì	n.	controversy, dispute, to dispute		5
协议书	xiéyìshū	n.	contract, protocol		5

访 fǎng — to visit, to inquire   言 149.4   3

访问	fǎngwèn	vb.	to visit, to call on, to interview	3
拜访	bàifǎng	vb.	to pay a visit, to call on	5
采访	cǎifǎng	vb.	to interview, to gather news, to hunt for and collect, to cover	4
出访	chūfǎng	vb.	to go and visit in an official capacity or for investigation	6

讲 jiǎng — to speak, to explain   言 149.4   2

讲	jiǎng	vb.	to speak, to explain, to negotiate, to emphasise, to be particular about, as far as sth is concerned, speech, lecture	2
讲课	jiǎng kè	vb.	to teach, to lecture	6
讲话	jiǎnghuà	n.	a speech, to speak, to talk, to address	2
讲究	-jiǎngjiu	vb.	to pay particular attention to, carefully selected for quality, tastefully chosen	4
讲座	jiǎngzuò	n.	a course of lectures	4
听讲	tīng jiǎng	vb.	to attend a lecture, to listen to a talk	2
演讲	yǎnjiǎng	n.	lecture, to make a speech	4

论 lùn — to discuss, view, theory   言 149.4   2

论文	lùnwén	n.	paper, treatise, thesis	4
辩论	biànlùn	n.	debate, argument, to argue over	4
不论	bùlùn	conj.	whatever, no matter what (who, how), regardless of, not to discuss	3
结论	jiélùn	n.	conclusion, verdict	4
理论	lǐlùn	n.	theory	3
评论	pínglùn	vb.	to comment on, to discuss, comment, commentary	5
讨论	tǎolùn	vb.	to discuss, to talk over	2
无论	wúlùn	conj.	no matter what or how, regardless of whether…	4
议论	yìlùn	vb.	to comment, to talk about, to discuss, discussion	4
争论	zhēnglùn	vb.	to argue, to debate, to contend, argument, contention, controversy, debate	4

设 shè — to set up, to arrange   言 149.4   3

设备	shèbèi	n.	equipment, facilities, installations	3
设计	shèjì	n.	plan, design, to design, to plan	3
设立	shèlì	vb.	to set up, to establish	3
设施	shèshī	n.	facilities, installation	4
设想	shèxiǎng	vb.	to imagine, to assume, to envisage, tentative plan, to have consideration for	5
设置	shèzhì	vb.	to set up, to install	4
设计师	shèjìshī	n.	designer, architect	6
建设	jiànshè	vb.	to build, to construct, construction, constructive	3
开设	kāishè	vb.	to offer (goods or services), to open (for business etc)	6

许 xǔ — to allow, to permit, to promise   言 149.4   2

许多	xǔduō	num.	many, a lot of, much	2
许可	xǔkě	vb.	to allow, to permit	5
不许	bùxǔ	vb.	not to allow, must not, can't	5
或许	huòxǔ	adv.	perhaps, maybe	4

也许	yěxǔ	adv.	perhaps, maybe		2
允许	yǔnxǔ	vb.	to permit, to allow		6
词	**cí**		**word, statement**	言 149.5	2
词	cí	n.	word, statement, speech, lyrics		2
词典	cídiǎn	n.	dictionary, also written 辞典 cídiǎn		2
词汇	cíhuì	n.	vocabulary, list of words (e.g. for language teaching purposes), word		4
词语	cíyǔ	n.	word (general term including monosyllables through to short phrases), term (e.g. technical term), expression		2
歌词	gēcí	n.	song lyric, lyrics		6
生词	shēngcí	n.	new word (in textbook), word that is unfamiliar or not yet studied		2
评	**píng**		**to discuss, to comment**	言 149.5	3
评	píng	vb.	to discuss, to comment, to criticize, to judge, to choose (by public appraisal)		6
评估	pínggū	vb.	to evaluate, to assess, assessment, evaluation		5
评价	píngjià	vb.	to evaluate, to assess		3
评论	pínglùn	vb.	to comment on, to discuss, comment, commentary		5
评选	píngxuǎn	vb.	to select on the basis of a vote or consensus		6
批评	pīpíng	vb.	to criticize, criticism		3
识	**shí**		**to know, to understand**	言 149.5	1
识	shí	vb.	to know, to understand, knowledge		6
识字	shízì	vb.	to learn to read		6
常识	chángshí	n.	common sense, general knowledge		4
认识	- rènshi	vb.	to know, to recognize, to be familiar with, to get acquainted with sb, knowledge, understanding, awareness, cognition		1
意识	- yìshi	n.	consciousness, awareness, to be aware, to realize		5
知识	- zhīshi	n.	knowledge		1
诉	**sù**		**to complain, to sue**	言 149.5	1
告诉	- gàosu	vb.	to press charges, to file a complaint		1
起诉	qǐsù	vb.	to sue, to bring a lawsuit against, to prosecute		6
投诉	tóusù	n.	complaint, to complain, to register a complaint (esp. as a customer)		4
译	**yì**		**to translate, to interpret**	言 149.5	4
翻译	fānyì	vb.	to translate, to interpret, translator, interpreter, translation, interpretation		4
诊	**zhěn**		**to examine patient, to diagnose**	言 149.5	5
诊断	zhěnduàn	n.	diagnosis, to diagnose		5
门诊	ménzhěn	n.	outpatient service		5
证	**zhèng**		**certificate, proof**	言 149.5	3
证	zhèng	n.	certificate, proof, to prove, to demonstrate, to confirm, disease, illness		3
证件	zhèngjiàn	n.	certificate, papers, credentials, document, ID		3
证据	zhèngjù	n.	evidence, proof, testimony		3
证明	zhèngmíng	n.	proof, certificate, identification, testimonial		3
证实	zhèngshí	vb.	to confirm (sth to be true), to verify		5
证书	zhèngshū	n.	credentials, certificate		5
保证	bǎozhèng	n.	guarantee, to guarantee, to ensure, to safeguard, to pledge		3

签证	qiānzhèng	n.	visa, certificate, to certify		5
身份证	shēnfènzhèng	n.	identity card, ID		3
诚	**chéng**		sincere, authentic	言 149.6	4
诚实	chéngshí	adj.	honest, honesty, honourable, truthful		4
诚信	chéngxìn	adj.	genuine, honest, in good faith, honesty, integrity		4
真诚	zhēnchéng	adj.	true, sincere, genuine		5
该	**gāi**		should, ought to	言 149.6	2
该	gāi	+ vb.	should, ought to, probably, must be, to deserve, to owe, to be sb's turn to do sth, that, the above-mentioned		2
应该	yīnggāi	n.	[as aux] ought to, should, must		2
话	**huà**		words, speech	言 149.6	1
话	huà	n.	words, speech, language, dialect		1
话剧	huàjù	n.	stage play, modern drama		3
话题	huàtí	n.	subject (of a talk or conversation), topic		3
的话	- dehuà	aux.	if (coming after a conditional clause)		2
电话	diànhuà	n.	telephone		1
对话	duìhuà	n.	dialogue		2
讲话	jiǎnghuà	n.	a speech, to speak, to talk, to address		2
神话	shénhuà	n.	legend, fairy tale, myth, mythology		4
说话	shuōhuà	vb.	to speak, to say, to talk, to gossip, to tell stories, talk, word		1
谈话	tán huà	vb.	to talk (with sb), to have a conversation, talk, conversation		3
通话	tōnghuà	vb.	to hold a conversation, to talk over the telephone, phone call		6
童话	tónghuà	n.	children's fairy tales		4
笑话	- xiàohua	n.	joke, jest		2
笑话儿	xiàohuàr	n.	(spoken) joke		2
打电话	dǎ diànhuà	vb.	to make a telephone call		1
普通话	pǔtōnghuà	n.	Mandarin (common language)		2
说实话	shuōshíhuà	vb.	to speak the truth, truth to tell, frankly		6
一句话	yī jù huà	phr.	in a word, in short		5
试	**shì**		to test, to try	言 149.6	1
试	shì	vb.	to test, to try, experiment, examination, test		1
试点	shìdiǎn	n.	test point, to carry out trial, pilot scheme		6
试卷	• shìjuàn	n.	examination paper, test paper		4
试题	shìtí	n.	exam question, test topic		3
试图	shìtú	vb.	to attempt, to try		5
试验	shìyàn	n.	experiment, test		3
笔试	bǐshì	n.	written examination, paper test (for an applicant)		6
测试	cèshì	vb.	to test (machinery etc), to test (students), test, quiz, exam, beta (software)		4
尝试	chángshì	vb.	to try, to attempt		5
考试	kǎoshì	vb.	to take an exam, exam		1
口试	kǒushì	n.	oral examination, oral test		6
面试	miànshì	vb.	to be interviewed (as a candidate), interview		4
诗	**shī**		poem, poetry	言 149.6	4
诗	shī	n.	poem, poetry, verse		4
诗歌	shīgē	n.	poem		5

诗人	shīrén	n.	bard, poet		4
详	**xiáng**		detailed, complete, thorough	言 149.6	5
详细	xiángxì	adj.	detailed, in detail, minute		5
询	**xún**		to inquire into, to ask about	言 149.6	5
询问	xúnwèn	vb.	to inquire		5
查询	cháxún	vb.	to check, to inquire, to consult (a document etc), inquiry, query		5
咨询	zīxún	vb.	to consult, to seek advice, consultation, (sales) inquiry (formal)		6
誉	**yù**		fame, reputation	言 149.6	6
名誉	míngyù	n.	fame, reputation, honour, honourary, emeritus (of retired professor)		6
说	**shuō**		to speak, to say	言 149.7	1
说	shuō	vb.	speak, to say, to talk, to explain		1
说法	-shuōfa	vb.	to expound Buddhist teachings		5
说服	shuōfú	vb.	to persuade, to convince, to talk sb over		4
说话	shuōhuà	vb.	to speak, to say, to talk, to gossip, to tell stories, talk, word		1
说明	shuōmíng	vb.	to explain, to illustrate, to indicate, to show, to prove, explanation, directions, caption		2
说不定	-shuōbudìng	vb.	can't say for sure, maybe		4
说明书	shuōmíngshū	n.	(technical) manual, (book of) directions, synopsis (of a play or film), specification (patent)		6
说实话	shuōshíhuà	vb.	to speak the truth, truth to tell, frankly		6
传说	chuánshuō	n.	legend, folklore, to repeat from mouth to mouth, they say that...		3
解说	jiěshuō	vb.	to explain, to comment		6
据说	jùshuō	vb.	it is said that, reportedly		3
听说	tīngshuō	vb.	to hear (sth said), one hears (that), hearsay, listening and speaking		2
小说	xiǎoshuō	n.	novel, fiction		2
再说	zàishuō	vb.	to say again, to put off a discussion until later, moreover, what's more, besides		6
比如说	bǐrúshuō	conj.	for example		2
很难说	hěnnánshuō	phr.	it's hard to say		6
就是说	jiùshìshuō	conj.	in other words, that is		6
一般来说	yībānláishuō	phr.	generally speaking		4
这就是说	zhèjiùshìshuō	phr.	in other words, that is to say		6
误	**wù**		mistake, error	言 149.7	3
误	wù	n.	mistake, error, to miss, to harm, to delay, to neglect, mistakenly		6
误会	wùhuì	vb.	to misunderstand, to mistake, misunderstanding		4
误解	wùjiě	vb.	to misunderstand, to misread, misunderstanding		5
错误	cuòwù	n.	error, mistake		3
失误	shīwù	n.	lapse, mistake, to make a mistake, fault, service fault (in volleyball, tennis etc)		5
语	**yǔ**		language, saying, expression	言 149.7	1
语法	yǔfǎ	n.	grammar		4
语言	yǔyán	n.	language		2
语音	yǔyīn	n.	speech sounds, pronunciation, colloquial (rather than literary) pronunciation of a Chinese character, phonetic, audio		4
成语	chéngyǔ	n.	idiom, proverb		5

词语	cíyǔ	n.	word (general term including monosyllables through to short phrases), term (e.g. technical term), expression		2
法语	fǎyǔ	n.	French (language)		6
汉语	hànyǔ	n.	Chinese (language)		1
华语	huáyǔ	n.	Chinese (language)		5
口语	kǒuyǔ	n.	colloquial speech, spoken language, vernacular language, slander, gossip		4
日语	rìyǔ	n.	Japanese (language)		6
外语	wàiyǔ	n.	foreign language		1
言语	yányǔ	n.	words, speech, (spoken) language		5
英语	yīngyǔ	n.	English (language)		2
西班牙语	xībānyáyǔ	n.	Spanish (language)		6
自言自语	zì yán zì yǔ	phr.	to talk to oneself, to think aloud, to soliloquize		6

诞 dàn — birth, birthday   言 149.8   6

诞生	dànshēng	vb.	to be born		6
圣诞节	shèngdàn jié	n.	Christmas season, Christmas Day		6

调 * diào, tiáo — to transfer, to move; to harmonize   言 149.8   3

调	diào	vb.	to transfer, to move (troops or cadres), to investigate, to enquire into, accent, view, key (in music), mode (music), tone (linguistics)		3
调	• tiáo	vb.	to harmonise, to regulate, to tune, to adjust		3
调查	diàochá	n.	investigation, inquiry, to investigate, to survey, survey, (opinion) poll		3
调动	diàodòng	vb.	to transfer, to manoeuvre (troops etc), movement of personnel, to mobilize, to bring into play		5
调研	diàoyán	vb.	to investigate and research, research, investigation		6
调节	diàojié	vb.	to adjust, to regulate, to harmonize, to reconcile (accountancy etc)		5
调解	• tiáojiě	vb.	to mediate, to bring parties to an agreement		5
调皮	• tiáopí	adj.	naughty, mischievous, unruly		4
调整	• tiáozhěng	vb.	to adjust, adjustment, revision		3
单调	dāndiào	adj.	monotonous		4
空调	kōngtiáo	n.	air conditioning, air conditioner (including units that have a heating mode)		3
强调	qiángdiào	vb.	to emphasize (a statement), to stress		3
协调	• xiétiáo	vb.	to coordinate, to harmonize, to fit together, to match (colours etc), harmonious, concerted		6

读 dú — to read, to study, to pronounce   言 149.8   1

读	dú	n.	comma, phrase marked by pause		1
读书	dú shū	vb.	to read a book, to study, to attend school		1
读音	dúyīn	n.	pronunciation, literary (rather than colloquial) pronunciation of a Chinese character		2
读者	dúzhě	n.	reader		3
朗读	lǎngdú	vb.	to read aloud		5
阅读	yuèdú	vb.	to read, reading		4

课 kè — lesson, course, classwork   言 149.8   1

课	kè	n.	subject, course		1
课本	kèběn	n.	textbook		1
课程	kèchéng	n.	course, academic program		3

课堂	kètáng	n.	classroom		2
课题	kètí	n.	task, problem, issue		5
课文	kèwén	n.	text		1
补课	bǔ kè	vb.	to make up missed lesson, to reschedule a class		6
功课	gōngkè	n.	homework, assignment, task, classwork, lesson, study		3
讲课	jiǎng kè	vb.	to teach, to lecture		6
上课	shàngkè	vb.	to go to class, to attend class, to go to teach a class		1
下课	xià kè	vb.	to finish class, to get out of class, (fig.) (esp. of a sports coach) to be dismissed, to be fired		1
谅	**liàng**		to excuse, to forgive	言 149.8	6
原谅	yuánliàng	vb.	to excuse, to forgive, to pardon		6
诺	**nuò**		to promise, to approve	言 149.8	6
承诺	chéngnuò	vb.	to promise, to undertake to do something, commitment		6
请	**qǐng**		to ask, to request, to invite	言 149.8	1
请	qǐng	vb.	to ask, to invite, please (do sth), to treat (to a meal etc), to request		1
请假	qǐng jià	vb.	to request leave of absence		1
请客	qǐng kè	vb.	to give a dinner party, to entertain guests, to invite to dinner		2
请问	qǐng wèn	vb.	may I ask...		1
请教	qǐngjiào	vb.	to ask for guidance, to consult		3
请进	qǐngjìn	vb.	please come in		1
请求	qǐngqiú	vb.	to request, to ask, request		2
请坐	qǐngzuò	vb.	please sit down		1
聘请	pìnqǐng	vb.	to engage, to hire (a lawyer etc)		6
申请	shēnqǐng	vb.	to apply for sth, application (form etc)		4
邀请	yāoqǐng	vb.	to invite, invitation		5
谁	**shéi / shuí**		who? whom? whose? anyone?	言 149.8	1
谁	shéi / shuí	pro.	who? whom? whose? anyone?		1
谈	**tán**		to talk, to chat	言 149.8	3
谈	tán	vb.	to talk, to chat, discuss, surname Tan		3
谈话	tán huà	vb.	to talk (with sb), to have a conversation, talk, conversation		3
谈判	tánpàn	vb.	to negotiate, negotiation, talks, conference		3
会谈	huìtán	n.	talks, discussions		5
座谈会	zuòtánhuì	n.	conference, symposium, rap session		6
谊	**yì**		friendship	言 149.8	5
友谊	yǒuyì	n.	companionship, fellowship, friendship		5
诸	**zhū**		various, all	言 149.8	6
诸位	zhūwèi	pro.	(pro.) everyone, Ladies and Gentlemen, Sirs		6
谋	**móu**		to plan, scheme	言 149.9	6
阴谋	yīnmóu	n.	plot, conspiracy		6
谓	**wèi**		to say, to name	言 149.9	4
无所谓	wúsuǒwèi	vb.	to be indifferent, not to matter, cannot be said to be		4
谐	**xié**		harmonious, humorous	言 149.9	6
和谐	héxié	adj.	harmonious, harmony, melodious		6

谦	**qiān**		humble, modest	言 149.10	6
谦虚	qiānxū	*adj.*	modest, self-effacing, to make modest remarks		6
谢	**xiè**		to thank, to decline	言 149.10	1
谢谢	- xièxie	*vb.*	to thank, thanks, thank you		1
感谢	gǎnxiè	*n.*	thanks, gratitude, to thank		2
警	**jǐng**		to alert, to warn	言 149.13	3
警察	jǐngchá	*n.*	police, police officer		3
警告	jǐnggào	*vb.*	to warn, to admonish		5
报警	bàojǐng	*vb.*	to sound an alarm, to report sth to the police		5
交警	jiāojǐng	*n.*	traffic police		3
民警	mínjǐng	*n.*	civil police, PRC police		6

谷 gǔ valley 150

谷	**gǔ**		valley, grain	谷 150.0	6
山谷	shāngǔ	*n.*	valley, ravine		6

豆 dòu bean 151

豆	**dòu**		bean, pea, bean-shaped	豆 151.0	4
豆腐	- dòufu	*n.*	tofu, bean curd		4
豆制品	dòuzhìpǐn	*n.*	legume-based product, soybean product		5
土豆	tǔdòu	*n.*	potato		5

豕 shǐ pig 152

象	**xiàng**		elephant, shape	豕 152.5	3
象征	xiàngzhēng	*n.*	emblem, symbol, token, badge, to symbolize, to signify, to stand for		5
大象	dàxiàng	*n.*	elephant		5
对象	duìxiàng	*n.*	target, object, partner, boyfriend, girlfriend		3
景象	jǐngxiàng	*n.*	scene, sight (to behold)		5
气象	qìxiàng	*n.*	meteorological feature		5
现象	xiànxiàng	*n.*	phenomenon		3
想象	xiǎngxiàng	*vb.*	to imagine, to fancy		4
形象	xíngxiàng	*n.*	image, form, figure		3
印象	yìnxiàng	*n.*	impression		3
豪	**háo**		grand, heroic	豕 152.7	5
自豪	zìháo	*adj.*	proud (of one's achievements etc)		5
豫	**yù**		relaxed, comfortable, at ease	豕 152.9	5
犹豫	yóuyù	*vb.*	to hesitate		5

豸 zhì badger 153

貌	**mào**		countenance, appearance	豸 153.7 5
礼貌	lǐmào	n.	courtesy, manners	5
面貌	miànmào	n.	appearance, face, features	5

貝 bèi shell 贝 154

贝	**bèi**		cowrie, shellfish, currency	贝 154.0 4
宝贝	bǎobèi	n.	treasured object, treasure, darling, baby, cowry, good-for-nothing or queer character	4
负	**fù**		to bear, to carry	贝 154.2 3
负	fù	vb.	to bear, to carry (on one's back), to turn one's back on, to be defeated, negative (math. etc)	6
负担	fùdān	n.	burden, to bear a burden	4
负责	fùzé	vb.	to be in charge of, to take responsibility for, to be to blame, conscientious	3
负责人	fùzérén	n.	person in charge	5
欺负	- qīfu	vb.	to bully	6
胜负	shèngfù	n.	victory or defeat, the outcome of a battle	5
财	**cái**		money, wealth, riches	贝 154.3 4
财产	cáichǎn	n.	property, assets, estate	4
财富	cáifù	n.	wealth, riches	4
理财	lǐcái	n.	financial management, finance	6
贡	**gòng**		to offer tribute, tribute, gifts	贝 154.3 6
贡献	gòngxiàn	vb.	to contribute, to dedicate, to devote, contribution	6
败	**bài**		be defeat, to damage	贝 154.4 4
败	bài	vb.	to defeat, to damage, to lose (to an opponent), to fail, to wither	4
打败	dǎbài	vb.	to defeat, to overpower, to beat, to be defeated	4
失败	shībài	vb.	to be defeated, to lose, to fail (e.g. experiments), failure, defeat	4
购	**gòu**		to purchase	贝 154.4 4
购买	gòumǎi	vb.	to purchase, to buy	4
购物	gòuwù	n.	shopping	4
采购	cǎigòu	vb.	to procure (for an enterprise etc), to purchase	5
收购	shōugòu	vb.	to purchase (from various places), to acquire (a company)	5
贯	**guàn**		to pierce through, to go through	贝 154.4 6
一贯	yīguàn	adj.	consistent, constant, from start to finish, all along, persistent	6
货	**huò**		goods, money	贝 154.4 4
货	huò	n.	goods, money, commodity	4
百货	bǎihuò	n.	general merchandise	4
售货员	shòuhuòyuán	n.	salesperson	4

贫	**pín**		poor, inadequate	貝 154.4	6
贫困	pínkùn	adj.	impoverished, poverty		6
责	**zé**		duty, responsibility, to reproach	貝 154.4	3
责任	zérèn	n.	responsibility, blame, duty		3
负责	fùzé	vb.	to be in charge of, to take responsibility for, to be to blame, conscientious		3
职责	zhízé	n.	duty, responsibility, obligation		6
指责	zhǐzé	vb.	to criticize, to find fault with, to denounce		5
负责人	fùzérén	n.	person in charge		5
账	**zhàng**		account, bill, debt	貝 154.4	6
账	zhàng	n.	account, bill, debt		6
账户	zhànghù	n.	bank account, online account		6
贷	**dài**		to lend, to borrow	貝 154.5	5
贷款	dàikuǎn	n.	a loan		5
费	**fèi**		to cost, to spend	貝 154.5	3
费	fèi	vb.	to cost, spend, fee, fare, be wasteful, surname Fei		3
费用	fèiyòng	n.	cost, expenditure, expense		3
花费	huāfèi	n.	expense, cost, to spend (time or money), expenditure		6
交费	jiāofèi	vb.	to pay a fee		3
经费	jīngfèi	n.	funds, expenditure		5
浪费	làngfèi	vb.	to waste, to squander		3
免费	miǎnfèi	vb.	(to be) free of charge		4
收费	shōufèi	vb.	to charge a fee		3
消费	xiāofèi	vb.	to consume, to spend		3
小费	xiǎofèi	n.	tip, gratuity		6
学费	xuéfèi	n.	tuition fee, tuition		3
消费者	xiāofèi zhě	n.	consumer		5
生活费	shēnghuófèi	n.	cost of living, living expenses, alimony		6
手续费	shǒuxùfèi	n.	service charge, processing fee, commission		6
贵	**guì**		expensive, noble	貝 154.5	1
贵	guì	adj.	expensive, noble, precious, (honourific) your		1
宝贵	bǎoguì	adj.	valuable, precious, to value, to treasure, to set store by		4
珍贵	zhēnguì	adj.	precious		5
贺	**hè**		to congratulate	貝 154.5	5
贺卡	hèkǎ	n.	greeting card, congratulation card		5
祝贺	zhùhè	vb.	to congratulate, congratulations		5
贸	**mào**		commerce, trade	貝 154.5	5
贸易	màoyì	n.	(commercial) trade		5
贴	**tiē**		to stick, to paste	貝 154.5	4
贴	tiē	vb.	to stick, to paste, to post (e.g. on a blog), to keep close to, to fit snugly, to subsidize, allowance (e.g. money for food or housing), sticker, m.w. for sticking plaster		4

补贴	bǔtiē	vb.	to subsidize, subsidy, allowance, to supplement (one's salary etc), benefit	5

资 zī — resources, capital   貝 154.6   3

资本	zīběn	n.	capital (economics)	5
资产	zīchǎn	n.	property, assets	5
资格	zīgé	n.	qualifications, seniority	3
资金	zījīn	n.	funds, funding, capital	3
资料	zīliào	n.	material, resources, data, information, profile (Internet)	4
资源	zīyuán	n.	natural resource, resource	4
资助	zīzhù	vb.	to subsidize, to provide financial aid, subsidy	5
工资	gōngzī	n.	wages, pay	3
投资	tóuzī	n.	investment, to invest	4
外资	wàizī	n.	foreign investment	6

赌 dǔ — to bet   貝 154.8   6

赌	dǔ	vb.	to bet, to gamble	6
赌博	dǔbó	vb.	to gamble	6

赔 péi — to compensate for loss   貝 154.8   5

赔	péi	vb.	to compensate for loss, to indemnify, to suffer a financial loss	5
赔偿	péicháng	vb.	to compensate	5

赏 shǎng — to bestow, to give   貝 154.8   4

赏	shǎng	vb.	to bestow (a reward), to give (to an inferior), to hand down, a reward (bestowed by a superior), to appreciate (beauty)	4
欣赏	xīnshǎng	vb.	to appreciate, to enjoy, to admire	5
赞赏	zànshǎng	vb.	to admire, to praise, to appreciate	4

赖 lài — to depend on   貝 154.9   6

赖	lài	vb.	depend on, hang onto a place, to blame, disclaim	6
依赖	yīlài	vb.	to depend on, to be dependent on	6

赚 zhuàn — to earn   貝 154.10   6

赚	zhuàn	vb.	to earn, to make a profit	6
赚钱	zhuànqián	vb.	to earn money, moneymaking	6

赞 zàn — to patronize   貝 154.12   4

赞成	zànchéng	vb.	to approve, to endorse, (literary) to assist	4
赞赏	zànshǎng	vb.	to admire, to praise, to appreciate	4
赞助	zànzhù	vb.	to support, to assist, to sponsor	4
称赞	chēngzàn	vb.	to praise, to acclaim, to commend, to compliment	4

赠 zèng — to give as a present   貝 154.12   5

赠	zèng	vb.	to give as a present, to repel, to bestow an honourary title after death (old)	5
赠送	zèngsòng	vb.	to present as a gift	5
捐赠	juānzèng	vb.	to contribute (as a gift), to donate, benefaction	6

走 zǒu run 走 156

走	**zǒu**		to walk, to go, to run	走 156.0 1
走	zǒu	vb.	to walk, to go, to run, to move (of vehicle), to visit, to leave, to go away, to die (euph.), from, through	1
走过	zǒuguò	vb.	to walk past, to pass by	2
走进	zǒujìn	vb.	to enter	2
走开	zǒukāi	vb.	to leave, to walk away, to beat it, to move aside	2
走路	zǒulù	vb.	to walk, to go on foot	1
走私	zǒusī	vb.	to smuggle, to have an illicit affair	6
拿走	názǒu	vb.	to take away	6
逃走	táozǒu	vb.	to escape, to flee, to run away	5
赶	**gǎn**		to overtake, to catch up with	走 156.3 3
赶	gǎn	vb.	to overtake, to catch up with, to hurry, to rush, to try to catch (the bus etc), to drive (cattle etc) forward	3
赶到	gǎndào	vb.	to hurry (to some place)	3
赶紧	gǎnjǐn	adv.	hurriedly, without delay	3
赶快	gǎnkuài	adv.	at once, immediately	3
赶忙	gǎnmáng	vb.	to hurry, to hasten, to make haste	6
赶上	gǎnshàng	vb.	to keep up with, to catch up with, to overtake, to chance upon, in time for	6
赶不上	- gǎnbushàng	phr.	can't keep up with, can't catch up with, cannot overtake	6
起	**qǐ**		to rise, to raise, to get up	走 156.3 1
起	qǐ	vb.	to rise, to raise, to get up, to set out, to start, to appear, to launch, to initiate (action), to draft, to establish, to get, m.w. for occurrences or unpredictable events: case, instance, m.w. for groups	1
起来	- qǐ lai	vb.	to stand up, to get up	1
起床	qǐchuáng	vb.	to get out of bed, to get up	1
起到	qǐdào	vb.	to have (a motivating etc) effect), to play (a stabilizing etc) role)	5
起点	qǐdiǎn	n.	starting point	6
起飞	qǐfēi	vb.	(of an aircraft) to take off	2
起码	qǐmǎ	adv.	at the minimum, at the very least	5
起诉	qǐsù	vb.	to sue, to bring a lawsuit against, to prosecute	6
发起	fāqǐ	vb.	to originate, to initiate, to launch (an attack, an initiative etc), to start, to propose sth (for the first time)	6
提起	tíqǐ	vb.	to mention, to speak of, to lift, to pick up, to arouse, to raise (a topic, a heavy weight, one's fist, one's spirits etc)	5
想起	xiǎngqǐ	vb.	to recall, to think of, to call to mind	2
一起	yīqǐ	adv.	in the same place, together, with, altogether (in total)	1
引起	yǐnqǐ	vb.	to give rise to, to lead to, to cause, to arouse	4
看起来	- kànqilai	adv.	seemingly, apparently, looks as if, appear to be, gives the impression that, seems on the face of it to be	3
对不起	- duìbuqǐ	phr.	unworthy, to let down, I'm sorry, excuse me, pardon me, if you please, sorry? (please repeat)	1
看不起	- kànbuqǐ	vb.	to look down upon, to despise	4
看得起	kàndeqǐ	vb.	to show respect for, to think highly of	6
了不起	• liǎobuqǐ	adj.	amazing, terrific, extraordinary	4

超	**chāo**		to exceed, to overtake	走 156.5	2
超	chāo	vb.	to exceed, to overtake, to surpass, to transcend, to pass, to cross, ultra-, super-		6
超出	chāochū	vb.	to exceed, to overstep, to go too far, to encroach		6
超过	chāoguò	vb.	to surpass, to exceed, to outstrip		2
超级	chāojí	adj.	super-, ultra-, hyper-		3
超市	chāoshì	n.	supermarket		2
超越	chāoyuè	vb.	to surpass, to exceed, to transcend		5
趋	**qū**		to hasten, to hurry	走 156.5	4
趋势	qūshì	n.	trend, tendency		4
越	**yuè**		to exceed, to climb over	走 156.5	2
越	yuè	vb.	to exceed, to climb over, to surpass, the more... the more		2
越来越	yuèláiyuè	adv.	more and more		2
超越	chāoyuè	vb.	to surpass, to exceed, to transcend		5
趣	**qù**		interesting, to interest	走 156.8	4
乐趣	lèqù	n.	delight, pleasure, joy		4
兴趣	xìngqù	n.	interest (desire to know about sth), interest (thing in which one is interested), hobby		4
有趣	yǒuqù	adj.	interesting, fascinating, amusing		4
感兴趣	gǎn xìngqù	vb.	to be interested		4
趟	**tàng**		a time, a trip	走 156.8	6
趟	tàng	vb.	to wade, to trample, to turn the soil		6

足 zú foot 足 157

足	**zú**		foot	足 157.0	3
足	zú	n.	foot, to be sufficient, ample		6
足够	zúgòu	vb.	to be enough, to be sufficient		3
足球	zúqiú	n.	soccer ball, a football		3
足以	zúyǐ	vb.	to be sufficient to..., so much so that, so that		6
不足	bùzú	adj.	insufficient, lacking, deficiency, not enough, inadequate, not worth, cannot, should not		5
充足	chōngzú	adj.	adequate, sufficient, abundant		5
满足	mǎnzú	vb.	to satisfy, to meet (the needs of), to be satisfied		3
十足	shízú	adj.	ample, complete, hundred percent, a pure shade (of some colour)		5
跃	**yuè**		to jump, to leap	足 157.4	6
活跃	huóyuè	adj.	active, lively, excited, to enliven, to brighten up		6
跌	**diē**		to fall	足 157.5	6
跌	diē	vb.	to fall, to tumble, to trip, (of prices etc) to drop		6
践	**jiàn**		to trample, to tread	足 157.5	6
实践	shíjiàn	vb.	practice, to put into practice, to live up to (a promise), to carry out (a project), practice		6

距	**jù**		to be at a distance of, distance	足 157.5	4
距离	jùlí	n.	distance		4
差距	• chājù	n.	disparity, gap		5
跑	**pǎo**		to run, to run away	足 157.5	1
跑	pǎo	vb.	to run, to run away, to escape, to run around (on errands etc), (of a gas or liquid) to leak or evaporate, (verb complement) away, off		1
跑步	pǎo bù	vb.	to run, to jog, (military) to march at the double		3
奔跑	bēnpǎo	vb.	to run		6
长跑	• chángpǎo	n.	long-distance running		6
逃跑	táopǎo	vb.	to flee from sth, to run away, to escape		5
跟	**gēn**		heel, to follow closely, with	足 157.6	1
跟	gēn	n.	heel, to follow closely, to go with, (of a woman) to marry sb, with, compared with, to, towards, and (joining two nouns)		1
跟前	gēnqián	n.	the front (of), (in) front, (in) sb's presence, just before (a date)		5
跟随	gēnsuí	vb.	to follow		5
高跟鞋	gāogēnxié	n.	high-heeled shoes		5
跪	**guì**		to kneel	足 157.6	6
跪	guì	vb.	to kneel		6
跨	**kuà**		to step across, to stride over	足 157.6	6
跨	kuà	vb.	to step across, to stride over, to straddle, to span		6
路	**lù**		road, path	足 157.6	1
路	lù	n.	road, path, journey, route, surname Lu		1
路边	lùbiān	n.	curb, roadside, wayside		2
路过	lùguò	vb.	to pass by or through		6
路口	lùkǒu	n.	crossing, intersection (of roads)		1
路上	- lùshang	n.	on the road, on a journey, road surface		1
路线	lùxiàn	n.	itinerary, route, political line		3
出路	chūlù	n.	a way out (lit. and fig.), opportunity for advancement, a way forward, outlet (for one's products)		6
道路	dàolù	n.	road, path, way		2
公路	gōnglù	n.	highway, road		2
马路	mǎlù	n.	street, road		1
铁路	tiělù	n.	railroad, railway		3
问路	wènlù	vb.	to ask for directions, to ask the way (to some place)		2
线路	xiànlù	n.	line, circuit, wire, road, railway track, bus route		6
一路	yīlù	adv.	the whole journey, all the way, going the same way, going in the same direction, of the same kind		5
走路	zǒulù	vb.	to walk, to go on foot		1
一路上	- yīlùshang	phr.	along the way, the whole way, (fig.) the whole time		6
一路平安	yīlùpíng'ān	vb.	to have a pleasant journey, Bon voyage!		2
一路顺风	yīlùshùnfēng	vb.	have a good trip (idiom)		2
高速公路	gāosù gōnglù	n.	expressway, highway, freeway		3
跳	**tiào**		to jump, to hop	足 157.6	3
跳	tiào	vb.	to jump, to hop, to skip over, to bounce, to palpitate		3
跳舞	tiào wǔ	vb.	to dance		3

跳高	tiàogāo	n.	high jump (athletics)		3
跳水	tiàoshuǐ	vb.	to dive (into water), (sports) diving, to commit suicide by jumping into water, (fig.) (of stock prices etc) to fall dramatically		6
跳远	tiàoyuǎn	n.	long jump (athletics)		3
踩	**cǎi**		**to step on**	足 157.8	6
踩	cǎi	vb.	to step on, to tread, to stamp, to press a pedal, to pedal (a bike), (online) to downvote		6
踏	**tà**		**to tread**	足 157.8	6
踏	tà	vb.	to tread, to stamp, to step on, to press a pedal, to investigate on the spot		6
踏实	- tàshi	adj.	firmly-based, steady, steadfast, to have peace of mind, free from anxiety		6
踢	**tī**		**to kick**	足 157.8	6
踢	tī	vb.	to kick, to play (e.g. football/ soccer)		6
蹈	**dǎo**		**to tread on, trample**	足 157.10	6
舞蹈	wǔdǎo	n.	dance (performance art), dancing		6
蹲	**dūn**		**to crouch, to squat**	足 157.12	6
蹲	dūn	vb.	to crouch, to squat, to stay (somewhere)		6

身 shēn body 158

身	shēn		body, life, oneself	身 158.0	1
身边	shēnbiān	n.	at one's side, on hand		2
身材	shēncái	n.	stature, build (height and weight), figure		4
身份	shēnfèn	n.	identity, aspect of one's identity (i.e. sth that one is – mayor, father, permanent resident etc), role		4
身高	shēngāo	n.	(a person's) height		4
身上	- shēnshang	n.	on the body, at hand, among		1
身体	shēntǐ	n.	the body, one's health		1
身份证	shēnfènzhèng	n.	identity card, ID		3
本身	běnshēn	pro.	itself, in itself, per se		6
健身	jiànshēn	vb.	to exercise, to keep fit, to work out, physical exercise		4
全身	quánshēn	n.	whole body, em (typography)		2
一身	yīshēn	n.	whole body, from head to toe, single person, a suit of clothes		5
终身	zhōngshēn	n.	lifelong, all one's life, marriage		5
转身	zhuǎnshēn	vb.	(of a person) to turn round, to face about, (of a widow) to remarry (archaic)		4
自身	zìshēn	n.	itself, oneself, one's own		3
躲	**duǒ**		**to hide**	身 158.6	5
躲	duǒ	vb.	to hide, to dodge, to avoid		5
躺	**tǎng**		**to recline**	身 158.8	4
躺	tǎng	vb.	to recline, to lie down		4

车 chē cart   车 159

车	**chē**		**cart, vehicle**	车 159.0	1
车	chē	n.	car, vehicle, machine, surname Che		1
车号	chēhào	n.	vehicle number (license plate number, taxi number, bus number, train car number)		6
车辆	chēliàng	n.	vehicle		2
车牌	chēpái	n.	license plate		6
车票	chēpiào	n.	ticket (for a bus or train)		1
车上	chēshàng	n.	in the car		1
车展	chēzhǎn	n.	motor show		6
车站	chēzhàn	n.	rail station, bus stop		1
车主	chēzhǔ	n.	vehicle owner		5
乘车	chéngchē	vb.	to ride (in a car or carriage), to drive, to motor		5
打车	dǎchē	vb.	to take a taxi (in town), to hitch a lift		1
倒车	• dǎo chē	vb.	to change buses, trains etc		4
倒车	dào chē	vb.	to reverse a car, to back a car		4
电车	diànchē	n.	trolleybus		6
堵车	dǔchē	n.	traffic jam, (of traffic) to get congested		4
火车	huǒchē	n.	train		1
开车	kāichē	vb.	to drive a car		1
客车	kèchē	n.	coach, bus, passenger train		6
快车	kuài chē	n.	express (train, bus etc)		6
列车	lièchē	n.	(railway) train		4
马车	mǎchē	n.	cart, chariot, carriage, buggy		6
慢车	mànchē	n.	local bus or train, slow train with many stops		6
骑车	qíchē	vb.	to ride a bike (motorbike or bicycle)		2
汽车	qìchē	n.	car, automobile, bus		1
上车	shàngchē	vb.	to get on or into (a bus, train, car etc)		1
停车	tíngchē	vb.	to pull up (stop one's vehicle), to park, (of a machine) to stop working, to stall		2
下车	xiàchē	vb.	to get off or out of (a bus, train, car etc)		1
修车	xiūchē	vb.	to repair a bike (car etc)		6
晕车	• yùnchē	vb.	to be carsick		6
停车场	tíngchēchǎng	n.	car park, parking lot		2
出租车	chūzūchē	n.	taxi, cab, rental car		2
电动车	diàndòngchē	n.	electric car, electric bicycle, electric scooter		4
公交车	gōngjiāochē	n.	public transport vehicle, town bus		2
机动车	jīdòngchē	n.	motor vehicle		6
开夜车	kāi yèchē	vb.	to burn the midnight oil, to work late into the night		6
自行车	zìxíngchē	n.	bicycle, bike		2
公共汽车	gōnggòng qìchē	n.	bus		2
轨	**guǐ**		**course, path**	车 159.2	6
轨道	guǐdào	n.	track (for trains etc), orbit (of a satellite), (fig.) a person's established path in life, desired trajectory (of a business or other endeavor)		6

					車 159.2	5
军	**jūn**		army, military			
军队	jūnduì	n.	army, troops			6
军舰	jūnjiàn	n.	warship, military naval vessel			6
军人	jūnrén	n.	serviceman, soldier, military personnel			5
军事	jūnshì	n.	military affairs, military matters, military			6
冠军	guānjūn	n.	champion			5
海军	hǎijūn	n.	navy			6
将军	jiāngjūn	n.	a general (military officer)			6
空军	kōngjūn	n.	air force			6
陆军	lùjūn	n.	army, ground forces			6
亚军	yàjūn	n.	second place (in a sports contest), runner-up			5
轮	**lún**		wheel, disk		車 159.4	4
轮	lún	n.	wheel, disk, ring, steamship, to take turns, to rotate, by turn, m.w. for big round objects: disk, or recurring events: round, turn			4
轮船	lúnchuán	n.	steamship, steamer, ocean liner, ship			4
轮椅	lúnyǐ	n.	wheelchair			4
轮子	lúnzi	n.	wheel			4
软	**ruǎn**		soft, flexible, pliable, weak		車 159.4	5
软	ruǎn	adj.	soft, (opp. 硬 yìng: hard)			5
软件	ruǎnjiàn	n.	(computer) software			5
转	* **zhuǎn, zhuàn**		to turn; to revolve		車 159.4	3
转	zhuǎn	vb.	to turn, to change, to shift, to pass on, to transfer			3
转	• zhuàn	vb.	to revolve, to turn, to circle about			6
转弯	zhuǎn wān	vb.	to turn, to go around a corner			4
转变	zhuǎnbiàn	vb.	to change, to transform, shift, transformation			3
转动	zhuǎndòng	vb.	to turn, to move, to flex, to turn sth around, to swivel			4
转告	zhuǎngào	vb.	to pass on, to communicate, to transmit			4
转化	zhuǎnhuà	vb.	to change, to transform, isomerization (chemistry)			5
转换	zhuǎnhuàn	vb.	to change, to switch, to convert, to transform			5
转让	zhuǎnràng	vb.	to transfer (ownership, rights etc)			5
转身	zhuǎnshēn	vb.	(of a person) to turn round, to face about, (of a widow) to remarry (archaic)			4
转向	zhuǎnxiàng	vb.	to change direction, fig. to change one's stance			5
转移	zhuǎnyí	vb.	to shift, to divert or distract (attention etc), to change, to transform, metastasis (medicine), to evacuate (people)			4
转动	• zhuàndòng	vb.	to turn, to revolve, to rotate			6
好转	hǎozhuǎn	vb.	to improve, to take a turn for the better, improvement			6
旋转	xuánzhuǎn	vb.	to rotate, to revolve, to spin, to whirl			6
轻	**qīng**		light, easy		車 159.5	2
轻	qīng	adj.	light, (opp. 重 zhòng), easy, gentle, soft, reckless, unimportant, frivolous, small in number, unstressed, neutral, to disparage			2
轻松	qīngsōng	adj.	light, gentle, relaxed, effortless, uncomplicated, to relax, to take things less seriously			4
轻易	qīngyì	adv.	easily, lightly, rashly			4
减轻	jiǎnqīng	vb.	to lighten, to ease, to alleviate			5
年轻	niánqīng	adj.	young			2

较	**jiào**		to compare, comparatively	車 159.6	3
较	jiào	*vb.*	to compare, to dispute, compared to, (before adj.) relatively, comparatively, rather		3
比较	bǐjiào	*vb.*	to compare, to contrast, comparatively, relatively, quite, comparison		3
辅	**fǔ**		to assist	車 159.7	5
辅助	fǔzhù	*vb.*	to assist, to aid, supplementary, auxiliary, subsidiary		5
辆	**liàng**		m.w. for vehicles	車 159.7	2
辆	liàng	*m.w.*	m.w. for vehicles		2
车辆	chēliàng	*n.*	vehicle		2
辑	**jí**		to gather up, to collect	車 159.9	5
编辑	biānji	*n.*	editor, compiler		5
编辑	biānjí	*vb.*	to edit, to compile		5
逻辑	- luóji	*n.*	logic (loanword)		5
专辑	zhuānjí	*n.*	album, record (music), special collection of printed or broadcast material		5
输	**shū**		to transport, to convey, to lose	車 159.9	3
输	shū	*vb.*	to lose, to transport, to donate, to enter (a password)		3
输出	shūchū	*vb.*	to export, to output		5
输入	shūrù	*vb.*	to import, to input		3
传输	chuánshū	*vb.*	to transmit, transmission		6
运输	yùnshū	*vb.*	to transport, to carry, transportation		3

辛 xīn bitter   160

辛	**xīn**		hot or pungent, hard, laborious	辛 160.0	5
辛苦	xīnkǔ	*adj.*	exhausting, hard, tough, arduous, to work hard, to go to a lot of trouble, hardship(s)		5
辣	**là**		peppery, pungent	辛 160.7	4
辣	là	*adj.*	peppery, pungent, hot (spicy), to burn		4
酸甜苦辣	suāntiánkǔlà	*phr.*	sour, sweet, bitter and spicy hot, fig. the joys and sorrows of life		5
辩	**biàn**		to dispute, to argue	辛 160.9	4
辩论	biànlùn	*n.*	debate, argument, to argue over		4

辵 chuò walk   辶辶 162

边	**biān**		side, edge, margin	辵 162.2	1
边	biān	*n.*	side, edge, margin, border, boundary		2
边境	biānjìng	*n.*	frontier, border		5
边缘	biānyuán	*n.*	edge, fringe, verge, brink, periphery, marginal, borderline		6
北边	- běibian	*n.*	north, north side, northern part, to the north of		1
东边	- dōngbian	*n.*	east, east side, eastern part, to the east of		1
海边	hǎibiān	*n.*	coast, seaside, seashore, beach		2
后边	- hòubian	*n.*	back, rear, behind		1
里边	- lǐbian	*n.*	inside		1

两边	liǎngbiān		n.	either side, both sides	4
路边	lùbiān		n.	curb, roadside, wayside	2
那边	- nàbian		n.	over there, yonder	1
南边	- nánbian		n.	south, south side, southern part, to the south of	1
旁边	pángbiān		n.	lateral, side, to the side, beside	1
前边	- qiánbian		n.	front, the front side, in front of	1
上边	- shàngbian		n.	the top, above, overhead, upwards, the top margin, above-mentioned, those higher up	1
身边	shēnbiān		n.	at one's side, on hand	2
外边	- wàibian		n.	outside, outer surface, abroad, place other than one's home	1
无边	wúbiān		vb.	without boundary, not bordered	6
西边	- xībian		n.	west, west side, western part, to the west of	1
下边	- xiàbian		n.	under, the underside, below	1
一边	yībiān		n.	one side, either side, on the one hand, on the other hand, doing while	1
右边	- yòubian		n.	right side, right, to the right	1
这边	zhèbiān		pro.	this side, here	1
左边	- zuǒbian		n.	left, the left side, to the left of	1

达 dá — to attain, to reach   辶 162.3   3

达成	dá chéng		vb.	to reach (an agreement), to accomplish	5
达到	dá dào		vb.	to reach, to achieve, to attain	3
表达	biǎodá		vb.	to express, to convey	3
传达	chuándá		vb.	to pass on, to convey, to relay, to transmit, transmission	5
到达	dàodá		vb.	to reach, to arrive	3
抵达	dǐdá		vb.	to arrive, to reach (a destination)	6
发达	fādá		adj.	developed (country etc), flourishing, to develop	3

过 guò — to pass, indicates past action   辶 162.3   1

过	guò	+	vb.	to pass, to cross, to go over, to celebrate, surname Guo	1
过	guo	+	aux.	[indicates a past experience or action, indicates a completion of action]	2
过来	- guò lai		vb.	to come over, to manage, to handle, to be able to take care of	2
过年	guò nián		vb.	to celebrate the Chinese New Year	2
过程	guòchéng		n.	course of events, process	3
过度	guòdù		adj.	excessive, over-, excess, going too far, extravagant, intemperate, overdue	5
过渡	guòdù		adj.	to cross over (by ferry), to pass from one form to another, transition, interim, caretaker (administration)	6
过分	• guòfèn		adj.	excessive, undue, overly	4
过后	guòhòu		n.	after the event	6
过敏	guòmǐn		vb.	oversensitive, allergic, allergy	5
过去	guòqù	+	vb.	to go over, to pass by	2
过去	guòqù	+	n.	(the) past, former times	3
过时	guòshí		vb.	old-fashioned, out of date, to be later than the time stipulated or agreed upon	6
过于	guòyú		adv.	too much, excessively	5
不过	bùguò		adv.	only, merely, no more than, but, however, anyway (to get back to a previous topic), cannot be more (after adjectival)	2
超过	chāoguò		vb.	to surpass, to exceed, to outstrip	2
错过	cuòguò		vb.	to miss (train, opportunity etc)	6

度过	dùguò	vb.	to pass, to spend (time), to survive, to get through		4
见过	jiànguò	vb.	have seen		2
经过	jīngguò	vb.	to pass, to go through, process, course		2
路过	lùguò	vb.	to pass by or through		6
难过	nánguò	vb.	to feel sad, to feel unwell, (of life) to be difficult		2
通过	tōngguò	prep.	by means of, through, via, to pass through, to get through, to adopt, to pass (a bill or inspection etc), to switch over		2
走过	zǒuguò	vb.	to walk past, to pass by		2
只不过	- zhǐbuguò	adv.	only, merely, nothing but, no more than, it's just that...		5

迁 qiān — to move, to shift — 辵 162.3 — 6

拆迁	chāiqiān	vb.	to demolish a building and relocate the inhabitants		6

迅 xùn — rapid, fast — 辵 162.3 — 4

迅速	xùnsù	adj.	rapid, speedy, fast		4

迟 chí — late, slow — 辵 162.4 — 4

迟	chí	adj.	late, slow, surname Chi		5
迟到	chídào	vb.	to arrive late		4
推迟	tuīchí	vb.	to postpone, to put off, to defer		4

返 fǎn — to return to — 辵 162.4 — 5

返回	fǎnhuí	vb.	to return to, to come (or go) back		5

还 * hái, huán — still, yet; to return, to pay back — 辵 162.4 — 1

还	hái	adv.	still, yet, in addition, even		1
还	• huán	vb.	to go or come back, to return, to pay back		1
还是	- háishi	adv.	or, still, nevertheless, had better		1
还有	háiyǒu	adv.	furthermore, in addition, still, also		1

近 jìn — near, close to — 辵 162.4 — 2

近	jìn	adj.	near, close to, approximately		2
近代	jìndài	n.	the not-very-distant past, modern times, excluding recent decades		4
近来	jìnlái	n.	recently, lately		5
近期	jìnqī	n.	near in time, in the near future, very soon, recent		3
近日	jìnrì	n.	(in) the past few days, recently, (within) the next few days		6
近视	jìnshì	n.	short-sighted, near-sighted, myopia		6
附近	fùjìn	n.	(in the) vicinity, nearby, neighbouring, next to		4
将近	jiāngjìn	adv.	almost, nearly, close to		3
接近	jiējìn	vb.	to approach, to get close to		3
靠近	kàojìn	vb.	(to be) near, to approach		5
最近	zuìjìn	n.	recently, soon, nearest		2

进 jìn — to go forward, to advance — 辵 162.4 — 1

进	jìn	vb.	to go forward, to advance, to go in, to enter, to put in, to submit, to take in, to admit, (math.) base of a number system, m.w. for sections in a building or residential compound		1
进步	jìnbù	n.	progress, improvement, to improve, to progress		3
进攻	jìngōng	vb.	to attack, to assault, to go on the offensive, attack, assault, offense (sports)		6
进化	jìnhuà	n.	evolution		5
进口	jìnkǒu	vb.	to import, imported, entrance, inlet (for the intake of air, water etc)		4

进来	jìnlái	vb.	to come in	1
进去	- jìnqu	vb.	to go in	1
进入	jìnrù	vb.	to enter, to join, to go into	2
进行	jìnxíng	vb.	to advance, to conduct, underway, in progress, to do, to carry out, to carry on, to execute	2
进展	jìnzhǎn	vb.	to make headway, to make progress	3
进一步	jìn yī bù	adv.	one step further, to move forward a step, further onwards	3
促进	cùjìn	vb.	to promote (an idea or cause), to advance, boost	4
改进	gǎijìn	n.	improvement, to improve, to make better	3
前进	qiánjìn	vb.	to go forward, to forge ahead, to advance, onward	3
请进	qǐngjìn	vb.	please come in	1
推进	tuījìn	vb.	to impel, to carry forward, to push on, to advance, to drive forward	3
先进	xiānjìn	adj.	advanced (technology), to advance	3
引进	yǐnjìn	vb.	to recommend, to introduce (from outside)	4
增进	zēngjìn	vb.	to promote, to enhance, to further, to advance (a cause etc)	6
走进	zǒujìn	vb.	to enter	2

连 lián — to link, to join, to connect ⾡ 162.4   3

连	lián	vb.	to link, to join, to connect, in succession, even, surname Lian	3
连接	liánjiē	vb.	to link, to join, to attach, connection, a link (on web page)	5
连忙	liánmáng	adv.	promptly, at once	3
连续	liánxù	adj.	continuous, in a row, serial, consecutive	3
连续剧	liánxùjù	n.	serialized drama, dramatic series, show in parts	3
接连	jiēlián	adv.	on end, in a row, in succession	5

违 wéi — to disobey, to violate ⾡ 162.4   5

违法	wéifǎ	vb.	illegal, to break the law	5
违反	wéifǎn	vb.	to violate (a law)	5
违规	wéiguī	vb.	to violate (rules), irregular, illegal, corrupt	5

迎 yíng — to welcome, to meet ⾡ 162.4   2

迎接	yíngjiē	vb.	to meet, to welcome, to greet	3
迎来	yínglái	vb.	to welcome (a visitor or newcomer), (fig.) to usher in	6
欢迎	huānyíng	vb.	to welcome, welcome	2

远 yuǎn — far, distant ⾡ 162.4   1

远	yuǎn	adj.	far, distant, remote, (intensifier in a comparison) by far, much (lower etc)	1
远处	• yuǎnchù	n.	distant place	5
远方	yuǎnfāng	n.	far away, a distant location	6
远离	yuǎnlí	vb.	to be far from, to keep away from	6
远远	yuǎnyuǎn	n.	distant, by far	6
长远	• chángyuǎn	adj.	long-term, long-range	6
跳远	tiàoyuǎn	n.	long jump (athletics)	3
永远	yǒngyuǎn	adv.	always, forever, eternal	2

运 yùn — to move, to transport ⾡ 162.4   2

运	yùn	vb.	to move, to transport, to use, to apply, fortune, luck, fate	5
运动	yùndòng	vb.	to move, to exercise, sports, exercise, motion, movement, campaign	2
运气	- yùnqi	n.	luck (good or bad)	4
运输	yùnshū	vb.	to transport, to carry, transportation	3

运行	yùnxíng	vb.	to move along one's course (of celestial bodies etc), (fig.) to function, to be in operation, (of a train service etc) to operate, to run, (of a computer) to run	5
运用	yùnyòng	vb.	to use, to put to use	4
运作	yùnzuò	vb.	to operate, operations, workings, activities (usu. of an organization), thread (computing)	6
运动会	yùndònghuì	n.	sports competition	4
运动员	yùndòngyuán	n.	athlete	4
好运	hǎoyùn	n.	good luck	5
命运	mìngyùn	n.	fate, destiny	3
幸运	xìngyùn	n.	fortunate, lucky, fortune, luck	3
亚运会	yàyùnhuì	n.	Asian Games	4

这 zhè — this, these — 辵 162.4 — 1

这	zhè	pro.	this, these, (commonly pr. zhèi before a m.w., esp. in Beijing), now	1
这边	zhèbiān	pro.	this side, here	1
这里	zhèlǐ	pro.	here	1
这么	zhème	pro.	so much, this much, how much?, this way, like this	2
这儿	zhèr	pro.	here (coll.)	1
这时	zhèshí	phr.	at this time, at this moment, (abbrev. of 这时候 zhè shíhou)	2
这些	zhèxiē	pro.	these	1
这样	zhèyàng	pro.	this kind of, so, this way, like this, such	2
这就是说	zhèjiùshìshuō	phr.	in other words, that is to say	6

迫 pò — to force, to compel — 辵 162.5 — 4

迫切	• pòqiè	adj.	urgent, pressing	4
被迫	bèi pò	vb.	to be compelled, to be forced	4
强迫	• qiǎngpò	vb.	to compel, to force	5
压迫	yāpò	vb.	to oppress, to repress, to constrict, oppression, stress (physics)	6

述 shù — to narrate, to state — 辵 162.5 — 4

描述	miáoshù	vb.	to describe, description	4

迷 mí — to bewilder, to be crazy about — 辵 162.6 — 3

迷	mí	vb.	to bewilder, to be crazy about, fan, enthusiast, lost, confused	3
迷人	mírén	adj.	fascinating, enchanting, charming, tempting	5
迷信	míxìn	n.	superstition, to have a superstitious belief (in sth)	5
歌迷	gēmí	n.	fan of a singer	3
球迷	qiúmí	n.	fan (ball sports)	3
影迷	yǐngmí	n.	film enthusiast, movie fan	6

适 shì — to fit, suitable — 辵 162.6 — 2

适当	• shìdàng	adj.	suitable, appropriate	6
适合	shìhé	vb.	to fit, to suit	3
适应	• shìyìng	vb.	to adapt, to fit, to suit	3
适用	shìyòng	vb.	to be applicable	3
合适	héshì	adj.	suitable, fitting, appropriate	2
舒适	shūshì	adj.	cosy, snug	4

送	**sòng**		to deliver, to carry	辵 162.6	1
送	sòng	vb.	to deliver, to carry, to give (as a present), to present (with), to see off, to send		1
送礼	sòng lǐ	vb.	to give a present		6
送到	sòngdào	vb.	to send to, deliver to		2
送给	sònggěi	vb.	to send, to give as a present		2
送行	sòngxíng	vb.	to see someone off, to throw someone a send-off party		6
发送	fāsòng	vb.	to transmit, to dispatch, to issue (an official document or credential)		3
赠送	zèngsòng	vb.	to present as a gift		5
逃	**táo**		to escape, to run away	辵 162.6	5
逃	táo	vb.	to escape, to run away, to flee		5
逃跑	táopǎo	vb.	to flee from sth, to run away, to escape		5
逃走	táozǒu	vb.	to escape, to flee, to run away		5
退	**tuì**		to retreat, to decline	辵 162.6	3
退	tuì	vb.	to retreat, to decline, to move back, to withdraw		3
退出	tuìchū	vb.	to withdraw, to abort, to quit, to log out (computing)		3
退票	tuìpiào	vb.	to bounce (a check), to return a ticket, ticket refund		6
退休	tuìxiū	vb.	to retire, retirement (from work)		3
选	**xuǎn**		to choose, to pick	辵 162.6	2
选	xuǎn	vb.	to choose, to pick, to select, to elect		2
选拔	xuǎnbá	vb.	to select the best		6
选举	xuǎnjǔ	vb.	to elect, election		6
选手	xuǎnshǒu	n.	athlete, contestant		3
选修	xuǎnxiū	vb.	(at a school) to take as an elective, an elective, elective (subject)		5
选择	xuǎnzé	vb.	to select, to pick, choice, option, alternative		4
当选	dāngxuǎn	vb.	to be elected, to be selected		5
评选	píngxuǎn	vb.	to select on the basis of a vote or consensus		6
挑选	tiāoxuǎn	vb.	to choose, to select		4
追	**zhuī**		to sculpt, to carve	辵 162.6	3
追	zhuī	vb.	to sculpt, to carve, musical instrument (old)		3
追究	zhuījiū	vb.	to investigate, to look into		6
追求	zhuīqiú	vb.	to pursue (a goal etc) stubbornly, to seek after, to woo		4
递	**dì**		to hand over, to pass on sth	辵 162.7	4
递	dì	vb.	to hand over, to pass on sth, to gradually increase or decrease, progressively		5
递给	dìgěi	vb.	to hand it (i.e. the aforementioned item) to (sb)		5
传递	chuándì	vb.	to transmit, to pass on to sb else, (math.) transitive		5
快递	kuàidì	n.	express delivery		4
逛	**guàng**		to stroll, to visit	辵 162.7	4
逛	guàng	vb.	to stroll, to visit		4
速	**sù**		fast, rapid, quick	辵 162.7	3
速度	sùdù	n.	speed, rate, velocity, (music) tempo		3
高速	gāosù	n.	high speed		3
加速	jiāsù	vb.	to speed up, to expedite		5

快速	kuàisù	*adj.*	fast, high-speed, rapid		3
迅速	xùnsù	*adj.*	rapid, speedy, fast		4
高速公路	gāosù gōnglù	*n.*	expressway, highway, freeway		3

通 tōng — to go through, to know well, to clear   辶 162.7   2

通	tōng	*vb.*	to go through, to know well, (suffix) expert, to connect, to communicate, open, to clear, m.w. for letters, telegrams, phone calls etc	2
通信	tōng xìn	*vb.*	to correspond (by letter etc), to communicate, communication	3
通报	tōngbào	*vb.*	to inform, to notify, to announce, circular, bulletin, scientific journal	6
通常	tōngcháng	*adj.*	regular, usual, normal, usually, normally	3
通道	tōngdào	*n.*	(communications) channel, passageway, alleyway	6
通过	tōngguò	*prep.*	by means of, through, via, to pass through, to get through, to adopt, to pass (a bill or inspection etc), to switch over	2
通红	tōnghóng	*adj.*	very red, red through and through, to blush (deep red)	6
通话	tōnghuà	*vb.*	to hold a conversation, to talk over the telephone, phone call	6
通行	tōngxíng	*vb.*	to go through, to pass through, to be in general use	6
通讯	tōngxùn	*n.*	communications, news story, dispatch	6
通用	tōngyòng	*vb.*	to use anywhere, anytime (card, ticket etc), to be used by everyone (language, textbook etc), (of two or more things) interchangeable	5
通知	tōngzhī	*vb.*	to notify, to inform, notice, notification	2
通知书	tōngzhīshū	*n.*	written notice	4
不通	bùtōng	*vb.*	to be obstructed, to be blocked up, to be impassable, to make no sense, to be illogical	6
畅通	chàngtōng	*adj.*	unimpeded, free-flowing, straight path, unclogged, move without obstruction	6
沟通	gōutōng	*vb.*	to join, to connect, to link up, to communicate	5
交通	jiāotōng	*vb.*	to be connected, traffic, transportation, communications, liaison	2
开通	kāitong	*vb.*	to open up (windows for air, ideas for discussion, transportation routes etc)	6
流通	liútōng	*vb.*	to circulate, to distribute, circulation, distribution	5
普通	pǔtōng	*adj.*	common, ordinary, general, average	2
普通话	pǔtōnghuà	*n.*	Mandarin (common language)	2

透 tòu — to penetrate, to pass through   辶 162.7   4

透	tòu	*vb.*	to penetrate, to pass through, thoroughly, completely, transparent, to appear, to show	4
透露	tòulù	*vb.*	to leak out, to divulge, to reveal	6
透明	tòumíng	*adj.*	transparent, open (non-secretive)	4

途 tú — way, road, path   辶 162.7   4

途径	tújìng	*n.*	way, channel	6
途中	túzhōng	*adv.*	en route, on the way	4
长途	chángtú	*adj.*	long distance	4
前途	qiántú	*n.*	prospects, future outlook, journey	4
用途	yòngtú	*n.*	use, application	4

造	zào		to make, to build	辵 162.7	3
造	zào	vb.	to make, to build, to manufacture, to invent, to fabricate, to go to, party (in a lawsuit or legal agreement), crop, m.w. for crops		3
造成	zàochéng	vb.	to bring about, to create, to cause		3
造型	zàoxíng	vb.	to model, to shape, appearance, style, design, form, pose		4
创造	chuàngzào	vb.	to create, to bring about, to produce, innovation		3
打造	dǎzào	vb.	to create, to build, to develop, to forge (of metal)		6
改造	gǎizào	vb.	to transform, to reform, to remodel, to remould		3
构造	gòuzào	n.	structure, composition, tectonic (geology)		4
建造	jiànzào	vb.	to construct, to build		5
制造	zhìzào	vb.	to manufacture, to make		3
逐	zhú		to pursue, to chase	辵 162.7	4
逐步	zhúbù	adv.	progressively, step by step		4
逐渐	zhújiàn	adv.	gradually		4
逻	luó		patrol	辵 162.8	5
逻辑	- luóji	n.	logic (loanword)		5
逼	bī		to compel, to pressure	辵 162.9	6
逼	bī	vb.	to force (sb to do sth), to compel, to press for, to extort, to press on towards, to press up to, to close in on		6
遍	biàn		everywhere, all over	辵 162.9	2
遍	biàn	adv.	everywhere, all over, m.w. for actions: one time		2
遍地	• biàndì	adv.	everywhere, all over		6
普遍	pǔbiàn	adj.	universal, general, widespread, common		3
道	dào		road, path, way	辵 162.9	1
道	dào	n.	road, path, way, principle, truth, morality, reason, skill, (class.) knowledge, method, Dao (of Daoism), to say, to speak, to talk, m.w. for long thin things (rivers, cracks etc)		2
道德	dàodé	n.	virtue, morality, ethics		5
道教	dàojiào	n.	Taoism, Daoism		6
道理	- dàoli	n.	reason, argument, sense, principle, basis, justification		2
道路	dàolù	n.	road, path, way		2
道歉	dàoqiàn	vb.	to apologize		6
报道	bàodào	vb.	to report (news), report		3
大道	dàdào	n.	main street, avenue		6
管道	guǎndào	n.	tubing, pipeline, (fig.) channel, means		6
轨道	guǐdào	n.	track (for trains etc), orbit (of a satellite), (fig.) a person's established path in life, desired trajectory (of a business or other endeavor)		6
街道	jiēdào	n.	street		4
楼道	lóudào	n.	corridor, passageway (in storied building)		6
难道	nándào	adv.	don't tell me ..., could it be that...?		3
频道	píndào	n.	frequency, (television) channel		5
渠道	qúdào	n.	irrigation ditch, (fig.) channel, means		6
通道	tōngdào	n.	(communications) channel, passageway, alleyway		6
味道	- wèidao	n.	flavour, smell, hint of		2
一道	yīdào	adv.	together		6

知道	- zhīdao	*vb.*	to know, to become aware of		1
遗	**yí**		to lose, to omit	辵 162.9	4
遗产	yíchǎn	*n.*	heritage, legacy, inheritance, bequest		4
遗传	yíchuán	*vb.*	heredity, to inherit (a trait), to pass on (to one's offspring)		4
遗憾	yíhàn	*n.*	regret, to regret, to be sorry that		6
遇	**yù**		to meet, to encounter	辵 162.9	4
遇	yù	*vb.*	to meet, to encounter, to treat, surname Yu		4
遇见	yù jiàn	*vb.*	to meet		4
遇到	yùdào	*vb.*	to meet, to run into, to come across		4
待遇	dàiyù	*n.*	treatment, pay, salary, status, rank		4
机遇	jīyù	*n.*	opportunity, favourable circumstance, stroke of luck		4
遭遇	zāoyù	*vb.*	to meet with, to encounter, (bitter) experience		6
遭	**zāo**		to meet, to encounter	辵 162.11	6
遭到	zāodào	*vb.*	to suffer, to meet with (sth unfortunate)		6
遭受	zāoshòu	*vb.*	to suffer, to sustain (loss, misfortune)		6
遭遇	zāoyù	*vb.*	to meet with, to encounter, (bitter) experience		6
遵	**zūn**		to observe, to obey	辵 162.12	5
遵守	zūnshǒu	*vb.*	to comply with, to abide by, to respect (an agreement)		5
避	**bì**		to avoid, to shun	辵 162.13	4
避	bì	*vb.*	to avoid, to shun, to flee, to escape, to keep away from, to leave, to hide from		4
避免	bìmiǎn	*vb.*	to avert, to prevent, to avoid, to refrain from		4
回避	huíbì	*vb.*	to shun, to avoid (sb), to skirt, to evade (an issue), to step back, to withdraw, to recuse (a judge etc)		5
邀	**yāo**		to invite, to request	辵 162.13	5
邀请	yāoqǐng	*vb.*	to invite, invitation		5

邑 yì　city　　β 163

那	**nà**		that, those, then (in that case)	邑 163.4	1
那	nà	+ *pro.*	that, those, commonly pr. nèi before a m.w., esp. in Beijing		1
那	nà	+ *conj.*	then (in that case)		2
那边	- nàbian	*n.*	over there, yonder		1
那里	nàlǐ	*pro.*	there, that place		1
那么	nàme	*pro.*	like that, in that way, or so, so, so very much, about, in that case		2
那儿	nàr	*pro.*	there		1
那些	nàxiē	*pro.*	those		1
那样	nàyàng	*pro.*	that kind, that sort		2
那会儿	nàhuìr	*n.*	at that time (in the past or the future)		2
那时候	- nàshíhou	*n.*	then, at that time, in those days (abbrev. 那时 nàshí: of course)		2
邻	**lín**		neighbour	邑 163.5	5
邻居	línjū	*n.*	neighbour, next door		5
邮	**yóu**		post office, mail	邑 163.5	3
邮件	yóujiàn	*n.*	mail, post, email		3

邮局	yóujú	n.	post office	4
邮票	yóupiào	n.	(postage) stamp	3
邮箱	yóuxiāng	n.	mailbox, post office box, email, email inbox	3
电子邮件 ·	diànzǐ yóujiàn	n.	email	3

郊 jiāo — suburbs, outskirts, open spaces 邑 163.6 5

郊区	jiāoqū	n.	suburban district, outskirts, suburbs	5

郎 láng — (arch.) minister, official, a youth 邑 163.6 4

新郎	xīnláng	n.	bridegroom, groom	4

部 bù — ministry, department, section 邑 163.8 2

部	bù	n.	ministry, department, section, part, division, troops, board, m.w. for works of literature, films, machines etc	3
部队	bùduì	n.	army, armed forces, troops, force, unit	6
部分	- bùfen	n.	part, share, section, piece	2
部门	bùmén	n.	department, branch, section, division	3
部位	bùwèi	n.	position, place	5
部长	bùzhǎng	n.	head of a (government etc) department, section chief, section head, secretary, minister	3
北部	běibù	n.	northern part	3
东部	dōngbù	n.	the east, eastern part	3
南部	nánbù	n.	southern part	3
内部	nèibù	n.	interior, inside (part, section), internal	4
全部	quánbù	adj.	whole, entire, complete	2
外部	wàibù	n.	external part, external	6
西部	xībù	n.	western part	3
胸部	xiōngbù	n.	chest	4
中部	zhōngbù	n.	middle part, central section	3
总部	zǒngbù	n.	general headquarters	6
大部分	- dàbùfen	n.	in large part, the greater part, the majority	2
一部分	- yībùfen	n.	portion, part of, subset	2
教育部	jiàoyùbù	n.	Ministry of Education	6
俱乐部	jùlèbù	n.	club (the organisation or its premises) (loanword)	5

都 * dōu, dū — all, both, entirely; city, capital 邑 163.9 1

都	dōu	adv.	all, both, entirely, (used for emphasis) even, already, (not) at all	1
都市	· dūshì	n.	city, metropolis	6
大都	· dàdū	adv.	almost all, for the most part, mostly (also -dōu), metropolitan, Dadu (capital of China during the Yuan Dynasty, 1280-1368, modern day Beijing	5
全都	quándōu	adv.	all, without exception	5
首都	· shǒudū	n.	capital (city)	3

酉 yǒu — wine 164

酒 jiǔ — wine, spirits 酉 164.3 2

酒	jiǔ	n.	wine (esp. rice wine), liquor, spirits, alcoholic beverage	2
酒吧	· jiǔbā	n.	bar, pub, saloon	4
酒店	jiǔdiàn	n.	wine shop, pub (public house), hotel, restaurant	2

酒鬼	jiǔguǐ	n.	drunkard		5
酒水	jiǔshuǐ	n.	beverage, a drink		6
白酒	báijiǔ	n.	baijiu, a spirit usually distilled from sorghum		5
红酒	hóngjiǔ	n.	red wine		3
啤酒	píjiǔ	n.	beer (loanword)		3
葡萄酒	- pútaojiǔ	n.	(grape) wine		5

配 pèi — to join, to fit 酉 164.3 3

配	pèi	vb.	to join, to fit, to mate, to mix, to match, to deserve, to make up (a prescription), to allocate	3
配套	pèi tào	vb.	to form a complete set, compatible, matching, complementary	5
配备	pèibèi	vb.	to allocate, to provide, to outfit with	5
配合	pèihé	adj.	matching, fitting in with, compatible with, to correspond, to fit, to conform to, rapport, to coordinate with	3
配置	pèizhì	vb.	to deploy, to allocate, configuration, allocation	6
搭配	dāpèi	vb.	to pair up, to match, to arrange in pairs, to add sth into a group	6
分配	fēnpèi	vb.	to distribute, to assign, to allocate, to partition (a hard drive)	3
支配	zhīpèi	vb.	to control, to dominate, to allocate	5

酱 jiàng — thick paste of fermented soybean 酉 164.6 6

酱	jiàng	n.	thick paste of fermented soybean, marinated in soy paste, paste, jam	6
酱油	jiàngyóu	n.	soy sauce	6
果酱	guǒjiàng	n.	jam	6

酷 kù — ruthless, strong 酉 164.7 6

酷	kù	adj.	ruthless, strong (e.g. of wine), (loanword) cool, hip	6
残酷	cánkù	adj.	cruel, cruelty	6

酸 suān — sour, tart 酉 164.7 4

酸	suān	adj.	sour, tart, sick at heart, grieved, sore, aching, pedantic, impractical, to make sarcastic remarks about sb, an acid	4
酸奶	suānnǎi	n.	yogurt	4
酸甜苦辣	suāntiánkǔlà	phr.	sour, sweet, bitter and spicy hot, fig. the joys and sorrows of life	5

醋 cù — vinegar, jealousy 酉 164.8 6

醋	cù	n.	vinegar, jealousy (in love rivalry)	6

醉 zuì — to be intoxicated 酉 164.8 5

醉	zuì	vb.	to be intoxicated, soaked in wine	5

醒 xǐng — to wake up, to be awake 酉 164.9 4

醒	xǐng	vb.	to wake up, to be awake, to become aware, to sober up, to come to	4
清醒	qīngxǐng	adj.	clear-headed, sober, awake	4
提醒	tíxǐng	vb.	to remind, to call attention to, to warn of	4

釆 biàn distinguish 165

采 cǎi — to pick, to pluck 釆 165.1 3

采访	cǎifǎng	vb.	to interview, to gather news, to hunt for and collect, to cover	4
采购	cǎigòu	vb.	to procure (for an enterprise etc), to purchase	5
采纳	cǎinà	vb.	to accept, to adopt	6

采取	cǎiqǔ	vb.	to adopt or carry out (measures, policies, course of action), to take	3
采用	cǎiyòng	vb.	to adopt, to employ, to use	3

释 shì — to explain, to release   采 165.5   4

解释	jiěshì	n.	explanation, to explain, to interpret, to resolve	4

里 lǐ — village   166

里 lǐ — lining, interior, inside   里 166.0   1

里	lǐ	n.	lining, interior, inside, internal, li: ancient measure of length, approx. 500 m	1
里边	- lǐbian	n.	inside	1
里面	lǐmiàn	n.	inside, interior	3
里头	- lǐtou	n.	inside, interior	2
城里	chénglǐ	n.	inside the city, downtown	5
公里	gōnglǐ	m.w.	kilometre	2
家里	jiālǐ	n.	home	1
哪里	- nǎli	pro.	where?, somewhere, anywhere, wherever, nowhere (negative answer to question), humble expression denying compliment	1
那里	nàlǐ	pro.	there, that place	1
手里	shǒulǐ	adj.	in hand, (a situation is) in sb's hands	4
心里	- xīnli	n.	chest, heart, mind	2
眼里	yǎnlǐ	n.	in one's eyes, in one's view	4
夜里	- yèli	n.	during the night, at night, nighttime	2
这里	zhèlǐ	pro.	here	1

重 * zhòng, chóng — heavy, serious; to repeat   里 166.2   1

重	• chóng	vb.	to repeat, repetition, again, re-, m.w. layer	3
重	zhòng	n.	heavy, (opp. 轻 qīng: light), serious, weight	1
重复	• chóngfù	vb.	to repeat, to duplicate	2
重建	• chóngjiàn	vb.	to rebuild, to re-establish, reconstruction, rebuilding	6
重新	• chóngxīn	adv.	again, once more, re-	2
重组	• chóngzǔ	vb.	to reorganize, to recombine, recombination	6
重大	zhòngdà	adj.	great, important, major, significant	3
重点	zhòngdiǎn	vb.	to recount (e.g. results of election), to re-evaluate	2
重量	zhòngliàng	n.	weight	4
重视	zhòngshì	vb.	to attach importance to sth, to value	2
重要	zhòngyào	adj.	important, significant, major	1
比重	bǐzhòng	n.	proportion, specific gravity	5
沉重	chénzhòng	adj.	heavy, hard, serious, critical	4
体重	tǐzhòng	n.	body weight	4
严重	yánzhòng	adj.	grave, serious, severe, critical	4
注重	zhùzhòng	vb.	to pay attention to, to emphasize	5
尊重	zūnzhòng	vb.	to esteem, to respect, to honour, to value, eminent, serious, proper	5

野 yě — field, plain   里 166.4   6

野	yě	n.	field, plain, open space, limit, boundary, rude, feral, wild, untamed (opp. 家 jiā: domestic)	6
野生	yěshēng	adj.	wild, undomesticated	6

量	* **liàng, liáng**		capacity; to measure	里 166.5	2
量	• liáng	vb.	to measure, to appraise		4
测量	• cèliáng	vb.	to survey, to measure, to gauge, to determine		4
产量	chǎnliàng	n.	output		6
大量	dàliàng	n.	great amount, large quantity, bulk, numerous, generous, magnanimous		2
含量	hánliàng	n.	content, quantity contained		4
衡量	• héngliáng	vb.	to weigh, to examine, to consider		6
尽量	jǐnliàng	adv.	as much as possible, to the greatest extent		3
力量	- lìliang	n.	power, force, strength		3
能量	néngliàng	n.	energy, capabilities		5
热量	rèliàng	n.	heat, quantity of heat, calorific value		5
商量	- shāngliang	vb.	to consult, to talk over, to discuss		2
数量	shùliàng	n.	amount, quantity		3
音量	yīnliàng	n.	loudness, volume		6
质量	zhìliàng	n.	quality, (physics) mass		4
重量	zhòngliàng	n.	weight		4
总量	zǒngliàng	n.	total, overall amount		6

金 jīn gold   钅 金 167

金	**jīn**		gold, metals in general, money	金 167.0	3
金	jīn	n.	gold, metal, money, gilded, highly respected		3
金额	jīn'é	n.	sum of money, monetary value		6
金牌	jīnpái	n.	gold medal		3
金钱	jīnqián	n.	money, currency		6
金融	jīnróng	n.	banking, finance, financial		6
黄金	huángjīn	adj.	gold, golden (opportunity), prime (time)		4
基金	jījīn	n.	fund		5
奖金	jiǎngjīn	n.	premium, award money, bonus		4
美金	měijīn	n.	US dollar ($)		4
现金	xiànjīn	n.	cash		3
押金	yājīn	n.	deposit, down payment		5
资金	zījīn	n.	funds, funding, capital		3
租金	zūjīn	n.	rent		6
奖学金	jiǎngxuéjīn	n.	scholarship		4
针	**zhēn**		needle, pin, tack	金 167.2	4
针	zhēn	n.	needle, pin, tack, needle like thing, acupuncture needle		4
针对	zhēnduì	vb.	to target, to focus on, to be aimed at or against, in response to		4
打针	dǎzhēn	vb.	to give or have an injection		4
方针	fāngzhēn	n.	policy, guidelines		4
钢	**gāng**		steel	金 167.4	5
钢笔	gāngbǐ	n.	fountain pen		5
钢琴	gāngqín	n.	piano		5

钟	**zhōng**		clock, o'clock	金 167.4	2
钟	zhōng	n	clock, o'clock, time as measured in hours and minutes, bell		3
钟头	zhōngtóu	n	hour		6
分钟	fēnzhōng	n	minute		2
闹钟	nàozhōng	n	alarm clock		4
鉴	**jiàn**		example, mirror	金 167.5	6
鉴定	jiàndìng	vb	to appraise, to identify, to evaluate		6
借鉴	jièjiàn	vb	to draw on (others' experience), to learn from (how others do things), lesson to be learned (by observing others)		6
铃	**líng**		bell	金 167.5	5
铃	líng	n	(small) bell		5
铃声	língshēng	n	ring, ringtone, bell stroke, tintinnabulation		5
钱	**qián**		coin, money	金 167.5	1
钱	qián	n	coin, money, unit of weight eqiv. 5g		1
钱包	qiánbāo	n	purse, wallet		1
价钱	jiàqián	n	price		3
金钱	jīnqián	n	money, currency		6
省钱	shěngqián	vb	to save money		6
挣钱	zhèngqián	vb	to make money		5
赚钱	zhuànqián	vb	to earn money, moneymaking		6
铅	**qiān**		lead	金 167.5	6
铅笔	qiānbǐ	n	(lead) pencil		6
铁	**tiě**		iron, arms, weapons	金 167.5	2
铁	tiě	n	iron, arms, weapons, hard, strong, violent, unshakeable, determined, close, tight (slang), surname Tie		3
铁路	tiělù	n	railroad, railway		3
地铁	• dìtiě	n	subway, metro		2
高铁	gāotiě	n	high speed rail		4
地铁站	• dìtiězhàn	n	subway station		2
钻	**zuān**		to drill, to bore	金 167.5	6
钻	zuān	vb	to drill, to bore, to get into, to make one's way into, to enter (a hole), to thread one's way through, to study intensively		6
铜	**tóng**		copper	金 167.6	6
铜牌	tóngpái	n	bronze medal, bronze plaque bearing a business name or logo etc		6
银	**yín**		silver, silver-coloured	金 167.6	2
银	yín	n	silver, silver-coloured, relating to money or currency		3
银行	• yínháng	n	bank		2
银牌	yínpái	n	silver medal		3
银行卡	• yínhángkǎ	n	bank card, ATM card		2
锋	**fēng**		point of spear, sharp point	金 167.7	6
先锋	xiānfēng	n	vanguard, pioneer, avant-garde		6

锅	guō		pot, pan	金 167.7	5
锅	guō	n.	pot, pan, boiler		5
电饭锅	diànfànguō	n.	electric rice cooker		5
铺	* pù, pū		shop, store; to spread	金 167.7	6
铺	• pū	vb.	to spread, to display, to set up, (old) holder for door-knocker		6
卧铺	wòpù	n.	a bed (on a train), a couchette		6
锁	suǒ		to lock up, to lock	金 167.7	5
锁	suǒ	vb.	to lock up, to lock, lock		5
销	xiāo		to melt, to cancel	金 167.7	4
销售	xiāoshòu	vb.	to sell, to market, sales (representative, agreement etc)		4
撤销	chèxiāo	vb.	to repeal, to revoke, (computing) to undo		6
促销	cùxiāo	vb.	to promote sales		4
推销	tuīxiāo	vb.	to market, to sell		4
错	cuò		mistake, wrong	金 167.8	1
错	cuò	n.	mistake, error, to be intricate, to dislocate, surname Cuo		1
错过	cuòguò	vb.	to miss (train, opportunity etc)		6
错误	cuòwù	n.	error, mistake		3
不错	bùcuò	adj.	correct, right, not bad, pretty good		2
没错	méi cuò	vb.	that's right, sure!, rest assured!, that's good, can't go wrong		4
键	jiàn		key, button	金 167.8	5
键	jiàn	n.	key (on a piano or computer keyboard), button (on a mouse or other device), chemical bond, linchpin		5
键盘	jiànpán	n.	keyboard		5
关键	guānjiàn	n.	crucial point, crux		5
锻	duàn		to forge metal, to temper	金 167.9	4
锻炼	duànliàn	vb.	to toughen, to temper, to engage in physical exercise, to work out, (fig.) to develop one's skills, to train oneself		4
镇	zhèn		to press down, to calm	金 167.10	6
镇	zhèn	vb.	to press down, to calm, to subdue, to suppress, to guard, garrison, small town, to cool or chill (food or drinks)		6
城镇	chéngzhèn	n.	town, cities and towns		6
镜	jìng		mirror, lens	金 167.11	4
镜头	jìngtóu	n.	camera lens, camera shot (in a movie etc), scene		4
镜子	jìngzi	n.	mirror		4
眼镜	yǎnjìng	n.	spectacles, eyeglasses		4

長	cháng		long	长镸	168
长	* zhǎng, cháng		to grow, to develop; long, length	長 168.0	2
长	• cháng	adj.	long, length, (opp. 短 duǎn: short), strong point		2
长	zhǎng	+ vb.	to grow, to develop		2
长	zhǎng	+ adj.	oldest, elder, chief, leader e.g. 秘书长 mì shū zhǎng - secretary general		6

长城	• chángchéng	n.	the Great Wall	3
长处	• chángchù	n.	good aspects, strong points	3
长度	• chángdù	n.	length	5
长短	• chángduǎn	n.	length, duration, accident, right and wrong, good and bad, long and short	6
长假	• chángjià	n.	long vacation	6
长久	• chángjiǔ	adv.	(for a) long time	6
长跑	• chángpǎo	n.	long-distance running	6
长期	• chángqī	n.	long term, long time, long range (of a forecast)	3
长寿	• chángshòu	adj.	longevity, live a long time	5
长途	• chángtú	adj.	long distance	4
长远	• chángyuǎn	adj.	long-term, long-range	6
长大	zhǎngdà	vb.	to grow up	2
班长	bānzhǎng	n.	class monitor, squad leader, team leader	2
部长	bùzhǎng	n.	head of a (government etc) department, section chief, section head, secretary, minister	3
厂长	chǎngzhǎng	n.	factory director	5
成长	chéngzhǎng	vb.	to mature, to grow, growth	3
处长	• chùzhǎng	n.	department head, section chief	6
船长	chuán zhǎng	n.	captain (of a boat), skipper	6
队长	duìzhǎng	n.	captain, team leader	2
会长	huìzhǎng	n.	president of a club, committee etc	6
家长	jiāzhǎng	n.	head of a household, family head, patriarch, parent or guardian of a child	2
局长	júzhǎng	n.	bureau chief	5
漫长	• màncháng	adj.	very long, endless	5
生长	shēngzhǎng	vb.	to grow	3
市长	shìzhǎng	n.	mayor	2
司长	sīzhǎng	n.	bureau chief	6
所长	suǒzhǎng	n.	what one is good at	3
团长	tuánzhǎng	n.	regimental command, head of a delegation	5
校长	xiàozhǎng	n.	(college, university) president, headmaster	2
延长	• yáncháng	vb.	to extend, to prolong, to lengthen	4
院长	yuànzhǎng	n.	the head of an institution whose name ends in 院 yuàn, chair of a board, president of a university, department head, dean, premier of the Republic of China	2
增长	zēngzhǎng	vb.	to grow, to increase	3
组长	zǔzhǎng	n.	group leader	2

門 mén gate 门 169

门	mén		gate, door	門 169.0 1
门	mén	n.	gate, door, opening, (m.w. for classes and languages), surname Men	1
门口	ménkǒu	n.	doorway, gate	1
门票	ménpiào	n.	ticket (for theatre, cinema etc)	1
门诊	ménzhěn	n.	outpatient service	5
部门	bùmén	n.	department, branch, section, division	3
出门	chū mén	vb.	to go out, to leave home, to go on a journey, away from home, (of a woman) to get married	2

大门	dàmén	n.	entrance, door, gate, large and influential family	2
敲门	qiāomén	vb.	to knock on a door	5
热门	rèmén	adj.	popular, hot, in vogue	5
入门	rùmén	n.	entrance door, to enter a door, introduction (to a subject), to learn the basics of a subject	5
上门	shàngmén	vb.	to drop in, to visit, to lock a door, (of a shop) to close, to go and live with one's wife's family, in effect becoming a member of her family	4
专门	zhuānmén	n.	specialist, specialized, customized	3

闪 shǎn — to dodge, to duck 門 169.2 4

| 闪 | shǎn | vb. | to dodge, to duck, lightning, surname Shan | 4 |
| 闪电 | shǎndiàn | n. | lightning | 4 |

闭 bì — to close, to stop up 門 169.3 4

闭	bì	vb.	to close, to stop up, to shut, to obstruct	6
闭幕	bìmù	vb.	the curtain falls, lower the curtain, to come to an end (of a meeting)	5
闭幕式	bìmùshì	n.	closing ceremony	5
倒闭	• dǎobì	vb.	to go bankrupt, to close down	4
封闭	fēngbì	vb.	to seal, to close, to confine, to seal off, to close down, sealed, confined, closed, unreceptive	4
关闭	guānbì	vb.	to close, to shut	4

闯 chuǎng — to rush, to charge 門 169.3 5

| 闯 | chuǎng | vb. | to rush, to charge, to dash, to break through, to temper oneself (through battling hardships) | 5 |

问 wèn — to ask, to inquire 門 169.3 1

问	wèn	vb.	to ask, to inquire	1
问候	wènhòu	vb.	to give one's respects, to send a greeting, (fig.) (coll.) to make offensive reference to (somebody dear to the person to whom one is speaking)	4
问路	wènlù	vb.	to ask for directions, to ask the way (to some place)	2
问题	wèntí	n.	question, problem, issue, topic	2
反问	fǎnwèn	vb.	to ask (a question) in reply, to answer a question with a question, rhetorical question	6
访问	fǎngwèn	vb.	to visit, to call on, to interview	3
顾问	gùwèn	n.	adviser, consultant	5
请问	qǐng wèn	vb.	may I ask...	1
提问	tíwèn	vb.	to question, to quiz, to grill	3
慰问	wèiwèn	vb.	to express sympathy, greetings, consolation etc	5
学问	- xuéwen	n.	learning, knowledge	4
询问	xúnwèn	vb.	to inquire	5
疑问	yíwèn	n.	question, interrogation, doubt	4

间 * jiān, jiàn — between, among; gap, to separate 門 169.4 1

间	jiān	n.	between, among, within a definite time or space, room, section of a room or lateral space between two pairs of pillars, m.w. for rooms	1
间接	• jiànjiē	adj.	indirect, second-hand (opp. 直接 zhíjiē: direct, immediate)	5
房间	fángjiān	n.	room	1
空间	kōngjiān	n.	space, room, (fig.) scope, leeway, (astronomy) outer space, (physics, math.) space	4

民间	mínjiān	n.	among the people, popular, folk, non-governmental, involving people rather than governments	3
期间	qījiān	n.	period of time, time, time period, period	4
人间	rénjiān	n.	the human world, the earth	5
时间	shíjiān	n.	time, period	1
夜间	yèjiān	n.	night-time, evening or night (e.g. classes)	5
之间	zhījiān	n.	between, among, inter-	4
中间	zhōngjiān	n.	between, intermediate, mid, middle	1
卫生间	wèishēngjiān	n.	bathroom, toilet, WC	3
洗手间	xǐshǒujiān	n.	toilet, lavatory, washroom	1

闲 xián — idle, unoccupied — 門 169.4 — 5

闲	xián	adj.	idle, (opp. 忙 máng: busy), unoccupied, leisure, enclosure	5
休闲	xiūxián	n.	leisure, relaxation, not working, idle, to enjoy leisure, to lie fallow	5

闹 nào — to make noise, to disturb — 門 169.5 — 4

闹	nào	vb.	to make noise, to disturb, to vent (feelings), to fall ill, to have an attack (of sickness), to go in (for some activity), to joke, noisy, cacophonous	4
闹钟	nàozhōng	n.	alarm clock	4
热闹	- rènao	adj.	bustling with noise and excitement, lively	4

闻 wén — to smell, (lit.) to hear, news — 門 169.6 — 2

闻	wén	vb.	to smell, (lit.) to hear, news reputation, surname Wen	2
新闻	xīnwén	n.	news	2

阅 yuè — to inspect, to review — 門 169.7 — 4

阅读	yuèdú	vb.	to read, reading	4
阅览室	yuèlǎnshì	n.	reading room	5

阔 kuò — rich, wide — 門 169.9 — 6

阔	kuò	adj.	rich, wide, broad, wealthy, long	6
广阔	guǎngkuò	adj.	wide, vast	6
宽阔	kuānkuò	adj.	expansive, wide, width, thickness	6

阜 fù — mound — 阝 170

队 duì — squadron, team — 阜 170.2 — 2

队	duì	n.	squadron, team, group	2
队伍	- duìwu	n.	ranks, troops, queue, line, procession	6
队员	duìyuán	n.	team member	3
队长	duìzhǎng	n.	captain, team leader	2
部队	bùduì	n.	army, armed forces, troops, force, unit	6
军队	jūnduì	n.	army, troops	6
排队	pái duì	vb.	to line up	2
球队	qiúduì	n.	sports team (basketball, soccer, football etc)	2
团队	tuánduì	n.	team	6
乐队	• yuèduì	n.	band, pop group	3

防 fáng — to protect, to defend — 阜 170.4 — 3

防	fáng	vb.	to protect, to defend, to guard against, to prevent	3

防范	fángfàn	vb.	to be on guard, wariness, to guard against, preventive	6
防守	fángshǒu	vb.	to defend, to protect (against)	6
防止	fángzhǐ	vb.	to prevent, to guard against, to take precautions	3
防治	fángzhì	vb.	to prevent and cure, prevention and cure	5
消防	xiāofáng	adj.	firefighting, fire control	5
预防	yùfáng	vb.	to prevent, to take precautions against, to protect, to guard against, precautionary, prophylactic	3

阶 jiē — step, stairs, rank — 阜 170.4 — 4

阶段	jiēduàn	n.	stage, section, phase, period	4
台阶	táijiē	n.	steps, flight of steps, step (over obstacle), fig. way out of an embarrassing situation	4

阳 yáng — sun, male principle, Yang — 阜 170.4 — 2

阳光	yángguāng	n.	sunshine	3
阳台	yángtái	n.	balcony, porch	4
太阳	tàiyáng	n.	sun	2
太阳能	tàiyángnéng	n.	solar energy	6

阴 yīn — cloudy, shady, Yin — 阜 170.4 — 2

阴	yīn	vb.	cloudy, shady, Yin (the negative principle of Yin and Yang), negative (electric.), feminine, moon, implicit, hidden, genitalia	2
阴谋	yīnmóu	n.	plot, conspiracy	6
阴天	yīntiān	n.	cloudy day, overcast sky	2
阴影	yīnyǐng	n.	(lit. and fig.) shadow	6

阵 zhèn — wave, spate, short period of time — 阜 170.4 — 4

阵	zhèn	n.	wave, spate, burst, spell, short period of time, m.w. for events or states of short duration, disposition of troops	4

阿 ā — pref used bef. names: ind. familiarity — 阜 170.5 — 4

阿姨	āyí	n.	maternal aunt, stepmother, childcare worker, nursemaid, woman of similar age to one's parents (term of address used by child)	4

附 fù — to add, to attach — 阜 170.5 — 4

附件	fùjiàn	n.	enclosure, attachment (email), appendix	5
附近	fùjìn	n.	(in the) vicinity, nearby, neighbouring, next to	4

际 jì — border, edge — 阜 170.5 — 2

国际	guójì	adj.	international	2
交际	jiāojì	n.	communication, social intercourse	4
实际	shíjì	n.	reality, practice, practical, realistic, real, actual	2
实际上	- shíjì shang	adv.	in fact, in reality, as a matter of fact, in practice	3

陆 lù — shore, land — 阜 170.5 — 4

陆地	lùdì	n.	dry land (as opposed to the sea)	4
陆军	lùjūn	n.	army, ground forces	6
陆续	lùxù	adv.	in turn, successively, one after the other, bit by bit	4
大陆	dàlù	n.	mainland China (reference to the PRC)	4

阻 zǔ — to hinder, to block — 阜 170.5 — 4

阻碍	zǔ'ài	vb.	to obstruct, to hinder, to block, obstruction, hindrance	5
阻止	zǔzhǐ	vb.	to prevent, to block	4

降	**jiàng**		to drop, to fall	阜 170.6	4
降	jiàng	vb.	to drop, to fall, to come down, to descend		4
降价	jiàng jià	vb.	to cut the price, to drive down the price, to get cheaper		4
降低	jiàngdī	vb.	to reduce, to lower, to bring down		4
降落	jiàngluò	vb.	to descend, to land		4
降温	jiàngwēn	vb.	to become cooler, to lower the temperature, cooling, (of interest, activity etc) to decline		4
下降	xiàjiàng	vb.	to decline, to drop, to fall, to go down, to decrease		4
限	**xiàn**		limit, bounds	阜 170.6	4
限制	xiànzhì	vb.	to restrict, to limit, to confine, restriction, limit		4
期限	qīxiàn	n.	time limit, deadline, allotted time		4
无限	wúxiàn	adj.	unlimited, unbounded		4
有限	yǒuxiàn	adj.	limited, finite		4
除	**chú**		to get rid of, to remove	阜 170.7	3
除	chú	vb.	to get rid of, to remove, to exclude, to eliminate, to wipe out, to divide, except, not including		6
除非	chúfēi	conj.	only if (..., or otherwise, ...), only when, only in the case that, unless		5
除了	chúle	prep.	besides, apart from (... also...), in addition to, except (for)		3
除夕	chúxī	n.	lunar New Year's Eve		5
拆除	chāichú	vb.	to tear down, to demolish, to dismantle, to remove		5
解除	jiěchú	vb.	to remove, to sack, to get rid of, to relieve (sb of their duties), to free, to lift (an embargo), to rescind (an agreement)		5
排除	páichú	vb.	to eliminate, to remove, to exclude, to rule out		5
消除	xiāochú	vb.	to eliminate, to remove		5
险	**xiǎn**		narrow pass, danger	阜 170.7	3
险	xiǎn	n.	narrow pass, danger, dangerous		6
保险	bǎoxiǎn	n.	insurance, to insure, safe, secure, be sure, be bound to		3
风险	fēngxiǎn	n.	risk, hazard		3
危险	wēixiǎn	n.	danger, dangerous		3
院	**yuàn**		courtyard	阜 170.7	1
院	yuàn	n.	courtyard, institution		2
院长	yuànzhǎng	n.	the head of an institution whose name ends in 院 yuàn, chair of a board, president of a university, department head, dean, premier of the Republic of China		2
院子	yuànzi	n.	courtyard, garden, yard, patio		2
出院	chū yuàn	vb.	to leave hospital, to be discharged from hospital		2
法院	fǎyuàn	n.	court of law, court		4
学院	xuéyuàn	n.	college, educational institute, school, faculty		1
医院	yīyuàn	n.	hospital		1
住院	zhù yuàn	vb.	to be in hospital, to be hospitalized		2
电影院	diànyǐngyuàn	n.	cinema, movie theatre		1
陪	**péi**		to accompany, to keep sb company	阜 170.8	5
陪	péi	vb.	to accompany, to keep sb company, to assist		5
陪同	péitóng	vb.	to accompany		6

陷	**xiàn**		to get stuck, to sink, trap	阜 170.8	6
陷入	xiànrù	vb.	to sink into, to get caught up in, to land in (a predicament)		6
缺陷	quēxiàn	n.	defect, flaw, physical defect		6
隐	**yǐn**		hidden, secret	阜 170.9	6
隐藏	yǐncáng	vb.	to hide, to conceal, to mask, to shelter, to harbour (i.e. keep sth hidden), to hide oneself, to lie low, to nestle, hidden		6
隐私	yǐnsī	n.	secrets, private business, privacy		6
隔	**gé**		to separate, to partition	阜 170.10	4
隔	gé	vb.	to separate, to partition, to stand or lie between, at a distance from, after or at an interval of		4
隔壁	gébì	n.	next door, neighbour		5
隔开	gékāi	vb.	to separate		4
随	**suí**		to follow, to go along with	阜 170.10	2
随	suí	vb.	to follow, to go along with, to allow, surname Sui		3
随便	suíbiàn	adj.	casual, random, as one wishes, as one pleases, anyhow		2
随后	suíhòu	adv.	soon after		5
随时	suíshí	adv.	at any time, at all times, at the right time		2
随手	suíshǒu	adv.	conveniently, without extra trouble, while doing it, in passing		4
随意	suíyì	adv.	as one wishes, according to one's wishes, voluntary, conscious		5
随着	suízhe	prep.	along with, in the wake of, following		5
跟随	gēnsuí	vb.	to follow		5
障	**zhàng**		to block, to hinder	阜 170.11	6
障碍	zhàng'ài	n.	barrier, obstruction, hindrance, impediment, obstacle		6
故障	gùzhàng	n.	malfunction, breakdown, defect, shortcoming, fault, failure, impediment, error, bug (in software)		6
隹	**zhuī**		**short-tailed bird**		**172**
集	**jí**		to gather, to collect	隹 172.4	3
集	jí	vb.	to gather, to collect, collected works, m.w. for sections of a TV series etc: episode		6
集合	jíhé	vb.	to gather, to assemble, set (math.)		4
集体	jítǐ	n.	collective (decision), joint (effort), a group, a team, en masse, as a group		3
集团	jítuán	n.	group, bloc, corporation, conglomerate		5
集中	jízhōng	vb.	to concentrate, to centralize, to focus, centralized, concentrated, to put together		3
收集	shōují	vb.	to gather, to collect		5
雄	**xióng**		male, masculine, grand	隹 172.4	5
雄伟	xióngwěi	adj.	grand, imposing, magnificent, majestic		5
英雄	yīngxióng	n.	hero		6

雨 yǔ rain 173

雨	**yǔ**		rain	雨 173.0 1
雨	yǔ	*n.*	rain	1
雨水	yǔshuǐ	*n.*	rainwater, Rainwater (one of 24 solar terms)	5
雨衣	yǔyī	*n.*	raincoat	6
暴雨	bàoyǔ	*n.*	torrential rain, rainstorm	6
下雨	xiàyǔ	*vb.*	to rain	1
暴风雨	bàofēngyǔ	*n.*	rainstorm, storm, tempest	6
雪	**xuě**		snow	雨 173.3 2
雪	xuě	*n.*	snow, surname Xue	2
冰雪	bīngxuě	*n.*	ice and snow	4
下雪	xiàxuě	*vb.*	to snow	2
雷	**léi**		thunder	雨 173.5 4
打雷	dǎléi	*vb.*	to rumble with thunder, clap of thunder	4
零	**líng**		zero, o	雨 173.5 1
零 | ○	líng	*num.*	zero, o, nought, zero sign, fractional, fragmentary, (opp. 整 zhěng: whole), odd (of numbers), (placed between two numbers to indicate a smaller quantity followed by a larger one)	1
零食	língshí	*n.*	between-meal nibbles, snacks	4
零下	língxià	*adj.*	below zero	2
需	**xū**		to need, to require, must	雨 173.6 3
需求	xūqiú	*n.*	requirement, to require, (economics) demand	3
需要	xūyào	*vb.*	to need, to want, to demand, to require, requirement, need	3
必需	bìxū	*vb.*	to need, to require, essential, indispensable	5
震	**zhèn**		to shake, to quake	雨 173.7 5
震惊	zhènjīng	*vb.*	to shock, to astonish	5
地震	• dìzhèn	*n.*	earthquake	5
露	* **lù, lòu**		dew; bare, open, exposed	雨 173.12 6
露	lù	*n.*	dew, syrup, medicinal liquid or lotion	6
露	• lòu	*vb.*	to reveal, to show	6
暴露	bàolù	*vb.*	to expose, to reveal, to lay bare	6
透露	tòulù	*vb.*	to leak out, to divulge, to reveal	6

青 qīng blue 青 174

青	**qīng**		blue, green	青 174.0 2
青	qīng	*adj.*	blue, green, black, young, Qinghai province	5
青春	qīngchūn	*n.*	youth, youthfulness	4
青年	qīngnián	*n.*	youth, youthful years, young person, the young	2
青少年	• qīngshàonián	*n.*	adolescent, youth, teenager	2
静	**jìng**		still, calm	青 174.6 2
静	jìng	*adj.*	still, calm, quiet, not moving	3

安静	ānjìng	*adj.*	quiet, peaceful, calm		2
冷静	lěngjìng	*adj.*	calm, cool-headed		4
宁静	níngjìng	*adj.*	tranquil, tranquillity, serenity, calm		4
平静	píngjìng	*adj.*	tranquil, undisturbed, serene		4

非 fēi wrong 175

非	**fēi**		to not be, not	非 175.0	1
非	fēi	*vb.*	to not be, not, non-, un-, wrongdoing, simply must		4
非常	fēicháng	*adv.*	very, very much, unusual, extraordinary		1
除非	chúfēi	*conj.*	only if (..., or otherwise, ...), only when, only in the case that, unless		5
辈	**bèi**		lifetime, generation	非 175.4	5
辈	bèi	*n.*	lifetime, generation, group of people, class, m.w. for generations, (literary) m.w. for people		5
一辈子	yībèizi	*n.*	(for) a lifetime		5
靠	**kào**		to lean against or on	非 175.7	2
靠	kào	*vb.*	to lean against or on, to stand by the side of, to come near to, to depend on, to trust, to fuck (vulgar)		2
靠近	kàojìn	*vb.*	(to be) near, to approach		5
可靠	kěkào	*adj.*	reliable		3
依靠	yīkào	*vb.*	to rely on sth (for support etc), to depend on		4

面 miàn face 176

面	**miàn**		face, side	面 176.0	1
面	miàn	+ *n.*	face, side, surface, aspect, outside, scale		2
面	miàn	+ *m.w.*	m.w. for flat things		2
面包	miànbāo	*n.*	bread		1
面对	miànduì	*vb.*	to confront, to face		3
面积	miànjī	*n.*	area (of a floor, piece of land etc), surface area, tract of land		3
面临	miànlín	*vb.*	to face sth, to be confronted with		4
面貌	miànmào	*n.*	appearance, face, features		5
面前	miànqián	*n.*	in front of, facing, (in the) presence (of)		2
面试	miànshì	*vb.*	to be interviewed (as a candidate), interview		4
面条	miàntiáo	*n.*	noodles		1
面向	miànxiàng	*vb.*	to face, to turn towards, to incline to, geared towards, catering for, -oriented, facial feature, appearance, aspect, facet		6
面子	miànzi	*n.*	outer surface, outside, honour, reputation, face (as in losing face), self-respect, feelings, (medicinal) powder		5
面对面	miànduìmiàn	*phr.*	face to face		6
表面	biǎomiàn	*n.*	surface, face, outside, appearance		3
层面	céngmiàn	*n.*	aspect, facet, level (political, psychological, spiritual etc), (geology) bedding plane		6
场面	chǎngmiàn	*n.*	scene, spectacle, occasion, situation		5
出面	chū miàn	*vb.*	to appear personally, to step in, to step forth, to show up		6
地面	• dìmiàn	*n.*	floor, ground, surface		4

对面	duìmiàn	n.	(sitting) opposite, across (the street), directly in front, to be face to face	2
方面	fāngmiàn	n.	respect, aspect, field, side	2
后面	- hòumian	n.	rear, back, behind, later, afterwards	3
画面	huàmiàn	n.	scene, tableau, picture, image, screen (displayed by a computer), (motion picture) frame, field of view	5
见面	jiànmiàn	vb.	to meet, to see each other	1
局面	júmiàn	n.	aspect, phase, situation	5
里面	lǐmiàn	n.	inside, interior	3
片面	piànmiàn	adj.	unilateral, one-sided	4
前面	- qiánmian	n.	ahead, in front, preceding, above	3
全面	quánmiàn	adj.	all-around, comprehensive, total, overall	3
上面	- shàngmian	n.	on top of, above-mentioned	3
外面	- wàimian	n.	outside, surface, exterior, external appearance	3
下面	- xiàmian	n.	below, next in order, lower level	3
表面上	- biǎomiàn shang	adv.	outwardly, superficially, on the face of it	6
多方面	duōfāngmiàn	adj.	many-sided, in many aspects	6
方便面	fāngbiànmiàn	n.	instant noodles	2
一方面	yīfāngmiàn	conj.	on the one hand..., on the other hand...	3
另一方面	lìngyīfāngmiàn	phr.	on the other hand, another aspect	3

革 gé leather 177

革	gé		leather, animal hides	革 177.0 5
革新	géxīn	vb.	to innovate, innovation	6
改革	gǎigé	n.	reform	5
鞋	**xié**		**shoes**	革 177.6 2
鞋	xié	n.	shoes	2
凉鞋	liángxié	n.	sandal	6
皮鞋	píxié	n.	leather shoes	5
球鞋	qiúxié	n.	athletic shoes	2
拖鞋	tuōxié	n.	slippers, sandals, flip-flops	6
高跟鞋	gāogēnxié	n.	high-heeled shoes	5

音 yīn sound 180

音	yīn		sound, noise, note	音 180.0 2
音节	yīnjié	n.	syllable	2
音量	yīnliàng	n.	loudness, volume	6
音像	yīnxiàng	n.	audio and video, audio-visual	6
音乐	• yīnyuè	n.	music	2
音乐会	• yīnyuèhuì	n.	concert	2
读音	dúyīn	n.	pronunciation, literary (rather than colloquial) pronunciation of a Chinese character	2
录音	lùyīn	vb.	to record (sound), sound recording	3
声音	shēngyīn	n.	voice, sound	2
语音	yǔyīn	n.	speech sounds, pronunciation, colloquial (rather than literary) pronunciation of a Chinese character, phonetic, audio	4

录音机	lùyīnjī	n.	(tape) recording machine, tape recorder	6
收音机	shōuyīnjī	n.	radio	3

頁 yè leaf 页 181

页 yè — page, leaf 頁 181.0 — 1
页	yè	n.	page, leaf, m.w. leaf, page, sheet	1
网页	wǎngyè	n.	web page	6

顶 dǐng — apex, crown of the head 頁 181.2 — 4
顶	dǐng	n.	apex, crown of the head, top, roof, most, to carry on the head, to push to the top, to go against, to replace, to be subjected to, m.w. for headwear	4

顺 shùn — to obey, to follow 頁 181.3 — 2
顺	shùn	vb.	to obey, to follow, to arrange, to make reasonable, along, favourable	6
顺利	shùnlì	adv.	smoothly, without a hitch	2
顺序	shùnxù	n.	sequence, order	4
一路顺风	yīlùshùnfēng	vb.	have a good trip (idiom)	2

项 xiàng — nape of neck, sum 頁 181.3 — 4
项	xiàng	n.	nape (of the neck), sum (of money), item, thing, (m.w. for items, clauses, projects, etc.), surname Xiang	4
项目	xiàngmù	n.	item, project, (sports) event	4

顿 dùn — to stop, to pause 頁 181.4 — 3
顿	dùn	vb.	to stop, to pause, to arrange, to lay out, to kowtow, to stamp (one's foot), at once, m.w. for meals, times	3
整顿	zhěngdùn	vb.	to tidy up, to reorganize, to consolidate, to rectify	6

顾 gù — to look after 頁 181.4 — 2
顾	gù	vb.	to look after, to take into consideration, attend to, surname Gu	6
顾客	gùkè	n.	client, customer	2
顾问	gùwèn	n.	adviser, consultant	5
不顾	bùgù	vb.	in spite of, regardless of	5
回顾	huígù	vb.	to look back, to review	5
照顾	-zhàogu	vb.	to take care of, to show consideration, to attend to, to look after	2
只顾	zhǐgù	adv.	solely preoccupied (with one thing), engrossed, focusing (on sth), to look after only one aspect	6

顽 wán — mischievous, obstinate 頁 181.4 — 6
顽皮	wánpí	adj.	naughty	6
顽强	wánqiáng	adj.	tenacious, hard to defeat	6

预 yù — to prepare, to advance 頁 181.4 — 3
预报	yùbào	n.	forecast	3
预备	yùbèi	vb.	to prepare, to make ready, preparation, preparatory	5
预测	yùcè	vb.	to forecast, to predict	4
预订	yùdìng	vb.	to place an order, to book ahead	4
预防	yùfáng	vb.	to prevent, to take precautions against, to protect, to guard against, precautionary, prophylactic	3
预计	yùjì	vb.	to forecast, to predict, to estimate	3

预期	yùqī	vb.	to expect, to anticipate	5
预习	yùxí	vb.	to prepare a lesson	3
预约	yùyuē	n.	booking, reservation, to book, to make an appointment	6
干预	gānyù	vb.	to meddle, to intervene, intervention	5

领 lǐng — neck, collar 頁 181.5 3

领	lǐng	n.	neck, collar, to lead, to receive, m.w. for clothes, mats, screens etc	3
领带	lǐngdài	n.	necktie	5
领导	lǐngdǎo	n.	lead, leading, to lead, leadership, leader	3
领取	lǐngqǔ	vb.	to receive, to draw, to get	6
领先	lǐngxiān	vb.	to lead, to be in front	3
领袖	lǐngxiù	n.	leader	6
白领	báilǐng	n.	white-collar, white-collar worker	6
本领	běnlǐng	n.	skill, ability, capability	3
带领	dàilǐng	vb.	to guide, to lead	3
蓝领	lánlǐng	n.	blue-collar, blue-collar worker	6
率领	lǜlǐng	vb.	to lead, to command, to head	5
占领	zhànlǐng	vb.	to occupy (a territory), to hold	5

频 pín — frequently, repeatedly 頁 181.7 5

频道	píndào	n.	frequency, (television) channel	5
频繁	pínfán	adv.	frequently, often	5
视频	shìpín	n.	video	5

颗 kē — m.w. for small spheres 頁 181.8 5

颗	kē	m.w.	m.w. for small spheres, pearls, corn grains, teeth, hearts, satellites etc	5

额 é — forehead, tablet, amount 頁 181.9 6

金额	jīn'é	n.	sum of money, monetary value	6
名额	míng'é	n.	quota, number of places, place (in an institution, a group etc)	6

题 tí — topic, subject 頁 181.9 2

题	tí	n.	topic, subject, question on a test or assignment, surname Ti	2
题材	tícái	n.	subject matter	5
题目	tímù	n.	subject, title, topic	3
标题	biāotí	n.	title, heading, headline, caption, subject	3
话题	huàtí	n.	subject (of a talk or conversation), topic	3
考题	kǎotí	n.	exam question	6
课题	kètí	n.	task, problem, issue	5
难题	nántí	n.	difficult problem	2
试题	shìtí	n.	exam question, test topic	3
问题	wèntí	n.	question, problem, issue, topic	2
议题	yìtí	n.	topic of discussion, topic, subject, issue (under discussion)	6
主题	zhǔtí	n.	theme, subject	4
专题	zhuāntí	n.	specific topic (addressed by a book, lecture, TV program etc), article, report or program etc on a specific topic	3

颜 yán — face, facial appearance 頁 181.9 2

颜色	yánsè	n.	colour, countenance, appearance, facial expression, pigment	2
五颜六色	wǔyánliùsè	phr.	multi-coloured, every colour under the sun (idiom)	4

風 fēng wind 风 182

风	**fēng**		wind, news, style	风 182.0 1
风	fēng	n.	wind, news, style, custom, manner	1
风暴	fēngbào	n.	storm, violent commotion, fig. crisis (e.g. revolution, uprising, financial crisis etc)	6
风度	fēngdù	n.	elegance (for men), elegant demeanour, grace, poise	5
风格	fēnggé	n.	style	4
风光	fēngguāng	n.	scene, view, sight, landscape, to be well-regarded, to be well-off, grand (dialect), impressive (dialect)	5
风景	fēngjǐng	n.	scenery, landscape	4
风俗	fēngsú	n.	social custom	4
风险	fēngxiǎn	n.	risk, hazard	3
台风	táifēng	n.	hurricane, typhoon	5
暴风雨	bàofēngyǔ	n.	rainstorm, storm, tempest	6
一路顺风	yīlùshùnfēng	vb.	have a good trip (idiom)	2

食 shí eat 饣食 184

食	**shí**		to eat, food	食 184.0 2
食品	shípǐn	n.	foodstuff, food, provisions	3
食堂	shítáng	n.	dining hall	4
食物	shíwù	n.	food	2
食欲	shíyù	n.	appetite	6
粮食	- liángshi	n.	foodstuff, cereals	4
零食	língshí	n.	between-meal nibbles, snacks	4
美食	měishí	n.	culinary delicacy, fine food, gourmet food	3
饮食	yǐnshí	n.	food and drink, diet	5
饭	**fàn**		cooked rice, meal	食 184.4 1
饭	fàn	n.	cooked rice, meal	1
饭店	fàndiàn	n.	restaurant, hotel	1
饭馆	fànguǎn	n.	restaurant	2
吃饭	chīfàn	vb.	to have a meal, to eat, to make a living	1
盒饭	héfàn	n.	meal in a partitioned box	5
米饭	mǐfàn	n.	(cooked) rice	1
晚饭	wǎnfàn	n.	evening meal, dinner, supper	1
午饭	wǔfàn	n.	lunch	1
早饭	zǎofàn	n.	breakfast	1
做饭	zuò fàn	vb.	to prepare a meal, to cook	2
电饭锅	diànfànguō	n.	electric rice cooker	5
饮	**yǐn**		to drink	食 184.4 5
饮料	yǐnliào	n.	drink, beverage	5
饮食	yǐnshí	n.	food and drink, diet	5
餐饮	cānyǐn	n.	food and beverage, catering, repast	5

饱	**bǎo**		to eat till full, satisfied	食 184.5	2
饱	bǎo	vb.	to eat till full, satisfied		2
饰	**shì**		decoration, ornament	食 184.5	5
装饰	zhuāngshì	vb.	to decorate, decoration, decorative, ornamental		5
饼	**bǐng**		round flat cake, cookie	食 184.6	5
饼	bǐng	n.	round flat cake, cookie, cake, pastry		5
饼干	bǐnggān	n.	biscuit, cracker, cookie		5
月饼	yuèbǐng	n.	mooncake (esp. for the Mid-Autumn Festival)		5
饺	**jiǎo**		dumpling	食 184.6	2
饺子	jiǎozi	n.	dumpling, pot-sticker (type of dumpling)		2
餐	**cān**		meal, to eat	食 184.7	
餐	cān	n.	meal, to eat, m.w. for meals		6
餐馆	cānguǎn	n.	restaurant		5
餐厅	cāntīng	n.	dining hall, dining room, restaurant		5
餐饮	cānyǐn	n.	food and beverage, catering, repast		5
快餐	kuàicān	n.	fast food, snack, quick meal		2
套餐	tàocān	n.	set meal, product or service package (e.g. for a cell phone subscription)		4
晚餐	wǎncān	n.	evening meal, dinner		2
午餐	wǔcān	n.	lunch, luncheon		2
西餐	xīcān	n.	Western-style food		2
早餐	zǎocān	n.	breakfast		2
中餐	zhōngcān	n.	lunch, Chinese meal, Chinese food		2
饿	**è**		to be hungry	食 184.7	1
饿	è	vb.	to be hungry, hungry, to starve (sb)		1
馆	**guǎn**		building, shop	食 184.8	1
宾馆	bīnguǎn	n.	guesthouse, lodge, hotel		5
餐馆	cānguǎn	n.	restaurant		5
场馆	chǎngguǎn	n.	sporting venue, arena		6
饭馆	fànguǎn	n.	restaurant		2
旅馆	lǚguǎn	n.	hotel		3
博物馆	bówùguǎn	n.	museum		5
大使馆	dàshǐguǎn	n.	embassy		3
体育馆	tǐyùguǎn	n.	gym, gymnasium, stadium		2
图书馆	túshūguǎn	n.	library		1
馒	**mán**		steamed bread	食 184.11	6
馒头	- mántou	n.	steamed roll, steamed bun, steamed bread		6

首 shǒu head 185

首	**shǒu**		m.w. for poems, head, first	首 185.0	3
首	shǒu	+ m.w.	m.w. for poems, songs etc		4
首	shǒu	+ n.	head, chief, first (occasion, thing etc)		6

首次	shǒucì	n.	first, first time, for the first time		6
首都	• shǒudū	n.	capital (city)		3
首脑	shǒunǎo	n.	head (of state), summit (meeting), leader		6
首席	shǒuxí	n.	chief (representative, correspondent etc)		6
首先	shǒuxiān	conj.	first (of all), in the first place		3
首相	• shǒuxiàng	n.	prime minister (of Japan or UK etc)		6

香 xiāng fragrant 186

香	xiāng		fragrant, sweet smelling	香 186.0	3
香	xiāng	adj.	fragrant, (opp. 臭 chòu: smelly), sweet smelling, aromatic, savoury or appetizing, (to eat) with relish, (of sleep) sound, perfume or spice, joss or incense stick		3
香肠	xiāngcháng	n.	sausage		5
香蕉	xiāngjiāo	n.	banana		3

馬 mǎ horse 马 187

马	mǎ		horse	馬 187.0	1
马	mǎ	n.	horse, surname Ma		3
马车	mǎchē	n.	cart, chariot, carriage, buggy		6
马路	mǎlù	n.	street, road		1
马上	mǎshàng	adv.	at once, right away, immediately, on horseback (i.e. by military force)		1
驾	jià		to harness, to drive	馬 187.5	5
驾驶	jiàshǐ	vb.	to pilot (ship, airplane etc), to drive		5
驾照	jiàzhào	n.	driver's license		5
驶	shǐ		to sail, to drive	馬 187.5	5
驾驶	jiàshǐ	vb.	to pilot (ship, airplane etc), to drive		5
行驶	xíngshǐ	vb.	to travel along a route (of vehicles etc)		5
驻	zhù		to halt, to stay	馬 187.5	6
驻	zhù	vb.	to halt, to stay, to be stationed (of troops, diplomats etc)		6
骄	jiāo		proud, arrogant	馬 187.6	6
骄傲	jiāo'ào	adj.	proud, arrogance, conceited, proud of sth		6
验	yàn		to test, to examine	馬 187.7	3
检验	jiǎnyàn	vb.	to inspect, to examine, to test		5
经验	jīngyàn	n.	experience, to experience		3
考验	kǎoyàn	vb.	to test, to put to the test, trial, ordeal		3
实验	shíyàn	n.	experiment, test		3
试验	shìyàn	n.	experiment, test		3
体验	tǐyàn	vb.	to experience for oneself		3
实验室	shíyànshì	n.	laboratory		3

骑	qí		to ride (horse, bicycle)	馬 187.8	2
骑	qí	vb.	to ride (horse, bicycle)		2
骑车	qíchē	vb.	to ride a bike (motorbike or bicycle)		2

骗	piàn		to cheat, to swindle	馬 187.9	5
骗	piàn	vb.	to cheat, to swindle, to deceive, to get on (a horse etc) by swinging one leg over		5
骗子	piànzi	n.	swindler, a cheat		5

骨 gǔ bone 188

骨	gǔ		bone, skeleton, frame	骨 188.0	4
骨头	- gǔtou	n.	bone		4

高 gāo tall 189

高	gāo		high, tall	高 189.0	1
高	gāo	adj.	high, (opp. 低 dī: low), tall, above average loud, surname Gao		1
高层	gāocéng	adj.	high level, high class		6
高潮	gāocháo	n.	high tide, high water, upsurge, climax, orgasm, chorus		4
高大	gāodà	adj.	tall, lofty		5
高档	gāodàng	adj.	superior quality, high grade, top grade		6
高等	gāoděng	adj.	high-level, higher (animals, education etc), advanced (math etc)		6
高度	gāodù	n.	height, altitude, elevation, high degree, highly		5
高峰	gāofēng	n.	peak, summit, height		6
高级	gāojí	adj.	high level, high grade, advanced, high-ranking		2
高价	gāojià	n.	high price		4
高考	gāokǎo	n.	college entrance exam		6
高尚	gāoshàng	adj.	noble, lofty, refined, exquisite		4
高手	gāoshǒu	n.	expert, past master, dab hand		6
高速	gāosù	n.	high speed		3
高铁	gāotiě	n.	high speed rail		4
高温	gāowēn	n.	high temperature		5
高兴	gāoxìng	adj.	happy, glad, willing (to do sth), in a cheerful mood		1
高于	gāoyú	adv.	greater than, to exceed		5
高原	gāoyuán	n.	plateau		5
高中	gāozhōng	n.	senior high school		2
高跟鞋	gāogēnxié	n.	high-heeled shoes		5
高科技	gāokējì	n.	high tech, high technology		6
高速公路	gāosù gōnglù	n.	expressway, highway, freeway		3
身高	shēngāo	n.	(a person's) height		4
升高	shēnggāo	vb.	to raise, to ascend		5
提高	tígāo	vb.	to raise, to increase, to improve		2
跳高	tiàogāo	n.	high jump (athletics)		3

鬼 guǐ — ghost — 194

鬼	**guǐ**		ghost, demon	鬼 194.0 5
鬼	guǐ	n.	ghost, demon, terrible, damnable, clever, sly, crafty, (suffix for sb with a certain vice or addiction etc), one of the 28 constellations	5
酒鬼	jiǔguǐ	n.	drunkard	5

魚 yú — fish — 鱼 195

鱼	**yú**		fish	魚 195.0 2
鱼	yú	n.	fish, surname Yu	2
鲜	**xiān**		fresh, bright	魚 195.6 4
鲜	xiān	adj.	fresh, bright, delicious, delicacy	4
鲜花	xiānhuā	n.	flower, fresh flowers	4
鲜明	xiānmíng	adj.	bright, clear-cut, distinct	4
鲜艳	xiānyàn	adj.	bright-coloured, gaily coloured	5
海鲜	hǎixiān	n.	seafood	4
新鲜	xīnxiān	adj.	fresh (experience, food etc), freshness, novel, uncommon	4

鳥 niǎo — bird — 鸟 196

鸟	**niǎo**		bird	鳥 196.0 2
鸟	niǎo	n.	bird	2
鸡	**jī**		chicken	鳥 196.2 1
鸡	jī	n.	chicken	2
鸡蛋	jīdàn	n.	(chicken) egg, hen's egg	1
公鸡	gōngjī	n.	cock, rooster	6
母鸡	mǔjī	n.	hen, don't know (humorous slang mimicking Cantonese 唔知)	6
鸭	**yā**		duck	鳥 196.5 5
鸭子	yāzi	n.	duck	5
烤鸭	kǎoyā	n.	roast duck	5

麥 mài — wheat — 麦 199

麦	**mài**		wheat, barley, oats	麥 199.0 6
小麦	xiǎomài	n.	wheat	6

麻 má — hemp — 200

麻	**má**		hemp, jute, flax, sesame	麻 200.0 3
麻烦	- máfan	adj.	inconvenient, troublesome, annoying, to trouble or bother sb, to put sb to trouble	3

黃	**huáng**	**yellow**		**201**
黃	**huáng**	yellow	黃 201.0	2
黃	huáng	*adj.* yellow, surname Huang		2
黃瓜	huángguā	*n.* cucumber		4
黃金	huángjīn	*adj.* gold, golden (opportunity), prime (time)		4
黃色	huángsè	*n.* yellow (colour), decadent		2

黑	**hēi**	**black**		**203**
黑	**hēi**	black, dark	黑 203.0	2
黑	hēi	*adj.* black, (opp. 白 bái: white), dark, sinister, secret, illegal, Heilongjiang province (abbreviation)		2
黑暗	hēi'àn	*adj.* dark, darkly, darkness		4
黑板	hēibǎn	*n.* blackboard		2
黑色	hēisè	*n.* black (colour)		2
黑夜	hēiyè	*n.* night		6
默	**mò**	silent, quiet	黑 203.4	4
默默	mòmò	*adv.* in silence, not speaking		4
沉默	chénmò	*adj.* taciturn, uncommunicative, silent		4
幽默	yōumò	*n.* (loanword) humour, humorous		5

鼓	**gǔ**	**drum**		**207**
鼓	**gǔ**	drum, to drum	鼓 207.0	5
鼓	gǔ	*n.* drum, to drum, to strike, to rouse		5
鼓掌	gǔ zhǎng	*vb.* to applaud, to clap		5
鼓励	gǔlì	*vb.* to encourage		5

鼠	**shǔ**	**rat**		**208**
鼠	**shǔ**	rat, mouse	鼠 208.0	5
鼠	shǔ	*n.* rat, mouse		5
鼠标	shǔbiāo	*n.* mouse (computing)		5

鼻	**bí**	**nose**		**209**
鼻	**bí**	nose	鼻 209.0	5
鼻子	bízi	*n.* nose		5

齊	qí		even	齐 210
齐	qí		neat, even	齊 210.0 3
齐	qí	adj.	neat, even, level with, identical, simultaneous, all together, to even sth out, surname Qi	3
齐全	qíquán	adj.	complete, comprehensive	5
一齐	yīqí	adv.	at the same time, simultaneously	6
整齐	zhěngqí	adj.	orderly, neat, even, tidy	3

齒	chǐ		tooth	齿 211
龄	líng		age, years	齒 211.5 5
年龄	niánlíng	n.	(a person's) age	5

龍	lóng		dragon	龙 212
龙	lóng		dragon	龍 212.0 3
龙	lóng	n.	dragon, imperial, surname Long	3

Pinyin Index

- Four columns of characters per page with Chinese, Pinyin and Radical Code.
- Entries ordered alphabetically by Pinyin. **Red-Brown** type shows Duo Yin Zi characters.
- Radical Code on right (e.g. 一 1.0) shows radical and extra strokes needed to write character.
- Use the Radical Code to then look up the character in the Main Entries section.
- Useful for when you know the Pinyin already.

子	Pinyin	Rad. Code	子	Pinyin	Rad. Code	子	Pinyin	Rad. Code	子	Pinyin	Rad. Code
阿	ā	阜 170.5	榜	bǎng	木 75.10	闭	bì	門 169.3	踩	cǎi	足 157.8
啊	a	口 30.8	傍	bàng	人 9.10	编	biān	糸 120.9	采	cǎi	采 165.1
挨	āi	手 64.7	棒	bàng	木 75.8	边	biān	辶 162.2	菜	cài	艹 140.8
挨	ái	手 64.7	包	bāo	勹 20.3	扁	biǎn	戶 63.5	参	cān	厶 28.6
矮	ǎi	矢 111.8	胞	bāo	肉 130.5	便	biàn	人 9.7	餐	cān	食 184.7
爱	ài	爪 87.6	薄	báo	艹 140.13	变	biàn	又 29.6	残	cán	歹 78.5
碍	ài	石 112.8	保	bǎo	人 9.7	辩	biàn	辛 160.9	惨	cǎn	心 61.8
安	ān	宀 40.3	宝	bǎo	宀 40.5	遍	biàn	辶 162.9	仓	cāng	人 9.2
岸	àn	山 46.5	饱	bǎo	食 184.5	标	biāo	木 75.5	藏	cáng	艹 140.14
按	àn	手 64.6	报	bào	手 64.4	表	biǎo	衣 145.3	操	cāo	手 64.13
暗	àn	日 72.9	抱	bào	手 64.5	别	bié	刀 18.5	草	cǎo	艹 140.6
案	àn	木 75.6	暴	bào	日 72.11	宾	bīn	宀 40.7	侧	cè	人 9.6
傲	ào	人 9.11	爆	bào	火 86.15	兵	bīng	八 12.5	册	cè	冂 13.3
八	bā	八 12.0	悲	bēi	心 61.8	冰	bīng	冫 15.4	厕	cè	厂 27.6
吧	bā	口 30.4	杯	bēi	木 75.4	饼	bǐng	食 184.6	测	cè	水 85.6
巴	bā	己 49.1	背	bēi	肉 130.5	并	bìng	干 51.5	策	cè	竹 118.6
拔	bá	手 64.5	北	běi	匕 21.3	病	bìng	广 104.5	层	céng	尸 44.4
把	bǎ	手 64.4	倍	bèi	人 9.8	拨	bō	手 64.5	曾	céng	日 73.8
爸	bà	父 88.4	备	bèi	夊 34.5	播	bō	手 64.12	叉	chā	又 29.1
罢	bà	网 122.5	背	bèi	肉 130.5	波	bō	水 85.5	差	chā	工 48.7
吧	ba	口 30.4	被	bèi	衣 145.5	玻	bō	玉 96.5	插	chā	手 64.9
白	bái	白 106.0	贝	bèi	貝 154.0	博	bó	十 24.10	察	chá	宀 40.11
摆	bǎi	手 64.10	辈	bèi	非 175.4	薄	bó	艹 140.13	查	chá	木 75.5
百	bǎi	白 106.1	奔	bēn	大 37.6	捕	bǔ	手 64.7	茶	chá	艹 140.6
拜	bài	手 64.5	本	běn	木 75.1	补	bǔ	衣 145.2	差	chà	工 48.7
败	bài	貝 154.4	笨	bèn	竹 118.5	不	bù	一 1.3	差	chāi	工 48.7
搬	bān	手 64.10	逼	bī	辶 162.9	布	bù	巾 50.2	拆	chāi	手 64.5
班	bān	玉 96.6	鼻	bí	鼻 209.0	步	bù	止 77.3	柴	chái	木 75.5
般	bān	舟 137.4	彼	bǐ	彳 60.5	部	bù	邑 163.8	产	chǎn	立 117.1
板	bǎn	木 75.4	比	bǐ	比 81.0	擦	cā	手 64.14	昌	chāng	日 72.4
版	bǎn	片 91.4	笔	bǐ	竹 118.4	猜	cāi	犬 94.8	偿	cháng	人 9.9
伴	bàn	人 9.5	壁	bì	土 32.13	才	cái	手 64.0	尝	cháng	小 42.6
办	bàn	力 19.2	币	bì	巾 50.1	材	cái	木 75.3	常	cháng	巾 50.8
半	bàn	十 24.3	必	bì	心 61.1	裁	cái	衣 145.6	肠	cháng	肉 130.3
扮	bàn	手 64.4	毕	bì	比 81.2	财	cái	貝 154.3	长	cháng	長 168.0
帮	bāng	巾 50.7	避	bì	辶 162.13	彩	cǎi	彡 59.8	厂	chǎng	厂 27.0

场	chǎng	土 32.3	处	chù	夂 34.2	弹	dàn	弓 57.8	顶	dǐng	頁 181.2
倡	chàng	人 9.8	触	chù	角 148.6	旦	dàn	日 72.1	定	dìng	宀 40.5
唱	chàng	口 30.8	穿	chuān	穴 116.4	淡	dàn	水 85.8	订	dìng	言 149.2
畅	chàng	日 72.4	传	chuán	人 9.4	蛋	dàn	虫 142.5	丢	diū	一 1.5
抄	chāo	手 64.4	船	chuán	舟 137.5	诞	dàn	言 149.8	东	dōng	一 1.4
超	chāo	走 156.5	串	chuàn	丨 2.6	当	dāng	小 42.3	冬	dōng	冫 15.3
朝	cháo	月 74.8	窗	chuāng	穴 116.7	党	dǎng	儿 10.8	懂	dǒng	心 61.13
潮	cháo	水 85.12	床	chuáng	广 53.4	挡	dǎng	手 64.6	冻	dòng	冫 15.5
吵	chǎo	口 30.4	闯	chuǎng	門 169.3	当	dàng	小 42.3	动	dòng	力 19.4
炒	chǎo	火 86.4	创	chuàng	刀 18.4	档	dàng	木 75.6	洞	dòng	水 85.6
车	chē	車 159.0	吹	chuī	口 30.4	刀	dāo	刀 18.0	都	dōu	邑 163.9
彻	chè	彳 60.4	春	chūn	日 72.5	倒	dǎo	人 9.8	斗	dòu	斗 68.0
撤	chè	手 64.12	纯	chún	糸 120.4	导	dǎo	寸 41.3	豆	dòu	豆 151.0
晨	chén	日 72.7	辞	cí	舌 135.7	岛	dǎo	山 46.4	督	dū	目 109.8
沉	chén	水 85.4	词	cí	言 149.5	蹈	dǎo	足 157.10	都	dū	邑 163.9
衬	chèn	衣 145.3	此	cǐ	止 77.2	倒	dào	人 9.8	毒	dú	毋 80.4
撑	chēng	手 64.12	刺	cì	刀 18.6	到	dào	刀 18.6	独	dú	犬 94.6
称	chēng	禾 115.5	次	cì	欠 76.2	盗	dào	皿 108.6	读	dú	言 149.8
乘	chéng	丿 4.9	聪	cōng	耳 128.9	道	dào	辵 162.9	堵	dǔ	土 32.9
城	chéng	土 32.7	从	cóng	人 9.2	得	dé	彳 60.8	赌	dǔ	貝 154.8
成	chéng	戈 62.3	粗	cū	米 119.5	德	dé	彳 60.12	度	dù	广 53.6
承	chéng	手 64.4	促	cù	人 9.7	地	de	土 32.3	渡	dù	水 85.9
程	chéng	禾 115.7	醋	cù	酉 164.8	得	de	彳 60.8	肚	dù	肉 130.3
诚	chéng	言 149.6	脆	cuì	肉 130.6	的	de	白 106.3	端	duān	立 117.9
吃	chī	口 30.3	村	cūn	木 75.3	得	děi	彳 60.8	短	duǎn	矢 111.7
持	chí	手 64.6	存	cún	子 39.3	灯	dēng	火 86.2	断	duàn	斤 69.7
池	chí	水 85.3	寸	cùn	寸 41.0	登	dēng	癶 105.7	段	duàn	殳 79.5
迟	chí	辵 162.4	措	cuò	手 64.8	等	děng	竹 118.6	锻	duàn	金 167.9
尺	chǐ	尸 44.1	错	cuò	金 167.8	低	dī	人 9.5	堆	duī	土 32.8
充	chōng	儿 10.4	搭	dā	手 64.10	滴	dī	水 85.11	对	duì	寸 41.2
冲	chōng	冫 15.4	答	dā	竹 118.6	的	dí	白 106.3	队	duì	阜 170.2
崇	chóng	山 46.8	打	dá	手 64.2	敌	dí	舌 135.4	吨	dūn	口 30.4
虫	chóng	虫 142.0	答	dá	竹 118.6	底	dǐ	广 53.5	蹲	dūn	足 157.12
重	chóng	里 166.2	达	dá	辵 162.3	抵	dǐ	手 64.5	盾	dùn	目 109.4
宠	chǒng	宀 40.5	打	dǎ	手 64.2	地	dì	土 32.3	顿	dùn	頁 181.4
冲	chòng	冫 15.4	大	dà	大 37.0	帝	dì	巾 50.6	多	duō	夕 36.3
抽	chōu	手 64.5	呆	dāi	口 30.4	弟	dì	弓 57.4	夺	duó	大 37.3
愁	chóu	心 61.9	待	dāi	彳 60.6	的	dì	白 106.3	朵	duǒ	木 75.2
丑	chǒu	一 1.3	代	dài	人 9.3	第	dì	竹 118.5	躲	duǒ	身 158.6
臭	chòu	自 132.4	带	dài	巾 50.6	递	dì	辵 162.7	额	é	頁 181.9
出	chū	凵 17.3	待	dài	彳 60.6	典	diǎn	八 12.6	恶	è	心 61.6
初	chū	刀 18.5	戴	dài	戈 62.14	点	diǎn	火 86.5	饿	è	食 184.7
厨	chú	厂 27.10	袋	dài	衣 145.5	店	diàn	广 53.5	恩	ēn	心 61.6
除	chú	阜 170.7	贷	dài	貝 154.5	电	diàn	日 73.1	儿	ér	儿 10.0
储	chǔ	人 9.10	单	dān	八 12.6	吊	diào	口 30.3	而	ér	而 126.0
处	chǔ	夂 34.2	担	dān	手 64.5	掉	diào	手 64.8	尔	ěr	小 42.2
楚	chǔ	木 75.9	胆	dǎn	肉 130.5	调	diào	言 149.8	耳	ěr	耳 128.0
础	chǔ	石 112.5	但	dàn	人 9.5	跌	diē	足 157.5	二	èr	二 7.0

发	fā	又 29.3	佛	fú	人 9.5	根	gēn	木 75.6	鬼	guǐ	鬼 194.0
乏	fá	丿 4.4	幅	fú	巾 50.9	跟	gēn	足 157.6	柜	guì	木 75.5
罚	fá	网 122.4	扶	fú	手 64.4	更	gēng	日 73.3	贵	guì	贝 154.5
法	fǎ	水 85.5	服	fú	月 74.4	更	gèng	日 73.3	跪	guì	足 157.6
發	fà	又 29.3	浮	fú	水 85.7	供	gōng	人 9.6	滚	gǔn	水 85.11
番	fān	田 102.7	福	fú	示 113.9	公	gōng	八 12.2	锅	guō	金 167.7
翻	fān	羽 124.12	符	fú	竹 118.5	功	gōng	力 19.3	国	guó	囗 31.5
凡	fán	几 16.1	府	fǔ	广 53.5	宫	gōng	宀 40.6	果	guǒ	木 75.4
烦	fán	火 86.6	腐	fǔ	肉 130.8	工	gōng	工 48.0	裹	guǒ	衣 145.8
繁	fán	糸 120.11	辅	fǔ	车 159.7	攻	gōng	攴 66.3	过	guò	辶 162.3
反	fǎn	又 29.2	付	fù	人 9.3	巩	gǒng	工 48.3	哈	hā	口 30.6
返	fǎn	辶 162.4	傅	fù	人 9.10	共	gòng	八 12.4	孩	hái	子 39.6
泛	fàn	水 85.5	副	fù	刀 18.9	贡	gòng	贝 154.3	还	hái	辶 162.4
犯	fàn	犬 94.2	复	fù	夂 35.6	沟	gōu	水 85.4	海	hǎi	水 85.7
范	fàn	艸 140.5	妇	fù	女 38.3	狗	gǒu	犬 94.5	害	hài	宀 40.7
饭	fàn	食 184.4	富	fù	宀 40.9	够	gòu	夕 36.8	含	hán	口 30.4
方	fāng	方 70.0	父	fù	父 88.0	构	gòu	木 75.4	寒	hán	宀 40.9
房	fáng	戶 63.4	负	fù	贝 154.2	购	gòu	贝 154.4	喊	hǎn	口 30.9
防	fáng	阜 170.4	附	fù	阜 170.5	估	gū	人 9.5	憾	hàn	心 61.13
仿	fǎng	人 9.4	该	gāi	言 149.6	姑	gū	女 38.5	汉	hàn	水 85.2
访	fǎng	言 149.4	改	gǎi	攴 66.3	孤	gū	子 39.5	汗	hàn	水 85.3
放	fàng	攴 66.4	概	gài	木 75.9	古	gǔ	口 30.2	航	háng	舟 137.4
飞	fēi	乙 5.2	盖	gài	皿 108.6	股	gǔ	肉 130.4	行	háng	行 144.0
啡	fēi	口 30.8	干	gān	干 51.0	谷	gǔ	谷 150.0	毫	háo	毛 82.7
非	fēi	非 175.0	杆	gān	木 75.3	骨	gǔ	骨 188.0	豪	háo	豕 152.7
肥	féi	肉 130.4	肝	gān	肉 130.3	鼓	gǔ	鼓 207.0	好	hǎo	女 38.3
废	fèi	广 53.5	感	gǎn	心 61.9	固	gù	囗 31.5	号	hào	口 30.2
肺	fèi	肉 130.4	敢	gǎn	攴 66.8	故	gù	攴 66.5	好	hào	女 38.3
费	fèi	贝 154.5	赶	gǎn	走 156.3	顾	gù	頁 181.4	耗	hào	耒 127.4
分	fēn	刀 18.2	干	gàn	干 51.0	刮	guā	刀 18.6	喝	hē	口 30.9
氛	fēn	气 84.4	刚	gāng	刀 18.4	瓜	guā	瓜 97.0	何	hé	人 9.5
纷	fēn	糸 120.4	纲	gāng	糸 120.4	挂	guà	手 64.6	合	hé	口 30.3
粉	fěn	米 119.4	钢	gāng	金 167.4	拐	guǎi	手 64.5	和	hé	口 30.5
份	fèn	人 9.4	岗	gǎng	山 46.4	怪	guài	心 61.5	核	hé	木 75.6
分	fèn	刀 18.2	港	gǎng	水 85.9	关	guān	八 12.4	河	hé	水 85.5
奋	fèn	大 37.5	糕	gāo	米 119.10	冠	guān	冖 14.7	盒	hé	皿 108.6
愤	fèn	心 61.9	高	gāo	高 189.0	官	guān	宀 40.5	贺	hè	贝 154.5
丰	fēng	丨 2.3	搞	gǎo	手 64.10	观	guān	見 147.2	黑	hēi	黑 203.0
封	fēng	寸 41.6	稿	gǎo	禾 115.10	管	guǎn	竹 118.8	很	hěn	彳 60.6
峰	fēng	山 46.7	告	gào	口 30.4	馆	guǎn	食 184.8	狠	hěn	犬 94.6
疯	fēng	疒 104.4	哥	gē	口 30.7	惯	guàn	心 61.8	恨	hèn	心 61.6
锋	fēng	金 167.7	歌	gē	欠 76.10	贯	guàn	贝 154.4	横	héng	木 75.11
风	fēng	風 182.0	格	gé	木 75.6	光	guāng	儿 10.4	衡	héng	行 144.10
奉	fèng	大 37.5	隔	gé	阜 170.10	广	guǎng	广 53.0	宏	hóng	宀 40.4
佛	fó	人 9.5	革	gé	革 177.0	逛	guàng	辶 162.7	洪	hóng	水 85.6
否	fǒu	口 30.4	个	gè	丨 2.2	归	guī	彐 58.2	红	hóng	糸 120.3
夫	fū	大 37.1	各	gè	口 30.3	规	guī	見 147.4	猴	hóu	犬 94.9
肤	fū	肉 130.4	给	gěi	糸 120.6	轨	guǐ	车 159.2	候	hòu	人 9.8

厚	hòu	厂 27.7	活	huó	水 85.6	甲	jiǎ	田 102.0	接	jiē	手 64.8
后	hòu	口 30.3	伙	huǒ	人 9.4	价	jià	人 9.4	揭	jiē	手 64.9
乎	hū	丿 4.4	火	huǒ	火 86.0	假	jià	人 9.9	结	jiē	糸 120.6
呼	hū	口 30.5	或	huò	戈 62.4	架	jià	木 75.5	街	jiē	行 144.6
忽	hū	心 61.4	获	huò	艹 140.7	驾	jià	马 187.5	阶	jiē	阜 170.4
壶	hú	士 33.7	货	huò	贝 154.4	艰	jiān	又 29.6	截	jié	戈 62.10
湖	hú	水 85.9	和	huo	口 30.5	坚	jiān	土 32.4	杰	jié	木 75.4
糊	hú	米 119.9	击	jī	凵 17.3	尖	jiān	小 42.3	洁	jié	水 85.6
胡	hú	肉 130.5	圾	jī	土 32.4	监	jiān	皿 108.5	结	jié	糸 120.6
虎	hǔ	虍 141.2	基	jī	土 32.8	肩	jiān	肉 130.4	节	jié	艹 140.2
互	hù	二 7.2	机	jī	木 75.2	间	jiān	门 169.4	姐	jiě	女 38.5
户	hù	戶 63.0	激	jī	水 85.13	减	jiǎn	冫 15.9	解	jiě	角 148.6
护	hù	手 64.4	积	jī	禾 115.5	剪	jiǎn	刀 18.9	介	jiè	人 9.2
花	huā	艹 140.4	绩	jī	糸 120.8	捡	jiǎn	手 64.7	借	jiè	人 9.8
划	huá	刀 18.4	肌	jī	肉 130.2	检	jiǎn	木 75.7	届	jiè	尸 44.5
华	huá	十 24.4	鸡	jī	鸟 196.2	简	jiǎn	竹 118.7	戒	jiè	戈 62.3
滑	huá	水 85.10	即	jí	卩 26.5	件	jiàn	人 9.4	界	jiè	田 102.4
划	huà	刀 18.4	及	jí	又 29.2	健	jiàn	人 9.9	今	jīn	人 9.2
化	huà	匕 21.2	吉	jí	口 30.3	剑	jiàn	刀 18.7	巾	jīn	巾 50.0
画	huà	田 102.3	急	jí	心 61.5	建	jiàn	廴 54.6	斤	jīn	斤 69.0
话	huà	言 149.6	极	jí	木 75.3	渐	jiàn	水 85.8	金	jīn	金 167.0
怀	huái	心 61.4	疾	jí	疒 104.5	箭	jiàn	竹 118.9	仅	jǐn	人 9.2
坏	huài	土 32.4	籍	jí	竹 118.14	舰	jiàn	舟 137.4	尽	jǐn	尸 44.3
欢	huān	欠 76.2	级	jí	糸 120.3	见	jiàn	見 147.0	紧	jǐn	糸 120.4
环	huán	玉 96.4	辑	jí	車 159.9	践	jiàn	足 157.5	劲	jìn	力 19.5
还	huán	辶 162.4	集	jí	隹 172.4	鉴	jiàn	金 167.5	禁	jìn	示 113.8
缓	huǎn	糸 120.9	几	jǐ	几 16.0	键	jiàn	金 167.8	近	jìn	辶 162.4
幻	huàn	幺 52.1	己	jǐ	己 49.0	间	jiàn	门 169.4	进	jìn	辶 162.4
患	huàn	心 61.7	挤	jǐ	手 64.6	江	jiāng	水 85.3	京	jīng	亠 8.6
换	huàn	手 64.7	给	jǐ	糸 120.6	将	jiāng	爿 90.6	惊	jīng	心 61.8
慌	huāng	心 61.10	季	jì	子 39.5	奖	jiǎng	大 37.6	睛	jīng	目 109.8
皇	huáng	白 106.4	寄	jì	宀 40.8	讲	jiǎng	言 149.4	精	jīng	米 119.8
黄	huáng	黄 201.0	技	jì	手 64.4	酱	jiàng	酉 164.6	经	jīng	糸 120.5
辉	huī	小 42.9	既	jì	无 71.5	降	jiàng	阜 170.6	井	jǐng	二 7.2
恢	huī	心 61.6	济	jì	水 85.6	交	jiāo	亠 8.4	景	jǐng	日 72.8
挥	huī	手 64.6	系	jì	糸 120.1	教	jiāo	攴 66.7	警	jǐng	言 149.13
灰	huī	火 86.2	纪	jì	糸 120.3	焦	jiāo	火 86.8	净	jìng	冫 15.6
回	huí	口 31.3	继	jì	糸 120.7	胶	jiāo	肉 130.6	境	jìng	土 32.11
悔	huǐ	心 61.7	计	jì	言 149.2	蕉	jiāo	艹 140.12	径	jìng	彳 60.5
毁	huǐ	殳 79.9	记	jì	言 149.3	郊	jiāo	邑 163.6	敬	jìng	攴 66.9
会	huì	人 9.4	际	jì	阜 170.5	骄	jiāo	马 187.6	竞	jìng	立 117.5
惠	huì	心 61.8	夹	jiā	一 1.5	脚	jiǎo	肉 130.7	竟	jìng	立 117.6
慧	huì	心 61.11	佳	jiā	人 9.6	角	jiǎo	角 148.0	镜	jìng	金 167.11
汇	huì	水 85.2	加	jiā	力 19.3	饺	jiǎo	食 184.6	静	jìng	青 174.6
绘	huì	糸 120.6	嘉	jiā	口 30.11	叫	jiào	口 30.2	究	jiū	穴 116.2
婚	hūn	女 38.8	家	jiā	宀 40.7	教	jiào	攴 66.7	纠	jiū	糸 120.2
昏	hūn	日 72.4	茄	qié	艹 140.5	觉	jiào	見 147.5	久	jiǔ	丿 4.2
混	hùn	水 85.8	假	jiǎ	人 9.9	较	jiào	車 159.6	九	jiǔ	乙 5.1

酒	jiǔ	酉 164.3	空	kōng	穴 116.3	类	lèi	大 37.6	邻	lín	邑 163.5
就	jiù	尤 43.9	恐	kǒng	心 61.6	泪	lèi	水 85.5	灵	líng	彐 58.4
救	jiù	攴 66.7	控	kòng	手 64.8	累	lèi	糸 120.5	铃	líng	金 167.5
旧	jiù	日 72.1	空	kòng	穴 116.3	冷	lěng	冫 15.5	零	líng	雨 173.5
居	jū	尸 44.5	口	kǒu	口 30.0	厘	lí	厂 27.7	龄	líng	齒 211.5
局	jú	尸 44.4	扣	kòu	手 64.3	梨	lí	木 75.7	领	lǐng	頁 181.5
举	jǔ	丶 3.8	哭	kū	口 30.7	璃	lí	玉 96.11	令	lìng	人 9.3
俱	jù	人 9.8	苦	kǔ	艸 140.5	离	lí	肉 114.6	另	lìng	口 30.2
具	jù	八 12.6	库	kù	广 53.4	李	lǐ	木 75.3	流	liú	水 85.6
剧	jù	刀 18.8	裤	kù	衣 145.7	理	lǐ	玉 96.7	留	liú	田 102.5
句	jù	口 30.2	酷	kù	酉 164.7	礼	lǐ	示 113.1	六	liù	八 12.2
巨	jù	工 48.2	跨	kuà	足 157.6	里	lǐ	里 166.0	龙	lóng	龍 212.0
拒	jù	手 64.5	会	kuài	人 9.4	丽	lì	丶 3.7	楼	lóu	木 75.9
据	jù	手 64.8	块	kuài	土 32.4	例	lì	人 9.6	漏	lòu	水 85.11
聚	jù	耳 128.8	快	kuài	心 61.4	利	lì	刀 18.5	露	lòu	雨 173.12
距	jù	足 157.5	筷	kuài	竹 118.7	力	lì	力 19.0	炉	lú	火 86.4
捐	juān	手 64.7	宽	kuān	宀 40.7	励	lì	力 19.5	旅	lǚ	方 70.6
卷	juǎn	卩 26.6	款	kuǎn	欠 76.8	历	lì	厂 27.2	录	lù	彐 58.5
卷	juàn	卩 26.6	狂	kuáng	犬 94.4	厉	lì	厂 27.3	路	lù	足 157.6
决	jué	冫 15.4	况	kuàng	冫 15.5	立	lì	立 117.0	陆	lù	阜 170.5
绝	jué	糸 120.6	矿	kuàng	石 112.3	俩	liǎ	人 9.7	露	lù	雨 173.12
觉	jué	見 147.5	亏	kuī	二 7.1	帘	lián	巾 50.5	律	lǜ	彳 60.6
角	jué	角 148.0	困	kùn	囗 31.4	怜	lián	心 61.5	虑	lǜ	心 61.6
均	jūn	土 32.4	扩	kuò	手 64.6	联	lián	耳 128.6	率	lǜ	玄 95.6
菌	jūn	艸 140.8	括	kuò	手 64.6	连	lián	辵 162.4	绿	lǜ	糸 120.8
军	jūn	车 159.2	阔	kuò	門 169.9	脸	liǎn	肉 130.7	乱	luàn	乙 5.6
咖	kā	口 30.5	垃	lā	土 32.5	恋	liàn	心 61.6	略	lüè	田 102.6
卡	kǎ	卜 25.3	拉	lā	手 64.5	炼	liàn	火 86.5	轮	lún	車 159.4
开	kāi	廾 55.1	落	là	艸 140.9	练	liàn	糸 120.5	论	lùn	言 149.4
刊	kān	刀 18.3	辣	là	辛 160.7	凉	liáng	冫 15.8	逻	luó	辵 162.8
看	kān	目 109.4	啦	la	口 30.8	梁	liáng	木 75.7	络	luò	糸 120.6
看	kàn	目 109.4	来	lái	木 75.3	粮	liáng	米 119.7	落	luò	艸 140.9
康	kāng	广 53.8	赖	lài	貝 154.9	良	liáng	艮 138.1	妈	mā	女 38.3
抗	kàng	手 64.4	栏	lán	木 75.5	量	liáng	里 166.5	麻	má	麻 200.0
烤	kǎo	火 86.6	篮	lán	竹 118.10	两	liǎng	一 1.6	码	mǎ	石 112.3
考	kǎo	老 125.0	蓝	lán	艸 140.10	亮	liàng	亠 8.7	马	mǎ	馬 187.0
靠	kào	非 175.7	懒	lǎn	心 61.13	谅	liàng	言 149.8	骂	mà	口 30.6
棵	kē	木 75.8	览	lǎn	見 147.5	辆	liàng	車 159.7	吗	ma	口 30.3
科	kē	禾 115.4	烂	làn	火 86.5	量	liàng	里 166.5	嘛	ma	口 30.11
颗	kē	頁 181.8	郎	láng	邑 163.6	疗	liáo	广 104.2	埋	mái	土 32.7
咳	ké	口 30.6	朗	lǎng	月 74.7	聊	liáo	耳 128.5	买	mǎi	大 37.3
可	kě	口 30.2	浪	làng	水 85.7	了	liǎo	亅 6.1	卖	mài	十 24.6
渴	kě	水 85.9	劳	láo	力 19.5	料	liào	斗 68.6	麦	mài	麥 199.0
克	kè	儿 10.5	牢	láo	牛 93.3	列	liè	刀 18.4	馒	mán	食 184.11
刻	kè	刀 18.6	老	lǎo	老 125.0	烈	liè	火 86.6	满	mǎn	水 85.10
客	kè	宀 40.6	乐	lè	丿 4.4	裂	liè	衣 145.6	慢	màn	心 61.11
课	kè	言 149.8	了	le	亅 6.1	临	lín	丨 2.8	漫	màn	水 85.11
肯	kěn	肉 130.4	雷	léi	雨 173.5	林	lín	木 75.4	忙	máng	心 61.3

盲	máng	目 109.3	漠	mò	水 85.11	牌	pái	片 91.8	铺	pū	金 167.7
猫	māo	犬 94.9	默	mò	黑 203.4	派	pài	水 85.6	葡	pú	艸 140.9
毛	máo	毛 82.0	谋	móu	言 149.9	盘	pán	皿 108.6	普	pǔ	日 72.8
矛	máo	矛 110.0	某	mǒu	木 75.5	判	pàn	刀 18.5	铺	pù	金 167.7
冒	mào	冂 13.7	母	mǔ	毋 80.1	盼	pàn	目 109.4	七	qī	一 1.1
帽	mào	巾 50.9	墓	mù	土 32.11	旁	páng	方 70.6	妻	qī	女 38.5
貌	mào	豸 153.7	幕	mù	巾 50.11	胖	pàng	肉 130.5	期	qī	月 74.8
贸	mào	贝 154.5	木	mù	木 75.0	跑	pǎo	足 157.5	欺	qī	欠 76.8
么	me	丿 4.2	目	mù	目 109.0	泡	pào	水 85.5	其	qí	八 12.6
媒	méi	女 38.9	拿	ná	手 64.6	炮	pào	火 86.5	奇	qí	大 37.5
梅	méi	木 75.7	哪	nǎ	口 30.7	培	péi	土 32.8	旗	qí	方 70.10
没	méi	水 85.4	纳	nà	糸 120.4	赔	péi	贝 154.8	骑	qí	馬 187.8
煤	méi	火 86.9	那	nà	邑 163.4	陪	péi	阜 170.8	齐	qí	齊 210.0
每	měi	毋 80.3	奶	nǎi	女 38.2	配	pèi	酉 164.3	企	qǐ	人 9.4
美	měi	羊 123.3	奈	nài	大 37.5	喷	pēn	口 30.9	启	qǐ	口 30.4
妹	mèi	女 38.5	耐	nài	而 126.3	盆	pén	皿 108.4	起	qǐ	走 156.3
门	mén	門 169.0	南	nán	十 24.7	朋	péng	月 74.4	器	qì	口 30.13
们	men	人 9.3	难	nán	又 29.8	碰	pèng	石 112.8	弃	qì	廾 55.4
蒙	mēng	艸 140.10	男	nán	田 102.2	批	pī	手 64.4	气	qì	气 84.0
盟	méng	皿 108.8	难	nàn	又 29.8	披	pī	手 64.5	汽	qì	水 85.4
蒙	méng	艸 140.10	脑	nǎo	肉 130.6	啤	pí	口 30.8	恰	qià	心 61.6
猛	měng	犬 94.8	闹	nào	門 169.5	皮	pí	皮 107.0	千	qiān	十 24.1
梦	mèng	木 75.7	呢	ne	口 30.5	脾	pí	肉 130.8	牵	qiān	大 37.6
迷	mí	辶 162.6	内	nèi	入 11.2	匹	pǐ	匚 23.2	签	qiān	竹 118.7
米	mǐ	米 119.0	能	néng	肉 130.5	偏	piān	人 9.9	谦	qiān	言 149.10
密	mì	宀 40.8	泥	ní	水 85.5	篇	piān	竹 118.9	迁	qiān	辶 162.3
秘	mì	禾 115.5	你	nǐ	人 9.5	便	pián	人 9.7	铅	qiān	金 167.5
棉	mián	木 75.8	年	nián	干 51.3	片	piàn	片 91.0	前	qián	刀 18.7
眠	mián	目 109.5	念	niàn	心 61.4	骗	piàn	馬 187.9	潜	qián	水 85.12
免	miǎn	儿 10.5	娘	niáng	女 38.7	漂	piāo	水 85.11	钱	qián	金 167.5
面	miàn	面 176.0	鸟	niǎo	鳥 196.0	票	piào	示 113.6	浅	qiǎn	水 85.5
描	miáo	手 64.9	您	nín	心 61.7	拼	pīn	手 64.6	欠	qiàn	欠 76.0
秒	miǎo	禾 115.4	宁	níng	宀 40.2	贫	pín	贝 154.4	歉	qiàn	欠 76.10
妙	miào	女 38.4	牛	niú	牛 93.0	频	pín	頁 181.7	枪	qiāng	木 75.4
灭	miè	火 86.1	扭	niǔ	手 64.4	品	pǐn	口 30.6	墙	qiáng	土 32.11
民	mín	氏 83.1	农	nóng	冖 14.4	聘	pìn	耳 128.7	强	qiáng	弓 57.9
敏	mǐn	攴 66.7	浓	nóng	水 85.6	凭	píng	几 16.6	强	qiǎng	弓 57.9
名	míng	口 30.3	弄	nòng	廾 55.4	屏	píng	尸 44.6	抢	qiǎng	手 64.4
明	míng	日 72.4	努	nǔ	力 19.5	平	píng	干 51.2	悄	qiāo	心 61.7
命	mìng	口 30.5	怒	nù	心 61.5	瓶	píng	瓦 98.6	敲	qiāo	攴 66.10
摸	mō	手 64.11	暖	nuǎn	日 72.9	苹	píng	艸 140.5	桥	qiáo	木 75.6
摩	mó	手 64.11	诺	nuò	言 149.8	评	píng	言 149.5	瞧	qiáo	目 109.12
模	mó	木 75.11	女	nǚ	女 38.0	坡	pō	土 32.5	巧	qiǎo	工 48.2
磨	mó	石 112.11	偶	ǒu	人 9.9	泼	pō	水 85.5	切	qiē	刀 18.2
膜	mó	肉 130.11	爬	pá	爪 87.4	婆	pó	女 38.8	且	qiě	一 1.4
末	mò	土 32.12	怕	pà	心 61.5	破	pò	石 112.8	切	qiè	刀 18.2
没	mò	木 75.1	拍	pāi	手 64.5	迫	pò	辶 162.5	侵	qīn	人 9.7
没	mò	水 85.4	排	pái	手 64.8	扑	pū	手 64.2	亲	qīn	立 117.4

勤	qín	力 19.11	绒	róng	糸 120.6	涉	shè	水 85.7	视	shì	見 147.4
琴	qín	玉 96.8	荣	róng	艸 140.6	社	shè	示 113.3	试	shì	言 149.6
倾	qīng	人 9.8	融	róng	虫 142.10	设	shè	言 149.4	适	shì	辵 162.6
清	qīng	水 85.8	肉	ròu	肉 130.0	谁	shéi	言 149.8	释	shì	采 165.5
轻	qīng	車 159.5	如	rú	女 38.3	伸	shēn	人 9.5	饰	shì	食 184.5
青	qīng	青 174.0	乳	rǔ	乙 5.7	深	shēn	水 85.8	收	shōu	攴 66.2
情	qíng	心 61.8	入	rù	入 11.0	申	shēn	田 102.0	守	shǒu	宀 40.3
晴	qíng	日 72.8	软	ruǎn	車 159.4	身	shēn	身 158.0	手	shǒu	手 64.0
请	qǐng	言 149.8	润	rùn	水 85.7	什	shén	人 9.2	首	shǒu	首 185.0
庆	qìng	广 53.3	弱	ruò	弓 57.7	甚	shèn	甘 99.4	受	shòu	又 29.6
穷	qióng	穴 116.2	若	ruò	艸 140.5	神	shén	示 113.5	售	shòu	口 30.8
秋	qiū	禾 115.4	洒	sǎ	水 85.6	审	shěn	宀 40.5	寿	shòu	寸 41.4
求	qiú	水 85.2	塞	sāi	土 32.10	升	shēng	十 24.2	授	shòu	手 64.8
球	qiú	玉 96.7	赛	sài	宀 40.11	声	shēng	士 33.4	瘦	shòu	广 104.10
区	qū	匸 23.2	三	sān	一 1.2	牲	shēng	牛 93.5	书	shū	丨 2.3
曲	qū	日 73.2	伞	sǎn	人 9.4	生	shēng	生 100.0	叔	shū	又 29.6
趋	qū	走 156.5	散	sǎn	攴 66.8	省	shěng	目 109.4	殊	shū	歹 78.6
渠	qú	水 85.9	散	sàn	攴 66.8	剩	shèng	刀 18.10	舒	shū	舌 135.6
取	qǔ	又 29.6	丧	sàng	十 24.6	圣	shèng	土 32.2	蔬	shū	艸 140.11
曲	qǔ	日 73.2	扫	sǎo	手 64.3	盛	shèng	皿 108.7	输	shū	車 159.9
去	qù	厶 28.3	色	sè	色 139.0	胜	shèng	肉 130.5	熟	shú	火 86.11
趣	qù	走 156.8	森	sēn	木 75.8	失	shī	大 37.2	属	shǔ	尸 44.9
圈	quān	口 31.8	杀	shā	木 75.2	师	shī	巾 50.3	暑	shǔ	日 72.8
全	quán	入 11.4	沙	shā	水 85.4	施	shī	方 70.5	薯	shǔ	艸 140.14
权	quán	木 75.2	傻	shǎ	人 9.11	湿	shī	水 85.9	鼠	shǔ	鼠 208.0
泉	quán	水 85.5	晒	shài	日 72.6	诗	shī	言 149.6	数	shù	攴 66.9
券	quàn	刀 18.6	山	shān	山 46.0	十	shí	十 24.0	术	shù	木 75.1
劝	quàn	力 19.2	扇	shān	戶 63.6	实	shí	宀 40.5	束	shù	木 75.3
缺	quē	缶 121.4	衫	shān	衣 145.3	拾	shí	手 64.6	树	shù	木 75.5
却	què	卩 26.5	闪	shǎn	門 169.2	时	shí	日 72.3	述	shù	辵 162.5
确	què	石 112.7	善	shàn	口 30.9	石	shí	石 112.0	刷	shuā	刀 18.6
群	qún	羊 123.7	扇	shàn	戶 63.6	识	shí	言 149.5	摔	shuāi	手 64.11
裙	qún	衣 145.7	伤	shāng	人 9.4	食	shí	食 184.0	帅	shuài	巾 50.2
然	rán	火 86.8	商	shāng	口 30.8	使	shǐ	人 9.6	双	shuāng	又 29.2
燃	rán	火 86.12	赏	shǎng	貝 154.8	史	shǐ	口 30.2	爽	shuǎng	爻 89.7
染	rǎn	木 75.5	上	shàng	一 1.2	始	shǐ	女 38.5	谁	shuí	言 149.8
让	ràng	言 149.3	尚	shàng	小 42.5	驶	shǐ	馬 187.5	水	shuǐ	水 85.0
扰	rǎo	手 64.4	烧	shāo	火 86.6	世	shì	一 1.4	睡	shuì	目 109.8
绕	rào	糸 120.6	稍	shāo	禾 115.7	事	shì	亅 6.7	税	shuì	禾 115.7
热	rè	火 86.6	勺	sháo	勹 20.1	似	shì	人 9.5	顺	shùn	頁 181.3
人	rén	人 9.0	少	shǎo	小 42.1	势	shì	力 19.6	说	shuō	言 149.7
忍	rěn	心 61.3	少	shào	小 42.1	士	shì	士 33.0	硕	shuò	石 112.6
任	rèn	人 9.4	绍	shào	糸 120.5	室	shì	宀 40.6	司	sī	口 30.2
认	rèn	言 149.2	舌	shé	舌 135.0	市	shì	巾 50.2	思	sī	心 61.5
扔	rēng	手 64.2	蛇	shé	虫 142.5	式	shì	弋 56.3	私	sī	禾 115.2
仍	réng	人 9.2	舍	shě	舌 135.2	是	shì	日 72.5	死	sǐ	歹 78.2
日	rì	日 72.0	射	shè	寸 41.7	柿	shì	木 75.5	四	sì	口 31.2
容	róng	宀 40.7	摄	shè	手 64.10	示	shì	示 113.0	寺	sì	寸 41.3

松	sōng	木 75.4	特	tè	牛 93.6	托	tuō	手 64.3	我	wǒ	戈 62.3
送	sòng	辵 162.6	疼	téng	疒 104.5	拖	tuō	手 64.5	握	wò	手 64.9
搜	sōu	手 64.9	梯	tī	木 75.7	脱	tuō	肉 130.7	卧	wò	臣 131.2
苏	sū	艸 140.4	踢	tī	足 157.8	哇	wā	口 30.6	乌	wū	丿 4.3
俗	sú	人 9.7	提	tí	手 64.9	挖	wā	手 64.6	屋	wū	尸 44.6
塑	sù	土 32.10	题	tí	頁 181.9	娃	wá	女 38.6	污	wū	水 85.3
宿	sù	宀 40.8	体	tǐ	人 9.5	袜	wà	衣 145.5	无	wú	无 71.0
素	sù	糸 120.4	替	tì	日 73.8	外	wài	夕 36.2	五	wǔ	二 7.2
肃	sù	聿 129.4	天	tiān	大 37.1	弯	wān	弓 57.6	伍	wǔ	人 9.4
诉	sù	言 149.5	添	tiān	水 85.8	湾	wān	水 85.9	午	wǔ	十 24.2
速	sù	辵 162.7	填	tián	土 32.10	完	wán	宀 40.4	武	wǔ	止 77.4
酸	suān	酉 164.7	甜	tián	甘 99.6	玩	wán	玉 96.4	舞	wǔ	舛 136.8
算	suàn	竹 118.8	田	tián	田 102.0	顽	wán	頁 181.4	务	wù	力 34.2
虽	suī	虫 142.3	挑	tiāo	手 64.6	晚	wǎn	日 72.7	悟	wù	心 61.7
随	suí	阜 170.10	条	tiáo	木 75.3	碗	wǎn	石 112.8	物	wù	牛 93.4
岁	suì	山 46.3	调	tiáo	言 149.8	万	wàn	一 1.2	误	wù	言 149.7
碎	suì	石 112.8	挑	tiǎo	手 64.6	亡	wáng	亠 8.1	吸	xī	口 30.4
孙	sūn	子 39.3	跳	tiào	足 157.6	王	wáng	玉 96.0	夕	xī	夕 36.0
损	sǔn	手 64.7	贴	tiē	貝 154.5	往	wǎng	彳 60.5	希	xī	巾 50.4
缩	suō	糸 120.11	铁	tiě	金 167.5	网	wǎng	网 122.0	息	xī	心 61.6
所	suǒ	戶 63.4	厅	tīng	厂 27.2	忘	wàng	心 61.3	悉	xī	心 61.7
索	suǒ	糸 120.4	听	tīng	口 30.4	旺	wàng	日 72.4	惜	xī	心 61.8
锁	suǒ	金 167.7	停	tíng	人 9.9	望	wàng	月 74.7	析	xī	木 75.4
他	tā	人 9.3	庭	tíng	广 53.7	危	wēi	卩 26.4	牺	xī	牛 93.6
她	tā	女 38.3	挺	tǐng	手 64.7	威	wēi	女 38.6	西	xī	襾 146.0
它	tā	宀 40.2	通	tōng	辵 162.7	微	wēi	彳 60.10	习	xí	冫 15.1
塔	tǎ	土 32.10	同	tóng	口 30.3	为	wéi	丶 3.3	席	xí	巾 50.7
踏	tà	足 157.8	童	tóng	立 117.7	唯	wéi	口 30.8	喜	xǐ	口 30.9
台	tái	口 30.2	铜	tóng	金 167.6	围	wéi	口 31.4	洗	xǐ	水 85.6
抬	tái	手 64.5	统	tǒng	糸 120.6	维	wéi	糸 120.8	戏	xì	戈 62.2
太	tài	大 37.1	痛	tòng	疒 104.7	违	wéi	辵 162.4	系	xì	糸 120.1
态	tài	心 61.4	偷	tōu	人 9.9	伟	wěi	人 9.4	细	xì	糸 120.5
弹	tán	弓 57.8	头	tóu	大 37.2	委	wěi	女 38.5	下	xià	一 1.2
谈	tán	言 149.8	投	tóu	手 64.4	尾	wěi	尸 44.4	吓	xià	口 30.3
坦	tǎn	土 32.5	透	tòu	辵 162.7	为	wèi	丶 3.3	夏	xià	夊 35.7
叹	tàn	口 30.2	突	tū	穴 116.4	卫	wèi	乙 5.2	先	xiān	儿 10.4
探	tàn	手 64.8	图	tú	口 31.5	位	wèi	人 9.5	鲜	xiān	魚 195.6
汤	tāng	水 85.3	徒	tú	彳 60.7	味	wèi	口 30.5	咸	xián	口 30.6
堂	táng	土 32.8	途	tú	辵 162.7	喂	wèi	口 30.9	嫌	xián	女 38.10
糖	táng	米 119.10	吐	tǔ	口 30.3	慰	wèi	心 61.11	闲	xián	門 169.4
躺	tǎng	身 158.8	土	tǔ	土 32.0	未	wèi	木 75.1	显	xiǎn	日 72.5
趟	tàng	走 156.8	兔	tù	儿 10.6	胃	wèi	肉 130.5	险	xiǎn	阜 170.7
掏	tāo	手 64.8	吐	tù	口 30.3	谓	wèi	言 149.9	县	xiàn	厶 28.5
桃	táo	木 75.6	团	tuán	口 31.3	温	wēn	水 85.9	献	xiàn	犬 94.9
葡	táo	艸 140.8	推	tuī	手 64.8	文	wén	文 67.0	现	xiàn	玉 96.4
逃	táo	辵 162.6	腿	tuǐ	肉 130.10	闻	wén	門 169.6	线	xiàn	糸 120.5
讨	tǎo	言 149.3	退	tuì	辵 162.6	稳	wěn	禾 115.9	限	xiàn	阜 170.6
套	tào	大 37.7	吞	tūn	口 30.4	问	wèn	門 169.3	陷	xiàn	阜 170.8

乡	xiāng	幺 52.0	胸	xiōng	肉 130.6	央	yāng	大 37.2	译	yì	言 149.5
相	xiāng	目 109.4	熊	xióng	火 86.10	扬	yáng	手 64.3	谊	yì	言 149.8
箱	xiāng	竹 118.9	雄	xióng	隹 172.4	洋	yáng	水 85.6	因	yīn	口 31.3
香	xiāng	香 186.0	休	xiū	人 9.4	羊	yáng	羊 123.0	阴	yīn	阜 170.4
祥	xiáng	示 113.6	修	xiū	人 9.8	阳	yáng	阜 170.4	音	yīn	音 180.0
详	xiáng	言 149.6	秀	xiù	禾 115.2	仰	yǎng	人 9.4	银	yín	金 167.6
享	xiǎng	亠 8.6	袖	xiù	衣 145.5	养	yǎng	八 12.7	引	yǐn	弓 57.1
响	xiǎng	口 30.6	须	xū	彡 59.6	氧	yǎng	气 84.6	隐	yǐn	阜 170.9
想	xiǎng	心 61.9	虚	xū	虍 141.5	样	yàng	木 75.6	饮	yǐn	食 184.4
像	xiàng	人 9.12	需	xū	雨 173.6	腰	yāo	肉 130.9	印	yìn	卩 26.4
向	xiàng	口 30.3	许	xǔ	言 149.4	要	yāo	襾 146.3	应	yīng	广 53.4
相	xiàng	目 109.4	序	xù	广 53.4	邀	yāo	辵 162.13	英	yīng	艸 140.5
象	xiàng	豕 152.5	绪	xù	糸 120.8	摇	yáo	手 64.10	赢	yíng	亠 8.15
项	xiàng	頁 181.3	续	xù	糸 120.8	咬	yǎo	口 30.6	营	yíng	艸 140.8
消	xiāo	水 85.7	宣	xuān	宀 40.6	耀	yào	羽 124.14	迎	yíng	辵 162.4
销	xiāo	金 167.7	悬	xuán	心 61.7	药	yào	艸 140.6	影	yǐng	彡 59.12
小	xiǎo	小 42.0	旋	xuán	方 70.7	要	yào	襾 146.3	应	yìng	广 53.4
晓	xiǎo	日 72.6	选	xuǎn	辵 162.6	爷	yé	父 88.2	映	yìng	日 72.5
效	xiào	攴 66.6	学	xué	子 39.5	也	yě	乙 5.2	硬	yìng	石 112.7
校	xiào	木 75.6	雪	xuě	雨 173.3	野	yě	里 166.4	拥	yōng	手 64.5
笑	xiào	竹 118.4	血	xuè	血 143.0	业	yè	一 1.4	勇	yǒng	力 19.7
些	xiē	二 7.5	寻	xún	彐 58.3	叶	yè	口 30.2	永	yǒng	水 85.1
歇	xiē	欠 76.9	循	xún	彳 60.9	夜	yè	夕 36.5	泳	yǒng	水 85.5
协	xié	十 24.4	询	xún	言 149.6	液	yè	水 85.8	用	yòng	用 101.0
斜	xié	斗 68.7	训	xùn	言 149.3	页	yè	頁 181.0	优	yōu	人 9.4
胁	xié	肉 130.4	讯	xùn	言 149.3	一	yī	一 1.0	幽	yōu	幺 52.6
谐	xié	言 149.9	迅	xùn	辵 162.3	依	yī	人 9.6	忧	yōu	心 61.4
鞋	xié	革 177.6	压	yā	厂 27.4	医	yī	匚 23.5	尤	yóu	尢 43.1
写	xiě	冖 14.3	押	yā	手 64.5	衣	yī	衣 145.0	油	yóu	水 85.5
械	xiè	木 75.7	鸭	yā	鳥 196.5	仪	yí	人 9.3	游	yóu	水 85.9
谢	xiè	言 149.10	牙	yá	牙 92.0	姨	yí	女 38.6	犹	yóu	犬 94.4
心	xīn	心 61.0	亚	yà	一 1.5	宜	yí	宀 40.5	由	yóu	田 102.0
新	xīn	斤 69.9	呀	ya	口 30.4	疑	yí	疋 103.9	邮	yóu	邑 163.5
欣	xīn	欠 76.4	烟	yān	火 86.6	移	yí	禾 115.6	友	yǒu	又 29.2
薪	xīn	艸 140.13	严	yán	一 1.6	遗	yí	辵 162.9	有	yǒu	月 74.2
辛	xīn	辛 160.0	延	yán	廴 54.4	乙	yǐ	乙 5.0	又	yòu	又 29.0
信	xìn	人 9.7	沿	yán	水 85.5	以	yǐ	人 9.3	右	yòu	口 30.2
星	xīng	日 72.5	炎	yán	火 86.4	已	yǐ	己 49.0	幼	yòu	幺 52.2
型	xíng	土 32.6	盐	yán	皿 108.5	椅	yǐ	木 75.8	于	yú	二 7.1
形	xíng	彡 59.4	研	yán	石 112.6	义	yì	丿 4.2	余	yú	人 9.5
行	xíng	行 144.0	言	yán	言 149.0	亿	yì	人 9.1	娱	yú	女 38.7
醒	xǐng	酉 164.9	颜	yán	頁 181.9	异	yì	廾 55.3	愉	yú	心 61.9
兴	xīng	八 12.4	演	yǎn	水 85.11	忆	yì	心 61.1	鱼	yú	魚 195.0
姓	xìng	女 38.5	眼	yǎn	目 109.6	意	yì	心 61.9	与	yǔ	一 1.3
幸	xìng	干 51.5	厌	yàn	厂 27.4	易	yì	日 72.4	予	yǔ	丿 6.3
性	xìng	心 61.5	宴	yàn	宀 40.7	益	yì	皿 108.5	宇	yǔ	宀 40.3
兄	xiōng	儿 10.3	艳	yàn	色 139.4	艺	yì	艸 140.1	羽	yǔ	羽 124.0
凶	xiōng	凵 17.2	验	yàn	馬 187.7	议	yì	言 149.3	语	yǔ	言 149.7

雨	yǔ	雨 173.0	择	zé	手 64.5	症	zhèng	疒 104.5	助	zhù	力 19.5
与	yù	一 1.3	责	zé	贝 154.4	证	zhèng	言 149.5	柱	zhù	木 75.5
域	yù	土 32.8	怎	zěn	心 61.5	之	zhī	丿 4.3	注	zhù	水 85.5
欲	yù	欠 76.7	增	zēng	土 32.12	只	zhī	口 30.2	祝	zhù	示 113.5
玉	yù	玉 96.0	赠	zèng	贝 154.12	支	zhī	支 65.0	筑	zhù	竹 118.6
育	yù	肉 130.4	扎	zhā	手 64.1	枝	zhī	木 75.4	著	zhù	艸 140.8
誉	yù	言 149.6	炸	zhà	火 86.5	汁	zhī	水 85.2	驻	zhù	马 187.5
豫	yù	豕 152.9	摘	zhāi	手 64.11	知	zhī	矢 111.3	抓	zhuā	手 64.4
遇	yù	辵 162.9	宅	zhái	宀 40.3	织	zhī	糸 120.5	专	zhuān	一 1.3
预	yù	页 181.4	债	zhài	人 9.8	值	zhí	人 9.8	转	zhuǎn	车 159.4
元	yuán	儿 10.2	展	zhǎn	尸 44.7	执	zhí	手 64.3	赚	zhuàn	贝 154.10
原	yuán	厂 27.8	占	zhàn	卜 25.3	植	zhí	木 75.8	转	zhuàn	车 159.4
员	yuán	口 30.4	战	zhàn	戈 62.5	殖	zhí	歹 78.8	庄	zhuāng	广 53.3
园	yuán	囗 31.4	站	zhàn	立 117.5	直	zhí	目 109.3	装	zhuāng	衣 145.6
圆	yuán	囗 31.7	张	zhāng	弓 57.4	职	zhí	耳 128.5	壮	zhuàng	士 33.3
援	yuán	手 64.9	章	zhāng	立 117.6	只	zhǐ	口 30.2	撞	zhuàng	手 64.12
源	yuán	水 85.10	掌	zhǎng	手 64.8	址	zhǐ	土 32.4	状	zhuàng	犬 94.3
缘	yuán	糸 120.9	涨	zhǎng	水 85.7	指	zhǐ	手 64.6	追	zhuī	辵 162.6
远	yuǎn	辵 162.4	长	zhǎng	长 168.0	止	zhǐ	止 77.0	准	zhǔn	冫 15.8
怨	yuàn	心 61.5	丈	zhàng	一 1.2	纸	zhǐ	糸 120.4	捉	zhuō	手 64.7
愿	yuàn	心 61.10	涨	zhàng	水 85.7	制	zhì	刀 18.6	桌	zhuō	木 75.6
院	yuàn	阜 170.7	账	zhàng	贝 154.4	质	zhì	厂 27.4	咨	zī	口 30.6
约	yuē	糸 120.3	障	zhàng	阜 170.11	志	zhì	心 61.3	资	zī	贝 154.6
乐	yuè	丿 4.4	招	zhāo	手 64.5	智	zhì	日 72.8	仔	zǐ	人 9.3
月	yuè	月 74.0	着	zháo	目 109.6	治	zhì	水 85.5	子	zǐ	子 39.0
越	yuè	走 156.5	找	zhǎo	手 64.4	置	zhì	网 122.8	紫	zǐ	糸 120.5
跃	yuè	足 157.4	召	zhào	口 30.2	至	zhì	至 133.0	字	zì	子 39.3
阅	yuè	门 169.7	照	zhào	火 86.9	致	zhì	至 133.3	自	zì	自 132.0
晕	yūn	日 72.6	哲	zhé	口 30.7	中	zhōng	丨 2.3	子	zi	子 39.0
云	yún	二 7.2	折	zhé	手 64.4	忠	zhōng	心 61.4	宗	zōng	宀 40.5
允	yǔn	儿 10.2	者	zhě	老 125.4	终	zhōng	糸 120.5	综	zōng	糸 120.8
晕	yùn	日 72.6	这	zhè	辵 162.4	钟	zhōng	金 167.4	总	zǒng	八 12.7
运	yùn	辵 162.4	着	zhe	目 109.6	种	zhǒng	禾 115.4	纵	zòng	糸 120.4
杂	zá	木 75.2	著	zhe	艸 140.8	肿	zhǒng	肉 130.4	走	zǒu	走 156.0
灾	zāi	火 86.3	珍	zhēn	玉 96.5	中	zhòng	丨 2.3	奏	zòu	大 37.6
再	zài	冂 13.4	真	zhēn	目 109.5	众	zhòng	人 9.4	租	zū	禾 115.5
在	zài	土 32.3	针	zhēn	金 167.2	种	zhòng	禾 115.4	族	zú	方 70.7
载	zài	戈 62.6	诊	zhěn	言 149.5	重	zhòng	里 166.2	足	zú	足 157.0
咱	zán	口 30.6	振	zhèn	手 64.7	周	zhōu	口 30.5	祖	zǔ	示 113.5
暂	zàn	日 72.8	镇	zhèn	金 167.10	粥	zhōu	米 119.6	组	zǔ	糸 120.5
赞	zàn	贝 154.12	阵	zhèn	阜 170.4	猪	zhū	犬 94.9	阻	zǔ	阜 170.5
脏	zàng	肉 130.6	震	zhèn	雨 173.7	珠	zhū	玉 96.6	钻	zuān	金 167.5
糟	zāo	米 119.11	争	zhēng	亅 6.5	诸	zhū	言 149.8	嘴	zuǐ	口 30.12
遭	zāo	辵 162.11	征	zhēng	彳 60.5	竹	zhú	竹 118.0	最	zuì	日 73.8
早	zǎo	日 72.2	整	zhěng	攴 66.11	逐	zhú	辵 162.7	罪	zuì	网 122.8
澡	zǎo	水 85.13	挣	zhèng	手 64.6	主	zhǔ	丶 3.4	醉	zuì	酉 164.8
造	zào	辵 162.7	政	zhèng	攴 66.4	煮	zhǔ	火 86.8	尊	zūn	寸 41.9
则	zé	刀 18.4	正	zhèng	止 77.1	住	zhù	人 9.5	遵	zūn	辵 162.12

昨	zuó	日 72.5	子	zǐ	子 39.0	族	zú	方 70.7
左	zuǒ	工 48.2	紫	zǐ	糸 120.5	足	zú	足 157.0
作	zuò	人 9.5	字	zì	子 39.3	祖	zǔ	示 113.5
做	zuò	人 9.9	自	zì	自 132.0	组	zǔ	糸 120.5
坐	zuò	土 32.4	子	zi	子 39.0	阻	zǔ	阜 170.5
座	zuò	广 53.7	宗	zōng	宀 40.5	钻	zuān	金 167.5
准	zhǔn	冫 15.8	综	zōng	糸 120.8	嘴	zuǐ	口 30.12
捉	zhuō	手 64.7	总	zǒng	八 12.7	最	zuì	日 73.8
桌	zhuō	木 75.6	纵	zòng	糸 120.4	罪	zuì	网 122.8
咨	zī	口 30.6	走	zǒu	走 156.0	醉	zuì	酉 164.8
资	zī	贝 154.6	奏	zòu	大 37.6	尊	zūn	寸 41.9
仔	zǐ	人 9.3	租	zū	禾 115.5	遵	zūn	辶 162.12
子	zǐ	子 39.0	族	zú	方 70.7	昨	zuó	日 72.5
紫	zǐ	糸 120.5	足	zú	足 157.0	左	zuǒ	工 48.2
字	zì	子 39.3	祖	zǔ	示 113.5	作	zuò	人 9.5
自	zì	自 132.0	组	zǔ	糸 120.5	做	zuò	人 9.9
子	zi	子 39.0	阻	zǔ	阜 170.5	坐	zuò	土 32.4
宗	zōng	宀 40.5	钻	zuān	金 167.5	座	zuò	广 53.7
综	zōng	糸 120.8	嘴	zuǐ	口 30.12			
总	zǒng	八 12.7	最	zuì	日 73.8			
纵	zòng	糸 120.4	罪	zuì	网 122.8			
走	zǒu	走 156.0	醉	zuì	酉 164.8			
奏	zòu	大 37.6	尊	zūn	寸 41.9			
租	zū	禾 115.5	遵	zūn	辶 162.12			
族	zú	方 70.7	昨	zuó	日 72.5			
足	zú	足 157.0	左	zuǒ	工 48.2			
祖	zǔ	示 113.5	作	zuò	人 9.5			
组	zǔ	糸 120.5	做	zuò	人 9.9			
阻	zǔ	阜 170.5	坐	zuò	土 32.4			
钻	zuān	金 167.5	座	zuò	广 53.7			
嘴	zuǐ	口 30.12	准	zhǔn	冫 15.8			
最	zuì	日 73.8	捉	zhuō	手 64.7			
罪	zuì	网 122.8	桌	zhuō	木 75.6			
醉	zuì	酉 164.8	咨	zī	口 30.6			
尊	zūn	寸 41.9	资	zī	贝 154.6			
遵	zūn	辶 162.12	仔	zǐ	人 9.3			
昨	zuó	日 72.5	子	zǐ	子 39.0			
左	zuǒ	工 48.2	紫	zǐ	糸 120.5			
作	zuò	人 9.5	字	zì	子 39.3			
做	zuò	人 9.9	自	zì	自 132.0			
坐	zuò	土 32.4	子	zi	子 39.0			
座	zuò	广 53.7	宗	zōng	宀 40.5			
准	zhǔn	冫 15.8	综	zōng	糸 120.8			
捉	zhuō	手 64.7	总	zǒng	八 12.7			
桌	zhuō	木 75.6	纵	zòng	糸 120.4			
咨	zī	口 30.6	走	zǒu	走 156.0			
资	zī	贝 154.6	奏	zòu	大 37.6			
仔	zǐ	人 9.3	租	zū	禾 115.5			

www.ingramcontent.com/pod-product-compliance
Lightning Source LLC
Chambersburg PA
CBHW081917090526
44590CB00019B/3385